NEW YORK 1900

METROPOLITAN ARCHITECTURE AND URBANISM 1890-1915

NEW YORK 1900

METROPOLITAN ARCHITECTURE AND URBANISM 1890-1915

by Robert A. M. Stern, Gregory Gilmartin and John Montague Massengale

First published in the United States of America in 1983 by
RIZZOLI INTERNATIONAL PUBLICATIONS, INC.,
300 Park Avenue South, New York, N.Y. 10010.
Copyright © 1983 Rizzoli International Publications, Inc.
Reprinted 1992

First paperback edition, 1995.

All rights reserved.
No part of this book may be reproduced in any manner whatsoever
without permission in writing from
Rizzoli International Publications, Inc.

Library of Congress Cataloging in Publication Data

Stern, Robert A. M.
  New York 1900.

  Includes bibliographical references and index.
  1. New York (N.Y.)—Buildings. 2. Architecture,
Modern—19th century—New York (N.Y.) 3. Architecture,
Modern—20th century—New York (N.Y.) 4. New York (N.Y.)
—City planning. 5. City planning—New York (State)
I. Gilmartin, Gregory. II. Massengale, John Montague.
III. Title.
NA735.N5S73   720'.9747'1   83-42995
ISBN 0-8478-0511-5
ISBN 0-8478-1934-5 (Paperback)

Designed by Martin Moskof, assisted by Susan Ritzau,
and George Brady

Set in type and printed by Eastern Press, New Haven, Connecticut
Reprinted by Edwards Brothers, Ann Arbor, Michigan

Distributed by St. Martin's Press

ACKNOWLEDGMENTS

Many people helped with *New York 1900*. We are most grateful to Christopher Gray, Director of the Office for Metropolitan History, who generously shared with us his wide knowledge of New York architecture and architectural sources. Erica Millar, Dan Schneider and Oscar Shamamian were invaluable research assistants. Cathy Martinez and Charling Chang Fagan and her entire staff at Columbia University's Avery Library gave every assistance. Curtis Channing Blake, Keith Morgan and Richard Oliver kindly allowed us to read their unpublished manuscripts, which have been cited in the appropriate footnotes.

For the photographic research, we must thank the patient staffs at New York City's two great collections, the New-York Historical Society and the Museum of the City of New York. Steve Miller and Jennifer Bright at the Museum of the City of New York, and Helena Zinkham at the New-York Historical Society were especially helpful. Esther Brumberg, former curator at the museum, lent her invaluable assistance in finding seemingly unobtainable photographs. Marty Messic and Steve Lewis spent long hours shooting the material used at Avery Library.

Finally, no book of this complexity can be published without a great deal of care by those in production. Amy Hatkoff heroically typed the first handwritten drafts; Kathy Kirchner typed and retyped later versions of the text with unflagging enthusiasm, never losing or mislocating even one of our thousands of footnotes; and Stanley Wilder White read the galleys, finding errors we had missed. Martin Moskof and Susan Ritzau designed the book, drawing it all together in an elegant, evocative and fresh manner; while Solveig Williams and Lynne Creighton-Neall at Rizzoli International Publications guided us through the writing, editing and printing. Our publisher, Gianfranco Monacelli, never flagged in his support or commitment to make *New York 1900* a work of permanent value.

Frontispiece: View of lower Manhattan ca. 1913, from a private collection

Contents

PREFACE	6	
AGE OF METROPOLITANISM	10	Stages of Metropolitanism
CIVIC STRUCTURE	26	City Planning, Transportation
CIVIC GRANDEUR	60	Civic Center, Buildings for Public Service, The Federal Presence, Schools, Culture and Learning, Churches, Monuments and Memorials, Recreation
PALACES OF PRODUCTION	144	Office Buildings, Banks and Commerce, Stores
PALACES OF PLEASURE	202	Theaters, Roof Gardens, Clubs, Coney Island
PALACES FOR THE PEOPLE	252	Hotels, Apartment Hotels, Apartments
METROPOLITAN NEIGHBORHOODS	306	Billionaire District, The West End, Morningside Heights, Suburbs
AFTERWORD	437	
PHOTOGRAPHIC SOURCES	439	
NOTES	440	
INDEX	490	

·BALVSTRADE·
Madison Square Presbyterian Church, northeast corner of Madison Avenue and Twenty-fourth Street. McKim, Mead & White, 1906. Detail of Elevation. OMH

Preface

This book is the middle volume of a three-part work devoted to the evolution of New York's architecture and urbanism in the Metropolitan Era, the three-quarters of a century from the Civil War's conclusion through the depression of the 1930s. Our intention is not to sit in judgment, but rather to let the period make a case for itself. In order to better recapture the ideals and flavor of the era, its buildings and places, we have illustrated the text with period photographs. These portray the city and its buildings as they were at the time and as the world outside New York first knew them. Similarly, we have emphasized original sources over subsequent scholarship and have quoted extensively from the literature of the period.[1]

The lively architectural scene after the Civil War gave birth to the nation's first generation of architectural critics; in view of the major role they play in this book a few words of introduction seem appropriate. Montgomery Schuyler was undoubtedly Metropolitan New York's foremost "architectural boulevardier" and America's most perceptive and broadminded critic.[2] Born in Ithaca, New York, in 1843, he arrived in the city twenty-two years later and found work as a journalist on Manton Marble's New York *World*. From 1885 to 1887 he was managing editor of *Harper's Weekly*, from 1883 to 1907 a member of the editorial staff and literary critic of the *New York Times* and from 1912 until his death in 1914 a critic for the New York *Sun*. Schuyler's architectural criticism was thus something of a hobby, yet he produced an extraordinarily copious *oeuvre* of far-reaching commentary, most of it for the *Architectural Record*. Although many of his writings were penned anonymously, others pseudonymously (some of the most sarcastic under the name Franz K. Winkler), his witty, urbane voice, crammed with obscure literary allusions, was always apparent.

In 1874–76 Schuyler worked with Henry Hobson Richardson and the latter's young draftsman, Charles Follen McKim, on the editorial staff of the *New York Sketch-Book of Architecture*. The sketchbook was a precursor of the architectural journals which, after 1880, became the principal sources of information on current building.[3] They published many of Richardson's Romanesque and Shingle Style projects, as well as photographs of the Colonial architecture which McKim and Schuyler saw as a threatened national heritage.[4]

Despite nostalgia for the pre-industrial past, Schuyler was the first American critic to consider bridges as works of architecture as well as engineering, and throughout his career he addressed the problem of the skyscraper as a distinctly modern and American building type. He wrote a number of times about the Chicago School of Modernists, and selective quotation has given him a reputation as an early disciple of Wright and Sullivan.[5] But for Schuyler, "the real radical defect of modern architecture in general, if not of American architecture in particular," was not an issue of style but of "the estrangement between architecture and building—between the poetry and the prose, so to speak, of the art of building, which can never be disjoined without injury to both."[6] While initially hostile to the American Classicism nurtured at the Ecole des Beaux-Arts in Paris, Schuyler, nonetheless, found the sought-for synthesis between "poetry and prose" in buildings such as Stanford White's Knickerbocker Trust Company and Robert D. Kohn's *Evening Post* Building—both designed by architects steeped in the Classical tradition.[7] He was able to perceive great architecture no matter its stylistic guise, yet his sympathies always harked back to the Romanesque Revival of his youth and the Gothic structuralism of his friend and mentor Leopold Eidlitz.

Russell Sturgis, Schuyler's colleague at the *Architectural Record*, had a far less catholic point of view. He was born in Maryland in 1838 of a Boston family which moved in 1850 to New York, where Sturgis attended the College of the City of New York (then known as the Free Academy). After studying architecture at the Academy of Fine Arts and Sciences in Munich, he returned to New York in 1862 to form a brief partnership (1863–68) with Peter B. Wight, whose National Academy of Design (1862) was a flamboyantly polychromed, Ruskinian interpretation of the Doge's Palace in Venice.[8] Sturgis's own buildings were far less pictorial; his designs for a number of rather dour buildings on the Old Campus at Yale were chiefly notable for the rigor with which their decoration articulated structure.[9]

In the 1870s Sturgis abandoned his architectural practice for a career of criticism and scholarship. An ardent Ruskinian, Sturgis's moralistic outlook pervaded even his encyclopedic *Dictionary of Architecture*[10] and four-volume *A History of Architecture*.[11] As Schuyler observed in his eulogy of Sturgis: "Nothing less than Ruskin's eloquence could . . . have inclined so large a proportion of the population of . . . New England towards the fine arts. Nothing else would have availed so much as the contention . . . that 'Art was the handmaid of Religion,' that aesthetics were, in fact, a subdivision of ethics, to reconcile the sensitive descendants of the Puritans to following their bent."[12] Sturgis's advocacy of Gothic structuralism pitted him squarely against the stylistic concerns of the American Renaissance; although both McKim and Mead were once draftsmen in his office, he rejected their later work, regarding the Renaissance as "the least interesting Italian work."[13] In return, Charles Baldwin, Stanford White's biographer, described Sturgis as "the most prolific of the petty despots who, after the example of Ruskin, set themselves up in this country as dictators in matters of art, subjecting artists and public to an intolerable tyranny."[14]

Marianna Griswold van Rensselaer was a member of New York's old aristocracy.[15] Born in 1857, she grew up near Washington Square and was educated by private tutors and European travel. Her first poems appeared in 1874 in *Harper's* magazine. Two years later she began writing art and architectural criticism for the fledging *American Architect and Building News,* the first architectural journal to succeed in establishing itself on American soil. Van Rensselaer found a wider audience among the readers of the *Century,* where her landmark nine-part series "Recent Architecture in America" began to appear in 1884. After the death of her husband, a mining engineer of Dutch-American lineage, her output increased, ranging in subject from gardening, landscape design, painting, history and architecture. She also published short stories and poems.

Van Rensselaer was one of the first of a new generation of American art critics to examine the parochial native art scene in the light of contemporary French work and uphold the Barbizon School as a model to technically deficient American artists.[16] She, nonetheless, hoped for the creation of a distinctly national school based on local subjects. Her architectural writings displayed a similar distrust of the picturesque and a belief that a more scholarly study of historical models would eventually produce a technically proficient American architecture. Van Rensselaer is best remembered, however, for authoring *Henry Hobson Richardson and His Works.* This still unsurpassed biography of the recently deceased Romanesque Revivalist was the first monograph published on an American architect.

After the premature death of van Rensselaer's son in 1894, she gradually abandoned her career as a critic for one of public service. In the same year she published a pamphlet, *Should We Ask For the Vote?,* which became one of the most widely read tracts of the anti-suffrage movement. For eight years she taught at the Neighborhood Guild on Delancey Street, and she served briefly as an inspector of the city's schools and president of the Public Education Association of New York. Her most monumental work of scholarship was the two-volume *History of New York in the Seventeenth Century* (1909), which occupied her for a decade. Van Rensselaer's position as a critic was summed up by Talbot Hamlin in 1936, two years after her death. "Her work is important as the almost perfect expression of a cultural breadth, a cultivated tolerance, and an artistic sensitivity which, united, were characteristics of the final flowering of nineteenth-century American life. Though not profound, her books are in general sound and, what is more, delightful reading. She not only expressed the new interest in art that was current in the educated American of the eighties and nineties, but she became one of its chief leaders. . . . She popularized taste and knowledge in the true way, by honesty of approach and beauty of style."[17]

The last of the critics extensively quoted in *New York 1900* is Herbert Croly (1869-1930), an astute observer and analyst of many fields. A philosophy graduate of Harvard College, he began to write for the *Architectural Record* and the *Real Estate Record and Guide* in 1900 after a year spent in Paris. In 1906 Croly retired from both journals to write *The Promise of American Life,*[18] which established his reputation as one of the most influential writers on American political thought. Supreme Court Justice Felix Frankfurter cited Croly's book as the original source for both Theodore Roosevelt's New Nationalism and Woodrow Wilson's New

Freedom, and Walter Lippman described Croly as the first important political philosopher to appear in America in the twentieth century.[19]

Croly went on to found the magazine *The New Republic,* later using it to play a major role in getting America to enter World War I. Croly broke with Wilson over the Treaty of Versailles, however, became less and less interested in politics during the Republican administrations of Warren G. Harding and Calvin Coolidge, and turned instead to the study of religion and metaphysics.

Croly, van Rensselaer, Sturgis and Schuyler are but a few of the distinguished writers whose names and words appear in this book. They were the beneficiaries of the era's sudden proliferation of architectural journals. The periodicals of the day gave voice to widely divergent points of view—from the hard-nosed business standards of the *Real Estate Record and Guide* to the aesthetic parochialism of Donn Barber's *New York Architect.* They provided detailed documentation of building programs and construction, and often provided trenchant criticism as well. The richness of this printed record was only exceeded by that of the buildings themselves. To resort to a tired but appropriate cliche, it was a golden age for architecture.

Preface Notes

1. We are nonetheless indebted to recent scholars. John M. Kouwenhoven's *Columbia Historical Portrait of New York* (New York: Columbia University Press, 1954) is the pioneering study of the city's urbanism. Grace M. Mayer's *Once Upon a City* (New York: MacMillan, 1958) and Gunther Barth's *City People, The Rise of Modern City Culture in Nineteenth Century America* (New York: Oxford University Press, 1980) are also remarkable works which concentrate on social rather than architectural history.
   Charles Lockwood's books *Bricks and Brownstone, The New York Rowhouse, 1783-1929, An Architectural and Social History* (New York: McGraw Hill, 1972) and *Manhattan Moves Uptown, An Illustrated History* (Boston: Houghton Mifflin, 1976) are invaluable accounts of events leading up to the Metropolitan Age, as is Edward K. Spann's *The New Metropolis, New York City, 1840-1857* (New York: Columbia University Press, 1981).
   A number of key works offer more specific views of New York's urbanism at the turn of the century: Harvey Kantor's *Modern Urban Planning in New York City, Origins and Evolution, 1890-1933* (Ph.D. diss., New York University, 1971) and "The City Beautiful in New York," *The New-York Historical Society Quarterly Bulletin* 57 (April 1975): 148-71; Christopher Tunnard and Henry Hope Reed, "The Vision Spurned: Classical New York," *Classical America* 1 (1971): 31-41 and 2 (1972): 10-19; Henry Hope Reed, *The Golden City* (Garden City, New York: Doubleday, 1959); and Mel Scott, *American City Planning Since 1890* (Berkeley: University of California Press, 1969).
   Our initial research for *New York 1900* appeared in an essay written for the centennial celebration of Columbia University's School of Architecture. See Robert A.M. Stern and Gregory Gilmartin, "Apropos 1900, New York and the Metropolitan Ideal," in Richard Oliver, ed., *The Making of an Architect, 1881-1981* (New York: Rizzoli, 1981), 49-85.
2. See William H. Jordy and Ralph Coe, eds., *American Architecture and Other Writings by Montgomery Schuyler* (Cambridge: Harvard University Press, 1961).
3. Jordy and Coe., eds., *American Architecture and Other Writings,* 7-9.
4. Montgomery Schuyler expressed similar sentiments in his article, "The Small City House in New York," *Architectural Record* 8 (April-June 1899): 357-88.
5. The main theme of Jordy and Coe's introductory essay is Schuyler's ambiguous attitude toward Modernism. Jordy and Coe, eds., *American Architecture and Other Writings,* 1-89.
6. Montgomery Schuyler, "The Point of View," *Inland Architect and News Record* 17 (February 1891): 5-6.
7. See his articles, "A Modern Classic," *Architectural Record* 15 (May 1904): 431-44; and "Some Recent Skyscrapers," *Architectural Record* 22 (September 1907): 161-76.
8. Jordy and Coe, eds., *American Architecture and Other Writings,* 4-7.
9. Montgomery Schuyler, "Russell Sturgis's Architecture," *Architectural Record* 25 (June 1909): 405-10; Vincent Scully, *American Architecture and Urbanism* (New York: Praeger, 1969), 101; and Jordy and Coe, eds., *American Architecture and Other Writings,* 5.
10. Russell Sturgis, *A Dictionary of Architecture and Building, Biographical, Historical and Descriptive,* 3 vols. (NY: Macmillan, 1901-02).
11. Russell Sturgis, *A History of Architecture,* 4 vols. (New York: Baker and Taylor, 1906-1915).
12. Montgomery Schuyler, "Russell Sturgis," *Scribner's* 45 (May 1909): 635-36. Also see Russell Sturgis, "Good Things in Modern Architecture," *Architectural Record* 8 (July-September 1898): 91-110.
13. Russell Sturgis, letter to Peter B. Wight, 1897, quoted by Charles Baldwin, *Stanford White* (New York: Dodd, Mead & Co., 1931; New York: Da Capo Press, 1971), 354.
14. Baldwin, *Stanford White,* 354.
15. James D. Van Trump, "An Introduction" to Marianna Griswold van Rensselaer, *Henry Hobson Richardson and His Works* (NY: Houghton Mifflin, 1888; Park Forest, Illinois: Prairie School Press, 1967); William Morgan, "Introduction to the Dover Edition," of van Rensselaer, *Henry Hobson Richardson and His Works* (New York: Dover, 1969), V-VI; and Cynthia Doering Kinnard, *The Life and Works of Marianna Griswold van Rensselaer, American Art Critic* (Ph.D. diss., John Hopkins University, 1977).
16. Kinnard, *Life and Works,* 55.
17. Quoted by Kinnard, *Life and Works,* 55.
18. Herbert Croly, *The Promise of American Life* (NY: Macmillan, 1909).
19. Both in a supplement to the *New Republic* (July 16, 1930) published after Croly's death. Quoted in Oswald Garrison Villard, "Herbert David Croly" in Harris E. Starr, ed., *Dictionary of American Biography* (New York: Charles Scribner's Sons, 1944), 21: 209-10.

Madison Square Garden, northeast corner of Madison Square at Madison Avenue and Twenty-sixth Street. McKim, Mead & White, 1890. CU

Age of Metropolitanism

If the people . . . actually knew what was good when they saw it, they would someday talk about Hunt and Richardson, La Farge and St. Gaudens, Burnham and McKim, and Stanford White when the politicians and millionaires were otherwise forgotten.
Henry Adams, *The Education of Henry Adams* (New York: Houghton Mifflin, 1918; Boston: Houghton Mifflin, 1961), 341.

Metropolitanism Architects, historians and the general public share a fascination with the turning point of the nineteenth into the twentieth century, a period known in France as the *fin de siecle* and *la Belle Epoque* and in America as the Mauve Decades and the Banquet Years.[1] Much of the allure of *la Belle Epoque* is surely rooted in nostalgia, an appropriate sentiment for the era of Marcel Proust, Henry James and Edith Wharton. Yet as the British architectural historian Andrew Saint has recently pointed out, the nostalgia for the particular spirit of 1900 goes beyond the search for "cultural coherence that has led people to idolize Periclean Athens or Florence under the Medici." More to the point, Saint writes, are "plain, perceptible facts of completeness and variety" which ensure the durability of the great cities of 1900 as cultural artifacts.[2] In short, we look back to turn-of-the-century London, Paris, Brussels, Vienna and New York in order to better understand their urbanism and to establish a standard against which to measure our own era.[3]

Unlike most great metropolises, which were also political capitals, New York achieved its stature purely on the basis of its geographical advantages, the energy of its citizenry and the vision of its artists and architects. While New York is such a central force in American thought that we tend to think it has always been a major metropolis, in fact its preeminence only dates from the latter half of the nineteenth century, when its great year-round port and splendid water and rail connections to the interior of the continent gave it an ideal situation in respect to both national and international commerce and fostered a period of staggering economic and physical growth.

New York City's population increased eightfold between 1825 and 1875, and when the city achieved its ultimate physical size in 1898 by annexing Brooklyn, the Bronx, Queens and Staten Island, its residents numbered 3.1 million, half of whom were foreign born.[4] By 1903 Herbert Croly observed that New York "is undoubtedly on the road to becoming the most national and the least suburban of American cities, the city to which men will be attracted in proportion as their enterprises, intellectual or practical, are far-reaching and important. . . . In the making of a metropolis, every part of the country must contribute a portion of its energies and talent."[5]

New York began to assume its position as a national center of commerce and culture around 1876. Enriched by the Civil War and Reconstruction, the city was in the thrall of what John DeWitt Warner termed "the centripetal tendency of wealth and art, the flow of each toward the point where the greatest amount of it is already gathered."[6]

Caught up in the burst of activity that followed America's Centennial, New York's artists and architects were acutely sensitive to the era's paradoxical process of expansion through consolidation and to its yearning for a national cultural expression. The Centennial sparked a sense of both a lost past and a bountiful future. America gave its newly rediscovered preindustrial artifacts archetypal status in the struggle to accommodate its heritage to the pressures of tremendous growth, hoping to transform the cultural and commercial programs of the day into glorious monuments commensurate with those of the past.[7]

The term Metropolitanism describes a complex geographic and social ideal in which the city supplied the same services and benefits as the nation as a whole. During the Metropolitan Age, which extended from the end of the Civil War to 1940, the city was perceived not as merely an economic necessity but as the highest representation of cultured life, and the destiny of cities was seen as inextricably linked to that of an optimistic and progressive civilization. "In order to be actually metropolitan," Croly wrote, "a city must not only reflect large national tendencies, but it must sum them up and transform them. It must not only mirror typical American ways of thought and action, but it must anticipate, define and realize national ideals. A genuine metropolis must be, that is, both a concentrated and selected expression of the national life."[8] This ideal fostered the interaction between the prevailing modes of architectural thought—the Classical, technological and vernacular—to produce an appropriately complex expression of the modern condition, one born of diversity, special interests, energy, vitality and a passion for excellence.[9]

The American metropolis developed into a hybrid urban form reflecting its pluralist, democratic society. The city encompassed within its boundaries the most disparate urban forms—from the densely textured canyons of the financial district to the Arcadian idyll of the suburbs—linked by the arteries of its mass transportation network. The city coalesced into a loose federation of sometimes overlapping but mutually dependent areas where specific activities were concentrated. The manufacturing, shopping, entertainment, urban and suburban residential districts were further refined by divisions of social and economic class. The localization of land uses evolved as an antidote to the "migratory" pattern of urban growth—described by the *Real Estate Record and Guide* in 1877 as "the complete devastation of resident [*sic*] localities within the city proper, through enlarged and extended mercantile occupation"—which had plagued Manhattan throughout most of the nineteenth century.[10]

The Three Stages of Metropolitanism

The architectural and urban history of New York in its Metropolitan Age extended through a cycle of three stages, each of which emphasized an aspect of the urban condition—cultural cosmopolitanism, political and economic consolidation, and functional pragmatism—present to a lesser degree in the other two. These stages also correspond to the general cycle of metropolitan growth advanced by Henry Isham Hazelton, who wrote in 1925 that "a metropolis grows first by its natural expansion, then leaps forward by adding large areas to itself, taking into the city overnight many villages and settlements; and thereupon, proceeds to consolidate its position by filling up the intervening area with rows of houses, stores and factories."[11] The first, or Cosmopolitan Era, of New York's Metropolitan Age extended from 1865 to 1890; the second period, the Composite Era, extended from 1890 to 1915; and the third, the Era of Convenience, from 1915 to 1940.

The Cosmopolitan Era, 1865-1890

At the start of the Cosmopolitan Era in 1865, the city was beginning to expand beyond its historic core on the southern tip of Manhattan. Portions of the Bronx were annexed in 1874, and men such as Frederick Law Olmsted, landscape architect of the nearly completed Central Park, were looking to the future: "The time will come when New York will be built up, when all the grading and filling will be done, and when the picturesquely varied, rocky formations of the Island will have been converted into formations for rows of monotonous straight streets, and piles of erect buildings. There will be no suggestion left of its present varied surface, with the single exception of the few acres contained in the Park. Then the priceless value of the present picturesque outlines of the ground will be perceived, and its adaptability for its purpose more fully recognized."[12]

The opening of the steam-powered, elevated railroads along Third and Sixth avenues in 1878 provided easy access to the upper island and for the first time gave low- and middle-income workers a reasonable alternative to the hopelessly overcrowded conditions of the tenement districts on the Lower East Side. The opening in 1880 of the Ninth Avenue El fostered the development of the Upper West Side, where a heterogeneous fabric of eclectic villas, townhouses and apartments provided the fullest domestic expression of Cosmopolitanism. Like the els, the Brooklyn Bridge transformed New Yorkers' sense of their city's geography. The completion of the bridge in 1883 was as important for New York as the opening of the transcontinental railroad in 1869 was for the nation as a whole.

As the city physically expanded, it simultaneously consolidated its role as the cultural, commercial and communications capital of the nation. The process of consolidation was fostered by a series of technological innovations in the late 1870s and early 1880s. In the 1870s the first, safe, passenger elevators signalled the dawn of the city's vertical growth. The Bell Telephone Company opened its first exchange in March of 1876, and in 1882 Thomas Edison began to supply the city with electricity. The completion of the Croton Aqueduct System in 1890 completed the technical armature necessary to support the tremendous growth the city would experience in the next ten years, when the population of Manhattan and the Bronx increased from 1.5 to 2 million.

The magnitude of New York's technological advances was paralleled by a tremendous growth in human resources resulting from the waves of immigration which touched its shores between 1880 and the First World War. Many immigrants chose to remain in the city, where they combined with the native stock to give New York the distinctly cosmopolitan character that was, and remains, its most obvious distinction. In 1893 John F. Sprague somewhat simplistically observed in *New York the Metropolis* that the eclecticism of the city's architecture was attributable to the diversity of the nationalities who "stay long enough to leave some impression of their manners and customs. Hence, with a great, throbbing, ever increasing, cosmopolitan population and a conglomeration of races and ideas, a diversity in the architecture is a natural result."[13]

The stylistic eclecticism that characterized the Cosmopolitan Era lacked a didactic or highly moralistic content, but was the product instead of a sensibility which sought the exotic and beautiful.[14] Inspired eclectic architects such as Frank Freeman, William A. Potter and Josiah Cleveland Cady designed works simultaneously rich in historical allusions and clearly specific to their own time. Their frequently astylar buildings represented one approach to the task of creating an American architecture, radically transforming and synthesizing historic precedents in an attempt to illuminate contemporary conditions. The architect A.D.F. Hamlin, a graduate of the Ecole des Beaux-Arts and a prominent teacher at Columbia College, in 1892 scathingly described the architecture of the Cosmopolitan City in terms that illustrated the Composite Era's preference for a more correct and homogeneous approach to style:

The most horrible compositions that disfigure our streets, the most *outré,* barbarous and illogical hotch-potches of mistaken design to be found in our cities, are quite as apt to be the work of intelligent men of fair general education, who are nevertheless possessed of the idea that "absolute originality" is the chiefest of architectural virtues, to be attained only by absolutely disregarding all historical precedent, as they are to be the productions of illiterate and philistic builders. The total absence in historic styles of anything exactly corresponding to the varied types of building which our everchanging conditions are constantly calling into being, while it has operated to prevent any mechanical copying or wholesale importation of those styles in recent years, has also retarded the convergence of American practice into anything like a national uniformity of type or character, except perhaps in the one domain of domestic architecture. Each designer makes use of the style which he imagines to best befit his special problem, or whose "grammar" he has most thoroughly mastered; as a rule, he uses it freely, adapting and modifying not always with the most perfect logic, but generally according to his lights. For this diversity of practice to crystallize into unity requires time. Mixture and fusion must precede the emergence of the crystal.[15]

New York's Cosmopolitan Era was preeminently one of independent monuments, the greatest of which was the Brooklyn Bridge. Providing the city with its first direct connection to a major land mass, the bridge tied together the two cities of Brooklyn and New York and opened up a vast area for residential development close to the business and governmental center of lower Manhattan. The bridge's poetry, however, resided in its ability to soar free of its context and be seen as an object apart, a freedom symbolically reinforced by the aspirational Gothic gateways of its piers. Functionally, the bridge's aloofness forced commuters to cope daily with its unconsidered connections to the cities at either end.[16]

New York's cosmopolitanism was reflected in the ambitions of its most influential citizens, the newly rich corporate barons. Like New York's artists and architects, they looked at the city in the light of European capitals and established a series of cultural institutions intended to catapult what seemed a provincial backwater into the realm of world class cities. The founding of the American Museum of Natural History, the Metropolitan Museum of Art, Carnegie Hall and the Metropolitan Opera reflected the cultural ambitions of the Cosmopolitan Era; yet these buildings betrayed an incomprehension of, or resistance to, the pro-

Metropolitan Opera House, northwest corner of Broadway and Thirty-ninth Street. J.C. Cady, 1883. View looking north on Broadway. MO

Brooklyn Bridge. John A. Roebling and Washington Roebling, 1867-83. A 1924 view looking southwest from Brooklyn. NYHS

cess of democratization which characterized the growing metropolis. Their cramped accommodations were inadequate to handle the potential crowds (for many years the museums were closed on Sundays, the only day most wage earners could attend), and the architectural expression of their facades ambiguously addressed the public realm.

The designs of the Metropolitan Opera House (opened in 1883) and Carnegie Hall (1891) were neither conventionally monumental nor expressive of their principal spaces. Both buildings were early examples of hybrid building types: Carnegie Hall included studios and offices, the Metropolitan Opera House contained commercial space and an apartment hotel. As Marianna Griswold van Rensselaer observed of the compromised program given to the architect of the Metropolitan Opera House, J.C. Cady, it would "manifestly be unjust . . . to ask for monumental grandeur in his House, or even for an adequate degree of external expressiveness. We can only congratulate ourselves that we have got as much as we have—an honest, unaffected, scholarly, dignified pile, as well designed in mass as was possible under the circumstances."[17]

William B. Tuthill's design for Carnegie Hall was more awkwardly massed. Tuthill offered splendid acoustics in the auditorium, but in the facades he achieved, at best, "dignity rather than beauty."[18] The hall's opening nonetheless announced a new era of eminence for New York, now prominent enough to secure the appearance of Peter Ilyich Tchaikovsky and Walter Damrosch as conductors at the opening performance. Three years later Henry J. Hardenbergh improved the building's appearance with the addition of a tower, though it in no way compensated for the lack of ample lobbies, a functional limitation reflecting the provincial world of the 1870s and 1880s.[19]

Stanford White's design for Madison Square Garden in 1887 and the competition for the new Cathedral of St. John the Divine in 1889 culminated the Cosmopolitan Era's hedonistic approach toward architectural style. Madison Square Garden—a wildly eclectic pleasure palace at an unprecedented scale that combined restaurants, theaters and a hall for horse shows—was perhaps the ultimate expression of Cosmopolitanism. Yet more than any other cultural institution of the post-Civil War era, the Garden's bold scale and carefully designed relationship to Madison Square established a dialogue with the larger public realm of the city.

Cathedral of St. John the Divine competition entry, north side of 110th Street between Morningside Drive and Amsterdam Avenue. William Halsey Wood, 1889. Perspective view from the southeast. CU

Cathedral of St. John the Divine competition entry, north side of 110th Street between Morningside Drive and Amsterdam Avenue. Carrère & Hastings, 1889. Perspective view from southeast. CU

The competition entries for the Cathedral of St. John the Divine epitomized Cosmopolitanism; the wide diversity of proposed styles and the eclecticism of the individual entries reflected an attempt to reconcile historical traditions to the unique situation of New York and an unprecedented program. The cathedral's mammoth size and towering height were a response to the increasingly vertical cityscape. Its eclectic design represented the ideal of an ecumenical Protestant cathedral. Intended to outstrip the lavish religious buildings of the Cosmopolitan Era—particularly the synagogues and St. Patrick's Cathedral—the Episcopal cathedral was meant to reassert the city's beleaguered Protestant culture. On the other hand, St. John the Divine affirmed the objective of assimilation to an Anglo-Saxon ideal; the chapels of its *chevet* were dedicated to the patron saints of the homelands of the city's immigrants. The cathedral was thus a turning point which predicted the ideal of homogeneity that characterized the Composite Era.

The Composite Era, 1890-1915

The period from 1890 to 1915 was one of economic expansion and consolidation. America's Imperial Age was marked by expansion abroad (the acquisition of the protectorates in the Caribbean and South Pacific) and intense geographical consolidation at home (the closing of the frontier and the growth of cities). Corporations were tapping the nation's major natural resources, establishing monopolies, and fueling a burgeoning, production-based economy on a scale hitherto unimagined. New York's fortunes rose with the nation's. "Suffice it to say," Croly wrote in 1903, "that the 'skyscrapers' of New York are as much filled with the offices of corporations, which conduct a business in other parts of the country, as Fifth Avenue is filled with the residences of capitalists who made their money in the West. New York is steadily attracting a large proportion of the best business ability in the country, not only as a matter of business convenience, but just as much because of the exceptional opportunity it offers to its favored inhabitants of making and spending money."[20]

The process of corporate, mercantile and institutional consolidation was mirrored by the creation of Greater New York in 1898. The event "touched public pride," Croly wrote, and resulted in an "awakening of municipal vanity. Thus neither is it fanciful to trace some connection between the aroused public spirit of the citizens of New York and the outburst of national feeling which accompanied and followed the Spanish War. For New York is national or nothing, and whatever intensifies and consolidates national life also quickens and consolidates the growth of public spirit in New York."[21] The city acquired a sense of itself as the representative American city comparable in its cultural and national significance to London or Paris. Moses King went further, describing New York as a "cosmopolis," a world capital.[22]

The Composite Era was the grandest manifestation of Metropolitanism in New York. Faced with the consequences of virtually uncontrolled social and physical growth, New Yorkers developed a new sensitivity to the role architecture and town planning could play in the quality of their day-to-day lives. By the mid-1890s a conception of the city emerged which James W. and Daniel B. Shepp described as "composite—a city made up of men and women from the uttermost ends of the earth, with their own peculiar habits and customs, all blending together into a more or less homogeneous whole."[23] The social ideal received its architectural expression in the revival of Classicism known as the American Renaissance, and was most vividly articulated in the realm of urban design by the City Beautiful movement.

Although the Cosmopolitan City had been a center of folk culture of all kinds—Marianna Griswold van Rensselaer described Cosmopolitan New York as a picturesque "composite of memories and artifacts"[24]—the kaleidoscopic diversity of culture and architecture in the 1870s and 1880s sparked a widespread fear for the loss of native American culture. "Look at the clubhouses of our Germans," van Rensselaer wrote in 1895. "Think of their musical societies, half artistic, half social in aim; read of their weddings and balls, where money is spent and diamonds are shown as profusely as on fashionable Fifth Avenue. And note the number of Teutonic or Hebrew-Teutonic faces in the finest carriages in Central Park. It will seem as though all of us Americans might be swept away and New York still exist, socially no less than industrially."[25]

Americans of the Composite Era regarded the preindustrial past as a stable icon in a world increasingly complicated by capitalism, social heterogeneity and an inharmonious democratic process. "The homogeneity so characteristic of American democracy at its best tends to disappear in the complicated hurly burly of the life of a great city," Croly remarked, "and the underlying separation of interest and point of view in its make-up comes plainly to the surface."[26] In reaction to the threat posed by cultural minorities, the old families joined the newly monied to reaffirm traditional values and their traditional role through the consolidation of power in betterment movements, such as the City Beautiful and in institutions such as the Opera, the Metropolitan Museum of Art and The New-York Historical Society.

The city began to develop a sense of its own history,[27] and a concern for the preservation of the past as pockets of its antiquity began to fall in the path of progress.[28] The threat to these neighborhoods and monuments encouraged some old-line New Yorkers to oppose the city's rebuilding so vehemently that it bypassed certain districts in its otherwise inexorable march north. Such was the case for the neighborhood north of Washington Square where, as van Rensselaer wrote in 1893, the "desecrated dwellings were being restored within and without, and a belief was gaining ground that, whatever may happen a little further up the avenue, this quarter-mile stretch will remain a good residence neighborhood." The local residents, of which she was one, "are proud of the aroma of fifty years antiquity which we breathe, and we delight to maintain that this is the only part of New York, outside of the tenement districts, where a 'neighborhood feeling' exists."[29]

Stretches of the natural landscape that defined the limits of the city were also threatened with development. Among these were the Palisades,[30] across the Hudson River in New Jersey, sections of which were ultimately preserved by the Rockefeller family from the ravages of quarrying. Other areas, particularly in the Bronx, were reserved by the city for parkland.

The call for a uniform Classicism was fueled by nostalgia for the social and architectural decorum of the nation's colonial and early Republican past, and by a growing conception that America was the heir to Western civilization. The latter view was even shared by some Europeans; the

English statesman and Prime Minister William Gladstone was said to have observed that "Europe may already see in North America an immediate successor in the march of civilization."[31] The Classical revival was a response to new wealth and to new building materials and methods, but it also embodied the principles of greatness and timelessness; it gave a national architectural style to America that could be the background for a great civilization.[32]

The intersection between an ideal of homogeneity and an insistently pluralistic reality determined much of the character of the Composite City. The tension between the aspirations of the City Beautiful movement, for example, and the rampant exploitation of economic forces, which produced both the skyscraper and the tenement, resulted in the urbanism which, like the columnar order of Classical architecture, was at once heterogeneous in its parts yet harmonious enough to establish an effect of overall composition. The Composite Era also reflected an interaction between international culture and national peculiarities and ideals. It did not put an end to New York's Cosmopolitanism—the diversity of its population could not be ignored nor fully assimilated into the Anglo-American tradition—but rather subsumed it in a higher ideal of civic homogeneity that, by virtue of its roots in broader Western European experience, was culturally accessible to all. In 1904 Hamilton Wright Mabie summed up contemporary feeling that

this great city of ours, with its diversities of race, of religion, of social, political and personal ideals—has a unity which the country has as yet failed to recognize, a genius which belongs to the future rather than to the past, and which, because it is of the future, is slow to reveal itself. We forget that New York is not only one of the first cities of modern birth, in magnitude of population and interests, but that it is also a city of a new type. Its very diversities are creating here a kind of city which men have not seen before; in which a unity of a more inclusive, if not a higher, order is slowly forming itself; a city the genius of which has the light of prophecy in it.[33]

The city focused its energies on the creation of a democratic public realm which all its citizens could enjoy. To the burdens of functional accommodation and structural stability, each work of architecture added a sense of responsibility for the expression of its purpose and the embellishment of the public realm. "It is not merely a demand for art objects in this *mis-en-scene* which prompts the effort to inspire a love of civic art," Gabrielle T. Stewart wrote in the *Architects' and Builders' Magazine* in 1903. "It is the moral suasion that goes with beautiful surroundings, the effect which a general replanning of the city, keeping its artistic merits well to the front, would have on all classes of citizens."[34] For a contemporary writer in *Harper's Monthly*, the movement demonstrated "the transition from individualism to civicism as the vital force."[35]

The intermingled social and aesthetic vision of the Composite Era was most clearly expressed in Edward Bellamy's popular novel *Looking Backward, 2000-1887*. The protagonist, Julian West, dreamt of a utopian future world in which the perfection of capitalism would transform society into a single, vast corporation. West described the city of the future:

At my feet lay a great city. Miles of broad streets, shaded by trees and lined with fine buildings, for the most part not in continuous blocks but set in larger or smaller enclosures, stretched in every direction. Every quarter contained large open squares filled with trees, among which statues glistened and fountains flashed in the late afternoon sun. Public buildings of a colossal size and an architectural grandeur unparalleled in my day, raised their stately piles on every side. Surely I had never seen this city nor one comparable to it before.[36]

The City Beautiful movement was the most direct attempt to realize such a vision. It culminated with the New York City Improvement Commission of 1904-07, which sought to carve a series of monumental, axially-organized public spaces out of the intractable city grid. The commission's goals were largely aesthetic; architectural ensembles were to be created at key points in the city while the remainder of the urban fabric was left to develop under the forces of real estate speculation. Although the 1907 city plan ultimately had little effect on the city's appearance, the architects of the Composite Era attempted to work pragmatically within the framework of capitalism to accommodate the needs of an expanding city to a monumental vision of urbanism.

At the same time the quaintly domestic social life of the Cosmopolitan Era was giving way to a more public and active social life. An anonymous writer in *Scribner's* detected "the growth in New York of the spirit of society . . . that instinct whose manifestations distinguish a great capital from a great centre of population merely, and are to be observed less in drawing-rooms than out-of-doors." New York had become a city of day and nighttime public promenades, of fashionable processions of carriages and pedestrians: "Now the *flâneur* seems at last to have made his appearance. New York . . . is at last taking on definite resemblance to that aspect of 'all the world' in virtue of which it is 'a stage.'"[37] While the rich enjoyed these processions which the poor could only observe with contempt or admiration, they were most important to the rising middle class, which lacked established traditions of its own. Van Rensselaer observed that in New York, the social life of the middle class

is aggravated not only by our large proportion of strangers, needing time to settle and throw out social roots, but, among strangers and natives alike, by the great cost of our soil. This means very high rents, and these mean boarding house life for multitudes of families who elsewhere would have homes of their own: it is said that half the houses within two blocks of Fifth Avenue between Thirty-fourth Street and Central Park are boarding houses of the better and more high-priced kinds. Then, by a natural reaction (or contamination), the easy-going pseudo-social life of the boarding house and cheap hotel aids our profusion of public pleasures in keeping many people contentedly adrift after they might have homes and begin to form genuine social ties. These people, and many others with small incomes who do have homes of their own (but most often in cramped, inhospitable flats), find their amusement in theatres and restaurants, and the motley pageants of the streets, or, if more soberly minded, in concert- and lecture-rooms and at church entertainments.[38]

The Composite Era brought a new sense of civic life as grand, popular theater. Restaurants, roof gardens and theaters proliferated and set the mood, but even ordinary shelters became more dramatic. A new type of hostelry, the apartment hotel, emerged to combine characteristics of the boarding house, apartment and grand hotel into a residential type perfectly suited to the transient class of upwardly mobile strangers who came to dominate the city. Restaurants, fountain courts and noon-time concerts became standard features in department stores and brought a sense of drama to the ordinary process of shopping, while public institutions such as railroad stations and banks dramatized their functions through celebratory architecture and thereby entertained the population as it went about its daily rounds.

The daily press quickly sensed that the city had been transformed not only socially but physically. The New York *World* pointed out that visitors passing through New York on their way to Chicago's Columbian Exposition in 1893 would see a vastly more beautiful city than those on their way to the Centennial Exhibition in Philadelphia in 1876, the city having transformed itself "from dreary monotonous ugliness to a beauty unmatched on this continent." This metamorphosis was attributable as much to simple business sense as to idealism. Builders had realized that "it costs little more to build after a good design than after a bad one, and the awakened desire for artistic comeliness in our dwellings and shops has, by encouragement, bred a race of competent architects among us who know how to secure beauty in a thousand inexpensive ways."[39] In 1904, the *Real Estate Record and Guide* boasted that between 1899 and 1903 an average of $120 million was spent each year on new buildings, an amount far in excess per capita than that spent in any other American city.[40] This phenomenon could be easily explained. Manhattan's long, narrow shape hindered the geographical expansion of commercial and residential districts, and much of the city's growth was thus accommodated by a continual process of rebuilding. Real estate values were driven to unprecedented heights and owners realized that a high standard of construction and design further enhanced the worth of their investment. "High-priced real estate demands buildings which are the best of their kind," the *Record and Guide* reported, "and little by little various types of buildings have been worked out which have established certain standards of design, of plan, of construction and of expense. These types of buildings are exceedingly various, and comprehend every kind of residence and business structure. They include, for instance, a standard type of office building, of loft building, of warehouse and factory, of hotel, of apartment hotel, of tenement and of private dwelling." The economic pressure was so intense that "expensive buildings are standardized in New York as they are no where else in the world, and because they are standardized they are built not merely by owners for investment but by builders in speculation."[41]

By 1890 the "sober autumnal colors" of the Cosmopolitan Era were giving way to a sparkling brightness.[42] The New York correspondent of the *American Architect and Building News* noted the sudden prevalence of light finishes,

almost gay in their pearly gray stone and pale cream-colored brick and terracotta. . . . The revolution in our idea of color is to be attributed to the growing influence upon the minds of our architects of the purest and best work of the Renaissance. . . . We have gained from our study of the past and from the refining influences of wider knowledge and broader sympathies, a power of distinguishing shades of color and shades of meaning, that were perceived and felt perhaps by past civilizations, but that have never before our time been so well understood and analyzed. Our aim is not to reconstitute any past epoch, but to take from that period the best, as we see it, and adapt it and refine it to our needs.[43]

The revival of Classicism in the plastic arts during the period 1890-1915 is commonly referred to as the American Renaissance, a term which carries with it, as does any manifestation of taxonomy in the arts, ambiguities and even the seeds of contradiction. The dominant stylistic trend of the American Renaissance has been labelled Scientific Eclecticism—the more or less archaeologically correct reproduction of elements and even entire compositions from the past, particularly from the Classical tradition.[44] As an anonymous reviewer of John Addington Symonds's *The Renaissance in Italy, The Fine Arts* (1877) discerned, the "mark" of the Renaissance lies in "the productions of the whole Western World." The lessons of Greek art and architecture, which Symonds felt lay at the core of the Italian Renaissance, were "travelling onward with ever-increasing vigor along a path which is constantly tending upwards, but whose end is lost in the dim distance of the future."[45]

While individual buildings were designed during the Cosmopolitan Era in a synthetic combination of styles, the Scientific Eclecticism of the Composite Era insisted on stylistic accuracy within a given work. The eclecticism lay on the urban scale, in the juxtaposition of buildings of different styles, because, as A.D.F. Hamlin observed,

There has thus far been found no style capable of immediate adaptation to all the variety of purposes and types of buildings of our day. And if there may be variety in the use of styles in different works by the same designer, still more must we look for variety in the works of different hands. It is hardly rational to demand uniformity in the use of historic styles in this age of rampant eclecticism in all fields of life and taste, of triumphant individualism, when authority sits so lightly on men's interests and lives; in this age of archaeology, when the different periods of history are made to live again in our imagination . . . in this age of rapid change and transition, when the garments of custom are outgrown in a day, and new discoveries overturn the established order with every decade. The universal adoption of any one historic style would be perfunctory. . . . Beyond the consistency of perfect natural harmony, which no one would claim for these juxtaposed examples of various styles, there is the higher consistency with the spirit of the time and with reason and propriety.[46]

Scientific Eclecticism was seen by its adherents as the logical next step for a nation deemed the inheritor of European civilization. Charles H. Reilly, the English apologist for American academic architecture pointed out that, "Travelled Americans have seen the monuments of the Old World and call for equal buildings at home."[47] Reilly wrote of McKim, Mead & White that since their Villard houses, "we may, perhaps, find a prototype, and generally an Italian one, for each of their larger structures. But there seems to me to be little harm in this when it is the *effect* which is copied rather than the exact *form*. The result with them has never been the lifelessness of an actual reproduction."[48] Indeed the firm's greatest works, such as the Low Library at Columbia University or Pennsylvania Station, illustrate the comment McKim made in a letter to Edith Wharton: "By conscientious study of the best examples of classic periods, including those of antiquity, it is possible to conceive a perfect result suggestive of a particular period, but . . . inspired by the study of them all."[49]

At least two other stylistic trends fell within the spirit of the term American Renaissance, if not within its literal meaning. One of these concerns us only minimally in this book: the search for a nonhistoricizing language exclusively expressive of contemporary conditions—a modernist architecture. This quest was best represented in contemporary American architecture by the works of Louis Sullivan and Frank Lloyd Wright. In one critical aspect, they shared an aspiration of the Scientific Eclectics: both groups sought to build an appropriate American architecture based on the compositional principles codified at the Ecole des Beaux-Arts in Paris. Rather than turning to the past for inspiration, however, Wright and Sullivan drew upon the theories of Viollet-le-Duc (a controversial teacher at the Ecole in the 1860s and a widely studied theorist) to synthesize the new structural possibilities of steel and reinforced concrete construction with a highly personal view of nature and an interest in various vernacular and regional architectures.

The second significant alternative to Scientific Eclecticism is more difficult to define. Known at the time as the Modern French style, it represented a view of Classicism as an on-going language. Whereas the spirit of Scientific Eclecticism was fundamentally archaeological, the Modern French was progressive, transforming the canonic elements of Classical architecture to express contemporary technology and taste. Architectural values were conceived of not as universally valid but rather at least partly relative. Charles Garnier, the French architect whose design for the Paris Opera House (1862–74) was one of the earliest and most influential examples of the style, summed up its sense of artistic freedom: "Regarding decoration as such, and regarding what ordering and style to adopt, there is no guide other than the inspiration and will of the one who is doing the building; the decorative art has such independence and freedom that it is impossible to submit it to fixed rules."[50]

To its critics, the Modern French was known as Cartouche Architecture because of its extensive use of that particular ornamental device as well as swags, garlands, festoons and a host of other overscaled motifs to enrich the facade.[51] The *Architectural Review* complained in 1897 that the style originated "from an abnormal and dropsical development of the keystone and the medallion, or heraldic escutcheon that invaded the field of architectural ornament like a bubonic plague."[52] To Montgomery Schuyler, an unsympathetic observer, it seemed "the negation of respose," connoting "something inflated and unrestrained."[53] Yet Modern French voluptuousness was perhaps an appropriate expression of a clientele that enjoyed excessive display, gastromony and girth.

While the methods of the Ecole des Beaux-Arts were theoretically divorced from issues of style, the Modern French mode dominated Parisian architecture in the 1890s. Many Americans were studying there at the time, and their eagerness to transport the style to New York sparked a battle of styles and a debate over the value of French architectural education and its appropriateness to American conditions. In an article in the *Architectural Record,* A.D.F. Hamlin praised the French for coming

nearer to a true reform in architecture than any other people. Starting with the elements of classic design, they had developed out of them a more or less rational and consistent system of treatment, in which they avoided on the one hand the academic stiffness of the Vignolesque school and on the other the extravagances of the Rococo. It had, and still retains, at least the merit of modernness and consistency, and is often used in such a manner as to acquit it of the reproach sometimes brought against it of artificiality and of want of relation to the system of construction employed. . . . The Ecole des Beaux-Arts has done much to unify the style and to give a thorough training to its practitioners and . . . it has proved the value of its instruction, independently of the special classicism it is supposed to inculcate, by such free and iconoclastic work as that of H.H. Richardson, who was trained in its ateliers, and by such buildings in Paris itself as the Trocadero and the metallic structures of the late Exposition. . . . The influence of the French School on American architecture, began in the persons of R.M. Hunt and H.H. Richardson, the pioneers of the American colony of architecture students in Paris. This influence was strongly stimulated by the Centennial Exposition of 1876, which started a veritable renaissance in American art.[54]

Ernest Flagg, a masterful interpreter of the Modern French vocabulary and one of the most articulate Americans to graduate from the Ecole des Beaux-Arts, persuasively argued for the pedagogical methods of the Ecole. "What the school does teach is a glorious Renaissance of the nineteenth century," he wrote in 1894.[55] Six years later Flagg expanded on the relationship between the education it offered and contemporary American practice, arguing that the circumstantial adaptability of the style offered the possibility of creating a specifically American modern architecture:

A revolution is in full progress among us, and it is beginning just where it ought to begin; that is, with the students. Let no one mistake the introduction of what appears to be modern French architecture as only a passing fancy to go the way of the "Richardsonian Romanesque," "Queen Anne" and "Italian Renaissance." It means much more than appears on the surface. The French resemblance is only an incident: it may indeed, soon pall and pass away, but the movement means that the principles which the French use are being introduced here, and these will last. . . . The movement means that our architects of the future will apply to the art in this country, the same logical reasoning, and that they will have the same careful preparation for the work that helps the Frenchman to lead the world in the fine arts. It also means that in the future the whole body of American architects are to work together along the same lines—to think in the same style. Thus we are about to enter upon a course which will make possible the evolution of a national style of our own, or perhaps enable us to set the fashion for the world.[56]

His argument was even persuasive enough to win over, at least for a moment, the editors of the *Architectural Record,* whose principal contributors, such as Schuyler, Sturgis and Croly, were loyal to the structural rationalism of Viollet-le-Duc or to Scientific Eclecticism:

We are so used to hearing about the "narrowness" and "clap trap" of the Ecole des Beaux-Arts and of the "official" style of modern French architecture that we are likely to forget or ignore the immense services rendered by that school to modern architecture, both in training of great French architects—not to speak of foreigners whom it has so generously received and liberally educated—and in the holding up of sound principles and generally wise and safe standards of taste. It was precisely during the reign of Napoleon and under the influence of this general awakening in architecture that the Ecole began to take the position of enlightened liberality and good taste, and that foreign, and especially American students, . . . began to frequent its courses.[57]

The Modern French style became so dominant in turn-of-the-century New York that George Maher, a modernist Chicago architect, accused New York of being a French city, with buildings which failed to "fit the design to the utilitarian idea." Maher cited the St. Regis Hotel as an example, claiming that it "destroys Americanism in the Americans who stop there. Before they know it they are talking French and shrugging their shoulders."[58] Yet as H.W. Desmond noted in the *Real Estate Record and Guide,*

If there be a distinctly modern style of value as fine art it is the French, however much one may be inclined to quarrel with it. In turning from the Romanesque and the Classic to the Modern French, American architects directed their thoughts, at any rate, from the dead to the living, from a style archaic and obsolete that had entirely passed from the world with the conditions that produced it, to a style "foreign" it may be, but alive, producing its examples and capable of contemporary explanation.

As a matter of fact, no style today is quite so "taking" with the crowd as the modern French. Its very defects are of the sort that attract the public.⁵⁹

Flagg described the more archaeological work of McKim and others who revived Roman Classicism at Chicago in 1893 as "fostered by a sickly sentimentalism,"⁶⁰ but Reilly spoke for the proponents of Scientific Eclecticism when he described the movement as "French classic, though it is classic pruned of recent French extravagancies—the *tour de force* and *l'art nouveau.*"⁶¹ Its advocates held a vision of "the splendid standards of Classic and Renaissance art" as magisterially correct. "Pity the artist," McKim wrote, "who does not feel humbled before its splendid examples of art."⁶² Because it was so clearly identified with a specific moment and place—Paris in *la Belle Epoque*—the Modern French was attacked as a foreign imposition on American practice, while Scientific Eclecticism was seen as a logical next step for a country deemed the inheritor of European civilization.⁶³

The Era of Convenience, 1915-1940

Greater New York grew at a tremendous pace during the Era of Convenience, forcing the city's architects and planners to balance the Composite Era's sense of the city as a monumental artifact with an increased awareness of the city's shortcomings as an environment in which to live and work. It was not so much that the emphasis shifted from the aesthetics of city design to the "science" of city planning, but that an attempt was made to accommodate the idealism of an older era to the very different problems of a newer, less innocent and therefore less self-confident time. Coordinated transportation systems, large-scale efforts to provide affordable housing for the lower classes and public places such as parks were all given more attention than they had been in the previous thirty or forty years. Declining immigration resulted in a reduced pool of cheap labor and forced a reconsideration of both the scale of buildings and public places and the problem of their physical maintenance. Labor-saving devices were introduced into the domestic realm on the same scale that they had been introduced into the office in the previous generation. Clothes washers and driers, electric irons, dishwashers and refrigerators, to name but a few, brought the domestic environment closer to the servantless utopia that had been a dream for almost a century.⁶⁴

The automobile and this new, liberated domesticity enabled a vast number of city dwellers to take full advantage of the opportunities inherent in the city's Metropolitanism. Ironically, the mobility brought by the self-sufficient home and the automobile shattered the Metropolitan scale of urbanism by opening a seemingly infinite region to urban and suburban development. The private automobile replaced the restrictive fixed-route, fixed-schedule transportation systems of the past with a sense of geographical freedom that subsumed the age-old order of town, village and countryside in a more or less continuous pattern of low-density suburban development. This suburban sprawl produced a new super-scale urbanism, described as Megalopolis by the planner Patrick Geddes, in which New York could only play a part, rather than the leading role.⁶⁵

While the servantless house and the automobile were the most visible expressions of the decline of the Metropolitan ideal, innovations in electronic communication were perhaps more profoundly destructive: radio, the talking movie and later television replaced the live theatre as a principal entertainment form, while improvements in telecommunications lessened the need for people to concentrate in a small area. Thus the phenomenon of technological innovation that raised the metropolis to its peak during the Composite Era ultimately caused its decline in the 1920s and 1930s.

New York's Era of Convenience was significantly dominated by legislative planning that began in 1916 with the enactment of laws to control land use and the height and bulk of buildings.⁶⁶ This reached a crescendo in 1929 with a sweeping reform of the laws controlling multiple dwellings and the first formulation of a comprehensive physical plan for the region.⁶⁷ The skills of "scientific" planning were combined with the City Beautiful movement's last burst of artistic passion, to produce a grand system of parks, parkways and planned enclaves of housing for the middle class and the poor in Manhattan, Brooklyn, the Bronx and Queens. The era closed with a grand world's fair, nervously enjoyed as the drums of impending world war beat increasingly loudly.

The canonical skyscraper was the era's most inspired building type. Initiated in the Composite Era by the Woolworth Building (1913), the type was established in the late 1920s by a cannonade of towers memorializing great corporations—McGraw-Hill, Cities Service, Chrysler, the Bank of Manhattan, the Radio Corporation of America—and the state of New York itself (the Empire State). These embodied at a metropolitan scale the synthesis of rational technology, romantic, symbolic aspirations, and decent, efficient accommodations for the day-to-day activities of business that architects had been struggling to achieve since the mid-1870s.[68] Architects in the Era of Convenience often attempted to apply the forms and efficiency of the skyscraper to complex institutional monuments such as James Gamble Rogers's Columbia Presbyterian Hospital (1927) and Coolidge, Shepley, Bulfinch & Abbott's New York Hospital (1933). Rockefeller Center (Reinhard & Hofmeister; Corbett, Harrison & Macmurray; Raymond Hood, Godley & Fouilhoux, 1931-40) marked the apotheosis of the symbolic and convenient skyscraper.[69] The most rationally planned complex of tall buildings, it offered a consolidated expression of its individual buildings and functions—from the private realm of the individual office to the public realm of the plaza and Radio City Music Hall—with careful attention paid to light and ventilation in the offices and efficient circulation within and between buildings.

Other achievements of the Era of Convenience, such as Robert Moses's parkway system on Long Island;[70] the large-scale housing projects of Andrew Jackson Thomas[71] and Clarence Stein;[72] the great skyscraper apartment houses such as the Ritz Tower, River House and the San Remo; and hotels such as the new Waldorf-Astoria combined the same characteristics. Theirs was a workable, manageable grandeur and a streamlined restatement of the values of the Composite Era in terms of the even more functional, if less confident, spirit of the post-World War I era. At the same time, these monuments marked an end to the Metropolitan ideal. Their Janus-like attitude was succinctly stated on the cornerstone of Caughey & Evans's Hampshire House on Central Park South, which proclaimed the hostelry's dedication to "yesterday's charm and tomorrow's convenience."

The spirit of Metropolitanism did not die with the stock market crash in 1929, though the twin-pronged attack of economic depression and the functionalist goals of European modernism effectively eroded its influence. Many projects built in New York in the 1930s reflected the compositional and stylistic values of the Metropolitan Era, among them the Menagerie (1934) which Aymar Embury II designed for Central Park,[73] Delano & Aldrich's Marine Air Terminal (1940) in Queens[74] and Francis S. Keally's Brooklyn Public Library (1941).[75] With the completion of the George Washington Bridge in 1931, however, a new sense of pragmatic materialism began to replace the monumental symbolism of the Metropolitan Era. While poetry had triumphed over logical planning at the Brooklyn Bridge in the early years of the Metropolitan Age, the opposite was true at the George Washington Bridge. The decision to abandon Cass Gilbert's design of romantically expressive masonry skin encasing the towers and expose the steel structure of the towers marked the end of an era of rhetorical poetics and the inauguration of matter-of-fact realism.[76] The synthesis of rationalism and romanticism inculcated at the Ecole des Beaux-Arts and nurtured in New York's Composite Era gave way to one of structural and social engineering—a philosophy born of American pragmatism though raised in Europe to the level of a moral issue amid post-World War I disillusionment. After 1945, when the city began to revive, an entirely new set of values would prevail, and the Metropolitan City would struggle for survival against the forces of megalopolitan giantism unleashed by the advocates of social and functional engineering.

Pennsylvania Station, Seventh to Eighth avenues between Thirty-first and Thirty-third streets. McKim, Mead & White, 1904–10. Waiting Room. NYHS

Civic Structure

Today there are no new worlds to find. Upon us is the responsibility never before laid on a people—building the world's capital for all time to come. What we do well will serve mankind forever; what we do ill will be a stumbling block until it is remedied. To none before us have been given such opportunities—to be used or wasted.
  John DeWitt Warner, "Matters That Suggest Themselves," *Municipal Affairs* 2 (March 1898): 123-32.

City Planning John DeWitt Warner's enthusiasm reflected the optimism that coursed through New York at the turn of the century. The social, political and economic consolidation of the city in the late 1890s sparked a vast outpouring of talent, energy and wealth which gave New York an architectural dignity and public expression to rival older world capitals. "There is a competition of cities," Charles Rollinson Lamb wrote, "of capitals as personifying countries. . . . It behooves us to realize that our representative city, New York, is under surveillance."[1]

If the idealism of the times ran high, it was checked by a daunting task; New York was still, in many ways, the most primitive of large cities. The great urban spaces of Europe—the boulevards of Paris, Vienna's Ringstrasse, London's Regent Street—were architectural harmonies imposed by fiat, the legacies of a royal past. As Charles Caffin noted in 1900, however, the fact that individualism was "the prevailing note in American character, the source of the nation's extraordinary development, and the foundation of our system of government" ran against the very idea of large scale public planning, though not of private benefaction.[2] Neils Gron, a foreign sociologist travelling to the United States, summed up New York's dilemma in the *New York Herald*: "Before I came to this country, and in all the time I have been here, it has never occurred to me to think of New York as being beautiful. Therefore, all this talk of beautifying New York seems strange to me. We expect of her power and magnificence, but not beauty. If a European came over here and found that New York was beautiful in the same way as the European cities he knew, he would be very much disappointed. I do not see how you can make New York beautiful in that way, with the laws and democratic spirit you have here. The kind of beauty that makes Paris charming can only exist where private rights and personal liberty are or have been trampled on."[3]

Individualism characterized the architecture of New York in the Cosmopolitan Era, the first major period of Metropolitan growth. Its stylistic eclecticism reflected a process of development by private exploitation of economic forces rather than public intervention, for city planning was an almost nonexistent discipline. But the example of the World's Columbian Exposition held in Chicago in 1892-93 caused a sudden flowering of the City Beautiful movement. After failed attempts ten years earlier to organize a fair in New York and the city's futile efforts to capture the Columbia Celebration for its own, the White City built in Chicago ironically represented the triumph of a vision of an imperialistic urbanism that was fostered by New York architects such as Richard Morris Hunt, George Post and McKim, Mead & White.[4]

The ideals and strategies first tested in plaster in Chicago were the logical tools with which to effect the consolidation of New York's diffuse urbanism. The forms of the Classical past were the most generally accessible physical expression of the national self-image; they connected contemporary experience with the high political ideals of the early Republic while stirring archetypal memories of Greece and Rome. Moreover, they seemed the only forms to have behind them a grammar and syntax that suggested strategies sophisticated enough to implement the kinds of planning reforms that had been discussed since the 1880s but were only now about to be realized.

The impact of the Chicago Fair took a number of distinct forms in New York: it legitimized the Classical approach to individual building design, encouraged those involved with important institutional buildings to see their responsibilities at a larger scale than that of the individual building, and fostered a gradual move toward comprehensive urban planning. While individual buildings such as McKim, Mead & White's Villard houses and the Century Club had anticipated the new Classicism, and their plan for Columbia University soon realized the Chicago Fair's sense of ensemble in permanent form, it was Richard Morris Hunt who set in place the mechanism for public action by founding the Municipal Art Society, a group of public-spirited architects, artists and reform-minded citizens soon joined

Proposed reading room for an elevated railroad station at Herald Square. National Sculpture Society, 1899. Perspective. CU

Proposed improvements, New York City Improvement Commission, 1904. General Plan. CU

by like-minded groups in a broad-based campaign for urban beautification.[5]

At the first meeting of the Municipal Art Society, the artist Edwin H. Blashfield issued a "Plea for Municipal Art" in which he urged New Yorkers to regard the Chicago Fair as a "colossal object lesson." "New York," Blashfield argued, "must wish that some grand buildings should be translated into enduring stone . . . the good time is coming. May not we . . . stand at the beginning of a movement in which architecture, sculpture, painting crystallized together as one immense factor, may be enlisted in the city's service to outlast the great exhibition."[6] Blashfield's aesthetic view, more a reaction to the fair's synthesis of architecture and decorative art than to the ensemble as an urban model, was symptomatic of the society's initial purpose: "to provide adequate sculptural and pictorial decorations for the public buildings and parks of the city of New York."[7] Their piecemeal efforts were decorative at best, and often grandiose, though rarely so eccentric as the National Sculpture Society's suggestion for a domed reading room at the elevated railroad station at Herald Square.[8] Quickly, however, a larger conception of the challenge emerged.

A growing tide of public sentiment for a comprehensive plan that would serve as a framework for private and public efforts at beautification was reflected in the founding of two magazines by the New York Reform Club: *Municipal Affairs* in 1897 and *Public Improvements* in 1901. In 1898, the year of the city's consolidation, the architect Julius Harder wrote in *Municipal Affairs* that "civic pride and interest in municipal affairs will in time evolve a logical city plan." Harder presented his own ideas in a plan for a new civic center located on an expanded Union Square, linked to major arteries by new diagonal streets which would serve to connect major transportation nodes with manufacturing districts. "The system of diagonal avenues results, aside from its practical and economical superiority, in conditions known as 'Vistas.' These occur not only at the actual point of intersection with others of their own kind, where the area of intersection necessarily becomes so large that its center may be occupied by a structure of importance, but also at their intersection with every street of the rectangular system by affording greater length of vision and bringing larger objects or an increased aggregate within the extended angle of sight. In general, the view, instead of terminating in a perspective

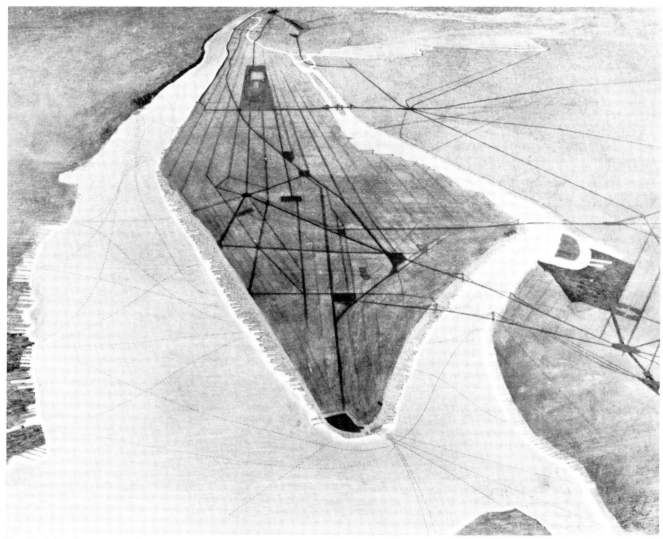

New York City Improvement Commission Plan, 1907. Bird's eye perspective looking north. CU

nothing, rests upon an object. These several objective points will be occupied by monumental structures, as the sites become proportionately valuable, through their importance commercially, so as to warrrant the erection of buildings of the first class upon them."[9]

The plan made it apparent that the introduction of any new streets that cut across the gridiron plan would be extremely disruptive to the city's fabric, and that the commercial nature of the city was at odds with the prevailing conception of a city as a monumental place. Harder attempted to defend the plan in terms of long-range public good: "While it is true that the execution of radical measures must result inevitably in greater restrictions upon individuals and corporations, and thus interferes with that liberty which is the essence of American institutions, the resulting increased value of the whole returns again to the greater number."[10]

Harder's plan also called for restructuring the gridiron plan in undeveloped areas of the city, creating a system of secondary avenues and small, square blocks open at the center to allow for service entries and sunlight. Though wildly ambitious, the plan was an early attempt in the City Beautiful movement to consider aesthetics in conjunction with health and sanitary requirements.[11]

From the first it was realized that Manhattan's gridiron plan worked against any conventional concept of the monumental. Ernest Flagg wrote of the commissioners who had drawn up the plan that was adopted in 1811: "To them the great city of the future was to be simply an enlargement of the primitive town of their own day . . . their one desire seems to have been to make use of every available square foot of land for strictly utilitarian purposes. . . . Of artistic thought there was not a suggestion."[12] Their plan, Flagg continued, had "lain like a huge gridiron on the city, binding it to hopeless monotony and humdrum commercialism of aspect, and acting as a barrier to any attempt to impart to the town that grand metropolitan air which distinguishes most of the great capitals of Europe."[13] But the gridiron was long established and unable to accommodate those points of congestion where building activity and land values were concentrated.

Flagg's own proposal for New York was just as ambitious as Harder's, although his approach to the modification of the grid was completely different. His plans called for a

Proposed parkway for Delancey Street. New York City Improvement Commission, 1904. Perspective view from the Williamsburg Bridge. CU

continuous greenbelt up the center of Manhattan modelled on Paris's Champs-Elysée or Berlin's Unter den Linden.[14] Flagg's nine-hundred-foot wide parkway between Sixth and Seventh avenues was to extend from Fourteenth Street to the Harlem River, sweeping away all in its path but the portion of Central Park which fell within its swath. Flagg viewed the park as an obstruction to the northward movement of development and traffic and wanted to sell the unused portion of the park to finance the scheme. But his objections to Central Park went deeper than the mere inconvenience caused by its interruption of the grid; a true disciple of the French rationalism, he objected to the park's artificial naturalism and what he deemed its suburban character, its rural space seen in contrast to the buildings surrounding it. Flagg's massive landscaped boulevard would have logically, if brutally, brought greenery in close daily contact with many citizens, yet the thought of digging up the park, which was already a popular and well used landmark, was surely nothing short of mad. Mad also, was his plan to demolish the Sixth Avenue department stores and the numerous theaters, hotels and apartment houses that stood in the way of the scheme. Amazingly, the plan was taken seriously; the *Real Estate Record and Guide* deemed it "the only really grandiose project yet suggested which possesses even the semblance of being practical."[15] Sympathetic discussion by critics such as Russell Sturgis attested to the community's receptivity to bold proposals and a sense of desperation in the face of what was coming to be perceived as irreconcilable differences between the Commissioners' Plan of 1811 and the ideals of the City Beautiful.[16]

The confusion of these uncoordinated schemes created a demand for a comprehensive plan that would consider all the problems of traffic, transportation and housing which plagued the newly consolidated city. Countless editorials in newspapers, particularly the *New York Times, New York Herald,* and *New York Tribune,* took up the call.[17] The *Times* proposed in 1902 the formation of a commission to draw up a city plan, suggesting that Charles F. McKim and Augustus Saint-Gaudens, New York residents who had worked on the McMillan Commission's city plan for Washington, D.C., act in similar capacities in New York.[18]

Seth Low's election as mayor in 1901 provided the movement with government recognition. Low, a member of the Municipal Art Society who had already demonstrated his commitment to the ideals of the City Beautiful on a large scale by commissioning McKim to design the new Columbia campus on Morningside Heights, was instrumental in establishing the Municipal Art Commission with a provision in the 1898 charter.[19] Later, in January 1903, a broad planning agenda was drawn up at a temporary conference organized at the mayor's request by the Municipal Art Society: its report has been characterized as "the first comprehensive survey of New York City's present and long-range improvement needs."[20]

In response, Low organized a New York City Improvement Commission which in 1904 presented a preliminary report enumerating a list of topics that a comprehensive plan must address "if New York is to take its place as one of the great Metropolitan Cities of the World." Principal among these were the "laying out of parks, streets and highways, the location of city buildings, [and] improvement of water fronts," features intended to fit together in such a manner "that all its parts shall be consistent, the one with the other, and form a homogeneous whole."[21]

While the report and its 1907 successor have frequently been compared unfavorably with Chicago's Plan of 1909, it was not without some audacious proposals, including an elevated highway along the Hudson River waterfront (not realized until 1931) and coordinated pier development in Chelsea which could combine the usual commercial facilities and the new elevated roadway with rooftop recreational parks. The acquisition of parkland was advocated, particularly in the rapidly developing sections of upper Manhattan and the Bronx; there were additional proposals for parks in the other boroughs where the development pressures were far less intense.

While no comprehensive, coordinated transportation plan was included in the report, a number of ingenious solutions to specific problems of congestion were proposed, among them a rather naive suggestion by Carrère & Hastings for a grade separation at the intersection of Forty-

Delancey Street, 1904. View looking toward the Williamsburg Bridge. CU

second Street and Fifth Avenue. More impressive were the proposals for various bridge terminals. A subway loop and terminal for the Queensboro Bridge and a transformation of Delancey Street at the foot of the Williamsburg Bridge into a landscaped parkway were complexly conceived responses to the problems brought about by traffic concentration at the bridges.

The commissioners also struggled to evolve a coherent plan for a civic center around City Hall, which the report emphatically described as "one of the few good monuments possessed by the City."[22] This observation in itself was important. For only fifteen years earlier the city fathers had proposed its demolition and replacement with a more commodious building that would meet the needs of an expanding bureaucracy. Nonetheless the report's basically aesthetic bent prompted Herbert Croly's scathing criticism: "The ugly actual cities of today make a livelier appeal to the imagination than does an ideal city, which in sacrificing its ugliness on the altar of civic art, sacrifices also its proper character and vitality.... The vision of a local pseudo-classic Beaux-Artist New Jerusalem... seems... a very insipid ideal. For me the skyscraper and the furnace-stack."[23]

The commission's life was extended for three years. In 1907 it submitted a final report, notorious for its emphasis on aesthetic issues at the expense of specific planning issues that directly affected the everyday lives of the bulk of the citizenry, such as zoning and housing standards.[24] Perhaps because the plan was so singleminded in its emphasis on the physical beautification of the city, it was not forgotten; its failings still seemed glaring enough in 1924 to merit Lewis Mumford's attention in his book *Sticks and Stones,* where it was castigated for its "pages and pages" devoted "to showing the improvement that would follow the demolition of the wall around Central Park—and the importance of clipped trees on the design of the grand avenues!"[25]

The city planner George B. Ford offered a somewhat more measured assessment of the report and the City Beautiful movement in a lecture delivered at Columbia University in 1911 that marked a milestone in the shift from the second to the third stage of Metropolitanism. "America," Ford stated ironically, "is the only country that has devoted its attention in planning its centers of population almost exclusively to the aesthetic side. In America the cry has been 'The City Beautiful.' Abroad it has been 'The City Logical, Convenient!'"[26]

The 1907 plan was not nearly so sweeping as Chicago's 1909 plan nor as comprehensive as its early formulation, and though its final publication was something of an anticlimax, it does bear some scrutiny. Many of its proposals were sound, and some prefigured improvements actually realized. The circular Bridge Plaza that would have united the Brooklyn approaches to the Manhattan and Brooklyn bridges, and the boulevard intended to link Prospect Park and the Brooklyn Municipal Center, were both worthwhile proposals, as was the plan's boldest stroke—the widening of Fifty-ninth Street into a topiaried boulevard connecting Central Park with the Queensboro Bridge, the conversion of Blackwell's Island into a park, and the conclusion of the axis with an *étoile* in Queens. Parkways connecting the parklands of the outer boroughs with the inner-city areas in Brooklyn and Manhattan were based on ideas initially proposed by Frederick Law Olmsted in the 1860s but enlarged to an appropriately metropolitan scale to form one of the plan's chief glories. While the overall intention was to foster the unity of the newly consolidated city, the individuality of each borough was expressed by symbolic gateways that were also functional and facilitated the flow of traffic at critical points of congestion.

The 1907 plan represented New York's most comprehensive effort to establish a civic identity akin to that of Paris or Vienna. Given the complexity of the problem, it is arguable that the plan failed because it was at once too early and too late. Too late, because by 1907 the great urban set pieces were in place or well underway: the public library, Grand Central and Pennsylvania stations, and the development of an "acropolis of learning" on Morningside Heights. Too early, because the grand scale of the parks, parkways and boulevards would not seem urgently needed until the automobile became an everyday thing thirty years later. It can be said, however, that the plan did represent a public affirmation of the need for an artistic response to a complex urban condition.

Proposed Bridge Plaza, Brooklyn. New York City Improvement Commission, 1907. Bird's eye perspective looking west. CU

The aesthetic concerns of the 1907 plan were countered in the same year by the founding of a Committee on Congestion of Population in New York. Benjamin C. Marsh, the committee secretary, shifted attention away from issues of beautification to "the securing of decent home conditions for the countless thousands who otherwise can only occasionally escape from their confining surroundings to view the architectural perfection and to experience the aesthetic delights of the remote improvements."[27]

In March 1908, the committee organized an exhibition on city planning at the American Museum of Natural History which came to be called the Congestion Show because of the many charts, maps and models that made all too vivid the enormous growth of cities in the previous twenty-five years.[28] Recognizing that the expanding subway system was fostering rather than relieving congestion and that it was allowing tenements to sprout in undeveloped areas of the city, the exhibit proposed a variety of solutions: among them the distribution of factories throughout the city in zones surrounded by working-class housing built with parks and recreational facilities, and the creation of model villages on unused parcels of land within the city limits. The exhibition brought before the public the shift from the aesthetic ideals of the City Beautiful of the previous decade to a new, more socially responsible, more scientific and pragmatic approach of the City Convenient.[29]

In a similar vein, the Russell Sage Foundation was founded in 1907 with a generous endowment committed to the improvement of the physical environment of the masses.[30] Its first project, the planned suburb of Forest Hills Gardens, Queens, was designed by Frederick Law Olmsted, Jr. and Grosvenor Atterbury as a realization of the model village concept forwarded at the Congestion Show. However, the foundation's eventual role in the creation of the Regional Plan Association hastened the demise of the Metropolitanism it had once nurtured by decentralizing political control of the metropolitan region.[31]

The development of mass transportation made possible the spread of tenements and the development of suburbs in the Bronx and on Long Island, sparking fears in Brooklyn for the borough's continued residential character and its individual identity within Greater New York. These concerns led a group of Brooklyn civic leaders and officials to commission Edward H. Bennett, collaborator with Daniel Burnham on the 1909 Chicago Plan, to prepare a city plan for Brooklyn. Bennett focused on the rejuvenation of the borough's downtown district, with a proposal for a new civic center around Borough Hall and Flatbush Avenue developed as the prime business and retail center (parks and shoreline drives were also proposed).[32] While the city's 1907 planning report had reflected an optimistic glorification of consolidation, the 1912 plan for Brooklyn, though still relying on the aesthetic strategies of the City Beautiful movement, reflected a growing recognition of dangers that accelerated development had brought.

The era of the Composite City was brought to a close in New York in 1911, when the city government turned its attention from issues of beautification to the problems brought about by the enormous height and bulk of the new skyscrapers and the incursions of manufacturing activities into prime residential and commercial neighborhoods, particularly in the vicinity of Fifth Avenue above Union and Madison squares.[33] The concerns of the new era had been foreshadowed by Croly, whose comments on the failure of the 1907 report had touched on the contradictory values of the times: "The interest of the real estate speculator demands congestion and concentration of business and population, which enormously increases real estate values along particular lines and at particular points, while the interest of the whole people in a beautiful and convenient city demands the distribution of population and business in the most liberal manner and according to an organic plan."[34]

De facto zoning in the form of protective convenants had existed in certain parts of the city long before the agitation for a comprehensive, municipally administered ordinance began. Large landholders imposed severe restrictions on the character of the development permitted on their property. The blocks just west of Fifth Avenue in the fifties, for example, had been owned in different parts by Columbia College and the Willetts and Stevens families, who left restrictive covenants which resulted in remarkably coherent blocks. Nonetheless, incompatible uses frequently

Proposed improvements to Fifty-ninth Street between Fifth Avenue and Queensboro Bridge. New York City Improvement Commission, 1907. Perspective from Fifth Avenue. CU

threatened such enclaves at their edges; livery stables were a common and particularly obnoxious building type plaguing fashionable residential neighborhoods.

Shops and other commercial establishments were also a problem: "the cheapest and commonest kind of retail business" at two of the four corners of Fifth Avenue and Forty-fifth Street prevented the street from becoming a fashionable residential street like those around it.[35] The construction of public facilities such as Grand Central Terminal in residential areas resulted in a major interruption in the surrounding neighborhoods. Not only did Grand Central introduce what the *Real Estate Record and Guide* labeled "discordant sights and sounds in the very heart of residence [sic] localities," it also closed ten streets, thereby producing a "notorious invasion of private rights and damage of neighborhood."[36] Before the 1890s, even hotels and apartment buildings were seen as dubious assets in the residential context. Despite these concerns, however, few property owners were willing to establish protective covenants, because the very stability they assured was seen in the long run as a drawback. New York real estate was first and foremost an asset; because of the seemingly inexorable northward growth of the commercial districts "all New York house-owners look forward to the period when their present residence localities will be required for the uses of business," according to the *Record and Guide*.[37] More than any other single factor, this idea of a "migratory method of growth" militated against the establishment of any kind of planning controls.[38]

In 1911 the Commission on Congestion of Population, created the previous year at Benjamin Marsh's entreaty, found that congestion was the result of towering office buildings and urged the immediate imposition of height restrictions, even before the preparation of a city plan.[39] The suggestion of legal controls met with wide support from the city's retailers, as the manufacturing district seemed to encroach inexorably on the fashionable residential and shopping districts north of Thirty-fourth Street and left the former shopping and residential district below Twenty-third Street reduced to an area devoted to manufacturing, mostly in the so-called needle trades. The *Real Estate Record and Guide* observed that if the garment factories established themselves between Thirty-fourth and Fifty-ninth streets "people living there would have to move out, abandoning their homes; the principal retail section would be ruined; the hotels would lose their guests, and New York City as a whole would receive a death blow."[40]

The Merchants Association, a coalition of commercial and civic groups brought together by the Fifth Avenue Association, organized a City Planning Exhibition held in 1913 at the New York Public Library.[41] The exhibit included material from two hundred cities and demonstrated a wide public support for city planning, later touring America and France.

By 1916 the city's major retailers resorted to more drastic action, forming a Save New York committee and declaring in advertisements their intention to save the city "from unnatural and unnecessary crowding, from depopulated sections, from being a City unbeautiful, from high rents, from excessive and illy distributed taxation."[42] Their remedy was to announce a boycott, effective February 1, 1917, of any manufacturer whose factory was located in a zone extending from Thirty-third Street to Fifty-ninth Street between Third and Seventh avenues.

The extra-legal actions of the Save New York campaign were largely successful in preventing new incursions and forcing established manufacturers to relocate, primarily to Long Island City and the district south of Pennsylvania Station. In the interim, however, the Board of Estimate adopted a zoning resolution which for the first time regulated the city's density. Prepared by the Commission on Building Districts and Regulations, headed by the lawyer Edward M. Bassett with George Ford as consultant, the resolution established three types of use districts—residential, business and unrestricted—and five categories of bulk districts. "What a few years ago would have been ridiculed as fantastic, arbitrary, and confiscatory," Robert H. Whitten observed in 1917, "is now welcomed by the property owners themselves as reasonable and absolutely necessary in the interest of public health, safety and general welfare and for the conservation of property values."[43]

The 1916 document typified New York in its provision

Proposed improvements to Fifty-ninth Street between Fifth Avenue and Queensboro Bridge. New York City Improvement Commission, 1907. Perspective view of the Manhattan entrance to the Queensboro Bridge. CU

for regulation of planning in the form of zoning without any overall plan except for the gridiron of the 1811 commissioners and the character of the city as it had pragmatically evolved. In order to render the resolution invulnerable to legal challenge, the land uses and building density legislated for an area were typically those already established in it—a fact which tended to preclude even sociologically desirable changes and to allow little latitude for the demands of the city's long term growth.[44]

The resolution's bulk restrictions were its most novel component. In addition to setting minimum standards for yards and courts, it limited the height of a building at the street line to a varying multiple of the street width. A building could be carried higher with a prescribed ratio of setbacks, and an area of the building one-fourth the size of the lot could be built to any height desired.

The establishment of a spatial envelope within which the building must fit was the culmination of efforts extending back into the 1890s to secure adequate light and ventilation in the new vertical city, and at the same time to recapture the sense of a coherent streetscape that had been lost in the highly individualistic post-Civil War and Cosmopolitan eras. The *Architectural Review* predicted in 1918 that "the actual result of putting these regulations into effect will be to make the streets of New York City both more beautiful and more harmonious. Providing, as it does, all encouragement and incentive for the use of towers and terraced roofs, it at the same time works toward a uniform cornice line, that in residential sections should gradually produce the same effect that is now so pleasantly obvious on the streets of Paris."[45] By fixing cornice lines and encouraging construction up to the street line, the 1916 zoning resolution had the effect of institutionalizing the street-oriented urbanism of the Composite Era and imposing a far greater degree of civic order than even the most visionary exponents of the City Beautiful movement could ever have hoped to achieve.

Transportation

No other city in the world is improving itself at the rate which New York is doing. We have under way tunnels, bridges, reservoirs, public buildings, new driveways and new parks, the total cost of which is literally stupendous. It is all improving the metropolis on a scale and at a rapid pace not equalled anywhere else in the world. Ten years hence New York will be transformed. Ours is a wonderful city to advance. From the *New York Sun,* quoted in the *American Architect and Building News* 73 (July 6, 1901): 5-7

New York City's transportation facilities were originally conceived of in strictly utilitarian terms, but the massive expansion and building program at the turn of the century coincided with a period of corporate bravado and aesthetic idealism which demanded a sense of civic grandeur in the projects. The great train stations, the bridges and the subway systems constructed at the time were designed not simply to allow movement through the city, but to celebrate it. Synthesizing the strategies of the American Renaissance and City Beautiful with the most recent advances in technology, architects in turn-of-the-century New York translated transportation problems of unprecedented magnitude into symbolic gateways that lent the city much of its public identity.

Railroads

Grand Central Terminal and Pennsylvania Station achieved an appropriate sense of public place through a remarkable reconciliation of traditional form with the techniques of modern production. Together, as Carl Condit observed, the two stations, "from their conspicuous architectural features to their hidden elements, possessed a grandeur and a power that placed them in the front rank of modern technical-artistic achievements. They are . . . the greatest architectural-engineering works ever undertaken in the United States. They are the centerpieces of a rail and waterway network of unprecedented magnitude and complexity."[46]

Grand Central Terminal, planned by Reed & Stem in association with Warren & Wetmore, was a more thoughtfully conceived piece of urban architecture than Pennsylvania Station.[47] Its underground corridors, which paved the way for future connections with neighboring hotels, restaurants and offices (many of them planned and developed by the railroad) as well as with the subway, established the

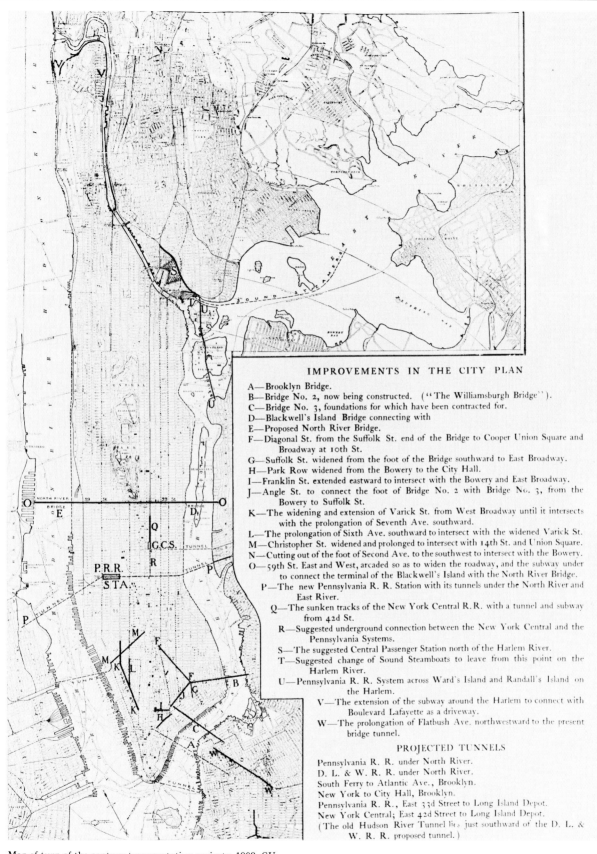

Map of turn-of-the-century transportation projects. 1903. CU

IMPROVEMENTS IN THE CITY PLAN

A—Brooklyn Bridge.
B—Bridge No. 2, now being constructed. ("The Williamsburgh Bridge").
C—Bridge No. 3, foundations for which have been contracted for.
D—Blackwell's Island Bridge connecting with
E—Proposed North River Bridge.
F—Diagonal St. from the Suffolk St. end of the Bridge to Cooper Union Square and Broadway at 10th St.
G—Suffolk St. widened from the foot of the Bridge southward to East Broadway.
H—Park Row widened from the Bowery to the City Hall.
I—Franklin St. extended eastward to intersect with the Bowery and East Broadway.
J—Angle St. to connect the foot of Bridge No. 2 with Bridge No. 3, from the Bowery to Suffolk St.
K—The widening and extension of Varick St. from West Broadway until it intersects with the prolongation of Seventh Ave. southward.
L—The prolongation of Sixth Ave. southward to intersect with the widened Varick St.
M—Christopher St. widened and prolonged to intersect with 14th St. and Union Square.
N—Cutting out of the foot of Second Ave. to the southwest to intersect with the Bowery.
O—59th St. East and West, arcaded so as to widen the roadway, and the subway under to connect the terminal of the Blackwell's Island with the North River Bridge.
P—The new Pennsylvania R. R. Station with its tunnels under the North River and East River.
Q—The sunken tracks of the New York Central R.R. with a tunnel and subway from 42d St.
R—Suggested underground connection between the New York Central and the Pennsylvania Systems.
S—The suggested Central Passenger Station north of the Harlem River.
T—Suggested change of Sound Steamboats to leave from this point on the Harlem River.
U—Pennsylvania R. R. System across Ward's Island and Randall's Island on the Harlem.
V—The extension of the subway around the Harlem to connect with Boulevard Lafayette as a driveway.
W—The prolongation of Flatbush Ave. northwestward to the present bridge tunnel.

PROJECTED TUNNELS

Pennsylvania R. R. under North River.
D. L. & W. R. R. under North River.
South Ferry to Atlantic Ave., Brooklyn.
New York to City Hall, Brooklyn.
Pennsylvania R. R., East 33d Street to Long Island Depot.
New York Central; East 42d Street to Long Island Depot.
(The old Hudson River Tunnel lies just southward of the D. L. & W. R. R. proposed tunnel.)

Grand Central Terminal, north side of Forty-second Street at Park Avenue. Bradford L. Gilbert, 1898–1900. View from north with exposed train tracks. MCNY

entire complex as a city in microcosm. *Architecture* called Grand Central and its related developments "probably the largest . . . and most successful combination of the esthetic and practical city building yet planned in America."[48] The complex stretched north of Forty-second Street for several blocks while its tracks spread almost as far east as Lexington Avenue. Its compact mass, elevated on a podium which allowed Park Avenue to flow around the building and its monumental public spaces, unconditionally established Grand Central as the symbolic gateway to the city.

The present Grand Central Terminal is the second building on the site. The original was erected in 1871, at the time of the consolidation of the New York Central lines. In 1898–1900 the station was extensively renovated and enlarged, although its inherent functional and symbolic inadequacies were still apparent.[49] Plans were already underway for its replacement when a serious accident on January 22, 1902, in the steam-filled Park Avenue tunnel, killed seventeen passengers and prompted the state to pass a law requiring the railroad to electrify its track south of the Harlem River. The same law permitted the city to allow the railroad the use of subsurface areas of the public streets in the terminal district. But the decision to build a new station was neither completely altruistic nor even functionally determined, since New York Central management realized that the impending tunnel construction under the Hudson River by the rival Pennsylvania Railroad would seriously challenge their dominance of the lucrative New York market.[50]

The genius behind the technological innovations of the new Grand Central was William J. Wilgus, Central-Hudson's chief engineer, who proposed a complete reconstruction of the terminal facilities. Sufficient data was prepared under his direction by January 15, 1903, for the railroad to solicit design proposals from a number of architects, including McKim, Mead & White of New York, Daniel Burnham of Chicago and Reed & Stem of St. Paul. McKim, already involved with the Pennsylvania Station design, passed the job of preparing the firm's submission to Stanford White, who proposed a fourteen-story building supporting a sixty-story tower. Crowned by a jet of steam driven three hundred feet into the air and illuminated red at night, the tower would have been the world's tallest and the city's most prominent landmark—if it had been built.[51]

Grand Central Terminal, north side of Forty-second Street at Park Avenue. Reed & Stem and Warren & Wetmore, 1903–13. View from Forty-second Street. MCNY

Reed & Stem were selected as winners of the competition, but after their plan and design were approved by the city in June 1903 they were "persuaded" by William K. Vanderbilt, Chairman of the Board of the New York Central, to relinquish their role as chief designers to Vanderbilt's cousin, Whitney Warren, and his partner, Charles D. Wetmore. In the final design of Grand Central, Reed & Stem contributed the articulation of Grand Central's elaborate circulation system, but it was unquestionably Warren who raised the complex to the level of compelling art.[52]

The main facade was one of the glories of the Modern French style in America. The three arched portals flanked by attached columns were clearly a triple repetition of the Arc du Triomphe du Carrousel at the Louvre in Paris and served as a symbolic triumphal arch for the railroad. Although Warren derived the elements of the composition from the Arc du Carrousel, he vastly increased their size while reducing the amount of detail. The majestic result showed the evolution of the Modern French taste since the completion of Warren & Wetmore's New York Yacht Club in 1899. The Yacht Club had three arched windows framed by pilasters, but its elaborate ornament almost overwhelmed the small building. In contrast, Grand Central had large masses with relatively small concentrations of ornament. Only Jules-Alexis Coutan's "monument to the glory of commerce as typified by Mercury, supported by moral and mental energy—Hercules and Minerva" was an exception.[53]

Inside, Warren reduced the wall to its essentials. The towering piers in the main concourse were immensely powerful, rising up without capitals to support a large but very simple entablature. They screened a Piranesian ramp system which guided the traveller down to the lower levels, and were crowned by a bold egg and dart cornice which in place of eggs had spotlights illuminating the astronomical mural painted on the vaulted ceiling with stars, lit from behind, to mark the constellations.

Reed & Stem's decision to elevate the central pavilion and its surrounding roadway was a stroke of genius. It was, however, initially abandoned by Warren who called for the terminal and office building to be set back behind a plaza facing Forty-second Street, with a second major square along its east facade on the future site of the Commodore Hotel. The viaduct in Reed & Stem's original proposal was not completed until 1919.[54] The system connecting northern

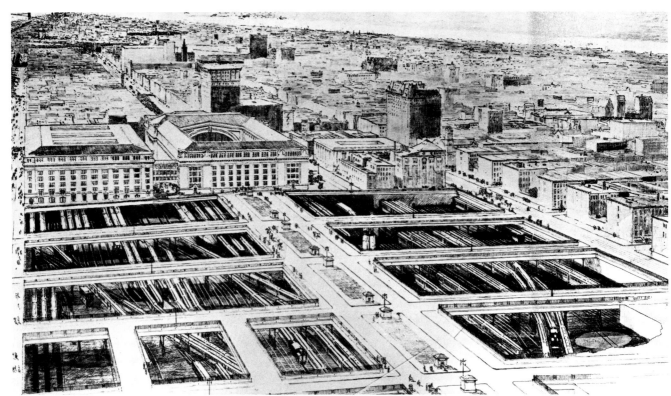
Grand Central Terminal, north side of Forty-second Street at Park Avenue. Reed & Stem and Warren & Wetmore, 1903–13. Perspective from north showing property available for air-rights development. MCNY

Grand Central Terminal, north side of Forty-second Street at Park Avenue. Reed & Stem and Warren & Wetmore, 1903–13. Sectional perspective. CU

Grand Central Terminal, north side of Forty-second Street at Park Avenue. Reed & Stem and Warren & Wetmore, 1903-13. Concourse. MCNY

Grand Central Terminal, north side of Forty-second Street at Park Avenue. Reed & Stem and Warren & Wetmore, 1903-13. Concourse detail. MCNY

Pennsylvania Station, Seventh to Eighth avenues between Thirty-first and Thirty-third streets. McKim, Mead & White, 1904–10. View from northeast. MCNY

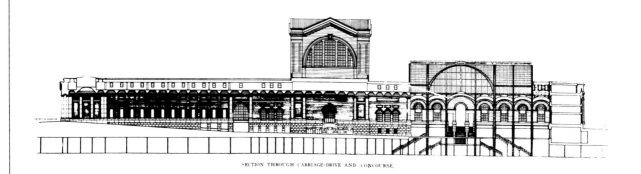

SECTION THROUGH CARRIAGE-DRIVE AND CONCOURSE.

Pennsylvania Station, Seventh to Eighth avenues between Thirty-first and Thirty-third streets. McKim, Mead & White, 1904–10. Section through Carriage Drive and Concourse. CU

and southern Park Avenue was not completed until 1928, when the final link was incorporated in Warren & Wetmore's twenty-eight-story tower for the New York Central Company, with two giant portals accommodating ramps to raise the Park Avenue traffic to the level of the viaduct.[55]

In addition to the variety of facilities available at the station, including those for dining, recreation and culture, the buildings that were constructed on the air rights (many connected to the station by underground concourses) included a post office, two hotels, a Y.M.C.A., private clubs, a major exhibition facility (Grand Central Palace) and numerous office buildings. Wilgus's concept for the development of air rights over the railroad tracks to the east, west and north of the terminal was as brilliant as the building itself. At the core of the development, known as *Terminal City*, was a bold conception of Park Avenue freed from the deleterious effects of belching steam and transformed into a broad boulevard with a mall through its center wide enough for pedestrians to stroll along surrounded by greenery.[56] The avenue was initially intended to be flanked by continuous blocks of five-story buildings that served as bases for thirteen-story towers to be set back a distance from the street. These height controls were supplanted by those of the zoning ordinance of 1916, which produced a nearly uniform cornice at the thirteenth story along the entire length of the avenue and transformed it into the most extensive expression of the ideals of the City Beautiful ever realized. The apartment houses and hotels that were built north to Forty-ninth Street together with the New York Central Building enabled the railroad to realize the Court of Honor concept originally conceived by Reed & Stem in 1903, although on a less ambitious scale.[57]

Pennsylvania Station's significance as an integrated work of architecture and engineering was never accompanied by the exploitation of the station's potential as an urban focus that marked Grand Central's *Terminal City*. McKim, Mead & White rose to the challenge to create an extraordinary monument for the city and the railroad by designing one of their most powerful buildings, but Pennsylvania Station was not blessed with Grand Central's dynamic location. From the first, it was seen as what the *Architectural Record* described as a "project of reclamation as well as 'reclame,'" an important step in the process of decentralization.[58] Together with the General Post Office at

40

Pennsylvania Station, Seventh to Eighth avenues between Thirty-first and Thirty-third streets. McKim, Mead & White, 1904-10. Concourse. NYHS

its rear, it was expected to foster a new civic center in the west-midtown area.[59] Yet aside from the hotel which the railroad built and operated on Seventh Avenue, and the department stores and hotels which clustered somewhat far away at Herald Square, the neighborhood languished.

Pennsylvania Station suffered as well from its own vastness: even though *Terminal City* was a much larger complex, Grand Central Terminal was a smaller depot than Pennsylvania Station. McKim, the partner in charge of the project, had only the precedent of Victor Laloux's plans for the Gare d'Orleans in Paris behind him as he explored the possibilities for multilevel design inherent in a station serving electrified equipment. (The design of Grand Central, begun after Pennsylvania Station, was moreover a terminal and not a station—trains did not continue there but terminated.)[60] The absence of steam engines allowed McKim to design the first great railroad station without the characteristic symbol of its nineteenth-century predecessors, the vast, glazed shed. Nevertheless, McKim did provide a glazed concourse, juxtaposed with a Classical waiting room loosely based on the Baths of Caracalla in Rome. Schuyler and others criticized the two different styles of the concourse and the waiting room, calling them contradictory.[61] But they could also be seen as an explicit statement of McKim's belief in the continuity of Classical form. Thomas Wolfe found it timeless:

The station, as he entered it, was murmurous with the immense and distant sound of time. Great, slant beams of moted light fell ponderously athwart the station's floor and the calm voice of time hovered along the walls and ceiling of that mighty room, distilled out of the voices and movements of the people who swarmed beneath. It had the murmur of a distant sea, the languorous lapse and flow of waters on a beach. It was elemental, detached, indifferent to the lives of men. They contributed to it as drops of rain contribute to a river that draws its flood and movement majestically from great depths, out of purple hills at evening.

Few buildings are vast enough to hold the sound of time, and . . . there was a superb fitness in the fact that the one which held it better than all others should be a railroad station. For here, as nowhere else on earth, men were brought together for a moment at the beginning or end of their innumerable journeys, here one saw their greetings and farewells, here, in a single instant, one got the entire picture of human destiny. Men came

Pennsylvania Station, Seventh to Eighth avenues between Thirty-first and Thirty-third streets. McKim, Mead & White, 1904-10. Arcade. CU

and went, they passed and vanished, all were moving through the moments of their lives to death, all made small tickings in the sound of time—but the voice of time remained aloof and unperturbed, a drowsy and eternal murmur below the immense and distant roof.[62]

McKim wrapped both halls in a low monumental building that formed a perimeter wall around the large block.[63] The waiting room rose above the center of the block, lit by eight enormous thermal windows visible from the street, while the concourse sat in a glazed court between the waiting room and the low building on Eighth Avenue. The passage from Seventh Avenue to the waiting room and concourse was a long, carefully modulated system of arcades and corridors that provided a sequence of spaces varying from low to high, narrow to wide, as circulation patterns required swift movement or allowed relaxation. Very clear on paper, and eloquent to those familiar with the station, the sequence was confusing to weary travellers like Arnold Bennett, the English novelist who is said to have remarked that "everything could be found there except the trains."[64] But the traveller arriving by taxi found the station uniquely convenient, with covered ramps (one for arriving and one for departing passengers) descending from the two Seventh Avenue corners to the level of the waiting room. The implication that these sunken drives were the canals of the new city was made explicit by the Venetian-style bridges which carried pedestrians into the building at its midpoint.

The blighting effect of the railroad on the cityscape resulted in a major project for civic improvement on the city's West Side, which continued to absorb popular attention long after the other proposals of the 1907 city plan had been forgotten. The West Side Improvement Project addressed the problem of the exposed tracks of the New York Central Railroad's freight division along the western edge of Riverside Park. The unsightly railroad, in addition to creating noise and fumes, cut the waterfront off from Olmsted's sensitively planned landscape and compromised the park's recreational value. The railroad's presence was even more untenable from Thirtieth Street south to Canal Street, where its tracks continued on grade down Eleventh Avenue and thus stymied the entire neighborhood's development.

The West Side improvement began as early as 1885,

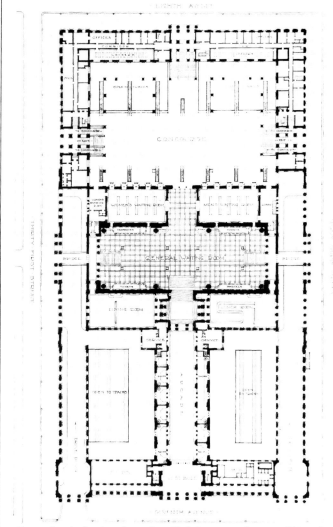

Pennsylvania Station, Seventh to Eighth avenues between Thirty-first and Thirty-third streets. McKim, Mead & White, 1904-10. Plan at street level. CU

Pennsylvania Station, Seventh to Eighth avenues between Thirty-first and Thirty-third streets. McKim, Mead & White, 1904-10. Pedestrian bridge over Carriage Drive. MCNY

when the city absorbed Twelfth Avenue into Riverside Park and first considered building a waterside roadway on reclaimed land beyond the railroad tracks.[65] In keeping with the spirit of the Composite Era, and its feeling for civic beautification, Peter B. Sweeney proposed in 1890 that the railroad tracks along the Hudson just west of Riverside Drive be covered over by an elevated, limited-access roadway between Seventy-second and Ninety-eighth streets. This roadway, designed by the architect Leopold Eidlitz, was modelled on London's Rotten Row with paths for pedestrians and equestrians in addition to traffic. Bordered by strips of greenery which continued the park's planting, the new roadway was to be built on landfill, the railroad tracks in part roofed over and elsewhere crossed by bridges.[66]

In 1899 Milton See proposed a more ambitious scheme to extend a four-hundred-foot wide terrace across the tracks from Seventy-second Street north to Spuyten Duyvil. The new terrace was to be treated not as an extension of Olmsted's naturalistic parkscape, but "as a great Italian garden," formally planted and edged with Classicizing arcades and balusters.[67] At 116th Street, See suggested an interior lagoon and boat landing for official visitors to the city, with a tree-lined boulevard passing in front of McKim's new campus for Columbia University and connecting Riverside and Morningside parks. The location of the lagoon foreshadowed the site and program intended for the Robert Fulton Memorial in 1909, another City Beautiful project to conceal the railroad.

The West Side improvement got under way in earnest in the second decade of the century, when preliminary negotiations were begun with the New York Central Railroad for covering its tracks and when a number of plans were drawn suggesting how the character of the reclaimed waterfront might be changed.

In 1900 the *Real Estate Record and Guide* called for the extension of Riverside Drive to the northern end of Manhattan "inasmuch as in the upper West Side there is the only remaining long strip of territory that is capable of development in character corresponding to that already made south of Claremont."[68] As originally laid out, Riverside Drive continued into Boulevard Lafayette, which unlike the drive below was flanked on both sides by buildings. The lack of a definitive city plan effectively stalled the development of properties above 138th Street, despite widespread agree-

Morris Park Station of the New York, New Haven & Hartford Railroad. Cass Gilbert, 1908. CU

ment that the Drive's rural character must be extended northward.

In 1913 Arnold W. Brunner and Frederick Law Olmsted, Jr. submitted a plan for the Drive's extension to Inwood, modifying the sharpest curves of Boulevard Lafayette and calling for the purchase for parkland of all properties to the west of the roadway, with the exception of the railroad tracks.[69] Brunner and Olmsted urged that the northern tip of Manhattan, treated with a prowlike concourse, be acquired as the site of "some great public building" and the proposed New York Central Railroad Bridge across the Spuyten Duyvil be relocated more economically, with an upper deck for traffic.[70] Although in 1917 the city and the railroad seemed close to an agreement to remove the tracks from the city streets and cover those in Riverside Park in exchange for adding more tracks, it was not until 1929 that tracks below Thirtieth Street were elevated and those from Thirtieth to Sixtieth streets depressed, and not until 1934 when Robert Moses built the Henry Hudson Parkway that the park was extended over the railroad, realizing a dream of fifty years while ironically throwing up a new barrier to the water in the form of the roadway itself.[71]

At the same time that railroad electrification initiated a transformation of the midtown area, brought about by the burial of the trains below Park Avenue and the establishment of a new focus of activity around Pennsylvania Station, it also extended the reach of New York's Metropolitanism. The New York, New Haven & Hartford, New York Central, and Long Island railroads electrified their lines to Westchester, Fairfield, Nassau, and Bergen counties and substantially improved their lines within the city proper by eliminating grade crossings and establishing commuter stations in the Bronx and Queens, where they already had rights of way through relatively unpopulated areas.[72] The improvements brought vast new areas within easy reach of midtown, which gradually diminished lower Manhattan's role as regional center.[73]

The New Haven Railroad's plan called for an ambitious upgrading of its passenger service on the Harlem River Branch, which connected Pelham Manor with the Park Avenue right of way to Grand Central.[74] Cass Gilbert was retained to design a series of stations at West Farms, Port Morris and other locations. Gilbert's stations at Baychester and Van Nest avenues were distinctly Dutch Renaissance in character while his Morris Park Station was almost Viennese.[75] Perhaps the loveliest of Gilbert's stations was on City Island: its low, hipped, tile roofs and random ashlar walls recalled Richardson's work for the Boston & Albany and other railroads.

The New York, Westchester & Boston Railroad was established in the waning of the Composite Era. Destined to play an important role in the development of the Bronx, the line was a stepchild of the New York, New Haven & Hartford Railroad that was based on two fatal premises. The first was that commuters would choose to save money by transferring to the subway to get from the South Bronx to the business sections of Manhattan rather than travel all the way to Grand Central on the more expensive railroad. The second was that the commercial district of New York would continue to migrate northward, so that the South Bronx would become a major center, as midtown had earlier. But the city's new zoning law, passed in 1916, slowed commercial and manufacturing growth north of Fifty-ninth Street, and by the 1930s the railroad was in bankruptcy.[76] Nevertheless, the New York, Westchester & Boston Railroad was conceived of as a first-class operation, and its stations offered sure testimony to a confident vision of the role of the suburb in the Metropolitan ideal. Considerable sums were spent on the Italianate and Spanish Renaissance stations and the company headquarters designed by Felheimer & Long in association with Allen H. Stem. The *Electric Railway Journal* described the stations as "the most attractive group of way structures possessed by any electric or steam railroad in the United States." It lauded the "progressive attitude of the company, which was ambitious to erect buildings which would add to rather than detract from the expected high-class suburban development of the territory."[77] The company's headquarters on Morris Park Avenue and 180th Street set the Arcadian tone carried out in the stations. Completed by the same architects in 1912, its twin towers framed an entrance loggia and were topped with spreading, red-tile roofs which suggested a picturesque

Competition entry for Uptown Terminal of the McAdoo Tunnels, Greeley Square at Sixth Avenue and Thirty-third Street. Howells & Stokes, 1908. Perspective. CU

villa rather than an office building.

While the authors of the New York City Improvement Commission's plan of 1907 were to some extent remiss in failing to prepare a coordinated transportation plan, there may well be a simple explanation in that such a plan, however informally arrived at, was already being implemented as two systems—one providing for regional rail transportation, and the other for an intra-city system that connected Manhattan with the outer boroughs. The implementation of these systems resulted in the many railroad improvements already discussed as well as the construction of the McAdoo Tunnels under the Hudson (the old "Hudson Tubes" now known as PATH), and the construction of the New York Connecting Railway's bridge across Hell Gate, which for the first time provided a land connection between the railroads serving New England, Long Island, Manhattan and the West.

The McAdoo system connected New Jersey with New York. Its central architectural feature was a large terminal and office building designed by Clinton & Russell for a block-long site on Church Street between Cortland and Fulton streets.[78] Completed in 1908, the Hudson Terminal consisted of a pair of Renaissance style, nineteen-story towers linked together below the street by a three-level rail terminal. (Originally, a grand bridge was to have spanned Dey Street and connected the buildings.) The terminal was the first to combine a major rail facility with a commercial real-estate development, but its almost complete absence of amenities for the commuter did not endear it to the public, though the sheer bulk and powerful massing of the buildings made the terminal one of the most impressive sights for travellers along the Hudson River. As plans were made in 1908 for the extension of the McAdoo Tunnels north to Greeley Square at Sixth Avenue and Thirty-third Street, a competition was held for an uptown terminal on the site eventually built upon by the Gimbel Brothers' department store. Howells & Stokes's proposal would have been one of the landmarks of the city: a ten-story base perhaps intended for the new store, with exuberant Modern French details including twin turrets and clock towers at the corners, abutted two thirty-five-story office slabs that were bridged together for their top ten floors to form an open courtyard in the sky—an image surely worthy of the visionary Italian architect Antonio Sant' Elia.[79]

Subways

Impressive though all of the rail termini and their feeder lines were, no rail improvement did so much to transform the city as the construction of the subway system, the first segment of which opened in 1904. The scale of the city had begun to change in the early 1870s, when the Ninth Avenue Elevated railway began service, although it was not until 1878 that the Third Avenue Elevated, the first full fledged, two track, trunk line, commenced operation between lower Manhattan and Yorkville. While the els relieved congestion, they brought blight with them. Their noise, the darkened streets beneath them, and the belching steam locomotives were widely criticized.

The era of elevated railroading reached its peak in 1903, when electrified service was extended along the full length of the east and west sides of Manhattan and into the Bronx and Brooklyn. Soon after, the completion of the first phase of the Interborough Rapid Transit (I.R.T.) subway system convincingly demonstrated the superiority of underground transportation.

The I.R.T. subway was foreshadowed as early as 1870, when Alfred Ely Beach opened an unusual and short-lived public underground transportation system that was powered by pneumatic air and ran under a short section of lower Broadway.[80] But even if the forces of Tammany Hall had not stopped Beach in order to preserve their control of the city's existing public transportation, it is doubtful that his pneumatic air system would have been practical. In 1891, the architect Alfred H. Thorp proposed a new system of elevated railways that was more prophetic for New York's subways. He suggested the construction of a continuous viaduct building along the city's waterfront combining rail transit at sixteen feet above the street level with an elevated boulevard sixteen feet higher still. On the landside he imagined new construction suitable to "retail shops of the best order, hotels, apartment houses, dwellings, etc., bordering as they would on a superb elevated boulevard, overlooking the rivers and shipping and yet entirely withdrawn from the bustle and traffic, and within easy access of rapid transit."[81] Thorp presented his scheme, which he described as a "girdle road," to the Rapid Transit Commission in 1895.[82]

J.J.R. Croes, a civil engineer, working in association with the architects Small & Schumann, carried Thorp's idea further, proposing routes often adopted by August Belmont's I.R.T. for the first subway. Croes called for a system that cut through built-up areas in the center of the blocks, arguing that such a route would be simpler, because of less interference with the utilities that lay buried in the streets. Although Croes appeared to have considered a subway in the city's center, together with his architectural collaborators he proposed as an alternative an enclosed steel viaduct that "with bridges with good design across the streets, will not prove as costly of construction and as objectionable to both property owners and travellers as either a steel viaduct in a street, or an underground tube anywhere."[83]

In 1897, the Rapid Transit Commission had definitely decided in favor of an underground system which would extend the sphere of the metropolis even further and more dramatically than the els had in the 1880s.[84] By 1899 the commission had agreed on a subway route proposed by William Barclay Parsons.[85] On February 24, 1900, the city signed a contract with the railway company.[86]

After many false starts, ground was finally broken for the city's first subway by Mayor Van Wyck and August Belmont, President of the Interborough Rapid Transit Company, in March 1900. The first phase of the subway was completed on October 27, 1904, and ran from City Hall up Fourth Avenue to Grand Central, across to Times Square, then north along Broadway to 145th Street.[87] Later in the year one section was extended to 157th Street and Broadway, and another to 145th Street and Lenox Avenue. By 1906 it would extend its full length along Broadway to Kingsbridge and under the Harlem River as far as 180th Street in the Bronx, and by 1908 to Brooklyn Heights.

While the subway was never conceived of as a civic ornament on a par with the East River bridges or the Carnegie libraries, it was not, however, intended to be merely transportation. Considerable emphasis was placed on the embellishment of the stations, viaducts and rolling stock. The principal architectural features of the subway were the small street-level structures designed by Heins & LaFarge. Most stations had steel and glass kiosks with a distinctly Parisian character, although they reflected the taste of the Beaux-Arts Baroque rather than the Art Nouveau of Hector Guimard's *Metro*.[88] Principal stations along Broadway—Bowling Green, 72nd, 96th, 103rd and 116th streets—and in Brooklyn and the Bronx were built with more substantial control houses of brick and stone that were set like garden pavilions in the landscaped median strip.[89]

Many of the stations did not compare favorably with earlier examples in Paris and Vienna, but most observers did not seem to notice. M.G. Cuniff, writing in *World's Work*, extolled that "For once on a great practical municipal undertaking, beauty has been made an important element in the work. Each station has a distinguishing color scheme . . . to aid travellers in identifying their destinations; and the decorations in Rookwood pottery, faience, and marble as well as tiling used in unprecedented quantities, offer a kaleidoscopic variety of color. Glass roofs provide the stations with plenty of light—which is diffused from the glazed tiles—and the platforms are broad enough to accommodate great crowds."[90] The *Real Estate Record and Guide* was even more emphatic in its praise: "the subway stations are excellent in the architectural propriety of their schemes of decorations. We suspect that the stairways will eventually prove to be too narrow; but there are no faults to find with the appearance of the stations. Something clean, neat and attractive was wanted; and the white tiles with colored borders serve the purpose admirably. The effect of this sort of thing upon popular taste is enormous; and since the example will be imitated thereafter, New York can congratulate itself on one specimen of 'Civic Art,' in which a very useful structure has been decorated with the utmost propriety."[91] Yet soon enough, the station's inadequacies were apparent, even to such boosters as the editors of the *Record and Guide:* "The experience of a week of subway operations has proved one defect beyond peradventure. The stations and their approaches have not been made as spacious as they should have been . . . the subway should have been designed to handle much larger crowds than the existing stations and their approaches can possibly accommodate. It is part of the permanent comprehensive transit system of the city. It will be carrying passengers when the central parts of Manhattan will be a ridge of skyscrapers, and when, owing to the concentration of business and residences, the traffic will be more dense by a good deal than it is at present. It will be found in the end that both in regard to its express service and in regard to its station accommodations, the subway has not been made sufficiently elastic."[92]

The handling of the station structure revealed an intense struggle for architectural expression between the engineers and the architects. The posts along the platform's edge were transformed into columns through a subtle manipulation of the profile at the base and capital, and the ceiling panel of each structural bay was relieved by wide ornamental moldings and rosettes. The walls of each station were carefully articulated in panels of glazed tile and terra cotta, with specially designed decorative panels made for each station depicting an historic building or event that would help the passengers (many of whom did not read English) identify the stations. The plaques at Fulton Street depicted the steamship Clermont, Grand Central had a New York Central locomotive, Columbus Circle, the Santa Maria, and so on. Unfortunately, as the *American Architect and Building News* quickly pointed out, the plaques as well as the station name panels "have . . . been placed where they are of least advantage to those who most need to consult them, the people in the cars."[93] The City Hall station was vaulted over in Guastavino tile, the ribs between the vaults sheathed in contrasting glazed tile to produce the line's grandest effect.[94] All in all, as an early promotional brochure stated, the decorations and in particular the illustrative panels were intended to be "instructive and decorative, as well as practical, and will have the effect on public taste just the same as anything else that tends to uplift and refine."[95]

No sooner had the subway begun to function than a controversy arose over the placement of advertisements on the walls. Whether Heins & LaFarge had anticipated the ads is unclear, although the company's right to display them was provided for in its contract with the city. Yet despite the era's general antagonism toward outdoor advertising, the

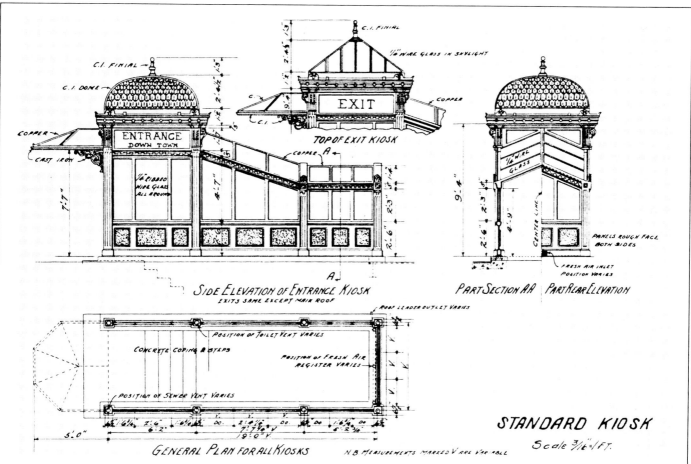

Standard kiosk, I.R.T. Subway. Heins & LaFarge, 1904. Plan, section and elevations. MCNY

I.R.T. Station, 116th Street and Broadway. Heins & LaFarge, 1904. MCNY

Whitehall Ferry Terminal, the Battery. Walker & Morris, 1907. Perspective. MCNY

American Architect and Building News felt that "worse things could happen than that the subway stations should in this way be converted into great popular schools of instruction in certain forms of mural decoration."[96] The *Real Estate Record and Guide* found the placards an "aesthetic . . . outrage."[97]

The civic sense evident in the new subway stations also characterized the design of the I.R.T. power station (1900–02), a vast facility which generated electricity for the network of substations scattered throughout the city. Its location at West Fifty-ninth Street and Eleventh Avenue placed it near the center of the I.R.T. system and allowed direct coal deliveries from ships in the Hudson River, but its presence threatened to permanently blight the neighborhood's development. At an early stage in the planning process Stanford White volunteered to design the facades and collaborate with the I.R.T.'s engineers on the utilitarian plan. He united the massive block in a continuous colonnade of banded pilasters framing arched windows, and covered the facades with delicate, French Renaissance details in a terra cotta that matched the buff-colored Roman brick. An attic story above the colonnade represented the enormous steel trusses which supported the facility's coal hoppers and chimneys. White also turned his attention to the chimneys, tapering them to suggest the entasis of a Classical column.[98]

The subway's capacity to stimulate underground linkages between buildings was immediately sensed. The first building to contain an "underground sidewalk" connecting to the subway was Clinton & Russell's Mercantile Building at the southwest corner of Twenty-third Street and Fourth Avenue, a building which, as the *Architects' and Builders' Magazine* rather bluntly observed, "attracts but little interest from the public eye unless its plainness is noted in contrast to the magnificent facade of the Metropolitan Life Building, on the opposite side of Twenty-third Street."[99] What was interesting about the Mercantile Building, however, was the fourteen-foot-wide, 165-foot-long passageway that connected the building's elevators at the rear of the lot with the subway platform at its front. The arcade, sheathed in white enamel brick and roofed over in glazed blocks that formed the sidewalk above, was entered by a broad, sinuously curved flight of stairs; along one side of its entire length shop windows opened on the first large basement store in New York.[100]

A second spurt of subway construction occurred at the close of the Composite Era. The Brooklyn Rapid Transit system (B.R.T.) grew out of the consolidation in 1900 of all the elevated lines in Brooklyn. In granting permission to the B.R.T. to construct a line in Manhattan, the city inaugurated what came to be called the Dual System of intra-city rail transit, providing for two lines, the I.R.T. and the B.M.T. (Brooklyn and Manhattan Rapid Transit Company). By 1917 the two linked the east and west sides of Manhattan with the Bronx, Brooklyn and Queens, but the inefficiencies in the Dual System and the addition of the city-owned Independent System soon made a mockery of the idea of coordinated subway transportation. Nonetheless, the incongruous turn of events could not have been anticipated by the city plans of 1904–07.[101] The B.M.T. combined a new concern for the convenience of passengers (the I.R.T. had been underdesigned and overcrowding was a serious problem from the beginning) with a less didactic and stylistically confused sense of aesthetics than the I.R.T.'s.

Though the architectural amenities of the B.M.T. were better than those of the original subway, they hardly approached the quality of contemporary work in London and Vienna.[102] In the underground stations, white glazed tiles were fitted along the side walls between a low cement base and high frieze of colored tiles containing station insignia. The use of representational plaques initiated in the original I.R.T. subway was continued in many of the stations, but the intricacies of panelling, string courses, and articulated column bases and caps were abandoned in favor of more easily maintained smooth surfaces and a more straightforward expression of the engineering.

Systems in Paris and Berlin influenced the design of the elevated portions of the line, particularly the portion that stretched along Queens Boulevard. The steel structure was "dressed" or sheathed in a sprayed concrete coating that transformed a usually dingy feature into an amenity. The alternation of smooth- and rough-coat surfaces and the extensive use of colorful glazed tiles inset for emphasis

St. George Ferry Terminal, St. George, Staten Island. Carrère & Hastings, 1907. Perspective. MCNY

helped articulate the basic structural organization.

Piers and Bridges

Soon after the Cosmopolitan Era began, New York City began to expand its boundaries, annexing parts of the Bronx in 1874. By 1883 the Brooklyn Bridge connected Manhattan Island to Long Island, enabling workers to easily go back and forth, but most travellers, whether tourist or commuter, and all freight still arrived by boat. The circumference of the city was lined by piers which serviced the shipping and ferry lines: the piers were often ramshackle structures, yet before the construction of the McAdoo Tunnels, the great railroad stations and the various bridges, they served as New York's principal gateways. Even later, many travellers continued to arrive by boat, including all those travelling by the Baltimore & Ohio, Erie, Lackawanna and other railroads which maintained ferry service from Manhattan to stations on the Hudson's west shore in New Jersey.

The 1904 *Report of the New York City Improvement Commission* called for "some uniformity of construction" to give the waterfront "an architectural appearance worthy of the City and in great contrast to the medley of different forms now existing" because of private development.[103] The suggestions of the powerless advisory committee were brief, but they did recommend that the individual companies which owned the piers be required to devote their roofs to public recreation facilities connected to one another by an elevated promenade.

Although the commission's proposals were never taken up in toto, the Whitehall Ferry Terminal was built in 1907 as a direct result of the plan. Recalling the commission's plea for recreational facilities incorporated into pier design, Walker & Morris designed a loggia facing the city and a roof garden with pergolas overlooking the bay.[104] Like Kenneth Murchison's Erie Ferry House at the foot of Twenty-third Street, also built in 1907,[105] and Snelling & Potter's Stapleton Ferry Terminal of 1908,[106] the Whitehall Terminal was influenced by the design of the Grand Palais of the Paris Exposition of 1900, translating the Modern French vocabulary into steel, copper and bronze. The most beautiful of New York's ferry terminals, however, was Carrère & Hastings's Staten Island Terminal, built in 1908 in St. George.[107] Its tapered stone pylons supported graceful metal keel-shaped arches which formed a canopy over the slip. The concourse behind was a metal shed supported on unadorned transverse arches, and had thermal windows at either end and metal walls panelled with etiolated pilasters.

The Chelsea piers were constructed in response to the 1907 city plan's plea for standardized pier construction. Nine piers were completed by the architects Warren & Wetmore in 1910. Stretching from Little West Twelfth Street to West Twenty-second, they were unified by a continuous two-story bulkhead along the streetfront which contained passenger lobbies, ticket booths and offices. Punctuating the street wall, the entrances to the shed-like piers were each proclaimed with a single vast arched window framed by massive piers and a pedimented roof topped with copper trophies. Warren & Wetmore invested the fashionable Modern French facades with a strikingly monumental grandeur and simplified but overscaled details. In part this reflected the utilitarian character of the program, but it also reflected their use of poured concrete for both the massive walls and sculptural details. The river facades, which sheltered open observation platforms, were contrastingly festive transformations of the utilitarian steel piers which lay behind the street facades, and greeted the arriving passenger with a flutter of pennants and trophies.[108]

Between 1903 and 1917 four major bridges were built in the city, the first since the Brooklyn Bridge was completed in 1883. The bridges combined pedestrian, vehicular, and rail transit in what were probably the most noticeable monuments to the new metropolitan scale. Like the piers along the waterfront, the bridges of the Composite Era were designed in collaborative efforts by engineers and architects. Although the bridges were great works of engineering, pressure was brought to bear on the administration of the newly consolidated city to ensure that they also be great works of architecture, worthy of the city's prominence. The idea was not to hide the marvels of engineering, but to complement them.

The most daring of the bridges of the Metropolitan Age,

Chelsea Piers, West Street between Little West Twelfth and West Twenty-third Streets. Warren & Wetmore, 1910. NYHS

not realized until the completion of the George Washington Bridge in 1931, was the Hudson River crossing first proposed in 1884 by the engineer Gustav Lindenthal. By 1890 plans had advanced sufficiently that the New York State Legislature passed a bill incorporating the North River Bridge Company for the purpose of building Lindenthal's design. The enormous bridge with its 2,860-foot-long span would have been 1,265 feet longer than that of the Brooklyn Bridge and would have gone further, as *Architecture and Building* said, "towards making the greater New York the foremost city of the world than any other event in the last twenty years."[109] Lindenthal's vision outstripped the imagination of his contemporaries, a problem that occurred again when he was City Bridge Commissioner and proposed a radical design for the Manhattan Bridge.

The Williamsburg Bridge was the first of the new East River bridges constructed to supplement the overtaxed Brooklyn Bridge. Designed in 1896–1903 by the engineer Leffert L. Buck, who had worked with Washington Roebling on the Brooklyn Bridge, it was intended to carry not only pedestrians and horse-drawn vehicles but also elevated trains and trolleys. Because of the width of the roadways required, it was decided steel towers would be more efficient than masonry.[110] Buck's purely utilitarian design was characterized by John DeWitt Warner in 1899 as a "surrender of the City Beautiful to the City Vulgar."[111] In the same year Buck first submitted plans for the Queensboro Bridge; the visual impact on the riverscape threatened by these two projects triggered a stream of protests. The public outcry prompted Mayor Seth Low to appoint Lindenthal as Commissioner of the Department of Bridges in 1902, and to regularly refer new bridge designs to the Municipal Art Commission for approval on the basis of their aesthetic effect.[112] Distressed by the unconsidered conditions of the approaches to the Williamsburg Bridge and by the squat proportions of its towers, Lindenthal usurped Buck's position and retained the firm of Palmer & Hornbostel as consultants, charging them with the task of "adding architectural grace to a work hitherto directed by the minds of engineers alone."[113] Because construction was already well under way, Palmer & Hornbostel proposed only modest interventions, including exuberantly modelled balconies and pinnacles on each tower that would be lit at night (the pinnacles were not built), two small monumental structures

Manhattan Bridge. Henry Hornbostel and Gustav Lindenthal, 1903. Model. MCNY

Manhattan Bridge. Carrère & Hastings and Leon Morsieff, 1904-09. Detail of tower and pedestrian walkway. MCNY

of masonry—one a comfort station, the other a tool house—and a number of minor decorative plaques based on initials of the bridge's name. Hornbostel also advocated widening Delancey Street, at the Manhattan end of the bridge, into a boulevard.[114]

Montgomery Schuyler opposed the awkward proportions of the towers, which abruptly changed profile as they rose above the roadway, and deplored their "uncouth and bandy-legged aspect which no cleverness in detail could redeem."[115] The best he could say on behalf of the bridge was "the ugliness of the Williamsburg has been the means of an increased appreciation of the beauty of the East River.[116]

By contrast, Schuyler wrote that the Queensboro and Manhattan bridges, opened within a year of one another in 1909 and 1910 respectively, gave "promise of a final and triumphant refutation of the official European criticism that 'public works in America are executed without reference to art.'"[117] Each was the result of collaborations between architects and engineers which produced a synthesis of contemporary technology and the Composite Era's concern for civic beautification.

Of the two, the Manhattan Bridge was surely the more grandiloquent monument to the city's recent consolidation. The first plans were drawn by R.S. Buck, but in 1903, after Lindenthal became Commissioner of Bridges, he redesigned the bridge in collaboration with Hornbostel. Lindenthal introduced controversial structural ideas like the use of eye-bar cables in place of conventional steel wires, thus making it possible to eliminate the stiffening truss that blocked the views from the roadways and stating a more eloquent dialogue between the roadway and the support.[118] He also proposed towers made up of four columns, which would permit the towers to pivot on their bases and compensate for the expansion and contraction of the cables. But a controversy arose over Lindenthal's technical innovations and Hornbostel's joint design, which called for the use of the space within the anchorage for meeting halls and for some delightful Modern French touches including urns and finials on each tower, was virtually ignored. When Lindenthal was dismissed in 1904 by the new mayor, George McClellan, a new design was drawn up by Leon Morsieff under the direction of George Best, the new bridge commissioner, and Carrère & Hastings were invited to replace Hornbostel as

Manhattan Bridge. Carrère & Hastings and Leon Morsieff, 1904-09. MCNY

architectural consultants.[119] The task remained the same: to produce a design that effectively defined the differences between architecture and engineering, producing a symbolic gateway for Brooklyn and Manhattan that would further reinforce the connections between two cities linked in an uneasy political marriage.

Schuyler felt that though the fundamental engineering of the bridge changed, Carrère & Hastings improved on, but did not depart from, Hornbostel's design for the towers and the anchorages. He approved of their substitution of an emphasized center for the more uniform expression of the three roadways that Hornbostel had proposed, and agreed to their retention of Hornbostel's powerful masonry anchorages, which he found "almost more than Roman. They wear, indeed, an aspect of Egyptian immobility."[120] The basic shapes of the Manhattan Bridge, called "A Bridge Beautiful As Well As Useful" by the *Architects' and Builders' Magazine,*[121] were carefully sculpted to achieve maximum expressiveness. Close attention was paid to the articulation of the distinctions between the cables which held the roadway in tension and the compressive capacities of the steel towers: the distinction between support and supported was made explicit in the manner emphasized by the French theorist of structural expression, Viollet-le-Duc. Carrère & Hastings introduced masonry above the roadbed, in the form of an exaggerated expression of the cable anchorage as saddles and of twin colonnades that formed a Court of Honor at the point of transition between the compressive and tensile portions of the structure.

The elliptical Court of Honor at the Manhattan end of the bridge had as its principal feature a triumphal arch based on the Porte St. Denis in Paris.[122] The court was reserved for vehicular traffic: street cars passed outside the plaza's colonnades, while the subway did not go onto the bridge until after passing under both the plaza and the arch. The Court of Honor was intended as a grand entrance to the city, but from the first it was dwarfed by the scale of the bridge and swamped by the traffic it served.

Though Lindenthal and Hornbostel's Queensboro and Hell Gate bridges may have lacked the grandeur of the Manhattan Bridge, they perhaps represented an even higher level of collaboration between engineer and architect. The Queensboro Bridge was the first major bridge in New York to depart from the cable suspension type initiated by

Manhattan Bridge. Carrère & Hastings, 1912. Court of Honor. MCNY

Queensboro Bridge. Henry Hornbostel and Gustav Lindenthal, 1909. MCNY

Roebling.[123] The first design for the bridge was prepared in 1899 by R.S. Buck, who proposed two cantilever spans of unequal length. The use of the cantilever principle made the issue of the anchorages less important than the overall handling of the structural cage which envelops the roadways and transfers the load from tower to tower. Lindenthal and Hornbostel developed Buck's basic design, manipulating the cross section to add an extra level of the roadway so as to narrow the overall width of the bridge and transform the passage across the river and the intervening island into a triumphal boulevard. They based their design on the Pont Mirabeau over the Seine at Neuilly, outside Paris, but they placed their truss above rather than below the roadway. The entrance to this avenue of steel was announced by two colossal bronze lanterns and two delightful cast-iron and terra-cotta kiosks leading to an underground terminal for the streetcars that crossed the bridge. Twin turrets marked the termination of the anchorage to crossing pedestrians and passengers on the elevated trains. The turrets, with their segmental arches and low domes, were elegant essays in the Modern French manner. The steel superstructure of the bridge began with a low arch across the roadway mounted with bronze commemorative plaques, and had four towers crowned by spiky finials which Hornbostel deemed "gaily capped."[124] The towers rested on masonry pylons of breathtaking slenderness, which could be achieved because of the self-buttressing nature of the cantilevered structure.

The treatment of the approach supports on the Queens side was elegant in a manner that simultaneously conjured up images of the Gothic, the work of Gustav Eiffel and the Art Nouveau. On the Manhattan side the steel was camouflaged in a granite and terra-cotta veneer with Guastavino arches carrying the roadway over an arcuated hypostyle hall of impressive proportions and no particular purpose.

Hornbostel's hand could be seen in every detail of the design, including the exquisitely worked out patterns of the rivets on the steel work. It was the detailed handling of the structure rather than the unexecuted approaches called for in the city plans of 1904 and 1907 that constituted the chief distinction of the design, an endlessly changing kaleidoscope of pattern that made every crossing a visually stimulating game.[125]

The Hell Gate Bridge was the largest steel-arch bridge

Queensboro Bridge. Henry Hornbostel and Gustav Lindenthal, 1909. Sectional perspective. MCNY

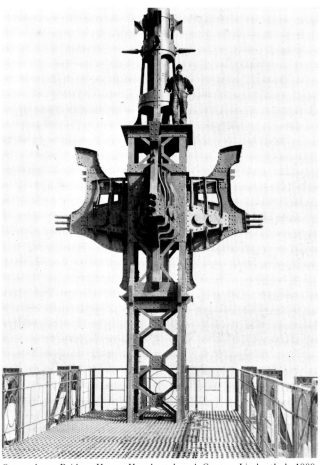

Queensboro Bridge. Henry Hornbostel and Gustav Lindenthal, 1909. Tower finial. MCNY

in the world when it was completed in 1914.[126] The only New York bridge designed and supervised by Lindenthal, it was Lindenthal's and Hornbostel's masterpiece. The gentle reverse curve in the top chord was particularly graceful in its expression of the transfer of forces to the masonry abutments and gave the bridge an uncommonly elegant silhouette against the sky. Hornbostel's original proposal for an effusive Modern French treatment of the flanking tower buttresses was rejected by the Arts Commission in 1907 because it was not "strictly utilitarian."[127] For the final design, which was not realized until 1914, he designed austere towers that buttressed and counterpointed Lindenthal's flowing arch with simple masses of stone only slightly cut back to reveal emerging pilasters. The viaduct over Wards and Randalls Islands was carried on even simpler, almost slab-like piers. Overhead electric wires were strung between tapered pylons with spherical finials that returned architecture to the pure Classicism of the Enlightenment.[128]

The Coming of the Automobile

The public transportation projects of the Composite Era were monuments to the Metropolitan ideal, consolidating the city physically as it had already consolidated politically. They represented, however, an increasingly outmoded technology. The development of the automobile, and later of the airplane, drastically altered the character of urban life. The former brought efficient personal transportation to the masses, the latter shattered inter-city distances and fostered an unprecedented decentralization of business. While these events belonged to the city's third stage of Metropolitanism, the Era of Convenience, they began to emerge shortly after 1900. The triumph of the airplane was foreshadowed in the visionary drawings of H.M. Pettit, whose fantastic skylines were dotted with flying machines, and that of the automobile by the gradual replacement of horse-drawn transportation by gasoline powered equipment.

As early as 1870 the horse was thought of as much in terms of recreation as transportation. When Olmsted first designed Central Park there were few saddle horses in the city except those kept by riding stables. His provision at a later stage of design of bridle paths and carriage drives was a major factor in stimulating interest in pleasure riding.[129] Both riding and driving through Central Park gave New

Hell Gate Bridge. Henry Hornbostel and Gustav Lindenthal, 1907–14. Perspective of 1907 scheme. CU

 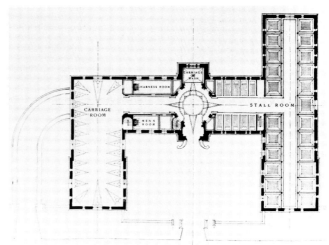

Stable of C.K.G. Billings, Speedway and 197th Street. Guy Lowell, ca. 1903. Perspective and plan. CU

Yorkers the chance to watch or participate in a parade of society, one which continued up Harlem Lane (now St. Nicholas Avenue) as far north as 168th Street. The completion of the Harlem River Speedway in 1898 finally realized the continuous carriage route to the island's northern tip which Olmsted had initially envisioned enabling one to proceed through either Riverside Drive or a chain of parks (Central, Morningside and St. Nicholas parks) and back by a route lined with greenery and little traffic to interfere. C.K.G. Billings's private stable (ca. 1903), located at the Speedway and 197th Street, was designed by Guy Lowell to serve the Billings's estate.[130] (Around 1909 the estate and adjoining acreage were purchased by John D. Rockefeller, Jr., who later donated the land to the city for use as Fort Tryon Park.) As designed by Lowell, the gracious facility had battered stucco walls and flaring shingled roofs surrounding three sides of a courtyard that was completed on the fourth by a low wall and latticed gates.

The Fifth Avenue Riding School, designed by C. Pfeiffer in association with the engineer F. Schuman, was one of the most fashionable of the city's riding establishments in the 1880s,[131] while Charles W. Romeyn's Dakota Stable (1885), occupying the entire block front on the south side of Seventy-fifth Street between Tenth Avenue and Broadway, was one of the largest.[132] The Dakota Stables were built by the Clark Estate as part of their program of improvements for the West End. Carriages were stored on the ground floor, horses stabled on the second and feed stored in the attic. A thirty-foot-square entrance court lined in white tile sat under the central entrance tower. The stable's ramps eventually proved too steep to allow its conversion as a garage and it was torn down in 1912.

Even though automobiles were coming into use at the turn of the century, few people took them seriously as dependable replacements for the horses and carriages that were the present means of daily transportation for the upper classes. In fact, some of the grandest stables were not built until after 1900. Frank Gould's stable (1901) on West Fifty-seventh Street, designed by York & Sawyer, consisted of a rusticated temple front leading to a triple height, top-lit riding ring in which horses could be exercised and lessons given.[133] Horgan & Slattery's Stable Building & Auction Mart for Fiss, Doerr & Carroll (1906) was even grander, consisting of a particularly unusual seven-story "horse hotel" adjoining a palatial sixty-seven-foot-wide arena running two hundred feet through the block between East Twenty-fourth and Twenty-fifth streets.[134] The arena was surrounded by galleries seating one thousand spectators. Spanned by a shallow caisson arch whose lower chord described an ellipse, it was lit by electricity as well as skylights and large windows at each end. The arena's facade at Twenty-fourth Street, in the full-blown Modern French style, consisted of two end pavilions supporting trophies and finials. Above and behind an arcaded stone screen wall rose the sweeping arch of the roof, punctured by a tall flagpole and containing a vast window in its tympanum.

The Tichenor-Grand Stable (1906) between Broadway and Central Park West, Sixty-first and Sixty-second streets, was the last of the great horse palaces, consisting of six stories of stabling facilities surmounted by a sky-lit show ring where horses were exercised and auctioned. Hill & Stout's Modern French facade was notable for its twin towers from which the stable floors, sheathed in metal, appeared to be stretched. At the top the arched truss of the riding hall was seemingly buttressed by the towers which were in turn crowned by domed finials.[135] Few stables were as grandiloquent or festive, however. Ludlow & Valentine's far more modest, two-story Standard Coach Horse Company (1902) at 41–43 West Sixty-third Street combined the nostalgically medievalizing architecture of the typical armories of the Cosmopolitan Era with a lighter, more Italian sensibility, embellished by a sculpted horse's head at the center of the facade.[136]

By 1906 the age of the horse was clearly waning and the garage, a new building type for the storage and maintenance of automobiles, began to develop. Many of the early public garages were conceived of as important civic buildings. None was grander than Snelling & Potter's three-story facility for Grahm & Goodman (1906) on West Ninety-third Street. Its reinforced concrete structure, sheathed in an elaborate Modern French brick and limestone facade with a high basement supporting flattened piers, rose to a complex

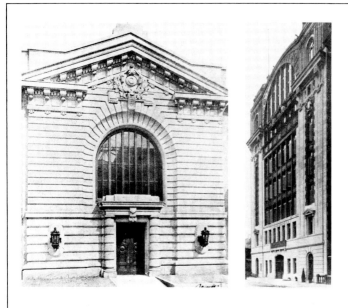

Riding Ring of Frank J. Gould, 219 West Fifty-seventh Street. York & Sawyer, 1901. CU

Tichenor-Grand Stable, West Sixty-first to West Sixty-second streets between Broadway and Central Park West. Hill & Stout, 1906. View from Sixty-first Street. CU

cornice climaxed at its center by a flagpole.[137].

By 1910 the effect of the new automobile era was beginning to be felt at all levels of the city, from the viaduct around Grand Central and the ramps at Pennsylvania Station, to the scale of the individual townhouse where Ernest Flagg was the first to recognize that the car was more than a replacement for the horse, but a convenience that could be stored in the house and used as frequently and as easily as an electric light or telephone.

Ernest Flagg's own house at 109 East Fortieth Street was the first to incorporate a garage. Designed in 1905, it seemed at first glance to be a conventional thirty-two-foot-wide, red brick and white marble townhouse with a *piano nobile* emphasized by a delicate iron balcony stretching across the three windows of the facade. But closer inspection revealed that the arched entryway, with elaborate iron gates, gave access to a *porte-cochère* with an elevator at the rear that could lower the car to a basement garage. Flagg adapted a Parisian model to American conditions, turning to the courtyard of a typical Paris *hôtel* for both the idea of the internalized *porte-cochère* and for the general organization of the plan and its complexly shaped spaces.[138]

As his house was being completed in 1907, Flagg was building the Automobile Club of America on West Fifty-fourth Street.[139] Compared to August Perret's Garage Ponthieu in Paris (1905-06), Flagg's retained a more explicit connection to Classicism, sheathing the structural frame in a taut, expressive skin of buff brick and subtly polychromed terra cotta without disguising the presence of the reinforced concrete structure. The decorated skin of the Automobile Club was manipulated to present the building's unusual, hybrid program, prophetic of mixed-use buildings of the Age of Convenience. Its ground floor was largely devoted to a washroom for cars and the elevators which carried them to garages on the upper floors, articulated with a repetitive pattern of metal-framed, infill windows. The *piano nobile*, sandwiched between the garage facilities, contained a large assembly room and a grill room for members' use. Its public character was articulated with a terra-cotta balcony and French doors elaborately framed in modelled terra cotta. The interiors of the public rooms relied on a more traditional Modern French vocabulary which sacrificed structural representation for familiarity.

Flagg's design would quickly seem naive. In 1913 Hubert Ladd Towle summarized the developing role of the automobile in an article entitled "The Automobile and Its Mission": five years earlier it had seemed a "transcendant plaything—thrilling, seductive, desperately expensive," but now it seemed to proffer an entirely new pattern of residential settlement.[140] In the interim Henry Ford had begun to mass produce cars on the assembly line. In 1916, at the dawn of the Age of Convenience, the Federal Roads Act initiated a national program of road building. The mobility of the automobile and a host of new technological advances—the telephone, radio, cinema and eventually television—conspired to produce a freedom of migration which never existed with the elevated, the railroad or the subway. Together they fostered a new concept of regional planning and a decentralization of the urban fabric. By 1955 Lewis Mumford summarized the effect of the automobile: "The distant dormitory areas of New York describe ever widening arcs," the result of planning "as if motor transportation existed in a social vacuum, and as if New York were a mere passageway or terminal for vehicles, with no good reasons of its own for existing."[141]

Automobile Club of America, 253 West Fifty-fourth and 248 West Fifty-fifth streets. Ernest Flagg, 1907. CU

Municipal Building, Centre Street at Chambers Street. McKim, Mead & White, 1907–14. A view from the southwest showing the Hall of Records (bottom left). NYHS

Civic Grandeur

Architecture, like government, is about as good as a community deserves.
Lewis Mumford, *Sticks and Stones* (New York: Boni & Liveright, 1924), 150-51.

Civic Center Design competitions for a new City Hall were held in 1888 and 1893. Although the building had been described when it opened in 1811 as "the handsomest structure in the United States; perhaps, of its size, in the world," it had been planned for a much smaller city and was incapable of absorbing the bureaucracy of metropolitan New York.[1] Moreover, the symbolism of the building and its surroundings were equally unsuitable for the metropolis. In 1811 no one had complained that the city fathers had saved some money by facing the northern side of the building in brownstone instead of the same marble as the other facades—the building stood on the outskirts of the city at Broadway and Chambers Street, and everyone figured the north side "would be out of sight to all the world" for years to come.[2] By the 1850s, however, the most fashionable residential neighborhoods were reaching as far noth as Central Park. In addition, the once lovely City Hall Park had been encroached on, first in 1875 by the construction of A.B. Mullett's enormous Second Empire style post office that completely filled the lower section of the triangular plot, and then in 1878 by the building of the notorious "Tweed" Courthouse directly to the north of City Hall. There was almost unanimous agreement that New York City needed to improve the conditions, but for years a debate raged on how to best deal with the problems.

In 1888 Charles B. Atwood won the first of the City Hall competitions with a scheme that would have flanked the two-story City Hall with seven-story end pavilions and connected the three sections with a covered arcade.[3] The new buildings were designed in a loosely interpreted French Classical style intended to complement the more scholarly design of the original structure, but the total effect was incongruous, made even worse by a tall bell tower on axis with the cupola of the City Hall intended to introduce a bold scale in keeping with the city's developing skyline.

The New York Chapter of the American Institute of Architects combined forces with concerned citizens to raise enough protest over the incursion of further buildings into City Hall Park that the project was stopped, but the sentiments of enlightened citizenry were only momentarily listened to by the politicians.[4] In 1891 Mayor Grant advocated the destruction of City Hall, which he found "doubtless a fine architectural model—a perfect picture of architecture you may say—but its interior arrangement is faulty in many ways and it is impossible to keep it in a decent sanitary condition."[5] Needless to say, the proposal to replace the City Hall sparked a heated debate. Most leading architects rallied to the cause of preservation, although some, such as Milton See and John R. Thomas, suggested that it might be relocated to a pastoral suburban location in order to make way for a more appropriately magnificent expression of municipality.[6] At one point, its destruction seemed so imminent that Columbia University dispatched two students to prepare a set of measured drawings for posterity.[7]

The State Legislature intervened, proposing that City Hall be preserved and a new municipal office building be raised outside the confines of City Hall Park.[8] In 1893 a competition was organized for a site at the northeast corner of the park, but according to an 1896 account in *Architecture and Building*, it "resulted in the submission of but a few plans, which lay for years on the top of an old safe in the Controller's office and at last accounts never had been opened, legislative action here having blocked the efforts of the city's officers."[9]

Late in 1893 the architects Richard Morris Hunt, Napoleon Le Brun and William Robert Ware, serving as advisors to the Municipal Building Commission, recommended City Hall's destruction in connection with a new competition for which they would serve as a jury.[10] After 134 entries were submitted and a jurors' report prepared, protest immediately arose over the failure of municipal nerve in the decision to build in the park. The *Architectural Record*, a leading critic of the project, expressed its hope that "like a former competition for the same building in which official laymen imposed their crude notion upon experts, it may come to nothing."[11]

New York City Hall competition entry, City Hall Park. Cram, Wentworth & Goodhue, 1893. Perspective view from Broadway. CU

The *Record's* wishes were fulfilled when the competition was marred by scandalous manipulations from Tammany Hall, and the State Legislature passed a law forbidding construction on the site of City Hall. The jury's report on the undistinguished though numerous entries was never officially accepted by the city, and the six finalists they had chosen had difficulty collecting the promised prize money.[12] Except for the scheme by Cram, Wentworth & Goodhue, none of the final six designs had achieved an appropriate civic expression.[13] Gordon, Bragdon & Orchard's design called for a vast French Renaissance palace,[14] while Brunner & Tryon proposed a far more grandiloquent Classical scheme with a central dome raised on a tall base ringed by Corinthian columns and smaller domes at each of the corners.[15] Cram, Wentworth & Goodhue's design offered a powerful, highly eclectic synthesis drawn from the work of Sir Christopher Wren, the English Baroque and fourteenth-century Sienna.

The flurry of confusion that accompanied the city's consolidation caused the plans for a new City Hall to be put aside until a sense of its symbolic function in Greater New York could be better articulated. But some city office space was still needed, and in 1897 John R. Thomas, one of the winners of the 1893 competition, was hired to adapt his City Hall design to a new Hall of Records to be built on the corner of Chambers and Centre streets.[16] Just as construction was starting in 1899, a Tammany administration was elected, and the new mayor hired the architects always used by Tammany Hall, Horgan & Slattery, to consult on the project. They proposed to save the city over a million dollars by using less marble and statuary, but when Thomas died in 1901 and Horgan & Slattery succeeded him, they submitted a plan for ornamental alterations that added one million dollars to the final cost of the building.[17]

Work continued until 1911, but when the Hall of Records opened in 1905 its program of decorative murals and sculpture was sufficiently realized to distinguish the design as the fullest government sponsored exemplar of the artistic collaboration that was a principal goal of the American Renaissance. Thomas's design exhibited the same sort of imposing French Classicism as Gordon, Bragdon & Orchard's City Hall proposal, but lightened in its mass and enlivened by an elaborate sculptural program that included at the cornice a row of heroic figures of former mayors and

Hall of Records, northwest corner of Centre and Chambers streets. John R. Thomas and Horgan & Slattery, 1899-1911. View from Centre Street. NYHS

governors carved by Philip Martiny. Thomas piled a three-story Corinthian colonnade on a two-story-high, triple-arched central entrance to form a slightly projecting frontispiece affixed to an elaborately detailed seven-story building crowned by a steeply pitched mansard roof. Inside, a lushly detailed central hall was dominated by a magnificent staircase leading to a colonnaded upper story that evoked the grand scale and opulence of Charles Garnier's Paris Opera. Schuyler found the Hall of Records "perhaps the most Parisian thing in New York," representing "the composite image" of the "broad, solid, ornate palaces, of an ample scale, which have been reared to accommodate the communal activities of the state or city." The skillfulness of its composition was particularly amazing, Schuyler pointed out, because Thomas "was so much a self-taught architect" who had never studied in Paris.[18]

Significantly, Thomas saw the Hall of Records not in isolation but as the wing of a projected group of governmental buildings stretching westward along the north side of Chambers Street to Broadway. Despite numerous alternate proposals, Schuyler reported, "the Hall of Records, by indicating its own supplement, has led the popular instinct to demand the completion of the scheme. . . . To provide in this manner for the extension of his own work is the greatest municipal service the architect of the Hall of Records had it in his power to render, even greater than the production of that handsome and dignified edifice, though this latter service is far from insignificant."[19] Plans for a building along Chambers Street intended to house a new County Courthouse were developed by Israels & Harder, who faithfully followed Thomas's design (which Harder had earlier worked on as an employee of Thomas).[20]

The success of the Hall of Records emphasized the need for a coordinated civic center plan, and reformers clamored for positive action.[21] Herbert Croly alleged that the city had "degraded one of the most spacious and delightful squares with which any City Hall in America was surrounded with an insignificant little park, over-run with buildings with no atmosphere, and no disposition of any kind to give space, distinction and dignity."[22]

The 1904 Report of the New York City Improvement Commission attempted to come to terms with the problem, emphatically giving its support for the retention of City Hall, which it described as "one of the few good monuments

Proposed Civic Center and Brooklyn Bridge Terminal, City Hall Park. Henry F. Hornbostel and George B. Post, 1903. Perspective. CU

possessed by the City."[23] While the 1904 report offered no specific suggestions for the civic center, its focus on the value of City Hall and appropriateness of its location, the need for a coordinated development plan, and on problems of congestion at the adjacent terminus to the Brooklyn Bridge, which dumped its traffic virtually on the doorstep of City Hall, all combined to trigger a sequence of events that led to the construction of the Municipal Building and a series of unrealized plans to unite new and existing facilities into a coherent civic center.

Five years earlier, George B. Post had proposed a sweeping new plan of diagonal avenues that would cut through the tangled street grid above City Hall and connect Park Row, Delancey Street and Union Square and facilitate north-south traffic movement while helping to prevent the repetition at the Williamsburg Bridge entrance of the congestion that plagued the Manhattan approach to the Brooklyn Bridge.[24] A principal feature of Post's proposal was the acquisition by the city of a large, irregularly bounded site north of Chambers Street for the establishment of "a great terrace" that would "make a most magnificent situation for a City Hall which would be adequate in size for the wants of Greater New York [and place] all the municipal buildings in a group, with the City Hall in the center."[25] While Post did not prepare a design for the project, he did illustrate his paper with a plan for a vast courtyard building to be located on the terrace whose principal approach would rise from Broadway via a block-wide ramped plaza to a terrace high enough to permit Centre Street to flow beneath it north from Park Row.

In 1903 Gustav Lindenthal, the Commissioner of the city's Department of Bridges, charged Post as consulting architect and Henry Hornbostel as designing architect with providing plans for a new terminal and restructured trolley loop at the Brooklyn Bridge and for a comprehensive organization of City Hall Park.[26] They proposed that the park be cleared of all buildings except City Hall, with city offices provided on the north side of Chambers Street in a new tripartite building incorporating Thomas's Hall of Records. Pedestrian bridges and a clocktower would connect this new building with the bridge, the park and a proposed 650-foot campanile-like municipal office tower. In contrast to earlier schemes that had called for the demolition or relocation of City Hall, Post and Hornbostel treated the building as a cherished cultural artifact. Its anachronistic small scale was enhanced by the proposed architectural backdrop, while the pyramid-topped skyscraper offered one of the earliest pure expressions of the symbolic role free-standing office towers might play. The project's five million dollar estimated cost defeated it, but the skyscraper and bridge across Chambers Street were reflected in the program of the 1907 Municipal Building Competition.[27]

A scaled-down version of the terminal project was prepared in 1905 by George E. Best, who had succeeded the controversial Lindenthal as Commissioner of Bridges.[28] Best eliminated the office tower and commissioned Carrère & Hastings to redesign the terminal building in a modified Renaissance vocabulary that was less sympathetic to the Hall of Records. The three million dollar project was never realized.

In 1907 the city revived in earnest the idea first proposed by Post and Hornbostel in 1903 of a municipal office building to complement City Hall. The irregular site was complicated, and the need for a building twenty to twenty-five stories high made the problem even more difficult. Entrants to the competition included Carrère & Hastings, Howells & Stokes, Clinton & Russell and McKim, Mead & White. Carrère & Hastings's scheme was a thirty-story French chateau, irregularly massed and elaborately roofed. Clinton & Russell and Howells & Stokes prepared less interesting schemes, the latter rejecting the complex geometry of the site in favor of a massive rectangular tower which rose to a gently set-back rooftop.[29]

The winners of the competition were McKim, Mead & White. McKim did not find the skyscraper form congenial and had been reluctant to enter the competition, so the building was designed by William Kendall, who was to become the firm's principal designer after McKim's death in 1909.[30] Although it drew heavily on the firm's earlier work—the layered stages of the tower from White's Madison Square Garden and Grand Central projects and the three-part organization from the Gorham Company Build-

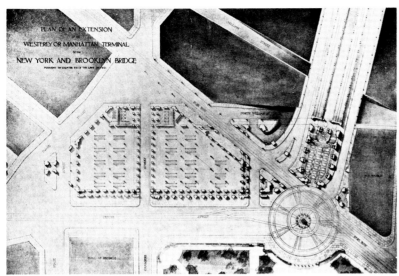
Proposed Brooklyn Bridge Terminal, Centre Street at Chambers Street. Carrère & Hastings, 1905. Plan of ground floor. CU

Proposed Brooklyn Bridge Terminal, Centre Street at Chambers Street. Carrère & Hastings, 1905. Centre Street elevation. CU

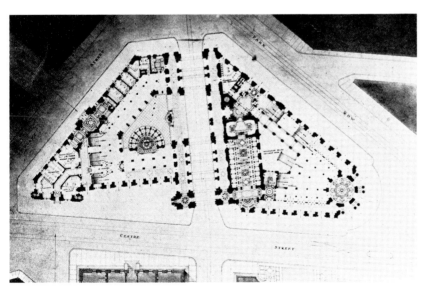
Municipal Building competition entry, Centre Street at Chambers Street. Carrère & Hastings, 1907. Plan of ground floor. CU

Municipal Building competition entry, Centre Street at Chambers Street. Carrère & Hastings, 1907. South elevation. CU

Proposed New York County Courthouse, east side of Madison Avenue between Twenty-fifth and Twenty-sixth streets. Howells & Stokes, 1909. Perspective view from Madison Square. CU

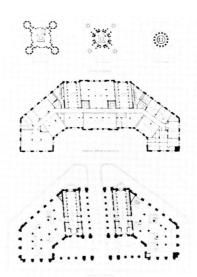

Municipal Building, Centre Street at Chambers Street. McKim, Mead & White, 1907–14. Plans of ground floor, typical office floor and tower. CU

ing—Kendall's design provided an early example of the skyscraper's potential to shape urban space. Seen from the southwest, the U-shaped mass deferred to City Hall by seeming to embrace it. At the top of the tower was an homage to the older building's cupola which gave the skyscraper the Imperial Roman overtones McKim had proposed as appropriate to the city's Metropolitan character.[31] At street level, a nobly proportioned arch permitted Chambers Street to run under the building, while an open hypostyle loggia at the south subway concourse sheltered travellers beneath vaults of Guastavino tile carried on intricately shaped piers. While the Municipal Building was in many ways little more than a glorified version of a commercial office building, its siting and the handling of its base and rooftop lantern, surmounted by Adolph A. Weinman's sculpture *Civic Fame,* all combined to raise the design to an appropriate symbolic level.

In the midst of the controversy surrounding the various threats to City Hall Park, the construction of the new Criminal Courts Building on Centre Street, from Franklin to White streets, went almost unnoticed. But upon its completion in 1894 by the architects Thom, Wilson & Schaarschmidt, it was immediately lambasted by the *Architectural Record* as "upon the whole quite the most discreditable edifice the city has ever erected. . . . The judges do not care about these things; the criminals dislike it, not because it is an ugly and vulgar building, but because it is a court of justice, and would dislike a better building quite as heartily; the criminal lawyers, if they be of the schuyster class, doubtless like it from natural affinity."[32]

The Criminal Courts Building was an anachronistic holdover from the Cosmopolitan Era in its loose approach to Classical prototypes and the strident polychromy of its granite, brownstone and brick facades. Although clearly based on Richard Morris Hunt's Lenox Library, the courthouse architects abandoned Hunt's studied, neo-Grec simplicity for an attempt at architectural bombast which, as the *Record* pointed out, made John Haviland's adjacent Egyptian style prison, known as the Tombs, take on "an aspect of new distinction since the advent of its disorderly neighbor."[33]

The need for larger courthouse facilities continued to grow. In 1909 the city decided to replace the Tweed Courthouse. Many sites, including Washington Square, were proposed before, amazingly, the selection process once again led to the north end of City Hall Park. The public and most of the profession found the notion untenable, although the *Architectural Record* thought that "in the interest of what is left of the park," a building that occupied "as narrow a fringe as possible" might not be too bad.[34]

While other sites were being considered, Howells & Stokes advanced a design for the new courthouse on the blockfront between the Appellate Courthouse and Madison Square Garden. They placed a nine-story tower containing the courtrooms on top of a much wider base housing offices and a library, in an exuberant combination of Classical motifs that would have made a remarkable transition between the chaste Classicism of James Brown Lord's Appellate Court and Stanford White's exotic pleasure palace.[35]

Another interim proposal was even more remarkable. In 1910 J. Riely Gordon designed a one-thousand-foot high courthouse for City Hall Park which he described as "clustered 'Pillars of Justice.'" The slenderness of Gordon's design was intended to save as much parkland as possible; as a result, the building would have been 350 feet taller than the Metropolitan Life Insurance Company Building, then the tallest in the world. The twenty-four-foot plinth, the base and the lower stories of Gordon's design were intended to house the County Clerk's office, while sixty circular courtrooms were accommodated in the shaftlike superstructure above. The frieze contained the law library while the judges' chambers were above in a 144-foot pedestal. Capping the entire composition, would have been a 192-foot-high statue of *Justice,* with a torch rising 1,064 feet above the city to act as a smokestack for the building. When illuminated at night, it would have the appearance of a "real, live, mammoth, flaming Roman torch . . . visible throughout Manhattan . . . and . . . at the same time the beacon light for vessels and the first indication of land from far out at sea."[37]

As a result of public opposition to the use of City Hall Park for building purposes, the law to permit construction

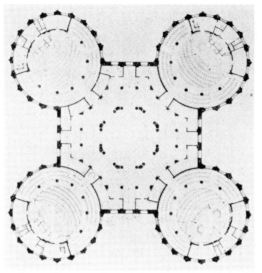

Proposed New York County Courthouse, Chambers Street facing City Hall Park. James Riely Gordon, 1910. Model and plan of typical courtroom floor. CU

of the courthouse was amended on October 12, 1911, to prohibit its location in the park and force the city to find an appropriate site elsewhere. A site was chosen in January 1912—bounded by Leonard, Lafayette, Baxter and Park streets in the heart of the area Post had suggested as a new civic center twelve years before—and in April, Guy Lowell was announced as the winner of a competition for the design of the new building.[38] The two-stage competition was complexly organized, with ten architects who placed in the first (open) stage pitted against twelve invited competitors in the second stage.[39] Lowell, who came from the former group, captured the jury's attention with a controversial but logical round building with a concentric plan eminently suited to the awkward site and the complexities of the building program.[40]

In January 1913 Lowell combined with the Committee on Civic Improvements of the New York Chapter of the American Institute of Architects to propose a scheme for grouping public buildings around a much larger site focusing on the courthouse. While the fate of the courthouse and the civic center at Foley Square was unresolved by the close of the Composite Era in 1915, an adjustment in the boundaries of the site and objections raised by the client in 1919 caused Lowell to change his design from a circle to a hexagon.[41] Difficulties in settling upon and paying for the site persisted and construction was not completed until 1926.[42]

While the Hall of Records reflected the bombast of *fin de siecle* Modern French design, James Brown Lord's building for the Appellate Division of the New York State Supreme Court, built in 1900 at the northeast corner of Madison Avenue and Twenty-fifth Street, appeared more like an imposing club.[43] The crusading journal *Public Improvements* praised "the first attempt in the city of New York to erect a building in which the utilitarian and artistic are so combined as to make one harmonious whole."[44] The Appellate Division, new to the state's court system, originally commissioned Lord to remodel for the court's temporary use the old Arnold Constable Building at Fifth Avenue and Nineteenth Street. On the strength of his work there, Lord was asked to prepare designs for a new building on a narrow lot (25 feet by 150 feet) on the corner of Twenty-fifth Street and Madison Square.

The principal features of Lord's design, aside from its dazzling whiteness, were the pedimented porch on Twenty-fifth Street, which led to a rotunda lit by a dome of grayish yellow glass, and the sculptural program that enlivened the building's elevations and skyline. The Appellate Court was the product of even more extensive collaboration of sculptors and architects than the Hall of Records. Ten figures which stood against the sky along the parapet were the work of eight sculptors, including Daniel Chester French, who sculpted *Justice,* flanked by *Study* and *Power* at the peak of the pediment, and Karl Bitter, who crowned the Twenty-fifth Street facade with the figure of *Peace*. The pediment was filled with Charles E. Neihaus's group, *The Triumph of Law,* while the courtrooms and interior passages were embellished by murals designed by Edward Simmons, Edwin H. Blashfield, Kenyon Cox, H. Siddons Mowbray and others, all working under the direction of John LaFarge.

The Appellate Court was the most important of a number of courthouses built by the city and state outside the civic center to meet the needs of the individual boroughs as well as the independent counties formed by the state government as new counterparts. Michael J. Garvin's 1906 design for the Bronx Borough Courthouse, on 161st Street between Brook and Third avenues, effectively mirrored the grandiloquence of contemporary public and institutional buildings in Manhattan.[45] A compact, almost vertical composition, the courthouse consisted of a high rusticated base supporting two stories and an attic. Above the deeply cut entrance arch, at eye level for passersby on the adjacent Third Avenue El, the leaf-crowned statue of *Justice* by G.E. Roine sat in a deep niche between Modern French variants of Doric columns.

H. Van Buren Magonigle's exuberantly Modern French design for the Gates Avenue Courthouse in Brooklyn, consisting of four Doric columns supporting a cornice between which were piled windows set in segmental arches, was rejected by the Art Commission in favor of the far more restrained, delicate design that was built.[46] Their action may have reflected the shifting taste of the day, or it may have stemmed from a concern for the scale of the existing

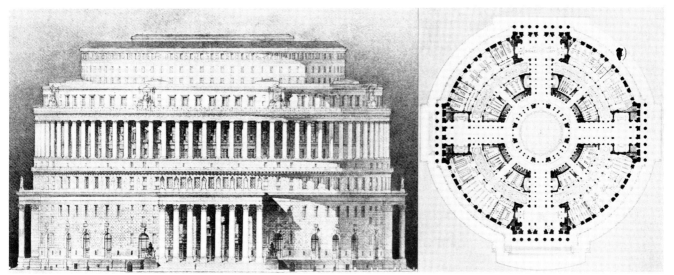

New York County Courthouse competition entry, Leonard and Park streets between Baxter and Lafayette streets. Guy Lowell, 1912. Elevation and plan of ground floor. CU

street on which the courthouse was to be built.

Given the municipal spirit of the Composite Era, the assumption might be made that the consolidation of the city would bring with it a need for new civic centers at the core of each of the outer boroughs to complement those in Manhattan. Yet initially little more was done than changing the name of Brooklyn's City Hall to Borough Hall. A competition was held for Brooklyn's Municipal Building in 1909, but the project was not realized until new designs were made in the 1920s.[47] Queens, which was only beginning to develop a sense of itself as something more than a scattering of villages, did not get a civic center until the 1930s. Nor did the Bronx, which built a borough hall in Crotona Park in 1895-97, designed by George Post, but waited until just before the First World War to consider the grouping of its public buildings along the Grand Boulevard and Concourse. Surprisingly, it was Staten Island, the most geographically remote of the boroughs that most coherently adapted the municipal spirit to a suburban situation. Carrère & Hastings were commissioned in 1906 to design a borough hall in Richmond, across the street from their St. George ferry terminal and not far away from their St. George branch building for the New York Public Library. Later they were to complete the ensemble with the Richmond County Courthouse (1913-1919).

The Richmond Borough Hall combined the efficient logic of the firm's traditionally sound planning with a Modern French vocabulary that transformed a modestly-sized building into a commanding gateway to the city's most unexplored borough.[48] A tall tower acted as a beacon of municipal greeting for the ferries as they approached from across the bay. At closer range, mansard roofs and the boldly scaled limestone and brick facade combined to form an appropriate impression of provincial monumentality. Carrère & Hastings skillfully adjusted the building—possibly based on the *Hotel de Ville* at Tours (1903), a monument of the Modern French style by the great teacher at the Ecole des Beaux-Arts, Victor Laloux—to a steeply sloping site by turning a monumental frontispiece with a raised Doric colonnade toward the harbor on the downhill side, while making the uphill side almost domestic in scale with French windows and a simply detailed entrance door placed directly below the clock tower.

The Richmond County Courthouse was stylistically miles apart from the exuberant Modern French style of the Borough Hall.[49] Built from 1913 to 1919, it reflected the evolution of Carrère & Hastings's work from a free, vigorously modelled Classicism to a more conservative and refined use of precedent, in this case derived from eighteenth-century France. Although Carrère & Hastings attempted to relate the two buildings scenographically by means of cornice alignments, the lower pitch of the courthouse roof, the boldly scaled portico and the uniform gray color set it apart and made it appear much grander.

Buildings for Public Service

In 1898 the *Real Estate Record and Guide* lamented the lack "of even one architecturally decent police station."[50] Of all the municipal departments, only the Fire Department seemed sensitive to its public image. As early as 1887 the Fire Department had retained Napoleon Le Brun to design a series of distinguished buildings that included the Old Slip Enginehouse in the Dutch Renaissance style[51] and the Richardsonian Romanesque headquarters at 157 East Sixty-seventh Street.[52] Le Brun designed other stations around town in the 1890s, culminating with the elaborate Engine Company Number 31 and Battalion Number 2 on Elm and White streets—a French Renaissance design built in 1895 on a newly widened street that was to become a major thoroughfare (Lafayette Street) connecting the unplanned village streets of downtown with the uptown grid.[53] The Elm Street Station set a new standard of quality for municipal architecture, although the *Record and Guide* thought its domestic character raised as many questions as it answered about civic art: "As a mansion say, on Riverside Drive, it would be entirely in place, and but for the large and numerous driveways which alone betray its actual purpose, would be accepted as an agreeable example of a rich and refined domestic architecture. But as a lodging for firemen and fire horses and fire engines, it is manifestly an extravagant absurdity."[54]

Hoppin & Koen's Engine Company Number 65 (1898)

New York County Courthouse, 60 Centre Street at Foley Square between Pearl and Worth streets. Guy Lowell, 1919-26. View from Centre Street. MCNY

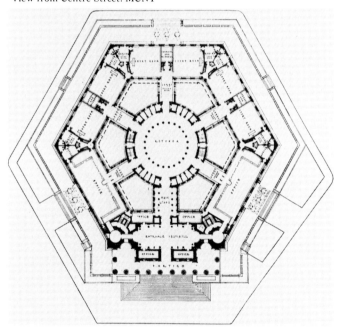

New York County Courthouse, 60 Centre Street at Foley Square between Pearl and Worth streets. Guy Lowell, 1919-26. Plan of ground floor. CU

Appellate Division, New York State Supreme Court, northeast corner of Madison Avenue and Twenty-fifth Street. James Brown Lord, 1900. View from Madison Avenue showing Madison Square Garden in the background. MCNY

Engine Company Number 31 and Battalion Number 2, northeast corner of Lafayette and White streets. Napoleon Le Brun & Sons, 1895. OMH

Engine Company Number 33, 44 Great Jones Street. Ernest Flagg and Walter B. Chambers, 1898. OMH

Water Tower Number 3 and Hook and Ladder House Number 24, 113 West Thirty-third Street. Horgan & Slattery, 1901. CU

on West Forty-third Street also failed to earn the full praise of the *Record and Guide*. Although its planar, Italianate facade, which complemented the nearby Century Club, represented a move toward a more suitably austere expression of municipality, "in the profound and the minute delicacy of its ornamentation, it is quite as unsuitable and as absurd as Le Brun's design. . . . Such things make the judicious grieve almost to the extent of longing for the old stupid engine houses. . . . For these are at least devoid of that pretentiousness which is a chief element in vulgarity."[55]

The consolidation of the city and the rise of civic spirit led to the construction around 1900 of several fire houses that brought an urban grandeur to neighborhoods otherwise untouched by any sense of monumental architecture. Ernest Flagg and Walter B. Chambers's design for Engine Company Number 33 (1898) at 44 Great Jones Street was the first and perhaps the most perfectly conceived of the city's Modern French station houses. It marked a distinct departure from the stations by Le Brun; overt historicism and elaborate decoration gave way to a functional grandeur arising from a special sensitivity to the expressive capacity of contemporary materials. The *Record and Guide* was quick to see its "advance in suitability upon its architecturesque predecessors."[56] The brick facade trimmed with limestone was simple and exuberant: a limestone base with two segmental arches providing access to the engine storage area supported a brick superstructure pierced by a bold, three-story central arch of limestone. The enormous arch was, as the *Record and Guide* observed, "entirely open, a mere sash frame, in fact, on which the intermediate floor lines are treated as transoms."[57] A metal cornice terminated the facade and provided an effective transition to a sloping roof cut by an ingenious skylight with movable shutters that compensated for the small window area provided by the arch to the top floor. A splendidly voluptuous cartouche at the crown of the arch supported a tremendous flagpole that pierced the skyline.[58]

Horgan & Slattery's Engine Company Number 72 (1900) at 22 East Twelfth Street was distinguished by an overscaled swan's neck pediment atop the central dormer, a motif that echoed, perhaps too faithfully, the pedimented porch of the adjoining tenement.[59] But Horgan & Slattery hit their stride as interpreters of the Modern French style with their Water Tower Number 3 and Hook and Ladder

Police Department Central Headquarters, Centre Street between Grand and Broome streets. Hoppin & Koen, 1909. View from the northeast corner of Centre and Broome streets. MCNY

Company Number 24.[60] Built in 1901 at 113 West Thirty-third Street, it was an unusually flamboyant building and also a compositional duality, with the appearance of two identical buildings set side by side. Unlike Flagg and Chambers's unified Great Jones design, here a limestone basement supported two great arches crowned by double split-pediments which triumphantly reached above the roofline.

At Engine Company Number 35 on East 114th Street, near Madison Avenue, Percy Griffin reinterpreted the same theme in a more explicitly archaeological manner, substituting a dignified, almost Roman Classicism for the syncopation and bravura of the Modern French designs.[61] Werner & Windolph's slightly larger Hook and Ladder Company Number 35 (1908) at 232 West Sixty-third Street, like their East Fifty-fourth Street Bath House, was bombastic, a tripartite composition in brick trimmed with limestone that made extensive use of Corinthian pilasters.[62]

Herts & Tallant's combined facility for Hook and Ladder Company Number 38 and Engine Company Number 88 could almost be confused with work by midwestern modernists such as George Maher.[63] Built in 1908 at 2223 Belmont Avenue in the Bronx, it was a starkly modelled brick box relieved only by undecorated limestone trim surrounding the openings. The windows of the second floor were dramatically set deep behind the facade in order to have them read as a cornice.

Even after 1900, distinguished Police Department buildings were few and far between.[64] Certainly the most dramatic was the new Central Headquarters at 240 Centre Street, a grand Baroque palace that majestically stood above the jumbled neighborhood around it.[65] Designed by Hoppin & Koen in 1909, it reflected the influence of the Modern French style but also the work of contemporary English architects such as John Belcher, John James Joass and Arthur Beresford Pite. Crowned by a too-small dome and squeezed into an irregular site that was eighty-eight feet wide at one end but only forty-six feet wide at the other, and that was too crowded by surrounding buildings to ever let one step back for a good view, the Central Headquarters was nevertheless a fine piece of urban design, which supplied the neighborhood with a secular focus and fulfilled Hoppin's intention "to impress both officer and prisoner . . . with the majesty of the law."[66]

Another station calculated to impress was Hunt &

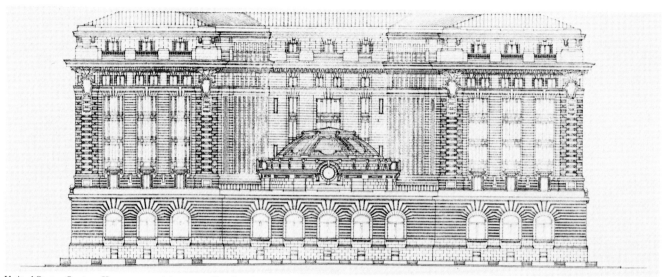

United States Custom House competition entry, Bowling Green and Bridge Street between State and Whitehall streets. Carrère & Hastings, 1899. State Street elevation. CU

Hunt's First Precinct House, also built in 1909.[67] An appropriately fierce version of the Palazzo Strozzi in Florence, the First Precinct occupied a site in what had been the watery center of Old Slip. Edward Pearce Casey's Thirteenth Precinct House was interesting principally because of its concrete construction in emulation of stone.[68] Casey used concrete not only for the floors, roofs and stairs, but also for the walls facing the courtyard and the street, which were made in separately cast blocks resembling cut stone. As Casey observed: "It is not necessary, or desirable, to imitate any particular stone, but it may be readily imagined that almost any texture, or degree of hardness or color, may be produced by the choice of the aggregates."[69]

Stoughton & Stoughton's Forty-first Precinct House was built within the greenery of Mosholu Parkway in the Bronx.[70] It was more a villa than a station house, with asymmetrical facades of dark red brick laced up in intricate patterns and great wooden brackets painted green supporting a roof covered in cobalt blue glazed Spanish tiles. The Forty-first Precinct was a new and more humane response to the problem of precinct house design: "Grass, flowers and vines will be added to form a more complete setting to these buildings, which, from their materials and style, seem as if they had always formed part of the landscape. They form a new departure in civic architecture—buildings of which the inhabitants of the neighborhood are justly proud . . . consorting well with their surroundings and being a dignified expression of their uses."[71]

The Federal Presence

Two of the greatest civic undertakings of the Composite Era were built not to serve the municipality but to reinforce its role as the leading American metropolis, representative of America's role in the world. These buildings were the United States Custom House (1907) and the United States Immigration Station at Ellis Island (1898).

The competition for the Custom House was announced in 1899.[72] Many leading architects including Cass Gilbert, Carrère & Hastings, Trowbridge & Livingston and Shepley, Rutan & Coolidge participated with schemes attesting to the hold of the Modern French style over American architects.[73] The *Architectural Review* observed that Carrère & Hastings's submission represented "the modern school of French architecture at its highest point."[74]

The jury, however, had a hard time choosing between Carrère & Hastings's design and Gilbert's, and invited the competitors into conference, suggesting that they form a partnership.[75] When that failed, the jurors chose Gilbert's design. Though his plans were quite similar to Carrère & Hastings's and each had an oval rotunda within a central light court, Gilbert's building was more powerfully massed, and his decision to thrust a monumental flight of stairs out onto the sidewalk (Carrère & Hastings kept their stairs within the building envelope) made it seem to connect more directly with the site, swallowing up the downward flow of Broadway and pulling it into the great rotunda.

The Custom House was the second in New York built exclusively for that purpose. The first was the small, Greek Revival temple at Wall and Nassau streets that Town & Davis designed in 1836. That building was outgrown within ten years, and in 1863 the Custom House was relocated in the former Merchants' Exchange Building, designed in 1842 by Isaiah Rogers. While Rogers's building, with its continuous Ionic colonnade raised on a massive base, was also conceived in symbolic rather than functional terms, its site on Wall Street was too inconspicuous for it to realize its full measure of grandeur. Gilbert's design, by virtue of its location, was far more compelling. Faced with a complex program for a working office facility, Gilbert did not set out to make an inhabited temple but rather to render a seven-story office building monumental through the manipulation of its scale and the introduction of sculpture. "It is a great Government building," Gilbert wrote after he won, "which, while having a practical purpose, should express in its adornment something of the wealth and luxury of the great port of New York, and have a dignity appropriate to a notable public monument."[76]

The site facing Bowling Green at the end of Broadway was difficult. Trapezoidal in plan, it had one long face toward the Battery, but its principal side was along Bowling Green, which could be seen at a great distance from uptown and therefore demanded a powerful facade. Though Gilbert

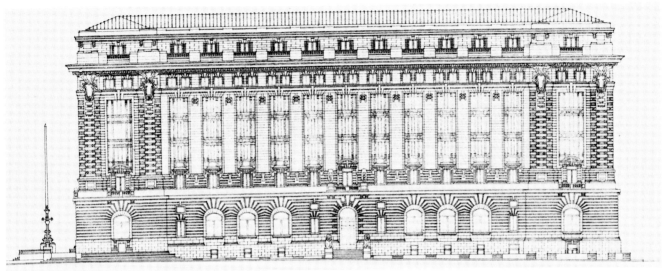

United States Custom House competition entry, Bowling Green and Bridge Street between State and Whitehall streets. Carrère & Hastings, 1899. Bridge Street elevation. CU

ironically turned the building's back to its source of wealth in the harbor, he acknowledged the ocean trade in the building's elaborate ornamentation with four sculptural groups by Daniel Chester French representing four continents, each symbolized by a woman surrounded by her icons. To the east, *Asia* sat on a throne of skulls, while a giant *Africa* slept in the west. In between were *North America,* clear eyed and forward looking, and a regal *Europe.* Atop the cornice stood twelve statues in period dress representing the great seafaring nations. Above it all, breaking the attic balustrade and crowning the facade, was a cartouche by Karl Bitter, consisting of the seal of the United States flanked by loosely draped, winged women—one holding the sheathed sword of peace and one the *fasces* of a strong nation—and topped by a federal eagle. Smaller decorative motifs were marine symbols such as dolphins and sea shells, while the head of Mercury, god of Commerce, was incorporated in the Corinthian capitals. The robust decoration was continued in the grand circulation spaces and the oval hall where clerks worked in great splendor.

Throughout the first half of the great period of European immigration, 1880-1920, human cargo was processed in less grand surroundings. First- or cabin-class passengers were met on board their ships by immigration inspectors who arrived and departed by cutters. However, the hordes of steerage-class travellers coming to New York—over twelve million between 1892 and 1925—were put ashore on Ellis Island, there to be examined and questioned. Even though the island was within sight of the towers of Manhattan, there was a long and tedious procedure to go through before the immigrants could officially enter the country.

The process was made somewhat more humane in 1897, when the old wooden buildings burned down and a competition was held for a new complex of buildings whose character and dignity would be in keeping with "the magnitude of the nation to which these structures were to be the entrance."[77] Boring & Tilton won with a scheme consisting of five buildings: a large reception center, hospital and surgeons' house, power house, kitchen and dining hall and bath and laundry. The main building was ample: 165 by 385 feet with a 62-foot-high ceiling and observation towers reaching to 100 feet. The towers helped to provide a picturesque skyline that established the complex in the flat expanse of the bay. At a closer scale, the main building's monumental portals were enriched with carvings of symbolically apt American eagles and a profusion of Modern French ornament. Ironically, the building intended as a gateway to America was one of the most vivid examples in New York of the influence of the Ecole des Beaux-Arts, where both Boring and Tilton had studied. Despite its flamboyant scenography, the main building was in reality an enormous "booking hall" that was able to process five thousand people per day (three thousand more in emergencies) while relatives watched from the visitors' gallery.

The opening of the new immigrant station passed almost without notice for most residents of the city. The *Architectural Record* observed "what a huge country this is getting to be, when what is really but a wicket or turnstile, whereby the incomers may be counted and sorted, is, by the actual requirements of its being, expanded to such proportions as these, and what a great thing it is, not only for America, but for humanity, that there should be so vast an asylum, or rather arena, opened for the crowded-out, the 'residuum,' of other lands."[78] Henry James demurred, finding Ellis Island

a drama that goes on, without a pause, day by day and year by year, this visible act of ingurgitation on the part of our body politic and social, and constituting really an appeal to amazement beyond that of any sword-swallowing or fire-swallowing of the circus. The wonder that one couldn't keep down was the thought that these two or three hours of one's own chance vision of the business were but as a tick or two of the mighty clock, the clock that never, never stops—least of all when it strikes, for a sign of so much winding-up, some louder hour of our national fate than usual. I think indeed that the simplest account of the action of Ellis Island on the spirit of any sensitive citizen who may have happened to "look in" is that he comes back from his visit not at all the same person that he went.

Before this door which opens to [the immigrants], there only with a hundred forms and ceremonies, grindings and grumblings of the key, they stand appealing and waiting, marshalled,

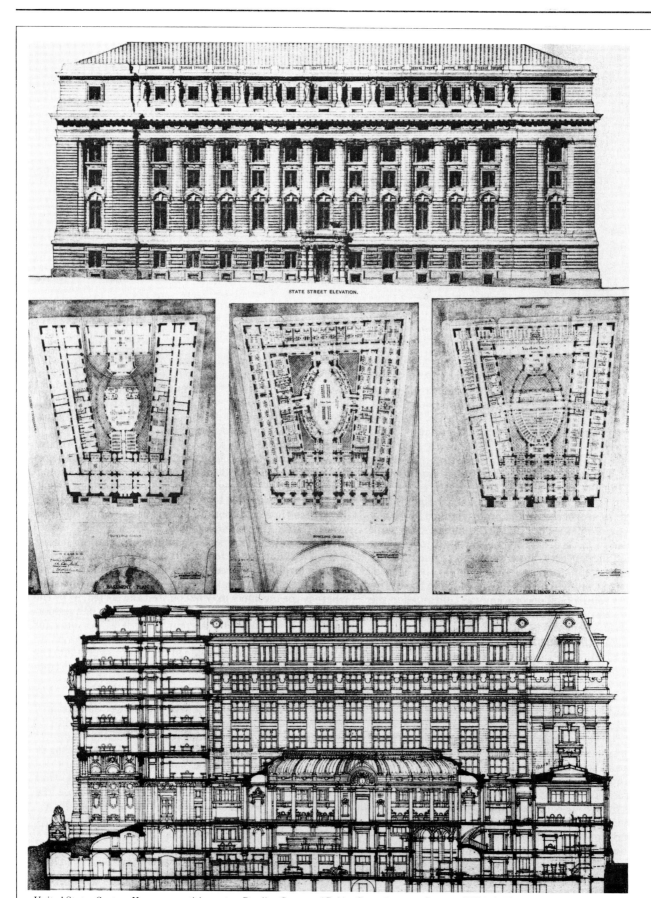

United States Custom House competition entry, Bowling Green and Bridge Street between State and Whitehall streets. Cass Gilbert, 1899. Plans of ground, first and second floors, State Street elevation and longitudinal section. CU

United States Custom House, Bowling Green and Bridge Street between State and Whitehall streets. Cass Gilbert, 1900-07. Rotunda. MCNY

United States Custom House, Bowling Green and Bridge Street between State and Whitehall streets. Cass Gilbert, 1900-07. View from Bowling Green. NYHS

United States Immigration Station, Ellis Island. Boring & Tilton, 1898. Immigrants departing for Manhattan. MCNY

United States Immigration Station, Ellis Island. Boring & Tilton, 1898. View looking west. NYHS

herded, divided, subdivided, sorted, sifted, searched, fumigated, for longer or shorter periods—the effect of all which prodigious process, an intendedly "scientific" feeding of the mill, is again to give the earnest observer a thousand more things to think of than he can pretend to retail.[79]

Schools

No public building type was less thoughtfully considered in the Cosmopolitan Era than the public school. As the *Real Estate Record and Guide* observed in 1890, "There are those who hold that for school buildings no design is called for more pleasing to the eye than that of the factory. . . . The idea of constructing such buildings with a view to making them an ornament to the city and a lasting pleasure to the beholder is one with which they [the bureaucrats of education] have no sympathy. They look upon the school-life of a child as a grinding, manufacturing process to which the factory style of building is eminently suitable."[80]

In the 1890s, the enormous influx of immigrant children and the civic spirit of the Composite Era produced widespread pressures for social and aesthetic reform of the school system.[81] By 1898, 85 percent of the city's population was foreign or had foreign-born parents, leaving the city's "salvation dependent upon the conversion of a daily arriving cityful of Russians, Turks, Austro-Hungarians, Greeks, Arabs, into good Americans," according to at least one educational reformer of the day, Adele Marie Shaw.[82] Her article about New York's public schools made it quite clear that the spirit of that reform was a combination of concern for the children's welfare and a fear of immigrant customs that made the school system almost independent of the parents: "For the first time in our history all children of school age are registered and cared for, all truants are followed up, all recreant parents coerced. . . . No one denies that New York's growth is abnormally large, its adoption of aliens abnormally confiding. If it hopes to Americanize a school population chiefly of foreign parentage it must use abnormal means. Last year one school had free baths; 1,000 baths were taken in that school in one week. Every school in the thickly settled districts should have free baths. If you sniff at 'frills' and say, 'Give them the three R's; let them get clean at home,' you forget that they will not get clean at home, and that if they stay unclean in school every child and every home is endangered."[83] Yet elsewhere in the article,

P.S. 165, West 108th Street between Amsterdam Avenue and Broadway. C.B.J. Snyder, 1898. View of the rear of the school on West 109th Street. NYHS

Shaw went on at great length about the importance of treating the children kindly, and said, "Make it all good, *no matter what it costs.*"[84] In fact, the city did spend a great deal of money on an enormous expansion of the school system, raising the public school building as well as the quality of education offered to a new level.

The first step for the Board of Education was to establish an architectural department, placing at its head as Superintendent of School Buildings C.B.J. Snyder, a dedicated architect with both administrative skills and design talent.[85] Snyder was a government bureaucrat who got things done while holding on to his ideals. During his many years in office he remained sensitive to the evolving technical and aesthetic issues of the day. As a result, the expansion of the city's school system between 1890 and 1915 mirrored, and in some cases pioneered, the most advanced theories of public education popular in the United States.

Snyder's first successes involved the improvement of general physical conditions in the existing schools. Under his direction, buildings adjacent to public schools were purchased and pulled down to give space for yards, to provide more light, and leave room for proper fire stairs and toilets.

By the mid-1890s, Snyder became increasingly involved with the design of new school buildings, introducing specialized facilities like laboratories, auditoriums, gymnasiums and playgrounds. His designs were easily distinguished from earlier New York City schools by the enormous double-hung windows used to give every classroom plenty of light and ventilation.[86] The over-scaled windows often gave a cozy domestic scale to the simply composed elevations. Placed in facades that had less wall surface than window area, they helped to produce geometric compositions that Snyder easily manipulated for Gothic, Jacobean, Colonial, and Modern French designs with a minimum of detail.

The public schools on Edgecombe Avenue, between 140th and 141st streets (1893),[87] and on St. Nicholas Avenue at 117th Street (1894)[88] were early examples of what John Beverly Robinson described in the *Architectural Record* as "the new order of things."[89] In these five-story buildings, Snyder employed the Dutch Colonial mode popularized by Robert W. Gibson's Collegiate Church in the West End to convey a sense of domesticity that helped elevate the schoolhouse to a level of architectural dignity comparable to that of the house.[90]

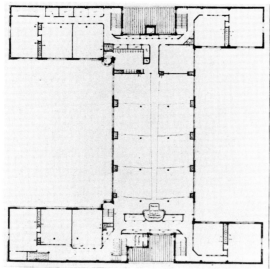

P.S. 165, West 108th Street between Amsterdam Avenue and Broadway. C.B.J. Snyder, 1898. Plan of typical floor. CU

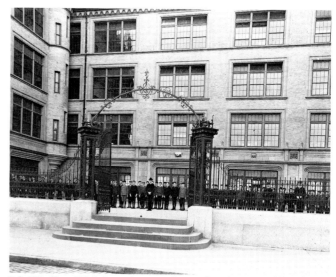

P.S. 165, West 108th Street between Amsterdam Avenue and Broadway. C.B.J. Snyder, 1898. View from West 109th Street. NYHS

At P.S. 165 on 108th Street, between Amsterdam Avenue and the Boulevard (as Broadway was called), Snyder introduced his greatest functional innovation, the H plan, in which two wings contained classrooms facing interior courts, while the center bar held a stack of flexible classrooms with walls which could be rolled back to provide a continuous open space for assemblies and games.[91] At Wadleigh High School for Girls, a more developed example of the H plan built near Seventh Avenue between 114th and 115th streets, Snyder introduced a note of monumentality with a hipped-roof square tower rising at one corner of the courtyard.[92]

Snyder was not always faced with tight inner city sites. At the corner of Andrews and Burnside avenues in the Bronx, he set P.S. 153 on a suburban plot surrounded by a generous lawn dotted with trees.[93] At first, Snyder proposed a school that assumed the character of a large country house or club. Though the Colonial cupola clashed with the English vernacular imagery of the building, it furthered the connections between the school as a representative of the newly consolidated metropolitan government and the disappearing village traditions.

The institution of a system of public high school education brought new demands on Snyder. His first effort, the DeWitt Clinton High School, built in 1906 on Tenth Avenue between Fifty-eighth and Fifty-ninth streets, was one of his most elaborate essays in the Dutch Colonial style.[94] At the time of its planning, Clinton was said to be the largest high school in the United States. The seventy-eight classrooms, fourteen laboratories, four study halls, two gymnasiums, and auditorium were organized on the H plan. The choice of the Dutch Colonial style for DeWitt Clinton came as the result of a suggestion "that the design of a school bearing the name of a man who had 'made history' should follow that which is associated with the early history of the city."[95] The principal interior spaces were handled in a Classical manner, with flattened arches, which helped to compartmentalize the long corridors, and a series of murals depicting Clinton's life flanking the proscenium in the auditorium.

The site for Morris High School (1901–04) at 166th Street and Boston Road in the Bronx was large enough to use an I plan (with much wider courts), and to locate a seventeen-hundred-seat auditorium in a separate wing at the back, with entrances from the school as well as from the street so that it could be used independently from the school on public occasions.[96] The long composition was dominated by a 189-foot-tall central tower with turrets containing ventilating shafts for the laboratories in the upper floors used for faculty research. Snyder's use of what was described as English Collegiate Gothic on the exterior of a science school assumed the same iconographic importance as C.C. Haight's similar work at Yale University's Scientific School and William A. Potter's Teachers College at Columbia University, helping to bridge the gap between the liberal arts traditions of Oxbridge and those in the new scientific disciplines.

In 1897 a competition was held for a new facility for Erasmus Hall High School in the still-independent city of Brooklyn. The consolidation of the two cities put the competition in limbo, but the published submissions reflected a new Classical approach and stood in clear contrast to Snyder's work at that time. Faced with an irregular mid-block site, the architects Mowbray & Uffinger proposed a group of pavilions linked in the manner of Jefferson's University of Virginia, with a courtyard or lawn open at one end to Flatbush Avenue and closed at the other by the main building containing the auditorium.[97] J.G. Glover (in association with H.C. Carrell) pursued a more compact plan, grouping taller buildings around a court with a monumental administration building containing the auditorium at the end.[98] Mowbray & Uffinger's scheme was vaguely Italian in style, perhaps reflecting Stanford White's new campus for New York University, but Glover's proposal was an overblown version of the neo-Grec that reflected Ernest Flagg's design for the Corcoran Art Gallery in Washington, D.C.

After the consolidation of the city, the design of the new building was turned over to Snyder, who transformed the central open space called for in the earlier schemes into a quadrangle surrounded by Collegiate Gothic classroom buildings and entered through a five-story-high tower facing Flatbush Avenue.[99] Only fragments of the original proposal were completed, because nostalgia forced the Board of

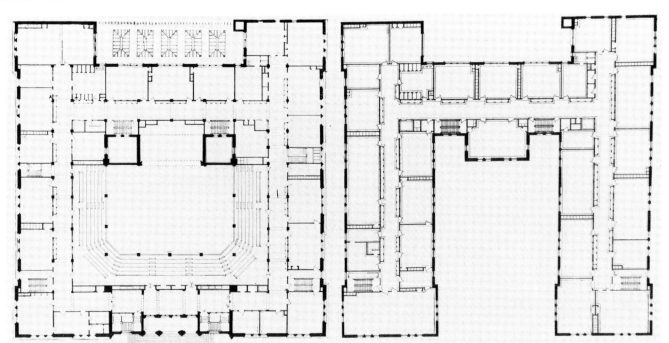

DeWitt Clinton High School, west side of Tenth Avenue between Fifty-eighth and Fifty-ninth streets. C.B.J. Snyder, 1906. Plans of second and third floors. CU

DeWitt Clinton High School, west side of Tenth Avenue between Fifty-eighth and Fifty-ninth streets. C.B.J. Snyder, 1906. Auditorium. CU

DeWitt Clinton High School, west side of Tenth Avenue between Fifty-eighth and Fifty-ninth streets. C.B.J. Snyder, 1906. MCNY

Morris High School, 166th Street between Boston Road and Jackson Avenue, Bronx. C.B.J. Snyder, 1904. NYHS

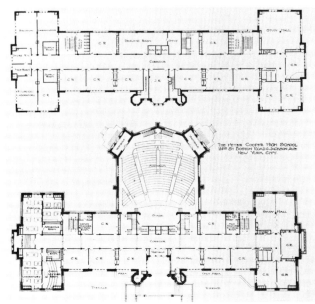

Morris High School, 166th Street between Boston Road and Jackson Avenue, Bronx. C.B.J. Snyder, 1904. Plans of first and typical floors. CU

P.S. 157, west side of St. Nicholas Avenue between West 126th and 127th streets. C.B.J. Snyder, 1899. NYHS

Education to preserve the original Dutch Colonial building of the Erasmus Academy. Nonetheless, the tower and the spectacular auditorium were effective testimony to Snyder's vision.

The various domestic modes that Snyder employed in the late 1890s all had sloping roofs which left ample space within for gymnasium, cooking and shop facilities, but they had the disadvantage of robbing the building of the rooftop playground space found in Snyder's earlier and grimmer castellated schools. By 1900 Snyder had devised a type of building that combined the advantages of a flat roof scheme with less forbidding though still monumental expression. Often built as freestanding buildings on generous sites in the less populated outer boroughs, this more monumental type was characterized by a simple double-loaded plan, a raised basement used as play space in bad weather, a convertible auditorium located nearer the top, and brick and limestone facades designed in a Modern French version of the English Baroque.

P.S. 124 on Fourth Avenue in Brooklyn was an early example of this distinctly civic type of schoolhouse.[100] The model was repeated in gentler versions elsewhere in Brooklyn at P.S. 137 (1901)[101] and P.S. 130 (1908).[102] P.S. 130 was built on Ocean and Fort Hamilton parkways in two stages, the first two floors preceding the last two by a couple of years.

Snyder's finest civic examples were found in Manhattan. His boldest essay in the Modern French style, Stuyvesant High (1905–06) 345 East Fifteenth Street, put the H plan to its most severe test.[103] The school's central entrance pavilion rose to an elaborate pediment emblazoned with its name on a plaque surrounded by garlands, festoons and other paraphernalia of the Modern French taste.

Snyder assimilated the lessons of his new style in a more natural way in more modest buildings like P.S. 21 (1906)[104] on Mott Street extending through to Elizabeth Street, and P.S. 66 (1909) on East Eighty-eighth Street.[105] P.S. 66 was distinguished by a rooftop pergola which was both ornamental and functional; P.S. 21 by a modified H plan built around an existing school which remained in use until the new facility was completed. In order to conserve space yet ensure adequate ventilation, the assembly room was set beneath a courtyard raised one-half level above the street. The courtyard was entered through a monumental

column screen stretched across a broad flight of steps. The school's skillfully composed facades combined red brick and limestone in a gently monumental, vaguely Georgian design. The same vocabulary was used in the miniscule P.S. 34 on Staten Island, a building with proportions based on those of the Petit Trianon but with a character more like that of a villa on Riverside Drive.[106] At P.S. 3 Snyder combined the domestic character of his earlier schools with a Modern French skyline, making a serious attempt to give the school a grand public character that was still sympathetic to the Federal style domesticity of its West Village neighborhood.[107]

Washington Irving High School (1913) was Snyder's last important high school.[108] Located on Irving Place in Manhattan, it was a vocational high school for girls. To justify the building's central location, Snyder was forced to pack a vast program onto a tight site, resulting in a nine-story, 150-foot-tall building that was dependent on elevators for vertical circulation. The complex program included facilities for a full complement of courses in domestic and office procedures as well as conventional subjects. William McAndrew, the first principal, called the curriculum fit "for college, for business and for matrimony."[109]

Snyder attempted to compensate for the austerity of the exterior expression and the sheer bulk of the mass with cozily domestic interiors. Inside the main entrance a foyer large enough for dances was finished in fumed oak. A fireplace opposite the entrance symbolized the central feminine values of home and hearth, and twenty mural paintings depicted scenes from Washington Irving's stories. On the floor above, Snyder planned the first theater in a New York high school and provided a gallery for socializing during intermissions. Dining was considered a part of the curriculum, for even while the student was in the dining room "she is under the scrutiny of competent teachers who correct any lapse of table manners and by this means instill knowledge of the refinements of daily life."[110] The building also contained rooftop play space and six gyms for sixty-four girls each. Other large high schools concluded the era—Bushwick High School in Brooklyn,[111] Flushing High School in Queens,[112] and Evander Childs in the Bronx[113]—but none were as innovative as Washington Irving High School.

Snyder's career was concluded with the Manhattan Trade School for Girls (1918) at Lexington Avenue and Twenty-second Street, an eleven-story school easily mistaken for an office or apartment building.[114] The designs for other trade schools were more successful. J.H. Freedlander's and Arthur Dillon's Baron de Hirsch Trade School sat far east on Sixty-fourth Street like a great Modern French mansion transplanted to a working-class district.[115] Pell & Corbett's School of Applied Design for Women was a twentieth-century temple, built in 1909 on the corner of Lexington Avenue and Thirtieth Street.[116]

The transformation of New York's public school system into a model of excellence did not preclude the development of a parallel network of private schools for the rich. Often begun as tutoring establishments, the private schools were lodged in brownstones until the 1890s, when they began to develop into major institutions incorporating sports facilities, auditoriums and libraries. Most of the schools followed their students to the Billionaire District, but two of the oldest, Trinity and Collegiate, rebuilt in the West End.

The Berkeley School on Forty-fourth Street between Fifth and Sixth avenues was the first important private school facility.[117] Designed by Lamb & Rich in 1890–91, the building's character expressed the transition from the freewheeling eclecticism of the Cosmopolitan Era to the more scholarly and condensed Classicism of the Composite. The richly colored facade of Indiana limestone, yellow brick and terra cotta had a wide frieze modelled on the Parthenon's and supported on four central columns. The upper floors provided rooms for boarders and a rooftop play area.

On the other side of Forty-fourth Street, Henry Rutgers Marshall's design for the Brearley School (1890) was more Richardsonian, with low springing entrance arch and deeply cut openings.[118] A short belt course visually connected its three-bay facade to the St. Nicholas Club on the east, and a taller belt course and a projecting cornice tied it to the Berkeley Lyceum on the west. In 1912, the Brearley School moved to a larger building on the southwest corner of Park Avenue and Sixty-first Street.[119] An eight-story slab

From far left:

Stuyvesant High School, 345 East Fifteenth Street. C.B.J. Snyder, 1906. View of main entrance on Fifteenth Street. CU

School of Applied Design for Women, northwest corner of Lexington Avenue and Thirtieth Street. Pell & Corbett, 1909. View from the southeast. MCNY

Berkeley School, 20 West Forty-fourth Street. Lamb & Rich, 1891. CU

Left: Brearley School, 9 West Forty-fourth Street. Henry Rutgers Marshall, 1890. Right: St. Nicholas Club, 7 West Forty-fourth Street. George E. Wood, ca. 1890. CU

St. Regis School, 55 East Eighty-fourth Street. Maginnis & Walsh, 1915. Eighty-fourth Street facade. CU

topped by a double-height loggia used for games, it was designed by McKim, Mead & White with a brick facade trimmed in marble that was an attempt to accommodate the period's new preference for cozy domesticity to the requirements of institutional identity and large scale construction.

Brearley had been founded by Samuel Brearley in 1884 to provide an education for girls equal in quality to that offered boys.[120] In 1892, Clara Spence founded her girls' school in a brownstone at 6 West Forty-eighth Street, admitting both boarding and day students.[121] In 1901 she moved the Spence School to a building at 26 West Forty-fifth Street designed by James B. Baker.[122] A full-dressed example of the Modern French, it had an elaborate Ionic porch, a mansard roof, and regularly spaced fenestration that made it look more like an apartment house than a school.

Collegiate, the oldest operating private school in the country, went in the opposite direction in the 1890s, closing its doors to girls when it opened its new building in the West End.[123] Trinity, established in 1709 as a charitable school by the Society for the Propagation of the Gospel in Foreign Parts, had stopped teaching girls in 1838, but after the school moved to the West End in 1895 they opened a sister school, St. Agatha's (1898) on West End Avenue at Eighty-seventh Street.[124]

Parochial schools built during the Composite Era were usually Classical. Elliot Lynch's design for the St. Stephen's Parish School was a poorly proportioned and monotonous version of the Modern French that was all too typical of the type.[125] Much more accomplished was the St. Regis School, designed by Maginnis & Walsh.[126] Extending from Eighty-fourth Street through to Eighty-fifth Street, between Madison and Park avenues, St. Regis was explicitly monumental and archaeological, recalling the work of McKim.

Culture and Learning

The post-Civil War pattern of growth and consolidation that affected the nation as a whole and in particular its principal city, New York, was best reflected in the city's cultural life. A host of new institutions was founded in the city during the Cosmopolitan Era; among them the Metropolitan Museum of Art (1869), the American Museum of Natural History (1870), and the Metropolitan Opera Company (1883). The city's principal college, Columbia, grew to function as a major university by merging with the College of Physicians and Surgeons in 1860 and establishing professional schools and affiliated colleges.

The architectural spirit of the Cosmopolitan Era was nowhere more clearly articulated than in the frequently monumental and always eclectic buildings constructed to house the new institutions in the 1870s and 1880s. The eclecticism of the Cosmopolitan Era tended to combine and synthesize historical styles in a romantic manner that equated novelty with genius and left the cultural ambitions of the corporate barons and the French-trained artists and architects they employed unfulfilled. Both groups were anxious not only to found and house cultural institutions but to emulate and rival the monuments of Europe, catapulting the new institutions and the city into positions of international prominence.

While the Metropolitan Opera House and Carnegie Hall did not expand significantly during the Composite Era, most of the city's museums, libraries and learned societies were dramatically transformed to achieve a scale commensurate with the vast throngs of the metropolis. New York's major cultural institutions, including the Metropolitan Museum of Art, the Brooklyn Institute of Arts and Sciences (Brooklyn Museum), the New York Public Library and the New-York Historical Society, established their present physical character during the floodtide of the American Renaissance in the years between 1890 and 1915. The single exception to the Classicism of these monuments was the American Museum of Natural History, which continued to grow according to its Richardsonian masterplan drafted by J.C. Cady in 1890.

The intensity of the era's building program can be interpreted in many ways. It can be argued that institutions supported by the established, largely Anglo-Saxon citizenry set out to build in a monumental way in order to reinforce the sense of American traditions in the face of the enormous wave of immigration from non-northern European countries (more than half of New York's population was foreign born in 1898),[127] because the palatial headquarters created for these institutions were surely intended to impress the new arrivals with the substance of established American institutions. But the institutional monuments can also be seen as appropriate expressions of the mood and aspirations of the new immigrants, who, realizing that they would never be able to fully assimilate their manners to those of native Americans, saw the institutions as places their children could not only enjoy at a distance but more importantly use in their efforts to share in the benefactions of the American way of life. Thus the construction of the cultural palaces of the Composite Era must ironically be seen, at least in part, as expressions of a pessimistic establishment and an optimistic proletariat.

The sense that the city's cultural institutions were tools for the education and assimilation of the metropolitan throngs was surely reflected in the construction of the first of the Composite Era's great museums, the Brooklyn Institute of Arts and Sciences. In 1892 the trustees of the institute, an umbrella group incorporating twenty-five learned societies, announced a competition for a colossal museum. Their conception was of a giant repository for all aspects of learning modelled on the Victoria and Albert Museum in South Kensington, London, an institution where art was valued for its educational and moral as well as purely aesthetic characteristics.[128] Not solely a museum of art, natural history and ethnology, it was also an institute where research and public education went hand in hand, clearly reflecting the spirit of the Composite Era.[129]

The idea for a new building had been under consideration since 1888, and in 1889 a site was selected at the edge of Prospect Park in the preserve overlooking Eastern Parkway which Fredrick Law Olmsted had designated for monumental buildings.[130] The competition documents for what would be the largest building of its kind ever built were prepared by Professor Alfred D.F. Hamlin of Columbia College, and Professors Franklin Hooper and W.H. Goodyear of the institute's Department of Architecture.

A jury consisting of A.D.F. Hamlin, Robert Swain Peabody and George L. Morse invited Louis De Coppet Berg, John M. Carrère, Albert E. Parfitt, William B. Tubby and Stanford White to compete, although the competition was open to all qualified architects. Three equal prizes of five hundred dollars were awarded to W.B. Chambers & J.M. Cromwell, William B. Bigelow, and McKim, Mead & White (ironically, Bigelow had briefly been a partner of McKim and Mead).[131] Chambers & Cromwell's rigorously composed scheme had steep mansard roofs and a central rotunda shrewdly calculated to invoke Sir Aston Webb's Victoria and Albert Museum, while Bigelow's scheme was far more complex in plan and section; unlike the others it respected the oblique angle which Washington Avenue formed on one side of the site. Bigelow placed the institute's auditorium behind a diagonal corner entrance and a vast memorial hall with a dome in emulation of St. Peter's Basilica in Rome above.

The selection of McKim, Mead & White's proposal was one of the first indications of the triumphant influence of the World's Columbian Exposition of 1892-93.[132] McKim took far less account than the other designers of the complexities of the institute's program and ignored the irregular geometry of the site. Instead he proposed a more coherently Classical image, larger than the program specified but suited to construction in segments. His square building with pavilions at each corner and domed pavilions at the center of each facade was linked to a central rotunda with a taller dome. Based on the elevations of McKim's Agriculture Building at the Chicago Fair, the facades were modulated with a pilastered order and a broken entablature that was to have supported sculptures by Daniel Chester French, Attilio Piccirilli and others. The Depression of 1893 delayed the start of construction until 1895, and only the two wings along Eastern Parkway and Washington Avenue, less than a quarter of the vast building, were ever completed.[133] But the promise of the institute catalyzed the development of the northern perimeter of Prospect Park, especially at Grand Army Plaza, where the Soldiers' and Sailors' Memorial designed by John Duncan was completed in 1892, shelters and entrance gates to the park designed by McKim's firm were built between 1889 and 1908, and a headquarters for the Brooklyn Central Library was planned in 1908.

The Metropolitan Museum of Art was less ambitiously conceived. Strictly intended as a repository for art rather than for all aspects of learning, it was founded in 1869 by the Art Committee of the Union League Club but did not get its own building until 1880.[134] The museum's first permanent home, in Central Park near Fifth Avenue at Eighty-second Street, was designed by Calvert Vaux and Jacob Wrey Mould, who conceived it as a freestanding pavilion in polychromed Ruskinian Gothic that related neither to the park nor to the nearby streets. It was extended to the south in 1888 with a building designed by Theodore Weston and in 1890-94 with an even less distinguished addition to the north by Arthur Tuckerman.[135] The two wings related closely to the polychromy and massing of Vaux's central pavilion, although they attempted to adapt it to the changing public image of a civic monument by incorporating Classical as opposed to Gothic details. The building's continued isolation from the urban context reflected the Cosmopolitan Era's ideal of individualistic monumentality as well as the museum's yet unclear conception of its public responsibilities. Under the directorship of Louis Palma di Cesnola, however, the museum's role was gradually extended from its clubbish origins to resemble that of the Victoria and Albert Museum, a transformation vividly proclaimed on May 31, 1891, when the Metropolitan first opened its doors on a Sunday and an estimated twelve thousand people crowded through the relatively small galleries, transforming the museum and its collections once and for all into a truly public institution, accessible to and patronized by a vast audience of working people.

In the Composite Era, the museum also strove to correct its lack of architectural connection to both Central Park and the city; in 1895 when Richard Morris Hunt's masterplan related the museum's front facade to the Avenue, and in 1905, when McKim included in a new masterplan a provision for an unrealized set of terraces and platforms in the park, creating a romantic dialogue between building and landscape antithetical to the objectivity of Vaux's pavilion, now concealed deep within the expanded museum.[136]

Hunt's boldly scaled, Greco-Roman entrance pavilion facing Fifth Avenue was completed after his death in 1895 by his son, Richard Howland Hunt, and George B. Post.[137] The dramatic scale of the new facade took full advantage of the opportunity, rare in New York, to set up a monumental vista by concluding the visual axis of a street—in this case Eighty-second Street. Hunt's facade was dominated by

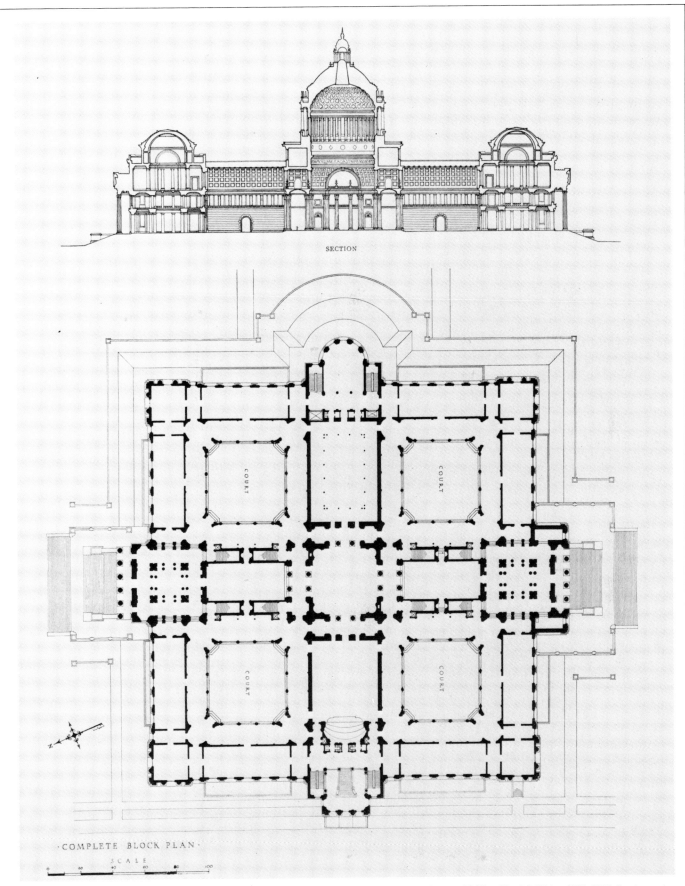

Brooklyn Institute of Arts and Sciences, southwest corner of Eastern Parkway and Washington Avenue. McKim, Mead & White, 1895–1915. Section and plan of ground floor. CU

Brooklyn Institute of Arts and Sciences, southwest corner of Eastern Parkway and Washington Avenue. McKim, Mead & White, 1895–1915. View from Eastern Parkway. CU

paired Corinthian columns on projecting bases supporting a broken entablature and massive blocks of rough stone intended to be carved into sculptural groups representing the arts of four great epochs. A tall attic and a low-hipped roof rising to three clerestories, the last two largely invisible from the street, completed the composition of the central pavilion. Giant glazed arches set between the paired columns provided light for the Great Hall within and a subtle reflection of that room's articulation. The central arch admitted the visitor to a vast Roman space. The arches of the facade were repeated within to subtly divide the 48-foot-wide, 166-foot-long room into three bays and support shallow-saucer domes invisible from the exterior. A gallery on the second floor offered Piranesian vistas through to the transverse galleries and, on the main axis, the grand staircase rose serenely beyond a screen of columns, inviting one into the heart of the museum's galleries.

Although Hunt's facade has been criticized as "textured and jumpy,"[138] it offered a lively, accessible grandeur that easily conveyed to the public the museum's role as an educational institution and an important civic monument. Its crescent shaped driveway and relatively narrow, steep stairs leading to a small porch—heavily criticized by the *Architectural Record* as a mockery of monumental design—were almost domestic in character and thereby undercut the design's monumentality and made the building seem more familiar and approachable. Hunt's desire that the museum be considered his personal monument was surely fulfilled in the small portion completed to his designs.

The Great Hall was all that was executed of Hunt's masterplan, which was perhaps grander than the trustees were able to imagine or afford. Extending as far south as Seventy-ninth Street and north to Eighty-fifth Street, it was articulated into pavilions linked by galleries with surrounding light courts, some of which were large enough to be developed as gardens. When J. Pierpont Morgan became president of the museum in 1904 and laid plans for the eventual donation of his collections to the museum, the need for new space once again became apparent. McKim, Mead & White, while designing Morgan's library on East Thirty-sixth Street, were invited to replace the younger Hunt and draft a new and more modest masterplan.[139]

The masterplan prepared by William Kendall, W. Symmes Richardson and Burt Fenner under McKim's

Brooklyn Institute of Arts and Sciences, southwest corner of Eastern Parkway and Washington Avenue. McKim, Mead & White, 1895–1915. Sculpture Hall. NYHS

supervision called for intermediary wings and pavilions along Fifth Avenue. Their simple massing and restrained detailing reinforced the flamboyance of Hunt's pavilion, establishing it as the jewel of the complex.[140] The first section was implemented in 1906 and completed in 1910; others followed so that by 1926 the Fifth Avenue facade stretched from Eightieth to Eighty-fourth streets. Unfortunately, plans for gardens and terraces facing Central Park, reminiscent of McKim's proposed terraces around the Washington Monument, were never executed. They incorporated Cleopatra's Needle, ornamental planting and flowers in what would have been the strongest incursion of the City Beautiful's romantic Classicism into the romantic naturalism of Olmsted's Central Park.

The growth of the library system in New York was largely fostered by private philanthropy. In 1895 the New York Public Library was formed by the consolidation of the Astor and Lenox libraries with the Tilden Trust. The new facility constituted one of the most important and best endowed book collections in the world. Since 1853 the Astor Library, a general reference facility open to the public at no charge, had been housed on Lafayette Street in a sober red-brick and brownstone Italianate building.[141] The Lenox Library was a specialized collection largely inaccessible to the general public. It was housed in a neo-Grec monument designed by Richard Morris Hunt in 1877 with gallery space as well as reading rooms and stacks. A design, in Royal Cortissoz's words, "of weighty scholarship, composed with a sort of impersonal sense of architectural law," it seemed to give architectural expression to its aloofness from the city's masses.[142] Even its commanding full-block site on Fifth Avenue between Seventieth and Seventy-first streets was at the time far removed from the populated section of the city. After Lenox's death, his trustees continued in the spirit of his acquisition and administration policies. Although the gallery was open to the public, the book collection remained closed.

The Tilden Trust was created as a result of Samuel Tilden's bequest of five million dollars "to establish and maintain a free library in the City of New York and to promote scientific and educational objects."[143] Ever since the incorporation of the Tilden Trust in 1887, there had been agitation for the construction of a library on the soon-to-be abandoned reservoir site on Fifth Avenue between

Metropolitan Museum of Art, Central Park facing Fifth Avenue at Eighty-second Street. Richard Morris Hunt, 1895–1902. A view from Fifth Avenue, showing Theodore Weston's 1888 wing behind and the first of McKim, Mead & White's additions along Fifth Avenue to the right. NYHS

Metropolitan Museum of Art, Central Park facing Fifth Avenue between Eightieth and Eighty-fourth streets. McKim, Mead & White, 1905. Perspective view of proposed carriage entrance and gardens. NYHS

Metropolitan Museum of Art, Central Park facing Fifth Avenue at Eighty-second Street. Richard Morris Hunt, 1895-1902. Great Hall. NYHS

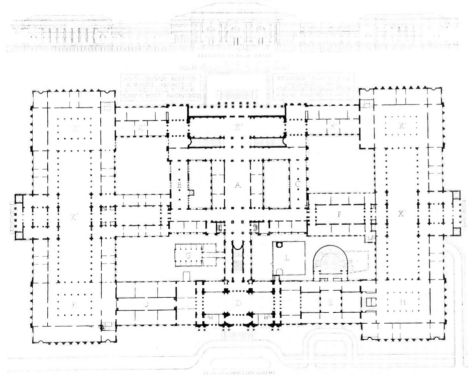

Metropolitan Museum of Art, Central Park facing Fifth Avenue between Eightieth and Eighty-fourth streets. McKim, Mead & White, 1905. Fifth Avenue elevation and plan of proposed additions. CU

Lenox Library, east side of Fifth Avenue between Seventieth and Seventy-first streets. Richard Morris Hunt, 1877. View from Fifth Avenue. NYHS

Proposed Tilden Trust Library, west side of Fifth Avenue between Fortieth and Forty-second streets. Ernest Flagg, 1891. Perspective view from Fifth Avenue. CU

Fortieth and Forty-second streets. The guiding genius behind the consolidation of the two libraries and the Tilden Trust was John Bigelow. As the first president of the New York Public Library, Bigelow would realize his dream of a central research facility of undisputed quality. In 1892 he wrote: "What the city wants is a library that shall possess sufficient vital force to become, reasonably soon, a repair for students from all parts of the world; to constitute an attraction to the literary and contemplative class, fitly corresponding with the incomparable attractions which she has always held out to men of affairs; to organizers of the material industries and interests of the nation."[144]

Anticipating the resolution of the Tilden Trust litigation, Bigelow commissioned plans from Ernest Flagg for a combined circulating and reference library in 1891.[145] The interior volumes of Flagg's project were so Roman in character that Arthur Dillon suggested in the *Architectural Review* that concrete would be the most appropriate form of construction. The plan, however, was ecclesiastical in inspiration, with a long nave filled with book stacks extending down the center of the site toward Sixth Avenue.[146] Flagg's plan took full advantage of the opportunity to combine the reservoir site with Bryant Park behind it. Setting his building far back from Fifth Avenue behind broad terraces and formally landscaped parterres, Flagg proposed a marriage of building and site which Dillon felt "would add much to the building and would make a park like which we have no good example."[147]

The consolidation of the two libraries and the Tilden Trust into a New York Public Library was consummated at last on May 23, 1895, and a year later the reservoir site was secured for the new building.[148] With all the pieces in place, in January 1896 the library trustees appointed John S. Billings as director, and he set out to define the character of the new institution and to organize a representative program for its building. Determined not to repeat the functional failures of the Boston Public Library, Billings invited Professor William Robert Ware of Columbia to assist in the preparation of schematic plans meant specifically to influence the *parti* of any design eventually prepared for the building. A competition was announced in May 1897 which included this basic organization among its requirements. In June 1897, while the competition entrants were at work on their designs, Billings presented the *parti* to members of the American Library Association for their professional criticism.[149] Billings's functional requirements were so specific that the trustees felt compelled to reassure architects and the public that they not only wanted a functional facility "but also an edifice that would stand as one of the chief monuments of the city."[150]

The competition was complexly organized. Six architects were selected from an open first stage to compete against six others invited by the trustees. Three designs from this second stage were submitted by a professional jury to the trustees; they in turn selected one name to forward to the Board of Estimate and Apportionment of the City of New York, which would actually construct the building.[151] The Jury of Award consisted of Billings, Ware and Bernard Green, engineer of the Congressional Library. Eighty-eight entries were received in the open first round, of which twenty-nine followed the Billings and Ware scheme quite closely.[152] Many of these entries were prepared by young architects, some still employed in offices other than their own. Quite a few of these were notable, particularly Brite & Bacon's very Roman proposal with a reading room based on the Pantheon,[153] and William W. Knowles's far more French proposal, which had a facade similar in some ways to Hunt's Metropolitan Museum, and a third-floor reading room based on the Baths of Diocletian.[154]

On July 28 twelve of the eighty-eight designs were selected and awarded four hundred dollars each to enter a second round, of which six survived: Joseph H. Freedlander; Haydel & Shepard; Hornbostel, Wood & Palmer; W. Wheeler Smith with Walker & Morris; Howard & Cauldwell; and Whitney Warren.[155] The following month the names of the six invited architects were announced: Cyrus L.W. Eidlitz; Carrère & Hastings; Charles C. Haight; McKim, Mead & White; Peabody & Stearns; and George B. Post.[156] In hindsight, the competition had succeeded in culling a veritable honor roll of emerging architectural talent in New York. Each of the twelve architects was paid eight hundred dollars to prepare a second design due on October

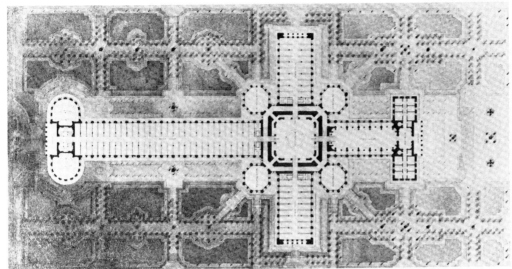

Proposed Tilden Trust Library, west side of Fifth Avenue between Fortieth and Forty-second streets. Ernest Flagg, 1891. Plan of ground floor. CU

20, 1897, and in November, the report of the jury was announced. First prize was awarded to the comparatively young firm of Carrère & Hastings, second place to Howard & Cauldwell, and third place to McKim, Mead & White.[157]

McKim had been reluctant to enter the competition, because he objected to the restrictions imposed by Billings's plan. Finally, he ignored it and substituted a different arrangement clothed in a rigidly Classical, colonnaded facade prophetic of Pennsylvania Station. The jury found that McKim did not give "sufficient weight . . . to the working necessities of the Library although its overall design evidenced such 'architectural ability' that it warranted third place."[158]

Carrère & Hastings's scheme not only defeated the McKim proposal on functional lines, but also drew attention to the Modern French style that was supplanting the hitherto dominant archaeological Classicism favored by McKim. Carrère & Hastings, Howard & Cauldwell, Wood, Palmer & Hornbostel, Walker & Morris, Haydel & Shepard, Joseph H. Freedlander and Whitney Warren had all submitted Modern French entries.[159] In Carrère & Hastings's hands, the style was to demonstrate its capacity for making grand civic architecture: the Public Library was New York's finest example of the Modern French approach to the problem of designing monumentally expressive and functionally rational public buildings.

The monumental elevations expressed the functions of the plan within. Pediments located the main reading rooms on the facade, the attic over the cornice indicated the picture galleries, the large scale windows on the Fifth Avenue facade housed administrative and utilitarian functions, and the vertical arrangement of narrow windows indicated the location of book stacks. The main reading room, located as Billings had requested at the rear and top of the building on the third floor, culminated a logical and impressive architectural progression from the principal entrance on Fifth Avenue. Ingenious scissor staircases on the Forty-second Street side provided more direct circulation and integrated the lending facility, included at the last moment as a result of the city's request with the reference facilities which were the heart of the building's purpose. An extensive use of metal and glass in the design of ceilings and book stacks helped establish a dialogue between traditional form and technological innovation.

The Public Library was the first important building in New York to provide its own monumental setting within the densely developed city fabric. Taking a cue from Hunt's Metropolitan Museum, then under construction, Carrère & Hastings capitalized on the library's site at the head of East Forty-first Street (admittedly, like East Eighty-second, a minor residential street, and not a great boulevard as one might expect in Paris). More importantly, as had been suggested by Ernest Flagg's earlier proposal, the library was set back from its bounding streets to provide for landscaped terraces and broad steps which stood in sharp contrast to the brownstone character of the neighborhood and the Victorian naturalism of Bryant Park immediately behind.

The construction of the Public Library was protracted and the building was not opened until 1911, during which period the architects refined their design and struggled with budget constraints.[160] By the time it opened the library had been the object of so much discussion that the event was somewhat anticlimactic.[161] Moreover, the Modern French style had begun to wane and the design perhaps seemed a bit old hat. Nonetheless, the assessment Arthur C. David made in 1910 still stands: "In the realism of the plan and in the mixture of dignity and distinction in the design, the New York Public Library is typical of that which is best in the contemporary architectural movement."[162]

Although consolidation brought about the unification of most public services, branch libraries in Brooklyn and Queens continued to be run by independent organizations that received financial subsidy from the municipal government.[163] In response to an increasing sense that consolidation was diminishing Brooklyn's cultural role, the public library system there began to explore the question of building a central facility to rival that of Manhattan. By 1905, a lively dispute had grown up about the proposed location for the library. A.D.F. Hamlin, of Columbia's School of Architecture, and John M. Carrère were asked to advise the library's trustees, and they recommended a site at the southeast corner of Flatbush Avenue and Eastern Parkway facing

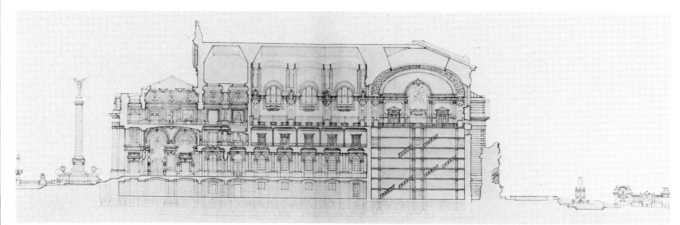

New York Public Library competition entry, west side of Fifth Avenue between Fortieth and Forty-second streets. Carrère & Hastings, 1897. Longitudinal section. CU

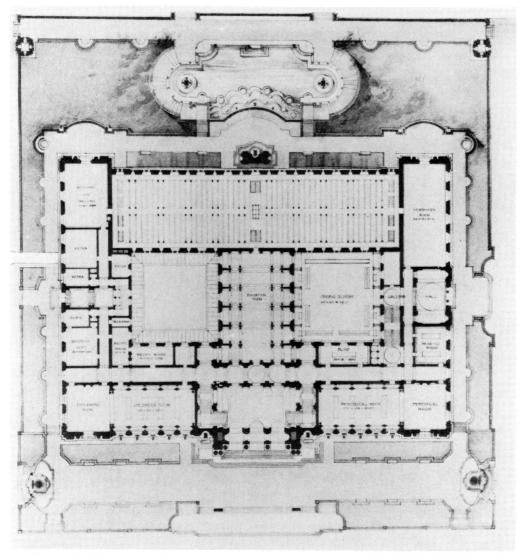

New York Public Library competition entry, west side of Fifth Avenue between Fortieth and Forty-second streets. Carrère & Hastings, 1897. Plan of first floor. CU

New York Public Library, west side of Fifth Avenue between Fortieth and Forty-second streets. Carrère & Hastings, 1897-1911. View from Fifth Avenue. NYHS

New York Public Library, west side of Fifth Avenue between Fortieth and Forty-second streets. Carrère & Hastings, 1897-1911. Lobby. CU

Proposed Brooklyn Central Library, Grand Army Plaza between Flatbush Avenue and Eastern Parkway, Brooklyn. Raymond F. Almirall, 1908. Perspective view from Grand Army Plaza. CU

Proposed improvements of Grand Army Plaza, Brooklyn. Raymond F. Almirall, 1908, Site plan. CU

Grand Army Plaza.[164] Hamlin, in order to demonstrate the feasibility of the site, assigned the problem to competitors for Columbia's post-graduate McKim Fellowship Competition the same year; the prize was won by Lucien E. Smith.[165] In 1907 the City Improvement Commission Plan designated Grand Army Plaza as an ideal location for public buildings, and the following year Raymond Almirall, a prominent Brooklyn architect, suggested a comprehensive treatment of the plaza in conjunction with the proposed Brooklyn Central Library.[166] Almirall's proposal called for a uniform cornice line around the plaza's perimeter, then lined with idiosyncratic buildings such as Francis H. Kimball's Montauk Club[167] and Frank Freeman's houses for Guido Pleisner[168] and George B. Shiebler.[169] Almirall also called for a colonnaded gateway echoing the ellipse of Grand Army Plaza and flanked by the library and zoological museum at the entrance to Prospect Park.

Almirall's design for the library was based on Lucien Smith's student project in many significant ways. Smith's scheme had arranged offices and stacks along the perimeter of the trapezoidal site and placed a domed reading room within the courtyard. Almirall developed this strategy retaining the basic *parti* but improving the somewhat awkward connections between its parts. The elevations were correspondingly similar, but Almirall's greatly heightened dome was better calculated to be seen in perspective. Construction on Almirall's design was begun but the project was stalled for lack of funds in the 1920s. When it was resumed in 1941, after Almirall's death in 1939, the portions he had built were torn down to their foundations and a new design by Githens & Keally was superimposed.[170]

The New York Public Library at Forty-second Street functioned principally as a reference center, leaving most circulation and lending to a handful of neighborhood branches built in the 1880s and 1890s. In 1887 George Vanderbilt had commissioned Hunt to design a small branch for the New York Free Circulating Library at 251 West Thirteenth Street, joining the Ottendorfer Branch on Second Avenue and the branch being built by Catherine Bruce on Forty-second Street.[171] In 1899 Herts & Tallant completed the Aguilar Free Library at 174 East 110th Street between Third and Lexington avenues, an independent library to serve immigrant Jews given by Grace Aguilar, a British novelist of Sephardic descent.[172]

By 1900 the demand for library services was rapidly escalating. From 1898 to 1903 the circulating department of the New York Public Library experienced a 30 percent increase in withdrawals for home reading.[173] The goal of building a series of branch libraries throughout the newly consolidated city went unrealized until 1901, when Andrew Carnegie offered to contribute $5,200,000 toward the construction of forty-two (eventually sixty-one) branch libraries, on sites paid for by the city. An advisory committee consisting of John M. Carrère, Charles F. McKim and Walter Cook was appointed to help formulate an architectural policy. Not surprisingly, their three firms were hired to do all the branches of the New York system, which included Manhattan, Staten Island, and the Bronx.[174] (A.D.F. Hamlin's position as advisor to the Brooklyn Committee steered most of the jobs in that borough to his former students J. Monroe Hewlett and J.T. Tubby.)[175]

Carnegie's bequest introduced the general public to a level of architectural excellence not customarily found in working-class neighborhoods.[176] Moreover, new buildings attracted readers who had never before gone to a library. When James Brown Lord's new Yorkville Branch opened in 1903 its book circulation leapt from 179,722 to 238,522; 40,600 readers used the library as compared with 12,319 previously.[177]

The instructions to the architects called for a standardized plan and a uniformity of character, materials and design. Maximum accessibility to the stacks was demanded, but also easy surveillance from the circulation desk. The reading room was to be at street level so that the library would advertise itself as such, the readers being visible through a showroom window. These instructions were ingeniously carried out in Manhattan, although constricted urban lots forced the typical plan type, intended for an open suburban site, to be rearranged vertically. This had been prefigured in Lord's Yorkville Branch at 222 East Seventy-ninth Street.[178] Though technically the first of the so-called Carnegie branch libraries, it had already been designed

Aguilar Free Library, 174 East 110th Street. Herts & Tallant, 1899. CU

Yorkville Branch, New York Public Library, 222 East Seventy-ninth Street. James Brown Lord, 1903. CU

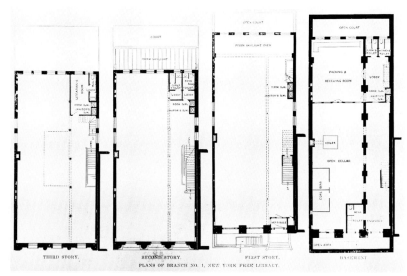

Yorkville Branch, New York Public Library, 222 East Seventy-ninth Street. James Brown Lord, 1903. Plans of basement, first, second and third floors. CU

when Carnegie made his gift. Typical of the Manhattan branches, it occupied a mid-block site on an important street. Lord set a colossal Ionic order atop a high rusticated basement in a Palladian design that was more imposing than most of the later Manhattan branches. Inside, he established the plan that was followed for most Manhattan branches: a ground floor entrance vestibule, circulation desk and reference area for adults, a children's reading room located on the second floor, and on the third floor a general reading room as far away from street noise as possible.[179] Lord's design also established the character of the Manhattan branch libraries: conceived as an elegant townhouse with light-filled rooms, it was an icon of humanistic reason and a refuge from the turmoil of the city.

McKim, Mead & White designed ten of the forty-two branch libraries built in Manhattan between 1902 and 1908. Their Chatham Square Branch on East Broadway was similar to Lord's Yorkville Branch but was less lavishly decorated, except for six Ionic columns which reduced the light available in the upstairs reading rooms.[180] In later branches, McKim abandoned the high Classicism of Greece and Rome, turning instead to the Italian Renaissance palazzo for inspiration. His Rivington Street Branch (1904–05) marked the transition toward a more domestic character.[181] A massive rusticated base supported two-story-high brick structural piers, flanking two brick Corinthian pilasters with limestone caps and base rising to a simple brick cornice trimmed in limestone. Delicate bronze panels and balconies set between the windows gave the building a decidedly cozy quality similar to the firm's Harvard Club.[182] The branch at 103 West 135th Street was one of McKim's more inventive designs, with the second floor treated as a glazed Palladian loggia, deliberately underscaled third-floor windows, and a red-tiled hip roof projecting beyond the facade to form a strong cornice line.[183]

Perhaps the firm's loveliest library was the restrained, Florentine design of St. Gabriel's Branch (1906–08) at 303 East Thirty-sixth Street.[184] Its heavily rusticated base and ashlar superstructure rose to an open loggia shaded by a projecting red-tile roof carried on sinuously curved iron brackets. Here, more than in their other branches, McKim and his assistant Kendall succeeded in bringing to the problem the same suavity and associational appropriateness that characterized their best townhouse work in the period; here, in a sense, the wisdom of the Renaissance was made available to all in a tough East Side neighborhood.

Babb, Cook & Willard's output was far less interesting. The firm, no doubt hired because of its close connections with Carnegie, was less comfortable with the Classical styles of the Composite Era than with the Richardsonian Romanesque of the 1880s.[185] Cook's Mott Haven Branch at 569 East 140th Street, corner of Alexander Avenue in the Bronx, was reminiscent of his design for Carnegie's own house, combining red-brick and white-limestone trim in a densely massed palazzo.[186] Instead of the Scottish-Georgian used for Carnegie, Cook and his partners seemed to have sifted the Italian Renaissance through a Bavarian sieve, providing a building that would look as apt on the Ludwigstrasse in Munich as in the Bronx.

Carrère & Hastings's work on Staten Island was much more successful.[187] The suburban locations of the small Tottenville and Port Richmond branches permitted the use of the more conventional Carnegie Library planning model used in the libraries he founded in towns and villages across the nation: in each a one-story pavilion housed the reading room and circulation desk, and toilets and offices occupied a lower projecting wing at the back. Both branches were lit with unornamented, arched windows set above book stacks which lined the walls. Pediments carried on brick piers with Doric columns *in antis* marked the entrances and helped establish a scale that mediated between the image of the suburban villa and the civic function of the library.

While the Brooklyn branches were also frequently set on generously sized suburban lots, large facilities were required to serve that borough's populous neighborhoods. The situation inspired such monumental designs as R.L. Daus's Flatbush and Greenpoint branches, two-story rectangular pavilions virtually identical in massing, although the former was executed in limestone, the latter in brick and marble.[188] Each was a rather lively example of the Modern French taste. A complex arrangement of roofs brought top light to the reading rooms through monitors, while the

Chatham Square Branch, New York Public Library, 31 East Broadway. McKim, Mead & White, 1903. MCNY

delivery desks were set in vaulted spaces of Roman inspiration.[189]

Walker & Morris's East Branch, with its high basement and main reading rooms raised two-thirds of a story above the street level, was equally dramatic.[190] Inside, the entrance lobby rose one-and-one-half stories to a skylight which brought light from a monitor on the ridge of the roof. The high windows of the reading room and the decision to set the library services one-half level below, allowed virtually every wall to be lined with books. A bay window at one end of the reading room was balanced by a fireplace inglenook in the children's reading room at the other end.

William Tubby's branch at Clinton and Union streets was particularly fine, though its one-story pavilion-like massing fit uncomfortably amid the brownstones and tenements.[191] The facades were articulated with alternating narrow and wide bays, and the wall surfaces enlivened by panelling, brick Ionic pilasters, white-marble columns and the brick and marble frieze of the cornice. The low vaulted space of the reading room inside, with its hanging lamps and skylights, was one of the most inviting of the branch library interiors.

The branch library program was an enormous success, bringing circulating libraries to most of the neighborhoods of the newly consolidated city in a short time. It also created a remarkably high, and to a considerable extent stylistically uniform, working symbol of the benefits of the new consolidation. In 1909, when the bequest was almost exhausted, the *Architectural Record* observed that "Whatever may be said of the propriety of the architectural garb in which their architects have clothed the fronts of these buildings, one cannot deny that they exercise a distinct influence on the public taste and make for a decided improvement on architecture."[192]

McKim, Mead & White's design for the J. Pierpont Morgan Library on East Thirty-sixth Street was similar in scale if not in purpose to the typical branch library.[193] Morgan was a shrewd and active art collector who amassed a vast treasure which not only filled his brownstone house at Thirty-sixth Street and Madison Avenue but also a house in England where he was forced to store many of his most valuable works because of a high tariff on art objects. In 1900, believing that the tariff situation would change, Morgan began to prepare for the "suitable disposition of the

St. Gabriel's Branch, New York Public Library, 303 East Thirty-sixth Street. McKim, Mead & White, 1908. MCNY

De Kalb Branch, Brooklyn Public Library, north corner of De Kalb and Bushwick avenues. William B. Tubby, 1905. MCNY

collections which would render them permanently available for the instruction and pleasure of the American people."[194] At first, Whitney Warren was asked to prepare designs for a relatively small building set in a garden on property Morgan was acquiring adjacent to his house. Warren's proposal was for a small but exuberant Modern French pavilion with a domed entrance that led past twin studies to a large room that would function as a library and museum.[195]

It is unclear why Morgan did not proceed with Warren, but in March 1902 he asked McKim to begin work on a new project which included not only the library but a house facing Park Avenue for his daughter Louisa Satterlee. His daughter's house, his own house and his son J.P. Morgan Jr.'s house were to be connected by underground tunnels. From the beginning, McKim's approach was icily monumental. His first proposal had a four-column Ionic portico; later that year, the final design, based on Annibale Lippi's Villa Medici of 1544, was settled upon. The library's principal feature was its deep porch, its roof supported on double columns set one behind the other. The scheme had three grandly scaled rooms—an entrance rotunda flanked on the east by a library lined with three tiers of books, and on the west by Morgan's study, a large room covered in red damask and furnished in the Renaissance style. McKim selected marble as the exterior material and persuaded Morgan that the blocks of stone be laid without mortar, in accord with the ancient Greek manner called *anathyrosis,* by which the stones were so closely fitted that even a knife blade could not pass between them.

The library was completed in 1907, three years after the Satterlee house, a limestone clad mansion with blocky massing and reticent detailing which deferred to its more precious neighbor to allow the library to assume the role of a freestanding pavilion in a garden. As distinguished as the library design was, its setting in a controlled architectural ensemble of suburban scale created a uniquely Arcadian idyll in the midst of the city's street grid.

The tendency in the Composite Era to monumentalize individual institutions extended even to the more modest fine art, historical and learned societies which had hitherto been content to carry on their proceedings in unassuming quarters that were frequently built for other purposes. In 1890, at the dawn of the Composite Era, the American Fine Arts Society held a competition for a new building to be

Morgan Library, 33 East Thirty-sixth Street. McKim, Mead & White, 1902–07. MCNY

erected at 212 West Fifty-seventh Street.[196] Atypically, the society was newly founded (1889) and building its first headquarters. Typically, however, its construction was made possible by a process of consolidation whereby a number of other organizations, including the Architectural League of New York (founded in 1881) and the Art Students League (founded in 1875) agreed to share its galleries, studios and classrooms. During the Composite Era, the Fine Arts Society became the scene of virtually every important exhibition of art and architecture held in the city. The annual exhibitions of the Architectural League held there were major events for the profession and the public at large. In 1892 the *American Architect and Building News* was able to observe that "architecture is rapidly becoming in this country a great and popular art," and as a measure of this turn of events, it cited the annual exhibitions of the Architectural League which were attracting greater crowds than all the annual architectural exhibits in Europe combined.[197]

The entries for the Fine Arts Society competition reflected the transitional state of American architecture in 1890. The Philadelphia architect Wilson Eyre submitted two proposals, one Classical and the other a Venetian Gothic palazzo.[198] Each had a low-keyed domesticity more representative of the spirit of the 1880s than of the new era. But H. Langford Warren's Romanesque design was composed with five arched arcades at the ground floor and an attic buttressed at each end by unbroken piers which reflected the new sensibility for urban grandeur.[199] Babb, Cook & Willard's submission, judging from Paul Gmelin's drawing of the principal doorway,[200] reflected the influence of McKim, Mead & White's Villard houses of 1887, as did Gilbert & Taylor's amateurish version of a Florentine palazzo.[201] The winning scheme by Henry J. Hardenbergh, in association with John C. Jacobson and Walter C. Hunting, managed to bridge the two eras.[202] Completed in 1892, it was a stately French Renaissance palace with three central panels dedicated to art, architecture and sculpture. The glazed and densely ornamented panels contrasted with largely blank end bays visually buttressing the facade, while a red-tile gable roof above the projecting cornice paralleled the facade and furthered its aura of imposing domesticity.

In 1900 the New-York Historical Society, which had been founded in 1804, announced its intention to seek a new, permanent home to meet its expanded role as both archive

Morgan Library, 33 East Thirty-sixth Street. McKim, Mead & White, 1902-07. Library. NYHS

and museum during the second century of its existence. The society sponsored a competition for a new headquarters to be erected on Central Park West between Seventy-sixth and Seventy-seventh streets. The problem was difficult, calling for a relatively small but imposingly monumental building that would include an auditorium and library as well as galleries and which would be built in stages as funds became available.

Howells & Stokes's restlessly composed Modern French submission showed little capacity for phased construction.[203] York & Sawyer's winning entry was by contrast icily cool, and the ascetic archaeology of the design was exacerbated by the decision to build it of hard gray granite.[204] The facades were based on McKim, Mead & White's Boston Public Library, substituting an Ionic colonnade above the high basement and framing the design with terminal pavilions to be built at a later date.[205]

Audubon Terrace was perhaps the grandest attempt to synthesize the artistic and philosophical goals of the American Renaissance. A veritable acropolis of academic institutions, Audubon Terrace was a concentration of cultural and educational facilities unique outside the context of a university.[206] The brainchild of Archer M. Huntington, a railroad magnate, philanthropist and distinguished scholar of Hispanic culture, its facilities were intended for the use of scholars and students, but were also open to the general public without charge. Audubon Terrace's architectural expression was compromised by its piecemeal development over a period of twenty-five years, yet it constituted one of the few architectural ensembles actually realized during the Composite Era.

The development of Audubon Terrace began in 1904 when Huntington began purchasing sections of Audubon Park, the former estate and game preserve of ornithologist John James Audubon.[207] Located on Broadway between 155th and 156th streets, the site overlooked Trinity Cemetery to the south and sat below a section of Audubon Park to the north which had remained undeveloped. The opening of the subway and the extension of Riverside Drive were already transforming Washington Heights' suburban character, and Huntington's purchase was perhaps motivated by a desire to preserve some part of the park from the encroaching apartment houses. In the same year, Huntington founded the American Hispanic Society, an institution

American Fine Arts Society, 215 West Fifty-seventh Street. Henry Janeway Hardenbergh, 1890–92. NYHS

Audubon Terrace, west side of Broadway between 155th and 156th streets. Charles P. Huntington. View from 156th Street, showing from left to right: American Geographical Society, 1911; Museum of the American Indian, 1925; American Numismatic Society, 1908; and the Hispanic Society of America, 1908. MCNY

meant to give public access to his extensive collection of Spanish art and books, and chose his cousin, Charles Pratt Huntington, as architect for the society's headquarters and most of the later buildings.

The Hispanic Society originally evoked a more Arcadian vision than later developments suggest.[208] A freestanding pavilion raised on a podium above 155th Street, it commanded a series of terraces and cascading steps which led from garden gates on 156th Street. Huntington designed the facades in a restrained Italian Renaissance style, uniting the composition with a colossal order of engaged Ionic columns set between massive piers. The architect sought, in his own words, "a style of architecture as massive and as serious as possible, while giving the character of a semi-public building, which was effected by classic lines of extreme simplicity, with the attempt to achieve good proportions and severe detail." Huntington felt this answered "the evident criticism of why a Spanish library and museum is not Spanish in the treatment of its exterior architecture."[209]

However, the main hall, a reading room with a second-story gallery housing the art collection, evoked an outdoor Spanish patio so successfully that Royal Cortissoz labelled the museum "a miniature Prado."[210] In a gesture typical of the Composite Period's quest for stylistic accuracy, the architect had spent seven weeks in Spain to obtain material for the interior design, and decorated the room's arcades with rich Plateresque reliefs and a tiled frieze representing scenes of the Spanish colonization of the New World.

The Hispanic Society's facades set the tone for the later buildings. In 1906 Archer Huntington became president of the American Numismatic Society and immediately donated the land and funds for a new building on the terrace, again designed by his cousin.[211] A small pavilion located fifty feet west of the Hispanic Society, it was planned from the start to connect the two buildings and to balance the composition with an extension of the Hispanic Society westward.

In 1909-11 Charles Huntington built the Church of Our Lady of Esperanza, the second Spanish Roman Catholic church in the city.[212] Originally entered through an Ionic portico approached by a flight of stairs from 156th Street, the church was later remodelled (1924) by Lawrence G. White, the son of Stanford White and a partner in his father's firm. White added a vestibule which accommodated the change of levels internally and brought the church's facade forward to the lot line. The renovation reflected a crucial change in the Huntingtons' architectural strategy. While the original buildings all faced north, the development of Washington Heights as a neighborhood of apartment buildings made such an outward looking focus increasingly unattractive. An attempt was therefore made to organize the courtyard internally, walling off the northern side and establishing an east-west axis from Broadway. The first building to reflect this change of heart was Huntington's American Geographical Society built in 1911 on the southwest corner of Broadway and 156th Street.[213] It replaced the society's similar but smaller Modern French building at 15 West Eighty-first Street, designed just ten years earlier by Howells & Stokes.[214] The design of the new Geographical Society was mirrored in Huntington's Museum of the American Indian at Broadway and 155th Street, opened in 1925.[215] The two buildings formed a small courtyard sunk below the level of Broadway; an iron grill and stairs articulated the transition to an inner court dominated by the Hispanic Society building. The northern edge of this court was finally closed by the Hispanic Society's Library (1923-30), designed after Charles Huntington's death by H. Brooks Price.[216] Price expressed Huntington's ubiquitous Ionic order indirectly, retaining its cornice but articulating the courtyard elevations of the library with simple panelling. His restraint served as an effective foil to a sunken sculpture court. Its heroically scaled equestrian statue of El Cid was by the philanthropist's wife, Anna Hyatt Huntington, who was also responsible for the library's bas-reliefs of Don Quixote and Boabdil and a series of smaller sculptural groups of wild animals.[217]

The program of education and assimilation implicit in the Composite Era's cultural palaces was evident in the major university campuses designed in the 1890s. Each was the result of expanding facilities and enrollments which required relocation from downtown. New York University's intention to move from Washington Square to a new site in the Bronx was announced when plans to merge with

Church of Our Lady of Esperanza, 624 West 156th Street. Charles P. Huntington, 1909-11. MCNY

New York University, University Avenue and West 181st Street, Bronx. McKim, Mead & White, 1895-1902. Hall of Fame and Gould Memorial Library. NYHS

Columbia College failed to materialize in 1892.[218] The proposed merger, though characteristic of the institutional consolidation which marked the Composite Era, was ironic in that the university had been founded in 1831 as a reaction to the rigorous, elitist and preprofessional curriculum of Columbia College. In 1835 New York University built a classroom building designed by Ithiel Town and Alexander Jackson Davis. Located on Washington Square, its grandeur and collegiate Gothic character "effaced and extinguished the architectural pretentions of anything Columbia had built up to that time."[219] After acquiring the Mali Estate on what was to become known as University Heights, in 1892 the university retained Stanford White to study the feasibility of reerecting the Washington Square building on the Bronx site. But in 1893 Helen Gould Shepard extended the benefactions of her recently deceased father, Jay Gould, and it became possible to consider the construction of an entirely new campus in the Bronx.

The masterplan prepared by White harked back to the Classicism of the early Republic: to Jefferson at the University of Virginia and, more directly, to Jean Jacques Ramée's plan for Union College in Schenectady. White proposed two U-shaped groups of classroom buildings disposed to either side of a central mall. At the head of the mall, the library sat on a bluff overlooking the Harlem River, Manhattan and the Hudson River beyond. At the other end of the mall was an existing sports field, and beyond it the dormitories adapted to the contour of the hill.

White chose a delicate palette for the buildings: variegated golden and buff Roman brick trimmed in limestone and buff terra cotta. The first building, the Hall of Languages, was completed in 1894,[220] site work began on the overall campus in 1895, and the first dormitory was completed in 1897.[221] The principal ornament of the campus, the Gould Memorial Library, was substantially finished in 1900, although work continued on the interior until 1902.

The library was smaller but no less Roman than McKim's at Columbia.[222] The projecting wings of its Latin cross plan housed administrative offices and eighteen seminar rooms. The central block contained a six-hundred-seat auditorium, and above, the Pantheonic reading room. The latter was a great domed rotunda, its walls lined with books behind an inner ring of columns washed with light from an oculus overhead. Outside, the principal feature of the building was the peristyle which encircled it at the edge of the bluff. The colonnade, which housed a Hall of Fame commemorating outstanding Americans, was conceived by University Chancellor Henry M. MacCracken as camouflage for the high foundations necessary on the steep hill.[223]

While the university had grand siting, especially in the piling up of its elements along the bluff, it was also, as Schuyler observed, very different from the pomp of McKim's Columbia: "in spite of the porticoes and the applied orders, and the saucer cupola, there is as much in the yellow brick and gray stone of Stanford White's masonry at University Heights as there is nothing in the Greco-Roman of his partner's on Morningside to recall the free and vernacular use of classic forms in Georgian and Colonial work. . . . By the homogeneousness of material between the principal building and its dependencies, these buildings really carry the 'collegiate' connotation which the subordinate buildings of Columbia so lack."[224]

The third major New York college campus to come into existence within the decade was City College, the only one to be publically financed and to offer free tuition, part of its role as "the crown and culmination of the system of the public schools."[225] Its former home, "a reminder of the day of small things," was a Gothic Revival building at Twenty-third Street and Lexington Avenue.[226] Designed by James Renwick, Jr., it had been rendered inadequate by half a century of expanding enrollments. In 1897 eight architectural firms were invited to compete for the design of a new campus to house six thousand students.[227]

George B. Post's prize-winning scheme took full advantage of the new site. Atop a promontory overlooking St. Nicholas Park, the site was as dramatic as New York University's, and the location as convenient to the populous sections of the city as Columbia's.[228] The campus consisted of five buildings forming a quadrangle divided by Convent Avenue. The principal building, a four-story wall of classrooms, followed the curve of St. Nicholas Terrace, and a vigorously modelled assembly hall seating 2,400 people sat

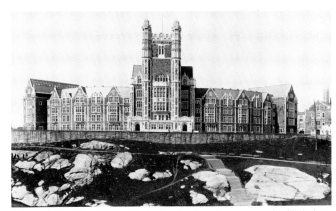

College of the City of New York, Amsterdam Avenue and St. Nicholas Terrace between 138th and 140th streets. George B. Post, 1905. View from St. Nicholas Avenue. NYHS

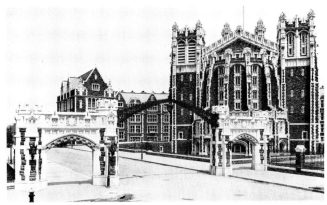

College of the City of New York, Amsterdam Avenue and St. Nicholas Terrace between 138th and 140th streets. George B. Post, 1905. Assembly Hall. NYHS

perpendicular to the chord of its arc. At the intersection of the two, a central tower housing the fan room and other mechanical functions gathered up the complex into a monumental whole. The buildings were sheathed in Manhattan schist, a rather coarse local stone excavated both on the site and from the construction of the I.R.T. subway. The apparent mass of the buildings was lightened by the use of white terra-cotta trim sandblasted to resemble marble. The stark contrast of black and white proved difficult for even the most sympathetic critics to accept, though the overall effect of the composition and its bold palette of materials evoked for Schuyler "the cloistrality and the charm . . . of its originals," the towers of Magdalen, Merton and St. John's at Oxford and Cambridge, "while, by dint of its superior scale and possibly of the very aggressiveness which comes from the contrast and conflict of the material, it has vigor, spirit and 'bite' beyond its originals."[229]

Despite the restricted budget and the coarse materials available, Post maintained a high degree of control over the project, down to the many small details which enlivened the composition—six hundred different grotesque figures graced the cornices, representing such diverse themes as the beginnings of higher education, and workers going about their trades. The irony that the more democratic City College eschewed the municipal Classicism of Columbia in favor of the cloistral English tradition—the public character usually preferred by the exclusive private universities— was not wasted on the *Architectural Record,* which concluded its assessment with the observation that "It remains to be said that in no other institution whatever could the 'fair humanities' of a picturesque and romantic architecture be more useful or more educative to those who are its occupants than precisely in the College of the City of New York."[230]

Churches

As the Cosmopolitan Era opened, New Yorkers witnessed the laborious completion of St. Patrick's, the Roman Catholic cathedral on Fifth Avenue between Fiftieth and Fifty-first streets. When first designed in 1850 by James Renwick, Jr., St. Patrick's was already a late flowering of the pious but rather dry scholarship of Pugin's Gothic Revival. By 1879, when the cathedral was dedicated, and by 1888, when its towers were complete, St. Patrick's stood as an architectural anachronism among the flamboyantly eclectic, astylar churches of Cosmopolitan New York, of which Temple Emanu-El (1868) was a prophetic exemplar.[231] Designed by Leopold Eidlitz and Henry Fernbach, it housed the city's most affluent Jewish congregation, and was an extravagant synthesis of Gothic and Saracenic motifs unified by the constructive principles of Viollet-le-Duc.

The addition of these two monumental houses of worship to Fifth Avenue's hitherto exclusively Protestant religious buildings testified to the city's growing cosmopolitanism. The ecclesiastical work of such brilliant eclectics as J.C. Cady, William A. Potter and R.H. Robertson was an expression of this diversity, synthesizing a panoply of associational styles within the general framework of the Richardsonian Romanesque. As Montgomery Schuyler observed of the 1880s, "Richardson's . . . Trinity Church in Boston . . . had a more immediate and general effect upon American architecture than any other ever erected in this country." But by the turn of the century, as Schuyler lamented in 1903, "the Romanesque revival has spent its force. There is hardly a parallel, even in our American way of treating architecture as a mere matter of fashion, to this 'movement' so sudden, so swift and so sweeping, which subsided as swiftly as it arose. And this is more the pity because the Romanesque, in the Richardsonian version of it, gave a more rational promise in church building than in almost any of its plans."[232]

A.D.F. Hamlin was less kindly disposed to the Romanesque churches of the Cosmopolitan Era: "They serve well the purpose for which they appear to have been solely designed—that of housing luxuriously the congregation, choir, clergy, Sunday school, and social activities of the parish. Seldom do they manifest the existence of any higher aim than this, or any adequate recognition of the value of simple dignity, sober decoration, and solid construction, in place of singularity and picturesqueness of design."[233]

Because of the religious associations of medieval architecture, relatively few churches reflected the general trend toward Classicism, although not all the new designs turned to the conventional Gothic style. For example, Robert W. Gibson's Collegiate Dutch Reformed Church (1892), executed in a distinctly Dutch Colonial mode, was a response to its congregation's particular history as well as a crystallization of a major style for the emerging West End neighborhood in which it was located.

In their Judson Memorial Church (1892), McKim, Mead & White attempted to address the issue of stylistic specificity with a design that was not Gothic but yet was appropriate to a church. They created, in Russell Sturgis's words, "a most able and most fortunate combination of Renaissance with an Italian round-arched earlier style," the Romanesque of San Miniato al Monte in Florence.[234] The change in taste and urbanism was evident in the firmness with which the Judson Church occupied its corner site facing Washington Square Park. The auditorium, a simple pedimented rectangular mass, was raised above the street by a tall basement with deeply cut, horizontally banded rustication, its solidity emphasized by the placement of the main entrance in the porchlike extension which connected to the tower. With its tiered arcades, the tower was the most literally Romanesque element of the design, which succeeded in synthesizing allusions to the presumptive faith of the Middle Ages and the more rationalistic post-Medieval world.

Nonetheless a trend toward purely Classical church design began to develop. Sometimes, as in the case of Gibson's Randall Memorial Church (1892), one of the first important Classical churches of the American Renaissance, it could be interpreted as a response to a particular physical context.[235] Set within the distinctly Classical context of Sailors' Snug Harbor on Staten Island, the Randall Memorial's bold pedimented porch led into a cruciform room crowned by a high Italian dome. In the case of various Christian Science churches, such as the First and Second Churches of Christ, Scientist, and in synagogues such as that of Congregation Shaaray Tefila, Classicism was also a response to theological and cultural issues. Classicism appealed to Christian Scientists because it so obviously bypassed the traditional mysticism of Gothic church architecture. Many of the city's established Jewish congregations adopted it for similar reasons, and also because Classicism invoked Solomon's Temple yet avoided the Oriental associations that were quickly becoming undesirable as mass migration from Eastern Europe altered the complexion of the Jewish community in New York.

Even the normally dour Presbyterians were once persuaded to clothe their worship in a purely Classical garment: McKim, Mead & White's short-lived Madison Square Presbyterian Church (it was dedicated in 1906 and demolished in 1913) was a remarkably pagan structure at the northeast corner of Twenty-fourth Street and Madison Avenue that faced Madison Square and the Metropolitan Life Insurance Tower. As the *Brickbuilder* put it the church, Stanford White's last great work, presented a difficult problem: "to erect a creditable church building in a spot backed by a fifteen-story skyscraper, with the possibility of a similar building on one side and a six-hundred-foot tower across the street."[236] Dr. Parkhurst, the church's minister, encouraged White to explore less austere forms than customarily found in Presbyterian church architecture. As a result, and in response to the limitations of the site, White developed a design with a cruiform plan entered through a boldly scaled portico and surmounted by a dome. White's highly polychromed building was even more evocative of early Christian architecture created under the influence of Imperial Rome than it was of the Renaissance. The exterior was sheathed in delicately colored buff brick and glazed terra cotta that enhanced the building's presence in relationship to the towering Metropolitan Life Insurance Building and helped distinguish it from other neighbors such as the recently completed Appellate Court. The pale green granite columns of the portico supported Corinthian capitals tinted blue, white and yellow; the pediment was filled with a frieze of white figures against a blue background with gilded details, while the exterior of the dome was clad in a pattern of green and yellow tiles and surmounted by a golden lantern. J. Monroe Hewlett found it "fortunate that the color has been applied with great reserve . . . so much so [that] on a bright day the color variation merely serves to impart a slight vibrant golden glow to the prevailing creamy

Judson Memorial Church, southwest corner of Washington Square South and Thompson Street. McKim, Mead & White, 1892. View from Washington Square. NYHS

Madison Square Presbyterian Church, northeast corner of Madison Avenue and Twenty-fourth Street. McKim, Mead & White, 1906. View from Madison Avenue. CU

Grace Church Mission Chapel and Dispensary, 406–14 East Fourteenth Street. Barney & Chapman, 1894. CU

tone of the building without in the least diminishing the quietness of the shade and shadow."[237] Inside, the use of color was equally evident, though the colors selected were more delicate, and subtly gradated to brighten toward the top of the dome.

Carrère & Hastings's West Park Presbyterian Church (1914) on West 174th Street and Wadsworth Avenue was a late example of the Classicizing trend in church design, although the English Mannerist inspiration of the firm's First Church of Christ, Scientist gave way to a more familiar Anglo-American Georgian vocabulary that recalled the London churches of Wren and Gibbs.[238] Carrère & Hastings deliberately exaggerated the scale and rhetoric of their prototypes, however, particularly in the extravagant bell tower that rose to almost three times the height of the church itself. The interior, delicately panelled and painted white, with a gallery at the rear, was even more explicitly indebted to Georgian examples.

While the new taste for Classicism did not overtake the traditional hold of Medievalism on the architecture of established religious groups, the sense of civic art that was so much a part of the American Renaissance had a profound effect on church designs of all styles, introducing a sense of urbanistic obligation into the design process that would reach its culmination in the design of the new St. Bartholomew's (1917) by Bertram Grosvenor Goodhue. Two church groupings by Barney & Chapman were among the earliest manifestations of the new sensitivity to site: Grace Church Mission Chapel and Dispensary (1894) at 406–414 East Fourteenth Street and Holy Trinity Church (1897) at 316 East Eighty-eighth Street each built in the heart of a densely populated working-class neighborhood. So successful were these from the sociological as well as urban design points of view that Schuyler was led to observe that though "architecture is not 'civics' . . . one may be allowed in an architectural review to express the wish that instead of two there might be twenty such centres of civilization on the East Side of New York."[239] Both of these churches were working-class branches of fashionable old-line congregations, the former an offshoot of Grace Church on Broadway, the latter of St. James's on Madison Avenue. Each included not only a church and rectory but also social service facilities.

The Grace Church Mission Center occupied a midblock site running through to Thirteenth Street. An elaborately decorated tower dominated the design, acting as the focus between the hospital and community buildings on the east and the chapel on the west. In emulation of a cloister, an arched passageway ran through the middle of the block to a south-facing playground courtyard along Thirteenth Street. The rectory at Thirteenth Street contained a clubhouse and parish building. The clubhouse was "an immensely interesting building, showing, as it does, what modern church work means in a crowded city like New York and in a densely populated neighborhood such as this one," the *American Architect and Building News* said. "In the building are about all the conveniences which could be asked for in the most carefully arranged fashionable club. Of course, its extent is limited . . . but parlors and a reading room as well as a gymnasium and an indoor swimming pool were included so that the . . . neighborhood will be convinced that the propaganda with which Grace Church is engaged in does not mean to exclude the enjoyment of healthful exercise and the luxury of a plunge."[240]

Although it did not run through the block, the site of the Holy Trinity complex was more spacious, extending some 250 feet along Eighty-eighth Street to allow the church to be oriented parallel to the street and behind a garden. To the west of the church and its gloriously proportioned tower, a cloister connected a small morning chapel with St. Christopher's house, which contained a large assembly room. Montgomery Schuyler observed in 1903: "There is nothing in New York which shows more admirably what has been called 'the willfullness and spontaneity of true Gothic'; which is so opposed to the conformity and regularity of true classic that no modern architect has succeeded, perhaps, in attaining high success in both." Schuyler felt that Holy Trinity's picturesque massing exhibited "such a strong and subtle artistic sense as is manifested in few indeed of the buildings of Manhattan."[241]

As the city grew and the character of neighborhoods changed, churches in particular found themselves robbed by surrounding tall buildings of the dignity which their own

Holy Trinity Church, 316 East Eighty-eighth Street. Barney & Chapman, 1897. CU

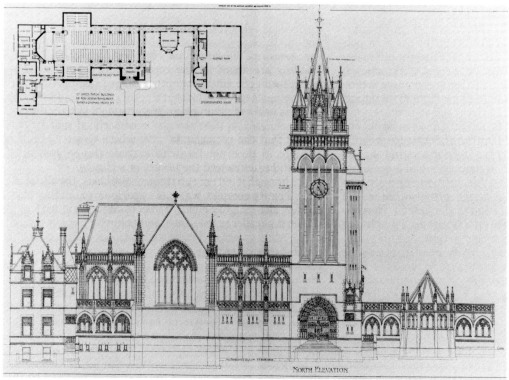

Holy Trinity Church, 316 East Eighty-eighth Street. Barney & Chapman, 1897. Elevation and plan of ground floor. CU

Broadway Tabernacle, northeast corner of Broadway and Fifty-sixth Street. Barney & Chapman, 1904. MCNY

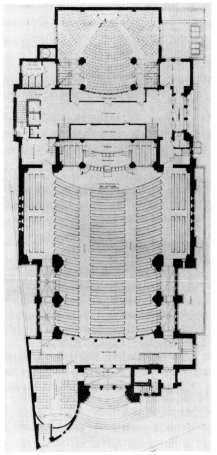

Broadway Tabernacle, northeast corner of Broadway and Fifty-sixth Street. Barney & Chapman, 1904. Plan of ground floor. CU

commanding size and ample light and air had previously afforded them in the community. At the same time, as *Architecture* observed in 1910, "Our metropolitan churches have become less and less houses of worship exclusively and more and more centers of social life. . . . They now include gymnasiums, athletic teams, clubs of various sorts whose obvious purpose is only slightly religious, but which have a real deep meaning in that they furnish a place of recreation in pure surroundings. . . . The buildings in which these great, modern, and heterogeneous activities are centered only partially resemble the parish churches of the past."[242] The new demands of an increasing social activism led to complexes like Holy Trinity, and also to such complex hybrid buildings as Barney & Chapman's Broadway Tabernacle (1904) at the northeast corner of Broadway and Fifty-sixth Street.

The Broadway Tabernacle, the city's first "skyscraper church," was a vivid solution to the problem of a too-small site and an unstable physical context. At first glance the Tabernacle seemed an accomplished but not remarkable design in the late French Gothic style, principally interesting for its accommodation to an irregular site. But as Schuyler observed, "the novelty . . . is not in the church but in the appendages. It is a frank attempt to take advantage of the new construction, not in the sacred edifice itself, but in its 'temporalities,' and to make up in the accommodation of these, by altitude, for the area that is lacking."[243] Put more directly, the bell tower was an office building with its own elevator and fire stairs, an ingenious solution to a difficult program including a church large enough for fifteen hundred worshippers, two smaller chapels, an auditorium for meetings, as well as facilities for a full fledged Sunday school program and a parish house for the pastor and his staff.

Barney & Chapman based their design on Richardson's Trinity Church in Boston. Protecting the land-locked flanks of the site by a judicious manipulation of the plan, they insured light to the north side of the church complex and sheltered the church complex "against whatever darkening skyscraper may come to be reared" along its edges. By stacking the extra-church facilities into a mini-skyscraper in the form of a giant tower at the crossing, a new, complex hybrid was born, uniting church, social hall and school in a simple, evocative envelope which, despite its Gothic style, was as densely composite as any Classical design by McKim.

The Gothic verticality of Barney & Chapman's Tabernacle proved a useful model for imposing visual unity on a hybrid building type, and pointed the way to a number of skyscraper churches of the 1920s—monuments to the metropolitanism of convenience and commercialism. Among them were: Bertram Grosvenor Goodhue's Office and Convocational Building projected for Madison Square; Tillion & Tillion's Manhattan Congregational Church at Broadway and Seventy-sixth Street; and Henry C. Pelton's, Burnham Hoyt's, and Allen & Collens's Riverside Church (1930) on Morningside Heights.[244]

A more characteristic strategy for anticipating urban growth and for coping with limited building sites was to place the parish facilities in a small building to one side of the church, thereby providing the church with its own context in perpetuity. This strategy was most successfully practiced by Cram, Goodhue & Ferguson in their highly inventive St. Thomas Church (1906-14), which replaced a previous church on the site designed by Richard Upjohn Sr. that burned in 1905.[245] A competition was held for a Gothic church large enough to seat seventeen hundred people, with a chantry for fifty to one hundred persons, a choir, a parish house and a rectory. Nine architectural firms were invited to compete: Parish & Schroeder; George B. Post; R.W. Gibson; C.C. Haight; Lord & Hewlett; Allen & Collens; Barney & Chapman; Carpenter & Blair; and Cram, Goodhue & Ferguson.[246] George Post's entry rather incongruously reiterated the facade of Notre Dame in Paris. Barney & Chapman's submission may have been the most lively, its bold corner tower a development of the firm's previous designs, while R.W. Gibson's was surely the most unorthodox, with an extraordinary three-bay facade facing Fifty-third Street and a vast semicircular auditorium. But Cram, Goodhue & Ferguson justifiably won the commission with the most important Gothic design since St. Patrick's. They proposed an asymmetrical building, shifting the axis of the nave with its narrow flanking aisles off the center of the site, and adding a gallery along the side street, behind the corner tower, to accommodate overflow crowds. As Schuyler put it, "The disposition is so unusual that the boldness of it would border on temerity did it not so clearly proceed from the fundamental disposition of the plan and were it not so clearly justified by the result."[247] Yet the symmetry of the individual elements of the plan gave the interior a traditional feel. Its chief beauty was the reredos designed by Goodhue and the sculptor Lee Lawrie. Offering relief from the massive solidity of the rest of the church, the exquisite details of Lawrie's sculptures and the canopies which framed them were subsumed into a rich yet delicate texture which seemingly dematerialized the altar.

The true distinction of St. Thomas, however, lay in its contribution to New York's composite urbanism. By designing an asymmetrical though carefully balanced facade with a single corner tower, the architects arrived at a sensitive response to the problem of a corner site. Since the facade, in effect, was a fragment of a traditional freestanding church with two towers, the church was thrown into a strong relationship with its neighbors. The asymmetry reinforced the integrity of the entire block and the tower provided a vertical termination to what was conceived of as a continuous street wall.[248] "In fact," Schuyler wrote, "if one were asked to designate one element which more than any other contributes to the distinction of the church among our essays in ecclesiastical gothic the world would have to say that more than any other it was composed in three dimensions. . . . Beyond question the new St. Thomas's is one of the chief architectural ornaments of New York."[249]

Cram, Goodhue & Ferguson employed a similar strategy of using ancillary facilities as a permanent foil to a church in their design for the South Church (1911) on the southwest corner of Eighty-fifth Street and Park Avenue. Relocated from the southeast corner of Madison Avenue and Thirty-eighth Street, the new facility marked the farthest extremity of Park Avenue's fashionable development.[250] An auditorium modelled vaguely on Ste. Chapelle in Paris occupied the corner, while a parish house and Sunday school were grouped around a courtyard to the side. The South Church showed the hand of Goodhue even more than St. Thomas: *Architecture* noted "the tremendous importance assigned to the vertical members and the contrast between the quiet and assured stability of the wall surfaces and the highly decorated, almost playful window treatments."[251]

Goodhue's Chapel of the Intercession, a large church erected in 1914 by Trinity Parish on the grounds of Trinity Cemetery at Broadway and 155th Street, had the advantage of a site immune from commercial encroachments. Its setting and scale were enhanced by a rectory and a large clubhouse attached to the long body of the church by an arcaded cloister. The complex was anchored to its site by the heaviness of the tower, placed to the side of the nave, and sporting on one of its corners a metal *flèche*. As C. Matlack Price observed, "A salient characteristic shared by each [of Goodhue's works] is the peculiar quality of Gothic employed for expression—a sort of Gothic at once rugged and refined; virile and massive without being heavy, and delicate without being trivial—and essentially scholarly without being archaeological."[252]

St. Bartholomew's decision to locate on Park Avenue, like South Church, was a reflection of the street's new fashionability. The congregation had been housed in a vaguely Romanesque church designed by James Renwick on Madison Avenue and Forty-fourth Street. Its chief distinction was the triple portal added by McKim, Mead & White in 1909, a scholarly adaptation of the portals of St. Gilles in Arles. The congregation's desire to incorporate the entrance in their new church set the tone for Goodhue's design, a monumental abstraction of Romanesque and Byzantine sources which epitomized his highly personal approach to historical styles.

The congregation originally considered developing part of the site to include a revenue-producing apartment house. At Goodhue's urging, however, the entire site was developed as a permanent foil to the church. The Community House was set at the rear of the lot behind a garden raised on a terrace. It mediated between the picturesque massing of the church and the residential side street. The composition was enhanced by Goodhue's subtle polychromy which mingled salmon colored brick and limestone and culminated in a dome sheathed in mosaic. St. Bartholomew's marked a unique synthesis in the city's ecclesiastical architecture, combining the picturesque ideals and the romantic eclecticism of the Cosmpopolitan Era with the sense of civic monumentality which marked the Composite Era.

St. Thomas Church competition entry, northwest corner of Fifth Avenue and Fifty-third Street. George B. Post, 1906. Perspective view from Fifth Avenue. CU

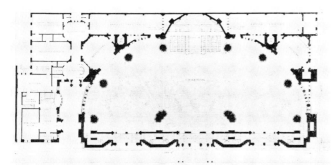

St. Thomas Church competition entry, northwest corner of Fifth Avenue and Fifty-third Street. Robert W. Gibson, 1906. Plan of ground floor. CU

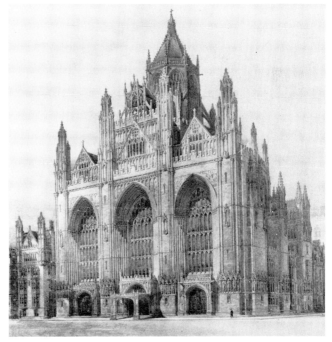

St. Thomas Church competition entry, northwest corner of Fifth Avenue and Fifty-third Street. Robert W. Gibson, 1906. Perspective view from Fifth Avenue. CU

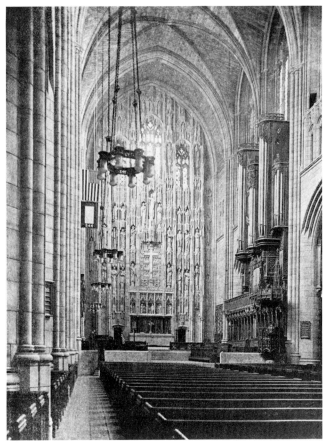

St. Thomas Church, northwest corner of Fifth Avenue and Fifty-third Street. Cram, Goodhue & Ferguson, 1906–14. Nave and reredos. CU

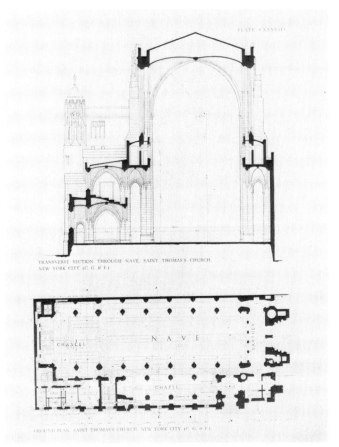

St. Thomas Church, northwest corner of Fifth Avenue and Fifty-third Street. Cram, Goodhue & Ferguson, 1906–14. Plan of ground floor and transverse section through nave. CU

Monuments and Memorials

The characteristic monument of the Cosmopolitan Era was dedicated to an individual hero rather than a political or social ideal. Perhaps because of lingering guilt over the city's ambiguous role in the Civil War, New York built comparatively few monuments to commemorate the war. Its first major commemorative monument, dedicated to Admiral Farragut, was not built until 1881, when two young artists, the sculptor Augustus Saint-Gaudens and the architect Stanford White, collaborated in the design of the statue and its base.[253] The combination of realism in the statue and abstraction in the details of its base marked the Farragut Memorial as a significant, if not fully synthesized reflection of French aestheticism and American realism. At the same time, the vaguely considered siting in a corner of Madison Square and the failure to establish a dialogue with the larger issues of landscape design made the Farragut Memorial a representative expression of the idiosyncratic public architecture of the Cosmopolitan Era.

"The New York people do not seem to be very happy in the selection of sites for their monuments. Even of the very best and most costly a large proportion are rendered comparatively insignificant by the position in which they are placed," the *American Architect and Building News* stated in 1881. Even the Farragut Memorial, it felt, "furnishes an example of some of the worst faults of the situation. Not only is it badly placed in itself, but the design of the figure with its pedestal is singularly at variance with its surroundings."[254] An anonymous writer to the magazine characterized the ensemble as "the image of a hero as an incident at the back of a sofa."[255] The exedral base combined with the frontal statue seemed pointless to many. Its placement in the square without any attempt to relate it to a building or a wall was questionable, especially when the garden in which it was set was described as "a dilapidated grass-plot, a few feet from the street, and overshadowed by waving foliage."[256]

While the Farragut Memorial was artistically innovative, its overall impact was slight compared to the construction in 1886 of the Statue of Liberty in New York Harbor.[257] The relationship between Frédéric Auguste Bartholdi's Statue of Liberty and Richard Morris Hunt's design for the base came closest to the spirit of monumentality that became the hallmark of the Composite Era. The base made

St. Thomas Church, northwest corner of Fifth Avenue and Fifty-third Street. Cram, Goodhue & Ferguson, 1906–14. View from Fifth Avenue. MCNY

St. Bartholomew's Church, east side of Park Avenue between Fiftieth and Fifty-first streets. Bertram Grosvenor Goodhue, 1919. View from Park Avenue showing Stanford White's portal. CU

St. Bartholomew's Church, east side of Park Avenue between Fiftieth and Fifty-first streets. Bertram Grosvenor Goodhue, 1919. View of crossing. MCNY

St. Bartholomew's Church, east side of Park Avenue between Fiftieth and Fifty-first streets. Bertram Grosvenor Goodhue, 1919. Perspective view from Park Avenue showing Goodhue's scheme for the crossing tower, which was redesigned and built by Mayers, Murray & Philip in 1930. CU

an appropriate transition between the extreme verticality of the statue and the low walls of the star-shaped fort which served as its site. Yet the monument's absolute isolation from the city, though poetic, exemplified the fundamental alienation between object and place that characterized the architecture of the Cosmopolitan Era.

It was not until the late 1880s that Americans became seriously interested in monumental commemorative architecture. The announcement of the results of the competitions for Grant's Tomb, Brooklyn's Soldiers' and Sailors' Monument, and the construction of a temporary arch over Manhattan's Fifth Avenue in honor of the centennial of Washington's inauguration marked the transition from the informality and individuality of the Cosmopolitan Era to the formality and communality of the Composite. *Building* magazine commented that:

In the natural order of the career of such a prosperous people, it is certain that they are turning to outward manifestations to commemorate the deeds of our great men, and to satisfy the natural human love of display, and the desire to beautify the public parks, squares and highways. The more this manifestation is shown, the greater is our responsibility. . . . To this end the monumental spirit latent in each true architect should be nourished by a faithful, earnest study of the purest classic work, to catch its spirit . . . in order that he may impart immortality to his completed design. Whatever may be larged against classic motives, forms and proportions for domestic work, it is obviously true, do not apply to monumental design. With all due regard to modern applications of mixed styles, we firmly believe that no monumental design will be thoroughly successful and effective that is not based on the spirit of such work.[258]

Although the competition results for a memorial to General Grant were announced in 1889, a site in Riverside Park at 120th Street had been chosen and Grant buried there in 1885.[259] Because no commission was awarded by the Expert Committee (which included the architects Napoleon Le Brun, William R. Ware, George B. Post and James E. Ware) a second limited competition was held, with John H. Duncan selected as winner.[260] Duncan's entry, based on Napoleon's Tomb at Les Invalides in Paris, consisted of a cube surmounted by a drum ringed by a colonnade and crowned with a stepped roof. More than any of the other

Admiral Farragut Memorial, Madison Square. Augustus Saint-Gaudens and McKim, Mead & White, 1881. A view which shows the tower of White's Madison Square Garden in the background. CU

Temporary Tomb of General Grant, Riverside Drive at West 122nd Street. Jacob Wrey Mould, 1885. NYHS

contestants, Duncan grasped the fundamental issue: to make a building that embodied not so much the character of Grant, a soldier who had outlived his reputation, but to create an American Valhalla, a shrine to American power. Not only was the design less restless and more formidably proportioned than the other entries, it also undertook a sophisticated dialogue with the dramatic site, incorporating a strong response to the obvious axis to the city to the south while introducing a secondary axis to the west in the form of a cascade of steps leading to the river's edge. Construction proceeded through the 1890s, and the tomb was dedicated in 1897.

Duncan's Grant Memorial was rivaled by his even more grandiloquent Soldiers' and Sailors' Memorial Arch in Grand Army Plaza in Brooklyn, a commission also won by competition.[261] Like the Centennial Arch, the Soldiers' and Sailors' Monument was in commemoration of the centenary of Washington's inauguration. Its cornerstone was not laid however, until October 31, 1889. The size and complexity of the design delayed its completion until 1892, while its ambitious sculptural program, largely the work of Frederick MacMonnies, was not completed until 1901.

Stanford White's Centennial Arch over lower Fifth Avenue was a more scholarly and less heavy-handed exploration of Classicism than Duncan's, and an even more significant indication of the taste of the Composite Era.[262] In honoring a public ideal—the commencement of our democracy—as well as a hero, it exemplified the new sense of national self-confidence that began to emerge at the time of the Centennial in 1876, in reaction to the cynicism and divisiveness of the post-Civil War era. The original arch, a temporary structure paid for by residents of the Washington Square neighborhood, was painted white, ornamented with stucco wreaths, and topped by a Colonial period, eight-foot-high statue of George Washington that was polychromed for the occasion. It offered a gentle, tentative intimation of civic grandeur that was uniquely appealing, especially in the evening, when incandescent lamps, among the first used outdoors, outlined its principal features against the darkening night sky.

Because of the enormous popularity of the arch, a committee was formed to raise $150,000 for construction of a permanent marble structure in Washington Square, slightly south of the original location.[263] But the *Real Estate*

General Grant National Memorial, Riverside Drive at West 122nd Street. John H. Duncan, 1890-97. A view which shows the Riverside Drive viaduct at 125th Street in the background. NYHS

Record and Guide suggested that the northward movement of the city's population made both locations unwise, calling into question the "proposition . . . to locate the arch in a section of the city that has seen its best days, and that twenty years from now will be changed in character—changed in such a way that no one will visit near it, except those whose personal interest bring them here."[264] Despite objections to the site, ground was broken in June 1890 for the permanent arch. Its popularity did much to establish the Classical ideal as the basis for virtually all commemorative architecture in the Composite Era.

Two more temporary arches were built in the 1890s. In 1892 Henry B. Herts, still a student at Columbia College, won a competition for the design of a memorial dedicated to Christopher Columbus.[265] Intended as a permanent memorial, it was only realized in a temporary version erected at Fifth Avenue and Fifty-eighth Street. According to the *Art Amateur,* Herts's Columbus Arch compared favorably with White's Washington Arch, a judgment not shared by the *American Architect and Building News* which did not "quite approve the polychromatic style adopted" and felt that it lacked the "poetry and refinement" of its immediate predecessor.

In 1899, the American victory at Manila and the swift, successful completion of the Spanish-American War led to the construction of an arch in honor of the war's great hero, Admiral Dewey.[266] Perhaps the most complex memorial ever proposed in the United States, it was built—if only in lath and plaster—at the height of American imperialism and the peak of the American Renaissance. Located in one of the city's most prominent intersections—where Broadway, Fifth Avenue and Twenty-fourth Street meet at Madison Square—the monument was a collaborative effort of the National Sculpture Society (whose second Vice-President, Charles Rollinson Lamb, modelled the monument on the Arch of Titus in Rome) and the American Society of Mural Painters, and served as a showcase for New York's artistic community. According to Russell Sturgis, the Dewey Arch "gave certain persons fresh grounds for belief that the plastic expression was the most natural expression of the art impulse of Americans."[267] Its success seemed to confirm that "New York has come to be recognized as the Great Art Center of America. Its schools of Art . . . have made a vast growth in the last decade, until there is no world center save

Washington Memorial Arch, Washington Square. McKim, Mead & White, 1889-92. A view looking south toward McKim, Mead & White's Judson Memorial Church. CU

Temporary Washington Memorial Arch, Fifth Avenue at Washington Square. McKim, Mead & White, 1889. View from Washington Square. MCNY

Prison Ship Martyrs' Monument, Fort Greene Park, Brooklyn. McKim, Mead & White and A.A. Weinman, 1908. NYHS

Paris which takes a higher stand in Art matters, and has before it a future of great promise. The Dewey Arch will evidence to the world the ability and fertility of sculptural and decorative talent in our New York Art Colony."[268]

As in the case of the Centennial Arch, the enormous popular success of the Dewey Arch led to a movement to finance its translation into more permanent materials. Fund raising progressed successfully until Dewey declared his candidacy for the presidency in the 1900 election, forcing the abandonment of the project and the return of $65,000 already in hand.[269] This was probably just as well, as it made it unnecessary for the city fathers to confront the problems raised by the awkwardness of its siting in the middle of an odd-shaped intersection and its relationship to traffic.[270]

McKim, Mead & White's Prison Ship Martyrs' Monument (1908) in Fort Greene Park, Brooklyn, was perhaps the most austere and most moving of the city's war memorials.[271] Set above three spacious terraces connected by broad flights of monumental stairs, the memorial consisted of a single, fluted Doric column that rose two hundred feet above the street to support an enormous bronze lantern sculpted by A.A. Weinman in the form of an urn.

H. Van Buren Magonigle and Attilio Piccirilli's Maine Monument was a memorial to those who lost their lives when the battleship Maine was blown up in Havana's harbor.[272] Won in competition, it was built at Columbus Circle in 1913. Magonigle's elegantly proportioned pedestal was surmounted by Piccirilli's somewhat underscaled and garishly gilded grouping depicting a triumphant Columbia in a shell-shaped chariot pulled by sea horses.

After the collapse of the project to make the Dewey Arch permanent, a fund-raising effort was made in 1901 on behalf of the construction of a Naval Arch at the foot of Broadway, thereby initiating a stream of proposals for the monumental embellishment of that site.[273] Ernest Flagg, architect of the new Naval Academy at Annapolis, was retained to design an arch intended to sit at the water's edge on axis with Broadway. Flagg's proposal would have been by far the most stylistically inventive of the arches built in the city, its single opening pushing upward into the attic. Three sculptural groups on the roof, with more at the base, and two lighthouses brought a conception of the waterfront that combined a Venetian sensibility with turn-of-century Parisian design.

New York, not to be outdone by Brooklyn's elaborate Soldiers' and Sailors' Memorial, formed a commission in 1893 to erect its own memorial in its own Grand Army Plaza at Fifty-ninth Street and Fifth Avenue. Almost from the first, the New York Federation of Fine Arts and the Municipal Art Society objected to the site, which they felt was inappropriate because the "skyscraper hotels" (the twelve-story Savoy Hotel and the fifteen-story New Netherland) that surrounded the plaza would dwarf the memorial.[274] Seven architects were invited in 1897 to compete for the commission in association with a sculptor of their own choice.[275]

Stoughton & Stoughton and Frederick MacMonnies, their collaborating sculptor, won the competition with a design for a column topped by *Victory* and flanked by equestrian groups.[276] But the argument about the site raged on for three more years, with increasing concern for the Monument Commission's failure to consider a comprehensive scheme for the entire plaza until 1900, when it agreed to move the site to Riverside Park.[277] First sited on what was known as Mount Tom, it was then resited at Eighty-ninth Street, and the monument was completely redesigned by Stoughton & Stoughton in association with Paul E.M. Duboy.[278] The new scheme was a sensitive response to the park's romantic landscape. Carefully positioned to lie on the axis of the stretch of Riverside Drive to the south, the monument crowned a promontory. The final design, not completed until 1902, evoked the Choragic Monument of Lysicrates in Athens, but with greater mass and *chiaroscuro*. The Eighty-ninth Street vista was terminated by a flagpole on the transverse axis of the monument, punctuating the view from the east across the Hudson River.

World War I fostered a final burst of sentiment for monumental commemorative architecture.[279] In 1919 Thomas Hastings designed an Arch of Freedom, executed again in temporary materials on the site of the Dewey Arch of twenty years earlier; while to the east, along the edge of

Dewey Arch, southwest corner of Madison Square. Charles Rollinson Lamb and members of the National Sculpture Society and the American Society of Mural Painters, 1899. A view looking up Fifth Avenue showing the Fifth Avenue Hotel to the left. NYHS

National Maine Memorial, Columbus Circle. H. Van Buren Magonigle and Attilio Piccirilli, 1913. CU

Soldiers' and Sailors' Monument, Riverside Drive at West Eighty-ninth Street. Stoughton & Stoughton and Paul E.M. Duboy, 1902. View from Riverside Drive. MCNY

Madison Square Park, he designed an Altar of Liberty which proved so popular that a campaign was waged to rebuild it in permanent materials.[280] In the same year, Helmle & Corbett designed an Arch of Democracy, for the intersection of Bedford Avenue and Eastern Parkway in Brooklyn, which was never executed.[281] Ware & Metcalfe's proposed Gateway of the Nation expanded on Flagg's earlier Naval Arch to combine an arch, a watergate and a Court of Honor that could serve as a military drillground in Battery Park at the foot of Manhattan.[282]

The early flurry of interest in commemorative monuments was not sustained. The World War brought a new sense of seriousness; war was no longer bully fun, the swaggering and splendid occasion it had seemed in 1899, but was instead a brutal and debilitating experience from which no nation was immune. Proposals such as the Gateway to the Nation or the Riverside Memorial, each of which included a vast outdoor amphitheatre, recognized the need for monuments which permitted community involvement and introduced a note of day-to-day practicality into a kind of project that had previously been seen in purely honorific terms.[283] But amphitheatres and drillgrounds did not go far enough, failing to express the new mood which called for a type of memorial which Charles Cornelius would label "utilitarian."[284] Henry Herts's and T. Markoe Robertson's proposed Victory Memorial captured the new mood, combining lofty sentiment and practicality in a proposal for the entire blockfront extending from Park to Lexington avenues between Forty-first and Forty-second streets.[285] The Victory Memorial was to have been three stories high, with the ground floor devoted to exhibition space, the basement to a huge sports complex, and the second floor an arena seating ten thousand. The third floor, in effect the hollow spaces between the vast trusses needed to span the arena below, was to have housed various meeting rooms, and the roof was reserved for recreational uses.

While the characteristic memorial of the Composite Era was large in scale and dedicated to an event of public significance, a number of smaller monuments convincingly caught the mood of the era, none more appropriately than the one dedicated to the architect Richard Morris Hunt, who had done so much to foster the revival of the Classical ideal in architecture and urban design. Hunt's death in 1895 produced a groundswell of sentiment among his fellow pro-

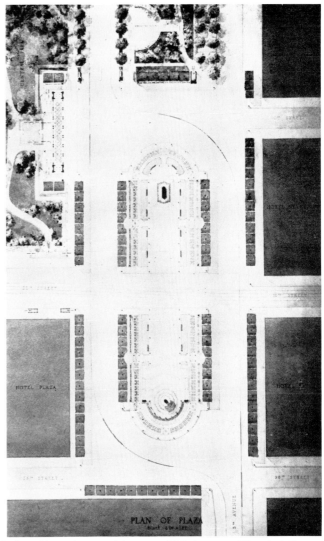

Pulitzer Fountain competition entry, Fifth Avenue at Fifty-ninth Street. Carrère & Hastings, 1913. Plan. CU

fessionals and others involved in civic reform to commemorate the nation's most prominent architect. Initially, the Architectural League suggested that one of Hunt's long dormant designs for a gateway to Central Park be built in his honor at Fifty-ninth Street and Fifth Avenue, but this idea was soon abandoned, partly because it was too expensive and partly because the idea of monumental gateways to the park had at least as many enemies as Hunt had friends.[286] Instead, the Municipal Art Society chose Daniel Chester French to create a memorial, and he in turn invited Bruce Price to collaborate in the design of the modest exedra which interrupted Central Park's Fifth Avenue wall between Seventieth and Seventy-first streets opposite Hunt's early masterpiece, the Lenox Library (torn down in 1912 for the Frick Mansion). Price's design paid loving homage to the neo-Grec vocabulary of Hunt's early work. Its specific location and uncompromised frontality contrasted with the casual placement of Stanford White's astylar "sofa" for the Farragut Memorial fifteen years earlier.

McKim, Mead & White's monument to Peter Cooper, in which they again collaborated with Saint-Gaudens, also reflected the shift of values from the Cosmopolitan to the Composite eras: Cooper sat inside a niche, protected at his rear by a screen wall, at his flanks by two Ionic columns, and above by a roof, all raised on a stepped base.[287]

One of the Composite Era's most extraordinary private memorials was the fountain and plaza at Fifty-ninth Street and Fifth Avenue which Joseph Pulitzer bequeathed to the city. Pulitzer's will called for a memorial to be named after himself and modelled on the grand Place de la Concorde in Paris. The New York City Improvement Plans of 1904 and 1907 recommended that the fifty thousand dollar bequest would be best spent at the intersection of Fifty-ninth Street and Fifth Avenue as part of the proposed widening of Fifty-ninth Street.[288]

A competition was proposed for the design of the new plaza, with a program expanded by the executors to incorporate a consideration of the site's function as a gateway to Central Park and to require the inclusion of a park shelter and subway station.[289] As a result, a somewhat self-indulgent memorial to a rich power broker developed into a major urban space with positive linkages to the new infrastructure made possible by the mechanical progress of the age. Carrère & Hastings's winning entry reflected the

Giovanni P. Morosini Mausoleum, Woodlawn Cemetery, Bronx. Jardine, Kent & Jardine, 1895. CU

Armour Mausoleum, Woodlawn Cemetery, Bronx. Renwick, Aspinwall & Owen, ca. 1900. CU

Grand Army Plaza's character as a transitional space between Fifth Avenue and Central Park, and Karl Bitter's statue, *Abundance,* on the south block neatly played off against Saint-Gaudens's statue of General Sherman already in place at the north. The design succeeded in tying together what had been an amorphous space, a ragged corner for the park, and an inconclusive termination to the lower half of Fifth Avenue. A low balustrade separated the fountain, the statue and its basin from the street, while Doric columns supported illuminated globes as well as bracketed torchieres which lit the plaza at night and provided its geometry with extra definition in the day.

More presumptuous, perhaps, were the mausoleums commissioned by the wealthy from the important architects of the day. The legacy of private men who imagined themselves princes of the city, they imitated memorials that only royalty had built before. The stage for building lavish mausoleums was set in 1876, when A.T. Stewart's body was scandalously disinterred and held for ransom. In reaction, William H. Vanderbilt decided that his family would need a more secure burial ground. In 1885 he commissioned Richard Morris Hunt to erect a secure family mausoleum both "roomy, solid and rich" and appropriate to the "plain, quiet unostentatious" Vanderbilts.[290] Hunt's design had a Richardsonian Romanesque facade based on the Church of St. Gilles in Arles, with a tomb chamber built into the hill and lit from above by a lantern. Built on a grassy knoll behind the Moravian Cemetery in New Dorp, Staten Island and landscaped by Frederick Law Olmsted, the tomb commanded a panoramic view of New York Harbor, where the family's fortune had begun.

Since 1840, the burial needs of Manhattan's upper classes had been filled by Greenwood Cemetery in Brooklyn.[291] Greenwood was one of the first naturalistically planted burial grounds in America. Its picturesque, English-influenced landscape, enhanced by Richard M. Upjohn's Gothic Revival gatehouses (1861), almost served as a public park. Although in the 1890s it was said that "all that wealth can command, everything that taste can suggest, all that local pride can bestow, has been lavished in the efforts to beautify this silent city," congestion in lower Manhattan and crowding at the ferry terminals made progress of funeral corteges to Brooklyn increasingly difficult.[292]

Woodlawn Cemetery was opened in 1865 by the Reverend Absalom Peter in the less congested northern reaches of the Bronx.[293] It was served by streetcars and railways and surrounded by relatively deserted avenues. "It is sufficiently remote from the island to be beyond the reach of its noise and the apprehension of disturbances from the extension of the city limits," the *New York Times* reported shortly after its opening. "It is essentially a rural cemetery and must remain so for years to come."[294]

As Woodlawn developed into the favored burial place for society's *400* in the Cosmopolitan Era, the increasingly dense congregation of individual monuments, each self contained and radically different in style, sparked a move toward the simplicity of Classical form. Jardine, Kent & Jardine's mausoleum for Giovanni P. Morosini (1895) exemplified the cosmopolitan approach to mortuary architecture which, as in ecclesiastical design, tended, because of its strong religious associations, to survive long after the Classical ideal was established in the city proper.[295] Morosini's Tomb was a cubic mass intersected by a Greek cross and capped by a low dome. Its austere exterior with overtones of Norman, Celtic, and Art Nouveau influences, was counterpointed by a Byzantine interior with *loculi* sheathed in marble and its floor and dome decorated with lush mosaics. Despite the tomb's romantic vocabulary, its independent, objective nature, intensified by a circular lawn, placed it at odds with the park-like setting and neighboring monuments.

In 1914 the *American Architect* decried the fact that until relatively recently, mortuary architecture had been characterized by "every form of sculptural vulgarity.... It is especially in the large, commercially operated cemeteries which invite wealthy patronage that unaffected reverence has too often been smothered by more or less vulgar ostentation."[296] Classicism seemed at least to offer a common language relating to individual tombs, as well as offering a variety of recognizable prototypes.

Classical memorials were occasionally erected as early as the 1880s. Jay Gould, one of the first plutocrats to build a

Bourke Mausoleum, Greenwood Cemetery, Brooklyn. Ernest Flagg, ca. 1902. CU

H.A.C. Taylor Mausoleum, Woodlawn Cemetery, Bronx. McKim, Mead & White, 1901. CU

mausoleum at Woodlawn, was interred in an awkwardly proportioned Ionic temple designed by H.Q. French.[297] By the turn of the century, however, Classicism dominated. Charles I. Berg's Coster Mausoleum[298] and Renwick, Aspinwall & Owen's Armour Mausoleum[299] were *tempietti* with short radiating arms containing the entrances and *sarcophagi*. The Armour Tomb's dome was cast in bronze and covered with a pattern of scales. Despite the Classical vocabulary, the vigorous accentuation of parts and rather top heavy proportions surely made the tomb as ostentatious and strident a display as the worst excesses of the Cosmopolitan Era.

Tombs of the Composite City tended increasingly toward a greater simplicity of massing and sparser ornamentation. Ernest Flagg's Bourke Mausoleum in the Modern French style was a rectangular mass, unarticulated on the sides, save for a continuous cornice and a compressed attic punctured to ventilate the tomb chamber.[300] A giant arch applied to the facade extended above the attic, framing a concave recess for the entrance and a vigorously carved tympanum.

Flagg's Modern French style lacked some of the sobriety of McKim, Mead & White's work at Woodlawn. The firm's Osborn and H.A.C. Taylor tombs were Classical *tempietti* with rich, garlanded friezes. The Goelet and Russell mausoleums looked back not to the Renaissance but to the more severe lines of Classical Greece and Rome; the former was an austere treasury with a tetrastyle Ionic portico, the latter an interpretation of the Tower of the Winds in Athens.[301] York & Sawyer's Millbank Memorial continued the trend toward the reduction of detail. A pink marble cube with corner piers framing Ionic columns in recessed porches, its sculpture was limited to bas-reliefs by Spicer Simpson over the entrance doors.

Perhaps the most moving of Woodlawn's mausolea was the tomb of William Bateman Leeds, designed by McKim's protege, John Russell Pope, around 1911.[302] Set on a square terrace, its unarticulated wall surface was cut back only at the entrance to create pilasters around the deeply recessed portals. Herbert Croly wrote in 1911 that its "permanent impression is due to the fundamental simplicity of the design, its beauty of form, the apt use of just a few incidental features and finally to what may be called its depth. . . . Its creator had ceased to think in terms of ordinary architectural incident and forms, and had imagined a monumental embodiment of the mystery of death."[303]

The new sense of restraint that came to characterize the city's memorial architecture by 1910 was also reflected in a number of tombs which relinquished the mausoleum type for an exedra, with the graves themselves marked only by flower beds. The Pulitzer Memorial by architect Duncan Chandler consisted of two stone benches flanking William Ordway Partridge's seated bronze figure with a high blank wall behind.[304]

Perhaps because of the lack of specifically religious sentiment expressed in Woodlawn's Neoclassical tombs, the cemetery's most extravagant memorial returned to Gothic. In keeping with the Composite Era's interest in stylistic accuracy, Hunt & Hunt's mausoleum for O.H.P. Belmont was a replica of St. Hubert's Chapel at Amboise, an exquisite fifteenth-century example of late French Gothic.[305] Although the exterior was limestone, its interior was cast in concrete, the floral moldings painted in naturalistic colors and then rendered by William Mackay to suggest the effects of age. Hunt & Hunt also commissioned Helen Maitland Armstrong to design a series of sixteen stained-glass windows, essays in archaicism that furthered the fiction of authenticity.

The city's major Jewish cemeteries, Salem Fields and New Union Field, both in Brooklyn, were characterized throughout their history by an eclectic approach to mortuary architecture, a situation which reflected the same search for an architectural heritage that marked the city's synagogue architecture. The wealthy German Jews patronized the architectural firm of Herts & Tallant. Their design for the Guggenheim Mausoleum at Salem Fields Cemetery was closely based on the Tower of the Winds in Athens, but its archaeological character was uncharacteristic of their approach to memorial design.[306] Herts & Tallant's Schnitzer and Woolner tombs were more typically eclectic. The vaguely Romanesque Schnitzer Tomb was a gabled mass of rough-cut cyclopean masonry which highlighted a single

Henry E. Russell Mausoleum, Woodlawn Cemetery, Bronx. McKim, Mead & White, 1894. CU

William Bateman Leeds Mausoleum, Woodlawn Cemetery, Bronx. John Russell Pope, 1911. CU

Schnitzer Mausoleum, Salem Fields Cemetery, Brooklyn. Herts & Tallant, ca. 1904. CU

Joel Goldenberg Mausoleum, New Union Fields Cemetery, Brooklyn. Herts & Tallant, ca. 1904. CU

Woolner Mausoleum, Salem Fields Cemetery, Brooklyn. Herts & Tallant, ca. 1904. CU

string course and the smooth granite arch over the entrance.[307] The Woolner family memorial consisted of a flat facade boasting interlaced floral ornament and curving profiles suggestive of the Art Nouveau. The Shonncer Tomb at Union Fields was more extreme in its abstraction, an astylar composition of ashlar masses barely relieved by abstract consoles carved in an Art Nouveau floral relief.[308] Perhaps Herts & Tallant's most revealing monument was the tomb of Joel Goldenberg, also at Union Fields.[309] Its battered walls, tapered doorway and simple cornice evoked an Egyptian mastaba. The entrance, however, was flanked by angelic guardians of paradise carved in low relief on the surface of the wall. Given the traditional Jewish stricture against the representation of the human figure, the building reflected the paradoxical status of the city's wealthy German Jews, suggesting an exotic cultural identity, apart from the mainstream yet attempting cultural assimilation.

Recreation

At the opening of the Age of Metropolitanism, the great parks were already in place. Central Park had been under construction since 1859 and was substantially complete by 1869; Prospect Park was finished in 1874. Although new parkland was acquired at Pelham Bay and in the northern Bronx in 1883, these sites were so far removed from the city's population that for years they were to function more as landbanks than as parks. Except for the slow completion of the Riverside Drive improvement after 1880, few new parks were constructed in that decade.[310] With the 1890s and the increasing focus on the city as a work of monumental art, more and more energy was expended on the improvement of existing facilities. Memorial sculptures were placed in Central Park, much to Olmsted's chagrin, for he considered monuments to individuals to be undemocratic.[311] He successfully banned memorials at Prospect Park, where energies were focused instead on the design of entrance gates and shelters.

In 1889 the firm of McKim, Mead & White was hired to design new entrances to Prospect Park at Grand Army Plaza, Ninth Street and Park Circle.[312] Those at the plaza presented the greatest challenge, not only because they were to function as the principal gates to the park, but also because they were to come to terms with the enormous scale of the elliptical plaza and relate to John H. Duncan's design

O.H.P. Belmont Mausoleum, Woodlawn Cemetery, Bronx. Hunt & Hunt, 1913. MCNY

Entrance to Prospect Park, Grand Army Plaza between Flatbush Avenue and Prospect Park West, Brooklyn. John H. Duncan, McKim, Mead & White and Frederick MacMonnies, 1889-94. A view showing Duncan's Memorial Arch, the four Doric columns by Duncan and White, and White's park shelters. MCNY

for the heroically scaled Soldiers' and Sailors' Monument which had just been chosen in competition. White, who was in charge of the project, was forced to include Duncan's design for two fifty-foot-high Doric columns supporting eagles by Frederick MacMonnies which flanked the main entrance to the park.[313] To help define the park's edge and reinforce the plaza's elliptical shape, White added two identical columns at the corners of Flatbush Avenue and Prospect Park West as well as a continuous balustrade with bronze urns. His two twelve-sided pavilions, roofed in thin Guastavino tile, supported on polished granite Tuscan columns, were more welcoming than either the columns or the eagles.[314]

The entrance at Park Circle (1890), though less grand, was equally memorable. In addition to twin pavilions, a pair of pedestals modelled by White on Michelangelo's base for the statue of Marcus Aurelius in Rome supported MacMonnies's brilliant sculptures, *The Horse Tamers* (more properly known as *The Triumph of Mind Over Brute Force*).[315] McKim, Mead & White continued to work in the park until 1917, supplying the designs for a Croquet Shelter (1904) and many pieces of Classical furniture, balustrades and pergolas.[316] These evocations of antiquity made explicit the dialogue between romantic Classicism and romantic naturalism which Olmsted and Vaux inherited from the late-eighteenth-century English landscape tradition. Other architects contributed to the dialogue, notably Helmle & Huberty, whose neo-Palladian Tennis House (1910)[317] and hauntingly lovely, terra-cotta faced Boathouse on the Lullwater (1905) were among the park's principal architectural features.[318]

Most of Central Park's major out-buildings, as well as the early pavilions of the Metropolitan Museum of Art, had been designed by Vaux in the 1870s in the High Victorian Gothic style. As early as 1863, however, Richard Morris Hunt had proposed a series of Classical gateways to the southern end of the park.[319] Vaux and Olmsted lobbied successfully against the construction, enlisting the aid of Clarence Cook in the *New York Daily Tribune* who labelled them "a barren spawn of French imperialism" at odds with the park's "purest and most elevated democratic ideas."[320] Hunt's project was defended by William J. Hoppin in the *New York Evening Post,* who noted that as the city developed northward, Central Park's character would inevitably

Boat House, east side of the Lullwater, Prospect Park, Brooklyn. Helmle & Huberty, 1905. View from the Lullwater. MCNY

become "more artificial and less rural; more of a garden and less of a park."[321] By the end of the nineteenth century, the Parks Commission was engaged in a continuous struggle to prevent new intrusions. Hunt's Fifth Avenue facade for the Metropolitan Museum (1902) and later McKim, Mead & White's masterplan for the museum (1905), which proposed a series of landscaped terraces to integrate the building into the landscape, unleashed a wave of proposals to embellish the park with Classical monuments.[322] Among the few changes carried out was the replacement of Vaux's rather awkward gas fixtures with the ubiquitous electric lamp standard designed by Henry Bacon in 1907.[323]

The Classicizing continued in Central Park long after the ideal of the City Beautiful had waned in the public mind. In 1917 a grand, strictly organized sunken garden and a colossal war memorial were proposed for the thirty-four-acre site of the former Lower or Croton Reservoir to the west of the Metropolitan Museum. The garden plan, drawn by Thomas Hastings, was immediately attacked in the press as elitist.[324] Its failure to gain popular support was particularly ironic as its northern end was conceived to frame MacMonnies's famous fountain, *Columbia Enthroned,* which had so captivated the public at the Chicago Fair in 1893.

Perhaps the last and most grandiloquent echo of the City Beautiful movement in New York City was John Russell Pope's 1925–31 proposal to cut a vast tree-lined parkway through Central Park.[325] Flanked by promenades and fountains, Pope's Boulevard of Art would have extended from the axis of his Theodore Roosevelt Memorial across the reclaimed site of the Croton Reservoir to the southern edge of the Metropolitan Museum. The ruthlessness of Pope's scheme reflected a sad loss of the sense of tact and decorum that had characterized McKim, Mead & White's intervention at Prospect Park.

While the major parks were being beautified, the newly consolidated city, goaded by social reformers such as Jacob Riis, set out to provide neighborhood oases in the working-class districts. These small parks were products of the "slum clearance" strategies of the day. Designed by the new generation of French-trained architects, the plans broke with the Victorian informality exemplified in the design of Union and Madison squares, and instead adapted the principles of French garden design to parks closer in scale to London squares. (Ironically, Bryant Park, behind Carrère &

Hudson Park, Hudson and Leroy streets. Carrère & Hastings, 1898. Belvedere and pool. NYHS

Recreation Pier, east end of East Third Street. Edward H. Kendall, 1896-98. Perspective view from East River. CU

Cosmopolitan magazine public baths competition entry. John Galen Howard, 1890. Perspective. CU

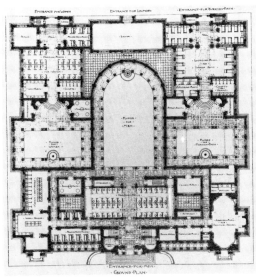

Cosmopolitan magazine public baths competition entry. John Galen Howard, 1890. Plan of ground floor. CU

Hastings's eminently Modern French style Public Library, remained a Victorian garden until it was redesigned in a more compatible style in 1934.)[326]

Carrère & Hastings's Hudson Park (1898), at Hudson and Leroy streets, was a reclaimed cemetery in the heart of a crowded tenement district. Its formal plan and very French rusticated limestone belvedere revolutionized the conception of park design.[327] Carrère & Hastings's introduction of Classical planning initiated a sociological and aesthetic controversy which, if only for a moment, brought back to sharp focus the moralistic undercurrent which one or another of the historical styles carried for many in the profession. Montgomery Schuyler took his case against the French style of park design to *Scribner's,* a nonprofessional journal; while he claimed to admire the contrast of Classical and naturalistic devices in Olmsted's plan for Central Park, he felt that the introduction of formal planning in the small city park robbed it of its capacity to contrast with the highly organized city around it, thereby preventing it from functioning as the necessary *rus in urbe* which made city life bearable, particularly for children and the elderly. For Schuyler, Hudson Park "so flouts this convention of the small city park that . . . it has the air of an attempt to expel nature with a fork."[328]

George F. Pentecost, Jr. defended the new formalism on the basis of context, writing in the *Architectural Record,* Schuyler's usual organ. While "fitness to the environment is the widest generalization of art," he argued, it was "positively frivolous" to imagine that a naturalistic environment can be convincingly evoked on a "small flat area symmetrically bounded on all four sides by solid rows of buildings, broad streets and sidewalks." For Pentecost, the issue was not one of sociology but of design: "Viewed from the standpoint of art works, New York squares and gardens could hardly be more disappointing. They are not works of art—they are simply breathing spaces conspicuous for their area. . . . The park should be a work of art—it should be valued in the proportion that it attains that end over and above the utilitarian ends."[329]

To supplement these neighborhood parks, recreational piers were constructed, although their usefulness was hampered by the increasing pollution of the rivers. In 1892 a law was enacted authorizing the Department of Parks to provide for piers combining facilities for the handling of merchandise on pier level with upper-floor recreation areas "wholly free to the inhabitants of the city."[330] This was not acted upon until 1896 when contracts were let for five piers with second-floor promenades for the citizenry. Each pier was designed in a distinct style: East Third Street was in the style of Louis XIV; East Twenty-fourth Street, Louis XVI; West Fiftieth Street, Colonial; West 129th Street, Romanesque; Christopher Street, "south Italian"; East 112th Street, "north Italian," a particularly appropriate choice, given its situation in a new riverfront park running between 111th and 113th Streets in what was described as "a really beautiful rural location" in what "is popularly known as Little Italy."[331] The piers were designed by Edward H. Kendall, who served between 1896 and 1898 as consulting architect for the Department of Parks. The East Third and East Twenty-fourth Street piers contained in addition glazed enclosures for winter use, while each pier typically had toilet facilities, a bandstand, and drinking fountains supplied with specially chilled water.[332]

Perhaps even greater than the need for breathing spaces for the city's working class was that of bathing facilities. Since indoor plumbing was still a rarity in most working-class tenement areas, many people went without bathing for months at a time. For aesthetic as well as hygienic reasons, public bathing facilities were a necessity.[333] In 1889 *Cosmopolitan* magazine initiated a competition for the design of public baths. Though the competition was open to all and the prize money relatively modest, the issues raised were so important that it attracted an eminent jury including R.M. Hunt, Cornelius Vanderbilt and A.F. D'Oench as well as the attention of a large segment of the architectural profession.[334] The first prize of two hundred dollars went to John Galen Howard, a recent graduate of the Ecole des Beaux-Arts who was later to become a leading architect in California.

By comparison with the second-prize scheme, a vaguely Richardsonian project by Lyman A. Ford of Boston, Howard's proposal was extraordinarily elaborate.[335] Like a

Sixtieth Street Public Bath, 232 West Sixtieth Street. Werner & Windolph, 1906. MCNY

Sixtieth Street Public Bath, 232 West Sixtieth Street. Werner & Windolph, 1906. Swimming pool and running track. CU

Roman bath, it was as much a social center as a hygienic facility, including plunges for men and women, a Turkish bath and meeting rooms. Though Howard's scheme was to set the standard for the best public baths of the early 1900s, it was not initially admired in all quarters. The editors of *Architecture and Building* promptly observed that "what poor people need first, and most, is a little place, well lighted and warm.... They do not need, in their winter bathhouses, tepidariums, or swimming tanks, or porticos or exercise halls; and the less magnificence is put into the new buildings, the more comfortable they will be for the people who use them, and the more profitable for those who own them."[336]

As if in response, in 1891 the Association for Improving the Condition of the Poor commissioned J.C. Cady to design a bathhouse on a twenty-five-foot-wide site on Centre Market Place near Broome Street on the Lower East Side. A modest facility, it contained twenty-five shower baths and five ordinary baths.[337] Although a few more public bathhouses were built by charitable organizations in the 1890s, especially in the densest slums of the Lower East Side, it was not until the turn of the century, when water pollution forced New York to abandon the floating baths it maintained on the East and Hudson rivers, that a serious effort was made to provide public indoor bathing and recreational facilities for the majority of the city's residents.[338] Public showering facilities for men and women were included in the pavilions erected in some of the larger neighborhood parks. Arnold Brunner's Florentine style pavilions in Seward and Jefferson parks were rather stiff examples of this type of facility.[339]

The enclosed public bathhouses of the early 1890s had been conceived of in purely hygienic terms, with no attempt to meet the recreational needs of the citizens. In 1906, a new kind of facility began to emerge that was stylistically and programmatically related to John Galen Howard's initial conception of seventeen years earlier. Built in large part as a result of public demand for a replacement for the floating baths, the new bathhouses almost always contained swimming pools as well as showering facilities. Many combined open air and enclosed areas for games as well as meeting rooms. Werner & Windolph's West Sixtieth Street baths were set on a constricted mid-block site.[340] Separate entrances for men and women led to ample locker and shower-

Public Baths, east side of Avenue A between Twenty-third and Twenty-fourth streets. William Martin Aiken and Arnold W. Brunner, 1906. View from Avenue A. MCNY

Public Baths, east side of Avenue A between Twenty-third and Twenty-fourth streets. William Martin Aiken and Arnold W. Brunner, 1906. Swimming pool. CU

ing rooms as well as to a swimming pool. Though small, the building was adequate to the needs of the four thousand people expected to use the facility each day.

Grander still were the baths designed in 1906 by William Martin Aiken and Arnold Brunner for a full-block site at Avenue A between Twenty-third and Twenty-fourth streets.[341] Aiken's and Brunner's facade, with its twin portals leading to waiting rooms for men and women, was surely one of the most imposing expressions of the City Beautiful—its low springing arches between paired Doric columns were more like portals to a great amphitheatre than frames around doors to a hygienic facility.

Other public bath structures, though usually smaller, and with showering facilities but no swimming pool, were no less elaborately conceived. Stoughton & Stoughton's baths at John Jay Park (1905–08) were a particularly elegant essay in the Modern French taste.[342] Also notable were York & Sawyer's identically planned 41st and 109th street facilities with their Modern French facades subtly individualized.[343] Some, such as Bernstein & Bernstein's Italianate public bath on Rutgers Place, provided rooftop recreational areas, in this case treated as a loggia set behind a screen of paired Corinthian columns.[344] Werner & Windolph's East Fifty-fourth Street Bath marked the culmination of the type, combining a gymnasium and the usual showering facilities in a monumentally scaled, vigorously modelled mid-block building crowned by an implied mansard roof concealing a rooftop recreation cage.[345]

By the First World War, advancing standards in tenement house design transformed the public bathhouse into a community recreation center with a swimming pool and indoor and rooftop gymnasia. William Emerson's West Twenty-eighth Street facility, though not particularly festive in character, surely went a long way, as the *Brickbuilder* observed, to "counteract the dangerous and confining circumstances of the tenement districts."[346] Like so many buildings at the end of the Composite Era, the Twenty-eighth Street baths provided a marked increase in services for the general public and a considerable decline in the quality of the buildings designed to house those services.

The continuing need for recreational centers still occasionally sparked instances of private philanthropy. Rice Memorial Stadium in Pelham Bay Park, by Herts & Robertson (ca. 1916), was given to the city by the widow of Isaac L.

Public Bath and Gymnasium, 348 East Fifty-fourth Street. Werner & Windolph, 1906. MCNY

Public Bath and Gymnasium, 348 East Fifty-fourth Street. Werner & Windolph, 1906. Gymnasium and running track. CU

Public Bath and Gymnasium, 348 East Fifty-fourth Street. Werner & Windolph, 1906. Men's shower room. CU

Rice whose Riverside Drive mansion had been designed by Herts & Tallant.[347] The stadium was the focal point of a complex of sports facilities including a 330-foot-long swimming pool. A one-hundred-foot-high white marble Doric column announced the complex, while the rim of the stadium itself was punctuated by Doric treasuries. In contrast to Herts's typically Modern French and Art Nouveau leanings, the stadium's relatively pure, Roman Classicism fitted its role as both a public monument and a private memorial.

Two large park projects combined recreational and educational facilities to a greater extent than usual: the New York Botanical Garden and the New York Zoological Park, both at Bronx Park. The Botanical Garden was incorporated in 1891. Patterned after the Royal Botanical Gardens at Kew, England, it set out to combine scientific scholarship with public information. Calvert Vaux and Samuel Parsons, Jr. selected a site in Bronx Park that included the Bronx River Gorge and a virgin hemlock forest.[348] As at Kew, the principal attraction was the glass house or conservatory, which was designed by William R. Cobb and erected by the Lord and Burnham Company in 1902. In keeping with its mission as a scientific institution, a museum building was erected in the same year which contained laboratories, classrooms, and a domed library as well as exhibition galleries. The competition for the museum building was won by Robert W. Gibson in 1898 with a pavilionated design featuring French mansard roofs, a central dome, and a colossal Corinthian order of engaged columns and pilasters.[349] Its French-influenced Classicism was a significant departure from Gibson's earlier eclectic work, suggesting the pervasiveness with which the Composite Period's conception of monumental building had taken hold. Both the museum and conservatory, however, were deeply criticized by the Fine Arts Federation, apparently because their academic planning was felt to be at odds with the park's natural informality.[350]

The New York Zoological Society was founded in 1895. Its Bronx Zoo was a revolutionary new conception, a marked contrast to the "small closed zoological gardens of Europe . . . a free Park, projected upon a larger scale than has ever been attempted before."[351] Unlike European models, it was not a menagerie for the public's amusement but was instead a research facility located on a large (250 acre) site far from the center of the city's population to achieve the

Elephant House, New York Zoological Park, Bronx Park, Bronx. Heins & LaFarge, 1911. Construction view of south facade. CU

sense of a natural haven and allow substantial outdoor ranges for the animals. The Bronx Zoo was also novel in that it was subsidized by the city; with no admission charged, it was clearly intended to serve every stratum of society, as long as they could get there.[352]

The zoo's original buildings were designed by Heins & LaFarge between 1899 and 1911 and represented a more sensitive response to the park context than did the Botanical Garden.[353] The major buildings were symmetrically disposed around Baird Court, a grassy mall dominated by the domed Elephant House, but additional animal houses were picturesquely arranged along the natural contours of the site. Each building was carefully individualized in massing and detail; the Lion House, in a fulsome Beaux-Arts Baroque, sat opposite the neo-Grec House for Primates.

The lofty dome of the Elephant House, combining late Roman and Byzantine motifs, was covered in brown and green glazed tiles. Entered through arched portals flanked by terra-cotta animal heads by A.B. Proctor and Charles B. Knight, the basilican interior was vaulted with Guastavino tiles whose soft brown and buff tones provided a sympathetic backdrop to the animals in their vast cages. The entire composition, particularly the polychromatic dome, had about it a suggestion of the romantic and picturesque no doubt deemed appropriate to its exotic inhabitants. The combination of axial and picturesque planning strategies reflected the sensitive adaptation of a formal Court of Honor to a sylvan, Arcadian setting.

Lion House, New York Zoological Park, Bronx Park, Bronx. Heins & LaFarge, 1903. Detail of main entrance. MCNY

View of Broad Street looking north from Beaver Street. On the west side of Broad Street between Exchange Place and Wall Street are the Blair Building (Carrère & Hastings, 1902-03), the Commercial Cable Building (George Edward Harding & Gooch, 1897) and the New York Stock Exchange (George B. Post, 1903). On the northwest corner of the intersection of Broad, Wall and Nassau streets is the Bankers Trust Building (1912) by Trowbridge & Livingston. NYHS

Palaces of Production

New York Harbor is loveliest at night perhaps. On the Staten Island ferryboat you slip out from the darkness right under the immense skyscrapers. As they recede they form into a mass together, firelined and majestic sentinel over the black goldstreaked waters. Their cliff-like boldness is the greater because to either side sweep in the East River and the Hudson River, leaving the promontory between. To the right stands the great stretch of the Brooklyn Suspension Bridge, its slight curve very purely outlined with light; over it luminous trams, like shuttles of fire, are thrown across and across, continually weaving the stuff of human existence. From further off all these lights dwindle to a radiant semicircle that gazes out over the expanse with a quiet, mysterious expectancy.
    Rupert Brooke, *Letters from America* (New York: Charles Scribner & Son, 1916), 5-6.

Office Buildings New York's first building to be constructed solely for use as office space was the Trinity Building at 111 Broadway, designed by Richard Upjohn and built by the Trinity Church as speculative office space in the 1840s.[1] The five-story Trinity Building was not nearly as tall as Upjohn's new Trinity Church, built across the street in 1846—its spire rose 284 feet to make it the highest structure in the city. Trinity's steeple and those of other churches dominated the skyline of the city until 1890, when the 309-foot-high Pulitzer Building[2] by George B. Post became the first secular building taller than Trinity. By 1897 so many more tall office buildings had risen that J. Lincoln Steffens was prompted to write in *Scribner's* that "the enterprise of business has surpassed the aspiration of religion."[3]

Steffens and others were convinced that no other city had ever undergone such a visible transformation in so short a time as New York in the last decade of the century.[4] "It is doubtful whether the change has been quite so rapid and radical in any of the older centers of population as in New York City," the *Real Estate Record and Guide* wrote in 1898.

Social life has been revolutionized; so has commercial enterprise. Wealth and population have increased beyond even the dreams of enthusiasts even thirty years ago. But in themselves, these are changes in the internal conditions of the city . . . he who would know what has been going on in New York life during the last thirty years cannot study any more illuminating page of history than the buildings of the city. From this point of view the most interesting chapter . . . is that concerning the office building and its development.[5]

New York's skyline before the invention of the elevator was, Montgomery Schuyler observed, "a 'purple line of humbler roofs' built to the limit as that limit was set by the power of ascension of the unassisted human leg."[6] Although a passenger elevator was used in New York at least as early as 1852 at the New York Crystal Palace Exhibition,[7] the full potential of the elevator was exploited first and most consistently in the office building, starting in 1870 with George Post's Equitable Life Assurance Building at 120 Broadway.[8] The Equitable Building had only five floors, but the extra-high stories lifted the peak of its mansard roof to 130 feet, almost twice the height of the average New York walk-up. Within five years, Post had completed the 230-foot-tall Western Union Telegraph Building at the corner of Broadway and Dey Street,[9] and Richard Morris Hunt had built the 260-foot New York *Tribune* Building on Park Row,[10] leading to conjecture that businessmen were beginning to build "up to the clouds and covering the ground with blocks that are a city in themselves."[11]

Despite the polemical tone of an article entitled "Height, the Architectural Feature of the Age," which stated as early as 1874 that "one might believe that the chief end of the present crop of buildings is the observation of comets," the transformation of the rest of the New York skyline between 1870 and 1890 was a gradual rather than a dramatic progression.[12] "When the Equitable Building was erected there was a general feeling that an extraordinarily high building had been added to New York's roll call of noble structures," the *Real Estate Record and Guide* declared in 1885,

and people came from far and wide to ascend its roof and look down from the dizzy height upon the marvelous stretch of scenery taking in the Bay, the Narrows, Staten Island, the North and East Rivers, and the major portion of New York and Brooklyn, with their countless piles of brick, stone and mortar. But even seven-story buildings have become wonders of the past, and an eight-story building is looked upon as a novelty no longer. Nine- and ten-story structures are now not infrequently built, and among those recently completed may be mentioned those of the Standard Oil Company's on Broadway, the Potter building on "Newspaper Row," the Mortimer building, adjoining the Stock Exchange, and the Astor building on Broadway, near Wall Street.[13]

Western Union Building, northwest corner of Broadway and Dey Street. George B. Post, 1873–75. View ca. 1875 looking south on Broadway from the City Hall Post Office, showing St. Paul's Chapel in the foreground and Trinity Church further downtown. AT&T

Tower Building, 50 Broadway. Bradford L. Gilbert, 1888–89. A 1905 view showing the once-towering Tower Building engulfed by surrounding office buildings. NYHS

In the business section on the Battery, entire blocks were soon filled by nine- and ten-story office buildings, yet because of the inherent structural problems of masonry-bearing wall construction above that height, few buildings rose higher than this new limit. A significant development was made in 1881 when Post, an engineer who became the most prolific commercial architect of the period, began construction on Bowling Green of the Produce Exchange, the first building in the world to have a structural system combining wrought iron and masonry.[14] Before the end of the decade a new stage in the development of the New York office building was reached, when the first example of the so-called Chicago system of construction—complete interior framing in metal without masonry bearing walls—was built in Manhattan. Appropriately named the Tower Building, it was designed and built at 50 Broadway by the architect Bradford L. Gilbert between June 1888 and September 1889.[15] Although the building was constructed on a small lot (21½ feet wide and 108 feet long) that limited the narrow structure to eleven stories, its metal skeleton made possible the tall, slender towers that followed, freed from the height restrictions of masonry construction.

Within a year Post's golden-domed Pulitzer Building had risen twenty-six stories to claim the title of "Tallest Building in the World." Chicago soon took that title, but enough tall buildings had been built in New York by 1894 that *Harper's Weekly* could report that "we are getting to be more accustomed to the lofty structures, and so conventional ideas, born of what we are accustomed to look at, are gradually being modified."[16] In fact, a new concept of urban form was emerging in lower Manhattan, based on the importance of height as the overriding image of New York City. When Post's St. Paul Building went up near the Pulitzer Building on Park Row in 1899, Manhattan again became home to the tallest building in the world, and others quickly followed to keep the distinction for New York throughout the Composite Era. The thirty-two-story Park Row Building rose nearby later in the year, and the forty-seven-story Singer Tower was finished in 1908. The fifty-two-story Metropolitan Life Tower was built in 1909, and the sixty-story Woolworth Building, known as the Cathedral of Commerce, was finished in 1913, the same year that the English poet Rupert Brooke offered his encomium to the Manhattan skyline, the office building's greatest monu-

A 1910 view looking east across City Hall Park, showing the Municipal Building (1907-15) by McKim, Mead & White under construction, and to the right the Pulitzer Building (George B. Post, 1890) and the *Tribune* Building (Richard Morris Hunt, 1873-76). NYHS

ment.

From the Tall Building to the Skyscraper

In 1897 Russell Sturgis summed up the opinion of those who were coming to realize that there was an inherent contradiction in the tall buildings built in the 1880s and 1890s: although they originally towered over their neighbors in relative isolation, they had been built as party-wall buildings and were becoming increasingly closed in as the city grew up around them. "A year or two of experience will show how far these high buildings are of business value when they cannot open side windows over their neighbors' property," Sturgis said. "It has been stated rather frequently in the newspaper press and elsewhere that these skyscrapers are only economically viable when they are isolated. That is to say, one sky-scraper is good, but two, close together, defeat each other's purpose; and of three in juxtaposition, the middle one is a pecuniary failure."[17] Yet R.H. Robertson's contemporary design for the 386-foot Park Row Building (1896-99) at 17-21 Park Row rose straight up from the street to a distinct cornice and had party walls on either side, as though the buildings along the streets of lower Manhattan which had lifted the cornice line of the walls defining the streets from five stories to eight stories to ten stories could continue their growth forever as technology improved.[18] Moreover, while Robertson implied that the street wall would eventually be twenty stories high, he also placed cupolas above the cornice which extended the outer bays of the facade up into the skyline and emphasized the freestanding quality of the Park Row Building as it towered over its neighbors. Mimicking the contradictory financial conception of the tall building pointed out by Sturgis, the design indicated a confused aesthetic conception which simultaneously proclaimed the Park Row Building's dual nature as a piece of infill in the urban fabric and as a tower soaring free of that fabric.

Although these towers silhouetted against the sky were initially called skyscrapers—a term with cloudy origins—as the city grew up around them, New York's architects began to recognize the distinctly different but complementary conditions of the infill office buildings and the freestanding tower, and to develop a new typology of the tall building. The infill building was used as the basic building block of the city, establishing a somewhat uniform and static base for the towers and skyscrapers which captured the essence of the tremendous height offered by the steel frame and the elevator to rise above the mass of the city and be permanently outlined against the sky. The most remarkable achievement of the new typology, and the form which proved most effective for the high-rise office building, was a hybrid which combined the infill building and the tower to create the true skyscraper. With a base locked into the block and the street wall, and a tower which stepped back to dramatically pierce the sky, the new skyscraper simultaneously met the traditional urban requirement for an homogeneous city fabric, the demands of a new metropolitan scale requiring a beautiful skyline, and both the tenant's and the neighbor's needs for adequate light and air in the office space and on the street.[19]

The hybrid was anticipated by two projects designed by the Chicagoan Louis Sullivan in 1891. The first was the Odd Fellows Temple, an unbuilt project which would have filled its corner lot to a height of ten stories and climbed twenty-five stories more in two setbacks.[20] The second was a theoretical design for a city filled with similar setback buildings crowned with crenellated, domed and steeply roofed towers.[21] But until the Era of Convenience, office buildings constructed in Chicago were usually modest designs in the form of only moderately tall infill buildings, because loose subsoil conditions restricted building heights, and Chicago builders and architects were uninterested in commercial monuments. In 1895 Schuyler

asked one of the successful architects of Chicago what would happen if the designer of a commercial building sacrificed the practical availableness of one or more of its stories to the assumed exigencies of architecture, as had often been done in New York. "Why the word would be passed and he would never get another chance to do so. No, we never try those tricks on our business men. They are too wide-awake." Another successful architect explained to me his procedure in designing a skyscraper. "I get from my engineer a statement of the minimum thickness of the steel post and its enclosure of terra cotta. Then I establish the minimum depth of floor beam and the minimum height of the sill from the floor to accommodate what must go between them. These are the data of my design."[22]

The "assumed exigencies" of New York architecture which Schuyler referred to arose from completely different circumstances. Despite the opinion of the Chicago architect he spoke to, the historically minded New York architects were not playing "tricks" on their clients. While the great monuments of the Chicago School were speculative office buildings with a utilitarian nature—clearly expressed by what was known as the Chicago Window, a horizontal unit which economically filled the space between the symbolically, articulated piers and spandrels of the Chicago Frame[23]—the great tall buildings designed by New York architects were more often headquarters for national and international corporations which wanted to make an impression in the nation's financial capital,[24] where the modest stylistic expression of the typical Chicago building would have been as inappropriate as its modest, mid-height infill form.

New York architects sheathed the New York office building in masonry walls intentionally designed to transform the new form of the tall building into extended versions of the familiar forms of European architecture. But because European buildings, with the exception of fortresses and churches, had also been limited to the height which a person could comfortably ascend by foot, there was no compositional or stylistic precedent for the tall office building with many identical floors repeated over and over, one on top of another. Although American architects and engineers quickly solved many of the practical problems involved in the construction of the tall building—the Pulitzer Building was completed less than a year after the much smaller Tower Building—the formal evolution of the massing and aesthetic expression of the true skyscraper was far more laborious.

In the vaguely Gothic *Tribune* Building, one of the first designs to revel in the aesthetic possibilities inherent in great height, Richard Morris Hunt "made groups of stories with piers and arches, so as to simulate the division of a lower building and to make the group of stories fulfill the same function of an organic member of the composition that the single story had previously performed," Schuyler wrote in a retrospective look at the development of the tall building in New York. He felt George Post went even further in the Western Union Building, treating the bulk of the floors in almost identical fashion and crowning the composition with a steep roof, a "recognition in the new architecture of the Aristotelian requirement in every work of art of a beginning, a middle and an end. Speaking the language of architecture, it was a division into base, shaft, and capital."[25] In later buildings, such as the Tower Building, the horizontal divisions of the middle floors were de-emphasized in favor of a vertical expression of the tall building. Despite the presence of the building's slab rising above its neighbors, Gilbert's handling of the street facade and his distinctive treatment of the side facades on the forward portions of the slab cleverly established an impression for passers-by on Broadway that above the height of the street wall the building was a freestanding tower.

Post's Romanesque style Union Trust Company Building, built in 1889-90 at 80 Broadway, was considerably wider and higher than the Tower Building, but Post's design more successfully balanced the urge for the soaring verticality of the freestanding tower with the realities of the building as a fragment of a city block.[26] Schuyler felt that the Union Trust first effectively made "the essential point . . . that there should be a triple division, and that the three parts should both assert themselves as parts and combine into a whole. . . . It is founded upon the analogy of a column, with its division into base, shaft and capital, and even conforms, as far as may be, to the proportions of the classic column."[27]

Paradoxically, the simultaneously massive and planar quality of the Romanesque style, which emphasized the presence of the wall, was more easily adapted to the problem of dividing the tall building facade into a columnar pattern than the Classical styles which dominated the Composite Era. McKim, Mead & White's design in 1894 for the moderately tall, nine-story Warren Building on the corner of Broadway and Twentieth Street had facades with five horizontal layers: despite some lovely details, the fragmented whole was less than the sum of its parts.[28] That was typical of early efforts to tackle the problem of the Classical expression of the tall building which caused Barr Ferree to observe in the year the Warren Building was completed that

Union Trust Building, 80 Broadway. George B. Post, 1889-90. NYHS

Mail and Express Building, 203 Broadway and 166 Fulton Street. Carrère & Hastings, 1891–92. Broadway entrance. MCNY

Mail and Express Building, 203 Broadway and 166 Fulton Street. Carrère & Hastings, 1891–92. Fulton Street entrance. NYHS

"the height of the building, instead of being treated as its most valuable property—which it clearly is from the mercantile standpoint—has been regarded as little more than disgraceful."[29] For the moment, it may have been just as well that the influential McKim, who stated more than once that he did not like tall buildings, did not want to tackle the problem of their design.[30] The task was left to younger architects such as Carrère & Hastings, who produced in the early 1890s a series of designs for the moderately tall office building that not only represented a high level of artistic expression but also made a pioneering contribution to the theoretical design of the tall office building.

Not surprisingly, Carrère & Hastings's earliest efforts were their least successful. Their first business building in New York, the Pierce Building, was a vertically extended palazzo, built in 1890 of buff brick and limestone on the northwest corner of Hudson and Franklin streets.[31] The architects divided the seven-story building with an attic story and three horizontal stories of two floors each, and then attempted, unsuccessfully, to unify the design with rustication, giant orders and Palladian motifs. Their Edison Building (1890–91) at 44 Broad Street was even more fragmented: the *Architectural Record* singled the building out as the first of a series of Architectural Aberrations which it began to illustrate and analyze in 1891.[32] (Montgomery Schuyler, who was probably the anonymous author of the series, was quick to point out in the *Record* that the term aberration was not necessarily a term of reproach but merely one describing a "deviation from the customary structure or type.")[33] The building's rich array of Classical elements confused the author, whoever he was: "So far as any principle of design can be detected in the front, indeed, it is to emphasize what is subordinate and slur what is principal. . . . The front . . . is not an architectural composition. Its stories are so many shelves loaded with architectural details."[34]

Carrère & Hastings's next commission, the *Mail and Express* Building, was a ten-story, L-shaped structure built in 1891–92 with entrances on Fulton Street and Broadway.[35] The architects succeeded in adapting Classical architecture to what was clearly a steel-frame building by making the facade appear to be an almost independent masonry wall screening a continuous grid of cast metal spandrels and muntins behind. Although the design marked no theoretical advance over Post's best work such as the Romanesque Produce Exchange Building, it was perhaps the first time that the principle of the separation of the wall from the structure had been applied to a purely Classical design. Hastings explained his thinking at the 1894 convention of the American Institute of Architects:

The mere theorist is apt to make too much of what he calls an "entirely new state of affairs." . . . The office building is only one step further in the general advancement. With the many difficulties before us, while endeavoring to design a lofty structure, we must . . . try to build in the most natural and logical way—adapting all precedents to this one new condition. . . . It would seem as if nature had come forward to provide us with comparatively new materials, in iron and steel, to assist us in this new kind of work. That these materials should play a most important part in our designing, it seems to me must be accepted. . . . We might use exposed iron in a partly decorative way to indicate the constructive members which are concealed of necessity, for fireproof reasons. I cannot imagine a more natural and beautiful solution than to treat these iron and steel constructions with curtain-walls, by honestly showing the iron or steel on the facade, with a filling-in of terra-cotta, brick or faience, with projections constructed in apparent iron and terra-cotta. . . . The utilitarian problem which confronts us is simply a bee-hive, or manifold collection of similar cells, with equal divisions, both lateral and perpendicular. As in all architectural study, our facades should, as much as possible, interpret this interior condition of things. . . . An equal distribution of openings, with ornament, may be *decoration,* but it is not *architecture.* . . . To secure . . . a large opening in contrast with a small one, or the grouping of openings together, and the proper color and variety in wall-surfaces, we must of necessity resort to combining some stories in one *motif.* In so doing, instead of filling in these large *motifs* with stone divisions, is it not more rational to allow the steel, iron or other construction of the interior floors and partitions to be apparent, instead of entirely masking them with masonry in the facade, and destroying the true values of

Manhattan Life Insurance Building, 66 Broadway. Kimball & Thompson, 1893. View looking northeast on Broadway, showing the Union Trust Building (George B. Post, 1889-90) and the American Surety Building (Bruce Price, 1894-95). CU

Home Life Insurance Building, 253 Broadway. Napoleon Le Brun & Sons, 1894. An 1897 view from behind City Hall. CU

Commercial Cable Building, 20–22 Broad Street. George Edward Harding & Gooch, 1897. CU

the openings.³⁵

Carrère & Hastings employed a more academic solution on the Broadway elevation of the *Mail and Express* Building, which was only twenty-five feet wide. They based the lower section on Philibert de l'Orme's entrance to the Chateau d'Anet (well known to all students at the Ecole des Beaux-Arts because it had been transported to the school's courtyard), but above the base the architects "tossed to the winds all theories which demand expression of the plan upon the facade or call for the limitation of ornament to the decoration of constructive parts," Francis Swales wrote in the British *Architectural Review*. "There is no suggestion of the iron structure of the building; there is only a plain wall of stone with openings for light or, where required, to assist the decorative balance. The decoration is constructed outside of and upon the wall, which serves as a background."³⁷

The Tall Building as Urban Infill

The *Mail and Express* Building initiated an approach to tall building design that dominated work throughout the late 1890s. In 1893 the architects Kimball & Thompson attempted to combine the motifs of the two *Mail and Express* elevations—the soaring verticality of the Broadway entrance, the masonry screen of the Fulton Street side and the piling up of layers in both—in the facades of the 348-foot-high Manhattan Life Insurance Building, the tallest building in the city.³⁸ Despite its great height, the building was a mid-block, infill building, constructed on lower Broadway near the Union Trust Building. The narrow composition was centered vertically and crowned by a massive cupola, divided horizontally primarily by two-story bands which included some attempts at a screen wall.

In 1894 Napoleon Le Brun & Sons completed another of the Classicizing infill towers, the seventeen-story Home Life Insurance Building at 253 Broadway between Murray and Warren streets.³⁹ The top was distinguished by a high mansard roof and a row of Ionic columns screening a loggia, and the base was rusticated and had elaborate applied ornament and columns, but the middle section consisted largely of unornamented windows grouped together towards the center, making the building one of the clearest examples of Schuyler's principle of the base, shaft and capital.

"Next . . . comes the Commercial Cable Building," the *Architectural Record* wrote in 1897. Because the tall (twenty-one-story) but narrow building crowned by a bulbous dome on Broad Street blocked several vistas, the *Record* called it "about the most obstreperous structure to which the new construction has given rise."⁴⁰ From Nassau Street, or across the street, the building looked like a soaring tower, but from Broad Street one could see that it was actually a mid-block slab which backed up to the only slightly taller Manhattan Life Building on Broadway.

In terms of height and bulk, the Park Row Building (1899) and Clinton & Russell's design for the twenty-seven-story building at 60–62 Wall Street (1905) culminated the development of the mid-block infill office building.⁴¹ The limestone base, unadorned brick shaft and limestone top of 60–62 Wall Street was a clear and straightforward application of Schuyler's column principle, but by 1905 it was clear that so long as the mid-block, infill type prevailed, the tall building was at best a pilaster, without the force or sculptural presence of a column. By the turn of the century, the tallest buildings were built at the corners of blocks, in a modified infill type, or as freestanding towers, while the mid-block infill type was stabilized at a relatively modest height, usually twelve or fifteen stories.

Many of the earliest mid-block, mid-height infill office buildings were designed by Clinton & Russell. Although their infill buildings had elevations which were relatively straightforward applications of the division of base, shaft and capital, Sturgis's rather harsh criticism of the Hudson Building, built in 1898 at 32 Broadway, at least served as an accurate physical description of virtually every one of their designs: "More objectionable is the insertion in the otherwise simple fronts of two horizontal stripes with a good deal of sculptured ornament in them, each stripe having the width of one story. Such a method of breaking up a lofty front is feeble, and seems the first suggestion that occurs to the puzzled designer without adequate resources. The value of this facade is in its rigid severity, its extreme plain-

Bayard Building, 65 Bleecker Street. Louis H. Sullivan and L.P. Smith, 1897. An 1898 view looking east on Bleecker Street. CU

Bayard Building, 65 Bleecker Street. Louis H. Sullivan and L.P. Smith, 1897. Cornice detail. CU

ness."[42] Ten years later, when Clinton & Russell built the Lawyers Title Insurance and Trust Company at 160 Broadway, one of their richest designs, they were still using the same *parti*.[43]

Warren & Wetmore's design for the fifteen-story, midblock Kean, Van Cortlandt & Co. Building (1903) on Pine Street had a bold screen of Ionic columns at the base supporting an "attic" floor, above which three flat bays of iron-clad windows set between brick piers rose seven floors to another "attic" and a projecting cornice carried on boldly scaled brackets.[44] Barr Ferree could not admire the design, but nevertheless found some interest in the "frank way in which it displays its Beaux Artism."[45]

Occasionally, an infill site was sufficiently wide and deep to encourage the development of light courts facing the street, as in Raymond F. Almirall's building for the Emigrant Savings Bank (1909-10) at 51 Chambers Street.[46] Atop a continuous 2½-story base containing a banking hall, two thirteen-story office wings rose to attics elaborately decorated in the Modern French style. Because the building ran through the block to Reade Street, the light court was repeated at the north, forming an H-shaped plan. The south court, located almost on axis with the City Hall cupola, was deep enough so that it did not block the silhouette of the dome against the sky.

Four infill buildings of the late 1890s and early 1900s were the most stylistically inventive and intellectually challenging tall building designs of the period: the Bayard Building (1897), the Little Singer Building (1902-04), the Blair Building (1902-03) and the New York *Evening Post* Building (1906). The finest was unquestionably the Bayard Building, designed by Louis Sullivan in association with Lyndon P. Smith.[47] Sullivan's only building in New York, it was a thirteen-story office building firmly embedded in its block of Bleecker Street between Broadway and Lafayette Street. Despite the fact that the Bayard Building was dwarfed by the towers farther to the south in the main business district, it met the maxim Sullivan presented in his essay "The Tall Building Artistically Considered": "It must be tall, every inch of it tall. The force and power of altitude must be in it. It must be every inch a proud and soaring thing, rising in sheer exaltation that from top to bottom it is a unit without a single dissenting line."[48]

Sullivan made a functional distinction in the facade of the Bayard Building that produced a lyrical composition: he distinguished between bearing and nonbearing columns, alternating thick and thin vertical lines which explained how the building was made. Each floor was marked by ornamented terra-cotta spandrels, but the horizontal spandrels were subordinate to the vertical piers, and the building truly soared from its sturdy base to the delicate cornice.

Contrary to subsequent architectural myths, Sullivan's work was well known and widely respected in New York. Russell Sturgis singled it out as one of the "Good Things in Modern Architecture,"[49] while the *Real Estate Record and Guide* offered a lengthy and sympathetic analysis of the building's structural expressionism, extolling the "invention, life, spirit and grace of detail, wrought in the most plastic of all building materials, that converts this front from an imperfect scientific demonstration into a work of art."[50] Schuyler considered the Bayard building

a very serious attempt to found the architecture of a tall building upon the facts of the case. The actual structure is left or, rather, is helped, to tell its own story. This is the thing itself. . . . Everywhere the drapery of baked clay is a mere wrapping, which clings so closely to the frame as to reveal it, and even to emphasize it. . . . If the building, apart from its wealth of decoration, recalls the works of contemporaneous engineering rather than of historical architecture, that also is "as it must be." The Bayard Building is the nearest approach yet made, in New York, at least, to solving the problem of the skyscraper. It furnishes a most promising starting point for designers who may insist upon attacking that problem instead of evading it, and resting in compromises and conventions.[51]

Though Sullivan's idiosyncratic decoration on the Bayard Building had little effect on New York architecture, his analysis of the design of the tall building surely influenced the French-trained architects who carried on the evolution of the New York skyscraper in the new century. Ernest Flagg's nearby Singer Building at 561-563 Broad-

Little Singer Building, 561-63 Broadway. Ernest Flagg, 1902-04. MCNY

way (called the Little Singer Building to distinguish it from Flagg's two other buildings for the Singer Manufacturing Company) was an L-shaped, twelve-story loft building constructed in 1902-04 with facades on Broadway and Prince Street.[52] Drawing upon the arguments of the French Rationalist architect Viollet-le-Duc and some of his proposed designs which used exposed iron and masonry in combination, Flagg set out to express the structure as directly as possible.[53] Although he was forced to cover the steel frame with fireproofing, he abandoned his usual representation of the Classical orders and set the glass back from the facade, sheathing the exterior with a metal lattice made up of decorative iron, terra cotta and glass and carrying Viollet-le-Duc's principles to a logical extreme. The intricate facade seemed as beguilingly transparent as a lace curtain, yet as solid as a thick masonry wall. In the *Architectural Record* Henry Desmond said of the designer of this "rational skyscraper" that "no other architect has ever so frankly accepted the situation which the skyscraper presents and submitted it to such brainwork. . . . The architect has clearly endeavored to permit the structure to design itself, confining his own role as much as posible to making the structural features as good looking as lay in his power. His problem as he understood it, was to protect a steel frame . . . and to let the building tell its own story as agreeably as it might."[54]

In massing and siting Robert D. Kohn's *Evening Post* Building (1906) at 20-24 Vesey Street was a typical side street, infill building of the period, breaking the cohesiveness of a brownstone row with a thirteen-story block.[55] Yet the distinctly Viennese Secessionist character of its ornament and the rational expression on the facade of the structure set it apart from more pedestrian designs. Three tiers of bay windows clad in copper and embellished with oval reliefs, based on the marks of well-known printers such as Elzevir, sat between flat piers sheathed in limestone that rose to an elaborately detailed copper mansard roof. Four heroic limestone statues, two by Gutzon Borglum and two by the architect's wife, Estelle Rumbold Kohn, rested in niches on brackets atop the piers at the point of transition to the roof representing the *Four Periods of Publicity*. Schuyler praised the elevation for its "flat front," calling it, like so many of his favorite designs, "the thing itself." He was particularly impressed by the structural framing, which

Evening Post Building, 20-24 Vesey Street. Robert D. Kohn, 1906. CU

Blair Building, 24 Broad Street. Carrère & Hastings, 1902-03. A 1905 view looking north on Broad Street showing the Commercial Cable Building (1897) by George Edward Harding & Gooch and the New York Stock Exchange (George B. Post, 1903) on the same block. NYHS

was "hardly draped, but articulated, developed and decorated in accordance with the facts of the case.... Instead of being concealed and confused, the essential structure is so emphasized that the spectator understands it better than he would have understood the mere steel frame before the architectural treatment of it was begun."[56]

Several critics compared the Bayard Building, the Little Singer Building and the *Evening Post* Building to Carrère & Hastings's Blair Building at 24 Broad Street.[57] "It would be interesting to transport [the Bayard Building] to Broad Street, set it up before Carrère & Hastings's Blair Building, and ask them to exchange views on each other's aspect," Barr Ferree wrote.

The architects of both structures studied at the Ecoles des Beaux-Arts in Paris; the Western architect has long been our most conspicuously individual practitioner; the New York firm is easily one of the most distinguished practitioners in the academic style. Their buildings are as far apart as the poles; both are fine examples of their kind; both well illustrate the characteristics of their designers. And both are vertical buildings. It is a triumph of principles over art; for Mr. Hastings has not pre-

viously given us a vertical high building, having contented himself with the repetitive method. Mr. Sullivan can not count Mr. Hastings as a disciple—they are much too far apart artistically for that—but at least he has pointed the way which Mr. Hastings has gladly taken in this most distinguished design. One has to compare it with the immediately adjoining Cable Building, to become aware of how much better things can be done to-day than were done a few years since.[58]

Desmond pointed out that the Blair Building was not so much an example of the Modern French style "as a demonstration of what might be derived from seasoned French training."[59] Carrère & Hastings substituted an applied skin for the Beaux-Arts ideal of articulated parts, concealing the actual structure of the building. But their design, as Desmond pointed out, "discloses, if it does not assert, the structural facts,"[60] treating the stone as an envelope over a barely concealed structural cage, an almost silent witness to the proceedings.

The most striking feature of the Blair Building's facades was a flatness in strong conflict with the prevailing mode of New York skyscraper design, which placed great

East River Savings Bank Building, northwest corner of Broadway and Reade Street. Clinton & Russell, 1911. CU

Broadway Chambers, northwest corner of Broadway and Chambers Street. Cass Gilbert, 1899. View from City Hall Park. NYHS

emphasis on the expression of weight. Carrère & Hastings did away with the conventional heavy stone cornices and the expression of the basement as a massive support, yet satisfactorily established the necessary connections to the ground and sky by treating the stone as a skin and judiciously using elaborately crafted decorative ironwork. The expressive possibilities of the Classical manner as applied to the problem of the tall building took on a new dimension, exhibiting a greater degree of abstract logic than any tall building to date. In the *Architectural Record,* Claude Bragdon called the Blair Building "the finest flower which has sprung skyward out of the Beaux-Arts hotbed,"[61] and Desmond declared that if "from the point of view of design, the skyscraper still awaits its creator, and if, for the time being, the public must be content in its tall buildings, with a denial, or at least a concealment, of the facts of structure, clearly, *en attendant,* the architects of the Blair Building have shown us a safe intermediate path to follow."[62]

In 1912 Carrère & Hastings extended their discourse in favor of the thin curtain wall in the United States Rubber Building, substituting a surface of largely unadorned flat piers that were clearly nonstructural.[63] The twenty-floor building had stores on the first and second floors, the United States Rubber Company headquarters on the six floors above, and rental office space filling out the remainder. The stores were marked by a recessed arcade set below a string course indicating the beginning of six floors of offices for United Rubber. The middle four floors of that grouping had strip windows in slight relief, the bottom floor had individual windows with free floating pediments, and the top story, separated by string courses above and below, had windows set in deep relief with columns *in antis.* The windows for the rental office space reverted to strip windows with dark metal spandrels, occasionally cut by marble spandrels which continued the surface of piers, emphasizing their nonstructural nature.

The Corner Infill Building

The United States Rubber Building stood on the southeast corner of Broadway and Fifty-seventh Street, easily visible from the north, where the nature of the marble sheathing wrapping around the corner made the thinness of the curtain wall even more evident. Together with the Blair Building on the corner of Broad Street and Exchange Place, it represented a distinctly different type than the office buildings discussed so far. While mid-block infill sites were the most typical condition in which tall buildings were built during the Composite Age, corner sites, though more costly to acquire, offered amenities such as additional light and air, more street frontage for lucrative shops, as well as greater prominence in the townscape and therefore increased identity. From the beginning of the Composite Era, designers of corner buildings wavered between an expression of the corner as merely a point connecting two street walls and an elaboration of the corner's potential for unique expression, often marked by a corner turret, as in the office building Robert Maynicke designed in 1897 for the southwest corner of Fifth Avenue and Twenty-second Street.[64] The Blair Building was a good example of the first concept, represented by others such as the St. Paul, Atlantic and Knickerbocker Trust buildings.

In the twenty-five-story St. Paul Building, George Post introduced a chamfered corner wrapped with a continuous layered facade like wallpaper.[65] Built in 1897–99 at the corner of Broadway and Ann Street, the St. Paul Building was the third on its site within a generation, replacing John Kellum's original *Tribune* Building, which had in turn replaced the burnt out ruin of P.T. Barnum's museum. Schuyler disliked Kellum's building, but did not feel that Post's piling up of layers in the new building marked an improvement: "The presentation of its stories as half stories and the inclusion of two of them in each apparent story . . . is done throughout the 'architecturesque' part of the work. . . . Doubtless the doubling of the stories 'gives scale, and a swaggering aspect to the structure, and avoids the squareness of the openings that would result from leaving the actual arrangement undisguised. But it is plain that even from the architecturesque parts, the facts have been suppressed instead of being expressed."[66]

The most common type of corner infill building constructed during the Composite Era was a simple rectangular box securely tied into the block and divided into the three

Royal Insurance Building, northeast corner of William Street and Maiden Lane. Howells & Stokes, 1907. MCNY

Washington Life Building, southwest corner of Broadway and Liberty Street. Cyrus L.W. Eidlitz, 1897-98. MCNY

parts suggested by Schuyler, usually in the form of a rusticated base in limestone or marble, an unadorned shaft, and a limestone or marble capital decorated with a colonnade or pilasters. The type was epitomized by the eighteen-story Atlantic Building by Clinton & Russell, the most prolific designers of corner infill buildings.[67] Constructed in 1901 on the corner of Wall and William streets, it had a static tripartite division somewhat enlivened at the top by exuberant Modern French ornament cast in terra cotta. Clinton & Russell's later East River Savings Bank Building, built in 1911 on Broadway at Reade Street, was much more severe, with pilasters in place of piers, quoins instead of rustication and minimal decoration.[68]

One of the best of the typical corner infill buildings was Cass Gilbert's earliest office building in New York, the eighteen-story Broadway Chambers, which won a medal for Gilbert in the 1900 Paris Exposition.[69] Built in 1899 on the northwest corner of Broadway and Chambers Street, it had terra-cotta and brick cladding, and a copper cornice that introduced a measure of polychromy absent in the more conventional masonry clad buildings of the 1890s.

By the time that McKim, Mead & White, with White in charge, designed the thirteen-story Knickerbocker Trust Company Building the type was well established, and White simply refined it with an elegantly restrained Classicism.[70] Only the four lower floors were built in 1902-04 on Fifth Avenue at Thirty-fourth Street; although all preparations were made for the eventual addition of the other nine floors, the building was never completed. But in 1906 White began the design of a similar twenty-story corner building for the Knickerbocker Trust Company, completed after his death by his junior partner W.S. Richardson and built in 1908-12 on Broadway at Exchange Place.[71] While the form and composition of the building broke no new ground, the editors of *Architecture* pronounced the details to be "of the same high order of excellence with most of McKim, Mead & White's work and leave little to be desired."[72]

One of the last of the rectangular corner infill buildings constructed in the Composite Era, the Astor Trust Building (1917) at 535 Fifth Avenue was even more restrained and elegantly detailed.[73] Designed by Montague Flagg, Ernest's younger brother, the nineteen-story box had a crisply carved, three-story, limestone base pierced by large arched windows marking a double-height banking hall, a granite shaft with a fenestration pattern emphasizing the solidity of the corners, and a darker capital cut into by a two-story colonnade and crowned by a neo-Grec cornice.

Although most of the corner buildings securely locked into the block were cloaked in Classical dress, they were occasionally constructed in other styles. Howells & Stokes's design for the seventeen-story Royal Insurance Company Building modified the Classical paradigm with an appropriately English flavor derived from the Edwardian Baroque of John Belcher and J.J. Joass.[74] Standing on the northeast corner of William Street and Maiden Lane, the building was clad in white Georgia marble, polychrome terra cotta in pale shades and soft-colored red bricks laid in a diamond diaper pattern which highlighted the white mortar and suggested a lightness complementing the other materials. The building's location allowed a rounded corner with a prominent entrance crowned by the lion and unicorn of the Royal Arms of the United Kingdom flanking a marble and bronze clock in place of the royal shield. The entry hall had ornamented plaster vaults, marble floors and wainscoting, and white oak, birch, East Indian mahogany and vermillion wood trim.

C.L.W. Eidlitz's design for the Washington Life Building, constructed in 1897-98 at 145 Broadway on the corner of Liberty Street, broke out of the static rectangular box of the typical Classical corner building to go further toward the expression of verticality.[75] Schuyler correctly observed that Eidlitz accomplished the feat primarily through massing:

The Washington Life Building . . . is acclaimed by everybody as one of the very best of the sky-scrapers, and it owes its whole effectiveness . . . to the introduction of the treatment of a visible roof. The base is without pretensions. . . . The shaft is reduced to its very simplest expression, a mere repetition of the openings of the tiers of cells, which leaves it as nearly as may be a plain shaft. The detail of the lower stories, successful in scale and careful both in design and execution, offers nothing striking. But

Proposed *Sun* Building, City Hall Park. Bruce Price, 1890. CU

American Surety Building, south corner of Broadway and Pine Street. Bruce Price, 1894-95. View looking northeast from the Trinity Church yard, showing George B. Post's Equitable Life Assurance Building (1810) across Pine Street from the American Surety Building. CU

Sketch for a New York office building. Bruce Price. CU

the steep wedge-shaped roof seems to have been designed "not laboriously but luckily." It gives character to the building below it and makes it a picturesque object equally in a near and in a distant view.[76]

D'Oench & Yost continued the theme of the steep roof on a corner tower in the twenty-one-story Germania Life Building, constructed in 1911 on the northeast corner of Fourth Avenue and Seventeenth Street.[77] Its enormous mansard was capped by an illuminated sign that ran along its entire southern ridge, a rare example of an instance where the building's unique form was not considered sufficiently symbolic of its principal tenant's identity.

A few of the corner buildings were treated as though they were freestanding towers engaged at their base by the wall of the street. Bruce Price first established the strategy in 1890 with a rather naive proposal for the New York *Sun* Building, a project intended not for a corner site but a mid-block one opposite City Hall.[78] Price based the design on the campanile in the Piazza San Marco, paying no attention to the problem of the adjoining buildings and vividly expressing the confusion between the physical facts of tall buildings as they were then understood and the desire to exploit for commercial purposes the symbolic possibilities naturally associated with buildings of great height. In 1894 Price won the competition for the American Surety Building at 100 Broadway, on the corner of Pine Street, and continued the same line of development, even going so far as to place the windows on each successive floor progressively further back in the masonry curtain wall to suggest the entasis of the *Sun* project.[79] "In this design Mr. Price eliminated the unpractical features of his first study, and lost some of its picturesqueness in consequence," Swales wrote in the *Architectural Review*:

The colonnade in the upper part was suppressed, and a row of pilasters extending through two storeys only was substituted; all the circular windows, with a single exception, gave place to practical square ones. In place of the square lantern stage and pyramidal roof there was only a screen wall pierced with circular openings, and capped with a *cheneau* rising above the main cornice. All of which tended to simplicity and added to the monumental character of the design; but the most important change was that in carrying down to the ground level the vertical lines

John Wolfe Building, southeast corner of Maiden Lane and William Street. Henry J. Hardenbergh, 1895. View from William Street. NYHS

Beaver Building, southwest corner of Pearl, Beaver and Wall streets. Clinton & Russell, 1904. NYHS

of the masonry between the windows of the upper storeys in place of the triple-arch treatment which followed the design of St. Mark's to—in this respect—a degree that was unsatisfactory both in design and practice.[80]

Although the top of the American Surety Building had facades on all four sides that clearly distinguished it from the typical corner building, Price's static elevations were perhaps the first example of the standard tripartite division taken up in two-sided corner buildings such as the Broadway Chambers or Price's St. James Building on Broadway at Twenty-sixth Street.[81]

In 1912 Trowbridge & Livingston built the thirty-one-story Bankers Trust Building, a campanile at the corner of Wall and Nassau streets.[82] Though securely attached to the block on its west side and separated from its neighbor to the north by only a tiny space, Bankers Trust rose above its neighbors to appear as a freestanding tower crowned by a large stepped, pyramidal roof, said to have been modelled on a portico at Palititiza in Macedonia, that became the bank's symbol.

The irregularly shaped blocks below City Hall occasionally produced V-shaped buildings that continued the street wall but from the right angle looked like proto-skyscrapers. The way that Henry J. Hardenbergh massed the John Wolfe Building at the intersection of William Street and Maiden Lane seemed to Schuyler "to substitute for the sense of something forced and arbitrary the sense of something continuous and growing."[83] Built in 1895, the slender, twelve-story, brick and limestone Dutch Renaissance style tower was refreshingly modest, with a vernacular style reminiscent of old New York that nevertheless maintained the distinctions between base, middle and top. As fascinating as Hardenbergh's Wolfe Building was, however, it seemed sentimental and idiosyncratic in comparison with Bruce Price's heroically scaled sketch project for a New York office building.[84] A slender, regularly fenestrated tower—a slab with rounded ends—rose fifteen floors from a broader, rusticated base to support a colossal arcade supporting a winged statue atop a conical roof. Clinton & Russell's Beaver Building (1904) was more conventional than Hardenbergh's or Price's designs.[85] The architects responded to the angular site at the intersection of Pearl, Beaver and Wall streets by rounding off the corner, but in all other

German American Insurance Building, northwest corner of Maiden Lane and Liberty Street. Hill & Stout, 1908. MCNY

German American Insurance Building, northwest corner of Maiden Lane and Liberty Street. Hill & Stout, 1908. Cornice detail. MCNY

Seligman Building, west corner of William and South William streets. Francis H. Kimball and Julian C. Levi, 1907. MCNY

respects the building was typical of the many infill structures they erected.

The twelve-story Seligman Building at the corner of William and South William streets, designed in 1907 by Francis H. Kimball and Julian C. Levi in an English variation of the Baroque style, displeased Schuyler.[86] He objected to the designer's efforts at modelling the composition, especially near the top where the *arris* of the corner was withdrawn to form a base for the corner tower crowning the design, and called the design the product of "mindless caprice, mere amentia, 'Amentia Americana.'" But Kimball and Levi must be given credit for coming to terms with its difficult site and the acute angle of the intersection of the two principal streets.

A V-shaped building completed the next year, the twenty-two-story German American Insurance Building, was designed by Hill & Stout to take advantage of its peninsular site at the intersection of Maiden Lane and Liberty Street and exploit the tower's possibility for soaring verticality and individual expression.[87] Above its three-story granite base, white porcelain brick pilasters rose uninterrupted for eleven floors, inset with glazed brick panels at every story. The top four floors were covered by terra cotta glazed in colors, capped by a magnificent terra-cotta overhanging cornice.

More common than the V-shaped, peninsular office buildings were those built along the end of typical orthogonal blocks with two corners. John Moser's theoretical design for the aptly named "Sky-scraper," designed in 1894, took advantage of the condition by breaking the building up into three towers analogous to Classical columns, with continuous paired shafts treated as double columns rising from a rusticated base to an elaborately modelled entablature and cornice.[88]

Hardenbergh's Whitehall Building, built in 1900, epitomized the three-sided office building.[89] The Whitehall had frontage on West and Washington streets as well as Battery Place; because it could be seen at a great distance across Battery Park, Hardenbergh substituted a bold composition for intricate detail. The center of the facade was recessed above the two-story basement and terminated by a sloping parapet suggestive of a pediment and embellished with a cartouche. The slightly projecting end bays were sheathed in broad stripes of yellow brick alternating with narrow

Whitehall Building, north side of Battery Place between West and Washington streets. Right: Henry J. Hardenbergh, 1900. Left: Clinton & Russell, 1910. NYHS

stripes of red brick, while the center was entirely sheathed in the red, resulting in a facade that appeared to shimmer in the marine light.

The effect of the nineteen-story Whitehall Building was enhanced in 1910 by the construction of a thirty-one story addition to the north designed by Clinton & Russell.[90] Though the addition was bulky and not particularly refined in its detail, viewed from the harbor its arched-end elevation towered above Hardenbergh's, extending the vertical axis and turning the entire composition into the base for the mountain of towers built north of the Battery.

Cass Gilbert's terra-cotta and limestone facade on the West Street Building (1905) at 90 West Street was a reinterpretation at a larger scale of his earlier Broadway Chambers which substituted a Gothic expression for a Classical one to introduce a measure of poetry hitherto absent from the tall building.[91] Rather than forming what Schuyler described as a "mere parallelo-piped," this U-shaped building faced three streets and rose above a row of two-story buildings to suggest a freestanding tower more convincingly than any earlier tall building in New York. Schuyler thought that its suggestion of a tower was enhanced by an intricately modelled six-story crown, which he found to be "distinctly 'the thing,'" and, more importantly, by the handling of the terra cotta clad facade which was organized as a plaiting of vertical piers rising uninterruptedly for 12 of the building's 20 stories, and recessed horizontal spandrels.[92]

William Welles Bosworth's American Telephone and Telegraph Building, built in 1914–17 at 195 Broadway between Dey and Fulton streets, grandly summed up the three-sided tall infill building.[93] A twenty-five-story block, it was treated as two distinct slabs fitted together. Echoing the nearby St. Paul Building of fifteen or so years before, Bosworth piled eight, three-story-high Ionic colonnades on top of a Doric base. At the northwest corner of the building a cupola modelled on the Mausoleum of Halicarnassus supported Evelyn Beatrice Longman's sculpture of the *Spirit of Communication,* a powerful, winged figure grasping electricity wrestled from the elements and transferring it through cables which swept down around his body to encircle the globe he stood upon. The Doric columns at the base were also used inside to create an extraordinarily powerful and unconventional hypostyle hall where massive, sculp-

West Street Building, 87 West Street. Cass Gilbert, 1905. MCNY

New York Life Insurance Building, 346 Broadway. McKim, Mead & White, 1896-99. View from the corner of West and Leonard streets. NYHS

tural columns formed a forest of polished marble.

Although the New York Life Insurance Building at 346 Broadway (an extension and remodelling in 1896-99 by McKim, Mead & White of a building designed by Griffith Thomas in 1870) completely filled its small block sandwiched between Broadway, Leonard, Catherine and Lafayette streets, the company's headquarters were too long and low to appear as a tower, and the architects treated it as an infill-type building.[94] Piling one story on top of another, they produced a composition rather like those of the loft buildings in the neighborhood with identical precast parts on every floor. "Theoretically, it is unsatisfactory because its treatment is that of three or four buildings of three storeys one upon the other," Swales wrote in 1908. "The objections are however, unsatisfactory.... Externally—and internally as far at least as the splendid banking-room and vestibules are concerned—it is the perfection of detail which captures one."[95]

The Trinity and United States Realty buildings at 111 and 115 Broadway had similar small sites between the Trinity Churchyard and Chambers Street. The Trinity Building, constructed on the site of New York's first office building, was designed by Francis H. Kimball and built in 1905 on a lot that was 264 feet long but less than 50 feet wide.[96] When the developers of the Trinity Building, the United States Realty Company, acquired a similar long, narrow site across Thames Street, they hired Kimball to design a companion building for their own use. In 1906 they widened the street and built the United States Realty Building, which shared the Trinity Building's problem of elevator area to floor area, limiting both to only twenty-one stories. Kimball placed the service cores along the thirty-foot-wide Thames Street, but while the majority of offices in the Trinity Building looked out on the churchyard, Kimball could only hope that tall buildings would never rise on the other side of the narrow Cedar Street to cut off the light in the United States Realty Building.

Kimball, who had been trained by the English Gothicist William Burges, designed both buildings in a vaguely Gothic style intended to complement Trinity Church. Yet despite a corner turret on the Trinity Building and the presence atop United States Realty of the Lawyers' Club, built with high, stained-glass windows which gave the suggestion of a cathedral, the curtain wall treatment of both narrow slabs

Trinity and United States Realty Buildings, 111 and 115 Broadway. Francis H. Kimball, 1905 and 1906. A 1913 view from the east after demolition of George B. Post's Equitable Building. MCNY

Trinity Building, 111 Broadway. Francis H. Kimball, 1905. Plan of first floor. CU

City Investing Building, south side of Cortlandt Street between Broadway and Church Street. Francis H. Kimball, 1908. Flagg's Singer Tower is visible behind. CU

gave none of the soaring quality of the Gothic Gilbert used on the West Street Building.

Kimball's City Investing Building, built in 1908 on the end of the block of Cortlandt Street between Broadway and Church Street, had too large a site to fill completely, since buildings then relied on natural ventilation and were more dependent on daylight.[97] He placed the service elements at the back of the building on the interior of the block and massed the building along Cortlandt Street with tall wings similar to those in Moser's proposal, although Kimball could not put a wing on the corner of Broadway and Cortlandt, where the Wessells Building stood, because the City Investing Company only owned the air rights to the lot and not the building itself.

After the junior partners at McKim, Mead & White convinced McKim to let the office enter the Municipal Building competition in 1907 under the supervision of William Kendall, the firm produced a dynamic variation on the infill type.[98] A freestanding building, it stood in relative isolation on the skyline, functioning as a tower with a strong vertical accent, a dramatically silhouetted crowning feature, a vastly enlarged rendition of Sir Christopher Wren's western towers at St. Paul's Cathedral in London capped by Adolph Weinman's statue *Civic Fame*. Yet the mass of the Municipal Building was dominated by its space-shaping qualities on City Hall Square where it accommodated a highly irregular site and made a remarkable culmination to the infill type. At street level, its vast entrance court, loggia and arch over Chambers Street appropriately conveyed, more convincingly than any other example, the capacity of the tall building for monumental expression.

The Skyscraper

The first buildings to convincingly express the romantic characteristics of the skyscraper were built on freestanding, V-shaped lots created by the intersection of Broadway with the city's grid of streets. The Fuller Building (1903), designed by D.H. Burnham and popularly known as the Flatiron Building, was only twenty-three stories high, but the unusual building lot allowed Burnham to give the building great drama.[99] Extending the building to the lot line on all sides, he lifted the building in an unbroken slab to produce a true, inviolable tower. Economy may have demanded that solution on such a small plot, but Burnham exploited

View ca. 1913 from the top of the American Telephone & Telegraph Building at 195 Broadway. The City Hall Post Office (A.B. Mullett, 1875) and the Tweed Courthouse (John Kellum, 1872) are visible in City Hall Park. To the west of the park is the Woolworth Building (Cass Gilbert, 1910-13) behind the Astor House and St. Paul's Chapel. North of the park are the Emigrant Savings Bank (Raymond F. Almirall, 1909-10) and the Hall of Records (John R. Thomas and Horgan & Slattery, 1899-1911). To the east, stand the Municipal Building (McKim, Mead & White, 1907-14), the Brooklyn Bridge Terminal, the Park Row Building (R.H. Robertson, 1876-99) and the St. Paul Building (George B. Post, 1897-99). AT&T

Fuller Building, Twenty-third Street between Broadway and Fifth Avenue. D.H. Burnham & Co., 1903. A 1903 view looking south from the intersection of Broadway and Fifth Avenue. NYHS

Times Tower, Broadway to Seventh Avenue between Forty-second and Forty-third streets. Cyrus L.W. Eidlitz, 1904. A view looking south showing left, the Olympia Theater (J.B. McElfatrick, 1895) and the Hotel Rector (D.H. Burnham & Co., 1910-11) and right, the Astor Hotel (Clinton & Russell, 1904). NYHS

the problem beautifully: the Flatiron Building was the first lyrical exemplar of the composite skyscraper. Particularly when seen from uptown, the apex of the triangle, which was only six feet wide, rendered the unencumbered tower more a thick wall than a volume.[100]

Despite the presence of much taller buildings around the rest of Madison Square, the building quickly grabbed a hold on the public imagination. Photographers such as Edward Steichen and Alfred Steiglitz fixed its image in the national psyche: a mystical tower, rising softly out of the haze, almost a part of the natural landscape. The Flatiron was not only a symbol of ethereal romance; tradition has it that the phrase "Twenty-three Skiddoo" derived from the shouts of policemen charged with clearing Twenty-third Street of gawkers who lingered at the base of the Flatiron waiting for the downdrafts created by the tower to lift the long skirts worn by the women of the time.

The Flatiron Building, the first really tall building north of City Hall, brought the city to the brink of its first skyscraper era. Eidlitz & MacKenzie's twenty-four-story Times Tower, completed in 1904, "scraped higher clouds" than any other building in New York because it stood on higher ground than the city's tallest building, the Park Row Building.[101] Like the Flatiron Building, the Times Tower had a small triangular site created by the intersection of Broadway with the city's gridded streets (on the newly renamed Longacre Square, where the *New York Times* had moved in emulation of the New York *Herald*'s similar move north from the towers of "Newspaper Row" on Park Row to Herald Square.) But C.L.W. Eidlitz's composition for the Times Tower did not have the Flatiron's soaring quality: the first sixteen stories were an ordinary, Italian Renaissance design, distinguished only by a trapezoidal plan, and on top of that mass sat an eight-story tower nearly half as large in plan, its point of transition barely acknowledged by a change in fenestration. An earlier design by Eidlitz that emphasized the tower by crowning it with a dome was more successful. Nonetheless, by placing a tower on a street defining base, Eidlitz succeeded in combining the two tendencies of the tall building into one composition, and thereby deserved credit for the construction of the first mature skyscraper.

The completion of the I.R.T. subway in 1904 that prompted the development of Times Square almost led to the building of a forty-story tower for the *New York American* on Columbus Circle.¹⁰² Proposed for the irregularly shaped block bounded by Fifty-eighth Street, Broadway and Eighth Avenue, Barney & Chapman's wildly extravagant design would have been one of the city's most visible landmarks. The base was a mass of columns, supporting a floor of giant caryatids, above which a shaft of piers rose to frame circular floors. A 555-foot-high clock tower, located at the southwest corner of the building, was the peak of a fantasy reminiscent of Mad King Ludwig's castle at Neuschwanstein.

The City Investing Company Building was built next to the ten-story headquarters of the Singer Manufacturing Company designed by Ernest Flagg in 1899.¹⁰³ "Comically, and in spite of the brandnewness and smartness of its modish Parisian detail," Schuyler wrote that year, "the Singer Building is a reversion, advantageous as it might be, on civic grounds, to restrict the height of all commercial buildings."¹⁰⁴ Flagg used this opportunity to register in stone the opposition to the tall building which he had expressed in print in 1896, when he proposed strict controls by the city on coverage for any towers rising above a suggested cornice height of one hundred feet.¹⁰⁵ The article was prompted by the appearance before the New York State Legislature in May 1896 of a bill controlling building heights. George Post supported the idea of controls at a meeting of the New York Chapter of the American Institute of Architects; after marshalling a number of practical arguments, he announced that "from an artistic point of view the gain to the city by the passage of such a law cannot be disputed, for even if the principal facades of a building towering above the surrounding house may be handsome its plain brick masonry on end and rear will always form a hideous mass. It can only be beautiful if treated as a tower, but such a facade would necessarily entirely lose its effect if connected continuously with another facade of approximately the same height."¹⁰⁶ Like Flagg, Post advocated a formula based on the width of the street and suggested a graded ratio.

While Post spoke in favor of height controls the *Real Estate Record and Guide* pointed out that his St. Paul Building was ironically an "object lesson . . . that is likely to bring the greater number of wavering or apathetic observers to his way of thinking. For the St. Paul is a crucial instance, not because it is a twenty-five story building merely or mainly, but because it is a twenty-five story building on a plot of moderate dimensions enclosed on two sides. Mr. Post might have had better conditions under which to make a 'reductio' or, rather a 'productio ad absurdum' of the permission to erect unlimited high buildings, but these will answer very well. It is not often that an architect has such an occasion to say 'I told you so' at his own expense, as it were."¹⁰⁷

The bill failed to gain sufficient support, but opposition to tall buildings continued, so that by 1899 disenchantment with the tall office building was firmly entrenched. As more and more tall buildings were built, height no longer seemed the mark of power it had traditionally been.¹⁰⁸ "Within the last two years," A.C. David noted in 1903,

the tendency toward the erection of "skyscrapers" has been checked by the very conditions these tall buildings have helped to create. Twenty-story structures could without inconvenience be built along the whole frontage of a street that was one hundred and fifty feet or more wide, but buildings twenty stories high on the narrow streets of New York's financial district, that were only adapted to four or five story buildings at the most, have proved to be a class of improvement, which for the sake of economy must be economically used. Even then, if a whole block could be covered over at one operation, the space could be so distributed into courts that the tenants of the rooms would at least on bright days be able to substitute sun for electric lights, but as these buildings cover only a small slice of the blocks on which they are situated, the twenty-story buildings erected are exposed to the danger of having essential portions of their light and air cut off by the erection of other twenty-story buildings on land immediately adjoining.¹⁰⁹

Schuyler stated the issue succinctly: "the problem of the skyscraper . . . is the skeleton of structure which has enabled builders to go, not as with the pioneers of the elevator architecture, but three times, four times, five times as

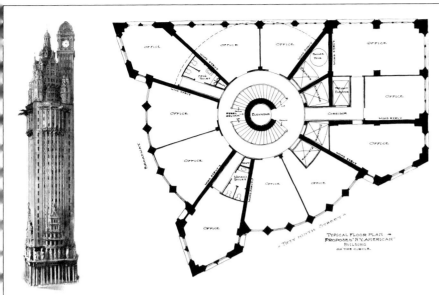

Proposed *New York American* Tower, south side of Columbus Circle between Broadway and Eighth Avenue. Barney & Chapman, 1904. Model and plan of typical floor. CU

high as builders went before; and while the Western Union and the Tribune Building towered only head and shoulders above their fellows, the newer skyscrapers stand waist deep, knee deep, ankle deep in such relatives as are left of the old-fashioned commercial buildings."[110] Clearly, as Charles Rollinson Lamb pointed out in *Municipal Affairs* magazine, with owners of existing buildings being forced to buy property around them to protect their light and air from the tall buildings sprouting up anywhere, a "reductio ad absurdim" would soon be reached "when all buildings are as tall as the tallest."[111]

After the frenetic pace of office-building construction in the 1890s, a temporary decline in the early years of the new century reduced opposition to tall buildings. Pressure resumed around 1907 when the construction of new, tall buildings along lower Broadway became so prevalent that the normally boosterish *Real Estate Record and Guide* proclaimed an "Invasion of New York City By Darkness," accompanying their claim with daytime pictures of streets darkened by the shadows of the tall buildings.[112]

Flagg again put forth an argument for controls, arguing that "our street facades have a ragged, wild Western appearance more suitable to a half-civilized community than to a city which claims rank with the other great capitals of the world. Great buildings, having one or two sides ornamented, rear their gigantic walls of naked brickwork far above adjoining buildings, and force their ugliness upon public view." Flagg was of course arguing a line that was almost wholly that of the French Academic tradition: "Only monuments and buildings of a public character, such as municipal buildings, churches, theatres and the like, should break the line of the street facade by going above its general height, and thereby obtain the setting and background which is their due."[113] Flagg was joined by many others. Schuyler bemoaned a city with "no skyline at all. It is all interruptions, of various heights and shapes and sizes, not even peaks in a mountain range, but scattered or huddled towers which have nothing to do with each other or with what is below."[114] More than anything else, Schuyler regretted the absence of any visible roof on most of the new tall buildings to give a building's silhouette its "form or comeliness. . . . The parallelopiped is not an architectural form, as any body will have impressed upon him by looking at the random row of parallelopipes in lower New York from across the East or North River. The practical owner may have had some reason who objected to his architect's design for a steeply-roofed ten-story building, upon the ground that 'That's all right on the Rhine, but it ain't business.' Nevertheless, he was insisting upon a defacement of the city, which is in great part wanton."[115] In 1904 Henry James discussed the problem somewhat more eloquently:

The "tall buildings," which have so promptly usurped a glory that affects you as rather surprised, as yet, at itself, the multitudinous sky-scrapers standing up to view, from the water, like extravagant pins in a cushion already overplanted, and stuck in as in the dark, anywhere and anyhow. . . . Crowned not only with no history, but with no credible possibility of time for history, and consecrated by no uses save the commercial at any cost, they are simply the most piercing notes in that concert of the expansively professional into which your supreme sense of New York resolves itself. They never begin to speak to you, in the manner of the builded majesties of the world as we have heretofore known such—towers or temples or fortresses or palaces—with the authority of things of permanence or even things of long duration. One story is good only till another is told, and sky-scrapers are the last word of economic ingenuity only till another word be written.[115]

Flagg devised a new plan, proposing that buildings be limited to one hundred feet high or a coverage of no more than three quarters of the entire plot, although a building on the remaining quarter could rise as high as practical, resulting in a skyline that would be a "tiara of proud towers."[117] "Without doubt the result would be a great improvement in the aspect of New York," Schuyler wrote. "The limitation to 100 feet, or eight stories, say, would automatically restore to our business streets the cornice line which in old times, before the passenger elevator, was automatically imposed by the five stories which were the maximum that a visitor or tenant could be expected to climb. And the new cornice line would be only half as high again as the old. For the rest . . .

Singer Tower, northwest corner of Broadway and Liberty Street. Ernest Flagg, 1905–08. View looking west on Liberty Street. NYHS

the regulation would make New York 'A City of Towers.'"[118]

The freestanding tower on the base was Flagg's solution to the problem of the tall building he had criticized so vehemently in 1896, when he had written that he believed "that almost the only advocate of high buildings are to be found among those who have a direct pecuniary interest involved."[119] And in a letter to the New York *Sun* the year before, Flagg had written, "Even if the tall buildings erected to-day are safe, I believe many of them will shortly become unsafe. As an architect I will never have anything to do with buildings of this kind. I believe there is no way to accomplish an artistic success where all laws of common sense are set at defiance. Just proportion is the first requisite of architectural design; how, then, can buildings which are out of all proportion to the width of the street be successful from the aesthetic standpoint? The solution of such a problem is a law against abnormal height."[120] Yet Flagg's change of heart, which the cynical might call "pecuniary," produced one of the most important developments in the evolution of the skyscraper. It simultaneously satisfied the need for dense concentrations of office space, the requirements for reasonable light and air inside the offices and on the street and the need for a permanent, visible and memorable icon that would function as a symbol of a corporation.

As plans were being made for the massive City Investing Building to rise next to his ten-story Singer Building, Flagg was given the commission to expand the small headquarters. Drawing on his ideal skyscraper type, Flagg used the old building as a base and placed a slender, sixty-five-foot square tower atop it.[121] Built in 1905–08, it was surmounted by a mansard rising to a nobly proportioned lantern that made it the tallest building in the world. Unfortunately, "the observation balcony seemed to have a strong appeal to those who were soured on life," according to the book *New York, The Wonder City,* and it soon became known as Suicide Pinnacle.[122]

A perfect marriage between Beaux-Arts rationalism and Modern French style, the Singer Tower had corners sheathed in the same brick and limestone used in the original building but dramatically contrasted with a central shaft of iron and steel, synthesizing the unifying structural expression of the frame with the humanistic imagery of the Classical tradition. The cladding was bold and unprecedented in a tall building, although it was related to Flagg's

Singer Tower, northwest corner of Broadway and Liberty Street. Ernest Flagg, 1905-08. Lobby. CU

City Investing Building, south side of Cortlandt Street between Broadway and Church Street. Francis H. Kimball, 1908. Lobby. CU

Little Singer Building, his New York Produce Exchange Bank Building (1905)[123] and Carrère & Hastings's Blair Building. Flagg expressed the skin differently than Carrère & Hastings had, however, contrasting the iron and glass skin with the masonry corners, where a technologically advanced wind brace system was used in the frame. The lobbies of the Singer Tower and City Investing Building were two of the first glories of the skyscraper era, indicative of those to come in the Era of Convenience.[124] The Singer Building lobby had a maze of piers in square bays supporting glass saucer domes: all the surfaces were covered with colored marbles and bronze ornament.

The Singer Tower was soon rivalled by a more traditional design by Napoleon Le Brun & Sons which nonetheless had lessons to offer about the base and shaft of the skyscraper type.[125] Le Brun's Metropolitan Life Tower (1909) was a boldly scaled campanile topped by an enormous roof and cupola which rose seven hundred feet to pass the Singer Tower as the tallest building in the world. Unlike the Singer Tower, which Schuyler called "merely an emergence, a peak in a mountain chain," it stood in comparative isolation on the corner of Madison Avenue and Twenty-fourth Street, north of the business district, the "cynosure of middle Manhattan."[126] Recalling Price's *Sun* Building project, the tower was closely based on the Campanile at the Piazza San Marco in Venice, a fact which Pierre Le Brun rather naively tried to deny by pointing to its jolt in scale and the punctuation of the surface with innumerable windows which considerably modified the original form. Yet unlike Price's campanile, the Metropolitan Life Tower was attached to an existing block of buildings designed by Le Brun in 1892 which insured the new tower's light and air. Viewed from Madison Square, it seemed to engage in a civilized conversation with the tower of Stanford White's Madison Square Garden two blocks to the north.

The ramifications of the new scale of the Singer and Metropolitan Life towers were quickly understood: the *Real Estate Record and Guide* immediately pointed out that "these two instances are peculiarly significant. In each . . . the holding corporations own very large plots, only a fraction of which will be covered by a tall tower, and by adopting this plan they secure many advantages." They were seen to be in sharp contrast with "the ordinary skyscraper" which "is generally designed somewhat as a tower, and . . . fre-

Metropolitan Life Tower, southwest corner of Madison Avenue and Twenty-fourth Street. Napoleon Le Brun & Sons, 1909. A 1909 view from the south end of Madison Square looking northeast, also showing the Metropolitan Life Building (Napoleon Le Brun & Sons, 1892), the Madison Square Presbyterian Church (McKim, Mead & White, 1906), the Appellate Division Courthouse of the New York State Supreme Court (James Brown Lord, 1900) and Madison Square Garden (McKim, Mead & White, 1890). MCNY

View of Madison Square looking south. To the left, on the southeast corner of Madison Avenue and Twenty-fourth Street, is the Metropolitan Life Tower (1909) by Napoleon Le Brun & Sons, next to the Metropolitan Life Building (Napoleon Le Brun & Sons, 1892) and across Twenty-fourth Street from Madison Square Presbyterian Church (McKim, Mead & White, 1906). To the right, at the intersection of Broadway and Fifth Avenue, is the Fuller Building (D.H. Burnham & Co., 1903). CU

Metropolitan Life Building, northeast corner of Madison Avenue and Twenty-third Street. Napoleon Le Brun & Sons, 1892. Main staircase. NYHS

quently is a tower as compared to low contiguous buildings, but . . . is not architecturally a complete tower . . . inasmuch as the rear and the sides of a building may some day be hidden by adjoining buildings."[127]

The *Architectural Record* proclaimed that the completion of the new towers marked the moment when the tall building broke "through another stratum of ether" and noted that "now we possess genuine tower architecture as an advertising feature on a rental basis . . . now we get to the point where the tower is practically the whole thing. . . . In many cases the lofty buildings are protected and isolated by their own surrounding property, but already in the case of the Singer Building the growth of the huge City Investing Company's Building has amalgamated itself with it, and as the white trimmings of the Singer Tower accords fairly well with that of its aspiring neighbor, the composite architecture is not without attraction, especially when viewed from a North River ferryboat."[128]

While the Singer and Metropolitan Life towers were under construction, Theodore Starrett proposed a one-hundred-story mixed-use building without setbacks or light courts that stacked layers of office space, industrial lofts, apartments, hotel, theater and shopping spaces under a rooftop amusement park, all separated by public plazas that came every twenty floors. "Our civilization is progressing wonderfully," Starrett wrote without any trace of irony. "In New York . . . we must keep building and we must build upward. Step by step we have advanced from the wooden hut to the 30-story skyscraper. . . . Now we must develop something different, something larger."[129] The *Real Estate Record and Guide,* perhaps frightened by the boldness and practicality of Starrett's project, suggested that "a corporation such as the Equitable Life Assurance Society, which owns a whole block, could erect a building which would be at once spectacular and profitable, by covering the outer rim of the block with a twenty-story structure, the intermediate section with a twenty-five story structure, and the center of the block with a tower as high as good elevator service would permit."[130] But the Equitable sold its property to a syndicate of developers including T. Coleman Dupont and Louis Horowitz, who instructed their architect Ernest R. Graham to pursue a different direction.

In 1912 they tore down George Post's venerable Equitable Building at 120 Broadway and replaced it with what

View looking northeast from the corner of Rector Street and Trinity Place. In the foreground is the Trinity Church steeple and, to the left, the Trinity Building (1905) by Francis H. Kimball. From the left, the towers visible are the City Investing Building (Francis H. Kimball, 1908), the Woolworth Building (Cass Gilbert, 1910-13), the Singer Tower (Ernest Flagg, 1905-08), the Equitable Building (Graham, Anderson, Probst & White, 1912-15) and the Bankers Trust Building (Trowbridge & Livingston, 1912). In front of the Equitable Building, on the southern corner of Broadway and Pine Street, is the American Surety Building (1894-95) by Bruce Price. CU

"King's Dream of New York." Rendering by Harry M. Pettit. From *King's Dream of New York,* 1911. CU

Woolworth Building, west side of Broadway between Barclay Street and Park Place. Cass Gilbert, 1910-13. MCNY

was unquestionably the bulkiest and densest office building ever, a forty-story structure with over 1.2 million square feet of rentable office space.[131] Packed into the small block between Broadway and Nassau Street, bounded by Pine and Cedar streets, the Equitable Building had a floor area almost thirty times its site area. Seen from the Trinity Churchyard, its vast height and visually unrelieved solidity not only dominated the comparatively slender Bankers Trust and Singer towers but also bulky slabs such as the Trinity Building.

Spurred on by the example of the Singer and Metropolitan towers, and alarmed by the proposed Equitable Building, agitation for skyscraper reform continued. In 1911 the *Real Estate Record and Guide* observed that "wholesale theft of daylight is the cause of over-supply of rentable space,"[132] and by 1913 the framework for the reforms of the 1916 Zoning Resolution was set.[133] But its enactment into law was preceded by the construction of the Woolworth Building, a masterpiece which culminated the development of the Composite Era skyscraper and anticipated the monuments of the Era of Convenience.[134]

While the Singer and Metropolitan towers had outlined a model for rational skyscraper development, their impractically slender towers and independently designed "bases" made them anomalies. Cass Gilbert's Woolworth Building, which climbed almost eight hundred feet to succeed the Metropolitan Life Tower as the world's tallest building in 1913, offered an even more convincing demonstration of the aesthetic power and potential urbanistic amenability of the base and tower formula. More than any of its predeccessors in New York, except for Sullivan's only modestly tall Bayard Building, the Woolworth Building convincingly inhabited its height.

Gilbert's early proposals, designed for a site at the southwest corner of Broadway and Park Place, called for a building with a stubby, stepped-back tower placed asymmetrically at the corner. But by 1911, the company had obtained more frontage on Broadway and the tower was positioned in the center of the eastern facade, where it began to take on its final form. The eighty-six-by-eighty-four-foot tower, which set back near the top, rose twenty-six stories above the building's twenty-nine-story base to produce a slightly squat profile that Gilbert's brilliant handling of the vertical ribs did much to help counteract.[135]

Facing City Hall Park and clad in glistening white terra cotta, the Woolworth Building replaced the Metropolitan Life Tower as the most conspicuous skyscraper in the city. Its location enabled it to rise in relative isolation from the buildings of the old city and to be seen at great distances across City Hall Park. As Schuyler put it, one of its "chief successes . . . is its success of 'scale.'"[136]

The Woolworth Building was remarkable for its free Gothic silhouette and detail, which elevated a rationally composed structural system to heights of lyricism seldom achieved in a commercial building. Truly a "Cathedral of Commerce," as the Reverend S. Parkes Cadman dubbed it,[137] the Woolworth Building set the standard for tall buildings for a generation, and Gilbert's Gothic style—"Woolworth Gothic," as it came to be known—replaced the Modern French as the most flexible and symbolically appropriate style for tall buildings. "A skyscraper, by its height which makes its upper parts appear lost in the clouds, is a monument whose masses must become more and more inspired the higher it rises," Gilbert wrote. "The Gothic style gave us the possibility of expressing the greatest degree of aspiration . . . the ultimate note of the mass gradually gaining in spirituality the higher it mounts."[138]

The Woolworth Building truly deserved the praise the *Architectural Record* had lavished on Gilbert's earlier West Street Building: "It is only in Gothic that one attains, to recur to Ruskin, 'those misty masses of multitudinous pinnacle and diademed tower' which can glorify the summit even of a practical and prosaic New York skyscraper."[139] Here, for the first time, was the complex, proud and soaring tall building that Sullivan and others had called for; here at last was a skyscraper in which base, shaft and capital were expressed and transformed to both the local and metropolitan scale of the city.

The interior spaces of the ground floor continued the splendid public scale initiated at the City Investing Building. Though gloomy by comparison with the marvelously lyrical lobby of the Singer Tower, the Woolworth Building's

Dry Dock Savings Bank, 333 Bowery. Leopold Eidlitz, 1875. MCNY

Bank for Savings, southwest corner of Fourth Avenue and Twenty-second Street. Cyrus L.W. Eidlitz, 1892. CU

double-height Gothic-style concourse was richly detailed with Sienna marble walls and a colorful but dimly lit mosaic ceiling supported on small brackets modelled by Donnelly & Ricci and depicting Gilbert, F.W. Woolworth and others involved in the building's construction. Although the Grand Foyer Hall and its great steps leading to the mezzanine-level shops constituted the principal interior space, the passages to the subway and the Rathskeller at the subway concourse level were nicely handled.

No building type more perfectly expressed America's boundless optimism on the eve of World War I than the New York skyscraper, nor so clearly articulated the American achievement in architecture.[140] H.P.A. Berlage, an eminent Dutch architect visiting New York in 1911, asked at a meeting of the Municipal Art Society: "Ought not, after all, the character of these titanic buildings to be that of a mass grouping, with omission of everything that can detract from this expression? For here we certainly have the concentration of the modern business life, and, therefore, also its architectural expression, so that these buildings could establish the architectural forms for the whole modern architecture."[141] A French engineer who visited New York in 1913 as a delegate to the International Congress of Engineers best captured that spirit: "The tall building has been explained as a scientific evolution, as a product of economic stress and scarcity of land. It has been admired, scoffed at, been justified and condemned. It has been likened to the castle of the robber baron. But I am not aware that it has been recognized for what it is and will be to posterity, namely, the material expression of the American of this generation."[142]

With the completion of the Woolworth Building the twentieth-century character of the Manhattan skyline was firmly established: "a mountain range of the mind," as Walter McQuade so eloquently put it, "an uncanny array of individual designs, a vision of power filed neatly into thousands and thousands of desk drawers, and a beautiful thing."[143]

Banking and Commerce

New York established itself as the nation's banking center by the Civil War, but most New York banks at the beginning of the Metropolitan Era maintained a modest architectural image. Although a number of monumental banks had been built on Wall Street during the Greek Revival, in the 1870s few banks emulated the French and English practice of building exclusively for their own use. Frequently located in converted residences, they forsook a public image for discretion. By the 1880s the high cost of land in the financial district encouraged bankers to build tall office buildings, reserve space for themselves on the ground floor, and simply rent out the rest of the building.[144]

Savings banks were the principal exception to this trend. They could afford to build for their own exclusive use because they were typically less centrally located. Moreover, because they dealt more directly with the general public than did the average commercial house, the savings banks felt it incumbent on themselves to convey a reassuring image of stability in a period of volatile economic conditions. Leopold Eidlitz's Dry Dock Savings Bank at 333 Bowery[145] and George Post's Williamsburg Savings Bank at 175 Broadway in Brooklyn,[146] both built in 1875, were early examples of monumental, isolated savings bank buildings. Eidlitz's design marked a high point of the Victorian Gothic in America, while Post reintroduced the Classical mode for the building type and provided an early premonition of the American Renaissance.

In the early 1890s the nation's economy was torn apart by the issue of free silver and teetered on the brink of total collapse, prompting a number of savings banks to build substantial headquarters which defiantly asserted their fiscal stability. "It has seemed necessary to make something of a show, to express in the building the fact that banks and other moneyed institutions are suffering, as it were, from the possession of too much cash, and are somewhat self conscious about it," A.C. David observed in the *Architectural Record*.[147]

In 1892 Cyrus L.W. Eidlitz, Leopold's son, designed the period's first important bank, the Bank for Savings at the southwest corner of Twenty-second Street and Fourth Avenue.[148] The Bank for Savings represented the transition from the free eclecticism of the Cosmopolitan Era to the

Brooklyn Savings Bank, northeast corner of Pierrepont and Clinton streets. Frank Freeman, 1894. NYHS

Classical rigor of the Composite. Although Romanesque in spirit, the elevations were symmetrically composed and sparingly detailed. The cross axial *parti* set a cruciform *piano nobile* atop a square base, providing even daylight in the main banking hall and articulating the location of individual offices along its edge. The entrances were relegated to the corners, where they accentuated the apparent solidity of the central mass. According to Schuyler, Eidlitz's design was "perhaps the most popular of recent buildings and the most classical piece of architecture in New York. . . . To attain in free architecture the distinctive charm of classic architecture, to gain purity without losing expressiveness is a rare, if not a unique achievement in contemporary work."[149]

Frank Freeman's Brooklyn Savings Bank, on the corner of Pierrepont and Clinton streets, was equally grand and more explicitly Classical: a bold, cross-axial, complexly massed composition in the neo-Grec style.[150] Its Classicism was quite unexpected from the architect whom Schuyler regarded as "our great authority on the Romanesque,"[151] but the neo-Grec allowed a freedom of proportions and details which Freeman brilliantly exploited to create a rich juxtaposition of scales.

McKim, Mead & White's Bowery Savings Bank (1894), the first truly sumptuous bank in New York, set a new standard of monumentality in bank design that was rarely equalled.[152] It occupied a difficult, L-shaped site; the main entrance was through a narrow, mid-block facade at 130 Bowery in the shadow of the elevated railway. A boldly proportioned temple front with two Corinthian columns *in antis* framed a high, arched vestibule to a colonnaded, barrel vaulted passageway which led to the main banking room. Located in a hipped-roof pavilion on the corner of Grand Street, this lavishly detailed, nobly proportioned Roman room was surely one of the glories of the period. An inner ring of marble Corinthian columns supported a richly modelled cornice and a deeply coffered, coved ceiling lit by a domed skylight, while the wall behind the colonnade was modelled with tabernacles and swags in high relief.

Although no other savings bank approached the Bowery in size or magnificence, a number of architects sought to echo its Classical splendor at a reduced scale. Robertson & Potter's New York Savings Bank on Ninth Avenue had a small bronze dome atop a chaste temple, a combination Schuyler found "not . . . so successful, because here the consecrated forms had to be adapted to practical requirements."[153] Helmle & Huberty's Greenpoint Savings Bank (1908) at Manhattan Avenue and Culver Street in Brooklyn achieved a more successful synthesis of a Doric temple front with a low dome of Guastavino structural title, enlivened on its inner surface by an intricate pattern in terra cotta and green.[154]

In his design for the Union Square Savings Bank (1907) at 20 Union Square, on the northeast corner of East Fifteenth Street, Henry Bacon adapted the robust Classicism and general *parti* of McKim's Knickerbocker Trust Company to a small corner site.[155] Four lushly modelled Corinthian columns supporting a cornice and balustrade formed a porch facing the square, while along Fifteenth Street pilasters alternated with tall windows.[156]

Mowbray & Uffinger's Dime Savings Bank in Brooklyn came closest to the splendor of White's vision.[157] Completed in 1907, the building occupied a triangular site on the northeast corner of Fleet Street at De Kalb Avenue. A dense, Ionic colonnaded screen on the exterior supported a simple dentilated cornice, chamfered at the corner to form the principal entrance. Within, a splendid hall beneath a low, leaded glass dome, though well detailed and built of fine materials, lacked the lushness of White's prototype.

In 1899 the Franklin Savings Bank held a competition for a new building to be built at the southeast corner of Forty-second Street and Eighth Avenue. Mowbray & Uffinger's unsuccessful entry attempted the type of synthesis between Roman precedent and Modern French detail that White hinted at in his Bowery Savings Bank, and Richard Morris Hunt achieved more explicitly in his Fifth Avenue facade for the Metropolitan Museum of Art.[158] Paired Ionic columns supported a cornice and attic, above which sat a small low dome on a drum. Triple windows set within arches lit the banking hall within. York & Sawyer's winning scheme (1899) further refined the synthesis.[159] A rusticated, temple-fronted strong box, it had triple windows

Bowery Bank, 130 Bowery. McKim, Mead & White, 1902. View from corner of Grand and Elizabeth streets. OMH

Bowery Bank, 130 Bowery. McKim, Mead & White, 1902. Banking Room. OMH

Bowery Bank. McKim, Mead & White, 1902. Banking Room. MCNY

National Park Bank, 214 Broadway. Donn Barber, 1904. Broadway facade. MCNY

punctuated with Ionic columns flanking the front door on Eighth Avenue and tapered Ionic pilasters along Forty-second Street. A grand Roman hall inside was roofed with a coffered, barrel vaulted ceiling carried on flattened piers.[160]

The increasing density of the financial district at the turn of the century had the ironic side effect of rekindling the economic viability of low, purpose-built commercial bank buildings. In order to maintain high rents, owners of tall office buildings were forced to buy adjacent lots to ensure adequate light and air for their tenants, and they were anxious to develop these mid-block sites with low buildings as a buffer against nearby skyscrapers.[161] The increasing verticality of the cityscape also tended to diminish the symbolic impact of the tall building. Schuyler observed in 1905 that "Altitude throughout the history of architecture has been a mark of pretentiousness," but that the situation was now reversed, and "a comparatively low building may on that very account be a comparatively 'swell' building."[162] As the *Real Estate Record and Guide* put it, the decision of a bank or newspaper to erect a low building exclusively for its own use "seems to convert the commercial enterprise into a public institution."[163]

C. L.W. Eidlitz's Liberty National Bank at 137 Broadway, a three-story bank building wedged within a twenty-five-foot-wide light court formed between two buildings, was an early, awkward example of this evolving genre.[164] Liberty National illustrated the crucial problem of the type: not only was it low, but its individual parts were smaller in scale than those of the neighboring skyscrapers.

De Lemos & Cordes's Speyer & Company (1901–03), was a larger facility located at 24–26 Pine Street.[165] Its three-story height ensured light and air to any adjacent building for years to come, a situation which Kean, Van Cortlandt & Company immediately capitalized on by constructing a tall building next door. According to A.C. David, De Lemos & Cordes's palazzo-like facade held "its own amid its exalted neighbors, and by a certain legitimacy of bearing without becoming either aggressively sumptuous or superfluously ornate."[166] Inside, its casually furnished, double height, top-lit banking hall revealed an almost domestic clutter that probably would never have been tolerated had Speyer & Company not been a private bank rarely visited by the general public.

Even more domestic in tone was Kirby, Petit & Green's four-story building for the Bush Terminal Company (1905) at Broad, Pearl and Bridge streets.[167] At the request of the client, Irving T. Bush, it was a Gothic design with a strong flavor of the Dutch architecture which had characterized the area when Manhattan was first settled. The reappearance of the Dutch style in the financial district prompted the *Real Estate Record and Guide* to nostalgically muse "How fine it would be if the whole section could be rebuilt in the same style."[168] Kirby, Petit & Green combined white granite and terra cotta, red and blue brick, and a red slate roof in a design that contrasted strongly in scale and character with the characteristically Classical work of the period.

Carrère & Hastings's Chubb Building (1899–1900) on South William Street was more stylistically advanced.[169] Though commissioned by an insurance company rather than a banking house, it belonged to the group of low, monumental buildings constructed in the financial district at the end of the century. A tautly detailed, brick box trimmed in limestone, it was one of the firm's most rigorous and restrained essays in the Modern French style. The fenestration expressed the plan: small rectangular windows on the first floor corresponded to office cubicles, while the open workroom on the second story, housing a cadre of clerks, was flooded with light by tall windows grouped on the South William Street facade. Carrère & Hastings made extensive use of exposed metal work at the Chubb Building, using paired colonnettes to support the decorated I-beams that spanned the second-floor window openings and pressed sheet metal lozenges tacked on to the cornice.

The National Park Bank on Broadway, Ann and Fulton streets was the largest and grandest of the monumental commercial bank buildings.[170] Donn Barber's Modern French design was one of the most inventive of any public building in New York. Abandoning the use of the orders, which had become the almost ubiquitous symbol of institutional dignity for bank buildings, Barber devised a tripartite division of the facades, with a colossally scaled arched opening flanked by battered, rusticated piers. The facades

National Park Bank, 214 Broadway. Donn Barber, 1904. Banking Room. NYHS

Chemical National Bank, 80 Chambers Street. Trowbridge & Livingston, 1907. Chambers Street facade. MCNY

Thirty-fourth Street National Bank, 305 West Thirty-fourth Street. Hiss & Weekes, 1905. CU

achieved a grandiose scale on the street and expressed the vaulted banking hall within. The arch was scarcely modelled except for a concave quadrant, a typical Modern French substitute for traditional moldings. Above the Broadway arch an attic stretched between bold cartouches, its mini-colonnade creating lively shadows and enhancing the arch's sense of lift.

The interior of the banking room was breathtaking. Albert Herter's murals depicting *Agriculture, Commerce* and *Industry* were but grace notes to what Schuyler termed a "noble apartment."[171] A stained-glass dome marked the crossing of the two axes of the T-shaped room, the arms of which were spanned by coffered barrel vaults suggesting a Renaissance church rather than a modern bank. Bronze and marble were intricately detailed to create a particularly rich effect, further enhanced by the lattice soffits and perforated webs of the exposed iron arches. The exquisitely decorated structure of the dome was ultimately derived from Labrouste's two libraries in Paris, and revealed to Schuyler "what an artist may do with modern engineering construction."[172] The National Park Bank was Barber's triumph and a worthy successor to Stanford White's work at the Bowery. "In spite of the reminiscence it affords," Schuyler wrote, "this work is of an unmistakable modernity.... So much of its effectiveness comes from the evidence it bears of being 'the real thing.'"[173]

Trowbridge & Livingston approached the difficult mid-block site of the Chemical National Bank with a strategy similar to White's at the Bowery Savings.[174] The lot was T-shaped, with frontages on Broadway and Chambers Street. The Broadway facade was a narrow, orthodoxly Classical temple front which led to a vestibule, a vaulted corridor and a spacious, lofty cruciform banking room with a more generous frontage on Chambers Street. The banking room was crowned by a metal and glass dome carried on pendentives. Most unusually, the interior forms were revealed on the Chambers Street facade. The metal skins of the vaults and dome rose behind a colonnaded stone wall, a highly innovative synthesis of Classical form and technological progressivism.

Trowbridge & Livingston also designed the headquarters of J.P. Morgan & Co. at Broad and Wall streets, the last of the Composite Era's great banking monuments in the financial district.[175] Completed in 1913 on the eve of World War I, its simplified Classicism was a perfect expression of the public persona of the highly independent capitalist who had dominated American finance and artistic patronage for twenty-five years. The architects were faced with a difficult site, an irregular pentagon with one reentrant angle and a requirement that the main entrance be placed at the acute angle formed by Wall and Broad streets. Moreover the site was so small that the architects were not allowed to waste any space in order to create a symmetrical banking room. The exterior was kept very severe, with windows deeply set in unornamented reveals. The atmosphere of the thirty-foot-high banking room was gentler. Within its necessarily peculiar shape, an exquisitely detailed marble and bronze screen wall defined the bank's hexagonal public area, dominated by a domed skylight overhead in the coffered ceiling. Trowbridge & Livingston kept the articulation of the walls to a minimum, alternating panels of marble with softly tinted mosaic arabesques depicting various industries.

After 1900 the commercial banks began to establish branch offices in the growing uptown business district and, later, in the smaller business districts which served the needs of residential neighborhoods throughout the consolidated city. Small neighborhood banks also abounded, and while these two types typically had small, mid-block sites, they were designed to be taken seriously as pillars of the community.

Donn Barber's Mutual Bank (1911) at 49 West Thirty-third Street combined the amplitude of the Speyer Building with the self-important Classicism of C.L.W. Eidlitz's Liberty Bank.[176] Barber composed a three-bay facade with engaged Ionic columns which suggested an entrance portico. The entrance was subtly emphasized by a wider intercolumnation; the arch of the doorway was correspondingly slightly larger than the windows which flanked it, thus infusing the monumental scheme with a surprisingly gentle and receptive air. Inside, a severely Roman atrium-like hall was lit from above by a flat skylight.[177]

Many of the branches, such as Harrie T. Lindeberg's

Knickerbocker Trust Company, northwest corner of Fifth Avenue and Thirty-fourth Street. McKim, Mead & White, 1902-04. CU

American Bank Note Company, 70 Broad Street. Kirby, Petit & Green, 1908. NYHS

Corn Exchange Bank on the south side of East Eighty-sixth Street between Lexington and Park avenues,[178] or his Bronx branch for the same bank,[179] presented dignified white marble facades with an icy elegance seemingly intended to contrast with the more rough and tumble buildings of the neighborhood. In each of his designs, Lindeberg substituted a Palladian window for the grander columns and pediments of the downtown banks, keeping the facade planar in Manhattan, while carrying the arch on Doric columns and setting back the doors and over-window to form a welcoming porch in the Bronx.

By 1910 a new hybrid type of bank building emerged with a ground-floor banking room and a superstructure of offices frequently reserved for the bank's exclusive use. Typically five to eight stories high, these buildings combined the symbolic identity of a low, monumental facility such as the Bowery Savings Bank with the increased efficiency and economic viability of a tall building. Hiss & Weekes's Thirty-fourth Street National Bank (1905) was an early example of the new hybrid.[180] Squeezed between brownstones on a typical twenty-five-foot lot, it provided a large hall at the back of the lot which contained the bank's activities. A block of offices, entered separately from the street, filled the front of the site and maintained the cornice line of the neighboring brownstones. The facade was based on a French Renaissance frontispiece, with a somewhat confused superimposition of orders. Renwick, Aspinwall & Tucker's Provident Loan Society of New York (1908) at the northwest corner of Twenty-fifth Street and Fourth Avenue[181] and McKim, Mead & White's five-story Second National Bank (1908) at the corner of Fifth Avenue and Twenty-eighth Street both provided rentable office space above the banking room, each referring to the palazzos of the great Italian Renaissance banking families as an appropriate prototype.[182]

McKim, Mead & White's Knickerbocker Trust Company has already been mentioned as an incomplete thirteen-story office building.[183] Ironically, Stanford White's design for its four-story base, the only portion completed, was as seminal for later bank buildings as his Bowery Savings Bank had been a decade earlier; the Knickerbocker Trust offered a cogent, consolidated expression of a single institution that was widely adapted for hybrid type bank buildings. Schuyler dubbed the Knickerbocker Bank a "Modern Classic," praising the consistency and clarity with which White allied a colossal columnar order with the building's actual vertical structure. Along the narrower Fifth Avenue frontage, four columns supported the cornice to form a shallow porch; along Thirty-fourth Street six pilasters provided less convincing visual support. A screen wall of glass and iron set behind the order flooded the robustly detailed interiors with light, "merging windows and wall together in one dark pattern of metal and glass between the marble columns."[184]

Kirby, Petit & Green's American Bank Note Company (1908) at 70 Broad Street and Joseph H. Freedlander's Importers' and Traders' National Bank (1908) at Broadway and Murray Street adapted the same formula to taller buildings, suppressing the expression of individual floors in favor of a monumental order of pilasters or columns framing a glass and metal infill. The site of the American Bank Note Company on a small block in the oldest section of the city was exposed to the street on three sides.[185] The tripartite organization of the facades presented a rusticated basement, three-story mid-section and a fully inhabitable attic above a cornice. At the entrance on Broad Street, a medallion surmounted by an eagle emphasized the centrally located door. Above that two Corinthian columns *in antis* rose three floors to the cornice, indicating the location of the principal work rooms of the company, while the attic contained executive offices and a private dining room.

The Importers' and Traders' National Bank had a small site facing City Hall Park which it had occupied since 1861.[186] Its decision to remain meant that the bank had to build upward, revolutionizing the traditional arrangement whereby clerks and executives conducted all their business within the banking room (while the Importers' and Traders' National Bank was a commercial bank, the American Bank Note Company was in the business of printing stock certificates and was only tangentially related to the realm of banking). Freedlander distributed the different functions on five floors, placing the director's office on the fifth and holding the sixth for future expansion. Services were clus-

Importers' and Traders' National Bank, southwest corner of Broadway and Murray Street. Joseph H. Freedlander, 1908. View from the northeast. MCNY

National City Bank, Wall Street to Exchange Place between William and Hanover streets. McKim, Mead & White, 1907. Perspective view from Wall Street. The lower arcade was built by Isaih Rogers in 1836–41. CU

tered together at the rear of the building to provide as much uninterrupted space as possible in the twenty-five-by-one-hundred-foot lot. The interiors were lavishly decorated in the Modern French style, but it was the severe grandeur of the white marble facades—which had four-story-high engaged Corinthian columns on the front and pilasters along the side, set on a rusticated base and rising to an elaborate cornice and balustrade—that give the bank a composite image necessary to reinforce its self-conception as a rock-solid institution.

In their Guaranty Trust Company at 140 Broadway York & Sawyer approached the hybrid type of bank and office building in a different way, clearly expressing the banking room.[187] Although only four floors of offices were superimposed on the banking room, the building was monumentally scaled, the equivalent of ten floors of the neighboring office building. The banking room was treated as a masonry building, with Ionic columns creating recessed porches between massive corner piers. Above an intermediary floor, the architects banded the office windows together vertically in a cage of metal and glass which seemed to slide behind an order of pilasters.

The headquarters of the National City Bank at 55 Wall Street, between William and Hanover streets, was the most unusual example of the hybrid type. It was a renovation and addition to Isaiah Rogers's Merchants' Exchange, a masterpiece of the Greek Revival and one of the "most costly and pretentious buildings . . . within . . . the United States" when it opened in 1841.[188] The original building was converted to the United States Custom House in 1863, but it was threatened with destruction when the federal government moved to Cass Gilbert's new Custom House on Bowling Green. Splendid though the building was, its four stories were too few to ensure an adequate rent roll, and its imposing Ionic colonnade was too weak to support the weight of an office tower that might have been built above.

The decision of National City Bank's president James Stillman to acquire the building was a major contribution to the preservation of the rapidly dwindling stock of historic buildings in lower Manhattan.[189] In 1901 he retained McKim, Mead & White to explore the possibility of building a skyscraper on top of the historic structure, but they later merely doubled its size by adding a superstructure as high as the building itself.[190]

The problem was a daunting one: to respectfully add to a building so complete in itself, and to create a new banking room the full size of the existing facility. While the *Architectural Record* was initially critical of McKim's decision to superimpose a Corinthian arcade above Rogers's Ionic order characterizing it as "rather an evasion than a solution," it was nonetheless grateful for the preservation of the old building and "obliged to the architects for working the least interference with the dignity of the old structure, and for giving an example of equal dignity in the new."[191]

McKim was most successful in the interior, where he transformed the original rotunda into a sixty-foot-high, cruciform banking hall with offices concealed on mezzanine floors in the corner piers. The hall featured a Corinthian order supporting a pilastered frieze executed in a soft gray monotone and was dominated by the flood of light which poured through the central oculus. The splendor of McKim's banking room, bolstered by sentiment on his behalf when illness forced his retirement from practice, won the critics over. Most importantly, the project was valued as an act of preservation and as the most fully developed expression of the commercial sector's willingness to embrace the era's artistic ideals. "While it was a proud day in the earlier life of the city of New York when the Merchants' Exchange opened its doors in 1841," the *Architectural Record* was moved to observe, "the day when the National City Bank shifted its scene of operations to the present larger and worthier edifice should be notable not only in the history of America's greatest banking institution, but should be equally remembered by New Yorkers and Americans as an occasion by which we have enriched our country by a monument worthy of our commercial enterprise."[192]

Banks were the most widespread and most public financial monuments in the Composite Era, but a number of key regulatory institutions also undertook to memorialize themselves at the turn of the century. The New York Clearing House Association, also known as the Associated Banks,

National City Bank, Wall Street to Exchange Place between William and Hanover streets. McKim, Mead & White, 1907. Banking Room. CU

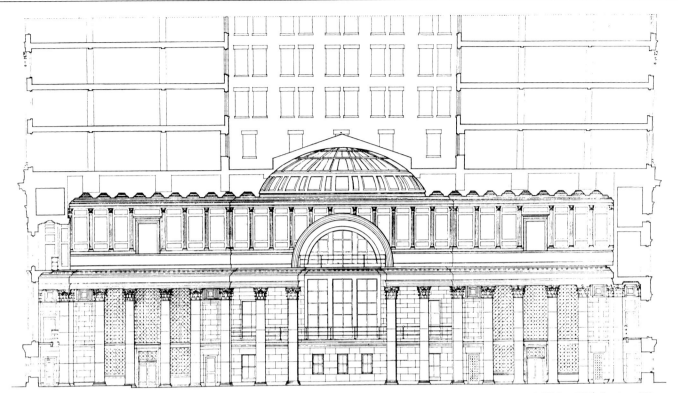

National City Bank, south side of Wall Street to Exchange Place between William and Hanover streets. McKim, Mead & White, 1907. Section. CU

was established in 1853 to facilitate the exchange of drafts on member banks.[193] In 1893 the New York Clearing House held a competition for a headquarters to be built on the north side of Cedar Street between Broadway and Nassau Street. Ernest Flagg's proposal was surprisingly restrained, displaying few of his characteristic neo-Grec or Modern French tendencies.[194] Flagg raised an Ionic temple front to the third floor, below a tall attic with paired pilasters supporting rooftop statuary, where it expressed neither the location of the great trading hall at the top nor the suite of meeting rooms on the second floor. Robert W. Gibson's winning proposal, built in 1894-96, took full advantage of the relatively isolated site.[195] A cruciform mass, the Clearing House was embellished along Cedar Street by a colossal Corinthian order supporting a high attic which contained the clearing room, lit by a dome set high on an octagonal drum. As the Classicist Henry Hope Reed has written, "Here was the architecture of Venice in all its opulence, more particularly that of the buildings of the 'Scuole' or religious guilds. Jewel boxes on small sites, they advertised the wealth and power of the members."[196]

After many years of discussion, the New York Stock Exchange decided in 1899 to rebuild the headquarters it had occupied on Broad Street since 1865. As the pioneering publicist Ivy Lee observed, the new headquarters "would be both monumental architecturally and equipped with every device that mechanics, electricity or ingenuity could supply, with every resource needed to transact the security trading for the commercial center of the world."[197] A competition was held, with a brief organized by Professor William Robert Ware of Columbia University and Charles W. Clinton of Clinton & Russell.

Heins & LaFarge's proposal was a mannered, fragmented essay in Classicism. Robert W. Gibson's design was grander, with a palatial board room better suited to casino gambling than the speculative adventures of the securities market.[198] The commission was won by George Post who offered a contrastingly powerful, consolidated image for the complex program of the Exchange, which included the principal board room for trading stocks, a smaller room for trading bonds, banking facilities, a suite for the Board of Governors, lounges and dining rooms for members and safe deposit vaults.[199]

The Broad Street facade was a boldly scaled hexastyle

Chamber of Commerce of the State of New York, northwest corner of Liberty Street and Liberty Place. James B. Baker, 1901. NYHS

Chamber of Commerce of the State of New York, northwest corner of Liberty Street and Liberty Place. James B. Baker, 1901. Chamber. MCNY

New York Clearing House, 77 Cedar Street. Robert W. Gibson, 1894–96. NYHS

temple portico set between two *antae* raised above the street. Fifty-two-foot-high Corinthian columns screened a continuous wall of glass, and a bold sculptural group in the pediment, designed by John Quincy Adams Ward and executed by Paul Wayland Bartlett, gave the Stock Exchange an air of magisterial calm as it presided over the financial world's most important intersection. Originally, the temple front was to express the location of the trading room on the second floor, so that the street level could be leased to a revenue-producing commercial bank. But the governors rethought this feature, which they feared would hamper the brokers' freedom of movement in times of panic, and reserved the ground floor for their own use.

Too much admired to be abandoned when the trading floor was lowered, the pediment and the glazed column screen were retained, thereby creating a stage-set quality not originally intended. To compensate for the seeming contradiction between plan, section and facade, Post treated the lower walls of the board room as a base for colossal Corinthian pilasters which echoed the columnar order of the facade. The pilasters, in turn, supported deep beams spanning the room to form coffers, the central one of which was top lit.

Appropriately, in 1900, the world of commerce set out to build two monuments to itself, a stock exchange of truly imperial swagger and a chamber of commerce, as richly ornamented as a jewel box. The New York Chamber of Commerce had been founded in 1768, but had never had its own building. Designed by James B. Baker, the Chamber was built in 1901 on the site of the former Real Estate Exchange at 65 Liberty Street, between Broadway and Nassau Street.[200] The arrangement of the facade permitted the location of a bank on the ground floor while a side entrance gave members access to a large vestibule where elevators and a monumental stairway led up to the main room or Chamber, as it is correctly called, the generous proportions and sumptuous detailing of which made it one of New York's greatest interior spaces. It measured sixty by ninety feet, and was covered by an extraordinary gilded and panelled ceiling with a skylight at its center fifty feet above the Chamber's floor.

The exterior of the Chamber, in some ways the nearest thing in New York to Charles Garnier's Paris Opera, was lavishly embellished with ornamental detail, emphasizing

R.H. Macy & Company, west side of Broadway between Thirty-fourth and Thirty-fifth streets. De Lemos & Cordes, 1901. A view which shows, to the right, McKim, Mead & White's *Herald* Building (1893). NYHS

such features as the oval windows that illuminated the interior of the Chamber. Four sculptural groups by Daniel Chester French—one of which depicted De Witt Clinton flanked by a crouched worker with a shovel representing his support of the Erie Canal and a female figure with fasces and orb representing Clinton's career in government—were placed at the top of the base between two of the six rhythmically disposed Ionic columns that represented the big room on the facade.

Stores

All America goes to New York for its shopping, when it can.... Humanity enjoys seeing the products of mankind, and the shops of New York, the resplendent lines of retail stores ... are always fascinating, alluring, irresistible.... The brightness of Broadway, the vivacity of lower Fifth Avenue, the sparkle of 23rd Street, are made up of the splendid temptations of the shop windows, and the groups of charming people who linger about them spell-bound.... What are the Paris boulevards, or even Regent Street, to this magnificent panorama of mercantile display? Moses King, *King's Handbook of New York City* (Boston: Moses King, 1893; New York: Benjamin Blom, 1972), 843.

The development of the department store was one of the hallmarks of New York's Metropolitan Age. The department store's encyclopedic collection of goods was aimed at luring women shoppers of all strata of society, but the significance of the new stores—popularly known as Big Stores—went far beyond greater efficiency of retailing. The Big Store was the archetypal symbol of the era's bourgeois culture and a prime force in the democratization of luxury. In the fluid society of the times, it gave apparel and household articles a new significance in defining social status, a trend accelerated by the department stores' invention of the fashion cycle. Women were increasingly becoming the directors of family consumption, but the department store, which typically included fountains, skylit rotundas, restaurants, nurseries, ticket booths, art galleries and theaters, reflected the transformation of shopping from a simple chore into a social and recreational activity indulged in for hours at a time as a respite from the confines of housekeeping and child-bearing. Gordon Selfridge, who opened a department store in London after gaining experience in America, observed of the Big Store's customers: "You know why

Siegel Cooper, east side of Sixth Avenue between Eighteenth and Nineteenth streets. De Lemos & Cordes, 1896. View from northwest with the Sixth Avenue El in the foreground. MCNY

they come here? It's so much brighter than their homes. This is not a shop—it's a community center."[201]

The era of the Big Store began when A.T. Stewart, the merchant who pioneered one-price, cash-only retail shopping, opened his palatial white marble building at Broadway and Chambers Street in 1848.[202] Stewart was a Scot who had arrived in New York in the 1820s, opening a dry-goods store on lower Broadway that measured a mere twelve by thirty feet. Stewart's reputation with his customers rested on the politeness and helpfulness of service; long after he had become a millionaire he continued to greet wealthy clients personally and to tour the selling floors to answer customers' complaints. Stewart's new "Marble Palace" was described by Philip Hone, the city's former mayor, as "spacious and magnificent beyond anything of the kind in the New World, or the old either."[203] Although Stewart set the monumental standard for later department stores, he was a more astute merchandiser than real estate visionary. The northward flow of the city's population was already in progress by the latter half of the nineteenth century, and in 1862 Stewart had to relocate his vast emporium. The new store, "a chaste and airy edifice of iron" filling the entire block between Broadway and Fourth Avenue, Ninth and Tenth streets, was designed by Stewart's favorite architect, John Kellum. Perhaps the first freestanding building erected as a modern department store, it boasted eight floors of two and one-half acres each, graced by an elegant rotunda that focused activity and introduced natural light into the heart of the building. But Stewart's move was again short-sighted; he failed to anticipate that many of the large and popular dry-goods businesses which appealed to a cost-conscious clientele would expand and relocate above Fourteenth Street along Sixth Avenue, a more central location made easily accessible to shoppers by the opening of the elevated railway in 1878, while the typical upper-class specialty dry-goods store of the post–Civil War era would locate along Ladies Mile, a stretch of Broadway extending from Stewart's at Astor Place northward to Madison Square.[204] The stores of Ladies Mile, such as Lord & Taylor at Broadway and Twentieth Street, designed by James H. Giles in 1869, were largely characterless loft spaces sheathed in pretentious cast-iron facades.[205]

The popular department stores of the Composite Era were more elaborate than those on Ladies Mile: vast Classical palaces, they were often clad in marble or granite with carefully designed interiors offering innumerable amenities. The Stern Brothers' store designed by William Schickel in 1893 was relatively modest in comparison to later Big Stores, its untutored Classicism more a reflection of the eclectic cast-iron architecture of the 1870s than an augur of the American Renaissance.[206] But its location at 32-46 West Twenty-third Street marked the first stage of yet another northern migration of the city's mercantile center. Stern Brothers' was the beginning of the end for Ladies Mile and also for Twenty-third Street's cachet as a fashionable residential quarter.

Most of the popular emporia were built along Sixth Avenue. In the 1890s the Siegel Cooper, Adams Dry Goods, Simpson Crawford and R.H. Macy companies all built monumental headquarters on prominent sites with continuous frontages on at least two and often three streets.[207] Their new accommodations were so vast that they contributed to the swift financial collapse of all of the stores except Macy's, the only one to continue operations after World War I. The arrival in New York of Siegel Cooper & Company, a Chicago firm, "stirred up the department storekeepers of New York to make their buildings as convenient as possible for a class of trade so intricate and enormous."[208] Siegel Cooper's was located on a full blockfront along Sixth Avenue and extended 460 feet down Eighteenth and Nineteenth streets. Designed in 1896 by De Lemos & Cordes, a firm that dominated New York's mercantile architecture in the 1890s, its size and amenities set the tone for a new scale of retailing enterprise and a new sense of the department store as a civic monument. Siegel Cooper's seemingly brought with it from Chicago a taste of the World's Columbian Exposition, transporting to New York the festive Classicism of its facades and an eighteen-foot-tall copy of Daniel Chester French's sculpture, *The Republic*. The original had dominated the Court of Honor at the Chicago Fair; its replica stood in the center of a fountain which marked the crossing of the store's two principal axes. "Meet me at the fountain" became a byword for one of the Composite Era's great meeting places. One could spend the day shopping, attending promotional yet edifying lectures and concerts, dining or having tea; as the store's advertisements proclaimed, it was "A City In Itself."

Simpson, Crawford & Company followed Siegel Cooper's example by locating on Sixth Avenue between Nineteenth and Twentieth streets in 1900.[209] Designed by William H. Hume & Son, the store's grim facades offered little hint of the delicate François I mode of its central glazed courtyard. It was De Lemos & Cordes's Adams Dry Goods Company (1900) and the firm's larger and more elaborate building for R.H. Macy & Company (1901) that established the Big Store as a type soon emulated in major American cities and in London. Adams & Company, as the store was popularly known, was located on the west side of Sixth Avenue between Twenty-first and Twenty-second streets.[210] Its Modern French ornament, rooftop pennants and tripods promised stylish goods and a grand occasion within. The boldly scaled entrances invited the pedestrian inside, while an engaged colonnade was raised high on the facade to announce the store to passengers on the elevated railroad. At the center, a glazed light well treated as a Court of Honor rose four floors through the building.

R.H. Macy & Company made the dramatic leap from Fourteenth Street to Thirty-fourth Street in 1901.[211] According to the *Architectural Record,* De Lemos & Cordes's design for the nine-story building stretched the Big Store to "the limit of useful and profitable height."[212] As a result, they had to develop sophisticated strategies to isolate potential fires and transport people swiftly and safely from floor to floor. Macy's red brick and limestone facades were a departure from De Lemos & Cordes's previous work and the overblown Classicism that had become the widely accepted standard for department stores. Despite sculptor J. Massey Rhind's heroic caryatids on the Thirty-fourth Street facade, the materials—the English Palladian details, the delicately modelled ornament of the store windows, canopy, clock, and in particular the stacked bay windows overlooking Broadway—gave the building a character closer to that of a great hotel than a store.

To compensate for the store's inability to buy the property at the busy Thirty-fourth Street corner, De Lemos & Cordes cut an open arcade lined with display windows between Broadway and Thirty-fourth Street, providing a short-cut through the block and further exposing the store's merchandise to public view. As was customary in department stores, restaurants were located on the less accessible top floor, so as to not take away valuable space from the more lucrative dry-goods sales and to minimize the smell of cooking in the selling areas. Macy's rooftop was designed for recreation, with a sixty-by-two-hundred-foot glass cover for exhibitions and special events.

While Macy's pioneered the move of retail trade to midtown, one last major department store was built on Ladies Mile in 1906, intended to capitalize on the construction of the subway under Fourth Avenue and the McAdoo Tunnels to New Jersey. John Wanamaker, a retailer from Philadelphia who acquired A.T. Stewart's store at Broadway and Ninth Street, built a new fourteen-story annex designed by D.H. Burnham & Company of Chicago on the block between Eighth and Ninth streets and Broadway and Fourth Avenue.[213] Wanamaker's annex had little of the bravura of the Sixth Avenue stores; a sober, Italianate design similar to Burnham's Marshall Field & Company store in Chicago, it resembled a warehouse more than a palace. The high ceilings and carefully crafted display cabinets inside set a tone of dignified elegance made more emphatic by a rotunda modelled on the one in the former Stewart store, but modified by tier upon tier of arches carried up eight floors to a domed skylight. Four more floors of offices and workshops were located above. On the second floor, a full auditorium provided space for public events featuring the organs and pianos in which the store specialized.

Gimbel's, another Philadelphia store, entered the New York market in 1911 with a store on Herald Square designed by Burnham.[214] At first glance the store seemed to belong to the genre of the Big Store, yet its interior revealed none of the special excitement of its predecessors. Gimbel's chief distinction was the remarkable speed of its construction, more a testimony to the pragmatism of the Era of Convenience which it helped usher in than to the enlightened aestheticism of the Composite Era.

The age of Big Store construction closed in 1913 with Stern Brothers' move from West Twenty-third Street to West Forty-second Street.[215] Though the location opposite Bryant Park was prominent and reflected the widespread

B. Altman & Company, east side of Fifth Avenue between Thirty-fourth and Thirty-fifth streets. Trowbridge & Livingston, 1906. MCNY

B. Altman & Company, east side of Fifth Avenue between Thirty-fourth and Thirty-fifth streets. Trowbridge & Livingston, 1906. Fifth Avenue entrance. MCNY

Windsor Arcade, east side of Fifth Avenue between Forty-sixth and Forty-seventh streets. Charles Berg, 1901. View from the southwest. NYHS

belief that West Forty-second Street would soon rival West Thirty-fourth Street as a shopping street, the store was too isolated from the popular shopping district at Herald Square and the smart shops along Fifth Avenue. The new store was designed by John B. Snook's firm, better known for its work in cast iron thirty years earlier. Its pilastered facade, a sober backdrop to the New York Public Library across the street, had a generously proportioned, simply lit vestibule at the main entrance which set the tone for the high ceilinged, well-lit and exceptionally open selling floors. A broad iron and glass canopy marked the carriage and automobile entrance on West Forty-third Street and deferred to that street's modest scale.

In the first decade of the twentieth century the various large specialty stores which still clustered along Ladies Mile moved northward. One of the first and most dramatic moves was B. Altman & Company in 1906 from Sixth Avenue between Eighteenth and Nineteenth streets into new, monumental headquarters at Fifth Avenue between Thirty-fourth and Thirty-fifth streets, diagonally across from the Waldorf-Astoria Hotel.[216] Designed in segments by Trowbridge & Livingston until the store filled the entire block in 1913, Altman's building was imposing and severe, an eight-story limestone palazzo distinguished by a glazed rotunda set within the building mass. Trowbridge & Livingston provided abundant display windows without sacrificing the image of monumental strength. In the *Architectural Record,* A.C. David praised Altman's "appearance of a fashionable store without any suggestion of mere ostentation."[217]

Benjamin Altman was the first to realize Fifth Avenue's potential as a shopping street for both the middle *and* upper classes, and also the first major retailer to move his store above Thirty-fourth Street: the new store set the stage for Fifth Avenue's transformation into the city's most prestigious shopping street. "The indirect effects . . . will . . . be still more considerable than the store itself," the *Real Estate Record and Guide* noted in 1904.

The peculiar importance of the Altman project consists in the fact that it is the first big store of a general character which has moved into middle Fifth Avenue. . . . A store such as this finds its customers among the whole mass of well-to-do people. The range and numbers of its frequenters is smaller . . . than that of

Tiffany & Company, southeast corner of Fifth Avenue and Thirty-seventh Street. McKim, Mead & White, 1906. View from the northwest. CU

Lord & Taylor, northwest corner of Fifth Avenue and Thirty-eighth Street. Starrett & Van Vleck, 1914. Wedgewood Room. MCNY

a department store.... Hitherto Fifth Avenue has been crowded not only with carriages; but with such stores as Altman's ... its sidewalks will become overflowing with foot-passengers as well as with footmen.... Broadway was and is crowded; but it was always too miscellaneous to be distinguished. Fifth Avenue is consistent and it is fashionable. It will contain nothing but hotels and shops—the most expensive in the city; and it will constitute the center of the distinctively metropolitan life of the metropolis—the life which is different from that which is to be found in any foreign capital or any other American city.[218]

Altman's was followed to Fifth Avenue by far less distinguished buildings, among them Hale and & Rogers's Renaissance style headquarters for James McCreery[219] and J.B. Snook's stiffly monumental store for W. & J. Sloane & Company at Fifth Avenue and Forty-seventh Street.[220] The completion of Sloane's in 1912 marked the furthest point to date of the northward expansion of the retail palaces, although the site itself, one half of the former Windsor Arcade, was not new to commerce.

The short-lived Windsor Arcade had been one of the grandest retail buildings ever constructed in the city.[221] Commissioned in 1901 to replace the Windsor Hotel after its destruction by fire, the Arcade was designed by Charles Berg as a temporary structure, a "taxpayer" housing art galleries, bookstores and other high quality, small scale retail establishments. The *Real Estate Record and Guide* felt that "the Windsor Arcade sums up and typifies this whole movement [uptown], and one can best describe what Fifth Avenue has become by sketching what the Arcade is and what it stands for.... Both the architecture and the arrangement of the Windsor Arcade makes one think of its prototypes on certain Paris boulevards. The design is smart, ornate and attractive—just conspicuous enough to advertise the popular purposes of the building, but not so conspicuous as to be vulgar and obtrusive."[222]

Lord & Taylor was the last of the large, elegant dry-goods emporia to locate on Fifth Avenue before the First World War.[223] While by no means as opulent or ambitious a project as Altman's, its ten-story building at the northwest corner of Thirty-eighth Street, designed by Starrett & Van Vleck, was more delicately scaled, with finely detailed display windows and a strong projecting cornice. The vaguely Italian Renaissance character of the design permit-

Abercrombie & Fitch, northwest corner of Madison Avenue and Forty-fifth Street. Starrett & Van Vleck, 1917. View of rooftop log cabin. CU

ted a simplified handling of the walls: the primary accents were the occasional balconies, a two-story pilaster screen at the top, and a chamfered corner which gave the building an image of solidity and became its most memorable feature.

Lord & Taylor marked the emergence of a more utilitarian and less artistically ambitious phase of specialty-store design, one characteristic of the shift from the monumentality of the Composite Era to the more pragmatic attitudes of the Era of Convenience. Typical of this type were LaFarge & Morris's Brooks Brothers (1917) at Forty-fourth Street and Madison Avenue[224] and Starrett & Van Vleck's Abercrombie & Fitch (1917) at Forty-fifth Street and Madison Avenue.[225] Abercrombie's dedication to the outdoor life led to a particularly inspired use of the roof, where shoppers could practice their fly-casting into a special water tank and test various kinds of sporting equipment. A twenty-by-fifty-foot log cabin with a wood-burning fireplace, perched on the roof, served as an office for northwoods guides to meet and arrange trips for would-be campers.

The emerging elegance of Fifth Avenue attracted jewelers and booksellers as well as department stores. Merchandisers expanded beyond over-the-counter retail sales into the manufacture of their own goods and needed facilities that combined the two functions. Stanford White's buildings for Tiffany & Company, at the southeast corner of Thirty-seventh Street and Fifth Avenue, and Gorham Company, one block south at the southwest corner of Thirty-sixth Street, were complex, mixed-use structures cloaked in unified exteriors.[226] C. Matlack Price reported in the *Architectural Record* that their example set off "a wave of ambitious alteration and construction from Madison Square to the Plaza."[227] T.P. O'Connor, an Anglo-Irish writer, observed that Tiffany's and Altman's "were palaces for the *magnifico* who ruled an Italian city and state in medieval times rather than a mere shop where the ordinary citizen or his wife could go and haggle about their wares."[228]

The Thirty-seventh Street location was the fifth site Tiffany's had occupied since the business was founded at 259 Broadway in 1837.[229] Completed in 1906, the store was modelled on the Palazzo Grimani in Venice. White camouflaged the building's seven stories with three tiers of paired Corinthian columns which inflated its scale and imposed a composite image on the hybrid program. The grandeur of the facades was carried into the showroom interior. The ceiling of the main floor was supported by gray Formosa marble Ionic columns, and the casework was fabricated of close-grained Philippine teak inlaid with steel and brass. As an afterthought, White provided on the top floor a vast hall used for exhibitions. Spanned by Guastavino tile arches and lit from above by a sixty-foot-long elliptical skylight, it was an elegant and spartan antidote to the opulence of the main hall at street level. White also designed a small garage for Tiffany's at 141 East Forty-first Street, with a brick and limestone facade that deferred to the residential character of the neighborhood.[230]

The Gorham Building was less dramatic than Tiffany's, with a traditional division into base, shaft and capital that lent it a gentler scale than Tiffany's unbroken column screen.[231] The main floor had Guastavino tile arches sheathed in delicate plaster reliefs resting on banded Ionic columns. Overall the building had an appropriately lighter and less opulent character than Tiffany's, suitable for Gorham's specialization in silver and gold. Tiffany's, though it included these among its wares, focused on diamonds and other gems.

Hill & Stout's Venetian Gothic palazzo for Wetzel & Company (1905), the gentleman's tailor at 2-4 East Forty-fourth Street, had some of the air of a private club but was notably exotic.[232] The choice of style was an act of deference to Leopold Eidlitz's Temple Emanu-El across the street rather than a reflection of the business within. A dressmaker's salon (ca. 1907) on Forty-sixth Street was conversely intended to be both elegant and familiar to its clientele. Warren & Wetmore employed a restrained Georgian Classicism that was unusual for the firm. "It would hold its own in Mayfair" as an elegant ornament, Swales felt, "but is not in any sense as typical of American shop-architecture as we should like it to be."[233]

A.C. David noted in 1907 that although the dry-goods and jewelry palaces of the first decade of the century lingered "in the minds of visitors to New York, and constitute a sort of selected and glorified vision of the thoroughfare,"[234]

Wetzel & Company, 2-4 East Forty-fourth Street. Hill & Stout, 1905. MCNY

Gorham Company, southwest corner of Fifth Avenue and Thirty-sixth Street. McKim, Mead & White, 1905. CU

Gorham Company, southwest corner of Fifth Avenue and Thirty-sixth Street. McKim, Mead & White, 1905. Salesroom. CU

they were only the principal monuments of the new Fifth Avenue, setting the tone for a host of more modest establishments that filled the interstices. Many of these new establishments were located in brownstones haphazardly renovated for commercial purposes.[235] The public's concern over the commercialization of the Avenue caused speculators and shopkeepers to make special efforts not to offend their clients, many of whom continued to live on the Avenue and in the neighboring side streets. Architects were often called on to design modest projects that would never have been given serious aesthetic consideration in other parts of the city. Shop owners selling furniture, pictures and rare books were particularly sensitive to the impression that their establishments made on the changing streetscape. H.F. Huber's workshop in a townhouse at 382 Fifth Avenue designed by James E. Ware & Son in 1904[236] and Duryea & Potter's showrooms at 463-67 Fifth Avenue were early exemplars of a commercial style that restated the elegance of a great palazzo at a modest, townhouse scale.[237] Alfred Taylor's conversion at 53 West Thirty-third Street was an even more ambitious, Classicizing design, with a bold scale comparable to contemporary work of McKim and others in the Billionaire District.[238] Robert D. Kohn's Modern French design for Theodore Kohn's jewelry store at 321 Fifth Avenue was a brownstone dramatically converted to a new scale by means of a bold composition and brilliant white stonework which contrasted sharply with the neighboring brownstones.[239] The design of individual small store fronts also received increasing attention. Delano & Aldrich's design for a store on East Thirty-second Street had French iron work which introduced a note of refinement that characterized the best store design in the second decade of the new century.[240]

By 1907 the first phase of Fifth Avenue's transformation was complete. What had been a quiet avenue of important residences punctuated by hotels and restaurants was now a great shopping boulevard. "The transformation of Fifth Avenue between 26th and 50th Streets, in a very real way symbolizes the transformation which has been taking place in the whole city of New York," A.C. David observed. "Since 1901 New York has become all the more distinguished among American cities for the concentration which has taken place therein, of wealth and business."[241] And Fifth Avenue, he felt, "has become the only American street

Schumann's Sons, 716 Fifth Avenue. Maynicke & Franke, 1909. MCNY

Black, Starr & Frost Company, southwest corner of Fifth Avenue and Forty-eighth Street. Carrère & Hastings, 1912. MCNY

devoted for over a mile of its length exclusively to retail trade of a high class which has taken on a specific character."[242] Like the Waldorf-Astoria Hotel, the fulcrum about which the new activity was balanced, Fifth Avenue provided "exclusiveness . . . for the masses, and the wonder is that the masses can pay the price. One gets the impression on Fifth Avenue that all the world is there, that all the world has more money than it needs, and that all the world rather likes to exhibit its superfluity."[243]

Tiffany's and Gorham's set the standard but not the tone for the smaller and in some ways even more lavish commercial palazzos which proliferated on the Avenue in the years between 1907 and the First World War. The most notable of these was the building Carrère & Hastings designed for Black, Starr & Frost at Forty-eighth Street.[244] The facades epitomized the tone of a great number of high-class specialty stores which eschewed the monumentality of Tiffany's for an understated, precious refinement. Although Black, Starr & Frost was only five stories tall, Carrère & Hastings's organization of the facades and their expression of the nonstructural decorative skin were indebted to the firm's contemporary United States Rubber Building. They captured the character of a jeweller's store, however, with delicate Italian Mannerist decoration.

Warren & Wetmore's building for Dreicer & Company (1907) at Fifth Avenue and Forty-sixth Street was slightly less imposing than Black, Starr & Frost's.[245] Black marble, enriched with brass Corinthian capitals on the ground floor, wood panelling and crystal produced an elegant interior. The use of Louis XV commodes and tables specially fitted with glass tops to display goods was an innovative replacement for more conventional casework.

Warren & Wetmore's store for Theodore B. Starr, Inc. (1911) in the lower two stories of an office building was delicately scaled, particularly in the light Adamesque interior similar to the firm's Ritz-Carlton Hotel a block away at Madison Avenue.[246] Maynicke & Franke's jewelry store for Schumann's Sons at 716 Fifth Avenue ended the century's first decade with an exuberant flourish. C. Matlack Price described it in the *Architectural Record* as "thoroughly French, from its flamboyant glass marquee to its twin terminal urns—a facade replete with those delightful architectural fantasia of which the keynote is irresponsibility and gaiety."[247]

The palazzo style was also adopted by art dealers who had earlier found more modestly "artistic" quarters in converted brownstones, but who now seemed intent on rivalling the imperial taste of their patrons. Carrère & Hastings's new building for M. Knoedler & Company at 556 Fifth Avenue, adjacent to the Dreicer Building, was perhaps the most discretely domestic example of the type.[248] In contrast, Duveen Brothers was the grandest art emporium in the city.[249] Located on the northwest corner of Fifth Avenue and Fifty-sixth Street, it was designed in 1911 by the architect Rene Sargent in association with Horace Trumbauer. A rusticated base on the narrow Fifth Avenue front supported an engaged temple front with high attic and mansard roof above, giving the building the character of a public institution.

Other retailers continued the palazzo tradition, none more elegantly than the Hardman Peck Company piano salesroom on Fifth Avenue designed by Harry Allan Jacobs in 1911.[250] A delicate, arcaded, second-floor loggia made a sensitive transition from the masonry wall above to the ground-floor showroom window. The interiors captured the flavor of a fashionable townhouse, exhibiting the company's wares in the sort of luxurious domestic setting for which they were intended.

Pressure mounted in the early 1900s for even further expansion of the shopping district above Forty-seventh Street. In 1907 A.S. Gottlieb designed a store for Cartier's at 712 Fifth Avenue, between Fifty-fifth and Fifty-sixth streets,[251] and soon after, in 1908, one of the houses of Marble Row was converted into a store and bachelor apartments.[252] Ernest Flagg's office building and store for Charles Scribner's Sons (1913) on Fifth Avenue between Forty-seventh and Forty-eighth streets[253] replaced Flagg's earlier headquarters for the firm at 153–157 Fifth Avenue,[254] completed just nineteen years before—sure testimony to the rapid march of commerce to upper Fifth Avenue.

Francis Swales found the first Scribner's "one of the earliest" of the small shop buildings "to possess any archi-

Scribner Building, 597 Fifth Avenue. Ernest Flagg, 1913. CU

Scribner Building, 153–57 Fifth Avenue. Ernest Flagg, 1894. OMH

tectural merit" and felt that "it would not be out of place in the Rue de la Paix."

It was one of the first to express an idea as to the proper treatment of a masonry front in which great holes must be made for light, and the largest of these holes in the ground story. At either end of the shop-front, entrances to the upper floors are arranged in pylon-like masses of stonework, pierced with windows of contrasting proportions of height to width. The fourth floor is treated as a deep frieze, while the horizontal value of the first story gives the impression of a truss spanning the shop-front, satisfies the eye if not the intellect as to strength, and has the appearance of transmitting the load placed upon it by the two piers between the second and third floor windows to the pylons of masonry at the side.[255]

The curved glass and iron marquee further compensated for the unresolved downward thrust of the masonry as it was transmitted to iron columns on the ground floor.

The new Scribner's Building went even further toward a frank expression of its nonload-bearing construction. Its facade was dominated by its two-story, extensively glazed store front. Flagg divided the lower floors of the facade into three bays, making the end two (one leading to the office building lobby, the other including a show window) quite narrow, and a center bay with a broad, flattened arch opening into the store. Flagg continued the three bays inside, terminating the vaulted, two-story central nave in a broad flight of steps that gave access to two mezzanine-level balconies. The bulk of the facade was executed in cast iron and glass, with two slender, banded Corinthian columns raised on high bases, helping to lift the broad architrave and a decorative banner announcing the Scribner name.

Henry Otis Chapman's adjoining buildings for Hoffstatter & Frères at the southwest corner of Fifty-third Street and Fifth Avenue pursued a Gothic line in deference to the Vanderbilt house next door and St. Thomas across the way. Chapman's Joseph Building and McKim, Mead & White's Ruszits Building at 7 East Forty-eighth Street pursued more familiar Classical themes. If the architects' efforts to inflate the typical rowhouses model to six or seven floors seemed forced, the stores were, nonetheless, observed in the *Brickbuilder* as "a commendable deference to architectural order almost without precedent in New York."[256]

Aymar Embury II summarized the situation in 1916:

The shopkeepers, in general, seem to realize that it is almost impossible to show enough of their goods in their windows to explain very fully the purposes of their shops, and they have endeavored to impress the buying public of the character of their shops by the architecture and general artistic handling of the building, using that as an index or expression of purpose of the goods within. This has definitely caused builders of the retail shop buildings to seek out good architects and good designs, so that the shop architects of New York have received an impetus apparent nowhere else in the world and which is bound to carry shop design very far.[257]

By 1917, however, the era of both the Big Store and the retail palazzo was drawing to a close, and with it that of Fifth Avenue between Thirty-fourth and Forty-seventh streets as an exclusive shopping street. Midtown Fifth Avenue's transformation into a middle-class shopping street, anticipated by Altman's in 1906, was fully realized in 1917 by the Woolworth Company's construction of an office building and retail store at the northeast corner of Fortieth Street.[258]

Madison Square Garden, northeast corner of Madison Square at Madison Avenue and Twenty-sixth Street. McKim, Mead & White, 1890. Roof Garden. CU

Palaces of Pleasure

Walk through the brightest regions of Upper New York, in the early evening, as their places of amusement open, as the garlands of fire bloom out upon Diana's Tower, as the great hotels and restaurants and theatres blaze their invitations in streams of golden light across the sidewalks, as luxurious carriages and well-tended horses fill the street, as the doors of one mansion and another swing back with the promise of dainty dining, and through the chinks of the curtains of countless quiet homes come rays like those of Christmas stars: if this is the only New York you see, and if you do not peer below the surface of some of its most glittering or most innocent-appearing spots, it may well amuse and please you: you may well admire the progress, the material development of the last twenty years, and praise our taste and civilization, our public spirit, our gaiety, hospitality, and kindness.

Marianna Griswold van Rensselaer, "People in New York," Century 49 (February 1895): 534-48

Theaters New York is identified with the image of the Great White Way, a glistening, scintillating night world that is a fairy-tale counterpart to its Babylon of skyscrapers. The glories of the Great White Way, which achieved almost mythic stature in Hollywood musicals of the 1930s, were a turn-of-the-century phenomenon.

The theaters of New York's Cosmopolitan Era were largely clustered along the Rialto—a stretch of Broadway between Fourteenth and Twenty-third streets which connected a rapidly fading center of fashion, Union Square, with the briefly ascendant Madison Square. Lit by gas, poorly ventilated, their exits largely unregulated by building codes, the theaters of the Rialto were prone to a series of disastrous fires in the 1880s. When rebuilt, they followed fashion northward, first hovering around Thirty-eighth Street before finally centering themselves near Long-acre Square (renamed Times Square in 1904 when the *New York Times* completed its tower at Forty-second Street and Broadway). The new theaters were safer than the old, primarily because they were lit by the electric light bulb, which architects soon discovered could unlock an almost limitless potential for advertisement and nighttime decor. The result, widely recognized by 1910, was the transformation of Broadway into the Great White Way.[1]

The establishment of the theater district reflected a new synthesis in the city's social makeup which embodied the concept of the melting pot. The Great White Way was patronized by two strands of society: an oligarchy of descendants of the monopolists who founded the city's great fortunes, and an increasingly dominant upper-middle class. The first group was gradually abandoning the ostentatious private social events so important to their parents' social stature and was often found seeking their pleasures outside the home. The second was partially drawn from first generation Americans of middle-European descent, and was effectively barred from the established clubs and the prestigious tiers of boxes at the opera house.

This synthesis was already evident by 1893, when the architect John B. McElfatrick replanned the Metropolitan Opera House after a catastrophic fire. Ten years earlier, the opera house had been built to provide box seats for the *nouxeaux riches* unable to acquire them at the lions' den of New York's old aristocracy, the Academy of Music on Fourteenth Street. The Academy quickly fell victim to the competition, and its company and audience consolidated with the Metropolitan. Even so, there were too few millionaires to fill three tiers of boxes, while there was an increasing demand for less expensive seats. McElfatrick removed one tier of boxes and added row seating to increase capacity.[2]

The new role of the middle class in patronizing theatres was most emphatically foreshadowed, however, by the opening of Stanford White's Madison Square Garden in 1890. Conceived by such prominent figures as Hiram Hitchcock, J. Pierpont Morgan, Andrew Carnegie, and White himself as a setting for the annual horse shows of the exclusive Equestrian Society, the Garden was intended as a pleasure palace for the oligarchy of wealth which considered a box at the opera and attendance at Wallack's Theater to be the twin badges of acceptance in the stratosphere of society. But such an elitist conception was doomed to financial failure, for the limited audience could not support the Garden's vast amphitheater. White, himself a shareholder, was soon put to devising spectacles for a popular crowd, and designed recreations of Shakespeare's house, the Globe Theatre, Goethe's House in Weimar, Dickens's Old Curiosity Shop, and a toy town for children modelled on old Nuremberg.[3] The Garden became the natural home of large-scale popular entertainments, inheriting the heterogeneous clientele of the first Madison Square Garden (converted by P.T. Barnum in 1873 from Commodore Vanderbilt's train sheds). It "appeared in answer to a genuine need, an oft repeated popular demand," Marianna Griswold van Rensselaer said.[4] The regular exterior, so unexpressive of the complex spaces within, reflected the coming of the Composite Era, yet the Garden's dominant feature, a tower evocative of the Giralda in Seville, looked back to the more romantic mood of the Cosmopolitan Era.

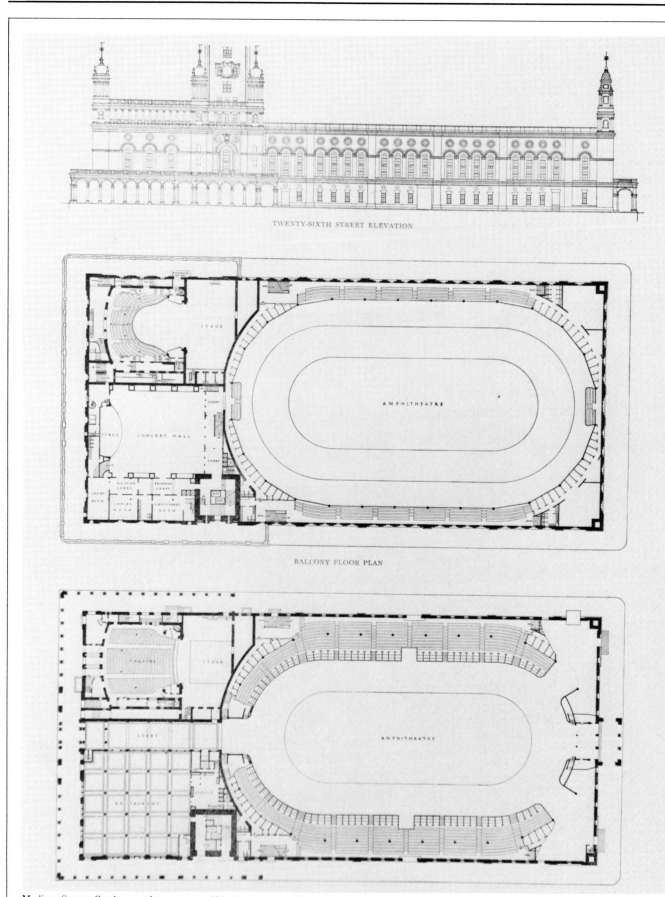

Madison Square Garden, northeast corner of Madison Square at Madison Avenue and Twenty-sixth Street. McKim, Mead & White, 1890. Plans of ground floor and balcony level. CU

Madison Square Garden, northeast corner of Madison Square at Madison Avenue and Twenty-sixth Street. McKim, Mead & White, 1890. Madison Avenue elevation. CU

Madison Square Garden, northeast corner of Madison Square at Madison Avenue and Twenty-sixth Street. McKim, Mead & White, 1890. Detail of arcade. CU

The theaters of the Metropolitan Age were characterized by two basic design strategies. The first was represented by the mute facades of Abbey's Theater at Thirty-eighth Street and Broadway and the Empire Theater on Broadway near Fortieth Street, both designed by John B. McElfatrick & Son.[5] The auditorium in each of these theaters, typical of the type, was concealed behind a conventional building that frequently housed the offices of the entrepreneurial manager and his staff. The Empire was also typical of many theaters in the Times Square area because its Broadway facade led only to a passageway to the auditorium; in order to save money, the main body of the theater was on a side street. Consequently, their mute facades relied almost exclusively on their marquees and playbills to convince the public of the drama and spectacle within.

The second design strategy treated the entire facade as a billboard advertising in permanent form the character of the transient delights and attractions within. This latter approach was glorified by the dominant theater architects of the period: Francis H. Kimball and Herts & Tallant. Kimball was a transitional figure whose work expressed the themes of the Cosmopolitan as well as the Composite Era. He came to New York in 1879 and formed a partnership with Thomas Wisedell to remodel the Madison Square Theater. This project was followed at once by Harrigan & Hart's, a red brick and terra-cotta essay in the Queen Anne style which Montgomery Schuyler found notable for its "air of domesticity and quaintness" and its expression of a "comfortable bourgeoisie."[6]

In 1882, Kimball & Wisedell designed the Casino, a theater with an exotic, individualistic, even hedonistic character that exemplified the values of the Cosmopolitan Era. The theater was built as a concert hall, but it found its destiny as the city's temple of light opera and burlesque. On its stage, the three Casino Girls beguiled young millionaires, Lillian Russell first captivated New York, and the Floradora sextet pranced, treated by the most dashing *bon vivants* to a ritual of public courtship. The common fate of the Floradora Girls—each, including the fabled Evelyn Nesbit, eventually married a millionaire—perfectly realized the myth of New York as the City of Opportunity.

The Casino's architecture ideally mirrored its function as a respectable seraglio at a public scale. Picturesquely

Casino Theater, southeast corner of Broadway and Thirty-ninth Street. Kimball & Wisedell, 1882. View from Broadway. MCNY

massed—a symmetrical unit on Broadway housed the stage, the swinging arc of the Thirty-ninth Street front expressed the auditorium behind, and a tower punctuated the Broadway corner—the Casino was a brilliant exception to the monotony of the brownstone cityscape. Its facades were covered in an eclectic mixture of Gothic and Islamic motifs, a synthesis described by Schuyler as "only an academic violation of the architectural unities."[7] The Casino was eventually cloaked in unsympathetic signs. Schuyler, commenting on their incongruity, found that the building's "degraded and vulgarized estate" provoked "not only weariness but resentment."[8]

Kimball's later designs were equally oblivious to the need to advertise a changing bill of fare, in part because several of the later theaters were built as the permanent home of a specific actor or one of the city's diminishing number of established stock companies; the performers rather than the repertory drew the audience. Kimball's New Fifth Avenue Theater of 1892, located on West Twenty-eighth Street near Broadway, and the 1891 Harrigan's Theater on Thirty-fifth Street between Fifth and Sixth avenues, both achieved the stature of public monuments.[9]

Their richly tapestried, eclectically Classicizing facades made them the city's first grand statements of the theater facade as billboard and conveyed a sense of personal showmanship within the taut, street-oriented urbanism of the Composite Era.

Harrigan's typified Kimball's work in the 1890s. The facade was vaguely reminiscent of a palazzo, and had a Classicizing symmetry which marked an abrupt change from the romantic exoticism of the Casino. A field of buff brick above a rather insubstantial base was striped with patterned bands of terra cotta and decorated by trophies around the windows, a second floor loggia, and an attic frieze sprouting a profusion of ornament. The frieze was perhaps Kimball's most brilliant stroke of decoration, a sinuously interlocking floral pattern entwining low relief portraits of Ned Harrigan in his most famous roles.

Most early attempts to incorporate electrical signs on theater facades lacked Kimball's architectural self-assurance. Oscar B. Hammerstein's Olympia Theater, built in 1895 on Broadway between Forty-fourth and Forty-fifth streets by John B. McElfatrick & Son, was the first of a series of buildings to emulate White's strategy at Madison

Olympia Theater, east side of Broadway between Forty-fourth and Forty-fifth streets. J.B. McElfatrick & Son, 1895. NYHS

Square Garden of housing a complex program within a compact shape.[10] The Olympia was the first theater located on Longacre Square and contained a theater, a concert hall, a restaurant and a glazed roof garden. Its electric sign gave more importance to Hammerstein's name than the theater's, reflecting the drawing power of the entrepreneur. Strung out in a long arch above the marquee, the sign tied together the complex's double entrance.

Save for its sign, the architecture of the Olympia failed to capture the delights offered within. In some respects, the building was positively grim, the clearest indication being the ill-conceived fire escapes that marred the building's sides. The facade was a colloquial restatement of Madison Square Garden that multiplied the parts such as the ground floor arcade and rooftop colonnade into a meaningless collage of detached elements lacking the specifically theatrical content—the story-telling cartouches—of Kimball's billboard theaters.

McElfatrick went on to design in 1904 a far tauter theatrical center, the Harlem Auditorium on 126th Street and Seventh Avenue. The complex contained a large theater, a restaurant, a cafe and a winter garden, and served as a social and cultural center for Harlem, a thriving neighborhood of largely German and German-Jewish descent. Its roof garden, used in summer for vaudeville and in winter as a ballroom, evoked the nostalgia of a German beer garden, and the private dining rooms were decorated as *rathskellers*, with heavy masculine color schemes and paintings of hunt scenes on the walls. The exterior eschewed the brilliant electrical displays of the Great White Way, considered inappropriate for a neighborhood theater. It proclaimed itself instead with a flurry of pennants on the roof, a temple-like glass and steel marquee and the word Auditorium permanently emblazoned on the frieze.[11]

The power and influence over a large audience exerted by theater owner-producers such as Hammerstein, David Belasco, Augustin Daly, Frederick Thompson, Florenz Ziegfeld and later the Shubert brothers made them the movie moguls of their day. Many of these theater impresarios were cultured, cosmopolitan men with a vast experience in many aspects of the performing arts. Some, like Hammerstein and Thompson, felt their skills extended to architecture and designed their own buildings. Frederick Thompson's New York Hippodrome, "the largest theatrical structure in the

New York Hippodrome, east side of Sixth Avenue between Forty-third and Forty-fourth streets. Frederic Thompson, 1905. NYHS

world," was meant to capture the most extravagant popular spectacles.[12] The name suggested Imperial Rome and its vulgar spectacles of life and death struggles between man and beast, and the "circus poster" style of decoration continued the imagery. The column capitals sprouted elephant heads, plaster horses galloped in the spandrels and live animals roamed in cages behind glass on the promenade level.

The Hippodrome carried the architectural use of electric lighting further than any other theater of the period, bringing to Manhattan the showmanship Thompson had earlier displayed at Coney Island's Luna Park. Its corner towers, modelled on Madison Square Garden's, supported glittering globes outlined in electric lights. Inside the auditorium the outlines of the dome were emphasized in bands of light. In addition, the stage, a vast apron projecting into the audience, boasted two circus rings. The entire apron could be lowered to the bottom of a water tank for naval pageants and aquatic displays. Annette Kellerman, the "million-dollar mermaid," would dive in and re-emerge, beguiling thousands in the process.

Hammerstein was the architect for the Manhattan Opera House built in 1907 on Thirty-fourth Street between Eighth and Ninth avenues.[13] The new opera house was intended to rival the Metropolitan, remedying its lack of back-stage facilities but continuing the process of democratization that had begun when the Metropolitan was set up in competition with the Academy of Music. It had fewer box seats than the Metropolitan, and interior decoration that catered to less patrician tastes with a fulsome, opulent display of plasterwork around the stage and proscenium boxes linked in giant aedicules with Modern French ornament. The exterior was contrastingly sober, a dignified temple of music eschewing all signs of commercial display.

The most distinguished theater architects of the Composite Era, the team of Henry B. Herts and Hugh Tallant, were more than any others responsible for transforming the side streets on either side of Broadway around Times Square into a glittering and festive world of theaters, an urban Coney Island. They created an original and seminal synthesis by combining the image of the theater as a public monument with that of the music hall. Drawing on the Modern French and Art Nouveau styles of the Paris boulevards, they achieved thoroughly integrated decorative pro-

New Amsterdam Theater, 214 West Forty-second Street. Herts & Tallant, 1903. Detail of entrance. NYHS

New Amsterdam Theater, 214 West Forty-second Street. Herts & Tallant, 1903. Smoking Room. MCNY

New Amsterdam Theater, 214 West Forty-second Street. Herts & Tallant, 1903. Auditorium. NYHS

grams. The effect was an un-Wagnerian *Gesamtkunstwerk;* rather than focusing attention exclusively on the stage, Herts & Tallant extended the atmosphere of the drama into the auditorium itself, enveloping the audience within a single, sensual experience.

The two partners were highly qualified to bring to New York a breath of the Parisian boulevard. Both were recent graduates of the Ecole des Beaux-Arts, familiar with the most up-to-the-minute thought in European design. Their original stylistic synthesis of European and American trends was justified, according to Abbott Halstead Moore, by the fact that "We are living in a period of transition such as never before occurred." Moore likened them to William Morris and Walter Crane, artists who "gave a fair and captivating form to the mood of their own time." The firm's refined work led Moore to speculate in 1904 that their office motto was *Le Beau C'est Le Vrai.*[14]

Herts & Tallant inaugurated their career in theaters in 1903 with two works of very different character—the New Amsterdam and Lyceum theaters. The New Amsterdam (on the south side of Forty-second Street, near Seventh Avenue) was immediately recognized as a rare New York manifestation of the Art Nouveau, but one that disdained the eccentricities of much of the French work and clung to a Classical grammar. The facade applied sinuous curves to a vast, compacted triumphal arch that fused the sculpture of George Gray Barnard (*Drama* enthroned, flanked by *Pierrot* and *Cupid,* a knight and a damsel) and a panoply of advertisements (an elaborate sign proclaiming the theater's name in Gothic script, with flanking cartouches below announcing the program for the day).[15] The iron and glass infill above the entrance suggested a bower within, and stated for the first time the theme of the interior decoration: the tea rose. The entire ensemble possessed the character of a poster, capturing the spirit of the light comedies offered inside.

In the auditorium itself, the flowing continuities of the Art Nouveau merged wall and ceiling in an encapsulation of space that anticipated the spatial theories of modernism. The tea rose was used everywhere as the basis for the decor—in stencil patterns, paintings, plaster work and wood carving—creating an atmosphere that was described as "picturesque, playful, teeming with movement and color."[16] The theater was the perfect stage set for the play with which it opened, *A Midsummer Night's Dream.*

Even as Herts & Tallant looked forward to future developments in architecture, they expressed a sense of continuity with the past in the underlying Classicism of their compositions and the intimations of the rococo in their decor. The elevator lobby, which gave access to the Aerial Theater above, was adorned with bas reliefs of scenes from classical drama, the foyer beyond with St. John Issing's scenes of old New York, and the tympanum at the end with an allegory of the present-day city, the word Progress written large above. The smoking room had sinuously intertwined ogee arches which merged into an oval dome and created a feeling of a heavy, Germanic medievalism which reflected the rising affluence of European-born Americans.

The Lyceum, also built in 1903, was the successor to a downtown theater known as the home of the drawing-room drama in New York. Although the new Lyceum was quite small and located on a side street (Forty-fifth Street near Times Square), the theater's facade made it New York's most monumental commercial theater. The grand conception of its Modern French front, with richly carved freestanding columns surmounted by flaming tripods and a boldly scaled glass and metal marquee outlined in lights, was designed to attract a "more cultured audience . . . and stand as a fitting frame for the conservative works of the most distinguished living dramatists."[17] The intimate auditorium and compressed foyers were decorated with a fulsome, almost over-ripe richness. The auditorium ceiling was deeply coffered and studded with lights, and the graceful curve of the proscenium tied together the enormous, domed hoods of the flanking boxes.

Herts & Tallant's most complex commission, however, was the Brooklyn Academy of Music, which they won in competition in 1904. The old academy building had been built in 1859 by Leopold Eidlitz and stood next to J.C. Cady and Henry Congdon's Brooklyn Academy of Design (1875) and across the street from the Mercantile Library (1867) by Peter B. Wight.[18] The picturesque Gothic Revival ensemble was a unique grouping of public buildings in the Cosmopolitan Era. As the center of local cultural life, the academy's destruction by fire in 1903 was a serious blow to Brooklyn's civic pride, particularly in light of the formerly independent city's recent consolidation and the recurrent fear that its individual identity would be subsumed by that of greater New York.

The new academy was a vastly more complex cultural center than any attempted in New York since Madison Square Garden. It contained an opera house, a theater, a lecture hall and offices for the Brooklyn Academy of Arts and Sciences—the building's prime tenant and sponsor of many of its activities. The building's separate functions were linked on the ground floor by a common lobby and above by a vast foyer adaptable for balls and banquets or promenades during intermissions.

Herts & Tallant's winning competition entry was a robust interpretation of Michelangelo's Campidoglio. But the facade was revised because of economic restrictions: the somber, monolithic mass relieved with sparkling terra-cotta polychromy that was built was an inventive reduction of the original scheme.[19] The academy's facades concealed the diversity of functions within, expressing a far different conception of a civic monument than its predecessor. It also avoided any hint of commercialism—the only sign was incorporated in the terra-cotta frieze.

The interiors of the Brooklyn Academy of Music were richly ornamented in plaster with tints of mauve, antique gold and ivory, and stencil patterns and murals by William DeLeftwich Dodge. Together they constituted a harmonious decorative ensemble that proffered a more evocative, sensual aspect than the trustees felt appropriate for the self proclaimed City of Churches. Herts was asked to clothe the nude plaster *putti* displayed on the Opera House ceiling, but when he protested in the Brooklyn newspapers a compromise was reached, and only those closest to the audience were altered.[20]

The partnership's most distinguished and comprehensive interior was the German Theater, a remodelling of the former Lenox Lyceum completed in 1908.[21] The theater's location on Madison Avenue near Fifty-ninth Street was unusual: away from the Broadway theater district but close to many clubs. The old Lenox Lyceum had an unusual polygonal plan, but the new theater did not require as much seating, and the extra space was given to a broad, spacious

Lyceum Theater, 149 West Forty-fifth Street. Herts & Tallant, 1903. MCNY

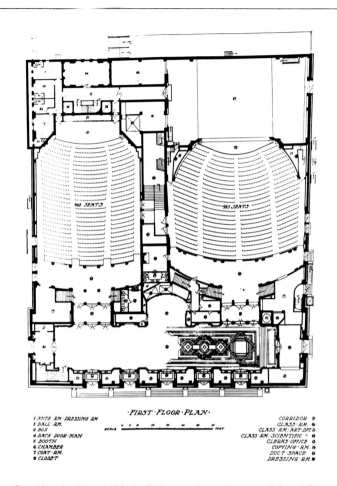

Brooklyn Academy of Music, Lafayette Avenue between Ashland Place and St. Felix Street, Brooklyn. Herts & Tallant, 1905-08. Plan of ground floor. MCNY

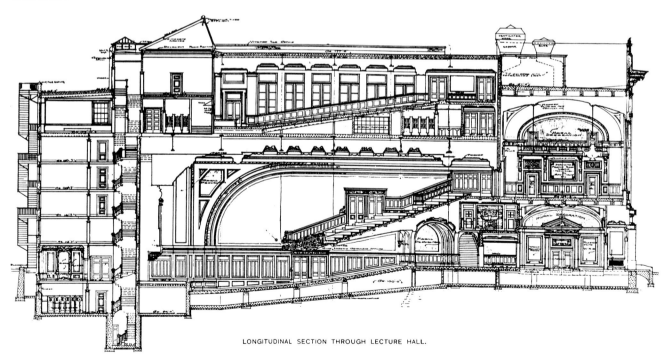

Brooklyn Academy of Music, Lafayette Avenue between Ashland Place and St. Felix Street, Brooklyn. Herts & Tallant, 1905-08. Longitudinal section through lecture hall. MCNY

Brooklyn Academy of Music, Lafayette Avenue between Ashland Place and St. Felix Street, Brooklyn. Herts & Tallant, 1905-08. NYHS

New German Theater, southeast corner of Madison Avenue and Fifty-ninth Street. Herts & Tallant, 1908. Auditorium. CU

New German Theater, southeast corner of Madison Avenue and Fifty-ninth Street. Herts & Tallant, 1908. Ladies' parlor. CU

promenade, a rare public amenity in New York theaters.

The German Theater's character was stamped by the collaboration of Herts & Tallant with Alphonse Mucha, the French Art Nouveau poster artist and muralist. The architectural forms of the auditorium were reduced to broad expanses of wall framed by flattened moldings that set off Mucha's stencil patterns and murals. The stencil patterns were generally based on abstracted plant forms, but medallions around the proscenium linked the German eagle with the American stars and stripes. Above the proscenium was Mucha's giant painting *The Quest for Beauty.* Flanking it were smaller representations of *The American Girl* and *The German Girl.* The symbolism captured the sense of the city's European immigrants and their descendants, suggesting that America was the inheritor of Western civilization and that its destiny was one they could increasingly participate in.

The ladies' parlors were extraordinarily sophisticated and virtually unique in New York as examples of the influence of the Glasgow School of Art Nouveau. Details such as bare electric light bulbs hanging from wire hoops, stencil patterns on the walls and curtains, segmental arches cut in thin planes of white-painted wood, and exposed tile surrounding the fireplace laid in a stack bond pattern were all integrated with custom-designed furniture.

Herts & Tallant's Gaiety Theater, built in 1908 on Forty-sixth Street just west of Broadway, restated the basic strategy of the facade at the Brooklyn Academy of Music. Triple arched openings set in an unadorned field of brick above a high base suggested a massiveness and grandness of scale which belied the theater's small size. The arches framed two stories of windows united by richly modelled terra-cotta tabernacles. But by following the prototypes of the Brooklyn Academy so closely, Herts & Tallant failed to incorporate signage into the Gaiety's compositional scheme, and its facade was soon obscured by a rude metal and glass marquee and an unsympathetic electric sign canted towards Broadway.[22]

The Folies Bergère, built in 1911 next to the Gaiety on Forty-sixth Street, was Herts & Tallant's clearest and most evocative statement of the facade as billboard and represented the culmination of their work. Save for the three arched doorways, the planar elevation was a blank wall tapestried in a Moorish pattern of ivory, gold and turquoise

Folies Bergère, 210 West Forty-sixth Street. Herts & Tallant, 1911. Proscenium arch. CU

Folies Bergère, 210 West Forty-sixth Street. Herts & Tallant, 1911. CU

terra cotta. The thin colonettes at the extremities of the facade suggested that the front was an abstraction of an honorific canopy carried in a triumphal procession, analogous to William DeLeftwich Dodge's heroic painted frieze depicting the *Triumph of Vaudeville*. Above the cornice, the pennants that so frequently fluttered above New York's palaces of amusement were translated into permanent fixtures as electric signs turned toward Broadway. The daily bill was announced by posters in oversized sentry boxes.

Except for the short-lived Koster & Bial's, the Folies Bergère was the first dinner-theater in New York. Its wide but shallow auditorium had all the interior arrangements of a theater, but the seating consisted of transverse rows of dinner tables, synthesizing the traditional music hall and the winter garden. The proscenium represented a garden trellis in *trompe l'oeil* perspective, with decoration which achieved a rococo preciousness in tones of mother-of-pearl, turquoise and antique gold, with salmon damask walls. Paintings by Dodge in the manner of Watteau to either side of the proscenium could be raised to reveal tiny auxiliary stages, heightening the magical spell of theatrical artifice.[23]

The Folies Bergère was Herts & Tallant's last major theater. They dissolved their partnership in 1911: Tallant joined the firm of Lord & Hewlett, while Herts continued on his own. In 1913, Herts built the Booth and the Shubert theaters, two separate buildings joined together and extending from Forty-fourth to Forty-fifth streets west of Broadway. Some of the brio and flamboyance that marked the firm's work seemed to have dissipated in Herts's solo efforts, yet the Booth and the Shubert were still exquisitely delicate essays in a simplified Italianate Mannerism.[24] By the time Herts completed the two theaters in 1913 the Great White Way had become a world of amusements, its streets so thronged with revellers that Herts had to provide a wide alley for carriage access, the legendary Shubert Alley.

Though Herts & Tallant were largely responsible for creating the character of the Broadway theater district, there were other projects attempting to transcend the commercialism of the day to create great cultural institutions. One such project was the New or Century Theater, the brainchild of a group of influential and wealthy New Yorkers including H.P. Whitney, H.R. Winthrop and Otto H. Kahn (who would later be involved in organizing the Metropolitan Square project to house the Metropolitan

Century Theater, Central Park West between Sixty-second and Sixty-third streets. Carrère & Hastings, 1906–09. View from Central Park West. NYHS

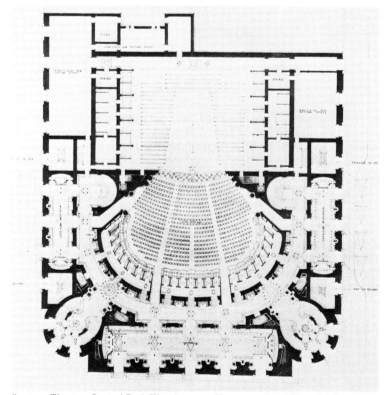
Century Theater, Central Park West between Sixty-second and Sixty-third streets. Carrère & Hastings, 1906–09. Plan of ground floor. CU

Opera).²⁵ They hoped to create an American equivalent of both Paris's *Opera Comique* and *Comedie Francaise,* to be supported not by ticket receipts or government subsidy, but by donations from public-spirited philanthropists like themselves. The venture constituted one of the most idealistic gestures of the American Renaissance, reflecting the genteel tradition that the public mind could be elevated through exposure to the most perfectly realized works of art.

Carrère & Hastings won the competition for the Century Theater. Opened in 1909, it was an overly monumental palace of the arts that was meant to compete in splendor with the public library and the city's great museums. The site was on Central Park West between Sixty-second and Sixty-third streets, next to Carrère & Hastings's and Robert Kohn's Ethical Culture Society, where a number of buildings formally and regally announced one's entry into the West End. The auditorium, modelled on the theater at Versailles, was richly marbled and gilded, its deeply coffered ceiling supported by columns so vast they dwarfed both audience and stage. A complicated system of monumental stairs and foyers, spiritual descendants of the public spaces of Garnier's Paris Opera, achieved an extravagance never possible in the tightly constricted lots of New York's commercial theaters.

Yet the Century, like Madison Square Garden, was doomed to financial failure, partly because the building's acoustics and sightlines were imperfect, partly because its elitist program of theatrical events failed to appeal to an increasingly democratic society, but most of all, because of the development of the city fabric. Fashion had firmly rooted on the East Side; Central Park West did not achieve its expected status as a second Fifth Avenue, and the park isolated the theater from much of its audience while its uptown location removed it from the fashionable hotels and restaurants.

Carrère & Hastings were also the architects of the Globe Theater, built in 1909 on West Forty-sixth Street. As in many theaters, the auditorium sat parallel to the sidestreet to allow larger backstage facilities. Carrère & Hastings deliberately masked the elevation's division into backstage and auditorium by stretching a stone facade across the entire streetfront. The taller backstage area was cloaked in brick; its diminutively scaled windows and the simplified details of its patterned brick frieze created the optical illusion that it lay far back from the street front. The facade itself was flanked by austere end pavilions. A high rusticated base supported an Ionic order of pilasters framing arched windows which gave access to a delicate wrought iron balcony overlooking the street. Between the pilasters the wall was completely obscured by cartouches and friezes in low relief. Despite its French compositional devices, the facade's decoration evoked an Italian Mannerist villa. Precious but relatively restrained, the Globe's facade eschewed signage to hint at, rather than proclaim, the frivolities within.²⁶

The era closed with a series of theaters which similarly avoided the aura of showmanship—small theaters, typified by Henry Miller's, Maxine Elliot's and the aptly named Little Theater—and sought a more private, genteel, even club-like atmosphere. In 1908 the great actress Maxine Elliott built her theater on Thirty-ninth Street, east of Broadway. The Chicago architects Marshall & Fox, Francophiles who built that city's most distinguished apartment houses with plans labelled in French, based its facade on the Petit Trianon at Versailles. An imposing monument despite its small size, the theater gingerly carried an electric sign at the very edge of its facade, while another, rented on Broadway, showed a hand pointing down the side street to Maxine Elliott's. The auditorium was in a subtly modelled, Louis XVI style, set for "only the highest and most refined type of modern comedy."²⁷

The reticence and refinement of Maxine Elliott's was even more characteristic of a genre of theaters suggestive of a clubbish or domestic environment. The Henry Miller Theater, designed in 1918 by Paul R. Allen and Harry Creighton Ingalls, had a discrete, Adamesque facade of warm brick and white marble with signs limited to quaint playbills crowned by broken pediments.²⁸ As in many New York theaters, the Henry Miller's axis ran parallel to the street, and the disposition of windows subtly conveyed the interior arrangement of offices in the mezzanine and the

American Theater, 644 Eighth Avenue. Charles Coolidge Haight, 1895. Roof Garden. MCNY

balcony above. The pedimented bays at either end in fact screened the alleyways required by the city building code as a precaution against fire. The interiors were still Adamesque but richer than the exterior. The panelled woodwork was painted in light, solid colors and antiqued to give an impression of age. The lounge evoked an English drawing room with an informal mixture of furniture, portraits, reading lamps and bibelots.

F. Burrall Hoffman's and Harry Creighton Ingalls's 1912 design for the Little Theater epitomized the trend for domestic imagery drawing on the Federal and Colonial periods, a movement in opposition to the theatrical palaces of the Great White Way.[29] The architects produced an elegant work for Winthrop Ames which suggested that Ames's patrons were "his guests for the nonce, in an old colonial house behind a garden wall, left behind in the march of progress, the simple front untouched and the interior remodelled by an amateur of the stage."[30] The use of carriage lamps, the disguise of the exits as a stable door, and potted plants on the terrace sustained the image of a great remodelled house. The facade was displayed at night by an integral lighting scheme which washed the surface with floodlights. The auditorium was perhaps unique in abandoning boxes and balconies for a single sloped floor of seats intimately focused on the stage. At intermission the guests retired to a tea room decorated as a private living room.

The bijou-like theaters of New York enjoyed only a brief heyday. The arrival in 1913 of the first Broadway theater built for motion pictures—Thomas Lamb's Strand Theater on Broadway and Forty-seventh Street—proclaimed the coming of age of a novel technology and the opening of a new era in theatre design.[31] The construction of legitimate theaters declined precipitously, as the period's architectural energies were spent on fabulous palaces for the movies, a mode of entertainment that would decentralize the Great White Way and contribute to the diffusion of the Metropolitan City.

Roof Gardens

In the days before air conditioning, theaters had to close during the heat of the New York summers, leaving theater owners with no profits, actors with no work, and glamor-seeking Gothamites and provincial tourists with little to do. But in 1882 the manager of the Casino Theater had the

Paradise Roof Garden, northwest corner of Seventh Avenue and Forty-second Street. Oscar Hammerstein, 1900. MCNY

inspired idea of starting an open-air theater on the roof of his building, thereby initiating a tradition of roof gardens that flourished until the 1920s, when Prohibition and air cooling combined to kill the idea.

The Casino Roof Garden was very simple—just tables and chairs, a few potted palms along the parapet, hanging lanterns, and a rag-tag orchestra that accompanied shrill-voiced chorines in the popular songs of the day. Its commercial success, however, prompted more elaborate versions. One of the earliest and best was on top of Madison Square Garden.[32] Perhaps best remembered because Harry K. Thaw shot Stanford White there in a dispute over the beautiful young Evelyn Nesbit, it was one of the most fashionable spots for New York's cafe society, composed of well-born young men of wealth who shunned their parents' elaborate entertainments for less formal evening pleasures frequently taken with women of great beauty but less "breeding."

The roof garden was surrounded by a colonnade of buff yellow brick and Pompeian white terra cotta punctuated by low towers. But it was the central tower, modelled after the Giralda in Seville, that "expressed perfectly the mood the Garden was intended to evoke, a mood demanding music,

dancing, parades of wooden soldiers, banners and the sounds of horses' hoofs."[33]

Other roof gardens were as exuberant as White's design, though rarely as tasteful. In 1900 Oscar Hammerstein opened the Paradise Roof Garden as an adjunct to his Victoria Theater at Forty-second Street and Seventh Avenue.[34] The Paradise was a theatrical extravaganza built like a stage set, with a liberal use of paint and canvas: in effect the stage performance spilled out onto the roof. The camera and the garish daylight gave a shabby air to the artificially rustic architecture and the dazed-looking sheep in the existing photographs, but the roof garden's combination of a soft starlit summer night, popular songs, a lively crowd, and, of course, food and drink must have provided a delightful and romantic escape from the city.

A light metal and glass roof covered a section of the Paradise, sheltering revelers from the rain. Later, at the Olympia, renamed the New York Theater, Hammerstein built another roof garden with a greenhouse-like cover that allowed year-round use—rain or shine, hot or cold.[35] He capitalized on the greenhouse effect by calling the roof garden the Cherry Blossom Grove, painting the steel

Astor Hotel, west side of Broadway between Forty-fourth and Forty-fifth streets. Clinton & Russell, 1904–09. Aerial perspective of Roof Garden. MCNY

framework green, using both natural and artificial plants, and combining decorative lights and painted landscapes to foster a theme of nature which was soon copied on other rooftops. Many, like Herts & Tallant's Aerial Theater on the top floor of the New Amsterdam Theater (1903), were so substantial that they could stay open year-round.[36] These more elaborate installations reduced to a minimum the differences between conventional theaters and rooftop gardens, but the price paid for this was usually a loss of that frivolous informality that had been the roof garden's special quality, particularly welcome in an era of starchy public occasions.

The most popular roof gardens were, like the Paradise or the American Roof Garden, a cross between a completely open roof and a permanently closed winter garden. As a result, according to a contemporary account, the connoisseurs, became "expert in the complicated draughtchart of the city . . . [and could] inform the curious, supposing it to be a torrid night, on which particular roof the sea or land breeze will be most refreshing; or on a cooler evening where ventilation is combined with protection; and at such times the program of the show is apt to be a secondary consideration."[37]

Just before World War I, managers such as Ziegfeld began to exploit the potential of the enclosed roofs during the winter months for late night, after theater entertainment (building laws did not permit the simultaneous operation of two theaters in one building), and showcased the leading talent of the day in a more intimate setting that permitted the audience to dine and explore the new, informal ballroom dancing being introduced by Irene and Vernon Castle. These rooftop entertainments were the precursors of the speakeasy night clubs that cafe society frequented during the Prohibition, when the inability to serve liquor legally denied the proprietors of these rooftop gardens their principal source of income.

Restaurants

As long as social life was dominated by the very rich, New York remained provincial, with entertainment largely confined to private homes or a handful of restaurants and hotels such as Delmonico's and the Hoffman House. However, the tremendous growth of the urban middle class in the Cosmopolitan Era brought with it a demand for more

restaurants. The most fashionable restaurants were on Fifth Avenue, while the gayest clustered around the theater district. Previously, only foreign restaurants had met daily needs, but the Composite Era saw the creation of the utilitarian and moderately priced American-style restaurant.

The fashionable Fifth Avenue restaurants imitated Delmonico's, New York's oldest. Founded in 1825 at the intersection of William and Beaver streets, Delmonico's had seven different locations over the years.[38] The Delmonico family tried two sites on Fifth Avenue before settling on a third: the first was at Fourteenth Street, the second at Twenty-sixth Street, and the third at Forty-fourth Street, in a building designed in 1897 by James Brown Lord, who four years earlier had built a new Delmonico's for men only at the original downtown site.[39] Delmonico's developed some competition in 1898, when Louis Sherry hired McKim, Mead & White to design an equally elegant restaurant on the opposite corner of Fifth Avenue and Forty-fourth Street.[40] Both had large main restaurants, private dining rooms, private suites for entertainment, ballrooms and "bachelor" apartments.

By 1884 the name Delmonico's had become synonomous with the mammoth dinner parties that epitomized the city's upper-class social life. A contributor to *Harper's Weekly* took a long backward glance that year: "Many persons who had been in the habit of regarding their dinners as a mere means of sustaining nature, and a scrupulous attention to dinner as unworthy of an earnest mind, learned for the first time at Delmonico's that dinner was not merely an ingestion, but an observance. . . . When we compare the commensalities of our country before the Delmonico period . . . with our condition in respect of dinner now, and think how large a share is due to Delmonico's, we shall not think it extravagant to call Delmonico's an agency of civilization."[41]

Sherry's continued in the same spirit, but with even more glitter. For two summers in the late 1880s Louis Sherry had worked as restaurant manager at the fashionable Hotel Elberon in New Jersey. His clients there promised to follow him if he went out on his own, and in 1890 he bought a private mansion on Fifth Avenue and Thirty-seventh Street and converted it to a restaurant. By the time he had prospered enough to hire Stanford White to design his twelve-story building on Forty-fourth Street he had also

Delmonico's, northeast corner of Fifth Avenue and Forty-fourth Street. James Brown Lord, 1897. View from Forty-fourth Street. NYHS

Sherry's, southwest corner of Fifth Avenue and Forty-fourth Street. McKim, Mead & White, 1898. Palm Room. OMH

stolen from Delmonico's a group known as the Patriarchs—twenty-five social figures picked by Ward McAllister to be the arbiters of his famous *400*. The most conservative members of society remained at Delmonico's, but the most ostentatious went to Sherry's. In 1903, C.K.G. Billings, heir to a Chicago utility fortune, gave a dinner for thirty-six guests mounted on horseback with a table and a champagne bucket hung on each horse. Two years later the architects Warren & Wetmore transformed Sherry's extravagant Louis XVI ballroom by planting a formal but temporary French garden reminiscent of Versailles for a dinner party given by James Hazen Hyde, the immensely wealthy heir to an insurance fortune.[42] The first dinner ball to be photographed, it was so costly and elaborate that gossip about the photographs forced the twenty-eight-year-old Hyde to resign from the directorates of forty-six major corporations and the vice-presidency of his family's Equitable Life Assurance Society. As a result of the scandal, most states enacted new laws governing insurance companies.

Stanford White complemented the ornate ballroom at Sherry's with a comparatively sober main restaurant panelled and pilastered in dark wood with gilt trim. An inventively original palm room was vaulted in latticework that gave an even lighter touch for less formal occasions. Suites of rooms upstairs allowed more private meals.

Other restaurants concentrated on Fifth Avenue also, like the Cafe Martin, in the former Delmonico's building on Twenty-sixth Street.[43] The most popular area for a night out on the town, however, was the theater district, where a different type of restaurant was found. While Louis Sherry and Ludivico Delmonico set out to rival the extraordinary opulence of some of their rich client's houses, they did so in a refined way, but many of the Broadway restaurateurs supplied the middle class with a taste of the splendor they could not find at home. Broadway's restaurants were as dramatic as the entertainments their patrons would later find at the theater. Theme restaurants were not uncommon—one of the most extraordinary was Murray's Roman Gardens, designed in 1907 by Henry Erkins.[44] The outside of the building, a remodelled public school originally designed by McKim, Mead & White, had a two-story imitation of the ancient *hôtel* of Cardinal de Rohan in Paris, which was enriched by the introduction of ornate niches filled with heroic-sized reproductions of allegorical and mythological

Sherry's, southwest corner of Fifth Avenue and Forty-fourth Street. McKim, Mead, & White, 1898. Palm Room. OMH

Murray's Roman Gardens, 228-32 West Forty-second Street. Henry Erkins, 1907. Main Dining Room. MCNY

Murray's Roman Gardens, 228-32 West Forty-second Street. Henry Erkins, 1907. Egyptian Dining Room. MCNY

figures, vines with decorative plants, and casts of classic sculptures from Paris. Inside, the fantasy was more distinctly Roman, although there were also Egyptian, Syrian, and Gothic motifs. The artificially lit atrium was the main dining room, intended to reproduce the garden of a villa in Pompeii, described as "the Newport of Rome."[45] Under a deep blue ceiling twinkling with electric stars, statues and victory trophies such as a Roman general might bring home with him on his return from his conquests were set among vines and bushes to further the garden effect.

The bulk of the city's popular restaurants featured European cuisine. Lüchow's was known for its fine German food and Wurzburger beer—"Down where the Wurzburger Flows" was a popular song about the restaurant—rather than its decor, which was comfortably Victorian. Founded in 1842 by Baron von Miehlbach, it was acquired in 1882 by August Lüchow, who turned it into one of the most fashionable restaurants of the Cosmopolitan Era. Because of its location at 110 East Fourteenth Street opposite Tammany Hall, it continued to function as an important dining place throughout the Composite Era long after fashion had moved further uptown.

Simpler foreign restaurants continued to be built and were lent distinction by their menu and their staff. Allaire's, on East Seventeenth Street, like the Hofbrau House at Broadway and Thirtieth Street,[46] had a German *bierhalle* band and rustic German furniture to go with its German food and waiters.[47] The two Mouquin's, one at Sixth Avenue and Twenty-eighth Street, and one downtown on Fulton Street, had French waiters, French musicians, French music, French decor and, of course, French food.[48] Eating there was often described as being like taking a trip to Paris. The Cafe Boulevard, at Second Avenue and Tenth Street, fed Hungarian food to over a thousand diners a day.[49] For only sixty cents, or a dollar on weekends, one could eat well while listening to a gypsy band. Whyte's Restaurant on Fulton Street, at the fringe of the downtown business district, was designed by Clinton & Russell in 1910 as a half-timbered English village inn.[50]

Childs, designed in 1900 by William Van Alen, later designer of the Chrysler Building, might be described as an American brasserie.[51] It was not a French cafe, a German *rathskeller,* or an English coffee house or tavern, but, by the opulent standards of the day, a simple restaurant where one

Childs, 47 East Forty-second Street. William Van Alen, 1900. MCNY

Lawyers' Club, 115 Broadway. Francis H. Kimball, 1912. Dining Room. CU

could eat comfortably without feeling extravagant. Childs, and other restaurants like it, were popular for white-collar lunches and dinners, or even simple midnight suppers after the theater. The decor of Childs was somewhat like a French brasserie with simple bentwood furniture, glistening floors of white mosaic tile, white marble wainscoting surmounted by mirrors, ceiling fans and simple pendant electroliers that became a standard for popular lunch rooms everywhere.

The Cafe Savarin was designed in 1915 by John J. Petit with a stripped-down, functional elegance that made it the epitome of this tradition.[52] A large restaurant that filled almost half the basement of the Equitable Building, the Cafe Savarin could seat a thousand diners in its three principal rooms. All three were finished with a blue, mat-glaze, six-inch tile, laid with continuous gray cement joints, and on the floor, light-gray, mat-glaze tiles laid within squares of dark gray bordering tiles with blue tiles at the intersections. Decorative faience plaques in low relief polychrome ornamented the rich blue piers relieving the monotony which might have resulted from the regular tile patterns, while a polychrome frieze incorporating the blue of the tile and the white of the plaster ceiling eased the transition from the wall. Bronze and opal glass cornices on the pillars and pilasters necessary for the structure coming down from above also served as indirect lighting that cast a pleasant diffused glow on the ceiling.

A restaurant at the top of the Equitable Building, the Bankers' Club, was a luncheon spot for the upper-middle-class businessmen no longer able to dine at their clubs, which had so often relocated uptown.[53] Although it was indeed a private club restricted to bank officers, its location in the heart of the banking district around Wall Street gave it a large and not particularly exclusive membership. Designed by the architect of the Equitable Building, Ernest R. Graham, and built in the same year, the Bankers' Club filled an entire floor of the enormous building with two dining rooms, a grill room, a lounge and service rooms. No other public rooms were needed, since the members only used the club for eating meals.

The Bankers' Club belonged to a type that the *Century* magazine termed "mid-air dining clubs."[54] Located in the tops of the downtown skyscrapers, they offered a convenient alternative to a restaurant for a Wall Street executive who wanted to entertain or eat alone near his office. The *Century* article illustrated the views of the Battery and New York harbor as seen from the different luncheon clubs. Looking out, it noted "all else (that is, heat, crowds, smell, dust, noise, struggle) seem beneath us . . . sinking back in the arms of a hospitable leather chair, one looks down on the city as a tired traveler might look down from a mountain crag."[55]

Most of the clubs were organized by profession. One of the most unusual designs was Francis H. Kimball's Gothic style Lawyers' Club, built in 1912 in the upper stories of the United States Realty Building.[56] Kimball was a pupil of the famous English Gothicist William Burges, and he spared no effort in creating a Gothic environment twenty-two stories above the ground. He often blocked the view with stained glass windows which portrayed the history of the law: he described the two-story window at the end of the main dining room by saying, "If it had been made in the Fifteenth Century, the people would have fallen down and worshipped it."[57]

The Income Tax law of 1913, World War I and Prohibition changed forever the character of New York's night-time amusement world. The very rich were rather less so, and anti-German feelings took a toll on foreign restaurants and beer halls. Most importantly, however, with liquor no longer available, restaurants and roof gardens could no longer survive and evening entertainment went undercover, literally diving underground. Night life burrowed into brownstone cellars in the 1920s, ending the grand tradition of public dining and late-night theatrical entertainment.

Clubs

The clubs are more frequented than ever, and there are more of them. No self-respecting society man limits his expenditure and attendance to a single one, as in the days of special rather than social enjoyment. Every division into which men may be separated has now its club. Even college fraternities have these

Union League Club, northeast corner of Fifth Avenue and Thirty-ninth Street. Peabody & Stearns, 1881. View from Fifth Avenue. NYHS

excuses for the assembling and association of their several New York alumni. The resemblance, both in social, and architectural importance, to Pall Mall and St. James's Street, is still rather faint, perhaps, but we are assuredly demonstrating, in far greater measure than ever heretofore, our inheritance of the English tradition in this respect. "The Point of View," *Scribner's* 7 (March 1890): 396.

In 1879 the Union League Club invited nine architectural firms to enter a competition to design the first building in New York to be erected specifically as a clubhouse.[58] The Union League dated from the Civil War, when political sentiments forced some of its members to break away from the older Union Club. Like most New York clubs, it had been housed in a converted mansion in the neighborhood around Madison Square.[59] This arrangement was adequate for the primarily domestic activities of the club, which served as a home away from home for young bachelors in temporary quarters and businessmen who worked too far from home to return for lunch—a new circumstance brought about by the rapid expansion of the city. But when the officers of the Union League announced the program for the large new clubhouse to be built on the corner of Fifth Avenue and Thirty-ninth Street, it was for a grander, more complicated and more public building than a house could accommodate.

The Union League Building Committee was concerned not only with the private comfort of its members, but also with the public expression of the clubhouse as civic ornament. The committee called for a "mixture of publicity and the privacy and comfort of a private home with somewhat of a pretentious show" that would make the Union League "conspicuous enough to invite public attention and criticism" without extending "an invitation to the casual stroller to walk in, as a museum or theatre might."[60] Their attitude reflected the image evolving in contemporary society of the private club as public monument. In a series of articles published by *Harper's Weekly* in 1890, Harry Loomis Nelson emphasized a correspondence between a city's cultivation and its clubs.[61] The civic importance of the club grew during the Cosmopolitan Era but found its full expression in the Composite Era, between 1890 and 1915.

Because the purpose-built clubhouse was a new type for New York, there was confusion among the architects in the Union League competition as to what an appropriate expression might be. The High Victorian, almost Queen Anne character of the facades of Peabody & Stearns's winning proposal were not quite congenial enough for the committee, but the club members did appreciate the expression of the largest public rooms on the elevation. The location of the library was clearly indicated by three large windows on Fifth Avenue and one on Thirty-ninth Street, the dining room was marked by high windows and a balcony, and the picture gallery and assembly hall, by arched windows.

The floor plans worked well, for Peabody & Stearns had drawn on their experience as house designers in the Queen Anne and Shingle styles to form discrete but open rooms which flowed quite easily from one to another. In fact, the organization of the club's rooms and circulation was surprisingly similar in all the competition entries, despite the novelty of the program. As in the typical London club, which surely served as a model for both architects and clubmen, the ground floor was primarily devoted to lounging rooms filled with comfortable leather armchairs arranged around hearths or great windows that permitted the members to observe the passing scene at a comfortable distance. The size and grandeur of the second floor, taller and more monumental than the first, also followed the London example, but the arrangement of the rooms was quite different from the paradigm. While the second floor of the typical London club contained more formal drawing rooms and a library, the Union League schemes had, in addition, two new rooms—a picture gallery and a public hall which in several of the schemes had a separate entrance.[62] Most entries also had a grand dining room near the top of the clubhouse, symbolizing the ceremonial role of dining in New York club life (and also keeping food odors from drifting up into the other rooms). That role was another New York innovation: London clubs relegated dining to a small, utilitarian room on the ground floor.

Although the Union League Club Building Committee chose Peabody & Stearns's proposal because they liked its integration of interior planning and exterior elevations, they preferred the more sober elevations drawn by Gambrill & Ficken and requested that Peabody & Stearns modify their building's flamboyant skyline. But the committee rejected more Classical designs by Richard Morris Hunt and McKim, Mead & Bigelow (Stanford White had not yet joined the firm) in which the expression of the smaller rooms was suppressed in favor of the ceremonial rooms. McKim, Mead & Bigelow divided their palazzo-like elevations into three tall stories of almost equal height that masked an interior section almost identical to that in Peabody & Stearns's entry. Hunt's entry was simultaneously less unified but colder and less domestic than McKim's, which had simple but delicate details. James Renwick tried to please all by preparing two sets of elevations for the same plans, one in a Classical style and one in Gothic.

Although McKim, Mead & Bigelow's and Hunt's palazzo-like designs were rejected by the Union League Building Committee, they were the harbinger of the most prestigious Composite Era clubs, which included some of the finest built expressions of the American Renaissance. But the history of the New York club is not solely limited to elitist institutions like the Union League Club. Clubs for ethnic minorities and business and community groups also flourished before the turn of the century, and played an important role in the ethnic diversification of the city by providing meeting places for upwardly mobile members from many different groups. Architecturally, these clubs were designed with a more modest character than the grand prototypes evolved at the Union League. Rather than being distinct civic monuments, they were often indistinguishable from other New York building types and thus sat more innocuously on the city streets than the palazzos erected for the great clubs of the Composite Era. The more modest clubs were often less fashionably up-to-date as well; they displayed the stylistic diversity of the Cosmopolitan Era well after the grander clubs had embraced the unified designs of the Composite Era.

Two clubhouse competitions, for the New York Athletic Club in 1886[63] and the Manhattan Athletic Club in 1888[64] attracted more picturesque schemes than the Union League competition. H. Edwards Ficken, who had teamed with Gambrill on the quiet elevations preferred by the Union League Building Committee, won the New York Athletic Club competition with a medieval fantasy based on

Union League Club competition entry, northeast corner of Fifth Avenue and Thirty-ninth Street. Richard Morris Hunt, 1879. Perspective. CU

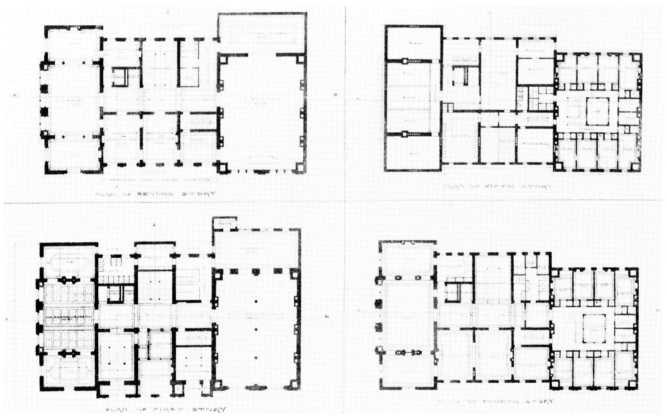

Union League Club competition entry, northeast corner of Fifth Avenue and Thirty-ninth Street. Richard Morris Hunt, 1879. Plans of first, second, fourth and fifth floors. CU

Progress Club, northeast corner of Fifth Avenue and Sixty-third Street. Alfred Zucker, 1890. View from Central Park. MCNY

the half-timber architecture of Alsace, although a different scheme was eventually built.[65] Some of that eclectic spirit was maintained in the various club types that evolved. The Grolier Club (a literary club which moved from rented rooms to a Romanesque-style clubhouse built for them in 1890 by Romeyn & Stever at 29 East Thirty-second Street[66] and then moved in 1916 to a Georgian design by Bertram Grosvenor Goodhue at 47 East Sixtieth Street),[67] the Caledonian Club (Alfred H. Taylor, 1898, at 846 Seventh Avenue)[68] and the Builders' League (John P. Leo, 1898, on West 126th Street)[69] all looked like small townhouses but were arranged for club activities; while the Catholic Club William Schickel & Co., 1892, at 120 West Fifty-ninth Street)[70] and the Colonial Club (Henry F. Kilburn, 1894, at 200 West Seventy-second Street—the first men's club in New York to allow women in the clubhouse as guests)[71] had facades with regular rhythms of evenly sized windows which gave them the appearance of apartment houses. The Mendelssohn Glee Club (1893, at 113 West Fortieth Street)[72] and the Bohemian Club (William C. Frohne, 1897, on East Seventy-third Street)[73] were even larger, with the dowdy institutional nature one might associate with a public building of the Cosmopolitan Era. Slightly more distinctive were the Progress Club (Alfred Zucker, 1890, at 1 East Sixty-third Street),[74] the Montauk Club (Francis H. Kimball, 1891, at Lincoln Place and Eighth Avenue, Brooklyn)[75] and the American Society of Civil Engineers (C.L.W. Eidlitz, 1892, at 220 West Fifty-seventh Street),[76] small palazzos which looked back to the coziness of the Cosmopolitan Era and forward to the explicit monumentality of the Composite Era.

The Progress, a prominent German Jewish club, was the first clubhouse in a decade to carry forward the spirit of McKim's Union League design. Zucker's elevations were naive representations of a palazzo, but the club did have a monumental presence and was perceived as a landmark: "Though the conveniences and requirements of members and individuals are not disregarded or even slurred, particular emphasis and consideration has been given to the collective or social phase of club life. As a result, the new clubhouse is more strictly palatial in character than perhaps any building yet erected in this country."[77] Kimball's Montauk Club reflected the new interest in condensed composition and specific imagery as well, although the Venetian palazzos it was modelled on also supplied a busy ornamental style suited to the taste of the Cosmopolitan Era.

The richer and more prestigious clubs followed the northward trend of fashion in the 1890s and built in the new neighborhoods where their members' houses stood, significantly contributing to the cityscape. Many of the clubs were designed by McKim, Mead & White, who had the double advantage of excellent social connections—White, for example, belonged to the New York Yacht Club, the Union, Metropolitan, Racquet & Tennis, Grolier, Players, City, Century and University clubs[78]—and a newly established reputation as the preeminent architects of the day. Their Classical designs for the Villard houses (1882-85) and the Boston Public Library (1887-98) were the most influential buildings of their time.

Although McKim, Mead & White's first club designs, like the Freundschaft (1889) at Park Avenue and Seventy-second Street,[79] and the Deutscherverein (1890) at 112 West Fifty-ninth Street,[80] represented a stylistic step backwards from the firm's impressively scaled Union League entry, their Century Association, designed in 1889 and constructed in 1890-91, established the paradigm for the monumental clubhouse of the Composite Era.[81] Located on the same block as C.L.W. Eidlitz's contemporary but *retardataire* Racquet & Tennis Club,[82] the Century was modelled on a sixteenth-century Veronese palazzo and continued the Renaissance associations of the firm's Classical work. The street elevation betrayed the fact that both McKim and White were responsible for the design of the club: the planar facade stretched across its mid-block site and the simple silhouette against the sky were characteristic of McKim's work, while the inventive and delicate ornament was more to White's taste.

Horizontal divisions in the elevation distinguished the uses of the different floors. Except for the loggia that mediated between the exterior and the interior, individual rooms were not expressed. A heavy rusticated base filled with service rooms on the lowest floor and lounging rooms

Century Association, 7 West Forty-third Street. McKim, Mead & White, 1891. A view of West Forty-third Street that also shows C.L.W. Eidlitz's Racquet & Tennis Club and R.H. Robertson's Academy of Medicine. CU

Metropolitan Club, northeast corner of Fifth Avenue and Sixtieth Street. McKim, Mead & White, 1894. A view from Grand Army Plaza that shows, to the left, Richard Morris Hunt's Elbridge Gerry mansion. MCNY

above supported a *piano nobile* where the central loggia separated the library and the dining room, two of the most important rooms in a social club dedicated to the arts. A gallery where members' works could be displayed was located in an extension behind the club, hidden from direct view yet easily accessible from the entrance hall. Its proximity to the entrance was accounted for by the fact that, like the gallery in the Union League Club, the Century gallery was open to the public, while the rest of the club was private.

A large stair connected the entry hall and the gallery. After the gallery the stair divided into two grand flights leading to a large hall which overlooked the double height entrance vestibule and gave access to lounges at the sides. A side stair then rose to the *piano nobile* and the dining room, the loggia used for summer dining, and the magnificent double cube space of the library.

The presence of a public gallery at the Century Association, like Stanford White's delicate ornamentation, was a remnant of the 1880s that gave way in the Composite Era to a more monumental civic scale on the exterior and greater exclusivity within. Despite the civic pretensions of the Composite Era clubhouse, the most prestigious clubs were conceived as ideal expressions of past values that were being threatened in the increasingly turbulent social world of turn-of-the-century New York, and they stood as bastions against the social diversification of the city. Unlike the Century Association, founded as a club for men of achievement, most of the exclusive clubs protected old privileges. "Endless, at all events, the power of one or two of these splendid structures to testify to the state of manners," wrote Henry James, "of manners undiscourageably seeking the superior stable equilibrium."[83]

By the 1890s membership in three or four clubs became common among men in New York society.[84] A typical day in the social ritual of a gentleman's club life began after a breakfast in bed and a slow rising, when he would walk to a nearby club to read the morning newspapers, collect the day's mail, and have a drink with his peers. Toward midday the clubman would proceed to Central Park for a ride on the bridle path, and then go home for a bath and preparations for lunch and social obligations in the afternoon. If there were no invitations for dinner, he could go back to the club to eat and pass the evening. In other words, the club took up all the slack in the clubman's life. Eating, drinking, and socializing in the proper setting with the proper crowd was its essence, although once within the confines of the clubhouse, watching the world outside pass by was always a popular activity. Most clubhouses were built on prominent thoroughfares, with lounging rooms looking out on the street, and members would pass the time by placing bets on who or what would go by next.[85]

Two clubs built by McKim, Mead & White soon after the Century exemplify the clubman's club. The Metropolitan Club, designed by White, was on the drawing boards while the Century was being finished, and carried the palazzo tradition to a considerably larger scale.[86] McKim's University Club, designed in 1896 and constructed from 1897 to 1900, combined features of Tuscan palazzos such as the Palazzo Strozzi and elements of Roman temples.[87] Even more than the relatively intimate Century Association, these two clubhouses determined the style of the grandest clubs that followed in the Composite Era.

The Metropolitan Club was often called the Millionaire's Club, because it was founded by J.P. Morgan after one of his friends had been blackballed at the Union Club. Located on Fifth Avenue across from the Grand Army Plaza entrance to the East Drive in Central Park, its flat marble facades were unusually free of ornament for a design by White. A ceremonial entry court at the eastern end of the club was screened from Sixtieth Street by a splendid gateway initiating a circulation sequence that was the dominant experience of the building. Inside, an opulent marble hall rose all the way through the clubhouse, like a palazzo *cortile* that had been glassed in and covered in luxurious materials. At the back of the hall a large, double staircase led up to a library and game rooms on the second floor and to another stair going to the dining room on the third floor. "In all the principal rooms," Schuyler remarked in one of his righteous moods, "there is a profusion and riot of decoration . . . [which] seems to contradict the dictum of Vespasian that cash is inodorous, for it exhales riches as, according to

Metropolitan Club, northeast corner of Fifth Avenue and Sixtieth Street. McKim, Mead & White, 1894. Plan of first floor. CU

Metropolitan Club, northeast corner of Fifth Avenue and Sixtieth Street. McKim, Mead & White, 1894. Main Hall. OMH

Cardinal Newman, the commonroom at Oriel College in his time exhaled logic."[88]

The University Club was originally located on Madison Avenue at Twenty-sixth Street. In 1894, the club's directors asked McKim to prepare plans for expansion onto the site of the Stokes house next door. The purchase of that site fell through, and several other proposals were put forward until 1896, when the club was able to purchase the lot at the northwest corner of Fifth Avenue and Fifty-fourth Street where the old St. Luke's Hospital stood before its move to Morningside Heights. Just six blocks south of the Metropolitan Club, it was in the midst of Vanderbilt Row, a perfect location for a club in the 1890s.

The solid block of the University Club was a firm palazzo that exuded confidence. The entire exterior, except for the cast bronze balustrades, was constructed of a light pink Milford granite that darkened over the years. Several sources were combined in a *pasticcio* that was one of McKim's most accomplished designs: references to Florentine palazzos such as the Strozzi and Medici palaces, the Sienese Palazzo Spannochi, and the Bolognese Palazzo Bocchi and Palazzo Albergati were used together with quotations from the Classical Temple of Mars Ultor and Mannerist and Baroque sources in a composition with a life of its own.[89] The result was original, but the appeal to authority in search of scholarly erudition was clearly shown when difficulties arose concerning the sculpted panels of Knoxville marble depicting the seals and mottos of the eighteen schools most represented in the club. To overcome the resistance of the club's building committee to the seals, McKim presented photographs showing the use of inscriptions on many Renaissance and Roman buildings including the Palazzo Spada, the Porta del Popolo, the Fontana dell'Acqua Paola, and the Porta Maggiore, and read a statement written by his assistant which cited further examples of the use of carved shields and inscriptions. The building committee yielded to such a venerable body of authority and accepted the shields carved by Kenyon Cox and Daniel Chester French.[90]

Unlike the Metropolitan, the University Club had no double-height space at the core of its plan, but rather separate square halls on the first, second and third floors. In plan it resembled a Renaissance *palazzo,* but in reality it lacked a generous *cortile.* The many rooms arranged around the hall (McKim managed to squeeze seven floors into what appeared to be a three-story clubhouse) were as rich as those at the Metropolitan, but less bombastic. The most important rooms, the library and main dining room, were finished with English oak panelling and owed a clear debt to the colleges of Oxford and Cambridge. Because the club owned a large collection of books, McKim lavished attention on the decoration of the library, a long groin-vaulted room with five transverse barrel vaults forming alcoves. The walls up to the springing of the vaults were covered with Classically ornamented bookshelves, and the plaster ceiling and canvas panels painted by H. Siddons Mowbray in the style of Pinturicchio's fresco vaults in the Borgia Apartments in Rome.[91]

A writer for the New York *Evening Post* marvelled over the University Club's appointments:

The third floor, with the exception of the council chamber, is devoted to pleasures of the table. A private dining room faces the avenue, decorated in green and gold . . . [it] extends along the whole street front. Like the library below, it is divided into three parts. The square end rooms have flat coffered ceilings; while that of the center portion rests upon a cove, supported by pilasters. This is the most ornate ceiling in the building, recalling in the boldness of its beams and mouldings, and the richness of gilding and color, one of the elaborate examples in the Doge's palace at Venice. The walls are panelled throughout with English oak, and in the frieze on the north side is the opening which forms the front of the musician's gallery, set back in a sort of mezzanine floor. This is a most sumptuous room, preserved however, from the tendency to be florid by the fine expanse of oak-wood. Above are the kitchens, and an open-air cafe is provided on the roof.[92]

A competition in 1901 for a new building for the Union Club, New York's oldest club, clearly demonstrated the acceptance of McKim, Mead & White's clubhouses as the proper prototype. The Union had outgrown its building on Fifth Avenue and Twenty-first Street and bought a large lot

233

University Club, northwest corner of Fifth Avenue and Fifty-fourth Street. McKim, Mead & White, 1900. View from Fifth Avenue. MCNY

University Club, northwest corner of Fifth Avenue and Fifty-fourth Street. McKim, Mead & White, 1900. Library. NYHS

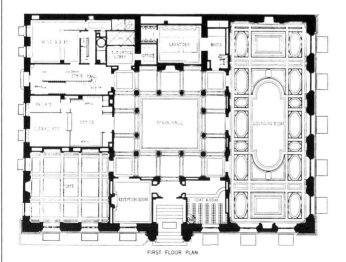
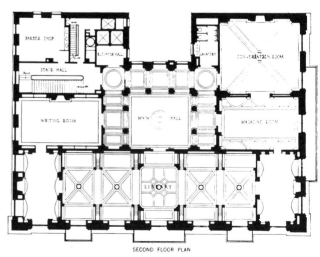
University Club, northwest corner of Fifth Avenue and Fifty-fourth Street. McKim, Mead & White, 1900. Plans of first, second, third and fourth floors. CU

University Club, northwest corner of Fifth Avenue and Fifty-fourth Street. McKim, Mead & White, 1900. Main Dining Room. MCNY

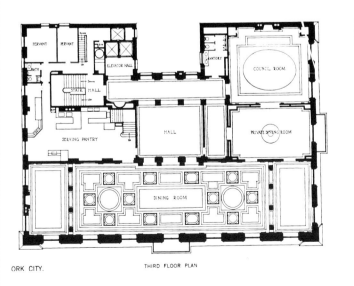

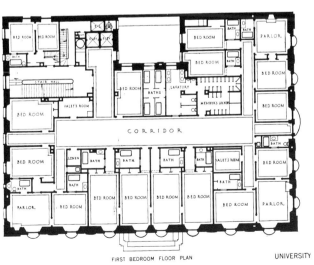

Union Club, northeast corner of Fifth Avenue and Fifty-first Street. Cass Gilbert and John DuFais, 1902. NYHS

Colony Club, 120 Madison Avenue. McKim, Mead & White, 1908. View from Madison Avenue. CU

on the corner of Fifth Avenue and Fifty-first Street. When the competitive designs for the club sometimes referred to as the Mother of Clubs came in, all were variations on the palazzo type. The winning entry was a very Italian design by Cass Gilbert and John DuFais.[93] Lounging rooms in the rusticated ground floor had simple but large arched windows that gave the members a good view of Fifth Avenue, while the more important rooms on the two main floors above had pedimented windows: those on the *piano nobile* alternated triangular and arched pediments. But other schemes combined other styles with palazzo compositions. Donn Barber's plans introduced a strong note of the Modern French taste to the palazzo: although the exterior was a synthesis of the two styles, the interior planning produced a carefully resolved axial composition that might have been a thesis project at the Ecole des Beaux-Arts.[94] The entries by Palmer & Hornbostel[95] and Barney & Chapman[96] had the monumental scale and massing of the palazzo type but were designed with a more domestic character that included their construction of red brick and limestone. Palmer & Hornbostel's facades were more accomplished, combining Georgian and Modern French motifs in an imposing yet intimate block.

The last club in the palazzo tradition by McKim, Mead & White was the new Racquet & Tennis Club on Park Avenue, designed by the office in 1916, after McKim and White were dead and Mead had retired.[97] It reflected the severity of the Palazzo Antinori in Florence, but the clubhouse was nevertheless a somewhat tired design done under the supervision of W.S. Richardson, best known for his fine business sense. A loggia at the center of the front elevation recalled the facade of the Century Club and pointed out the vast size of the Racquet Club, which extended a full block along Park Avenue. The blank arches at the top of the club, which masked various racket courts, were an attempt to ameliorate the scale, but the single rhythm and almost identical size of the facade elements did not help. The interiors were as bland as the exterior, with the exception of three wood panelled rooms: perhaps the finest of those three, appropriately, was the locker room. Also unusual was the entry hall, which connected to a covered drive at the back of the club that ran between Fifty-second and Fifty-third streets. But the hierarchy of the many openings to the hall was confused, particularly because the stair followed a circuitous route, and the circulation suffered from the same lack of strong vertical connections in the stair halls as the firm's designs for the Metropolitan and University clubs.

Although the Colony Club was built in 1916 in a loosely Colonial style that one might expect from its name, it continued the civic scale introduced to the clubhouse by McKim, Mead & White.[98] Designed by the Georgian specialists Delano & Aldrich, who succeeded McKim, Mead & White as the leading clubhouse architects, the red-brick building on the northwest corner of Park Avenue and Sixty-second Street fit in well with its neighbors. Together with Delano & Aldrich's Third Church of Christ Scientist and the block of Georgian-style houses on Park Avenue between Sixty-eighth and Sixty-ninth streets, the Colony contributed to the surprisingly modest and domestic character of the avenue of the sixties, which contrasted distinctly with the grand limestone and marble blocks of hotels and apartments below Sixtieth Street. But the Georgian elements of the Colony Club were stretched over too large a structure, because of the many different functions required in a modern clubhouse. A ballroom and a reception room that could be entered by a side entrance on Sixty-second Street, a swimming pool in the basement, a gymnasium and running track, squash courts, separate dining rooms for members and nonmembers, twenty bedrooms and twelve maid's rooms all swelled the clubhouse to over twice the size of the original club. The organizational clarity of interior planning suffered from the greatly increased size.

All in all, the new Colony was considerably less successful than the original clubhouse that the club had outgrown. The original building was also in a Colonial style, but it was a smaller and more delicate design that reflected a more modest tradition of clubhouse planning that had also been established by McKim, Mead & White. The first clubhouse in New York built for women, it was designed in 1904 by White and constructed in 1905-06 at 120 Madison Avenue, just above Thirtieth Street.[99] The six-story Georgian building ran one hundred feet along Madison Avenue, but was still less than half the size of Delano & Aldrich's later Colony Club and maintained an intimate, domestic scale that was considered appropriately for "venerably connected and socially prominent ladies."[100] The deep-red bricks were laid with the headers showing, a practice usually reserved for nonbearing construction. White was severely criticized in the architectural journals for an immoral use of material, but he redeemed himself somewhat by having the brick inside the relieving arches of the blind arcade laid diagonally to suggest the nonbearing capacity of these panels.[101] The brick was an uncommon type, with an irregular surface that gave the wall an uneven texture that caught glancing light. Darker bricks were laid in diaper patterns in the spandrels of the blind arcade and the panels of the attic floor.

The Colony was large enough to provide meeting, dining, reading and athletic facilities, but the character of the interior was as domestic as the exterior. White collaborated with Elsie de Wolfe on the decor, just two or three years after she had left the stage to begin a career in interior decoration. Most of the public rooms combined French decoration with Colonial furniture, although the club members were particularly proud of the Mediterranean fantasy in the basement-level pool room, described by *Indoors and Out:* "The ceiling of ground glass is covered with a lattice. Grapevines are twined thickly over the lattice, their broad leaves and big clusters of fruit a most natural looking arbor. Electric lights are arranged above the glass ceiling in such a way as to send through it and the vines a soft yellow light, like sunlight filtered through foliage. The walls are all lined with mirrors which create an amazing effect of spaciousness. As one glances about the room the single pool is multiplied many times and the eye looks down a long vista of vine-covered, sun-lighted arbors and marble basins."[102]

The first of the more domestic, red-brick and limestone designs was McKim's Harvard Club, which was also the first of several clubs built on Forty-fourth Street between Fifth and Sixth avenues.[103] The earliest of three sections was completed in 1894, and was a small but relatively formal building intended to evoke fond memories of college life in Cambridge. But the clubhouse had little of the spirit of McKim, Mead & White's palatial designs: although it was built of Harvard brick and modest in overall size, the limestone details were grandly scaled and gave the facade a

Harvard Club, 27 West Forty-fourth Street. McKim, Mead & White, 1900. View of entrance from Forty-fourth Street. CU

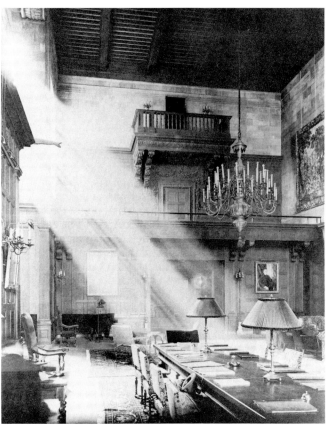

Harvard Club, 27 West Forty-fourth Street. McKim, Mead & White, 1902. Harvard Hall. CU

public scale. Later additions—the majestic Harvard Hall, a triple-height, wood-panelled room that extended the club through the block to Forty-fifth Street, and an aesthetically unfortunate six-story section added to the west side of the club after McKim's death—vastly increased the size of the building without greatly increasing its formality.[104]

McKim, Mead & White's brick and limestone Lambs' Club, designed by White in 1903 and constructed in 1904–05 one block west of the Harvard Club on Forty-fourth Street, was a theater club founded in 1874 in emulation of a similar club in London.[105] A five-story building on two city lots, the clubhouse had a lovely domestic character: only the large windows on the second and third floors, the marble lambs' heads on the third and fourth floors, and the flagpole on the fourth floor flanked by marble rampant lambs and ornament suggested that the building was more public than an important small house. The windows on the second floor lit a large banquet hall, and the smaller windows on the third floor the library. Behind the library was a small theater panelled in dark oak trimmed with gilt and finished with dark green curtains.

The first clubhouse designed by the Georgian specialists Delano & Aldrich was for the Knickerbocker Club, built in 1914 at the corner of Fifth Avenue and Sixty-second Street.[106] The graceful, Federal-style Knickerbocker was as taut and refined as their Colony was overblown and bloated. One might possibly argue that the clubhouse reflected the taste of the members of the exclusive club, who considered themselves more patrician than the members of other clubs, but the Colony was the women's social equivalent of the Knickerbocker. The Knickerbocker, however, did not provide as many facilities as the Colony Club, because it had a smaller membership and virtually all its members belonged to other, larger clubs as well. The women did not have that option, and when the Colony Club moved to a new clubhouse the members made it larger than the first but tried to keep the old scale.

A few clubs only required small clubhouses but wanted a grand image. A competition in 1899 for a new home for the New York Yacht Club, the elite yacht racing club of the country, produced one of the most exuberant and eccentric small buildings in New York. The entries by Warren & Wetmore[107] and Howard, Cauldwell & Morgan[108] both had overscaled, Modern French facades pierced by three large,

New York Yacht Club competition entry, 37 West Forty-fourth Street. Warren & Wetmore, 1899. Elevation. CU

New York Yacht Club, 37 West Forty-fourth Street. Warren & Wetmore, 1899. View from Forty-fourth Street. MCNY

arched windows filled at the bottom with plug-in elements representing ship's sterns, but only Warren & Wetmore's winning design had the wonderful brashness which the Old World often ascribes to the New. As built, Whitney Warren's first major commission had bulbous galleons dripping seaweed afloat on a sea of dolphins, scaly brackets, and a fantastic Neptune keystone. Inside the club, one was immediately confronted by a dramatic marble staircase which ascended rapidly to an axial hall terminated by a toplit rotunda centered on the silver America's Cup trophy. The model room next door had elaborately carved woodwork, incised with seashells and mythical sea creatures, which floated on a continually moving surface created by a profusion of moldings and scale wooden models of members' boats. The whole was a masterpiece of bravado, with more than a little tongue in cheek. The *Architectural Review* agreed in substance, although not in the ultimate judgment: "While there was some semblance of reserve in the exterior of this most interesting building, there is little of this quality visible so far as the interior is concerned. The riot of swags and spinach, icicles and exotic vegetation that is in progress in the chimney-piece of the model room, for example, takes away one's breath. Surely this is not architectural design."[109]

The most prestigious of the turn-of-the-century Jewish clubs was the Harmonie, first located in a converted house on Forty-second Street that Herts & Tallant remodelled in 1898.[110] Their design hinted at the Art Nouveau, but also had a solid German burgher character that the Harmonie members apparently wished to leave behind, because in 1904 the Harmonie bought land on Sixtieth Street, across the street from J.P. Morgan's Metropolitan Club, and hired the Metropolitan's architect to design a grander but considerably smaller building. White's design had a three-story marble base and colossal terra-cotta pilasters above, but the building did not have a very grand presence on the street. The facade was too flat and too high on its narrow side street site to establish its own identity, though it functioned admirably as a backdrop for the Metropolitan's entry court.

Donn Barber's Lotos Club was larger than the Harmonie, yet like the Harmonie it lacked individual presence. A club for journalists and men interested in literature, the Lotos moved in 1909 from a converted townhouse to its new clubhouse at 110 West Fifty-seventh Street because it

New York Yacht Club, 37 West Forty-fourth Street. Warren & Wetmore, 1899. Model Room. CU

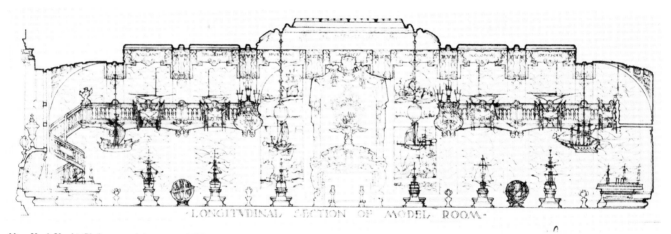

New York Yacht Club competition entry, 37 West Forty-fourth Street. Warren & Wetmore, 1899. Transverse and longitudinal sections of Model Room. CU

needed larger facilities for its many members and frequent dinners.[111] The lower floors of the new club were filled with public rooms, the third, fourth and fifth floors with bedrooms, and the top floor primarily devoted to dining. The arrangement was similar to White's *parti* for the Harmonie, which had a dining room on the sixth floor and bedrooms on the fifth, but the *parti* was used more successfully in clubhouses tall enough to take on the character of a tower such as the original Yale Club, an eleven-story building on a narrow site across the street from the Harvard Club.[112] Built in 1901 by Tracy & Swartwout, the Yale Club had three floors of dining rooms on top, well above the surrounding buildings. The two bottom stories were filled with public rooms and offices, and the remaining floors given over to bedrooms. In 1915, having designed the clubhouse so that it could be converted to apartments, the Yale Club moved to an even taller but similarly arranged tower near the recently completed Grand Central Terminal. The new twenty-one story tower, designed by James Gamble Rogers (who later designed most of the Yale colleges), was conveniently located near the trains to New Haven, and even had an underground connection to the station.[113]

Tower clubhouses, built with floors of bedrooms sandwiched between club rooms and aerial dining rooms, were particularly appropriate for large social organizations that were less exclusive than the Union or Metropolitan clubs. The most architecturally distinguished stood on West Fortieth Street opposite Bryant Park and the new New York Public Library. The Republican Club, built in 1904 at 56 West Fortieth Street, was fittingly designed by New York's leading bank architects, York & Sawyer.[114] Its muscular facade had fiercely correct High Renaissance details that tied it to the Medicis and their republic. Henry J. Hardenbergh's design for the New York Club (1906) at 20 West Fortieth Street had more eclectic detailing.[115] The enormous, attenuated arcade on the second floor perhaps represented the Classicism of New York's Composite Era, but the bold gables, quoins and voussoirs recalled the city's Dutch heritage. The Engineer's Club was designed by Whitfield & King, who won half of a competition held by Andrew Carnegie for two buildings constructed in 1906 for several engineering groups.[116] The clubhouse at 32 West Fortieth Street was connected with a tower built by James Gamble Rogers at 25 West Thirty-ninth Street that housed the

New York Yacht Club, 37 West Forty-fourth Street. Warren & Wetmore, 1899. Detail of Model Room. CU

New York Yacht Club, 37 West Forty-fourth Street. Warren & Wetmore, 1899. Detail of facade. CU

New York Club, 20 West Fortieth Street. Henry J. Hardenbergh, 1906. View from New York Public Library. CU

Masonic Temple, northwest corner of Lafayette and Clermont avenues, Brooklyn. Lord & Hewlett, 1909. Clermont Avenue elevation. CU

headquarters for the American Institute of Electrical Engineers, the American Society of Mechanical Engineers and the Institute of Mining Engineers.

H.P. Knowles's 1909 design for the facade of the Masonic Hall tower at 46 West Twenty-fourth Street was festive but not very accomplished.[117] Inside, the individual Gothic, Jacobean, Renaissance, Colonial, Grecian Ionic, Grecian Doric, French Ionic, French Doric, and Corinthian meeting rooms formed one of the most unusual collections of rooms of the period. "There is something about the building of a great secret order which demands the bizarre," said *Architecture*, "and the treatment of the eleven lodge rooms of similar dimensions and character of furnishing in the same style would result in an appalling monotony. The architect has very wisely chosen to write in a daring way a brief history of architecture as seen from his standpoint, but the fact that they are all considered from an individual angle, and that the same mind has dominated the styles, (instead of being dominated by them) has resulted in a series of rooms quite different in design, of every period, and yet of singular unity of character."[118]

James Riely Gordon won the competition for the enormous Lodge Number 1 of the Benevolent Protective Order of Elks with a much more restrained scheme.[119] The tower, built in 1911, had a sober shaft of plain brick and a five-story Classical base of cut stone. All the important public rooms except the Lodge Room were on the first two floors (the roof had a solarium and a terrace, but the dining rooms were on the ground floor), which were opulent yet restrained. But the extravagant Lodge Room, which filled the rest of the five-story base, was designed in an eye popping version of Beaux-Arts Baroque. For large trusses, twenty-five by seventy-five feet, were required to support the eight floors of bedrooms above the Lodge Room. Gordon arranged the upper floors in a U shape with a small central light well, so that the trusses were buried in the long walls that formed the light well and the parallel walls at the perimeter of the building, and windows could be placed between the webs of the trusses.

Donn Barber faced a similar problem in his design for the Central Branch of the Young Women's Christian Association.[120] The Central Branch was built in 1920 next to Barber's earlier Y.W.C.A. National Board Building on the northwest corner of Lexington Avenue and Fifty-second

Engineer's Club, 32 West Fortieth Street. Whitfield & King, 1906. Perspective view from Bryant Park. CU

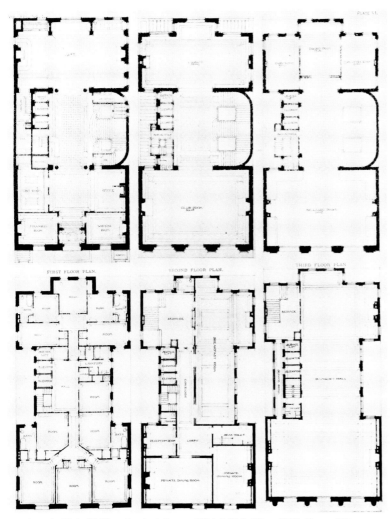

Engineer's Club, 32 West Fortieth Street. Whitfield & King, 1906. Plans. CU

Street; together the buildings filled the Lexington blockfront between Fifty-second and Fifty-third streets. The important branch required an extra large assembly hall convenient to the entrance, and the floors above were carried by two enormous trusses spanning the hall. Barber suspended the swimming pool between the trusses, and framed the rest of the building normally.

The decoration of the Central Branch was dignified but simple, typical of the atmosphere that the numerous Ys built during the Composite Era aspired to. Their character changed from the assertiveness of R.H. Robertson's Romanesque design for a Y.M.C.A. (1885) at 7 East Fifteenth Street,[121] to that of large but modestly detailed pallazzos, such as Parish & Schroeder's West Side Y.M.C.A.[122] and Louis Allen Abramson's Central Y.W.H.A.,[123] which quietly emulated the great clubhouses.

Boring & Tilton's Eastern District Y.M.C.A. in Brooklyn, built in 1906 at Marcy Avenue and South Street, was a large and well equipped palazzo with complete group facilities—a theater, meeting rooms, classrooms, a gymnasium and a pool—and bedrooms where one could stay for $2.50 to $5 per week (meals were $3.50 extra per week).[124] H. Van Buren Magonigle's Elks Clubhouse (1912) at 144 South Oxford Street in Brooklyn, was smaller but grander, a Florentine palazzo in brick.[125] But Lord & Hewlett's Brooklyn Masonic Temple on the northeast corner of Lafayette and Clermont avenues was even grander, a true palace for the people.[126] "The Masonic Temple is quite the most dignified and impressive piece of architecture which has been done in the past two years," *Architecture* proclaimed in 1909:

and it seems almost safe to assume that . . . it will win . . . the gold medal of the Architectural League. I do not recall any other building which expresses so completely the high purpose and aims of a great secret society like the Masons, and it is as beautifully thought out in every particular as it is perfect in general conception. The color of the brick work is delightful, the method of using colored terra cotta in the columns, the capital, the belt courses and in the cornice is the best of modern times; one is tempted to say the best of all time. The building is, I suppose, Greek. I say this grudgingly, for it is so thoroughly modern in its handling that it seems to me really American of the highest type rather than a derivative from some ancient architecture.[127]

Luna Park, Coney Island, Brooklyn. Frederic Thompson, 1903. NYHS

Manhattan Beach Hotel, Coney Island, Brooklyn. J. Pickering Putnam, 1877. A view that shows the Manhattan Beach Ampitheater, center, designed by Francis H. Kimball in 1885. NYHS

Coney Island

Even before the opening of New York's first roof garden in 1882, amusements at the Centennial Celebration in Philadelphia led to the development of Coney Island as a summer retreat from Manhattan. Through much of the nineteenth century Coney Island had been notorious as a refuge for criminals, who congregated in the wooden shantytowns of the island's West End, but in 1875, when Culver's Railway connected Coney Island to the Prospect Park section of Brooklyn, its development as a resort began in earnest. In 1876 the Hotel Brighton opened on the island's eastern tip, followed in the next few years by the Manhattan Beach and Oriental hotels. As Julian Ralph remembered the resort: "There, many of us first saw an abundance of electric lights, newly popularized at the Philadelphia Centennial and, as if to impress upon us the part which that world's fair played in enlarging all our comforts and elegances, there rose above our heads on Coney Island the tall skeleton tower which had been the highest object at the Centennial, and we were pulled to and fro, on the Marine Railway, by locomotives from the same exposition."[128]

John G. Prague's Hotel Brighton was typical of the new resort: a vast Stick Style palace with a long, low-slung mass asymmetrically punctuated by mansard-roofed towers and deep porches that caught the ocean breezes and served as outdoor promenades.[129] The hotel seafronts were laid out as vast lawns, with a boardwalk at the edge of the surf. Guests were serenaded from bandstands, the largest of which was the Manhattan Beach Amphitheater by Francis H. Kimball, a vast permanent tent raised on a circular shingled base.[130] The Manhattan Beach Hotel, which catered to transients, was famous for its night-time fireworks displays over the ocean.[131]

The hotels drew part of their clientele from the fashionable set that patronized the nearby Gravesend and Brighton Beach Racetracks and part from the wealthy middle-class families who summered within commuting distance of Brooklyn and New York. In 1896 Julian Ralph described Coney Island as "the first made-to-order resort in America; the first resort which, instead of developing its own capital, had capital brought to it and lavished upon it in the manner in which so many great nineteenth century enterprises, banking upon certain prosperity, have leaped from nothing into full fledged perfection."[132] The vast amounts of capital

Luna Park, Coney Island, Brooklyn. Frederic Thompson, 1903. NYHS

invested in the hotels resulted in a major feat of contemporary technology. In 1888, when the Hotel Brighton was undermined by shore erosion, it was raised off its pilings, set atop 120 railway cars, and moved inland from the encroaching waves.[133] The hotels were doomed, however, when horse racing was banned in New York State in 1909. Although the racetracks substituted automobiles, the hotels lost many of their clients.

Until the 1890s the eastern end of Coney Island was dominated by a disorganized group of amusement shows, rude taverns, beer gardens and bathing establishments. But the great popularity of the Midway Plaisance, an amusement park at the 1893 World's Columbian Exposition in Chicago that was isolated from the more educational displays in the Court of Honor, catalyzed the development of Coney Island as a scene of popular amusements and set the *leitmotif* for much of its architecture. With the opening of George Tilyou's Steeplechase Park in 1897, the amusements began to attract a more respectable, middle-class crowd. Steeplechase Park was a vast, fenced enclosure, ultimately stretching across fifteen acres and centered on a huge iron shed which sheltered concessions from bad weather. Steeplechase was named after its most popular ride, a mechanical racetrack with wooden horses which ironically echoed the entertainment of the island's hotel crowd.[134]

The success of Steeplechase Park, which fenced out the island's more disreputable sideshows and provided family entertainment, led to the construction of two more enclosures: Luna Park and Dreamland. Luna Park was the brainchild of Frederick Thompson, the entrepreneur later responsible for the New York Hippodrome. Opened in 1903 and expanded a year later, Luna Park was a fantastic *mélange* of plaster and lath towers, by day somewhat seedy, but at night dazzlingly outlined in electrical light. Albert Bigelow Paine described the scene at twilight: "Tall towers that had grown dim suddenly broke forth in electrical outlines and gay rosettes of color, as the living spark of light travelled hither and thither, until the place was transformed into an enchanted garden, of such a sort as Aladdin never dreamt."[135] The eclecticism of Luna Park's architecture reflected Thompson's belief that "In building for a festive occasion there should be an absolute departure from all set forms of architecture . . . [the architect] must dare to decorate a minaret with Renaissance detail or to jumble Romanesque with *l'art nouveau* . . . keeping his line constantly varied, broken, and moving, so that it may lead gracefully into the towers and minarets of a festive skyline. . . . I have tried to make [Luna Park] as much a part of the carnival spirit as the bands, flags, rides, and lights."[136]

Thompson's ensemble was deliberately picturesque and exotic, with extensive Japanese gardens, arcaded walkways, and a re-creation of the Mughal marketplace in Delhi, complete with elephants. The same sense of illusion pervaded the amusements. The most popular attraction was a simulated rocket trip to the moon.[137]

Thompson's financial success at Luna Park lay not only in his brilliant showmanship but also in the development of sanitized amusements to redeem Coney Island's *risqué* reputation and lure the respectable middle class. As the distinguished architecture critic Barr Ferree wrote in 1904, it demonstrated "that not only can Coney Island be good, but that goodness pays, and pays handsomely."[138]

Luna Park's lessons were picked up at Dreamland, opened in 1903 by Senator J.R. Reynolds, a prominent real estate investor. Conceived by architects Kirby, Petit & Green in the heyday of the American Renaissance, Dreamland was the most ambitious attempt the city had seen to create a permanent World's Fair and to apply the aesthetic strategies of the City Beautiful to the realm of popular amusements. While Luna Park captured the ethos of the Chicago Exposition's raucous Midway, Dreamland harked back to its formal Court of Honor, organized around a central lagoon and a sunken plaza where chariot races were staged. The entire park was dominated by a monumental tower which lent the complex both a symbolic focus and an advertising image. Ferree labelled the ensemble "a mimic White City" which illustrated "the value of architecture as aid to civic betterment."[139]

Despite the coherence of Dreamland's academic plan, building materials and color, the individual facades lining the lagoon displayed an eclectic diversity. As Ferree observed, "they exhibit so much variety that they might well have been built by a dozen architects, instead of being the designs of a single group intent on producing a single whole."[140] Kirby, Petit & Green in fact synthesized their Classical prototype with the sense of pictorial showmanship first realized at Luna Park. The facade of Andrew Mack's Fishing Pond featured the vast prow of a ship suspended over the entrance, its mid-air passage between fortified pylons guided by plaster mermaids. Next to it a miniature version of the Doge's Palace housed the Canals of Venice, a boatride through a *papier-mâché* evocation of that city. A Japanese pavilion, designed as a teahouse, was incongruously used to exhibit an airplane. A Tudor hospital displayed infants in incubators. Old Nuremburg was a small scale re-creation of a medieval street, peopled with midgets.

These buildings stood abruptly juxtaposed to Dreamland's other, Classical, facades. The Fall of Pompeii, an Ionic colonnade framed by pavilions, sheltered Charles M. Shean's fresco of the Bay of Naples, while Vesuvius's eruption was scenographically reenacted inside. The facade of Wormwood's Monkey Theater bore a colonnade of date palms in colored relief. Kirby, Petit & Green's most imaginative facade was surely the Electricity Building, which housed the generating station for Dreamland's night-time electrical displays. Framed by Modern French pylons, its round doorway was the center of an abstraction of the armature of a dynamo emitting gilded rays of light.

Dreamland was never as popular as Luna Park—its rides and illusionistic journeys always had an aspect of *déjà vu* when compared to Frederick Thompson's—and when it burned in 1911 it was already experiencing financial difficulties. The architecture too was perhaps less successful at conveying the idea of relaxed inhibitions. But ironically, Kirby, Petit & Green succeeded in creating a microcosm of New York's urbanism in the Composite Era—its eclecticism seeking historical accuracy, its individual parts cohering into a Classical vision.

Luna Park, Coney Island, Brooklyn. Frederic Thompson, 1903. NYHS

Dreamland, Coney Island, Brooklyn. Kirby, Petit & Green, 1904. CU

Dreamland, Coney Island, Brooklyn. Kirby, Petit & Green, 1904. Entrance to Creation. NYHS

Plaza Hotel, west side of Grand Army Plaza between Fifty-eighth and Fifty-ninth streets. Henry Janeway Hardenbergh, 1907. View from Fifth Avenue. MCNY

Palaces for the People

The moral in question, the high interest of the tale, is that you are in the presence of a revelation of the possibilities of the hotel—for which the American spirit has found so unprecedented a use and a value; leading it on to express so a social, indeed positively an aesthetic ideal, and making it so, at this supreme pitch, a synonym for civilization, for the capture of conceived manners themselves, that one is verily tempted to ask if the hotel-spirit may not just be *the American spirit most seeking and most finding itself.*
Henry James, *The American Scene* (New York: Harper & Bros., 1907; Bloomington: Indiana University Press, 1968), 102.

Hotels New York's great hotels were perhaps the clearest record of its pluralistic society. Vast pleasure palaces that served the visitor and the resident, established wealth and the rising middle class, they were a creation of the physical and social mobility of nineteenth-century urban life. Improved transportation, of course was one factor in the evolution of the grand hotel. Better ships fostered travel across the Atlantic to Europe and along the coast, and the rapid expansion of the railroads vastly increased inter-city travel: in 1883 the *Hotel Gazette* estimated that 200,000 travelling salesmen were riding the rails around the country to peddle their wares.[1] But the large, luxury hotels which replaced the inns and boarding houses of the eighteenth century were also the first physical manifestation of the public culture created in the cities of the Metropolitan Era. New cultural demands produced hotels filled with vast halls for promenading, lounging, and dining in public—communal activities which flourished more rapidly in the volatile democratic society of America than in the more established social structure of Europe; consequently, the large luxury hotel was an American invention. "The American hotel is to an English hotel what an elephant is to a periwinkle," the British journalist George Augustus Sala wrote in 1861. It is "as roomy as Buckingham Palace, and is not much inferior to a palace in its internal fittings. It has ranges of drawing rooms, suites of private rooms, vast staircases and interminable layers of bedchambers."[2]

New York's first great hotel was the Astor House, designed in 1836 by Isaiah Rogers, who was also the architect of America's first great hotel, the Tremont House in Boston.[3] The five-story Greek Revival style hostelry, built of Quincy granite, filled the entire Broadway blockfront between Barclay and Vesey streets and was immediately recognized as one of the most impressive piles in the city. Even before its completion the New York *Evening Post* reported that its "appearance far surpasses expectation; for size and solidity no building in the United States will compare with it."[4] But its conveniences were even more impressive: fifteen years after its opening, the *Home Journal* declared that it had been "such a bold stride in advance of the time to build so vast and complete a hotel that the time has scarcely yet caught up with it."[5] The hotel had 309 rooms and was the first in New York to offer bathing and toilet facilities on every floor, a real novelty at a time when even the finest mansions lacked such comfort. The lobby constantly bustled with the arrival and departure of guests, and men often congregated around the entrance to watch the commotion.

Rivals to the Astor House opened farther north on Broadway in the following decades, but as late as 1853 it was "still the best hotel in the country . . . in the opinion of large numbers of competent judges," according to the *Home Journal*.[6] Its glory was fading, however, as fashion moved north, and a new generation of luxury hotels opened on Broadway between Canal and Fourteenth streets. "During the last eighteen months nearly half a dozen new hotels, of differing sizes, have been opened in various parts of the city," wrote the *New York Herald* in August 1852, and "now nearly half a dozen more are ready to be opened in a very few weeks."[7]

In September 1859 Amos F. Eno anticipated fashion by opening the Fifth Avenue Hotel on Madison Square.[8] Because its location on Twenty-third Street was generally considered too far uptown to be successful, the hotel was known as Eno's Folly, but the very presence of the hotel attracted interest in the neighborhood, which was soon established as the city's most fashionable. The Fifth Avenue Hotel was the most modern and luxurious in the city, with the first passenger elevator in New York and a grand entrance hall—160 feet long and 27 feet wide, rising to a height of 15 feet above the marble floors. A sitting room to one side was known as the Amen Corner, because Senator Thomas Platt, leader of the Republican Party, held court there. In 1900 Platt managed to get rid of the reform-minded and troublesome Governor Theodore Roosevelt by arranging for him to become the Republican Vice-Presidential

253

Fifth Avenue Hotel, southeast corner of Madison Square at Broadway and Twenty-third Street. William Washburn, 1859. A view from Madison Square that also shows the Hoffman House to the right. NYHS

candidate—a few months later William McKinley was assassinated and T.R. became President. For the next half century many of the most important social occasions in the city took place at the hotel.

William Washburn's vaguely Italianate design was a six-story marble palace, but it was nevertheless a monument to a gentler past and not nearly so flamboyant as the nearby Hoffman House, built soon after for a more democratic crowd.[9] With opulent interior appointments, including an elaborate bar where Bougereau's *Satyr and the Nymphs* looked out over the patrons, the Hoffman House more accurately reflected post-Civil War taste. Further up Fifth Avenue at Forty-ninth Street, well above the business and entertainment districts of the time, the Windsor[10] and Buckingham[11] hotels opened in 1873 to cater to a family trade.

In 1889 an editor of the *Real Estate Record and Guide* bemoaned the lack of "a really great hotel" and observed that the Hoffman and Windsor hotels were architecturally "not much more than barns, and the most ignorant countryman, however much he may be delighted with the Hoffman House bar, could not stand very much in awe of the Hoffman House building." In fact, as the editor succinctly stated, "There is nothing distinctive, nothing Metropolitan" about any of the hotels.[12] A decade later, however, the situation had changed dramatically. "The hotels of New York have grown *passi passu* with the growth of the city," as William Hutchins observed in 1899 in the *Architectural Record*. "Each stage of the increasing wealth and comfort of the country was represented by hotels in which the highest point of that wealth and comfort was marked."[13] Hutchins was writing at the end of a decade in which changes in social customs, economic prosperity, and advances in construction and technology—the elevator, the telephone, electric lighting, etc.—had combined to produce the largest and most lavish hotels thus far in the city's history.

The grandest of the new hotels to be built in the 1890s was the Waldorf-Astoria, built at Fifth Avenue and Thirty-fourth Street. One year later, the Savoy and New Netherland hotels opened on opposite corners of Fifth Avenue and Fifty-ninth Street. As a group, the hotels reinforced Fifth Avenue's importance as a focus of glamour and power for a decade to come, defining fashion's northern and southern boundaries. Ironically, their buildings were somewhat old fashioned, vast turreted chateaux that looked back to the architecture of the Cosmopolitan Era just ending as much as they partook of their own Composite Era. An admiring writer described one of those hotels in terms that described them all: "Tesselated pavements, marble columns, groined, fluted and quartered ceilings; veneerings of precious stones, statuary and paintings, Pompeian conceits in color and subject, tapestries superb enough for an oriental queen, and a glitter of gold and silver in crystal, are all baptized in a flood of delicate colors as a thousand jets of flame flow softly through colored stars and flash their splendors through overhanging pendants and candelabra."[14]

The Waldorf-Astoria was actually two hotels, the Waldorf and the Astoria, that were joined together: the first opened in 1893 and the latter in 1897.[15] The Waldorf was built by William Waldorf Astor, who was preparing to settle in England where he could buy himself a title (he ultimately became a viscount). Astor razed his father's house on the northwest corner of Fifth Avenue and Thirty-third Street and overshadowed his despised aunt's house next door on the avenue with a massive ten-story hotel crowned by turrets and enormous gables rising another three or four stories. Aunt Caroline's son, John Jacob, decided it would be fun to demolish *his* mother's house and build stables to stink up William's resplendent hotel. But since they were in business together—their joint fortune estimated at two hundred million dollars—John Jacob reconsidered and joined his cousin William Waldorf in the hotel business. John wanted to name his part of the hotel Schermerhorn for his mother's family, but William persuaded him to call the new, taller section the Astoria, after the dream city John Jacob I had hoped to develop in his fur-trapping empire. Their contract specified that the ground-floor connection between the two hotels could be sealed off if the alliance became unsupportable.

Both hotels were designed by Henry J. Hardenbergh. Montgomery Schuyler found the architecture of the ensemble "an interesting exemplification of how fast we have

Waldorf-Astoria Hotel, west side of Fifth Avenue between Thirty-third and Thirty-fourth streets. Henry Janeway Hardenbergh, 1897. View from Fifth Avenue. MCNY

Waldorf-Astoria Hotel, west side of Fifth Avenue between Thirty-third and Thirty-fourth streets. Henry Janeway Hardenbergh, 1897. Peacock Alley. MCNY

Plaza Hotel, west side of Grand Army Plaza between Fifty-eighth and Fifty-ninth streets. Henry Janeway Hardenbergh, 1907. Men's Cafe. MCNY

moved in these things," the Waldorf being "already antiquated by its towering neighbor."[16] The Astoria continued the German Renaissance associations of the Waldorf, but in an exuberant yet symmetrical composition that treated the original hotel as an end pavilion of the much larger ensemble containing 1,300 bedrooms and 40 public rooms. Schuyler praised Hardenbergh for rendering "a very considerable public service.... A systematic attempt was made to secure in a hotel decoration that had a more artistic value and a more serious purpose than the journey work which it had been the rule to employ."[17] Another writer for the *Architectural Record* found that in comparison to earlier hotels "simplicity and classic taste is taking the place of mere gorgeous underplanned decoration."[18] But the Waldorf-Astoria nonetheless had an opulent, fulsome ambiance: the exterior reflected the stylish eclecticism of the Cosmopolitan Era, while the interior anticipated the purer Classicism of the Composite Era.

Different public rooms were each designed in a distinct historical style. The cafe on Thirty-fourth Street was "finished in English oak in the style of the German Renaissance, with Flemish decoration," while the style of the dining room along Fifth Avenue was described as "Italian Renaissance. The magnificent pilasters and columns are carved from marble from northern Russia. The panels of the silk hangings are rose pompadour."[19] The Astor Gallery on the floor above was a rococo interpretation of the Hotel Soubise in Paris, built between the periods of Louis XV and Louis XVI. But the hotel's *piece de resistance* was the enormous ballroom, ninety-five feet long and three stories high. The ballroom was surrounded by tiers of boxes, its yellow walls relieved by ivory trim and decorative panels painted in rose and gold and covered by a ceiling painted by Edwin H. Blashfield to represent *Music and Dance*.

"On the ground floor, the corridors and ladies' parlor, and smoking rooms, and cafes and dining rooms, with music, and crowds, and chatter, present to the student of contemporary manners an interesting and ever changing kaleidoscope," Robert Stewart reported in *Munsey's*. Every night people who couldn't afford the tariffs would loiter in front of the windows along Fifth Avenue, watching the guests down oysters and champagne amid the pomp and glamour inside. But at least as popular was the main hall, known as Peacock Alley. "The young women arrayed

Plaza Hotel, west side of Grand Army Plaza between Fifty-eighth and Fifty-ninth streets. Henry Janeway Hardenbergh, 1907. Tea Room. MCNY

St. Regis Hotel, southeast corner of Fifth Avenue and Fifty-fifth Street. Trowbridge & Livingston, 1904. Perspective view from Fifth Avenue. MCNY

St. Regis Hotel, southeast corner of Fifth Avenue and Fifty-fifth Street. Trowbridge & Livingston, 1904. Palm Room. MCNY

along the Thirty Fourth Street corridor wear a more or less conscious attitude of expecting you to ask them to dance," Stewart continued. "At home it would be shocking, but in frivolous New York they are here for a good time and mean to have it."[20]

The Waldorf-Astoria was also famous for the astounding comfort of its accommodations. "Think of it!" Stewart exclaimed, "You arrive tired, dusty, irritable. Your bag is whisked out of your hand, and you are conducted through a brilliant hall. . . . Presto! You find yourself in a bijou of a suite, with your trunks awaiting you, with a bed which simply beseeches you to lie on it, and with a porcelain tiled bathroom all your own. You press one button in the wall; electric lights flash up. You press another; a maid or valet . . . knocks to unpack your luggage and help you to dress. You press a third; a hall boy appears, like the slave of Aladdin's lamp, to execute any possible command monsieur may issue, from fetching a glass of iced water to ordering a banquet served up to you."[21] An army of servants was required to provide all these services: thousands of guests stayed every night in the Waldorf, but thousands more men and women waited on them, requiring a tremendous but efficient organization.[22] Henry James marveled at the way the seamless organization complemented the gathering of the cosmopolitan crowd: "Here was a social order in positively stable equilibrium. Here was a world whose relation to its form and medium was practically imperturbable; here was a conception of publicity *as* the vital medium organized with the authority with which the American genius for organization, put on its mettle, alone could organize it. The whole thing remains for me . . . a gorgeous golden blur, a paradise peopled with unmistakable American shapes, yet in which, the general and the particular, the organized and the extemporized, the element of ingenuous joy below and of consummate management above, melted together and left one uncertain which of them one was, at a given turn of the maze, most admiring."[23]

The Holland House, a few blocks away on the southwest corner of Fifth Avenue and Thirtieth Street, was perhaps the city's grandest hotel before the addition of the Astoria Hotel to the Waldorf so transformed its neighbor.

Designed by Harding & Gooch in 1891, the Holland House was large, with 350 bedrooms, and had many technological marvels.[24] "Although so immense and preeminent," *King's Handbook of New York* said in 1893, "the exceeding delicacy of its architectural details, and the fineness of its design, make this one of the most attractive and beautiful secular structures on this avenue of palaces."[25] The ground floor was filled with public rooms in various Classical styles, yet the whole did not equal the great forward leap of the Waldorf-Astoria, particularly in the way the Waldorf-Astoria stirred the public imagination as a center of glamorous city life.

Another group of luxury hotels, nearly thirty blocks north on Fifth Avenue, marked the same transitional period. Grouped around the plaza at the southeast corner of Central Park were the Savoy, New Netherland and Plaza hotels: the Savoy and the New Netherland both opened in 1892 on opposite corners of Fifty-ninth Street, but the Plaza Hotel, across the plaza to the west, had a complicated history that illustrated the transformation of the grand hotel. The Savoy, on the southeast corner of Fifth Avenue, was a twelve-story, almost Classical building designed by Ralph S. Townsend,[26] while the New Netherland, on the northeast corner, was a vaguely Romanesque design by William H. Hume that stood 234 feet high, making it, at that time, the tallest hotel in the world.[27]

The Plaza was begun in 1883 as a family apartment hotel, designed by Carl Pfeiffer in a busy version of the Queen Anne style.[28] But the builders, Phyfe & Campbell, ran into financial problems, and after five years of litigation the New York Life Insurance Company foreclosed on the mortgage and hired McKim, Mead & White to transform the half-built structure into a luxury hotel in the Classical style. "The Plaza Hotel," *King's Handbook* said of McKim, Mead & White's design, "is one of the most attractive public houses in the wide world, and represents the highest possibilities attained in the art of constructing and keeping great modern caravanseries. . . . It shows rich and tasteful effects . . . and the simple beauty of Italian Renaissance architecture. . . . A large part of the main floor is finished with choice marble mosaic pavements, silvered ceilings,

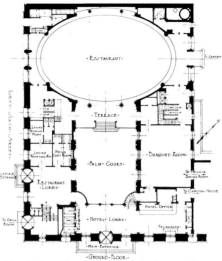

Ritz-Carlton Hotel, west side of Madison Avenue between Forty-sixth and Forty-seventh streets. Warren & Wetmore, 1910. Plan of ground floor. CU

enfoliated bronze columns, counters of Mexican onyx, woodwork of mahogany, and fine paintings. Here are the reception rooms, with their Gobelins tapestries; and the great lounging room, where ladies and gentlemen meet, amid Persian rugs, dainty tables, rich easy-chairs, costly paintings and other attractive features."[29] By 1905, however, the building was outdated and it was decided, H.W. Frohne wrote in 1907, "to replace the hotel, which had lived but a small part of its effective life, by a new one which should be as much superior to its predecessors as the latter was to some of the old down-town establishments of before the war."[30]

The recovery of the economy at the turn of the century produced a boom in the construction of grand hotels. Not only did upper- and middle-class social life continue to increasingly function at public restaurants and private receptions and dances requiring large halls and ballrooms, but a mania developed for English style living. It became fashionable to build a country house for a permanent residence, while keeping a place in the city for the winter season. For those who could not afford to or simply didn't want to maintain two houses, it was acceptable to take a suite of rooms in a stylish hotel. Various Goulds and Solomon Guggenheim, for example, lived in suites at the new Plaza, along with Europeans of tenuous royal descent (although genuine monarchs on visits to New York stayed at the Plaza), and the hotel became an important center for fashionable meals, as well as important balls and cotillions. The hotel's location was partially responsible for the distinction, but it was clearly its architecture that made it the new leading hotel of New York. The owners of the Plaza surpassed the Waldorf-Astoria by hiring the Waldorf's architect to design his masterpiece.

Hardenbergh did not abandon the chateauesque domesticity of his earlier work, but the overall composition and detailing of the Plaza Hotel were far more disciplined and ordered than at the Waldorf-Astoria. The details of the Plaza hinted at the style of Francois I, but they were deliberately restrained and concentrated at the mansard roof, where the filigree softened the skyline silhouette. The simple mass below presented Hardenbergh's clearest statement of the tripartite skyscraper formula, with a rusticated limestone base alluding to traditional masonry construction and an unarticulated shaft sheathed in terra cotta. The result was a masterful combination of *gemuetlichkeit* and Classical rigor.

Although the exterior suggested a square plan organized around an interior court, the hotel was in effect an incomplete fragment of the block. Like Hardenbergh's other hotel plans, his interior arrangements at the Plaza had little formal interest and were merely an economical ordering of numerous functions. But the decoration of the rooms was the most refined that had been seen in New York hotels. The most conspicuous feature was the Tea Room, modelled on the Carlton Tea Room in London. Filled with palm trees and capped by a glass dome described as "a mosaic of myriad colors," the Tea Room's space was visually extended through the use of mirrors and glass doors leading into the restaurant.[31] The Men's Cafe at the northeast corner was decorated in German Renaissance style, with dark wood panelling, brass chandeliers, tapestries and elaborate wooden trusses supporting the ceiling. The most sumptuous interior, however, was the dining room on the corner of Fifty-eighth Street, overlooking Vanderbilt's château. Elaborately gilded and mirrored, with brocaded curtains, crystal chandeliers, and a deeply coffered ceiling, the room was reserved for the hotel's permanent residents.

While the Waldorf-Astoria remained a fashionable hotel, it was beginning to seem somewhat outlandish as architecture: "over florid in treatment and inharmonious in structure . . . an ambiguous combination of a First Empire palace and a summer hotel . . . its furniture and decoration . . . certainly reminiscent of that pompous period of French supremacy; its corridors . . . suggestive of Saratoga."[32] The vastness, which had once seemed so impressive, now compromised its function as an exclusive "club" for the rich. It was waggishly remarked that the Waldorf "provides exclusiveness for the masses," and the Plaza became the preeminent hotel of the day.[33]

Another hotel, the St. Regis, was opened in 1904 for those "who were rich, and who were or wanted to be fashionable, but [who wanted a hotel] which would also be

Ritz-Carlton Hotel, west side of Madison Avenue between Forty-sixth and Forty-seventh streets. Warren & Wetmore, 1910. View from Madison Avenue. MCNY

Hotel Renaissance, southwest corner of Fifth Avenue and Forty-third Street. Right: Clarence Luce, 1894. Left: Howard & Cauldwell, 1898. View from Fifth Avenue. CU

Hotel Imperial, southeast corner of Broadway and Thirty-second Street. McKim, Mead & White, 1890. NYHS

Astor Hotel, west side of Broadway between Forty-fourth and Forty-fifth streets. Clinton & Russell, 1904–09. NYHS

Astor Hotel, west side of Broadway between Forty-fourth and Forty-fifth streets. Clinton & Russell, 1904–09. Art Nouveau suite. MCNY

somewhat quieter and more exclusive. The St. Regis is the only hotel which has been designed throughout particularly for the purpose of supplying the wants of a richer class," Arthur C. David pointed out in the article "The Best Type of Metropolitan Hotel." The standards of the rich man's townhouse, he continued, "have been transferred to a hotel, and have in some respects been transcended." The desire for a domestic atmosphere affected the choice of location on the corner of Fifth Avenue and Fifty-fifth Street in the midst of the most exclusive residential district, accessible to theaters and shops yet "plainly withdrawn from the ordinary places of popular resort."[34]

The young firm of Trowbridge & Livingston won the competition for the St. Regis commission with an accomplished design that used a vocabulary of ornamental details based on contemporary French practice to set a new standard for the luxury hotel. The public rooms were relatively small in comparison with those of the city's great hotels, but Trowbridge & Livingston compensated with an extraordinary richness of materials and a variety of ingenious strategies that visually extended the spaces. The main dining room overlooking Fifth Avenue, evocative of the Hall of Mirrors at Versailles, was seemingly doubled in length by a huge mirror filling the southern wall. The Palm Room, by now a virtually inevitable feature of all Metropolitan Age hotels, was also panelled with mirrors. Murals by Robert Van Vorst Sewell in the lunettes above depicted the life of Psyche, while three stained glass domes admitted light. The building's metalwork was especially distinguished, most notably the two revolving doors at the main entrance, freestanding bronze baldachinos in the lobby. Also notable was the doorman's sentry box that stood under the marquee.

Warren & Wetmore's design for the Ritz-Carlton continued the evolution of the discreet, deliberately understated luxury hotel.[35] Completed in 1910, it filled the western blockfront of Madison Avenue between Forty-sixth and Forty-seventh streets with a sixteen-story predominantly red-brick box above a limestone base with regularly repeated doorways along Madison Avenue that attempted to suggest a typical row of London houses.

The interiors were known for their "good taste" and innumerable conveniences; when the famous chef Escoffier came to work at the hotel, the elegant elliptical restaurant quickly became the most fashionable spot for young socialites. The delicate Adam style Classicism was enormously influential on hotel designers all over America and came to be known as Ritz Hotel Adam. The sense of refined domesticity was continued throughout the hotel: the bedrooms, arranged in suites, were painted in pale shades of blue, gray, rose and green and furnished with delicately scaled reproductions. In addition, they included elaborate locking systems with remote controls at the desk and bedside to release locked doors, and subtle lighting that included early experiments with indirect sources hidden in coves.

Though the Ritz-Carlton was among the city's most luxurious hotels, it reflected a tradition of more modest hotels such as the Hotel Imperial (McKim, Mead & White, 1890, Broadway and Thirty-second Street),[36] the Hotel Renaissance (Clarence Luce, 1894, Fifth Avenue and Forty-third Street),[37] the Manhattan Hotel (Henry J. Hardenbergh, 1897, Madison Avenue and Forty-second Street)[38] and the Hotel Navarre (Barney & Chapman, 1900, Seventh Avenue and Thirty-eighth Street).[39]

McKim, Mead & White's Hotel Imperial was perhaps grander in name than reality, but it was one of the most Classical hotels of its time. A nine-story hotel, one of the young firm's comparatively few tall buildings, it was Stanford White's free interpretation of a Florentine palazzo, with extensive rustication on the upper floors and a two-story base sheathed in marble and punctuated by broad windows along the sidewalk. Hardenbergh's Manhattan Hotel was less Classical, yet it did indicate several years before the Plaza that his taste was becoming less inclined toward the picturesque. At sixteen stories, it was the tallest hotel in the city, and it was grand in its facilities as well as its size. The interiors exhibited the discreet but rich sense of materials which was Hardenbergh's trademark, and the extensive use of dark wood anticipated his later work at the Plaza, yet the Manhattan could not rival the size and number of social spaces at the later hotel.

The Hotel Renaissance, Luce's four-story yellow-brick superstructure set atop a two-story marble base and crowned by a richly modillioned terra-cotta cornice, was notably deferential to McKim, Mead & White's Century Club on the other side of Forty-third Street. Howard & Cauldwell's 1898 addition, on the other hand, was deliberately anticontextual, a piece of a recent Paris boulevard defiantly transferred to an exceptionally narrow lot along a minor side street.[40] The editors of the *Real Estate Record and Guide* thought the effect of the new design, "like the effect of all the juxtapositions of pretentious and architecturesque buildings on Forty-third Street, is what they call in New England, 'unneighborly,' and enhances the general impression of the vicinage of being an architectural museum rather than an architectural quarter." The editors wryly observed that these things "are managed better in France" where consideration for "the unities . . . goes so far towards making Paris a city, and the neglect of which goes so far towards keeping New York a mere agglomeration."[41] Improbable though the addition to the Hotel Renaissance was, as much because of its size as because of its design, it was notable as an early manifestation of the *fin de siecle* Francophilia of New York's architecture: it was, as the *Record and Guide* pointed out, "quite the most Parisian thing in New York. The air of reproduction is everywhere evident, and also the air of being completely up-to-date." It has in New York "an imported and exotic air. As it could not be indigenous it can never become vernacular."[42]

Howard & Cauldwell's flamboyant French design foreshadowed a new species of popular hotels that soon clustered around Times Square, vast amusement palaces that catered to crowds with scenographic interiors that mirrored the theatricality of the Great White Way. The pattern was set by the Astor Hotel, on the west side of Broadway between Forty-fourth and Forty-fifth streets, designed by Clinton & Russell in 1904.[43] Because of its elaborate facilities for public entertainment—it had enormous dining and ball rooms and an extensively developed rooftop with winter gardens and outdoor planting—it was, to some extent, perceived as a replacement for the Waldorf-Astoria.

The Astor was a fully developed example of the Modern French style; its brick and limestone facade terminated in a balcony at the eighth floor that was accessible to guests in summer. The balcony also served as a transition to the elaborate green-copper mansard roof, which like the balcony below was outlined by dozens of lampstands creating a

Hotel Belmont, west side of Park Avenue between Forty-first and Forty-second streets. Warren & Wetmore, 1906. Dining Room. CU

Hotel Rector, southeast corner of Broadway and Forty-fourth Street. D.H. Burnham & Co., 1910-11. View from Forty-fourth Street. CU

memorable nighttime silhouette while illuminating the roof garden. Surprisingly, the mansard roof also sheltered the hotel's cavernous ballrooms, where high ceilings and large spaces could be easily accommodated without the interruption of structural columns.

The Astor's interiors were a catalogue of historical styles, with evocations of the past and exotic locales which reflected the influence of theme restaurants. Certain rooms were characterized by the widespread interest in New York's early history and in the vanishing monuments of Manhattan's past. The basement included the Old New York Lobby and the American Indian Grill Room, the latter decorated with bows and arrows and Indian headdresses. The main lobby incorporated four murals by William De Leftwich Dodge depicting *Ancient and Modern New York*. The lobby floor contained Chinese alcoves, a Flemish smoking room and a Pompeian billiard room, but its principal feature was an *orangerie* where ingenious scenographic and lighting effects were used to transform an interior room into a vision of the Mediterranean. The Hunt Room was of a more masculine sixteenth-century German Renaissance, enlivened with stag horn electroliers and a continuous frieze depicting hunting scenes—its deer in full relief sported genuine antlers.

The ballrooms and meeting rooms under the mansard roof also reflected the thematic approach of the lobby areas, and included a small meeting room in the Colonial style named College Hall, an Oriental room, a series of Art Nouveau rooms with elaborate panelling and leaded glass, and three small rooms each designed as a yacht's cabin with window pictures by C.T. Chapman representing a cruise from Larchmont to New York. By 1909 the hotel had become so successful that a large addition was built at its west side that increased not only guest accommodations but also public facilities, including a new ballroom relocated to a more conventional street level location.[44]

The Astor's success led to the construction of a number of other Broadway hotels, including the Knickerbocker at Forty-second Street and Broadway,[45] designed by Trowbridge & Livingston in a manner heavily influenced by Clinton & Russell and by Hardenbergh's Hotel Manhattan.

At the Knickerbocker the architects attempted to design a popular hotel without resorting to the rather theatrical effects employed at the Astor. To achieve a sense of luxury at a relatively modest cost, they commissioned a series of mural paintings, the most notable being *Old King Cole* by Maxwell Parrish, and set above the principal bar. The Knickerbocker's facades, like the Astor's, were in a brick and limestone French Renaissance style, with a high-pitched roof that lacked the theatrical swagger of the swelling mansard. Its Forty-second Street entrance, however, was graced with an elegant iron canopy. The Knickerbocker never caught on as a hotel, and with the coming of Prohibition, it was converted to an office building in 1920.

D.H. Burnham's design for the Hotel Rector (1910-11, Broadway and Forty-fourth Street) marked the last full statement of the Modern French hotel.[46] A replacement for the famed Rector Restaurant on the same site, its sixteen-story limestone and brick facade combined the polychromatic richness of the Astor with the simple, unbroken lines of the St. Regis. The Broadway entrance led not to the hotel but to its principal public feature, a 700-seat restaurant in a vast room interrupted by four structural columns. The restaurant was raised one story above the grade-level entrance to allow the extensive kitchen natural light and ventilation; one entered a sunken vestibule within the space of the dining room, checking one's coat before ascending a theatrical flight of steps into the dining room proper. Appropriately the most sumptuous room in the hotel, it was painted off-white, extensively gilded, and had red velvet hangings that caused the *American Architect* to label it one of "the most riotous interpretations of Louis XV."[47] The hotel lobby was more restrained. A domed rotunda opened into its barrel vaulted space that had polychrome limited to richly veined marble walls and the cool white plaster vaults.

By 1911 the Rector, Astor and Knickerbocker hotels had created something of an architectural ensemble clustered around Times Square. Together their facades of brick and limestone provided an effective foil to Cyrus Eidlitz's limestone Times Tower, whose unique siting, shape and silhouette guaranteed its role as the district's symbolic focus. As a group, the hotels began to suggest the vernacular

Biltmore Hotel, Vanderbilt to Madison avenues between Forty-third and Forty-fourth streets. Warren & Wetmore, 1913. View from Forty-fourth Street. CU

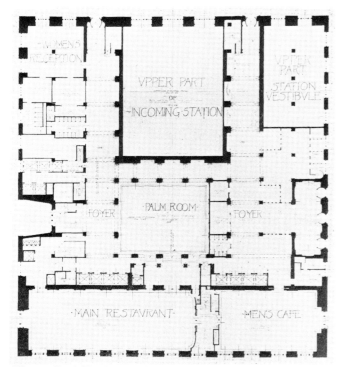

Biltmore Hotel, Vanderbilt to Madison avenues between Forty-third and Forty-fourth streets. Warren & Wetmore, 1913. Plan of ground floor. CU

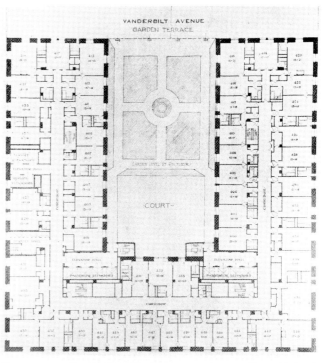

Biltmore Hotel, Vanderbilt to Madison avenues between Forty-third and Forty-fourth streets. Warren & Wetmore, 1913. Plan of typical floor. CU

Biltmore Hotel, Vanderbilt to Madison avenues between Forty-third and Forty-fourth streets. Warren & Wetmore, 1913. Palm Room. MCNY

style which ten years earlier the *Real Estate Record and Guide* had believed unattainable.

The general trend of hotel design in the decade before America's entrance into World War I was toward size, pure and simple, combined with convenience. Many of the best hotels, located near the newly completed railroad complexes of Grand Central Terminal and Pennsylvania Station, were so vast as to be considered cities within the city. Most were near Grand Central, where they could provide ready access not only to the railroad but also to fashionable shops, the growing number of midtown offices, and, via subway, the business center in lower Manhattan.

The Hotel Belmont (1906) was the first and most lavish of the hotels which clustered around Grand Central.[48] Located across from the terminal on the west side of Park Avenue, it was designed by Warren & Wetmore, whose family connections with Cornelius Vanderbilt, President of the New York Central Railroad, got them the commission for not only the terminal but for many of the surrounding buildings as well. They compressed 750 rooms in a slab that rose uninterrupted for twenty-three floors, making it the tallest hotel in the city. Despite the efforts to embellish the facade with an elaborate, if ludicrously overscaled cornice and an iron and glass marquee, the architects did not seem able to overcome the impersonality of the Belmont's size. Even the interior public spaces, despite the careful orchestration of the plan and the full-blown repertoire of classical forms, seemed coldly grand. Warren & Wetmore's Vanderbilt Hotel (1912), ten blocks south on Park Avenue, was an improvement over the Belmont's facade.[49] The architects used design techniques such as light courts to break up the exterior slab, varying the brick color and introducing delicately scaled Adamesque detailing to lighten its apparent mass. Inside, as well, the discrete space making of the Belmont's public rooms gave way to a more open plan, with the lobby floor treated as one amply lit room under a vaulted ceiling, with plants and screens used to articulate various areas for dining and lounging.

The Biltmore (1913), also designed by Warren & Wetmore, was the most complexly planned of New York's station hotels.[50] Built above the tracks of the Incoming Station of Grand Central Terminal, the Biltmore included within its base station facilities such as waiting rooms, train platforms, and a pedestrian concourse leading to the main terminal as well as to the subway. Because the entire basement of the hotel was devoted to the trains, facilities such as the kitchen and laundry had to be located above grade, leading to the hotel's innovative massing, with a seven-story base containing ground level shops, lobbies and restaurants and a separately articulated eighteen-story superstructure containing guest rooms and crowned by the large banquet facilities.

As Theodore Starrett pointed out in *Architecture and Building,* the Biltmore was conceived of as a machine.[51] Though its public spaces were broken up and lobbies were ingeniously spread over a number of levels—the result of functional demands on the cross-sectional organization—arriving guests flowed through it with uncommon ease. The character of the public rooms—with the exception of the rather excessively decorated banquet rooms—was a gentle, restrained Classicism, a far cry from the fully orchestrated baroque of the firm's Belmont Hotel. Frankly commercial and public in character, unlike their more domestic Ritz-Carlton, the Biltmore was comfortable and endearing, but not truly elegant.

The Biltmore was far more endearing than Warren & Wetmore's subsequent Commodore Hotel (1919), which carried out similar ideas at even greater scale.[52] The hotel had two thousand guest rooms and vast public facilities, and provided complex linkages with Grand Central, the subway (parts of which were located directly below) and the elevated roadway which routed the traffic of Park Avenue around the terminal. Unfortunately, what the Commodore possessed as an ideal location in relation to travel convenience, it lacked in charm; its lobby, imagined as an Italian courtyard, had little of the scenographic bravura of earlier hotel lobbies. The biggest hotel in New York, it was a commercial hotel for businessmen and conventioneers that never captured the loyalty of New Yorkers as a meeting place.

Two important station hotels were built in conjunction with the opening of Pennsylvania Station and the extension of the McAdoo Tunnels (Hudson Tubes) to Herald Square. The first of these, the McAlpin (1904) designed by F.M. Andrews & Company, anticipated the Biltmore as "a commercial hotel with all the glitter of the more essentially 'smart' hotels."[53] It included a rooftop health club and solarium for men (women's facilities were on a separate floor), sample rooms for commercial travellers, and, as "a unique tribute to the Metropolis, a 'Silent Floor' reserved for guests whose visit to New York requires them to sleep in the day time hours."[54] What the architectural design of the McAlpin may have lacked in distinction it made up for in the lavishness of its interior appointments. Notable was the extensive use of gilding and mirrors as well as the series of twenty-six tapestries depicting the history of New York which were designed and woven especially for the hotel by the Herter Brothers.

The problem confronting McKim, Mead & White in the design of the Hotel Pennsylvania (1919) was daunting: "to produce the largest hotel building in the world in the greatest hotel city and in so doing to translate into concrete expression the ideals and the enthusiasm of the great railway system as owner and the Statler Company as lessee and operator."[55] The Hotel Pennsylvania, like the General Post Office by the same architects, was intended to enhance the setting of the railroad station. The hotel was set back fifteen feet from the building line in order to initiate a sense of a forecourt or plaza in front of the station. The four-story base sheathed in limestone and the portico of six Ionic columns at the entrance brought the character of the station across Seventh Avenue, but the failure to extend the vocabulary to adjacent buildings and the almost ceaseless flow of traffic prevented the establishment of any sense of the monumental forecourt comparable to that which developed to the north and south of Grand Central Terminal.

Apartment Hotels

A type of hybrid hotel developed in the 1870s and flourished between 1890 and 1910.[56] Called the apartment hotel, this new form of accommodation supplied the services of a hotel to permanent or long term residents and helped forge a sociological link between the Cosmopolitan Era, which disdained apartment houses, and the Age of Convenience, which saw people flocking to them. The apartment hotel was initially intended for bachelors and young families as

Hermitage Hotel, 592 Seventh Avenue. Robert D. Kohn, 1907. NYHS

Hotel Somerset, 150 West Forty-seventh Street. Frederick Browne, ca. 1900. CU

Bachelor Apartments, 15 East Forty-eighth Street. Lienau & Nash, ca. 1900. CU

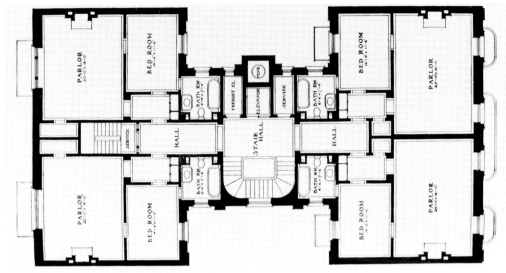

Bachelor Apartments, 15 East Forty-eighth Street. Lienau & Nash, ca. 1900. Plan of typical floor. CU

yet unable to afford a house or staff of their own. As the city's middle class grew, however, the apartment hotel became a feature of metropolitan life which lasted until rapid rail transit made year-round, country-style suburban living accessible to city workers.[57] Apartment hotels were also a response to a loophole in the city's building laws which controlled the height of residences (houses and apartment houses—that is suites of rooms with kitchens) but not of hotels.

Apartment hotels met a real need in the expanding city. As E.T. Littell observed in a paper read in 1876 before the Eighth Annual Convention of the American Institute of Architects, "In all great centers of population there comes a certain period of growth when, by reason of the increasing value of real estate and the weight of taxation, the rental of a domicile becomes so great that the [middle] class . . . is forced by gradual process into the suburbs and into the country, leaving the rich and the poor together to form the city population. . . . Notably this is the case in New York; and the people upon whom the pressure falls with the most severity are, *first,* the bachelors; *second,* the young married couples; *third,* those [the elderly] whom the decline of life has left with few or none around them."[58]

Littell proposed two solutions, which he called "club chambers" and "apartment houses." Club chambers housed fifty or sixty persons in two-bedroom suites, and best served bachelors. Apartment houses, as Littell viewed them, were in effect residential hotels which met the need for young or old childless married couples to live economically. The apartments consisted of a hall, a parlor, a dining room, a bathroom and bedrooms, "with possibly a five-by-eight cooking closet furnished with a gas range," but without amenities typical of the house such as an elaborate kitchen or a laundry. A restaurant would be provided in the building "from which meals should be forwarded, in felt-lined boxes, to the private dining rooms of the tenants."[59]

Apartment hotels based on Littell's model flourished in the west midtown area and the West End during the Composite Era. Usually modest in size, they were typically infill buildings with a single exposed front facade elaborately decorated to make a distinct contribution to the rich texture of the newly vertical mid-Manhattan townscape.

Israels & Harder designed several mid-block hotels, including the Warrington (161 Madison Avenue),[60] the Devon (70 West Fifty-fifth Street)[61] and the Arlington (Twenty-fifth Street near Broadway).[62] Their Holland Hotel at 66–68 West Forty-sixth Street was a restrained composition of alternating limestone string courses and red brick panels enlivened by unusual recessed bay windows.[63] H.B. Mulliken's Iroquois Hotel on West Forty-fourth Street was a particularly chaste example of the apartment hotel in the midtown area. Its generally bland exterior was relieved by a large iron and glass canopy which protected guests as they alighted from cabs.[64] Frederick Browne's Hotel Somerset at 150 West Forty-seventh Street was built with an enormously scaled column screen at the entrance that was reiterated at the roof, suggesting that the lessons of Howard & Cauldwell's bold addition to his Hotel Renaissance were not ignored.[65] Charles I. Berg's Hotel Touraine, just west of Fifth Avenue on Thirty-ninth Street, was a more robust exemplar of the popular Modern French taste.[66] Its boldly rusticated base, twin columns of iron-sheathed bay windows and paired brackets supported a balcony cornice at the base of an elaborate mansard roof that was pierced by dormers and sported a rooftop garden. Renwick, Aspinwall & Owen's larger and somewhat more subdued Mansfield Hotel on Forty-fourth Street west of Fifth Avenue enjoyed a suitably elegant plan, not only in its public spaces but also in the ample residential suites.[67]

The Prince George was the most elaborate of the mid-block apartment hotels.[68] Designed by Howard Greenley, it was completed in 1905 on a 200-foot-wide site extending through the block to Twenty-seventh Street. On the Twenty-eighth Street facade, Greenley skillfully adapted the robust forms of the Modern French vocabulary to the narrow New York street by flattening the profiles of the individual elements of the facade. His division of the composition into two, giving the impression of two buildings side by side, helped reduce the building's scale in relationship to its neighbors. Inside, the tea room had mosaic tile floors, an arched lattice ceiling and Viennese bentwood furniture which offered a refreshing break with the generally heavy

Carlyle Chambers, southwest corner of Fifth Avenue and Thirty-eighth Street. Herts & Tallant, ca. 1900. CU

Hotel Essex, northeast corner of Madison Avenue and Fifty-sixth Street. Howard, Cauldwell & Morgan, 1901. CU

Mills House Number One, south side of Bleecker Street between Thompson and Sullivan streets. Ernest Flagg, 1896. View from Bleecker Street. NYHS

interiors of the typical public rooms of the day.

Ludlow & Valentine's Seymour Hotel was only slightly smaller.[69] While the bulk of the hotel was on Forty-fifth Street, a twenty-five-foot-wide sliver to the west of the New York Yacht Club faced Forty-fourth Street. The Seymour's principal facade was relatively flat, except for a modelled arched pediment at the entrance which was restated at the eighth floor as an elaborately modelled swan's neck pediment carried on robust brackets. Lienau & Nash's bachelor apartments at 15 East Forty-eighth Street were far more restrained, eschewing the typical red brick and limestone patterning of the Modern French prototypes in favor of an attempt at a dignified English Georgian, perhaps in response to the more solidly residential neighborhood east of Fifth Avenue.[70]

Robert D. Kohn's Hermitage Hotel, built in 1907 on Seventh Avenue south of Forty-second Street, was a more inventive design.[71] Described by Montgomery Schuyler as "a place where you can leave traces of your own inhabitancy and of your intention to resume habitation, with the certainty of not finding it too much 'swept and garnished' for alien occupancy before your return," the Hermitage was designed specifically for bachelors, with single room accommodations, a public restaurant and grill, and lounging and writing rooms on the second floor "in the manner of a club." Kohn's facade was lauded by Schuyler as "a mere envelope, but an envelope that fits, like the sculptured drapery through which the structure of the nude is felt." Schuyler particularly admired the two-story base, where four sandstone columns with squat proportions and pronounced entasis clearly stood out from the structural piers behind them and framed a light metal and glass infill of bay windows: "They are masks . . . but they are not the less impressive and hardly the less expressive for that. They reveal even while concealing."[72] A seven-story shaft with vertically panelled brickwork reflecting the structural bays and the room arrangements within was topped by a corbelled balcony which marked the transition to a mansard roof punctuated with three dormers. The detailing throughout consisted of abstracted traditional forms, reflecting the influence of the Art Nouveau and progressive Viennese Classicists such as Otto Wagner and Josef Plecnik.

Some of the apartment hotels were quite large, frequently occupying corner sites which allowed for inventive unit planning and individual expression in the facades. Particularly noteworthy in the midtown area were Mulliken & Moeller's Hotel Cumberland at Broadway and Fifty-fourth Street[73] and Harry Allan Jacobs's Hotel Seville at Madison Avenue and Twenty-ninth Street, which had an elaborately modelled facade with Modern French motifs.[74] Herts & Tallant's vaguely Hawksmoorian Carlyle Chambers occupied a corner at Fifth Avenue and Thirty-eighth Street.[75] Howard, Cauldwell & Morgan's Essex, located at the corner of Madison Avenue and Fifty-sixth Street, was by no means as flamboyant as their earlier Hotel Renaissance, although the elaborate Serlian dormers made a memorable skyline.[76]

The Gotham Hotel (1905) was the most glorious of the apartment hotels.[77] Twice as tall as its neighbor to the south, the University Club, it was designed in a similar Italian Renaissance vocabulary to harmonize with McKim, Mead & White's most admired clubhouse. Hiss & Weekes respected the club's set back, taking advantage of the sliver of exterior space as an outdoor dining terrace defined by a balustrade, canopy and plantings, and accessible to the main restaurant through French doors which continued the arches of McKim's ground floor. (These features disappeared when Fifth Avenue's traffic lanes were widened in 1911.) The arches of the club's third floor were sympathetically restated; string courses and balconies were used to carry across its horizontal divisions. The Gotham was also intended to complement Trowbridge & Livingston's St. Regis across Fifth Avenue, with which it formed a symbolic gateway to the Central Park hotel district. While the St. Regis had originally been planned as an apartment hotel but never functioned as such, the Gotham started out as an apartment hotel and gradually became more and more transient as the elaborate provisions for permanent family life failed to attract clients. In addition to the usual restaurants and lobby, special dining facilities were provided for children and family servants, while special elevators connected the hotel's kitchen with small pantries in each apartment so that families need not necessarily dine outside their apart-

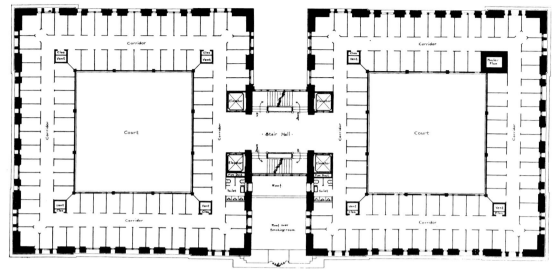

Mills House Number One, south side of Bleecker Street between Thompson and Sullivan streets. Ernest Flagg, 1896. Plan of typical floor. CU

ments and the odor of food would not clog the public halls.

The two Mills Houses, designed by Ernest Flagg in 1896, were the most unusual of the apartment hotels.[78] They were not intended for the usual family clientele, but for working-class bachelors who could not afford to live alone or even to board with families. Palatial in scale, with tiny bedrooms but modern sanitary facilities, as well as lounges, restaurants and smoking and reading rooms, they were a product of the vision of Darius O. Mills, the philanthropically-minded proprietor who expected them to yield a modest 5 percent profit. While hardly in the same class as the Gotham Hotel, they were, in their way, equally grand, causing *Scribner's* to label the first Mills House "A Palace at Twenty Cents a Night."[79]

Mills House No. 1 (1896) occupied the full blockfront along the south side of Bleecker Street between Thompson and Sullivan streets. The building consisted of two ninety-by-ninety foot twelve-story blocks linked by a glazed stair hall. Each block contained about 750 bedrooms as well as elevators and toilets. The bedrooms either faced the street or a large interior courtyard lit by a skylight. The palatial impression of the facades was echoed throughout by the grouping of windows, reducing the impression of the cellular organization within, and through the introduction of an elaborately modelled and boldly scaled frontispiece set between the two blocks at the entrance on Bleecker Street. A bold cornice of copper carried on wrought-iron brackets fittingly climaxed the sophisticated Indiana limestone facade.

Apartments

The burden of Mrs. Manson Mingott's flesh had long since made it impossible for her to go up and down stairs, and with characteristic independence she had made her reception room upstairs and established herself (in flagrant violation of all the New York proprieties) on the ground floor of her house; so that as you sat in her sitting room window with her, you caught . . . the unexpected vista of a bedroom with a huge low bed upholstered like a sofa, and a toilet-table with frivolous lace flowers and a gilt-framed mirror.

Her visitors were startled and fascinated by the foreignness of this arrangement, which recalled scenes in French fiction, and architectural incentives to immorality such as the simple Americans had never dreamed of. That was how women with lovers lived in the wicked old societies, in apartments with rooms on one floor, and all the indecent propinquities that their novels described. Edith Wharton, *The Age of Innocence* (New York: D. Appleton & Company, 1920), 28-29.

The earliest multiple dwellings in New York were simply empty houses rented to poor families left behind as the fashionable neighborhoods developed further and further to the north on Manhattan Island. The city's booming population placed tremendous pressure on the price of land accessible to the commercial districts, and the poor, least able to pay the cost of commuting on the new forms of transportation, were forced to live in greater and greater numbers in the old single-family houses. As early as 1833, however, speculators learned that more money could be made by building tenements designed to allow the landlord to pack in more tenants than could easily be squeezed into a converted house.[80]

Those tenements were mean affairs, inherently limited by their construction on twenty-five- by-one-hundred- foot lots, the New York City standard devised for single-family houses that had been used in determining the dimensions of the city grid. Only those who couldn't afford any better lived in these tenements; not only did they usually lack modern conveniences, but because of the city's booming population and the rapidly increasing land costs it produced, the lots were developed at as high a density as possible. Light wells were not even considered, and several rooms on each floor had no windows for daylight or fresh air.

In 1870, however, Rutherford Stuyvesant opened the Stuyvesant Apartments, a tenement in configuration, though the first apartment house designed for the middle class.[81] Stuyvesant's impeccable social position lent the project some social cachet, as did his choice of architect, Richard Morris Hunt, who was just beginning to establish his position as the most fashionable architect of the time. Before the building at 142 East Eighteenth Street was even finished, several prominent people subscribed for apartments there.[82]

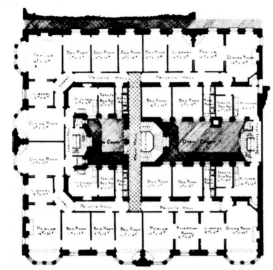 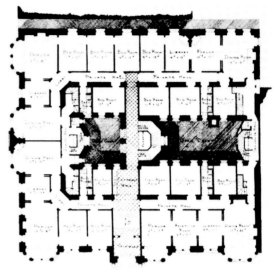

Hoffman Arms, northwest corner of Madison Avenue and Fifty-ninth Street. Charles W. Romeyn & Company, 1884. Plans of first floor and upper floors. CU

As Edith Wharton's well known description of Mrs. Mingott's shocking situation indicated, however, most New York families with any social aspirations still would not live anywhere but a house, no matter how humble. "No one would be so foolish to imagine," *Scribner's* commented in 1874, "that the general introduction of apartment houses would straightaway inaugurate a domestic and social millenium,"[83] yet by 1893 *King's Handbook of New York* was able to report that apartment houses "hold more than half of the middle-class population of Manhattan Island. Real estate is so valuable and consequently rents so high that to occupy a house is quite beyond the reach of a family of ordinary means, and the suburbs on account of their inaccessibility are out of the question. Consequently apartments and flats have become a necessity, and a system of living, originally adopted for that reason, has become very much a virtue. Apartment life is popular and to a certain extent fashionable. Even society countenances it, and a brownstone front is no longer indispensable to at least moderate social standing. And as for wealthy folk who are not in society, they are taking more and more to apartments."[84]

The Development of the New York Apartment House

By the late 1870s, the limitations of the narrow lot tenement had become clearly evident, and a movement for the reform of that building type became interwoven with a more general movement for the amelioration of a host of social conditions that plagued the poorest classes. The Tenement House Law of 1879 mandated the use of a plan that because of its shape—narrow at its center to allow light wells at either side—was known as the Dumbbell plan. Simultaneously, the middle class was coming to accept the inevitable consequences of Manhattan's ever increasing congestion. There was only a limited amount of land available, yet more and more people wanted it. Moreover, the very rich had not yet accepted the apartment house (they would not until after the turn of the century), and the astounding prices they were paying for house sites were driving all prices to unheard of levels. As a commentator for *Building* magazine pointed out, "Exclusiveness here is the only mark of social distinction; hence both those who have acquired wealth and seek such distinction are in active competition for homes in the narrow and geographically limited region of fashion."[85] By living in multiple dwellings, the middle class could aspire to the more prestigious districts. But by 1882 the apartment house had become so respectable that it could improve neighborhoods. *Harper's Monthly* reported scores of apartment houses being built near saloons, stables, tenements and rookeries, "occupied by refined, fastidious people" who would never have thought of living in such a district as a single family.[86]

Many of these buildings were little more than glorified tenements. The Stuyvesant, for example, looked better than the average tenement, was built with better materials and had more space per occupant—there were only two apartments per floor—but the rooms were still poorly lit and badly ventilated. There was a demand to be filled, however, and developers slowly raised their standards. In 1871 Dr. David H. Haight rebuilt a mansion at Fifteenth Street and Fifth Avenue and created the first apartment house in New York with an elevator, capable of commanding rents of $2-3,000 a year.[87] By 1886 Chas. F. Wingate reported in *Building* that conveniences such as elevators and economies of construction had made apartment buildings an improvement over private houses. Maintenance was easier and cheaper, although the class of tenant Wingate was writing about was rarely doing the work himself: "To the householder the principal saving from living in flats is in the wages, waste and worry of servants. A family who would require from four to eight servants in an ordinary dwelling can easily get along with half that number in an apartment house. This means a saving of about five hundred dollars a year for each servant dispensed with, to say nothing of mental wear and tear and avoidance of 'aggravation.'" Moreover, Wingate continued, "Anyone accustomed to living in flats and who has thoughts of returning to a separate dwelling, will be struck with the contrast in the proportion of rooms, the height of ceilings and the size of windows. As has been frequently pointed out, the floor space in a flat is much larger than in private houses of the same grade or scale of rent, and there is also much greater area in every way."[88]

Hoffman Arms, northwest corner of Madison Avenue and Fifty-ninth Street. Charles W. Romeyn & Company, 1884. Perspective. CU

Wingate also pointed out that there was safety in numbers, and that women in particular were more secure in a large apartment building than a private house. The Cosmopolitan Era, and the great public hotels, had transformed public opinion about communal living: there was still a problem of association with the concept of the tenement and the poor, but that was partially dealt with by simply changing the name to French Flat. Although the buildings were clearly inferior to contemporary French tenements, the terms were devised to give them the social cachet necessary to compete with the brownstone. Parisian apartments, which had developed from a long tradition of dense urban living, were the grandest in the world, and it was not uncommon for Parisians to feel they were enhancing their status by moving out of private houses into apartments.[89] As more and more architects followed Hunt to the Ecole des Beaux-Arts, French architecture became increasingly well known and popular on this side of the Atlantic. A number of turn-of-the-century articles and books documented the history of the French apartment house for American architects.[90]

Hunt's Stuyvesant Apartments were perhaps the first American building to be called a French Flat, but it was succeeded in popular usage by the term "apartment house." In 1877, the *Real Estate Record and Guide* called the apartment house a development of the tenement,[91] although in a slightly more candid moment they had earlier admitted that they were really only "the tenements of the rich."[92] The chateauesque Berkshire (Carl Pfeiffer, 1883, at Madison Avenue and Fifty-second Street),[93] the Hoffman Arms (Charles Romeyn, 1884, Madison Avenue and Fifty-ninth Street)[94] and the Osborne (James E. Ware, 1885, Seventh Avenue and Fifty-seventh Street)[95] were all grand and imposing on the street and in their lobbies, but they simply placed too much bulk on their lots and were poorly laid out.

The year after the Osborne was completed, H.W. Fabian published an essay in *Building* that called for bulk and height controls for apartment house construction. "Though formerly but little system prevailed in the erection of apartment houses in a block, as regards their relation to one another, a systematic arrangement will undoubtedly become a feature of the future, and in addition to a reasonable proportion between the width of streets and the heights of buildings, the ideal of future development may be described in the formula 'One block, one house.'" Fabian was not only explicit in his call for the "abolishment of the twenty-five foot lot principle," but also in his belief that the "workingman's home of the future" should contain no kitchen (food would be prepared in a communal restaurant), and heating and laundry facilities should be centrally provided. Fabian also advocated that the house be rented fully furnished and that elevators be provided so that the houses could be stacked, though the overall height of the building "of course . . . should not exceed a certain proportion to the width of the street."[96]

New York architects began to look back to Hunt's criticism of the competition held in 1879 for the design of a model tenement that had produced the dumbbell type. Commenting on James E. Ware's winning entry, a three court dumbbell scheme, Hunt prophetically pointed out that the problem could not be tackled within the constraints imposed by the narrow, twenty-five by one-hundred-foot lot, and that in any case, the dumbbell type would be better replaced by a model with one large courtyard.[97]

Hunt was familiar with the courtyard apartment from his days at the Ecole des Beaux-Arts. In Paris and other European cities where the apartment house had been established earlier than in New York, two basic planning types had been developed, the courtyard and the tenement. The courtyard apartment house was based on a socially cooperative idea of collective habitation: apartments formed a barrier around a courtyard, which thereby became a private realm reserved for the tenants exclusively. The tenement was collective but not cooperative in its implications: in it, the individual character of the dwelling was deemphasized in favor of the public aspects, as represented in the street facades and the circulation spaces—lobbies, stairways and corridors which were often quite grand and were thought of as extensions of the street.

As early as 1877, Alfred T. White, a Brooklyn businessman interested in housing reform, had hired the architects William L. Field & Sons to build the first courtyard apartment house in the metropolitan area.⁹⁸ The project, the Home Buildings at Baltic and Hicks streets in Brooklyn, was probably influenced by model working-class developments of the 1860s in London, such as those built by Sir Sidney Waterlow's Improved Model Dwelling Corporation.⁹⁹ In 1879, White built a second and more important development, the much larger Tower complex. Designed by Field for an adjoining lot bordered by Hicks, Baltic and Warren streets, it consisted of three six-story buildings set around a large courtyard, and two rows of two-story cottages built along a mews, the entire group housing 260 families. The Home Buildings and the Tower apartment houses all featured open stairs on their fronts, and perimeter galleries leading to shallow, floor-through apartments that faced on the court. All rooms had outside windows, and each apartment had a water closet, although communal bathing facilities were located in the basement.

With these projects, White, whose motto was "philanthropy plus 5 percent," introduced the concept of limited dividend housing, later to be carried forward by the City and Suburban Homes Company and many subsequent sponsors of working-class housing. White sponsored a third project in Brooklyn in 1890, the Riverside buildings at Columbia Place, again designed by Field.¹⁰⁰

The introduction of the courtyard *parti* in Brooklyn established in the metropolitan area a new type of multifamily accommodation with distinct advantages over the tenement. The court was a social amenity, which not only supplied reasonable amounts of light and air to the apartments, but provided a communal oasis away from the teeming streets of a poor section of Brooklyn. Children could play under the watchful eyes of their families, with the children of other families whom the parents knew and with whom they shared a sense of identity. At night and on weekends, the parents could also relax under the trees in the courtyard. The individual floor-through apartments, of course, also had their advantages. Being double-sided, they probably felt psychologically more like a house than any apartment that the tenants had been able to afford before. In the days before air conditioning, such considerations, combined with those relating to contemporary theories of disease, gave apartments special significance.

The courtyard model was also used for wealthier families. Although none of the tenants of the Dakota Apartments, built in 1882 on Central Park West between Seventy-second and Seventy-third streets, were members of New York's society's *400,* they were rich—they had to be to be able to afford to live in New York's most luxurious apartment house. Henry J. Hardenbergh's design for the Dakota, like his subsequent plans for the Waldorf-Astoria, was New York's first convincing expression of a new form of urban living.¹⁰¹

The image of the Dakota was a splendid and exact expression of the Cosmopolitan Era's tendency to combine monumentality and domesticity. A great, broad pile of tawny brick trimmed in stone, the Dakota sat behind a moat, guarded by iron railings and crowned by a vigorous roofscape worthy, if not of Blois or Chambord, at least of some outsized mid-Victorian hunting lodge in England, France or Germany. Though each stack of apartments was virtually identical from top to bottom, different window shapes and the selective use of balconies gave the facades a subtle liveliness and variety that lent a measure of individuality to each apartment without compromising the total image. In 1886 H.W. Fabian labeled the Dakota, the "most excellent of any of the kind in New York . . . with its lofty and handsomely ornamented roof [it] proclaims afar the palatial character of all its rich and comfortable dwelling suites."¹⁰²

In plan, the Dakota was a paradigm of its type. Its courtyard functioned admirably as a *cour d'honneur* for all users of the building. Broad enough to accommodate carriages, embellished by a fountain and guarded from the street by a concierge, the courtyard was entered through a majestically proportioned gateway.¹⁰³ Other notable organizational features included the use of an entry system to enhance a sense of privacy, the setting of first-floor apartments well above street level to ensure visual privacy, the introduction of "moats" along all street frontages to increase safety and supply light and air for basement spaces, and the provision of collective spaces (a restaurant, a ballroom and a suite of guest rooms).

Dakota, northwest corner of Central Park West and Seventy-second Street. Henry Janeway Hardenbergh, 1882. View from Central Park. MCNY

East River Houses, 507–23 East Seventy-seventh Street. Henry Atterbury Smith, 1909. View from southeast. CU

In 1887 the architects and builders Hubert, Pirsson & Company proposed a courtyard apartment building for the middle class, to be built on the site of the original Madison Square Garden (McKim, Mead & White's Garden was built instead).[104] Sponsored by William H. Vanderbilt, this premonitory project combined distinctly individual accommodation in a unified mass. Hubert's plans called for a thirteen-story building running along the perimeter of a full city block, to consist of six layers of "small two-story houses, each 22 x 50 feet, and set one on top of another." The idea, which Hubert claimed was aborted by the passage of the height control law, was based in part on his belief that "the French, except perhaps for the very poorest classes, do not live in apartments, but in *small, private dwelling houses, built on one level on the top of one another* and reached by a narrow ascending street."[105] Shops were to have been located on the ground floor and to have extended the full depth of the site, their roofs forming the floor of the eighty-foot-wide courtyard. The 240 "houses" would have been connected at their parlor levels by fourteen-foot-wide "aerial sidewalks" cantilevered beyond the building line by four feet. Pairs of elevators at each of the four corners of the building were to provide vertical circulation for tenants and guests, while dumbwaiters situated between each pair of apartments would have handled deliveries and garbage removal. "The aerial sidewalk arrangement," Hubert and his partners wrote, "by making the public access to the houses absolutely open and free, carries out to the utmost the French idea, that the public hall and stairs are a mere continuation of the public street, and that each apartment is in all of its essentials a separate and individual home."[106]

Only sketch plans remain for Hubert's dramatic Madison Square Garden proposal. Nonetheless its synthesis of the duplex unit (with its sense of domesticity) and the courtyard (with its specifically public character) made it a unique statement, and one that would be taken up in various ways by the architects in the Composite Era and afterward.

Hubert's use of the duplex apartment unit was a brilliant response to the typical, affluent New Yorker who echoed Edith Wharton's response to the "indecent propinquities" of living on a single floor. The duplex was introduced by Hubert, Pirsson & Company in the cooperatively financed and maintained apartment houses called Hubert Home Clubs. The first of these, built in 1883 at 121 Madison Avenue, consisted of stacked duplex apartments, with two separate elevator cores serving five apartments per floor.[107]

Few apartment buildings were built in the early 1890s. The general economic slump of the time was the main reason for this, but the imposition of height controls in 1888 was also partially responsible. The height control legislation was continually refined during the 1890s, so that by 1901 nonfireproof residential buildings were limited to 85 feet, while fireproof structures could go as high as twelve stories provided they did not exceed 150 feet on a street 80 feet wide, or ten stories and 125 feet on a street 68 feet wide.

As the economy began to revive in the late 1890s, three apartment building types prevailed: courtyard apartments occupying very large sites; smaller elevator apartment buildings (frequently with duplex units); and conventional walk-up apartments. The last two were both legally defined as tenements, though the term apartment house was used to describe those intended for the more affluent tenant.

The Courtyard Apartment

The most important work of the 1890s was the design of working-class apartments. By 1893, according to a Board of Health census, over one million New Yorkers—70 percent of the population—lived in multiple-family dwellings, four-fifths of which were tenements, mainly dumbbells.[109] But the inadequacies of the dumbbell tenement—overcrowding, small light wells, badly lit rooms and communal toilets and sinks—had become all too apparent to a number of architects and social reformers, who set out to improve conditions. In 1894, the architect Ernest Flagg wrote an important article in *Scribner's* outlining the evils of the tenement and proposing a courtyard building that would occupy four lots, one-hundred by one-hundred feet. Although the core was so small that it was hardly a courtyard in the sense that would have been understood by the designers of the best courtyard apartments already existing in New York, it at least provided adequate light and air to all apartments. Flagg's model tenement house was divided by fire walls into four sections and had stairways at each corner of the courtyard.[110]

Flagg's chance to test his square plan came in a competition sponsored in 1896 by the Improved Dwelling Council, an organization devoted to the construction of better tenements which still returned a profit. Contestants were required to design a building for an entire city block and use interior courts no smaller than nine hundred square feet. In addition, the apartment houses had to be as economical in area as dumbbell tenements, and every apartment facing the long avenues had to be planned with an entrance from the side streets so that all the frontage on the ground floors would be available for stores.[111]

With only a few alterations, Flagg's 1894 scheme fit the requirements perfectly, and both he and James E. Ware received prizes. Flagg's model tenement was soon built by the newly formed City and Suburban Homes Company, a limited-profit development company specifically devoted to the building of houses for wage earners. In 1897 the company commissioned him to design a complex of model tenements to house 373 families on West Sixty-eighth and West Sixty-ninth streets between Amsterdam and West End avenues.[112] In 1900 Flagg designed a development of eleven six-story walk-up tenements constructed on a large parcel of land on Tenth Avenue, between West Forty-first and West Forty-second streets. These were notable in that the sponsorship of the New York Fireproof Tenement Association introduced a new and highly significant note of concern into the project.[113] The City and Suburban Homes Company's second project, on East Sixty-fourth Street between First Avenue and Avenue A (York Avenue), was built by Ware. Like Flagg's tenements, these were six story walk-ups, but they showed improvements in the organization of the interior plan.[114]

The competition of 1896, the two built examples of new ideas, and the continual proselytizing by Flagg and others for reform, led to the implementation of the so-called New Law of 1901, which encouraged large lot development and doubled the basic lot width from twenty-five feet to fifty feet while holding land coverage to 70 percent. This combination of factors gave birth to a truncated version of the courtyard apartment.[115] The most notable were the East River Houses, also known as the Cherokee Flats or Cherokee Apartments.[116] Working-class housing that was even more suc-

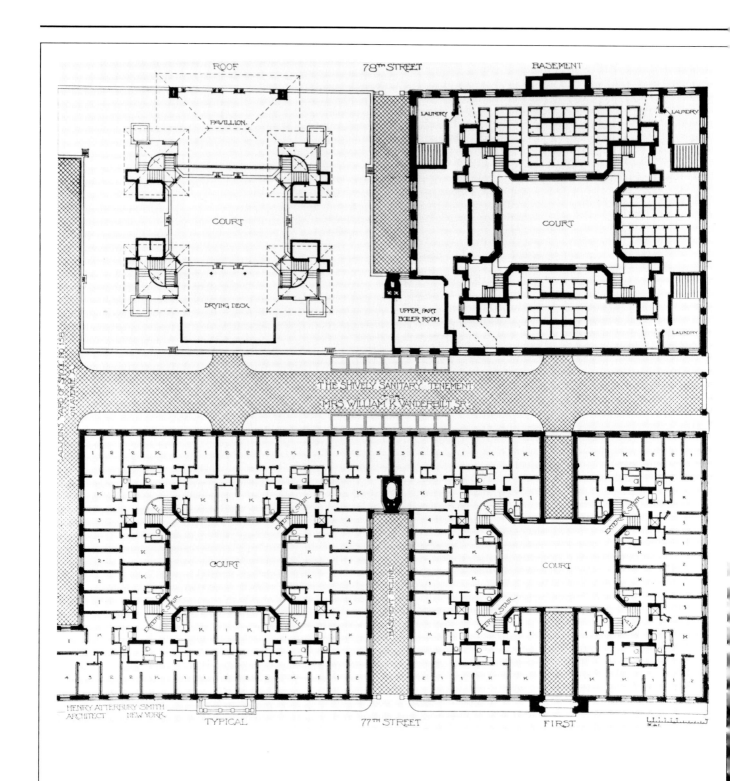

East River Houses, 507–23 East Seventy-seventh Street. Henry Atterbury Smith, 1909. Plans of a typical floor, basement and roof. CU

East River Houses, 507–23 East Seventy-seventh Street. Henry Atterbury Smith, 1909. Chimney detail. OMH

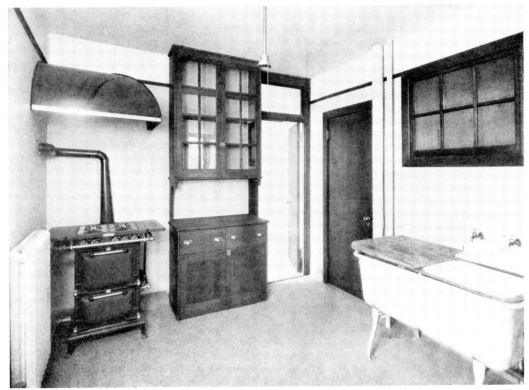
East River Houses, 507–23 East Seventy-seventh Street. Henry Atterbury Smith, 1909. Typical kitchen. OMH

998 Fifth Avenue, northeast corner of Fifth Avenue and Eighty-first Street. McKim, Mead & White, 1910. View from Fifth Avenue. MCNY

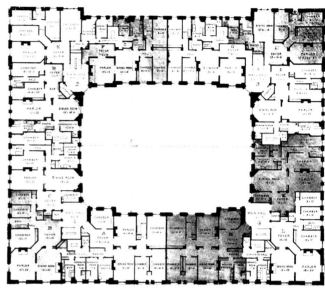

Graham Court, east side of Seventh Avenue between 115th and 116th streets. Clinton & Russell, 1901. Plan of a typical floor. CU

cessful than Flagg's group for the City and Suburban Home Company, these apartments were designed by Henry Atterbury Smith, and built under the sponsorship of Mrs. William K. Vanderbilt in 1908 and 1909. The group of four buildings, housing a total of 384 families, was sited along Cherokee Place between East Seventy-seventh and Seventy-eighth streets facing John Jay Park. Although the courtyards around which the apartments were grouped were only marginally larger than the light wells of speculatively built hollow-core tenements, they nevertheless ensured cross ventilation in all apartments and broke down the scale of the development.

Using a relaxed variation on a Florentine Renaissance vocabulary, Smith was able to infuse the Cherokee Flats with considerable grace and intimacy. A number of attractive features were introduced to modify the austerity of the overall massing. The tunnels leading to the interior courts from the street, lined in Guastavino tile, not only connected the courtyards with the street but also established a grid of pedestrian circulation through the block. Delicate glass and iron pergolas at the roof sheltered stairs left open to enhance the movement of air through the buildings, wrought-iron seats at the landings were provided for those made weary by the climb, and triple-hung windows opening onto open wrought-iron balconies were included in each apartment. In fact, the fine sense of detail rivaled (and in some ways exceeded) that of contemporary luxury apartments. The gentle scale, which resulted as much from the decision to build walk-ups and from the intimate relation to John Jay Park as it did from the delicate handling of the forms, made the complex a very special oasis in the city.

Two other examples of the truncated courtyard apartment house were built not for the poor but the rich. Harde & Short's Alwyn Court (1908) and McKim, Mead & White's 998 Fifth Avenue (1912) both had such small courts that they were, in effect, tenements as much as courtyard apartment houses. Yet each was finely detailed, designed to meet a demand that would grow after the war for a new type of apartment. The upper- and upper-middle classes no longer considered the apartment hotel the most fashionable alternative to a private house, and began to move to vast apartment houses in the fashionable neighborhoods. As the *Real Estate Record and Guide* commented, "We must learn to take a very large view of New York, for it is to be the foremost city of the world. The leading families in America are adopting a standard of living which includes more than one home. There is a country home and also a city home. The real homestead is in the country. There's where the family's treasures are. For the city home, apartments are coming to be preferred over the private dwelling, for one reason, because a private dwelling may not be obtainable in the particular neighborhood where the family wishes to reside in town. The really high-class apartment offers to tenants of wealth and standing the choice of the finest locations in Swelldom."[117]

The principal feature of the Alwyn Court was not the court but the generous and geometrically intricate plans, the elaborate interior appointments including fine panelling, extensive closets (an innovation of the era) and a central vacuum system, all encased in an extraordinarily intricate French Renaissance style tapestrylike wall of terra cotta. The palatial manner of the building was intended to impress the visitor and the passerby with the status of the inhabitants. But *Architecture* magazine remarked somewhat sarcastically that "one does not know which to admire most completely, the infinite patience of the draughtsman who worked out the detail or the consummate skill displayed by the terra cotta company who executed it. The design, if made by a pastry cook, would be of the highest excellence, but it can hardly be considered at all in the light of architecture although the detail of the entrance has considerable charm."[118]

McKim, Mead & White's design for 998 Fifth Avenue was more chaste, presumably because its very exclusive clientele was thought to be more refined than the upper-middle-class tenants in the Alwyn at 180 West Fifty-eighth Street.[119] Above the granite base, the facades were sheathed in limestone carved with Italian Renaissance details. The twelve-story building with an almost square plan only filled half the block-front along Fifth Avenue, but the floors were cleverly arranged so that all the various duplex and simplex units except one had only servant's and service rooms on the

Graham Court, east side of Seventh Avenue between 115th and 116th streets. Clinton & Russell, 1901. Rendering. CU

Graham Court, east side of Seventh Avenue between 115th and 116th streets. Clinton & Russell, 1901. Courtyard. CU

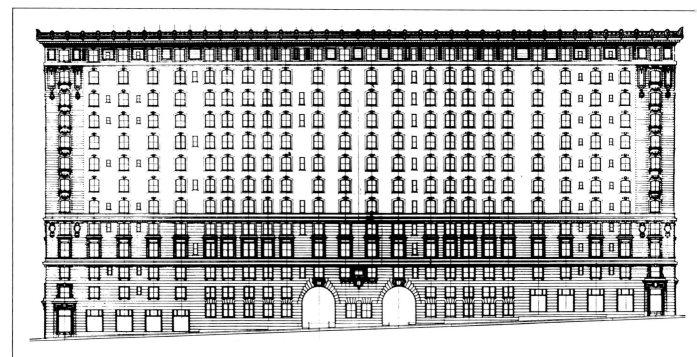

Belnord, Broadway to Amsterdam Avenue between Eighty-sixth and Eighty-seventh streets. H. Hobart Weekes, 1908. Eighty-sixth Street elevation. CU

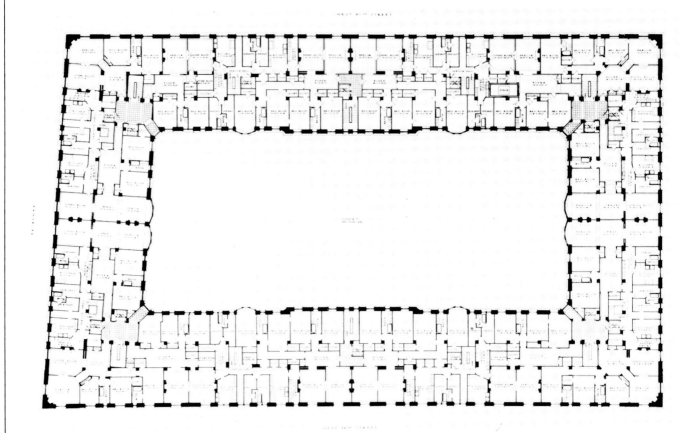

Belnord, Broadway to Amsterdam Avenue between Eighty-sixth and Eighty-seventh streets. H. Hobart Weekes, 1908. Plan of typical floor. CU

Astor Court, east side of Broadway between Eighty-ninth and Ninetieth streets. Charles Platt, 1916. View from Broadway. CU

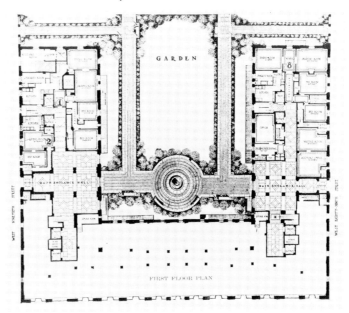

Astor Court, east side of Broadway and Eighty-ninth and Ninetieth streets. Charles Platt, 1916. Plan of first floor. CU

Cooperative Building, 25 West Sixty-seventh Street. Sturgis & Simonson, 1901. Painter's studio. CU

Cooperative Building, 25 West Sixty-seventh Street. Sturgis & Simonson, 1901. Dining room. CU

Bryant Park Studios, southeast corner of Sixth Avenue and Fortieth Street. Charles Rich, 1901. A.A. Anderson's studio. CU

Bryant Park Studios, southeast corner of Sixth Avenue and Fortieth Street. Charles Rich, 1901. View from Sixth Avenue. CU

court. The success of the building was ensured when the rental agent, Douglas L. Elliman, persuaded Senator Elihu Root to move into the building by offering him a cut-rate rental: fifteen thousand dollars per year instead of twenty-five thousand dollars. Once Root, who had earlier established the respectability of a Park Avenue address when he built his house there in 1903, moved to 998, others immediately followed.

Although the New Law of 1901 was general enough to allow different building types, it was clearly influenced by an interest in the true courtyard apartment on a large scale. The wave of building that swept over New York after the turn of the century brought with it a new type of courtyard apartment, built for the middle class on the West Side in the image of a palace. Three of the most outstanding examples of the palatial courtyard apartment house were built by the Astor family: Graham Court, designed by Clinton & Russell and built in 1901; the Apthorp, designed by the same architects and built in 1908; and Astor Court, designed by Charles Platt and completed in 1916.

Graham Court, located on a two-hundred-by-two-hundred-foot lot on Seventh Avenue between West 116th and 117th streets in Harlem, was an eight-story Florentine palace with a splendid arch on Seventh Avenue giving access to a landscaped court with elevators at each of the four corners going up to the ninety-six apartments above.[120] The Apthorp, built on a full-block site from Broadway to West End Avenue between Seventy-eighth and Seventy-ninth streets, though similar to Graham Court, was much larger and had even more luxurious apartments.[121] However, the increased density unfortunately produced a stark, almost gloomy courtyard, too narrow for its height and too often shrouded in shadow.

The Belnord (not built by the Astors) was another impressive example of the palatial courtyard type.[122] Designed in 1908 by H. Hobart Weekes, it occupied a full block between Broadway and Amsterdam Avenue, from Eighty-sixth to Eighty-seventh street. The Belnord's block was larger than the Apthorp's, resulting in a courtyard that was bigger, better proportioned and more generously planted, although the detailing of the building's facade was not nearly as elegant.

Astor Court was perhaps the loveliest of all the courtyard apartments built between 1900 and the First World War.[123] Located on the east side of Broadway between West Eighty-ninth and Ninetieth streets, it was distinguished by an almost plain Italianate facade of red brick. The Broadway frontage at grade was given over to shops, and the courtyard and apartments were entered from the cross streets, with the courtyard treated not as a *cour d'honneur* but as a garden.

Duplex and Studio Apartments

The comparatively narrow, moderately tall (usually twelve story) duplex apartment house was one of the principal ornaments of the Composite Era, combining highly individualized accommodation in a compact mass that was both a distinct representation of the collective identity of the inhabitants and a fragment of the larger cityscape. These duplex apartments were originally built for artists to live and work in: their attraction was a double-height "studio" space with oversized windows facing north. The studios were designed to function as both workplace and living room, but one critic coyly described how the studio apartment found a wider audience: "Mrs. Apartment Seeker has been to a tea or a reception at Mr. Artist's studio apartment and has seen his magnificent studio as part of an apartment, to him a necessity. Such an attractive plan for his 'soirée' and so appropriate for the display of his pictures and work. How lovely it would be for her to give such teas and musicals, how effective. She immediately starts looking for one, and that room will be the main consideration of renting an apartment; only those will be looked at which have a studio."[124] Soon, as the *Architectural Review* pointed out: "So many other people have taken studio apartments that, it is safe to say, the artists are in the minority in some buildings at least. Probably in the last analysis the motive is in most cases the same that has brought the big living room into favor in moderate-size houses—a desire for simplicity and breadth, for at least one room big enough so that one does not feel restricted."[125]

The studio apartment building was introduced to New York by a landscape painter, Henry W. Ranger, and a builder, William J. Taylor. "Ranger was paying $2,000 a year, or something like it, for an apartment in which to live," the *New York Times* reported in 1909, "But he couldn't paint in his apartment and was, therefore, compelled to pay $700 a year rent for a studio. Worse than that, his studio was not suited to the display of his pictures, which he was therefore compelled to exhibit elsewhere."[126] Ranger prepared a complete set of drawings for a building where artists could live, work and display their work. After being turned away by one contractor, Ranger went to Taylor; together with the architects Sturgis & Simonson they built the Cooperative Studio Building at 25 West Sixty-seventh Street in 1901.[127] The design had an ingenious cross sectional arrangement that kept costs down and maximized the use of space: two duplex apartments were located at the front or back of seven floors, and smaller, simplex apartments were located in a rear extension with slightly higher ceilings in the studios, so that while there were fourteen floors at the front there were only ten at the rear. Deed restrictions were negotiated for properties on Sixty-eighth Street, ensuring good light for the artists' studios on the north side of the Cooperative Building. The southern part of the building was rented out, producing a twenty-three percent return on the artists' investment.

Several other studio buildings followed on Sixty-seventh Street, designed by different combinations of the same group of architects: in 1903, Simonson, Pollard & Steinam designed 29-33 West Sixty-seventh,[128] in 1905 Steinam & Simonson completed the Central Park Studios (numbers 11-15)[129] and Pollard & Steinam designed the Atelier building (39-41 West Sixty-seventh Street),[130] in 1906 Pollard & Steinam designed 35 West Sixty-seventh (never built)[131] and in 1918 George Mort Pollard built the Hotel des Artistes on the corner of Sixty-seventh and Central Park West.[132] The facades of the buildings worked well together, creating an intimate enclave just off the park. Only the Hotel des Artistes, however, could stand very well on its own. Its facade, slightly reminiscent of an Elizabethan manor house, had a rich limestone base and carved figures representing the arts. Inside, most apartments had English Renaissance style panelling in the living and dining rooms. But there were no kitchens, because food was prepared in a central kitchen, connected to the apartments by electric

Gainsborough Studios, 222 Central Park South. Charles Buckham, 1908. View from Central Park. CU

Gainsborough Studios, 222 Central Park South. Charles Buckham, 1908. Plans of typical floors. CU

Studio Building, 44 West Seventy-seventh Street. Harde & Short, 1909. View from Manhattan Square. MCNY

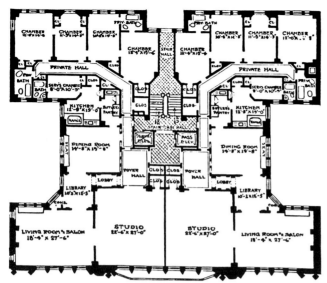

Studio Building, 44 West Seventy-seventh Street. Harde & Short, 1909. Plan of typical floor. CU

The Mayfair, 471 Park Avenue. Charles Buckham, 1908. View across Park Avenue. MCNY

dumbwaiters. The "hotel" (the building was always a cooperative apartment house) also contained a restaurant, a theater, a ballroom, a swimming pool and squash courts.

Other studio apartment houses were built to take advantage of open spaces on the city's grid. The Bryant Park Studios, designed around 1901 by Charles Rich, were located on the southeast corner of Sixth Avenue and Fortieth Street, looking out over the small park.[133] Built from an artist's point of view by A.A. Anderson, a painter who had lived in Paris for many years, it had a generous and functionally organized plan. Anderson's own apartment was lavish, with elaborate doorways and architectural tableaux such as a Turkish corner, no doubt as useful as a backdrop for a portrait as it was valuable for conversation.

In 1906 the National Arts Club opened a fifteen-story studio building on Nineteenth Street, directly south of two houses at 14 and 15 Gramercy Park that had been converted into their clubhouse.[134] The building was planned by George B. Post & Sons so that part of each floor was given over to two small apartments, while every other floor had two duplex apartments with double-height studios facing north, looking out over the low clubhouse to Gramercy Park. The Studio Building, designed by Harde & Short in 1909, was at 44 West Seventy-seventh Street, on the southern boundary of Manhattan Square (the park surrounding the Museum of Natural History).[135] Two more studio apartments were built on Central Park South—the Gainsborough Studios at 222 Central Park South, designed by Charles Buckham and completed in 1908,[136] and another building by Buckham, 36 Central Park South, completed in 1912.[137] The Gainsborough's facade was one of the most distinguished of all the studio buildings. Bas-reliefs and a bust of Sir Thomas Gainsborough above the Ionic portal, as well as the oversized windows, marked it as an artist's building, skillfully crowned by mosaics and a flurry of ornament at the top. Cass Gilbert's 200 West Fifty-seventh Street[138] joined several studio apartment houses designed by Pollard & Steinam on that wide street.[139]

Duplex apartments intended for conventional family life included 471 Park Avenue, designed by Charles Buckham and completed in 1908,[140] and two of the most elegant apartment houses of any type, the identical cooperatives at 131–135 East Sixty-sixth Street and 130–134 East Sixty-seventh Street designed by Charles Platt in 1906.[141] Platt's

131–35 East Sixty-sixth Street. Charles Platt, 1906. Studio in Apartment C. CU

131–35 East Sixty-sixth Street. Charles Platt, 1906. Stairway in Apartment C. CU

powerful Italian Renaissance palazzo sheathed in a warm gray limestone was commanding in its simplicity. Because the double-height studios faced the court between the two buildings, Platt was able to group the windows facing the street into an even rhythm; the resulting facade was a sheer cliff unbroken except by a projecting cornice and two-story-high Ionic columns carrying a split pediment at the entrance. Inside, perhaps in deference to the building's address on the fringes of the Billionaire District, each apartment contained a kitchen and a bath as well as at least one servant's bedroom, while one of the apartments had no studio space at all. A critic for the *Architectural Record* "accustomed to the ordinary New York house" found the effect of the duplex apartment with double-height studio "exhilarating. It provoked such a feeling of amplitude. It was supplied with such an abundance of light and air. It was so big and yet so intimate, so spacious and yet so economical, and the studio made a most admirable living room."[142]

The Improvement of the Tenement

The Cooperative Studio Building revived a tradition of cooperative apartments that had died with the financial failure of the Hubert Home Clubs.[143] Most of the studio apartment houses that followed, including all the artists' buildings on West Sixty-seventh Street and the upper-middle class apartment houses on East Sixty-seventh Street, continued the legacy, reflecting a feeling of social insecurity that affected apartment house design during the prosperity of the first two decades of the twentieth century. As the city grew and the familiar neighborhoods of rowhouses gave way to the more impersonal apartment house, there was a desire to ensure sociological as well as economic homogeneity. By 1909, the *Real Estate Record and Guide* could comment that the term "Club Building" was "becoming the generic name for a special class of house in which and by which there is an attempt made, first through the choice of a particularly refined neighborhood; second, by the exceptional beauty and homelike attractions of the inward parts of the house itself; and third, by providing or insuring neighbors of quality, to fill the social void between the isolated and unlovely life in a promiscuously populated flat and the highest standard of living known to mankind—a house all to oneself and his own, in a choice quarter with old neighbors."[144]

1 Lexington Avenue, Lexington Avenue and Gramercy Park. Herbert Lucas, 1910. View from Gramercy Park. MCNY

Cornwall, northwest corner of Broadway and Ninetieth Street. Neville & Bagge, 1910. View from Broadway. OMH

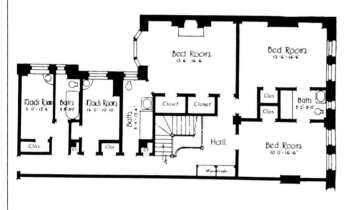

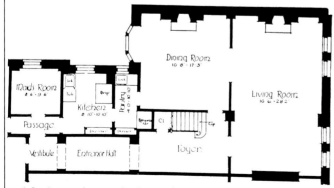

1 Lexington Avenue, Lexington Avenue and Gramercy Park. Herbert Lucas, 1910. Plans of typical apartment. CU

Home Club, 11–15 East Forty-fifth Street. Gordon, Tracy & Swartwout, 1906. MCNY

Colosseum, southeast corner of Riverside Drive and 116th Street. Schwartz & Gross, 1910. View from Riverside Drive. MCNY

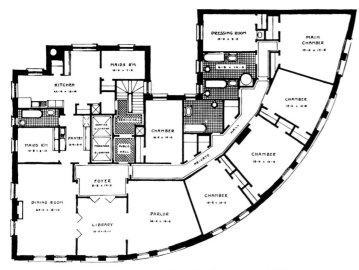

Colosseum, southeast corner of Riverside Drive and 116th Street. Schwartz & Gross, 1910. Plan of typical floor. CU

An article in the *Architectural Record,* commenting on the practice of many of these Club Buildings of keeping some apartments as rental properties to help defray expenses, made clear the sociological basis of Club Buildings when it suggested that unless the "cooperators unite to constitute themselves a vigilance committee, some day there will elude the vigilance of the janitor and the real estate agent a 'peroxide Juno' . . . or a hooknosed tenant, of the kind of hooknose you know and apprehend."[145] Nonetheless, because a distinguishing feature of the Club Buildings was that they were built by their future tenants, it is fair to say that from an architectural as opposed to a sociological point of view, the cooperative and home club ideas led to a substantial improvement in quality over the typical speculative apartment house of the day, bringing to the design of the apartment house "the same interest, which accounts in such large measure for the good results in [the] country house architecture" so widely admired. In particular, it was felt that the "one feature still lacking in the design of apartment buildings is that which in country houses suggests the domestic side of life."[146]

Three of the new Club Buildings were built around 1910 on Gramercy Park, approximately twenty-five years after the construction of the cooperative Gramercy Park Apartments.[147] The developers and future residents of 24 Gramercy Park included Richard Watson Gilder, editor of the *Century* magazine, Jules Guerin, an architectural illustrator, John B. Pine, treasurer of Columbia University and Herbert Lucas, the building's architect.[148] Lucas's design was loosely Colonial in character, with red-brick walls relieved by white-stone trim that were as much a reference to its Greek Revival style neighbors as to the then fashionable associations between a beneficent domesticity and the Anglo-American Georgian styles. Inside the duplex apartments, the Colonial theme was carried out with white woodwork, open fireplaces, and generous use of columns to articulate the spaces. Each apartment opened onto balconies overlooking the park.

J. Riely Gordon's design for the Gramercy Park Club was reminiscent of late French Gothic styles.[149] Its nearly white terra-cotta skin was in bold contrast to the dark red, brick and brownstone neighbors, including the earlier Gramercy Park Apartments at Number 34. In 1910 Lucas followed with a third Club Building on Gramercy Park, One Lexington Avenue, at the northeast corner of Lexington and Twentieth Street. It had none of the charm of his earlier buildings, but was a coldly competent limestone palazzo, somewhat enlivened by projecting balconies.[150]

The most architecturally distinguished example of the type was designed by Tracy & Swartwout in the heart of the club district at 11 East Forty-fifth Street.[151] Completed in 1906, this towering Florentine palazzo housed only six families and was fittingly called the Home Club. The ground floor had a drive-in court, and the next floor was given over to two very lofty dining and drawing rooms. The next five floors were very large, floor-through apartments, while a duplex filled the top two floors.

After the passage in 1901 of the New Law, a seemingly endless succession of apartments were built in Manhattan and, to a lesser extent, in the Bronx and Brooklyn, which continued to maintain a more suburban scale until after the First World War. Memorable though the duplex and courtyard types were, the predominant apartment house of the Metropolitan Age was the more conventional tenement. Certain architects became specialists in the field: the work of many, such as Neville & Bagge, Schwartz & Gross, and Gaetan Ajello was generally distinguished more by its ability to maximize rentable space than by any other notable characteristic. Nonetheless their work determined the block to block texture of the Composite City, just as the work of those architects who turned out the seemingly endless rows of brownstones that dominated the post-Civil War era formed the background of the Cosmopolitan City. When these apartment house designers were faced with difficult conditions, like the site of Neville & Bagge's El Nido Apartments at 116th Street and Seventh Avenue in Harlem, they gave ample proof of their ingenuity.[152] Nonetheless, the repetitiousness of most of their buildings, designed with modest variations which gave each building some individuality, helped the speculative sector flesh out the civic ideals of the American Renaissance with considerable panache, and formed the key to the stability of *fin de siecle* urbanism.

Early rationalization of the speculative apartment house was credited to Neville & Bagge. According to Charles H. Israels, though "it may be impossible to point to any work of this firm which is superlatively excellent, they have succeeded by their numerous examples in raising the standard of an entire neighborhood from one of debasement to at least of respectability."[153] Neville & Bagge used three basic *partis*—central courts, courts opening to the street, and courts opening to the back—with all the courts built to the minimum legal size determined by the New Law of 1901. Because of their minimal size, the central courts were perhaps the least desirable. The Netherlands, built in 1909 on West Eighty-sixth Street near Riverside Drive, was typical, with exceedingly long entry halls and numerous bedrooms placed on a dim courtyard that was twelve stories deep but only thirty-one feet square.[154] Yet other windows on the mid-block building were even more poorly situated, only a few feet away from the adjoining buildings. The Reed House (1906) at West 121st Street and Broadway had the advantage of a corner site, but the central court was even smaller than at the Netherlands because Neville & Bagge divided it almost in half with the stair and elevator rather than placing the circulation at each corner.[155]

The apartment houses with courts opening to the back of the lot were also corner buildings, such as 590 West End Avenue, built on the corner of Eighty-ninth Street in 1916[156] and 789 West End Avenue corner of Ninety-ninth Street in 1916,[157] and shared the problem of minimal light wells which depended on the arrangement of the adjoining buildings. Much more successful were the corner apartment houses with courts opening to the street. The Cornwall (1910) on the northwest corner of Broadway and West Ninetieth Street was typical of that type.[158] The rather luxurious entry and lobby were on the side street, and the ground floor frontage along Broadway was given over to stores. Circulation at the back of the court and in the center of the building rose to a plain hall serving only three apartments, one in each wing, and a less desirable apartment at the back. The Cornwall, like the Dorchester at Riverside Drive and Eighty-fifth Street and 801 West End Avenue at Ninety-ninth Street, was a red-brick building with limestone trim and bases.[159] All the facades were heavy, with fussy details and rather graceless proportions.

Schwartz & Gross brought a more sophisticated sense of composition to the problem of the speculative apartment house. While their work in the 1920s included upper-class apartment houses such as 55 and 101 Central Park West and 1185 Park Avenue, they established their practice with more modest efforts for the middle- and upper-middle classes in the West End, Morningside and Washington Heights. The most elegant were the Colosseum, built in 1910 at 435 Riverside Drive,[160] and a similar building across West 116th Street, 440 Riverside Drive.[161] Both pulled back from 116th Street in broad sweeping curves that enhance the street's role as an approach to Columbia University's main gate. But the awkward division of the Colosseum's plan ignored the hierarchy implied in the building's facade and employed a long, narrow and dark hallway characteristic of the firm's work. Although the brick and stone facades of the twelve-story apartment house at 509 Cathedral Parkway (West 110th Street) were among the more dignified in the neighborhood, the dense units were no better planned than those in the surrounding buildings.[162] The same could be said of the Marc Antony and the Prince Humbert, built in 1911 on adjoining lots at 514 and 520 Cathedral Parkway.[163] The brick pattern along the street was quite attractive, but the plans were contorted. Even their design for Heathcote Hall, a truncated courtyard apartment built in 1911 at 609 West 114th Street, had the characteristic long and narrow hall.[164]

Rouse & Sloan and its successor firm, Rouse & Goldstone, were the upper-class equivalents of Neville & Bagge. The Wyoming, an early (1907) design located at Fifty-fifth Street and Seventh Avenue, displayed the firm's standard *parti:* light courts along the street carved into the building's mass and "gave the appearance of a group of massive towers," which the *Architects' and Builders' Magazine* noted was "heightened by the use of mansard roofs."[165] The Riviera Apartments (1910, Riverside Drive between 156th and 157th streets) developed the strategy at a much larger scale with one hundred and fifty apartments in four towers hugging the edges of an irregular site.[166] The *parti* was carried to its highest expression in the Montana Apartments, built in 1913 at 375 Park Avenue, where the Steinway Piano factory had formerly filled the block between Fifty-second and Fifty-third streets.[167] Rouse & Goldstone's imposing Italian Renaissance design was broken into three pavilions by deep light courts which opened onto Park Avenue. A three-story limestone base and an elaborate cornice tied the construction together at a roof canted over the central pavilion to suggest a pediment. At the ground floor, the central pavilion was carved out to form a sheltered driveway large enough for three or four cars to wait for passengers. The top (thirteenth floor) was devoted exclusively to servant's bedrooms and bathrooms, while a large restaurant, entered from the lobby, was run exclusively for the tenants and their guests.[168]

A tendency toward the Georgian styles that were felt to express domesticity grew in apartment design in the decade leading up to America's entry into the First World War. This was an understandable reaction to the bombast of the *Belle Epoque* apartments in the West End such as the Dorilton and the Ansonia. The finest examples of the Georgian apartments were often found in the smaller buildings on the side streets in the older neighborhoods. Browne & Almiroty's Sumner Apartments at 31 West Eleventh Street[169] and Walker & Gillette's Studio Apartments at 144 East Fortieth Street[170] had enlarged but modest and refined versions of working-class tenement plans. Frederick J. Sterner's picturesque Studio Apartments at 132 East Nineteenth Street used white stucco trimmed with brick to suggest Twickenham of the early-nineteenth century or the Chelsea of Voysey and Mackintosh.[171]

Sometimes, as in the case of Tracy & Swartwout's Astor Apartments (1915) at 305 West Forty-fifth Street, the size of the building was great enough to produce a palatial image—there was even room for a landscaped courtyard—yet the side street location seemed to demand a more modest Georgian expression.[172] Charles Platt, working with a full blockfront on Broadway a year later, produced in the previously mentioned Astor Court Apartments a new synthesis between the big scale, courtyard *parti* of the Italian villa and the gentleness and gentility of expression of the red-brick Georgian: "Here we find perhaps the closest suggestion of domestic occupancy that has thus far been accomplished, and as this suggestion is so admirably adapted to much smaller facades, we hope that it marks the beginning of a new era in apartment house design."[173]

Wyoming, southeast corner of Seventh Avenue and Fifty-fifth Street. Rouse & Sloan, 1911. CU

Montana, east side of Park Avenue between Fifty-first and Fifty-second streets. Rouse & Goldstone, 1913. View from Park Avenue. MCNY

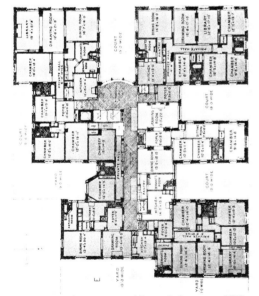

Wyoming, southeast corner of Seventh Avenue and Fifty-fifth Street. Rouse & Sloan, 1911. Plan of typical floor. CU

Montana, east side of Park Avenue between Fifty-first and Fifty-second streets. Rouse & Goldstone, 1913. Lobby. MCNY

William A. Clark house, northeast corner of Fifth Avenue and Seventy-seventh Street. Hewlett & Hull and Henri Deglane, 1907. View across Fifth Avenue from the southwest. NYHS

Metropolitan Neighborhoods

"Sir, let us take a walk down Fifth Avenue." To be sure Dr. Johnson never said that. But neither did he say "Sir, let us take a walk down Fleet Street," as has been confessed by the person who for many years imputed that invitation to him on the cover of a London magazine. And the more modern formula is the more attractive, as will be admitted by all who have seen both thoroughfares in recent years. In fact . . . that part of Fifth Avenue to which I shall direct your attention has become really and unfailingly amusing.

Franz K. Winkler (Montgomery Schuyler), "Architecture in the Billionaire District of New York City," *Architectural Record* 11 (October 1901): 679–99.

Billionaire District The evolution of Fifth Avenue offers the most accurate portrait of the city's growth from the Knickerbocker Era of Washington Irving and the childhood of Henry James to the close of the Metropolitan Era. Though Fifth Avenue was included in the Commissioners' Plan of 1811, it was not opened until 1824 and was not developed with substantial buildings above Fourteenth Street until the 1850s.[1] Compared with Broadway or Wall Street, Fifth Avenue was so inconsequential that Charles Dickens did not even mention it in his description of New York in 1842. But from the 1850s on, when the city began to implement in earnest the Commissioners' Plan, Fifth Avenue emerged as the nexus of fashion.

"The supremacy of Fifth Avenue is natural and demonstrable, not accidental or artificial," said the *Real Estate Record and Guide* in 1878. "Aside from the preeminent claims of Fifth Avenue as the natural center of the island, occupying an elevated and commanding position" there were other considerations that focused fashion along its length; principally, the fact that a concentration of industry along the East and Hudson rivers pushed the upper classes to the island's center. It was with only a little exaggeration that the *Record and Guide* called Fifth Avenue "the via maxima of the metropolis and of the continent; destined in time perhaps to assert its superiority over any fashionable thoroughfare the world can produce."[2]

In the 1870s old New York society lived near Washington Square at the lower end of Fifth Avenue, while the newly rich lived uptown on Murray Hill, anchored by the two Astor houses on Fifth Avenue at Thirty-third and Thirty-fourth streets and A.T. Stewart's marble mansion across the street. The most fashionable churches and clubs that served the neighborhoods lined the blocks of Fifth Avenue in between. Richard Upjohn's Church of the Ascension stood at the corner of Tenth Street, the Fifth Avenue Presbyterian Church was at Nineteenth Street, Marble Collegiate Church at Twenty-ninth Street, and Leopold Eidlitz's Temple Emanu-El at Forty-third Street. New York's first club, the Union Club, had a mansion at Twenty-first Street, and the Knickerbocker Club stood on the corner of Twenty-eighth Street, near the Calumet clubhouse on Twenty-ninth. The increasingly public social life was also served by the fashionable hotels, restaurants and theaters that were grouped on Fifth Avenue around Madison Square.

But the virtually insatiable demands for office and retail space made another northward migration of fashion inevitable. In the beginning, the commercial buildings had clustered around the wide cross-streets at Fourteenth, Twenty-third, Thirty-fourth, and Forty-second streets, but they were already expanding, most notably at Union Square and near Forty-second Street, where the new Grand Central Terminal stood.[3] In the 1880s Henry J. Hardenbergh's design for the Western Union Building (1884) was built on Madison Square, in the very heart of the fashionable district, and McKim, Mead & White's American Safe Deposit and Columbian Bank (1882), an early essay in Classicism as applied to the problem of the tall building, rose above Fifth Avenue at Forty-second Street, further isolating residential sections and accelerating the northern migration of fashion.

Members of New York society preferred to live surrounded by their peers and easily succumbed to the pressures of economic development. In 1893, for example, one of August Belmont's sons sold the house at the northeast corner of Fifth Avenue and Eighteenth Street he had inherited from his father.[4] In the 1850s the lot had been worth $40,000, but Belmont sold it only forty years later for $615,000. The house was immediately torn down, to be replaced by a denser development, and Belmont bought a new lot on the corner of Fifth Avenue and Eighty-first Street for $215,000. Yet only sixteen years later, in 1910, that lot was sold to the Century Holding Company, which tore down Belmont's new house and hired McKim, Mead & White to design the apartment building known as 998 Fifth Avenue, the first apartment house in New York where the fashionable rich lived.

After 1870, when the city condemned the land at the

Marble Row, northeast corner of Fifth Avenue and Fifty-seventh Street. Robert Mook, 1869. An 1894 view from the southwest. BB

southeast corner of Central Park and laid out the open space that would later be called Grand Army Plaza, the ten blocks of Fifth Avenue below the park slowly became the most prestigious residential district in the city. One indication was the construction of several of the most fashionable churches there. In 1870 St. Thomas's moved from their church at Broadway and Houston Street, which they had occupied since 1826, to a new Gothic structure on the northwest corner of Fifth Avenue and Fifty-third Street designed by Richard Upjohn.[5] In 1872 the Collegiate Reformed Protestant Dutch Church built a church at Fifth Avenue and Forty-eighth Street, one of four churches in Manhattan that constituted a single parish of the oldest ecclesiastical organization in the city.[6] The Fifth Avenue Presbyterian Church, located at Nineteenth Street since 1852, moved to Fifty-fifth Street in 1875, and St. Patrick's Cathedral, under construction at Fiftieth Street since 1858, opened in 1879.[7]

In 1869 Mrs. Mary Mason Jones built Marble Row, speculative housing for the rich, at the northeast corner of Fifth Avenue and Fifty-seventh Street, designed by Robert Mook.[8] Mrs. Jones, whose banker father had paid fifteen hundred dollars for the site in 1825, had unshakeable faith in the future of the area. She was portrayed as Mrs. Manson Mingott by her niece Edith Wharton in *The Age of Innocence:*

> It was her habit to sit in the window of her sitting room on the ground floor (imprisoned by her obesity), as if watching calmly for life and fashion to flow northward to her solitary doors. She seemed in no hurry to have them come, for her patience was equaled by her confidence. She was sure that presently the hoardings, the quarries, the one-story saloons, the wooden greenhouses in ragged gardens, and the rocks from which goats surveyed the scene, would vanish before the advance of residences as stately as her own—perhaps (for she was an impartial woman) even statelier; and that the cobblestones over which the old clattering omnibuses bumped would be replaced by smooth asphalt, such as people reported having seen in Paris.[9]

Mary Mason Jones's patience was rewarded in 1879, when the Vanderbilt family, heirs to a fortune that was reputedly the greatest in the world, began a lavish building

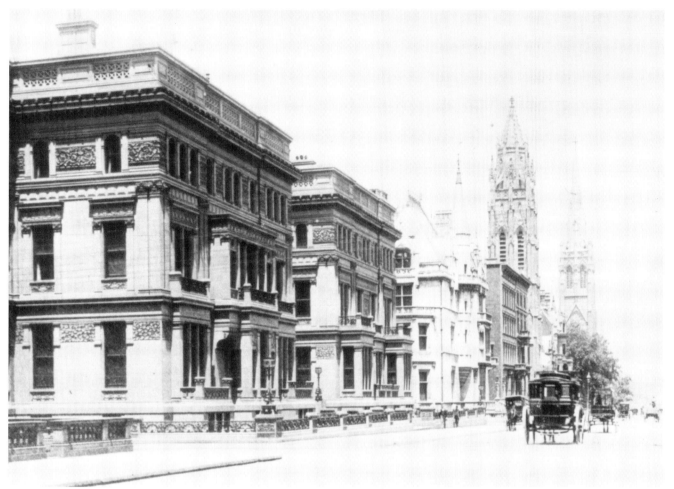

William Henry Vanderbilt, Elliot F. Shepard and William D. Sloane houses, west side of Fifth Avenue between Fifty-first and Fifty-second streets. John B. Snook and Charles Atwood, 1879-82. A view from the southeast showing the William Kissam Vanderbilt house and addition as well as St. Thomas and the Fifth Avenue Presbyterian churches further north on Fifth Avenue. NYHS

program that soon gave the ten blocks of Fifth Avenue below Central Park the popular name of Vanderbilt Row. The founder of the fortune, Commodore Cornelius Vanderbilt, had lived in a rowhouse at 10 Washington Place, and his eldest son, William Henry Vanderbilt, in a mansion built in 1867 at Fifth Avenue and Fortieth Street. When the Commodore died in 1877 he left a contested will that was settled out of court in April 1879, leaving William Henry and his two elder sons, Cornelius Vanderbilt II and William Kissam Vanderbilt, with the bulk of the money.[10] In August 1879 George B. Post filed plans at the New York City Buildings Department for a new house on land Cornelius II owned at 1 West Fifty-seventh Street, directly across the street from Marble Row.[11] Completed in 1882, Post's house for Cornelius II had a combination of late Gothic and early Renaissance details, mingled in a manner reminiscent of French chateaux.

Only a few days later in August 1879, William Henry Vanderbilt filed applications with the Buildings Department for two houses designed by John B. Snook, who had designed William Henry's first house, and Charles Atwood, an architect who at the time was working for the Herter Brothers—a firm of decorators and cabinetmakers.[12] The two houses, separated by a glazed atrium that served as a common entrance, filled the blockfront on the west side of Fifth Avenue between Fifty-first and Fifty-second streets; Vanderbilt lived in the house on Fifty-first Street, and his two daughters—Mrs. Elliot F. Shepard and Mrs. William D. Sloane—lived with their families in the house on Fifty-second Street. Snook and Atwood intended the neo-Grec, cubic houses to be built of Ohio freestone with lavish details carved in red and black marble, but Vanderbilt insisted they use the more common brownstone for everything.[13] Nevertheless, even before the Vanderbilts took up residence in January 1882, Montgomery Schuyler wrote that "in size and color these are the most 'important' dwellings which have been built in New York since the 'palatial' mansion in white marble of Mr. Stewart."[14]

In December 1879 William Kissam Vanderbilt and his architect, Richard Morris Hunt, filed the plans for a house on Fifth Avenue across Fifty-second Street from the house built for William Kissam's sisters by their father.[15] While William Henry Vanderbilt's houses combined characteristics of the dour brownstones of the Civil War period with the

Charles L. Tiffany house, northwest corner of Madison Avenue and Seventy-second Street. McKim, Mead & White, 1882–85. An 1885 view from the southeast. NYHS

eclectic freedom of the Cosmopolitan Era, and Cornelius Vanderbilt II's residence added the Cosmopolitan elements of contrasting materials and a picturesque skyline, Richard Morris Hunt's design for the William Kissam Vanderbilt house revealed an archaeological rigor that prefigured the sensibility of the Composite Era.

W.K. Vanderbilt's wife Alva was an ambitious woman who wanted a house that would make everyone, particularly those at the top of New York society, take notice. The people who mattered most to Alva realized that a powerful new force had entered New York social life when her announcement of a ball to be held in the house on March 26, 1883 forced the acknowledged queen of New York society, Mrs. William Astor, to call on the Vanderbilts for the first time, so as not to be left out of the party. "Like an Oriental Dream, The Scene in Mr. W.K. Vanderbilt's Beautiful House Last Evening . . . the Wealth and Grace of New York in Varied and Brilliant Array" the headline in the *New York Herald* announced the next day, while the article went on to report that the costume ball was "probably never rivalled in republican America and never outdone by the gayest court of Europe."[16] Many of the guests dressed up as kings and queens—Mrs. Paran Stevens, who lived in Marble Row, dressed as Queen Elizabeth I, and Cornelius Vanderbilt came as Louis XVI, although his wife appeared as "Electric Light." As the guests wandered through the rooms many of them realized that a new era had arrived on Fifth Avenue that night. Wealth and fashion were united with a decor derived from the past that, however ostentatious, displayed a patina of "good taste." For those with adequate means and awareness of the new fashion, the era of commonplace, nearly identical brownstone houses and of cluttered, overfurnished Victorian rooms was soon replaced by one of the ever-more luxurious mansions designed in period styles, their rooms filled with treasures from the past coordinated in selection and placement.[17]

Schuyler compared the W.K. Vanderbilt house to other domestic architecture in New York, and pronounced it "brilliantly successful." "It is emphatically a building in design," he wrote. "The style of the work is fifteenth-century French Gothic, or rather transitional, the style of the Palais de Justice and the Hotel du Bourgtheroulde at Rouen, of the Hotel Cluny at Paris, and of part of the Chateau of Blois."[18]

Other critics and architects were even more impressed

Henry Villard houses, east side of Madison Avenue between Fiftieth and Fifty-first streets. McKim, Mead & White, 1882-85. View across Madison Avenue from the southwest. CU

by Hunt's new Chateau style. Charles McKim liked to stroll past the house after a hard day's work, because he was refreshed by just looking at it.[19] The critic Royal Cortissoz called Hunt "a poet as well as an architect" for designing "a tour de force.... a lyric inspiration.... an isolated triumph of lightness and vivacious beauty.... It stands alone in all America."[20] Herbert Croly judged the Vanderbilt house the best of all Hunt's houses, a design of "ease ... grace and ... urbanity."[21] People of wealth and fashion soon paid the design the honor of trying to reproduce it.

On Madison Avenue at Sixty-eighth Street, Hunt built three houses for Henry G. Marquand, a banker and developer for whom he had already built Linden Gate in Newport, and for whom he was in the process of designing the Marquand Chapel at Princeton University and the Guernsey Building at 160-64 Broadway.[22] Begun in 1881 and completed three years later, the houses were different in style from the Vanderbilt chateau but still looked back to the French Renaissance. At the same time, Stanford White was building the Charles L. Tiffany house (1882-85) a few blocks north on Madison Avenue at Seventy-second Street.[23] While the classical elements of Hunt's chateaux were harbingers of the Composite Age, White's composition for the Tiffany house, inspired by the German Renaissance, was one of the quintessential statements of the Cosmopolitan Era. Russell Sturgis found it "probably the most successful attempt in recent times to give in a dwelling the high-pitched, soaring character affected by the German town houses in the sixteenth and seventeenth centuries."[24] But the *Real Estate Record and Guide* thought it belonged in the country, calling it a "princely chateau" because "it resembles one more than a mansion or a palace. It is, indeed, in the rural style of architecture. The only regret is that it does not stand in the centre of several acres of ground. This house has, by the way, increased the value of the surrounding property, as all fine improvements must do."[25]

Tiffany wanted a large house with separate apartments for himself, his daughter and her family, and his son, Louis Comfort Tiffany, and his family. Charles left the details to be decided by his son in conjunction with Stanford White. A drawing by Louis seems to have formed the basis for White's design,[26] but there is no doubt at all about the identity of the designer of Louis's own apartment.[27] Louis's brilliant proto-Art Nouveau interiors were eclectic but in an

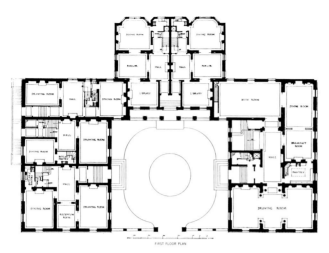

Henry Villard houses, east side of Madison Avenue between Fiftieth and Fifty-first Streets. McKim, Mead & White, 1882–85. Plan of first floor. CU

unusually original interpretation that was consistently applied in each room.

Although the massing of the Tiffany house was picturesque, the way in which White unified three large apartments in one house was prophetic of the architecture of the Composite Era. Another project in the office of McKim, Mead & White at the same time, the Villard houses (1882–85), was even more prophetic.[28] A brownstone interpretation of Italian Renaissance palazzos, most specifically the Cancelleria in Rome, the Villard houses were the first important expression of the Classicism and conceptual unity of the Composite Era.

Henry Villard was a railroad entrepreneur who in April 1881, a year and a half before the first of the new Vanderbilt houses was finished, bought the eastern blockfront of Madison Avenue between Fiftieth and Fifty-first streets, only one block over from Vanderbilt Row.[29] He soon announced his plans to build several houses that would be entered through a garden rather than directly from the street. "In the center of the block," Villard said in an interview in the *Real Estate Record and Guide,* "is to be a fine fountain, one of the ornaments of the city."[30] Feeling that the group house would make a finer urban ensemble than an ordinary block of rowhouses, he suggested that similar developments be built in other new areas of the city. But it was the style of the Villard houses rather than their planning that made them an important factor in the history of New York architecture: those who built their own house seemed to prefer a more individual image, while developers continued to build in the conventional rowhouse pattern.[31]

A year after he bought the lot, Villard hired his friend and relative Charles McKim to design the houses. Eventually, however, the job was assigned to an associate at McKim, Mead & White, Joseph Morrill Wells, who was credited with the final design.[32] Wells hid six houses behind a uniform facade that gave the appearance of one mansion, covering the whole in a correct classical design, an underscaled interpretation of the Cancelleria in Rome that was surprisingly cozy. There was no classical precedent for the material, but Wells had specified limestone—Villard, like W.H. Vanderbilt, wanted brownstone.[33]

Two Miles of Millonaires

The location of the Villard houses near Vanderbilt Row was just one indication that the Vanderbilts had firmly established the area as one of the most prestigious residential districts in the city. In 1884 John D. Rockefeller bought and remodelled a brownstone house at 4 West Fifty-fourth Street, and the neighborhood soon included the houses of Harry Payne Whitney, Charles Harkness, Jay Gould, Collis P. Huntington, Henry M. Flagler, Benjamin Altman, Robert Goelet, Solomon Guggenheim, Russell Sage and others of the richest of New York's self-proclaimed capitalist princes.[34] With the departure of St. Luke's Hospital and Columbia College for Morningside Heights in the early 1890s, the side streets became solidly built up with smaller but still grand rowhouses. As early as 1892, however, when Cornelius Vanderbilt II enlarged his house on the corner of Fifty-seventh Street so that it extended along Fifth Avenue to Fifty-eighth Street and filled the entire southern edge of Grand Army Plaza, his mansion faced a plaza dominated by some of the largest and grandest hotels in New York, brand new buildings indicating commercial pressures already pushing residential development still further to the north. Further south on Fifth Avenue, the St. Regis Hotel was built on the corner of Fifty-fifth Street in 1904, and the Gotham, an apartment hotel, was constructed across the Avenue from the St. Regis in 1905. Together with the Cartier Building between Fifty-fifth and Fifty-sixth streets (712 Fifth Avenue, A.S. Gottlieb, 1907) and the Windsor Arcade between Forty-sixth and Forty-seventh (Charles I. Berg, 1901), they marked a commercial encroachment into the neighborhood which the Vanderbilts tried to resist.[35] When William K. Vanderbilt sold a plot diagonally across Fifth Avenue from his to Morton F. Plant in 1902, he made Plant sign an agreement that the site would remain residential for twenty-five years.[36] By 1916, however, so many houses on Fifth Avenue between Forty-second and Fifty-ninth streets had been converted to commercial space that Plant built a new mansion designed by Guy Lowell, at 1051 Fifth, on the corner of Eighty-sixth Street, and sold the house back to Vanderbilt.[37] Having specified the residential restriction in the first place, Vanderbilt had the right to break it: although

Cornelius Vanderbilt II house, Fifth Avenue between Fifty-seventh and Fifty-eighth streets. Richard Morris Hunt and George B. Post, 1879–83 and 1892. A 1906 view from Grand Army Plaza showing the Fifth Avenue Presbyterian Church and the Gotham Hotel further south on Fifth Avenue. MCNY

View of Prospect Hill, circa 1884, from Park Avenue and Ninety-forth Street, showing the Central Park Reservoir and the Ruppert house on the left. NYHS

he paid one million dollars, a very high price for a house, he promptly made his money back by leasing the mansion to Cartier's for one of the highest rentals on Fifth Avenue. Cartier's, needing more space than they had at 712 Fifth Avenue, was glad to pay for the prime location.

As soon as Olmsted & Vaux began their work on Central Park in 1859, journalists and social commentators had predicted that Fifth Avenue along the park would one day become the most fashionable residential district in the city. In 1862 Anthony Trollope observed on his visit to New York that "the present fashion of Fifth Avenue about Twentieth Street will in course of time move itself up to the Fifth Avenue as it looks, or will look, over the Park at Seventieth, Eightieth, and Ninetieth Streets."[38] Central Park was finished in 1876, in time for the American Centennial, but while most of the land along its eastern edge was owned by that time by members of New York society, few of them were as yet ready to move there.

An article published in 1879 in the *Real Estate Record and Guide* reported that New York's millionaires in the next twenty years would "be found [building] east of the Central Park." But it admitted that "a visit to that region, where building activity is greatest, will convince anyone that these new houses do not represent the coming era of prosperity, but rather that which is passing away. The new buildings are mainly of the brown stone front variety, such as characterized the most desirable houses erected during the last quarter of a century."[39]

The area above Fifty-ninth Street suitable for fashionable residences was circumscribed to the west by the permanent barrier of the park and to the east by the open cut of the railroad along Park Avenue and also by a vast tenement area known as the East Side. Marianna Griswold van Rensselaer was among the first to point out that while there was "no true 'leisure class' in New York," with "even our wealthiest men . . . busy workers," a physical expression of the extremes of wealth and poverty could be seen in the distinction between the "central strip" of fashionable development "running from end to end of the island, and stretching into certain lateral quarters, which the well-to-do possess" and "all those shabby quarters of the East side and the West wherein the majority of the well-to-do never set a foot."[40]

The Upper East Side had been established as a middle- and working-class neighborhood as early as 1834, when the New York & Harlem Railroad opened a line that ran from City Hall to Eighty-sixth Street, with local stops along the way. By 1837 the line extended to the formerly remote village of Harlaem (where Harlem stands today). In 1858 horse-drawn trolleys ran up Second Avenue as far north as 122nd Street and along Third Avenue as far as Eighty-sixth Street; by 1878 the Third Avenue Elevated Railway ran to 129th Street. Most of the development consisted of row after row of brownstones, built by speculators for sale to the middle class, interspersed with tenements that housed working-class families employed in the numerous breweries and light industrial businesses in the neighborhood.[41]

The city guided the growth of the Upper East Side by leasing or giving away land in the area to hospitals, schools and museums.[42] In 1866 twenty lots on Eighty-first and Eighty-second streets between Madison Avenue and Park Avenue were leased to the Roman Catholic diocese for an industrial school run by the Sisters of Mercy, and eighteen lots on East Seventy-seventh Street between Park and Lexington avenues were signed over to the German Hospital for fifty years at one dollar per year. In 1868 the New York State Legislature closed Hamilton Square, a small park laid out in the Commissioners' Plan of 1811 between Fifth and Third avenues and Sixty-sixth and Sixty-ninth streets, and in the 1870s the city leased or sold the land on Lenox Hill to a host of institutions, including Mount Sinai Hospital, Hahnemann Hospital, the Normal College, and homes run by the Association for the Improved Condition of Deaf Mutes, the Sisters of Mercy and the Ladies' Baptist Home Society. In 1868 the state legislature also ordered the commissioners of Central Park to set aside a site on Fifth Avenue between Eighty-first and Eighty-fourth streets for the New-York Historical Society, but when the society declined to move from their building on East Eleventh Street, the commissioners offered the land to the new Metropolitan Museum of Art, which moved there in 1880.

A block by block survey of Fifth Avenue published by

the *Real Estate Record and Guide* in 1889 showed that the development of the Upper East Side was in clusters,[43] leaving many sections completely barren, as a reporter who called himself the "Wanderer" (and may have been Montgomery Schuyler) pointed out in a different issue of the *Record and Guide:*

It is peculiar to New York that wherever an eligible location is selected by some far-seeing builders on which to make improvements, they are always followed by other builders whose attention has thereby been called to the site as an inviting field for their labors. This is especially to be observed on passing by the very high ground—about the highest in New York—between Ninety-first and Ninety-second streets, Fifth and Fourth avenues. Around the blocks comprised within this limited region there are numerous improvements, completed, which were undertaken only last year, not to speak of the somewhat earlier improvements in that neighborhood, such as the large residences of Messrs. Ruppert, Eliot and Untermeyer, the one on Fifth avenue and Ninety-third street, the other on Park avenue and Ninety-fourth street, and the last named on Ninety-second street, near Fifth Avenue.[44]

The early development of Prospect Hill was typical of the Upper East Side. Formerly called Mount Pleasant, Prospect Hill was named because it was the highest point on the east side of Manhattan and provided wonderful views to New Jersey and the Long Island Sound. Once dominated by Archibald Gracie's country house, Prospect Hill became more established when the New York & Harlem Railroad opened a station and the Mt. Pleasant Hotel was built, so that passengers could spend a day by the river. Rowhouse settlement started in the late 1850s, when the horse-drawn trolleys on Second Avenue provided less expensive commuting. By the 1880s the expensive lots along Fifth Avenue were mainly reserved for grand houses, but as these were under construction, the Wanderer pointed out, more ordinary brownstones were built on the side streets and along Madison Avenue, where the stores also congregated. One architect and developer, Thomas Graham, built rowhouses in the neighborhood (on Ninety-second Street between Fifth and Madison avenues), along with the "first apartment hotel on the east side."[45] But the Third Avenue El and the open trench for the sunken tracks in the middle of Fourth Avenue, deceptively renamed Park Avenue between Forty-third and Ninety-sixth streets in 1888, served as a barrier for development of fashionable housing to the east, where smaller rowhouses and tenements were built down the hill to the factories and breweries along the East River.

The boom along the section of Fifth Avenue that faced the park began in 1890, when more houses were built in Manhattan than in any previous year.[46] Not only were the new houses built almost exclusively for the rich, they were built at a time when taste shifted dramatically from the idiosyncratic individuality of the Cosmopolitan Era to a new sense of stylistic unity rooted in the Classical taste. The result was a substantial new district, unlike any other, which developed so quickly that by 1898 Fifth Avenue between Murray Hill and Ninetieth Street was described in an article entitled "Two Miles of Millionaires" as "the backbone of New York, the spinal column" of geography, wealth and fashion.[47] By 1902 "the very rich from all over the country [were] flocking to New York, and securing dwellings regardless of cost," and Herbert Croly noted that it was "definitely settled that there was only one section of the city in which people who were both rich and fashionable would live."[48] Croly expanded the area that Schuyler called the Billionaire District until it included not only the area east of the park but also south of it to about Thirty-sixth Street between Madison and Sixth avenues.

A typology of houses began to emerge on Fifth Avenue in the early 1890s. "Nearly all the pretentious houses—those that merit to be called 'mansions'—are on the corners," the *Real Estate Record and Guide* reported at the start of the decade.[49] Some built later on, like Cornelius Vanderbilt II's chateau in its final form, would fill an entire blockfront, but there were never more than a handful of these—the Vanderbilt, Carnegie and Frick houses in the Billionaire District, and the Schwab mansion in the West End. Much more common were corner houses that filled more than one lot, like the Tiffany house. Single-lot corner houses, such as Marquand's own house in the group of three he built, were also numerous and worked very well. The shallow rooms could all be lit with large windows along the street, rather than on light wells, and if the entry was placed in the long facade facing the side street, the room at the corner had a double exposure. On Fifth Avenue, that meant that the principal rooms could be given a view of the park. Narrower houses filled in the mid-block sections, usually with their entrances placed to one side so as not to interfere with the bowed facade which swelled the interior space and nominally increased the amount of light and view.[50]

Different styles began to emerge as well, represented in both planning types. Each style conveyed a distinct meaning by historical association, and sometimes by association with some great figure in contemporary society. The French Gothic or Chateau style, which Hunt and C.P.H. Gilbert specialized in, had the example of the Vanderbilts behind it as well as the example of the nobility of France. The Italian Renaissance style, a specialty of McKim, Mead & White, drew its strength from its association with the architecture of the Medici and other noble families of great wealth and power, while the red brick and limestone Anglo-American Georgian, pioneered by McKim, Mead & White and successfully adopted by Delano & Aldrich, had behind it the weight of American colonial traditions and upper-class English taste. Only the Modern French and the Arts and Crafts movements, the least archaeological of the styles, had little specific precedent behind them. The critics of the Modern French condescendingly labelled it Cartouche Architecture, but in the hands of skilled graduates of the Ecole des Beaux-Arts it combined the authority of historical example with a sense of modernity. The even freer Arts and Crafts was most appreciated by those who admired the nonconformist trends in late nineteenth-century English design.

Chateau Style

Richard Morris Hunt was the acknowledged master of the Chateau style. When Vanderbilt hired George B. Post to enlarge his house in 1892, the architect brought in Hunt, his former teacher, to consult with him on the design.[51] The result was a more classical and less picturesque mansion— even the facades of the original house were altered. Russell Sturgis, who was not a Classicist, complained that "there is not the boldness of relief, the free disengagement of pavilion or tower from the general mass, the frank use of projection in plan or of broken sky-line which the immense facilities at the architect's command might, perhaps, warrant us in asking. The tower which forms the northeastern angle of the main structure is certainly admirable in its proportions, taken by itself, but it is hardly distinguishable from the mass of the building, and is immeasurably less effective than it would have been with a little more detachment from that mass."[52] Sturgis was much more pleased by the interior of the house, which had decorations by John LaFarge, Augustus Saint-Gaudens and William H. Low. Post used the vast number of the rooms to try many different styles— Gothic, French Renaissance, Louis XIV, Louis XV, Louis XVI and even Moorish in the smoking room. The Vanderbilt's conception of their own importance was shown by the inclusion of a State Room.

Like the Vanderbilt mansion, Hunt's house for Elbridge T. Gerry, built in 1891-94 on the corner of Sixty-first Street, was decidedly less picturesque than his designs of the 1880s.[53] The entrance facade on Sixty-first Street was a symmetrical composition that recalled the transitional French Renaissance work of the Louis XII wing of the Chateau de Blois, an essentially Classical design built by craftsmen trained in the Gothic tradition. The stone ornament on this facade was far more lavish than on the corner tower or the Fifth Avenue elevation. Schuyler judged the Gerry mansion "the most interesting and the most successful" of Hunt's later houses, "so distinctly an ornament to the city as to be one of the public possessions."[54]

An even more Classically composed design was the double-house four blocks to the north on the corner of Sixty-fifth Street that Hunt built in 1893 to 1895 for Caroline Webster Schermerhorn Astor and her son, Colonel John Jacob Astor IV.[55] Mrs. Astor had reigned over New York society from her brownstone palace at 350 Fifth Avenue on the corner of Thirty-fourth Street.[56] When her nephew replaced his parents' house next door with the large Waldorf Hotel, the noise of the construction encouraged the William Astors to follow fashion's northward flow, replace their own

Caroline Webster Schermerhorn Astor and John Jacob Astor IV house, northeast corner of Fifth Avenue and Sixty-fifth Street. Richard Morris Hunt, 1891-95. An 1898 view looking north on Fifth Avenue. MCNY

Mrs. Josephine Schmid house, southeast corner of Fifth Avenue and Sixty-second Street. Richard Morris Hunt, 1895. View across Fifth Avenue from the northwest. MCNY

Mrs. Josephine Schmid house, southeast corner of Fifth Avenue and Sixty-second Street. Richard Morris Hunt, 1895. Entry elevation and plan of first floor. CU

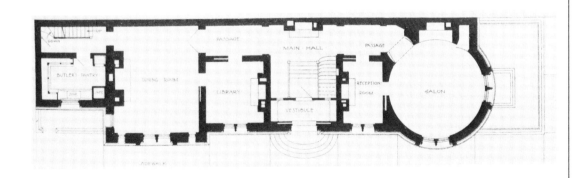

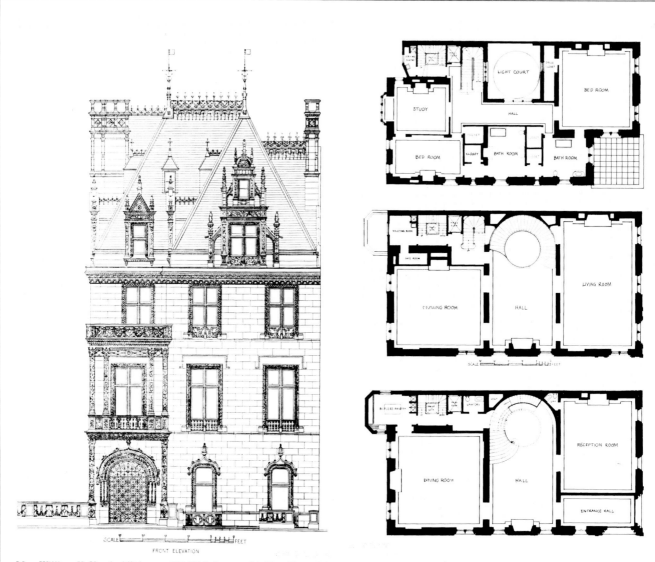

Mrs. William K. Vanderbilt house, 666 Fifth Avenue. McKim, Mead & White, 1905–06. Front elevation and plans of first, second and third floors. CU

house with a hotel (the two were later merged and became the Waldorf-Astoria), and build anew on upper Fifth Avenue. Her husband (William Astor) died in 1892, but Mrs. Astor continued with the project.

The Astor mansion was designed in a French Renaissance style based on later, more Italianate models than the Gerry house. The details were more Classical, and the outline against the sky less picturesque. The tripartite, symmetrical division of the limestone facade echoed the neo-Grec Classicism of Hunt's nearby Lenox Library and reflected the increasing influence of academic composition on all styles. This trend away from picturesque asymmetries toward more Classical composition was partially a result of Hunt's lifelong campaign for the academic principles of the Ecole des Beaux-Arts and must have seemed like sweet vindication to him. Yet, ironically, Hunt never built a Classical house in the city, reserving the "grand manner" for his public buildings.

Hunt's other Fifth Avenue residences of the 1890s, the Schmid mansion on the southeast corner of Sixty-second Street and Fifth Avenue, built in 1895,[57] and the Lawrence house, 969 Fifth Avenue at Seventy-eighth Street (1891)[58] were more medieval chateaux of similar character. The house for Mrs. Josephine Schmid was long and narrow: twenty-five feet wide on Fifth Avenue and one hundred feet long on Sixty-second Street. The *parti* was standard for its type, although the round salon on the corner was an unusual touch well suited to the Chateau style.

Several architects continued Hunt's Chateau style. Rose & Stone showed little of his facility in their dour Isaac Brokaw residence (1 East Seventy-ninth Street, 1899), perhaps being more influenced by the work of H.H. Richardson.[59] In their house for Gertrude Rhinelander Waldo (1897) at 867 Madison Avenue, Kimball & Thompson looked to the same sources as Hunt but surpassed the master in exuberance and charm.[60] In 1905 McKim, Mead & White were commissioned by Mrs. William K. Vanderbilt, Jr. to add one more monument to Vanderbilt Row, a house at 666 Fifth Avenue intended to complement Hunt's house next door for W.K. Vanderbilt.[61] White's design used a center hall *parti* that had become the standard in the Anglo-American Georgian houses that were more typical of the firm, but White cut a porch out of one corner on the third floor and used steep roofs with large chimneys and dormers to give the house a picturesque mass.

C.P.H. Gilbert was one of the most prolific designers in the Chateau style.[62] Two notable early designs were the Isaac D. Fletcher house at 2 East Seventy-ninth Street, completed in 1899,[63] and the Frank W. Woolworth residence (1901) at the corner of Fifth Avenue and Eightieth Street.[64] Like the Schmid house, both had corner sites with narrow frontages on Fifth Avenue and long ones on the side street. Several blocks to the north, at Fifth Avenue and Ninety-second Street, Gilbert built a larger corner house for Felix Warburg and his four sons.[65] Warburg was a Kuhn, Loeb & Company partner who had married the daughter of Jacob Schiff, a German who succeeded Abraham Kuhn and Solomon Loeb as the head of the powerful banking house. Before the mansion was completed in 1908, Warburg's father-in-law tried to persuade his young partner to change Gilbert's Gothic chateau to a Classical palazzo like the one he had bought in 1903. Schiff, conscious of anti-Semitism, thought the French Gothic style was too ostentatious, and refused to visit the house until his daughter Frieda became ill (but the day after his visit he sent her a warm letter and a check for twenty-five thousand dollars as a house gift). The *Real Estate Record and Guide* found the six-story, limestone mansion with fifteenth-century detail "magnificent."[66] Several of the main rooms on the second floor ran the width of the house, which stood on a double lot fifty feet wide on Fifth Avenue.

The Chateau style was not restricted to Fifth Avenue mansions: a number of quite interesting representatives of the style were found in smaller houses on the side streets. C.P.H. Gilbert's rowhouse for E.C. Converse (3 East Seventy-eighth Street, 1899) was a symmetrical composition with a spare use of Gothic ornament.[67] Israels & Harder's later design for Edward Thaw's house (1905) on East Eighty-ninth Street[68] was more archaeologically correct, but Kirby, Petit & Green's even later house for Mrs. H.B. Gilbert (1911) was a marvelous combination of abstract composition and ornate detail.[69]

Italian Renaissance

"The millionaire is as little of a revolutionist in social as in political matters," Herbert Croly wrote in 1902.

He confines his enterprise to business. In intellectual, artistic and moral affairs he lives by tradition alone. His attitude is a curious compound of somewhat contradictory motives. His very deep seated desire for excellence in whatever he does or has, is diverted by his lack of social self-confidence into these traditional and conventional channels; and the result is a social type entirely different from the *parvenu* of literature. He does not try to cover up his sense of his own newness merely by vulgar ostentation, or as he perhaps would in an older and aristocratic country, by an attempt to buy his way into society. What society he wants, he has; for the rest he prefers to remain a businessman. But he does wish to emancipate his children and his fellow-countrymen from the reproach of being raw and new; and consequently he tries in every way to bring to bear upon them historical and traditional influences. He wants them to acquire and to realize more of a past than a few hundred years on a new continent can afford; and he wants to make that past something to be seen and felt. So he distributes enormous sums of money for educational purposes; he and his family are frequently abroad; he often becomes an ambitious collector of pictures and "objets d'art"; and particularly in all aesthetic matters, he wants things with a European reputation. . . . One must, says Mr. Paul Bourget "recognize the sincerity, almost the pathos of this love of Americans for things about which there is an atmosphere of time and stability."[70]

Croly went on to say that the American millionaire solved the problem of an appropriate house as he would solve any problem he was unfamiliar with, by hiring an expert: "The method often results in the making of houses which are extraordinarily complete and beautiful. There are several American designers . . . who are capable of using the rich and splendid materials of the past with so just a sense of their values that the rooms they decorate and furnish obtain the fresh and complete propriety of a new creation. For the old materials are used in new combinations and in rooms of different atmosphere and proportions; and unless, as frequently happens, they are to appear completely out of place, the effect they produce must be moderated in the direction

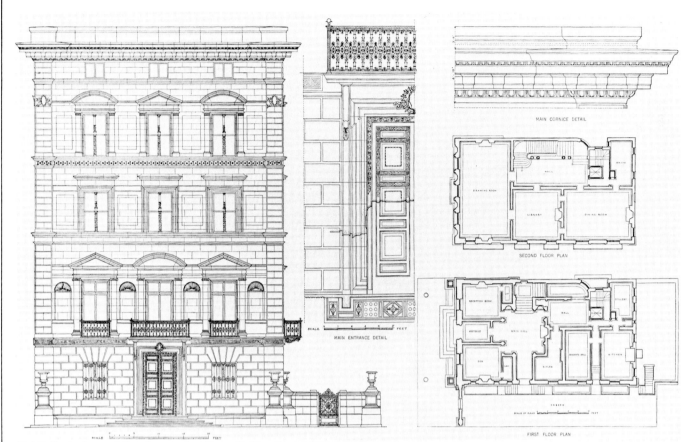

H.A.C. Taylor house, 3 East Seventy-first Street. McKim, Mead & White, 1894-96. Front elevation, plans of first and second floors, and details. CU

John Innes Kane house, 610 Fifth Avenue. McKim, Mead & White, 1904-08. Entrance hall. CU

Joseph Pulitzer house, 9 East Seventy-third Street. McKim, Mead & White, 1901-03. View from the southwest. CU

of simplicity and even homeliness."[71]

Although Croly did not uncritically accept the phenomenon of the millionaire and his house, he supported the movement toward restraint and elegance, which he found was best satisfied at a large scale by the architecture of the Italian Renaissance. Like most critics, he traced the style's revival in America back to McKim, Mead & White's Villard houses and the Boston Public Library (1887-98).[72] In 1894-96 the firm built the second Italian Renaissance house in New York, the H.A.C. Taylor house at 3 East Seventy-first Street.[73] Modelled on the Palazzo Bartolini-Salembini in Florence, the Taylor house was more historically accurate in its massing and exterior materials than the Villard houses. Although the house had one more floor than its model, McKim added rustication and a prominent ashlar treatment of the wall to compensate for the greater height. The interiors, like those in the Villard houses, were original and eclectic. McKim's John Innes Kane house was more severe, with smooth and undifferentiated ashlar masonry on the upper walls broken only by a minimal string course and simple window surrounds capped by bold architraves.[74] Built on the corner of Fifth Avenue and Forty-ninth Street at the bottom of Vanderbilt Row, the Kane house had shallow rustication and paired pilasters on the ground floor which recalled Baldassare Peruzzi's design for the Palazzo Massimo alle Colonne in Rome (1535), but the rest of the palazzo was a *pasticcio* of the Italian Renaissance.[75]

Although Stanford White's design for Joseph Pulitzer's house at 9 East Seventy-third Street, built between 1901 and 1903, was more flamboyant than the typical McKim design, it was nonetheless a scholarly work based on two Venetian palazzos by Baldassare Longhena, the Palazzo Pesaro (1676) and the Palazzo Rezzonico (1667).[76] But White severely reduced the strongly modelled figures in the spandrels and keystones of Longhena's Baroque design, uncharacteristically emphasizing the building's mass over its surface decoration. One explanation for the design's unusual degree of plasticity (unusual for White or any of his partners in the firm at the time), was Pulitzer's near blindness: he demanded plaster models as the design developed so that he could judge the house by touch. As his blindness increased he became more sensitive to noise, and his room was built with double walls for sound protection.[77]

In 1907 Delano & Aldrich completed a modest palazzo

Robert S. Brewster house, southeast corner of Park Avenue and Seventieth Street. Delano & Aldrich, 1907. A 1907 view looking southeast on Seventieth Street showing the Union Theological Seminary across Park Avenue. CU

John S. Phipps house, 6 East Eighty-seventh Street. Grosvenor Atterbury, 1903–04. A 1903 view from the northeast. CU

for Robert S. Brewster at 100 East Seventieth Street, on the corner of Park Avenue.[78] Although Delano said that "an attempt was made to build a house of no particular historic style or epoch," the design was an almost pure expression of the Florentine Renaissance.[79] In the same year, Harry Payne Whitney, a son of William C. Whitney and the husband of Cornelius Vanderbilt's daughter Gertrude, moved into 972 Fifth Avenue, a house between Seventy-eighth and Seventy-ninth streets which his uncle Oliver had commissioned McKim, Mead & White to design together with an adjoining house to be rented or sold.[80] The house, designed by White, had simple massing relieved by a swell front on Fifth Avenue, an exposed garden wall along the side and delicately scaled, elaborate ornament. The facade was a more refined version of the numerous swell-front houses built by developers on the Avenue, but the interiors displayed White's sure touch for decoration.

Even though the Whitney house was designed well after the H.A.C. Taylor house, it was a transitional Classical design that reflected the taste of the Cosmopolitan Era as much as that of the Composite. It might be called Italianate rather than Italian, like the Edward J. Berwind house on the corner of Fifth Avenue and Sixty-fourth Street (Nathan C. Mellen, 1896),[81] and smaller Italianate townhouses built in the Billionaire District in the late 1890s by Henry F. Kilburn,[82] the Boston firm of Peabody & Stearns,[83] Parish & Schroeder[84] and Schickel & Ditmars.[85]

In 1896 McKim began designing a more correct Italian Renaissance rowhouse, built for Levi P. Morton at 681 Fifth Avenue.[86] Its severe facade contrasted sharply with the houses to either side, but after the turn of the century the Morton house influenced the construction of rowhouses with archaeologically accurate details throughout the Billionaire District. Several were designed by Charles Platt, whose early work was perhaps even more scholarly than McKim's. Platt started by remodelling two brownstone rental properties for the Vincent Astor Estate Office. The first was completed in 1906 at 844 Fifth Avenue, next door to Mrs. William B. Astor's chateau.[87] The Astor Estate Office wanted to enlarge and modernize the brownstone in order to increase the rent, but not wanting to spend a great deal of money, they insisted that the old floor levels be maintained. Platt extended the floors toward the street and built a new limestone facade with a rusticated pattern, classical mold-

Thomas Fortune Ryan art gallery, 3 East Sixty-seventh Street. Carrère & Hastings, 1913. MCNY

Otto Kahn house, northeast corner of Fifth Avenue and Ninety-first Street. J. Armstrong Stenhouse and C.P.H. Gilbert, 1918. A 1918 view looking along Ninety-first Street from Fifth Avenue showing the James A. Burden house beyond. MCNY

ings and a shield in the center of the composition. He used the same solution in 1911 at 7 East Sixty-fifth Street.[88]

Other Italian Renaissance rowhouse designs built after 1900 were Grosvenor Atterbury's John S. Phipps house (1903-04) at 6 East Eighty-seventh Street,[89] York & Sawyer's William A. Cook house (East Seventy-first Street, 1912-13)[90] and Hewitt & Bottomley's Wolcott G. Lane house (15 East Seventy-fourth Street, 1914).[91] One of the most charming of the Italian Renaissance rowhouses was also one of the smallest: the private art gallery Carrère & Hastings built for Thomas Fortune Ryan at 3 East Sixty-seventh Street in 1913.[92] In 1916, McKim, Mead & White began a much more severe design, the Thomas Newbold house (1916-18) at 15 East Seventy-ninth Street.[93] Above a horizontally rusticated base, the house had a patterned facade similar to Platt's Astor houses, complete with a cartouche over the large center window.

While the Newbold house was under construction, J. Armstrong Stenhouse and C.P.H. Gilbert were building the last of the great Italian Renaissance palazzos in New York, the Otto Kahn mansion at 1 East Ninety-first Street.[94] Appropriately, the Kahn house was a more faithful copy of the Cancelleria than the first palazzo built in New York, the Villard houses. The limestone facade was closer in color to the original, and the simple rectangular mass was more authentic. The Kahn mansion even had two entrances, although unlike the Cancelleria, where one of the two gates led to a courtyard and the other to a church inside the palazzo, the two were only the opposite ends of a powerfully spatial carriageway cut into the mass of the house. Yet the elaborately asymmetrical arrangement of rooms and light courts behind the cool, ordered facade was faithful to the spirit of the original, if not to its organization.

Modern French

John Carrère and Thomas Hastings introduced the Modern French townhouse to New York in the early 1890s. The style became enormously influential, particularly at the end of the decade, not only for the formidable mansions and houses built by the rich, but also for the speculative rowhouses in the Billionaire District built for the rich. "Even the speculative builders spare neither money nor pains in the attempt to make the dwellings they put upon the market tempting to fastidious customers," Herbert

Richard M. Hoe house, 9 East Seventy-first Street. Carrère & Hastings, 1892. View from the southeast. CU

Dr. Christian A. Herter house, 819 Madison Avenue. Carrère & Hastings, 1893. Front elevation. CU

Croly wrote in 1902. But, he continued, "if the means which they adopt to this end are frequently grievous and disheartening the fault is as much their customers' as their own."[95] These were the buildings that Montgomery Schuyler described in 1901 as rowhouses "of the newest fashion, which all exhibit the swell front which has suddenly invaded all the fashionable quarters and which is so apt to get the unskillful or the unwary into trouble."[96]

Carrère & Hastings's first and most modest Manhattan house was built in 1892 at 9 East Seventy-first Street. It was commissioned by Richard Hoe, an inventor and manufacturer of printing equipment and a noted bibliophile.[97] Hastings, the firm's designer, produced an interesting elevation dominated by a strong geometric composition that displayed a careful balance of verticals and horizontals. Unlike the swell-front houses which Schuyler singled out for criticism, the Hoe house had carved stone details subordinated to the overall design yet still rich—colored marble columns and lintel made a porch at the front door, and planar keystones and shallow cornhusk carvings framed the deep revealed windows. Most important was the tripartite division of the facade, which emphasized the middle two stories between a strong cornice and a decorative course above the rusticated base. Carrère & Hastings continued the horizontal lines of the neighboring Richardsonian rowhouse, but the handling of the details had far more to do with memories of uniform Parisian streets than the typical condition in New York.

Carrère & Hastings's second New York house was built at 819 Madison Avenue for Dr. Christian A. Herter, a physician, biochemist and author of numerous medical books and pamphlets.[98] The house was finished in the same year as the Hoe house, but its *Régence* facade was considerably more prophetic of future development. The elevation repeated the tripartite system used in the Hoe house; the two center floors of living quarters were emphasized by colossal Corinthian pilasters. Herter requested an office and waiting room on the ground floor and an extensive laboratory on the top, and the composition followed quite naturally.

Carrère & Hastings's next townhouse commission, the first H.T. Sloane house (1893–94) at 9 East Seventy-second Street, continued the tripartite system and the Classical order of the Herter house, but the architects inflated the facade with voluptuous sculptural details to make the

H. T. Sloane house, 9 East Seventy-second Street. Carrère & Hastings, 1893–94. CU

Mrs. Ernesto G. Fabbri house, 11 East Sixty-second Street. Haydel & Shepard, 1899–1900. MCNY

M. Newborg house, 50 East Fifty-second Street. J.H. Freedlander, 1904. Entrance hall. CU

Stable and artist's studio for C. Ledyard Blair, 121-23 East Sixty-third Street. Trowbridge & Livingston, 1901. CU

Sloane house one of the most compelling and vigorous examples of the Modern French style in New York.[99] The pilasters grew into columns, a heavy cartouche appeared over the front door, and consoles, garlands, and floral embellishments grew in the second and third stories. The exuberant spirit of its facade was carried into the richly articulated interior. A *porte cochère* led to an arcaded Court of Honor and the main entrance, from which a stair swept up in a great arc to a grand salon, stretched the full fifty feet across the facade.

The Herter and Sloane houses presented the two main tendencies that the Modern French style would follow. The Herter house was relatively restrained and had more direct historical precedent—in the *Régence* style of the eighteenth century—than the bombastic Sloane house, which was one of the most explicit examples of a tendency in the Modern French toward bravado that caused the *Architectural Review* to denigrate the style as Cartouche Architecture: "Originating from an abnormal and dropsical development of the keystone and the medallion, or heraldic escutcheons, it has invaded the field of architectural ornament like a bubonic plague. The cartouche is even more offensive than the perpetual garland in that it can and does appear in so many places."[100]

The economic recession that followed the Panic of 1893 stopped most building in the Billionaire District until almost the end of the decade. When construction resumed the flamboyant Cartouche or Beaux-Arts Baroque style was initially more popular than the more restrained variant of the Modern French. One of the most delightful Beaux-Arts Baroque houses was designed by Haydel & Shepard for Mrs. Ernesto G. Fabbri and built in 1899-1900 at 11 East Sixty-second Street.[101] Even more flamboyant was J.H. Freedlander's design for the M. Newborg house (1904) at 50 East Fifty-second Street, in which the architect compensated for the narrow lot by making the narrow house taller than its neighbors.[102] The elongated facade of the Newborg house was covered with strongly contrasting elements—bold stone bollards on the steps, a light iron and glass marquee over the arched door, a deeply rusticated base below a smooth stone facade covered with elaborately carved ornament, including ornate grotesques and four consoles supporting a heavy balcony—and each floor had a completely different pattern of openings. Even grander was the stable and artist's studio for C. Ledyard Blair at 121-123 East Sixty-third Street designed by Trowbridge & Livingston.[103] A double-width building, its high basement supported two stories of residential accommodation and a steeply pitched mansard punctuated by two bull's eye windows which combined with the recessed, arched loggia at the center to give the facade a distinctly anthropomorphic character.

The most ostentatious Beaux-Arts Baroque house was built on the northeast corner of Fifth Avenue and Seventy-seventh Street for Senator William A. Clark of Montana.[104] When it was completed in 1907 at a cost of about five million dollars exclusive of its furnishings, the Clark house was believed to be the most expensive private city residence ever erected in the United States. It served its purpose as a highly visible monument to the wealth of its owner, who owned enough of his home state to make him worth more than one-hundred million dollars and was determined to make an impression in New York.

The original designs for the house were made by Lord, Hewlett & Hull before the turn of the century, but Clark thought that the plans were too modest. So the drawings were sent for criticism and suggestions to the French architect Henri Deglane, designer of the Grand Palais at the 1900 Universal Exposition in Paris, who substantially increased the ornament. The composition united two pavilions with a tower. The main block, on the corner of Seventy-seventh Street and Fifth Avenue, contained the principal reception rooms and bedroom suites. The dining room, kitchen, and smaller reception rooms for the bedroom suites were placed in the other pavilion, connected to the main block of the house by a corridor centered on a two-story rotunda in the lower part of the tower. The rotunda was a sculpture gallery that opened on four sides to the corridor, a picture gallery in the main pavilion, a conservatory on Seventy-seventh Street and the dining room in the small pavilion.

The cupola, lifted well above the roof so that it was easily seen from Central Park and other relatively remote locations, was castigated by the *Architectural Record* as

E.K. Dunham house, 35 East Sixty-eighth Street. Carrère & Hastings, 1899-1901. CU

Mrs. Frederick Edey house, 10 West Fifty-sixth Street. Warren & Wetmore, 1903. CU

inappropriate to a dwelling and the most "meaningless and fatuous feature . . . [to be found] even in the wildest vagaries of our domestic architecture.[105] The magazine published the Clark house as the twenty-first in its series of Architectural Aberrations, noting that "a casual criticism in a weekly paper not long ago observed that the Clark house . . . would have been an appropriate residence for P.T. Barnum." The "ferocity" of the stone cutting, the *Record* continued,

is, in fact, so unmitigated that the basement seems to have had as its prototype rather a log-cabin than any extant construction of masonry. . . . A certified check to the amount of all this stone carving, hung on the outer wall, would serve every artistic purpose attained by the carving itself. . . . the Copper King and his architect seem unaware that boldness and brassiness are going out of fashion in house building, and that modesty and a sense of home-like seclusion are coming in. The Clark mansion would have been centrally "in it" half a dozen years ago, when it was projected. But it will be hopelessly "out of it" when it comes to be completed, and antiquated and old-fashioned while it is still brand new. Which will be the most just and severe Nemesis that could possibly overtake an edifice which could at no time have any better claim upon anybody's attention than that it was in the height of the mode.[106]

Yet as *Architecture* observed, "the measure of its success as one of the important architectural monuments of the city must depend upon the skill with which the architectural elements and enrichments of the later period of the French Renaissance have been utilized, modified and combined in the production of a modern palace; and is quite independent of the question as to whether a modern palace of vast scale and lavish enrichment is an appropriate residence for an American citizen."[107]

In contrast with the Clark house, Carrère & Hastings's Modern French design for the E.K. Dunham house (1899-1901) at 35 East Sixty-eighth Street, was judged "full of good design and well placed detail" by the *Architectural Review,* which labelled the house "rococo."[108] The *Architectural Record,* which had been critical of earlier Modern French work, was pleased to call the design "to the attention of the large tribe of bunglers who are busy disfiguring our street with rude extravagances of the 'French Style,'" and grudgingly acknowledged that "the exuberance is handled with skill and discretion, and very clearly avoids defects of over-muchness inevitable in this sort of work when produced by designers of less experience. Indeed, there are only a few architects in the United States who have acquired an idiomatic mastery of this style."[109]

In the Dunham house, Carrère & Hastings effectively adapted the inflated, overscaled character and effusive ornament of the Modern French style to a surprisingly modest building. As a result the highly individual design of the Dunham house commanded a distinct presence while conforming to the Parisian conception of the city as a coherent entity realized incrementally over time. Like the less bombastic Hoe house, the Dunham residence was composed with proportions and divisions intended to reinforce the continuity of the street wall.

Countless similar examples were built around the same time, such as Carrère & Hastings's L.H. Lapham house (1902) at 15 West Fifty-sixth Street,[110] a speculative house (1902) at 8 East Eighty-third Street designed by Janes & Leo,[111] George Q. Palmer's house (1904) designed by his cousin George Carnegie Palmer (of Palmer & Hornbostel) at 1 East Seventy-third Street,[112] C.P.H. Gilbert's Stuart Duncan house (1 East Seventy-fifth Street, 1904),[113] and the houses by the still young firm of Warren & Wetmore for Mrs. Frederick Edey (10 West Fifty-sixth Street, 1903),[114] and G.H. Warren (924 Fifth Avenue, 1905).[115]

In 1899 Ernest Flagg and his junior partner Walter B. Chambers completed the Oliver Gould Jennings house at 7 East Seventy-second Street, next door to the H.T. Sloane house.[116] The Jennings house was a natural complement to its neighbor, looking like an end pavilion for the wider and more plastic composition by Carrère & Hastings. Individual details—from the extravagant copper crest on the bulbous mansard roof, to the vermiculated courses at the base of the limestone facade—were quite fantastic, yet the whole was subordinate to the Sloane house.

Around the turn of the century the same architectural

Oliver Gould Jennings house, 7 East Sixty-second Street. Ernest Flagg and Walter B. Chambers, 1899. CU

Marble Twins, 645-47 Fifth Avenue. Hunt & Hunt, 1905. MCNY

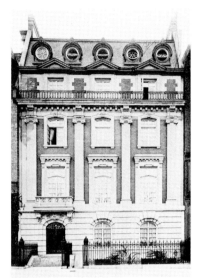

Jacob Schiff house, 967 Fifth Avenue. Charles C. Thain, 1903. CU

sensibility of the Composite Era, which had caused the popularity of the Italian Renaissance, began to push the best of the Modern French architects towards more refined and historically correct designs. Although developers and *nouveaux riches* like Senator Clark continued to build in the Cartouche style, Carrère & Hastings, Warren & Wetmore and Flagg designed their most important commissions in a more restrained variant of the Modern French. Flagg's design for his brother-in-law Arthur Scribner's house (39 East Sixty-seventh Street, 1903-04) had swags hung below the fourth floor and the cornice, but the total effect was kept in check by the simplicity of the window designs and the plain ashlar of the superstructure.[117] Flagg's brick and limestone house for his other brother-in-law, Charles Scribner, was at 9 East Sixty-sixth, next door to Richard Howland Hunt's flamboyant William J. Schieffelin residence (5 East Sixty-sixth Street, 1900).[118] Its location highlighted the restrained and Classical version of the Modern French style that Flagg was beginning to master with a shallow, dentilated cornice carrying a balcony rail at the fifth floor and ornamental cartouche panels set above the second-floor pedimented French windows.[119]

The use of brick and limestone at the Charles Scribner house was one indication that the simpler, domestic qualities usually associated with the Anglo-American Georgian style were beginning to influence the development and style of the Modern French townhouse. Carrère & Hastings had already combined the boldly scaled elements of the Modern French with distinctly Georgian influences in the F. Burral Hoffman house, built in 1898 at 58 East Seventy-ninth Street,[120] and at least one speculative builder followed that direction in almost identical houses designed by Charles Brendon at 32 East Fifty-first Street (1901)[121] and at 39 East Seventy-seventh Street (1902).[122] Flagg's Albert Gould Jennings residence (2 East Eighty-second Street, 1903)[123] was another brick and limestone variation on the Modern French style, but Carrère & Hastings's mansion for Mrs. Charles H. Senff (1900)[124] was a more influential one. Though it was built at Madison Avenue and Forty-first Street, not in the Billionaire District but in the still-fashionable Murray Hill section, the restrained Senff house was notable for its recall of the French red-brick and stone architecture of Jules Hardouin Mansard's Cour de Marbre at Versailles and the late French Renaissance Place Henry VI in Paris. The style's planar walls and simple classical details were well suited to the more archaeological aspect of the Modern French style.[125]

In 1903 the builders John T. and James A. Farley built a brick and limestone double-width rowhouse at 967 Fifth Avenue, on the same block as the Clark mansion then under construction.[126] The *Real Estate Record and Guide* judged the house "in all respects equal to those built specially for millionaire owners, and found that as an instance of commercial building this . . . marks an epoch."[127] In comparison with the flamboyant swell-front houses more often built by developers, the rowhouse, which was bought by Jacob Schiff, was distinguished by its restrained elegance. Charles C. Thain's design revived the Louis XVI Classicism Carrère & Hastings had used a decade earlier at the Herter house.

Later in 1903 Hoppin & Koen employed the same motifs of red brick and limestone, tripartite division and applied pilasters in their Louis XVI style J.F.D. Lanier house.[128] Three years later they composed a very similar facade for R.T. Wilson's house at 15 East Fifty-seventh Street, but built the all-limestone design in the Adam style, described as "the English Louis XVI"[129] by a contemporary critic who reported that "Mr. Hoppin went to London to study the work of the Adam Bros. before designing the interiors, the style of which has been carried throughout every apartment in the house."[130]

Hunt & Hunt's rowhouses, known as the Marble Twins (1905) at 645-647 Fifth Avenue, were another variation on French neoclassicism, with a vermiculated base, two-story pilasters, and a bold attic-story and cornice.[131] Carrère & Hastings's Geo. L. Rives residence at 69 East Seventy-ninth Street was more subtle. "The triple division of a five-story facade, with the central member consisting of the second and third story tied together by pilasters, dates from French examples of the end of the 18th century; and these French examples have a good claim to be considered as the source of the most appropriate conventions for domestic

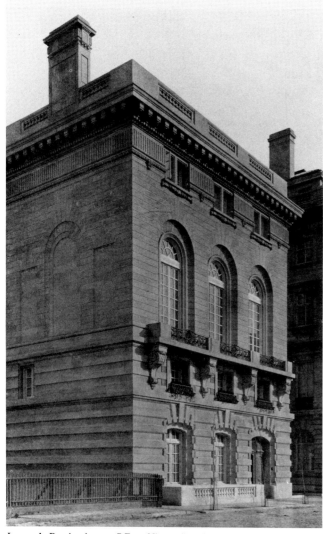

James A. Burden house, 7 East Ninety-first Street. Warren & Wetmore, 1903–05. CU

street architecture," the *Architectural Record* said of the Rives house in 1909. "The facades of the old buildings on the Place Vendome in Paris, have simplicity without attenuation, and dignity without pretension. At the same time the design of each individual house had no meaning or propriety except in relation to its neighbors. Modern French architects have sought seduously to improve on this early model, but it may be doubted whether their improvements have been worth the ingenuity expended upon them. The houses on the Place Vendome are wholly admirable types of a gentleman's city residence, and Messrs. Carrère & Hastings have shown their usual good sense in adapting the design to the conditions of a contemporary private residence in New York."[132]

Modern Renaissance

The Rives house was a rather academic representative of the more restrained tendency of the Modern French style. But two houses designed in 1903 by Warren & Wetmore combined some of the restraint and archaeological sensibility of Carrère & Hastings's Herter house with the bold scale and inventiveness of their Sloane house, creating a new mode known as Modern Renaissance. Warren & Wetmore's house for Mrs. M. Orme Wilson, built on a triple lot at 3 East Sixty-fourth Street, was in the overscaled and astylar tradition of the Modern French taste, but the power of its sparse yet sculptural details, with simple profiles, seemed less bombastic than other houses.[133] Their contemporary design for the James A. Burden house had more historical precedent, yet its spirit and execution were equally bold.[134] Built at 7 East Ninety-first Street, the house might be best described as a Modern French interpretation of an Italian palazzo: the mass and the simplicity of the details were from the Italian Renaissance, but the plastic modelling of the details, particularly the openings around the windows, the inventiveness of the ornament, as in the entablature, and the insertion of a service floor between the ground floor and the *belle étage* were all distinctly French.

Burden was the founder of an iron foundry in Troy, New York that grew into the enormous American Machine and Foundry Company, but the house was paid for by his father-in-law, W.D. Sloane. Sloane also hired Carrère & Hastings to build a house next door at 9 East Ninety-first Street for his other daughter, Mrs. John Henry Ham-

Mrs. M. Orme Wilson house, 3 East Sixty-fourth Street. Warren & Wetmore, 1903–04. MCNY

Henry Phipps house, northeast corner of Fifth Avenue and Eighty-seventh Street. Trowbridge & Livingston, 1905. View from the southwest. MCNY

mond.[135] Even though Hastings used no specific prototype, his translation of the Italian Renaissance was less original than Warren & Wetmore's: the scale was more conventional, the fenestration pattern more ordinary, and many of the ornamental details fussier. Yet the muscular Ionic columns and curved pediments on the *piano nobile,* the deeply revealed openings, the massive quoins, the imposing cornice and the planar walls gave the simple mass a plastic firmness revealing a sense of the Modern French. Like the Burden house, the Hammond house had French-style interior decorations.

Carrère & Hastings were less concerned with correctness of detail than McKim, whom Hastings referred to as "Mr. Beautiful Facade."[136] Hastings, known as "Mr. Good Plan," believed "that his first duty was that of making the building serve in the most economical manner possible the function, or the combination, for which it was constructed," according to the *Architectural Record.* "Otherwise he would inevitably drift into the position of a man who applied an aesthetic cosmetic to the face of a building whose plan and structure were devised by an engineer. The plan of a building is inevitably its dominant aspect, and a practical people like the Americans will not put up with wasteful and inconvenient layouts.... The first and most important result of the [Beaux-Arts] school training which the present generation of American architects has been receiving is the restoration of the plan to its proper position in a general architectural method."[137] While Carrère & Hastings were influenced by the restraint inherent in the elevations drawn by McKim, Mead & White and incorporated that attitude into their later designs, their belief in the importance of the plan and its expression in a unified composition kept them from adopting the archaeological aspect of the older firm's work. Instead, the designs of Carrère & Hastings and other Beaux-Arts trained architects who followed them developed the style known as Modern Renaissance: just as Beaux-Arts planning was a synthesis of antique Roman planning sifted through the sieve of the Ecole, the facades of Modern Renaissance houses were freely handled Renaissance houses informed by twentieth-century influences.

"The importance of Carrère & Hastings cannot be understood unless a careful explanation is attempted, both of the significance of the example set by McKim, Mead & White, and the significance of the improvement made thereupon by Carrère & Hastings," the *Architectural Record* wrote in 1910.[138]

All architecture since the Renaissance has been imitative in method and alien in origin. Good architecture has consisted, first, in the selection of those forms best suited to the local purposes, and then in the peculiarly consistent, idiomatic, realistic, and beautiful rendering of the adopted style. The distinction of modern French architecture is due to the fact that for some centuries French architects have on the whole been more consistent, more capable and more intelligent in their imitation than have the architects of other countries, and whatever distinction American architecture has any chance of attaining must depend upon the display of similar merits.[139]

James Gamble Rogers's design for the Edward S. Harkness house[140] and Trowbridge & Livingston's Henry Phipps mansion[141] were early examples of the Modern Renaissance style. Harkness was a Standard Oil heir and director who knew that he didn't want a house as ostentatious as Senator Clark's Cartouche style mansion, just being finished as the Harkness house started construction. Harkness hired Rogers, whom he knew from Yale University, where Harkness was a trustee and Rogers was the campus architect (Rogers later designed the Gothic and Colonial style buildings for the house system donated by Harkness). "It was the wish of the client," reported the *New York Architect,* "and the aim of the architect to design a dignified house that would not in an ostentatious way indicate its costliness, a feature unfortunately prominent in many of our pretentious city residences."[142] Harkness and his new wife Mary Stillman filled the house with a distinguished art collection that they later donated to the Metropolitan Museum.

Like many Modern Renaissance houses, both the Harkness and Phipps houses were located on prominent corners. The Harkness house was a simply massed palazzo at 1 East Seventy-fifth Street that was entered on its long side on the side street. The Phipps residence at 1 East Eighty-seventh

Street was built on a considerably larger lot, and Trowbridge & Livingston set the house back behind a terrace with a driveway surrounding a fountain. The bulk of the house was as simply massed as the Harkness house, although there was a low *orangerie* at the eastern end of the plot screening out the neighbors. Both houses were built of marble, but while Rogers leaned towards the Italian Renaissance for inspiration, Trowbridge & Livingston looked more to the example of French country houses of the late eighteenth century.

In 1910, when the *Real Estate Record and Guide* reported on the progress of "New Palaces on Fifth Avenue," several were corner houses in the Modern Renaissance style.[143] One was Carrère & Hastings's almost Italian design for Edwin Gould (936 Fifth Avenue, 1910),[144] whose scandalous brother George had already torn down his chateau at Fifth Avenue and Sixty-seventh Street and replaced it with a Modern Renaissance house by Horace Trumbauer.[145] "If we are still using in America many styles of design hardly on speaking terms with each other," *Architecture* commented,

at least for New York City houses we have found a style at once characteristic, suitable and beautiful, and most of the larger houses recently erected in this city have been designed in this style. It has its genesis in the French of the periods of Louis XV and Louis XVI, and is strongly affected by the admiration for the Italian Renaissance ever present in American architects of today. These influences have resulted in a style which at first glance appears to be French, and upon closer inspection evidences its American genesis. The residence for Mr. George J. Gould . . . exhibits these qualities in their best expression, a restrained, refined, and educated piece of design. The . . . decorative members . . . are kept very flat, with the result that the surface has sufficient play of light and shade to keep it from being tiresome without the exaggerated lines which result in restlessness.[146]

The grandest of the new palaces described by the *Real Estate Record and Guide* was Trumbauer's James B. Duke house at Fifth Avenue and Seventy-eighth Street, next to the Harry Payne Whitney house.[147] Trumbauer had a large lot to work with—72 feet by 140 feet—so like Trowbridge & Livingston he looked to the eighteenth-century French country house for inspiration and designed an abstracted, overscaled version of the Chateau Labottier in Bordeaux by Laclotte. In order to get the proper proportions, the service rooms were placed in the basement and the servant's bedrooms under the low roof, so that the public rooms could be placed on the ground floor around a grand hall and the eight large bedrooms on the second floor. The Louis XVI public rooms were less austere than the limestone facade.

As the Duke house was being finished in 1912, Henry Clay Frick was beginning construction of the largest and most elaborate Modern Renaissance mansion in New York.[148] Frick was an ex-business partner of Andrew Carnegie: each disliked the other, but Frick was a brilliant manager who increased the production and profits of the Carnegie Steel Company forty-fold in a dozen years (it was also Frick who oversaw the Carnegie Company's infamous Homestead War in an attempt at union busting). The problems between the two men led to their selling out to J.P. Morgan's United States Steel Trust in the largest industrial sale to date. While Carnegie took his profits and built his house uptown, Frick leased William H. Vanderbilt's house at 640 Fifth Avenue. Twenty years earlier he and Andrew Mellon had examined Fifth Avenue mansions and estimated maintenance costs: Vanderbilt's was then the most luxurious in the city and they reckoned that it would require an income of about one thousand dollars a day. In 1906, while living at 640 Fifth Avenue, Frick bought the vast site of the Lenox Library for $2,250,000. At the top of Lenox Hill, it was one of the most prominent lots in Manhattan, the only elevated property on Fifth Avenue besides Carnegie's. Frick had been acquiring art under the tutelage of the English dealer Joseph Duveen, who persuaded him that cost was not to be considered in acquiring great art, and urged him to build a house suitable for his future collection. In 1907 Frick paid six-hundred thousand dollars for another fifty feet to the east of his lot, and, at Duveen's suggestion, hired Carrère & Hastings.

Although Frick eventually built a three million dollar

C. Ledyard Blair house, southeast corner of Fifth Avenue and Seventieth Street. Carrère & Hastings, 1917. View from the northwest. MCNY

Henry Clay Frick house, Fifth Avenue between Seventieth and Seventy-first streets. Carrère & Hastings, 1912-14. A 1913 view of the Frick house under construction showing the interior courtyard. MCNY

house, Hastings's first few projects overestimated even Frick's architectural pretensions. Early drawings show a distinctly French interpretation of the Palazzo Farnese in Rome, with a rusticated nine-bay arcade across the first floor, alternating pediments over the windows on the second floor, plain square window frames on the third and bold quoins at the corners. An entrance porch supported by hermes was to stand on Seventy-first Street and a long gallery for pictures would have occupied the eastern edge of the central courtyard.

The accepted scheme had a more French character, with a front portico based on one at the Louis XVI style Hotel du Chatelet, and an axial Beaux-Arts plan. The main block of the house ran from Seventieth to Seventy-first streets, set back from Fifth Avenue behind a broad terrace. A *porte cochère* on Seventieth Street opened onto a small court intersected by the entry hall: from that point one could proceed through the house on foot, alongside the house in a courtyard surrounded by arcades (one of which bisected the entry hall), or continue into the courtyard by carriage. A perpendicular axis at the end of the court bisected the west gallery, the focal point of the large garden on Fifth Avenue.

Before Frick died in 1919, he asked Hastings to design an extension for two galleries that would fill the passage from the back courtyard to Seventy-first Street. Hastings planned two new units, distinct in form and detail from the earlier construction. The first was an oval gallery prefaced by a hall intended to serve as the entrance for the museum Frick envisioned. The second gallery, a one-story Doric structure, was to stand just to the east. Only the latter gallery was built, completed in 1923 and used for the first Frick Art Reference Library.[149]

Hastings must have been pleased when C. Ledyard Blair asked him to design a house for the lot on the corner of Fifth Avenue and Seventieth Street, opposite the open end of the Frick garden.[150] Given the opportunity to complete the architectural setting for the main facade, Hastings responded with a Modern Renaissance elevation well suited to its prominent neighbor. A rusticated ground floor supported a seven-bay center framed by fluted Corinthian pilasters on the pavilions at each end. The subtle indentation of the central bays, which became more obvious above the cornice in the setback of the attic story, resembled the tripartite division of the Frick house, and the very flat Louis XVI

Henry Clay Frick house, Fifth Avenue between Seventieth and Seventy-first streets. Carrère & Hastings, 1912-14. View from Central Park. CU

details—the embedded panels of vases, swags and candelabra—continued the decorative scheme. Only the Tuscan columns with entablature blocks bearing a frieze of *bucranea* and rosettes at the front door offered much three dimensional relief. The elegant refinement of the flat block could have resulted in a long, boring elevation in the hands of a less talented designer.

The plan filled the long and narrow lot, 150 feet by 30 feet. A curved stair screened by paired columns at the rear of the almost central oval entry led up to a large gallery that separated the dining and drawing rooms. Each of the latter rooms was built to the full depth of the house. Although they sat in the two-bay end pavilions, each room was three bays long, contradicting the indentation of the Seventieth Street elevation. Reception rooms, bedrooms and service rooms were arranged economically on the other floors.[151]

Anglo-American Georgian

"Ten years ago the larger private residences in New York were almost exclusively designed in a bastard combination of French and Italian and the refined qualities of both schools were lost in elaboration of overscaled ornament," *Architecture* pronounced in 1911.

It was the triumph of Beaux Arts architecture, as it is sometimes understood, rather than of that sane and conservative design which the French graduates of the Beaux Arts employ for residential or monumental buildings as opposed to the exuberant fancy which the same architects lavish upon their nonpermanent exhibition buildings. The country as a whole is once more settling down into more sober realms of art; every style is being treated with more dignity and restraint, and we are losing the attitude of mind which regarded the early Colonial architecture of this country as something to be admired but not imitated.

The great firm of McKim, Mead & White never hesitated to borrow where they pleased and have executed with equal facility and success works in the most diverse styles, but from the beginning they have mingled with the great volume of work executed by their office occasional tonic doses of Colonial in which is shown sympathy with the Colonial methods such as has been granted to few other American architects. Perhaps their Colonial work has been no better executed than their Italian or Spanish, but to the writer, at least, it seems more sympathetic, approaching nearer to a rational ideal of architecture as it should be held in this country, and to the supreme expression of the conditions and needs of American life.[152]

The rise in national spirit following the Centennial that fed the flowering of the American Renaissance naturally produced an interest in the events and artifacts of Colonial times. Among the first to look back to Colonial architecture were Charles McKim, William Mead, William Bigelow and Stanford White, the four young architects who set out in 1877 on what they afterwards called their "celebrated" trip to Marblehead, Salem, Newburyport and Portsmouth, where they made sketches and some of the earliest measured drawings of Colonial houses. Mead later reported that it was that sketch trip which caused the office to turn toward Classicism.[153]

In 1882, the same year they designed the Villard houses, McKim, Mead & White also designed the H.A.C. Taylor house in Newport, the first Colonial Revival building in the country.[154] In 1894, when they designed the H.A.C. Taylor house at 3 East Seventy-first Street, they also designed for Taylor the first Georgian Revival building in the city, a double house fronting on Seventy-second Street behind his house.[155] The double house at 2-4 East Seventy-second Street was built in a style similar to the three Federal rowhouses Charles Bulfinch built in Boston for Harrison Gray Otis at the beginning of the nineteenth century in a chaste red brick and stone style that has also been described as American Adam.

As they were completing the Taylor houses in 1896, McKim, Mead & White began the design of another Federal style double house, built in 1896-98 for James J. Goodwin at 9-11 West Fifty-fourth Street.[156] "The Georgian epoch, pure and simple, is revived in the . . . two houses, Nos. 9 and 11," Russell Sturgis wrote at the turn of the century. Unlike the six-bay Taylor houses (three bays each) the Goodwin houses were "forced into one by the placing of a projecting porch with Ionic columns in the middle of the whole five-windowed front. The house, No. 9, which evidently possesses two of the five windows in each tier, has its door piece flat and, therefore, subordinate."[157] Yet despite that unorthodox feature, the ornamental details brought McKim, Mead & White's second Federal rowhouse close to the spirit of the third Harrison Gray Otis house.

But it was not until the construction in 1899-1902 of Babb, Cook & Willard's very large mansion for Andrew Carnegie that the Georgian style began to be taken seriously as a suitably impressive alternative to the Modern French and Italian Renaissance styles.[158] Despite its enormous size and its prominent isolation in a large private garden running a block along Fifth Avenue from Ninetieth to Ninety-first streets, the Carnegie mansion was intended to be more modest and more obviously domestic in character than smaller mansions, such as the Phipps house a few blocks south at Eighty-seventh Street. Schuyler reported that Carnegie told his architects he "did not want a palace,"[159] but asked for "the most modest, plainest, and roomy house in New York."[160]

Although the dour Scottish-Georgian manse was less monumental and exuberant than a Modern French design, Babb, Cook & Willard's heavy-handed details, influenced by the Modern French taste, kept the house from being a perfect exemplar of Anglo-American Georgian. Ironically it was left to the leading Modern French architects Carrère & Hastings to design the house that, perhaps more than any other, led to the popular acceptance for residential urban design of the Anglo-American Georgian style. Their red brick house on Park Avenue for Senator Elihu Root was built in 1903-05 in an English Regency style that struck one critic as the "embodiment of well proportioned dignity."[161] "It is a significant fact that the house of one so prominent in national life as Mr. Root should be strikingly free from the profusion of ornament and meretricious finery which blazes forth from the facades erected by many notable citizens," according to the magazine *Indoors and Out*:

But it will be remembered that it was the owner of this house who, a year ago uttered a most reasonable voice on an occasion when architects of the country and their distinguished guests were assembled in Washington. He selected "The Simple Life" as the subject of an address in which he gave unstinted praise to the Jeffersonian simplicity that molded in purest form the White House, Mt. Vernon, Monticello, and the early mansions of

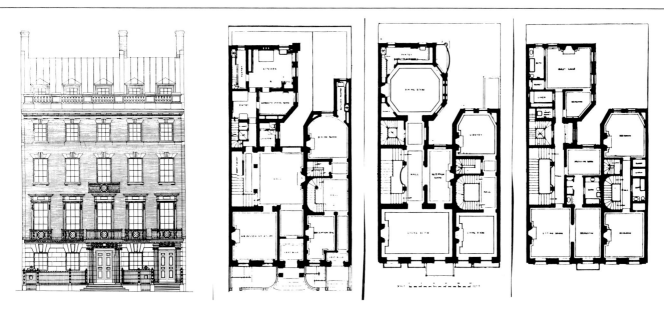

James J. Goodwin house, 9-11 West Fifty-fourth Street. McKim, Mead & White, 1896-98. Front elevation and plans of first, second and third floors. CU

Andrew Carnegie house, southeast corner of Fifth Avenue and Ninety-first Street. Babb, Cook & Willard, 1899-1902. View from Fifth Avenue looking along Ninety-first Street. MCNY

Elihu Root house, southeast corner of Park Avenue and Seventy-first Street. Carrère & Hastings, 1903–05. View across Park Avenue. CU

Willard Straight house, northeast corner of Fifth Avenue and Ninety-fourth Street. Delano & Aldrich, 1914. View from Fifth Avenue. CU

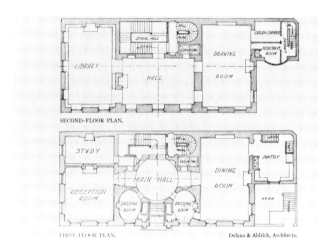

Willard Straight house, northeast corner of Fifth Avenue and Ninety-fourth Street. Delano & Aldrich, 1914. Plans of first and second floors. CU

Charleston, Annapolis and other centers of Colonial times. In the restrained and dignified design of his own house he has again emphasized an appreciation of the consummate taste which American gentlemen of a century ago expressed in the rearing of their homes. The scene has shifted from the river banks of primitive Virginia to a metropolis speeding to become the center of the world; but chastity, dignity and reserve still remain eternal truths of art, and refined intelligence in building a home is quick to do them homage.[162]

McKim, Mead & White's house for Philip A. Rollins, built a bit earlier—1900–03—on the southwest corner of Madison Avenue and Seventy-eighth Street, was not only smaller but less inventive.[163] Compared to the severe, abstracted and planar facades of Carrère & Hastings's design, which had brick and mortar colors calculated to emphasize the header pattern and complemented by the bluestone base and limestone trim, McKim, Mead & White's design was more obviously archaeological, looking to the work of Bulfinch. Edwin Outwater's John W.A. Davis house, built in 1904 on the northwest corner of Lexington Avenue and Sixty-fifth Street, was more typical of what Schuyler described as Old New York, giving the impression a house had migrated uptown from Washington Square.[164]

With the exception of a handful of Georgian houses on Park Avenue that followed the example of the Root house, the only Georgian mansion to be built between 1903 and the World War was the Willard Straight House.[165] Completed in 1914 at 1130 Fifth Avenue on the corner of Ninety-fourth Street, it was designed by the young firm of Delano & Aldrich, who were to become the preeminent advocates of the Georgian taste. With its simple details, planar walls and bull's eye windows in the attic story, the Straight house was essentially a Modern Renaissance house in Georgian dress. Schuyler, and apparently many millionaires and their architects, found the Georgian styles less appropriate for the grand mansions along the avenues than for the modest rowhouses of the side streets. "The habitat of the bourgeois house extends . . . from the Fifties to the Eighties," Schuyler wrote in 1906. "And it is surely a good thing that a burgess much short of being a millionaire should yet have his home made to order.[166]

Some of the Georgian rowhouses were bigger in scale and more ostentatious than the "bourgeois" model Schuyler

Paul Leicester Ford house, 37 East Seventy-seventh Street. Henry Rutgers Marshall, 1900–01. CU

Charles Dana Gibson house, 127 East Seventy-third Street. McKim, Mead & White, 1902–03. CU

favored, combining the characteristic red brick and limestone of the Georgian with boldly swelling fronts embellished in a French manner with columns, pilasters and quoins. These were frequently built near Fifth Avenue in those blocks that Schuyler felt to be given over "by common consent . . . to houses of palatial pretensions."[167] Numbers 19 East Eighty-sixth Street[168] and 133 East Sixty-second Street[169] were representative of Georgian houses that seemed to Schuyler very Parisian, while 63 East Seventy-ninth he called "late of London," because it had no "positive architectural quality."[170] Charles Platt's largest townhouse, built for John T. Pratt in 1915 at 7 East Sixty-first Street, was a five-bay, five-story dwelling best described as Federal style with Italian Mannerist details.[171] Henry Rutgers Marshall's house for Paul Leicester Ford (1900–01) at 37 East Seventy-seventh Street was a simple brick box that also had bold Italian Renaissance ornament.[172] Though the house was not on a corner, Marshall took advantage of the setbacks of the neighboring brownstone to fill the west end with windows and convey the impression of a freestanding house. For Hugh D. Auchincloss's house (1902–03) at 33 East Sixty-seventh Street, Robertson & Potter took advantage of a similar site. A comparison of the presentation drawings for the house, published in 1902, and the house as built makes clear the shift from the lush, fundamentally French feeling of so much turn-of-the-century work, no matter what style, toward a more reserved, Anglo-Saxon approach.[173]

Schuyler's expectations of a Georgian style expressive of a comfortable bourgeoisie was best fulfilled in the narrow (sixteen to twenty foot) rowhouse. Stanford White's design for his close friend Charles Dana Gibson, built in 1902–03 at 127 East Seventy-third Street, quickly established the type.[174] The house for the artist and cartoonist had a central entrance on the ground floor enhanced by a simple porch and surmounted by a version of the tripartite Palladian or Serlian window that denoted the principal living space on the larger second floor. The rest of the facade was very flat, with little detail or ornament: the upper-floor windows had no true architraves, merely stone lintels, and even the arched window had no archivolt but a simple series of brick voussoirs held in place by a keystone made, appropriately, of limestone.

The paradigm was used in numerous versions by

Charles Hudson house, 3 East Seventy-sixth Street. Brite & Bacon, 1899. CU

developers and architects such as Pickering & Walker,[175] Albro & Lindeberg,[176] George B. de Gersdorff,[177] Ernest Flagg and Walter B. Chambers,[178] Percy Griffin,[179] Charles Romeyn[180] and Grosvenor Atterbury.[181] But no architects of the era better handled the Georgian and more consistently produced work that suggested quiet wealth than Delano & Aldrich. Just as their house for Willard Straight summarized the trend at mansion scale, their houses for Allen Wardwell, Howard Gardiner Cushing, Marion Hague and Marshall J. Dodge did so at the scale of Schuyler's comfortable bourgeoisie. The four-and-one-half-story Wardwell house, at 127 East Eightieth Street,[182] and the J. Marshall Dodge house at 37 East Sixty-eighth Street,[183] were stripped to the barest essentials, relying on the proportions of the windows and the fine brickwork to give them character. The brickwork at the Cushing house at 121 East Seventieth Street[184] and the Hague house, further east at Number 161,[185] was somewhat more elaborate, though only in the Cushing house did Delano resort to the traditional repertoire of cornice moldings and pedimented door heads to enliven the composition and make it more stylistically specific.

A few architects such as Frederick J. Sterner, Brite & Bacon and Kirby, Petit & Green combined the domestic spirit of the Anglo-American Georgian with earlier English and Dutch sources for a richer but still intimate character. Brite & Bacon's house for Charles Hudson, built in 1899 at 3 East Seventy-sixth Street, used tapestry brick and limestone trim in a symmetrical facade crowned by four classical urns.[186] The three-sided projecting bay combined leaded-casement windows in the two upper floors with an elegant Classical doorway. Kirby, Petit & Green's residence for Irving T. Bush at 28 East Sixty-fourth Street was flamboyantly Jacobean, with a high, almost Flemish gable, strapwork ornament, and elaborately leaded casement windows in a three-sided bay that ran almost the full width of the house and rested on a bracketed cornice supported by paired Doric columns.[187] Schuyler felt that the bay was too massive for the columns carrying it, and that the deeply recessed entrance was Stygian in its darkness. Moreover, he found the entire facade "questionable as a city street front. As one pavilion in the garden front of a Jacobean mansion, fronting a terrace with peacocks, say, and a lake, it would be as entirely in place as it is entirely out of place in a New York

Irving T. Bush house, 28 East Sixty-fourth Street. Kirby, Petit & Green, 1905. View showing Seth Low's house (30 East Sixty-fourth Street, Theodore Weston, 1881–82) with lamps indicating Mayor Low's residence on the corner of Madison Avenue. MCNY

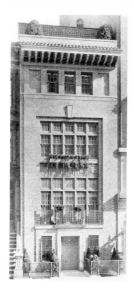

E.T. Cockcroft house, 59 East Seventy-seventh Street. Albro & Lindeberg, 1907. CU

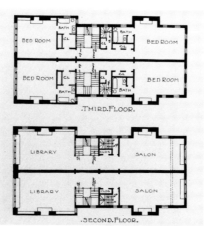
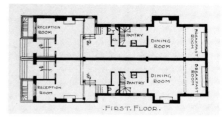

Rowhouses, 105–07 East Seventy-third Street. Grosvenor Atterbury, 1903. Plans of first, second and third floors. CU

side street. It has not been adapted so much as conveyed." Nonetheless, he admired its detail and its picturesqueness: "in its entirety [it is] something to look at and to make a picture of. And though this measure is not so rare as it was ten years ago, it is not yet so common that we can afford to ignore an example of it when it comes our way."[188]

The New New York House

Schuyler praised the variety of styles used in what he described as the New New York House for breaking down the monotony of New York's repetitive streets filled with brownstones: "the new architecture gives an added zest to life in New York, inasmuch that there is many a single block front in Manhattan of 1911 that has more architectural interest than any fifty blockfronts of the brownstone period."[189] Yet a common feature of virtually all the New New York houses was what was known as the American basement plan.[190] American basement plan houses had no front stoop, as in old New York houses, because they were entered only a step or two above the sidewalk. While brownstones had the kitchen in the front of the basement and the dining room in the rear, in the new houses the living and dining rooms were placed together on the second floor, separated by the center staircase. On the ground floor, a reception hall or foyer was on the street side, and the kitchen was on the garden, connected to the dining room by a dumbwaiter.

Arts and Crafts

After the turn of the century, brownstones all over the city were remodelled, with their stoops cut off, floors rearranged, and, sometimes, all new facades put on. The red brick Georgian styles were one of the most common for the new facades, although others were also used, as in Charles Platt's remodelling of the two brownstones for the Astor Company. The freely eclectic Artistic style evolved in the West End twenty years earlier was successfully revived for a number of more modern and abstract Arts and Crafts style houses.[191] In 1907 Albro & Lindeberg remodelled a brownstone at 59 East Seventy-seventh Street for E.T. Cockcroft, combining the second- and third-floor windows in one panel to enlarge the apparent scale of the house without resorting to the rhetoric of columns and pilasters.[192] They centered the entrance in the composition, set a keystone above the

Frederick J. Sterner house, 154 East Sixty-third Street. Frederick J. Sterner, 1914. CU

principal window panel, and layered the brick in superimposed panels for a rich effect. Walker & Gillette's renovation of a brownstone at 53 East Sixty-first Street exhibited some of Albro & Lindeberg's direct approach, although the rusticated brick base, the marble door surround and brackets supporting a balcony in front of the *Serliana* which illuminated the living room, gave the design the flavor of an Italian villa that was delightfully enhanced by the unorthodox, wide brick band and projecting cornice crowning the composition.[193] Schuyler noted that the use of stucco was

a novelty in a city house front, though common in the suburbs. . . . This front is of no style. . . . It is merely the putting together of materials in the most straightforward manner and in accordance with a scheme derived from nothing but the requirements, practical and architectural, of the particular structure. But this work, being done by a sensitive and trained hand, has resulted in a very artistic and a very individual expression and, though of no style, very distinctly has style and is clearly one of the best of the recent things.[194]

In the same spirit of cozy domesticity, Frederick J. Sterner transformed the Italian palazzo into a rustic villa style. After converting the exteriors of a group of houses on East Nineteenth Street,[195] Sterner undertook a more ambitious but similar project on East Sixty-third Street in 1914. His own house at 154 East Sixty-third Street had an open atrium that separated his architectural offices at the rear from his private quarters on the street.[196]

Grosvenor Atterbury designed a new pair of houses at 105–107 East Seventy-third Street with large windows similar to those used by Albro & Lindeberg.[197] The slightly projecting balconies and the somewhat elaborate bracketing system were the only breaks permitted in an otherwise smooth and unassuming facade. As *Architecture* magazine observed:

The characteristic feature of modern work is the dependence placed upon materials and color in place of basing the design upon proportions alone. We are using materials far more rationally than has been done for at least two hundred years and every building in which simple brick courses and panels take the place of elaborate carving, is a step forward. We have no name for this as yet, but we may be sure that it some day will be named,

Bertram Grosvenor Goodhue house, 106 East Seventy-fourth Street. Bertram Grosvenor Goodhue, 1909. CU

A 1900 view of Fifty-fourth Street just west of Fifth Avenue showing 7 West Fifty-fourth Street, the James J. Goodwin house at 9-11 West Fifty-fourth Street and the University Club on the corner. CU

and . . . while simple and inexpensive to the last degree [will shine out] as infinitely the superior in thoughtfulness and the real fundamentals of architecture to its limestone and marble neighbors in spite of the expensive character of their ornament and materials.[198]

Schuyler, who found the houses evocative of the work in London's studio quarter of Chelsea, was critical of Atterbury's use of small lights to make up the large window walls: "Our grandparents used the largest panes of glass they could afford."[199]

Bertram Grosvenor Goodhue's own house (1909) at 106 East Seventy-fourth Street was a brownstone renovation with bold brick and limestone Gothicizing elements that made it "more suggestive of the artistic leanings of a travelled individual of culture than of an active practitioner of the profession of architecture," according to the *Architectural Review*.[200] Schuyler found its "picturesqueness so unforced as to seem instructive and unconscious. . . . A smug successful grocer might not find himself at home behind this front but an artist would find himself entirely so."[201]

Vanderbilt Row Rowhouses

Some of the earliest and finest examples of the New New York House were built in the side streets around Vanderbilt Row. A few of the streets had been lined with brownstones and livery stables which were torn down or remodelled to make way for new townhouses, while other streets were left with large plots of open land when institutions such as Columbia University, the Catholic Female Orphan Asylum and St. Luke's Hospital moved out.[202] When St. Luke's left West Fifty-fourth Street in 1896, the *Real Estate Record and Guide* reported that "on the south side of Fifty-fourth Street, as well as the north, new dwellings are going up, and even new fronts are being adjoined to old dwellings merely in the interest of architecture." Yet despite the example of the University Club on the corner of Fifth Avenue and the work of graduates of the Ecole des Beaux-Arts who "might be expected to show the desire for ensemble in an unusual degree," the *Record and Guide* lamented the miscellaneous character of the new townscape.[203]

In 1900 Russell Sturgis documented the houses of Fifty-fourth Street in an article he entitled "The Art Gallery of New York Streets."[204] He began with two vigorous examples of the Modern French house, 46 West Fifty-fourth Street, which he found "singular in its independence"[205] and 7 West Fifty-fourth, "another simple and direct conception."[206] But Sturgis most admired McKim, Mead & White's double houses for James Goodwin at Numbers 9 and 11, completed in 1896, because of their innovative revival of "the Georgian epoch, pure and simple."[207] The facades of the Goodwin houses influenced two brownstone conversions: Palmer & Hornbostel's house at 18 East Fifty-fourth Street[208] and C.P.H. Gilbert's 26 East Fifty-fourth Street.[209] Both combined the red brick and limestone Georgian palette with vigorously modelled and overscaled ornamentation that originated in the Modern French.

Sturgis found the rest of the work on the other side of Fifth Avenue less interesting. McKim, Mead & White's William H. Moore residence at 4 East Fifty-fourth Street, a remodelling begun in 1900, was a five-story, double-width townhouse with a massive balcony at the *piano nobile* and a strong cornice which had a palatial scale representative of McKim's cool, scholarly manner.[210] He was more favorably disposed to McKim's facade at 19 East Fifty-fourth Street, which he called "rejuvenated classicismo."[211] Like the Moore house, this was an Italian palazzo at the scale of a large rowhouse—Sturgis deemed it similar to contemporary *villini* built in Florence. Like so many of McKim's houses, it represented his preference for archaeological correctness rather than formal innovation.

After the turn of the century East Fifty-first Street between Fifth and Park avenues was transformed from a street of brownstones to more up-to-date houses. The Georgian mode prevailed in the first block to the east of Fifth Avenue: Percy Griffin designed an elegant three-bay house that stood at Number 5,[212] and William Strom built a generously proportioned double-width house for Mrs. Charles Dickey at Numbers 25 and 27 that included an unusual, delicately detailed conservatory bay-window over the entrance porch.[213] Further east, York & Sawyer designed three Modern French townhouses at Numbers 31, 33 and 35,

W.E.D. Stokes house, 4 East-Fifty-fourth Street. W.E.D. Stokes, 1900. CU

Rowhouses, 31–35 East Fifty-first Street. York & Sawyer, 1908. CU

each identical except for the handling of the entrance canopies.[214]

Modest Georgian townhouses jostled vast Modern French and Italianate palazzos along West Fifty-sixth Street. The L.H. Lapham house at Number 15 was an exuberantly French design by Carrère & Hastings that was slipped between two brownstones, one of which was shortly replaced by A.N. Allen's 17 West Fifty-sixth Street in the Georgian mode.[215] Mrs. Frederick Edey's house, across the street at Number 10 by Warren & Wetmore, was uncharacteristically stiff sitting between a brownstone and McKim, Mead & White's double-width Georgian H.B. Hollins house at Number 12.[216] At the northwest corner of Fifth Avenue, Horace Trumbauer built a palazzo for the Duveen Brothers' gallery,[217] while further west at 30–32, C.P.H. Gilbert constructed a vast palazzo for Henry Seligman, replacing two brownstone houses.[218]

Seventieth Street

East Seventieth Street had a piecemeal development pattern typical of the rest of the Billionaire District.[219] It ran across the peak of Lenox Hill, part of a thirty-acre tract formerly owned by the Scottish immigrant Robert Lenox. After Lenox's death his son began selling off lots, and at the end of the Civil War there were eleven buildings on the street, all sandwiched between the railroad on Park Avenue and the horse trolley on Second Avenue. By the time World War I began, the Frick mansion stood at the western end of the street, and the blocks between the mansion and the Third Avenue Elevated Railroad were completely built up with brownstones interspersed with new houses constructed by prominent families.

Frick bought the former site of the Lenox Library in 1908, but waited until 1912 to start construction, when he was apparently satisfied that the neighborhood would be suitable.[220] In the meantime, several small but distinguished houses were built on the block, like the first one, Thornton Chard's Italian Renaissance rowhouse for Dave Hennen Morris (19 East Seventieth Street, 1909).[221] But the completion of the Frick mansion in 1914 prompted the construction of some grand houses on the block: in the same year Carrère & Hastings began C. Ledyard Blair's Modern Renaissance residence on the corner opposite the Frick house, and Dr. W.B. James started to build an Italian Renaissance design by Trowbridge & Livingston at 9 East Seventieth Street that was described by the *Real Estate Record and Guide* as "one of the largest private houses in the city. . . . in height . . . second only to John D. Rockefeller's house on West 54th Street."[222]

When the railroads along Park Avenue were changed from steam power to electric traction in 1904, the broad avenue became one of the most desirable addresses in the city,[223] and in 1907 Delano & Aldrich completed the elegant Robert S. Brewster house on the southeast corner of Park Avenue and Seventieth Street.[224] Three years later the Union Theological Seminary on the southwest corner of Park and Seventieth sold its campus and moved to Morningside Heights,[225] and the investment banker George Blumenthal, a partner at Lazard Freres, bought a large plot on the corner and hired Trowbridge & Livingston to design an elegant palazzo.[226] Next door at 21 East Seventieth, Frederick J. Sterner built an enormous townhouse in a modern Jacobean style for Stephen C. Clark, heir to the Singer Sewing Machine Company.[227] Twin oriels flanked the entrance, counterpointing the otherwise strict symmetry of the brick facade trimmed in limestone, and the delicate leading of the windows brought the scale of the glass into almost perfect harmony with the scale of the brick. The house featured the courtyard that Sterner included between the front and back of many of his townhouses. In 1916 Gerrish Milliken, later president of the Milliken textile firm founded by his father, bought 721 and 723 Park Avenue, two brownstones on the opposite side of Seventieth Street, and converted them into a single house.[228]

The north side of the block between Madison and Park avenues was the site of the Presbyterian Hospital, which did not move to Washington Heights until 1928. Consequently, these houses stood surrounded by brownstones and institutional buildings until after the war.[229] Nearer to Lexington Avenue, however, smaller rowhouses were built in the same period. Delano & Aldrich designed one of their small Federal style houses for Howard Gardner Cushing, built in 1910 at

Left: Howard Gardner Cushing house, 121 East Seventieth Street. Delano & Aldrich, 1910. Right: Samuel Trowbridge house, 123 East Seventieth Street. Trowbridge & Livingston, 1902-03. NYPL

Dave Hennen Morris house, 19 East Seventieth Street. Thornton Chard, 1909. MCNY

Number 121. Next door at 123, Samuel Trowbridge, one of the partners in the firm responsible for the James and Blumenthal houses, built his own house in 1902.[230] A few doors away, on the corner of Lexington Avenue, the architect Grosvenor Atterbury transformed an ordinary brownstone with a charming profusion of bays, oriels and balconies.[231] The remodelling was completed for his father in 1909, but Atterbury moved into the house himself after his father's death in 1914.

The architect James Gamble Rogers grew up in a brownstone on the other side of Lexington Avenue, at 164 East Seventieth Street, which he remodelled in 1911.[232] Another Federal style rowhouse by Delano & Aldrich, built for Miss Marion Hague in 1911, stood nearby at Number 161, near a freestyle remodelling at Number 164 by William Emerson,[233] and across the street from Edward Pearce Casey's unusual Tudor residence at 154 East Seventieth for Stephen H. Brown, Governor of the New York Stock Exchange.[234] But some of the most elegant buildings on the block were the stables designed by C.P.H. Gilbert for Daniel G. Reid (170 East Seventieth Street, 1901-02),[235] Jules S. Bache (163 East Seventieth Street, 1902)[236] and Henri P. Wertheim (165 East Seventieth Street, 1902).[237]

Park Avenue

When Elihu Root began construction in 1903 of his house on the southeast corner of Park Avenue and Seventy-first Street,[238] on the same block where Gerrish Milliken later assembled his brownstone palace, it marked an important step in the transformation of the avenue from an unimportant street of ordinary tenements and modest rowhouses to one of the city's most fashionable boulevards, second only to Fifth Avenue.[239] The potential for a grand, 140-foot-wide boulevard was first established in the 1880s when the hilly topography of Park Avenue between Fifty-sixth and Ninety-sixth streets forced the New York Central Railroad to dig a deep cut for its new tracks and cover them over for long stretches. Although breaks in the cover were numerous enough to call into question the propriety of continuing the name Park Avenue north of Grand Central Terminal, and belching steam engines made the boulevard a smoky one, the landscaping of the avenue progressed in slow but steady stages, and the trains were electrified in 1904. Two years later the *Real Estate Record and Guide* reported that

The development of Park avenue above 59th street will bear watching during the next few years. When the New York Central announced that it was going to run electric instead of steam cars through the tunnel, it was generally supposed that the avenue would become available as a site for expensive residences, and certain lots were bought and one or two houses built on that assumption. But the tendency to use the avenue in this way has not gained any headway; and recently there have been indications of another tendency in an opposite direction. Two sites between 60th and 80th streets have been bought, which will be improved by large fireproof apartment houses; and it looks as if any property on Park avenue in the residential section which is available for reimprovement would be used in this manner. The avenue can never become a handsome thoroughfare devoted to private residences, because so many of the corners are already improved with apartment houses, which are too expensive to be thrown into the scrap heap, and then the East Side really needs a thoroughfare in which apartment houses of largest size can be erected. Madison avenue is not well adapted to the purpose, because the lots are shallow. The corners are strongly held. Lexington avenue will doubtless be lined with many such buildings; but it is not wide enough to permit the erection of apartment houses of the largest size. Park avenue will be quieter than either Lexington or Madison avenue, and it is so wide that a twenty-story building could be erected, if desired. Such buildings are needed, because of the large and increasing numbers of people who want to live in that part of the city. These people may prefer private houses; but in the course of time all but the very wealthy will be forced to put up with apartments. The area in which such people care to live is very much restricted and there seems at present to be no chance of making it larger.[240]

In 1917 the *Real Estate Record and Guide* again surveyed the development of Park Avenue north of Forty-second Street—"one of the most remarkable sectional developments in the city in the past fifteen years"—and confirmed its earlier predictions.[241] South of Fifty-ninth

Percy Pyne house, northwest corner of Park Avenue and Sixty-eighth Street. McKim, Mead & White, 1910–12. Sixty-eighth Street elevation, entrance details and plans of first and second floors. CU

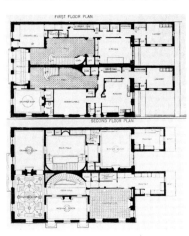

Double house for Geraldyn Redmond and the Countess de Laugier Villars, 701–703 Park Avenue. McKim, Mead & White, 1913–15. View across Park Avenue and plans of first and second floors. CU

Street was solidly built up with apartment houses, while north of that district was a mixed development of mansions and "high class" apartments. Lenox Hill was covered almost exclusively with fashionable houses built around Root's house, but "the first of the high class apartments to be built on Park Avenue was one on the northwest corner of 61st street [540 Park Avenue, by William A. Boring] which was finished in 1909" and was highly successful, so that by 1917 most of the desirable corners along the avenue had been taken by apartment houses.[242] The first apartment house on Fifth Avenue above Fifty-ninth Street, McKim, Mead & White's 998 Fifth, was not completed until 1912 (when Root ironically moved out of his Park Avenue house and into Number 998, thereby establishing the social acceptability of the apartment house for the most socially conscious), and the transformation of the more solidly built-up Fifth Avenue into a street of apartment houses was a slow and gradual process which was not fully underway until the 1920s. Thus Park Avenue offered a uniquely concentrated glimpse of the Composite Period's conception of urban life for the rich, and its transformation from the mansion to the palatial apartment house.

The restrained character of the Root house was a harbinger of the mansions that would follow it on Park Avenue. Three years later, McKim, Mead & White started the design of a large house for Percy Pyne that was built between 1910 and 1912 three blocks to the south at 680 Park Avenue.[243] McKim had been given the commission by his friend and Pyne's uncle H.A.C. Taylor in 1906, but when McKim retired from the firm the design of the brick and marble house was taken over by Kendall.[244] *Architecture* magazine commented that the

residence of Mr. Percy R. Pyne is by no means an extraordinary conception that has been determined by conditions of living in New York regardless of the wishes or desires of the architects, but in the adjustment of the various portions to the whole scheme its architects have apparently been as free from the spirit of imported traditions as if these traditions had never existed.... After all it is from the detail that this building may best be remembered, and as in all McKim, Mead & White's work it is kept in very low relief, simple in modeling and in close adherence to the spirit, if not to the actual forms from which it has been derived. The usual three divisions of base, shaft and

Arthur Curtiss James house, northwest corner of Park Avenue and Sixty-ninth Street. Allen & Collens, 1916. CU

cap of our buildings have been retained, the base emphasized in the customary way by building it of marble, while the cap is divided from the shaft by a simple label mold. The base is, though rusticated, extremely flat, and strong moldings above the base are not used, their place being taken by a plain band with an exquisitely decorated fret. The window openings in the principal story are without trim, except for a suggestion of a brick arch, while those of the third story have a white architrave and cornice above; yet the second story is dominant as befits its position. The method of accentuating the entrance door by filling the whole brick arch with white is as delightful as it is unusual and the porch marking the entrance door is perhaps the feature of the building. The ionic columns are exquisitely detailed, while the entablature above them, covered with decoration, is so frankly and gracefully treated that its elaboration in no way conflicts with the extreme simplicity of the building itself.

So few of the New York residences appear like homes that, when one finds a house like this, one feels as if a day of Thanksgiving should be proclaimed.[245]

In 1917 Walker & Gillette completed a mansion on the opposite end of the block at Sixty-eighth Street for Henry P. Davison,[246] and in 1918 Delano & Aldrich added a more chaste mixture of the Federal and Greek Revival styles in the William Sloane house at 686 Park Avenue.[247] In 1926 McKim, Mead & White completed the block with a house for Oliver D. Filey, Pyne's son-in-law, in Pyne's former garden next door on Park Avenue: taken as a group, the houses formed the city's first blockfront of Colonial Revival buildings.[248]

Two of the most unusual mansions on Park Avenue (or elsewhere) stood nearby on Sixty-ninth Street. A double house for Geraldyn Redmond and the Countess de Laugier Villars was constructed in 1913–15 on the northeast corner of Park Avenue and Sixty-ninth Street.[249] Designed by Kendall for McKim, Mead & White, it resembled a vastly enlarged French Renaissance gatehouse. Directly across Park Avenue on part of the former campus of the Union Theological Seminary stood Allen & Collens's Arthur Curtiss James house, another surprisingly eclectic design that could only have been built in the period before World War I when the rules of academicism were loosened.[250] Covered in Knoxville gray marble, the eccentric house was intended to convey the spirit of the English Renaissance.

Reginald de Koven house, 1025 Park Avenue. John Russell Pope, 1913. View of the Great Hall. CU

Reginald de Koven house, 1025 Park Avenue. John Russell Pope, 1913. CU

John Russell Pope designed a more characteristic Elizabethan style house for Reginald de Koven, built in 1913 on the east side of Park Avenue between Eighty-fifth and Eighty-fourth streets.[251] Two large bay windows on Park Avenue marked the room de Koven called the Great Hall, which had at one end a double-storied stone mantel and a replica of a plaster ceiling from the Reindeer Inn at Banbury, England, and at the other a carved oak screen and minstrel gallery modelled on the Great Hall at Hatfield House. The stairhall was carved and painted in the manner of the staircase at Knowle Park, but some rooms came from later periods. Woodwork in the style of Sir Christopher Wren was used in the library, connected with a dining room with woodwork adapted to frame a set of French paintings owned by de Koven. I.N. Phelps Stokes's design for John Sherman Hoyt was more Tudor, although its strongest association was with contemporary College Gothic.[252] Built in 1917 at Park Avenue and Seventy-ninth Street, it was one of the last large corner houses constructed in Manhattan.

Several Modern Renaissance designs were also built on Park Avenue. In 1910 Hunt & Hunt built a large corner house at Eighty-fifth Street that was stiff and unengaging.[253] Oakleigh Thorne's house, built in 1911 on the northeast corner of Seventy-third Street and Park Avenue, was originally designed by Albert Joseph Bodker in a more Italian manner with a tile roof and *sgrafitto* decorations on the studio walls.[254] The somewhat reduced version of the house was made in the French manner to complement some rooms and furniture acquired by Mrs. Thorne. "Certainly," Matlack Price wrote, "this is not 'American architecture,' but it is an evidence that a connoisseur possesses not only keen architectural appreciation but also a desire that such perfection as was attained in France may serve as a model and incentive in this country."[255]

Schuyler described one of the modern Renaissance houses—the Jonathan Bulkley house on the northeast corner of Park and Sixty-first Street—as more "a palazetto than a palazzo . . . deliberately 'underscaled' . . . in opposition to the current method, apparently derived from the Beaux Arts, of deliberately overscaling the detail."[256] Built by James Gamble Rogers in 1910–11, the Bulkley house was modest in size, only seventy by thirty feet and relatively low. Schuyler found it "at present so lonesome that at the first glance it has the air rather of a clubhouse than of a dwelling.

903 Park Avenue. Warren & Wetmore, 1912. View from Park Avenue and Seventy-ninth Street. NYHS

But a second glance not only corrects the misapprehension, which would in any case be impossible if the house were surrounded by others of like pretentiousness, but also shows that it is one of the most successful examples in New York of domestic architecture of the palatial kind, upon which the architect and the owner are entitled to unreserved congratulation."[257] Although Schuyler was confident that enough townhouses had been built along Park Avenue to guarantee its "manifest destiny" as a "thoroughfare of palaces," the completion of a spate of apartment houses, albeit palatial ones, began to suggest that the permanent character of the street was not yet clearly established.[258]

The announcement in 1909 of plans to build apartment buildings at 829 Park Avenue and 925 Park Avenue had caused the *Real Estate Record and Guide* to advance the argument that "the really 'modern' fashionable boulevard is by the very nature of things compelled to exemplify the new as well as the old standards of living, and on Park Avenue at the present moment may be seen under construction, simultaneously, both co-operative and individual houses of the highest type in their respective classes."[259] Delano & Aldrich's 925 Park Avenue at the northeast corner of Eightieth Street was a distinguished design: it housed twenty-one duplex apartments and a small number of triplex and simplex units in a fourteen-story palazzo with Modern French tendencies in the generously proportioned arches that unified the two lowest floors, the elaborate ironwork on the balconies, and the bold cartouche centered on the Park Avenue facade.[260] While the three lower floors of the building, where the triplex apartments were located, were sheathed in Indiana limestone, the remainder of the building was cloaked in terra cotta.

This luxurious apartment house was built by William J. Taylor, who had reintroduced the cooperative Home Club apartment to New York in 1901. While 925 Park Avenue was still under construction, Taylor broke ground for 929 Park (Pickering & Walker) and 563 Park (Walter Chambers).[261] As the stone courses dividing the red brick facades every two floors indicated, 563 Park Avenue had duplex apartments, although they were limited to the units actually facing Park Avenue on the west side of the building. But 563 Park Avenue was just one of several cooperative, duplex apartment houses built on Park Avenue in an effort to

563 Park Avenue. Walter Chambers, 1909–10. View across Park Avenue. CU

635 Park Avenue. J.E.R. Carpenter, 1912. Plan of typical floor. CU

attract more affluent tenants.[262]

A few months after 998 Fifth Avenue was completed in 1912, Park Avenue got its first truly upper-class apartment, built at 903 Park Avenue on the northeast corner of Seventy-ninth Street.[263] Designed by Warren & Wetmore, it had only one apartment per floor. The rents were nine to ten thousand dollars per year, the most expensive being the penthouse rented by Carll Tucker, treasurer of the Maxwell Motor Company.

Another apartment house built in the same year, J.E.R. Carpenter's 635 Park Avenue, was smaller than 903 Park but marked some advance in planning.[264] The thirteen-room apartments on each floor were divided into three sections: public, private and service. The public and private rooms were easily separated if desired, while the service rooms were convenient to both. In addition to that functional consideration, particular care was given to the proportions of the rooms and the minimization of corridors, although family members had to cope with a dreary hall leading to the bedrooms. Carpenter went on to specialize in the design of upper-class apartments, such as 960 Park Avenue[265] and 907 Fifth Avenue,[266] which won a Gold Medal from the American Institute of Architects in 1916. These and many limestone-clad Park Avenue apartment buildings he built after World War I were marked by a restrained Classicism intended to epitomize good taste.

As the war ended, Warren & Wetmore completed the construction of a massive courtyard apartment house at 270 Park Avenue that set the pattern for post-war development of the avenue below Fifty-ninth Street.[267] Built over the train yards of Grand Central Terminal, 270 Park Avenue was constructed on a newly created lot that precluded the need for assembling parcels of land from various lots. Between Fifty-ninth and Eighty-sixth streets, the restrained designs of the prolific firms of J.E.R. Carpenter, Emery Roth, Schwartz & Gross and Rouse & Goldstone embodied the principles of the 1916 zoning resolution to achieve a remarkably coherent and consistent urban ensemble.

925 Park Avenue. Delano & Aldrich, 1909-10. Perspective. CU

The West End

What a great work it is that has been undertaken and is now accomplishing between the Park and the Hudson. It is an attempt made, not at all upon philanthrophic and benevolent grounds, but as a mere matter of commercial supply and demand, to do a work of the greatest possible philanthropy and benevolence. . . . [The West End] is a new city, to all intents and purposes, and not an extension of the old. "The Architecture of the West Side," *Real Estate Record and Guide* 40 (September 10, 1887): 1150.

In the 1880s the area between Central Park and the Hudson River, from 59th to 110th streets (except for the streets west of Broadway and south of 70th Street), became known as the West End. Born at the Centennial, it underwent numerous periods of growth and prosperity before attaining its present form in the early 1930s. These cycles of growth and rebuilding left it with a heterogeneous collection of buildings which formed the best record of the diverse architectural and social history of the Metropolitan Era, most representative of the urbanism of the period.

The transformation of the West End into a distinct and fashionable residential quarter was slow. As late as 1877 the *Real Estate Record and Guide* bemoaned that it was not yet established as a desirable neighborhood, despite natural advantages and man-made improvements such as the Boulevard and Columbus Circle, the latter "laid out on a far more magnificent scale than the Fifth Avenue Plaza." Hampered by its isolation from the main line of city development northward along Fifth Avenue, and cut off from the East Side by Central Park, the West End seemed destined to become "the cheap side of the city."[268]

The development of the West End began in earnest on December 20, 1879, when Edward S. Clark (who would shortly build the Dakota apartments and numerous rowhouses on Seventy-third Street) read a paper entitled "The City of the Future" before a group of real estate investors known as the West Side Association. Clark painted a verbal panorama of a new section of the city that would combine apartment houses with single-family dwellings suitable for housing different economic classes: "Some splendidly, many elegantly, and all comfortably . . . the architecture should be ornate, solid and permanent, and . . . the principle of economic combination should be employed to the greatest possible extent."[269] The architectural and sociological diversity of the west side of Manhattan from 72nd to 110th streets was a compelling fulfillment of Clark's vision. Not an extension of an older section of the city, like the Billionaire District, the West End was a new enclave that could almost be regarded as a suburb of the existing city.

Great hopes were held for the West End from the first, even though its progress was halted time and again by the quixotic economic conditions of the post-Centennial years. Initially there was hope that the West End would become, like West Philadelphia, a city of cottages.[270] Here was to have been, as Schuyler observed in 1899, "an opportunity for a quarter of small houses. So much land was thrown open to settlement by the completion of the elevated railroad" that it was possible to develop houses for people for whom "no provision had been made during the brownstone period," people whom circumstances had "driven to New Jersey, to the uttermost parts of Brooklyn, and [who] toward the close of the brownstone period began to take refuge in flats. The social philosopher and the Philadelphian agree that it is good for a citizen to live in his own house, and the West Side seemed to offer the New Yorker his chance."[271] Yet the cozy neighborhood of cottages never developed. The opening of the Ninth Avenue El in 1880 brought about a more diverse neighborhood of houses, apartment houses and family hotels sharing the gardens and drives of Central and Riverside parks.[272] The El (running along Columbus Avenue with stops at 66th, 72nd, 86th, 91st and 104th streets), the landscaped Boulevard, the transverse road through Central Park at 72nd Street, Manhattan Square (where the Museum of Natural History was under construction), and the high *corniche* of Riverside Drive overlooking lushly planted parklands along the Hudson constituted the major circumstances of planning which shaped the West End, acting as focal points to which early development gravitated.[273] As if to crystallize the sense of the West End as a new city, the major avenues above Fifty-ninth Street were rechristened: in 1880, Eleventh Avenue became West End Avenue and Bloomingdale Road became the Boulevard (it was renamed Broadway in 1898) and in 1883 Eighth Avenue was renamed Central Park West. As the neighborhood grew in the late 1880s and early 1890s, its eclecticism (both the diversity of architectural styles and the juxtaposition of apartments, rowhouses, tenements and freestanding villas) was one of the phenomena that triggered the movement toward the homogeneous urbanism of the City Beautiful in the mid-1890s.[274] The West End's eclecticism was itself a reaction to the uniformity of the brownstone era. Edith Wharton's well known characterization in *A Backward Glance* of New York in the 1870s perhaps went too far in its condemnation of brownstone as a building material—Wharton lambasted it as "the most hideous stone ever quarried"—but her sense of the older city as a "cramped horizontal gridiron of a town without towers, porticoes, fountains or perspectives, hidebound with deadly uniformity of mean ugliness"[275] was partially answered by the shorter blocks and varied silhouettes of the West End district.

In 1885 the *Real Estate Record and Guide* observed that "Everything seems still to be in a state of architectural flux . . . the old brownstone front, repeated through so many dreary miles below Central Park has fallen at last into hopeless discredit."[276] But "it was the development of the West Side that struck the first blow at the tyranny of the brownstone front," Schuyler noted. "The immigrants to the new quarter insisted on the confession in their house fronts that they were individuals and that their houses were their own."[277] The mansions and rowhouses built in the West End during the Cosmopolitan Era spoke of a pluralistic society, the rowhouses in particular reflecting a dialogue between the uniformity of the row and the need for an individual expression for each house. Their compact, picturesque massing evoked a suburban ideal and expressed a disenchantment with the industrialized city; their eclectic syntheses of historical styles recalled the Old World, belying the newness of the locale.[278] These associations, and the confident individualism of the rowhouses, perfectly suited the aspirations of the city's burgeoning, upwardly mobile professional classes. In Schuyler's words, the West End provided "the expression of a 'comfortable bourgeoisie' . . . often heightened into the expression of something more artistic."[279]

John Matthews house, northeast corner of Riverside Drive and Ninetieth Street. Lamb & Rich, 1891. View from Riverside Drive. MCNY

Samuel G. Bayne house, southeast corner of Riverside Drive and 108th Street. Frank Freeman, 1892. CU

However, subsequent development did not fulfill Schuyler's expectation that the West End would become a quarter for those of "moderate means."[280] As Edward Tuckerman Potter and Frederick Law Olmsted had already observed, the standard size of a Manhattan lot, twenty-five by one hundred feet, put the price of land beyond the reach of the wage-earner class.[281] As a result the West End became largely a neighborhood of upper-middle class professional and business men, and was called an "American Belgravia" by a critic in *Munsey's*.[282] The typical house was large but more modestly scaled than those in the Billionaire District, to which the architecture of the West End was endlessly compared in the 1890s. No comparison was more pointed than the *Real Estate Record and Guide*'s statement that "looked at as a whole the west side is architecturally superior to the east side; but, on the other hand, it is equally certain that in single examples of solid, costly, pretentious, if not artistic dwellings, the east side has distinctly the advantage."[283]

A fashion for building artistic houses, modest but intimate private houses designed by architects in an urban mode equivalent to the Shingle Style cottages of the suburbs and resorts, began around 1880. The artistic city house usually filled a gap in a brownstone row, requiring that the architect "insert a front which did not contradict its surroundings nor assert itself at their expense, but deferred to them and conformed to them as far as it could without stultifying itself."[284] The rowhouse development of the West End was typically carried out on a larger scale, however. As the *Real Estate Record and Guide* put it: "A favorite scheme with investors seems to be a row of five twenty-foot houses, varied and individual, but so far connected in design as to show they are fronts of one project."[285]

While rowhouses were beginning to fill up the side streets and to line West End Avenue, Riverside Drive remained largely undeveloped.[286] Yet the Tweed Administration's decision to construct Riverside Drive was always recognized as central to the West End's success. Opened in 1880, though not extended by viaduct over the Harlem Valley until 1900, the Drive combined grand monuments and terraces with an informal curvilinear roadway and naturalistic plantings. This juxtaposition of Classical and naturalistic elements reflected the same rich, cosmopolitan approach found in the earlier Central Park: city and country

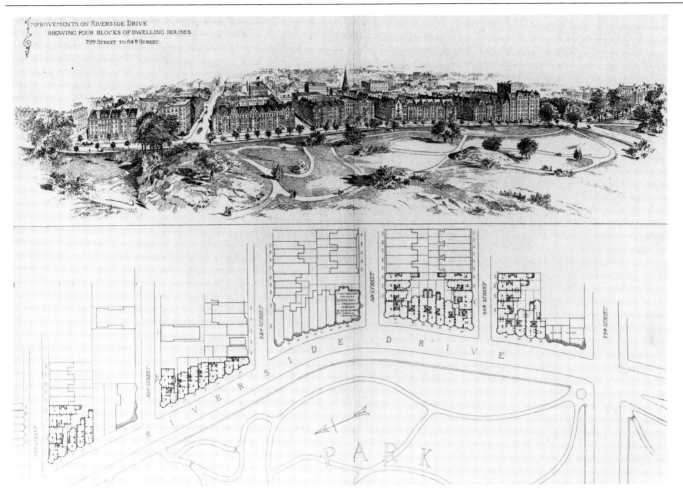

Improvements on Riverside Drive between Seventy-ninth and Eighty-fourth streets. Clarence True, 1898. Aerial perspective and site plan. CU

stated as thesis and antithesis, with neither predominating.

In the late 1880s a series of large townhouses and a few freestanding villas were built on the Drive, particularly in the high eighties and nineties. Schuyler found this a "fortunate" circumstance, which suggested that the buildings along Riverside Drive might commit it "to a suburban rather than a strictly urban character."[287] The first of these freestanding villas—Cyrus Clark's turreted, decidedly Romanesque granite house at the southeast corner of Ninetieth Street, designed by Henry F. Kilburn in 1889—was typical of those Schuyler and others hoped would eventually line the Drive.[288] The Clark mansion was both cottage and castle. Its rustication, machiolations, and corner tower lent it a baronial grandeur akin to Cady's contemporary facade for the Museum of Natural History, while its deep porches and asymmetrical entrance facade responded to the river views and the internal plan.

Lamb & Rich's house for John Matthews (1892) carried this sense of the picturesque villa even further.[289] With extensive porches, pronounced tile roofs and numerous turrets, the house can best be described as a rambling, Richardsonian Shingle Style cottage whose shingles, clapboard and pebble-dashed stucco were translated into glacial stonework, brick and terra cotta. Its aura of permanence and great age, belying the infancy of the neighborhood, was abetted by the decision to retain the plot's ancient trees, and by the contrasting delicacy of the exquisitely lacelike foliage patterns of its wrought-iron fence.

Frank Freeman's house for Samuel G. Bayne on the south side of 108th Street was the last of the Cosmopolitan Era's urban villas on Riverside Drive.[290] Freeman's design was more compact than that of Lamb & Rich's house and more specifically indebted to Henry Hobson Richardson, with a pyramidal massing designed for the corner perspective and an extensive use of ribbing, decorative brick patterns, and polychrome masonry. The geometrical patterns and almost Sullivanian floral motifs which enriched the riverside facade reflected a hedonistic sense of opulence that epitomized the social climate of New York's Cosmopolitan Era.

Not everyone could afford a villa, however, and rowhouses were built on Riverside Drive to meet the needs of the less affluent. Clarence True, a builder-architect who designed and constructed numerous houses in the West

Rowhouse, southwest corner of West End Avenue and Seventy-sixth Street. Lamb & Rich, 1891. A view from West End Avenue showing rowhouses by Lamb & Rich to either side. NYHS

Rowhouse, southwest corner of West End Avenue and Seventy-sixth Street. Lamb & Rich, 1891. Perspective view of stairhall. CU

End, was largely responsible for setting the character of the lower part of the street in the 1890s. In his 1889 prospectus, he recalled that the stretch of Riverside Drive from Seventy-ninth to Eighty-sixth streets was facing imminent development with flats until he "secured all the available property south of Eighty-fourth Street, and by covering it with beautiful dwellings insured a most promising future."[291] In 1899 True published a plate in *Architecture and Building* entitled "Improvements on Riverside Drive" which showed a development stretching from Seventy-ninth to Eighty-fourth streets.[292] The rowhouses frequently mingled Jacobean, French Gothic and Dutch Renaissance motifs in combinations of bow fronts, bay windows, elaborate gables and corner towers which maximized views of the Hudson River, mediated between the orthogonal street grid and the curvilinear roadway, and created the most varied and picturesque streetfront in the city.

Many of True's generously proportioned houses on the Drive, such as those on the north corner of Seventy-sixth Street (1896–98) and the south corner of Seventy-seventh Street (1891–92), were wider than the standard twenty-five-foot lot, a luxury made possible by the frequent shallowness of the lots and the large scale of True's operation.[293] They were in effect party-wall mansions. True was also widely credited with popularizing the American basement plan, which featured a grade level entrance instead of a traditional stoop, a reception room on the ground floor, and a more private and spacious parlor occupying the building's full width on the floor above.[294]

Perhaps more than any other firm, Lamb & Rich brought to the city house the disciplined individuality that characterized the shingled suburban villa of the Cosmopolitan Era. They captured some of the flavor of their Matthews villa in a group of four houses built in 1888–89 at 35–38 Riverside Drive.[295] The two center houses, both with bowed fronts, shared a heavily corbelled fourth-floor balcony. The steeply pitched roof above, with crow-stepped gables, was punctuated by ingenious turreted dormers. The houses at either end, whose narrower bow fronts broke through the roof line to form turreted towers with loggias on the top story, framed the group. The evocative architectural imagery combined Classicizing elements (as in the shell motif of the paired doors at the corner) with a heavily Germanic, medieval aura, as though a Rhineland castle had been domesticated to allow its new tenants to picture themselves at once as sixteenth-century burghers and nineteenth-century commercial barons.[296]

Lamb & Rich's most significant group of rowhouses was built in 1891 along the west side of West End Avenue between Seventy-sixth and Seventy-seventh streets and a short way in on the side streets.[297] Although six of the houses on the avenue created a symmetrical composition, they were richly varied in type: the center two were three stories with gables, the flanking pair were four stories, and the pair beyond were again three stories but with dormers. Contrasting buff and red brick were also used to give the houses a sense of individuality which almost denied that they were constructed as a row. The large house on the corner of West End Avenue and Seventy-sixth Street broke from the mold of the party-wall rowhouse. A one-story annex with a terrace above separated it from the rowhouses along Seventy-sixth Street and suggested a freestanding mansion, deliberately fostering the heterogeneity of building types which had come to characterize the West End.

While the small city house was undoubtedly the principal feature of the West End's development in the 1880s and early 1890s, the neighborhood's character was considerably enhanced by the construction of upper-middle-class apartment houses along Central Park West, hotels along the Boulevard and tenements for wage earners along Central Park West and Columbus and Amsterdam avenues. Edward Clark realized his own vision of an economically and typologically mixed community in his development of land he owned on Seventy-second and Seventy-third streets, when he built two rows of houses along the north side of Seventy-third Street running east and west from Columbus Avenue, tenements on Columbus Avenue, and crowned the group with the construction of the Dakota apartment house on Central Park West.

Clark's architect, Henry J. Hardenbergh, adapted the typical *parti* of the brownstone to the new aesthetic of individuality, designing townhouses prophetic of the future

Left: Hotel Majestic, southwest corner of Central Park West and Seventy-second Street. Alfred Zucker, 1889. Right: Dakota apartments, northwest corner of Central Park West and Seventy-second Street. Henry Janeway Hardenbergh, 1882. View from Central Park. MCNY

of the West End.[298] The elevations were simplified, abstracted French Gothic built of olive sandstone, red and buff-colored brick, materials chosen to harmonize with the Dakota. Unified by a continuous stone base and an identical third story, the *piano nobile* was marked by a rippling play of recessions and projections, with oriels, bay windows and porches. Above, a continuous pitched roof was interrupted with gables, dormers and, to accent the corner pavilions, full fourth floors with hipped roofs. Hardenbergh's sophisticated dialogue between what Schuyler described as "civicism" and individualism was widely emulated but rarely equalled in the work of speculative builders.[299]

The vast bulk of the luxurious Dakota apartments on Central Park West loomed over the neighborhood and served as a symbolic gateway to the West End. The Dakota "fixed the status of the neighborhood, and prevented it from degenerating as it might easily have done, under the pressure of owners in haste to realize their own investment, into a quarter of cheap flats."[300] By placing the tenements in the shadow and noise of the Ninth Avenue El, the luxurious Dakota apartment house facing the park, and rowhouses on the side street, Clark established the hierarchy of the typical West Side neighborhood.

As the Dakota proclaimed, Seventy-second Street was the principal approach to what had come to be described as "The New City."[301] The only grade level vehicular crossing through Central Park, its tone was set at the park's center where the roadway crossed the axis of the Mall at the Bethesda Fountain and Terrace, the principal formal element in Olmsted's design. Once outside the park, Seventy-second Street returned to the grid, framed by the Dakota and Alfred Zucker's imposing Hotel Majestic of 1889. In its heyday, the street beyond was the most fashionable in the West End. Controlled by restrictive convenants, its rowhouses were set behind lines of elm trees in tiny grassed-in plots which linked the verdant landscapes of Central and Riverside parks. The individual houses along Seventy-second Street, however, were for the most part architecturally undistinguished; the *Real Estate Record and Guide* labelled them "pretentious . . . unartistic, and sometimes positively vulgar . . . [a] triumph of contract architecture . . . now a Renaissance front, and now a Gothic, and now a Moorish."[302] By the early 1890s, the street was decried as a lost opportunity. It was this perception of individuality run amok more than anything else that provoked a reaction against the eclecticism of the West End, and which led to attempts to create a more ordered yet rich and heterogeneous environment on a large scale.

It was not that the individual buildings of the Cosmopolitan Era were rejected—Schuyler found its rowhouses "without doubt the most interesting examples of domestic architecture New York has to show"[303]—but that a new feeling for stylistic uniformity and an interest in planned development emerged to forge a new urbanism. This was achieved through a large scale of development and the use of restrictive covenants between a builder and prospective buyers, thereby guaranteeing that the builder would erect on a given street only houses of a specific character, width and height.[304] Nonetheless, the character of the buildings was still highly individual and often idiosyncratic. By the mid-1890s many began to feel that the Romanesque style used in most public buildings was too universal, and that the eclectic combinations of the houses, though cozy and familiar in character, did not seem distinctly expressive of the local scene. As a result, a sense of the West End not only as a "new city," but more particularly as a "new New Amsterdam" began to emerge, encouraged no doubt in part by the burgher scale of the houses already built and in part by the many residents who represented the old Knickerbocker families and sought to stamp the community with a sense of their past, thus counteracting the European culture flaunted by the newly rich robber barons. Sensing that the old traditions were dying out, they set out to revitalize them in this new section of the city.

The Dutch Colonial Revival was initiated by McKim, Mead & White in 1885 with a row of five houses at the southwest corner of West End Avenue and Eighty-third Street.[305] Schuyler described them as "models of the second rate genteel houses" of the end of the nineteenth century and judged them superior to the city's Federal era rowhouses for their "power of composition, and for uniting the members of a 'row' into an architectural unity."[306] Along

Collegiate Reformed Dutch Church, northeast corner of West End Avenue and Seventy-seventh Street. Robert W. Gibson, 1892. View from West End Avenue. CU

the side street, houses with crow-stepped gables alternated with units whose roofs ran parallel to the street. The latter type sheltered wood-framed loggias beneath their eaves and featured gently swelling bays which allowed diagonal views down the street to the river. The long ridge of their roofs was terminated on the corner house, where a Dutch gable rose out of its hipped roof and the loggia wrapped around the corner to form a picturesque, turreted tower. The composition of the larger corner house wove together the different strands of the design, and the horizontal banding of two tones of brick united the individual dwellings into a single, variegated mass.

The Dutch Revival was immediately taken up by Frederick B. White, a young architect who died in 1886 when he was twenty-four, shortly after he had completed a row of eight houses on the northwest corner of West End Avenue and West Seventy-eighth Street.[307] These were clearly a reaction to the decorative excesses of the Cosmopolitan Era; the *Real Estate Record and Guide* lauded their "'conscientiousness'—freedom from all meretricious tricks of ornament," and found them "neat, substantial and chaste in design . . . and yet decidedly elegant."[308] White's houses married conventional plans of the English basement type to an ingeniously varied massing and facades that synthesized Dutch and Romanesque allusions. Though individually asymmetrical, the houses facing Seventy-eighth Street were linked by a central crow-stepped gable and deeply recessed Syrian arches which shaded entrances to two units. The octagonal tower of the large corner house dominated the intersection.

The sense of the West End as a new New Amsterdam was most vividly articulated by Robert W. Gibson's Collegiate Dutch Reformed Church at West End Avenue and Seventy-seventh Street, completed in 1892, which linked the broad traditions of a congregation founded in New Amsterdam with the new spirit of Metropolitanism.[309] Despite its modest height, the powerful stepped gable, the rigorous articulation of the masses separating church from school and providing a modest suggestion of a cloister, and the vividly colored combination of brick, stone, terra cotta and Dutch tile contributed to the building's commanding presence. In the interior the need to provide unobstructed sight lines for each parishioner led to a novel solution in which columns supporting the roof timbers were confined to the

Rowhouses, southwest corner of West End Avenue and Eighty-third Street. McKim, Mead & White, 1885. CU

Rowhouses, west side of West End Avenue between Eighty-fourth and Eighty-fifth streets. Frank Miles Day, 1894. View from West Eighty-fifth Street. CU

edges of the room where they screened the aisles from the auditorium proper. Gibson's church was closely inspired by the Meat Market in Haarlem, the Netherlands. It was a more literal adaptation of Dutch sources than previously seen in New York, reflecting the increasingly "scientific" eclecticism that came to dominate the architecture of the Composite Era later in the 1890s.

The complex of seven houses that Clarence True built in 1889 at the northwest corner of Ninetieth Street and West End Avenue was a late example of Dutch motifs, combining crow-stepped gables with Flemish strapwork. The *Real Estate Record and Guide* acclaimed the group as True's masterpiece.[310] But the most significant domestic exemplars of the Dutch Revival were Frank Miles Day's richly polychromed rowhouses for R.G. Platt (1894) on the west side of West End Avenue between Eighty-fourth and Eighty-fifth streets.[311] The avenue facade was composed as a symmetrical group beneath highly elaborated gables, but along Eighty-fifth Street the units of the composition were allowed to break apart to accommodate additional houses, two of them charmingly grouped beneath a single gable. Day's houses were unique for their combination of precisely observed historical details and picturesque massing; they represented the Composite Era yet simultaneously looked back to the romantic Cosmopolitanism in which the West End's architecture was steeped.[312] While the Dutch Revival waned in the late 1890s when the Modern French style achieved its dominance, the Dutch contribution to the character of the West End was recognized by Heins & LaFarge at the turn of the century in their I.R.T. subway kiosk at Seventy-second Street, the gateway station to the West End.[313]

At the close of the Cosmopolitan Era, the West End was flourishing, but the individualistic eclecticism of its domestic architecture impaired the sense of an overall fabric. This was less true, however, of its principal institutions. The West End's churches, schools, hospitals and museums were generally robust examples of the Romanesque Revival popularized by H.H. Richardson, and their stylistic consistency was such that Schuyler, writing in 1891, characterized the West End as a "new and strange city. . . . So strange and exotic of aspect is this quarter that a New Yorker of 1880 even, who might be suddenly dropped into it, would never recognize it as part of the downtown brownstone city that

367

A ca. 1910 view of Sherman and Verdi squares at Broadway and Seventy-second Street. Center: I.R.T. Subway Kiosk, Heins & LaFarge, 1904. Left: Henry F. Kilburn's Colonial Club (1894); the St. Andrews Hotel (1897) by Andrew Craig; beyond, the turret of R.H. Robertson's Rutgers Presbyterian Church (1890); and the Ansonia (1899–1904) by W.E.D. Stokes and Graves & Duboy. Clinton & Russell's Apthorp (1908) is visible in the distance at Broadway between Seventy-eighth and Seventy-ninth streets. Right: Janes & Leo's Dorilton (1902) at the northeast corner of Broadway and Seventy-first Street. MCNY

he knew. The West Side is not in any strictness a Romanesque town, to be sure, but the prevailing and pervading architectural element which gives it its character is undeniably Romanesque."[314]

As late as 1888 the *Real Estate Record and Guide* decried the paucity of churches in the West End, observing that many new residents had no alternative but to continue attending parishes on the East Side or downtown.[315] A host of new churches was constructed around 1890, as parishes expanded their existing facilities, followed their congregations westward, or established uptown branches. Among these the most striking example of Richardson's influence was William A. Potter's design for St. Agnes Chapel, won in competition in 1889.[316] Its picturesque composition was a learned response to Richardson's Trinity Church in Boston, while the tower looked back to the Albany City Hall. Schuyler described St. Agnes as "one of the finest works of the revival . . . an example of 'Richardsonian Romanesque' of which Mr. Richardson might have been proud."[317] Potter's forms, however, were more geometrical, less ornamental and hence less archaeological; Schuyler considered the church in some respects an "advance" over its prototypes.[318]

Although most of the West End's churches were located on major corners, St. Agnes had a mid-block site which ran from Ninety-first to Ninety-second streets west of Columbus Avenue. A fifty-foot-wide strip of land to the east was part of the Croton Aqueduct System and presumed permanently vacant, allowing Potter an unusual opportunity to design an almost freestanding building in the midst of the urban grid. Potter set the parish house behind a small garden on the west side of the Ninety-second Street frontage; the church was seemingly set in a courtyard carved out of the city block.

St. Agnes was an uptown branch of the venerable Trinity Parish, and in 1895 Trinity School moved into an adjacent building at 139 West Ninety-first Street designed by Charles Coolidge Haight.[319] Haight's Collegiate Gothic design, a U-shaped building framing a small forecourt on the street, presaged the best of C.B.J. Snyder's public schools. Less remarkably picturesque than St. Agnes, it had a relationship to the street characteristic of the Composite Era, creating an awkward and abrupt adjacency to Potter's parish house.

Two new church buildings were built near Broadway

St. Agnes Chapel, Columbus to Amsterdam avenues between West Ninety-first and Ninety-second streets. William A. Potter, 1889. View from Ninety-second Street. NYHS

and Seventy-second Street, the fashionable heart of the West End district. The Rutgers Presbyterian Church at Broadway and Seventy-third Street, designed by R.H. Robertson in 1890, was a low, simple composition executed in three tints of rough-faced sandstone.[320] Oriented to the orthogonal street grid, it took advantage of the eccentric angle of Broadway to project an almost freestanding tower at the south in front of the facade. But as was the case at a number of Robertson's churches, the tower was never completed. Two blocks south, at Broadway and Seventy-first Street, Charles Coolidge Haight's brick and stone Christ Church was warmer in color and texture.[321] The church's massing was typical of the Cosmopolitan Era; the Latin cross plan ignored the peculiarity of Broadway's diagonal, although the rectory, designed three years later by Rose & Stone, helped tie the church into the block fabric and formed a delightful small courtyard.

Christ Church, Rutgers Presbyterian and St. Agnes were rather literal transcriptions of suburban church types, executed with little accommodation to Manhattan's street grid. By the 1890s, although the Romanesque still dominated ecclesiastical architecture, a number of churches suggested a more sensitive approach to the urban context, compacting the massing and imagery of freestanding churches so as to better adapt themselves to the constricted lots of the city. Henry F. Kilburn's West End Presbyterian Church on the northeast corner of Amsterdam Avenue and 105th Street and his Park Presbyterian Church on the northeast corner of Amsterdam Avenue and Eighty-sixth Street followed similar strategies.

West End Presbyterian was a parish organized in 1888 which completed its church two years later.[322] The interior angles of the church's cruciform plan were filled by corner entrances, the parish house and a dramatic tower at the intersection, thus establishing a continuous streetwall while still articulating the individual parts on the facade. Built of light yellow brick striped with horizontal terra-cotta bands, the design was a delicate, eclectic combination of Romanesque and Renaissance motifs. Park Presbyterian Church was even more stylistically synthetic.[323] Kilburn used a deep-hued reddish brownstone with tinted mortar to accentuate its massiveness, and juxtaposed heavy rustication to floral reliefs of extreme delicacy. The church filled its site to the lot lines, but Kilburn's gables and towers pro-

New York Cancer Hospital, Central Park West between 105th and 106th streets. Charles Coolidge Haight, 1885–90. View from Central Park West. CU

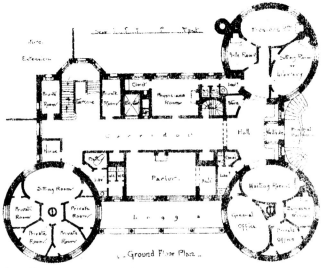

New York Cancer Hospital, Central Park West between 105th and 106th Streets. Charles Coolidge Haight, 1885–90. Plan of ground floor. CU

duced a varied and picturesque skyline expressive of the internal organization.[324]

St. Paul's Methodist Episcopal Church at the northeast corner of West End Avenue and Eighty-sixth Street represented a turning point in the West End's church architecture from the astylar eclecticism of the Cosmopolitan Era to the more condensed imagery of the Composite Era.[325] Designed by R.H. Robertson in 1895, it referred, as did Stanford White's Judson Memorial Church, to the early Italian Renaissance as a transitional moment embodying both the presumptive religious faith of the Middle Ages and the rational enlightenment of the modern era. Despite its Classicizing details, the avenue facade was, in Schuyler's words, "unscrupulously picturesque."[326] One of its two towers was tall and octagonal, the other short and square, set at forty-five degrees to the body of the church. Schuyler described the church as "an extreme example of free classic in ecclesiastical work."[327] Fond though he was of St. Paul's, Schuyler was not certain whether the "jolly aspect" he perceived in its design was "appropriate."[328] The Classicizing tendency of St. Paul's would not come to full flower until after the turn of the century, when Central Park West became the city's most representative street of churches.

Haight's Cancer Hospital (1885–90) was the nation's first facility devoted exclusively to that disease.[329] Located on Central Park West between 105th and 106th streets, it had a battlemented, individualistic Romanesque design which, like the Seventy-seventh Street facade of the Natural History Museum, epitomized the monumental spirit of the Cosmopolitan Era. The picturesque imagery was married to an inventive plan: the fifty-foot-wide round towers that dominated the hospital's massing were determined by contemporary sanitary beliefs, which held that germs collected in corners. The wards were located in the towers, which on the ground floor were ingeniously divided up into oval and polygonal offices, with ancillary spaces located in the central block. The brown stone and red brick exterior evoked the Chateau de Chambord with steeply pitched slate roofs and Gothic dormers.

The Association Residence for Aged Respectable Indigent Females, one of the city's oldest and best endowed institutions for housing the poor, stood nearby, at Amsterdam Avenue between 103rd and 104th streets.[330] Richard Morris Hunt's design, begun in 1881–83 and expanded twenty years later, was appropriately more domestic in character than the Cancer Hospital. Its long, mansard roof fronted on the avenue and was punctuated with dormers and gabled pavilions in an abstracted French Gothic vocabulary.

The most conspicuous monument of the West End's Cosmopolitan Era was the American Museum of Natural History, founded in 1869.[331] In 1874, when the middle-class residential character of the West End was still a matter of speculation, the museum laid the cornerstone of its first permanent home on the site of Manhattan Square. The square had been included in the Commissioners' Plan of 1811 and was later intended as an extension of Central Park, but it was an obvious site for the new museum. The original building, designed by Calvert Vaux and Jacob Wrey Mould, was a Ruskinian Gothic design which balanced their Metropolitan Museum of Art across Central Park. In 1890 Josiah Cleveland Cady of Cady, Berg & See completed a section on Seventy-seventh Street of a vast new masterplan which called for a square building linked at the center of each side to a monumental central tower.[332] Schuyler observed in 1897: "The Romanesque which [Cady] has chosen for his style is by no means the aggressive and importune phase of that style. It is carried out with . . . decorum and moderation."[333] Cady's facade was a rigorously symmetrical five-part composition with twin towers flanking a central block and terminal pavilions whose corner turrets were capped by conical roofs and ringed with heraldic eagles. The vigorous massing and the use of both rock faced and smooth granite of a warm, red tint enlivened what was at the time the longest facade in New York. Cady's decorative details and turrets, finials and towers lent the museum baronial splendor and a somewhat martial air which belatedly reflected the same spirit that had labelled Clark's nearby apartment house, the Dakota, because it lay so far from the settled city.

Cady's proposed museum typified the monuments of the Cosmopolitan Era in its picturesque exterior wedded to

American Museum of Natural History, Manhattan Square, Central Park West to Columbus Avenue between Seventy-seventh and Eighty-first streets. Cady, Berg & See, 1890. View of Seventy-seventh Street facade with the Ninth Avenue El in the foreground. MCNY

Nathan Straus house, 27 West Seventy-second Street. John H. Duncan, 1896. In the background are Hardenbergh's West Seventy-third Street rowhouses. CU

River Mansion, southeast corner of Riverside Drive and 106th Street. Robert D. Kohn, 1900. View from 106th Street. CU

a conventional plan and in its awkward relationship to the Manhattan Square site and to Central Park. Too large to be comprehended as a freestanding building, it nonetheless eschewed any articulation of the city block, leaving narrow, vestigial slivers of the original Manhattan Square. In the Composite Era, Trowbridge & Livingston attempted to address Central Park in their 1911 masterplan, which proposed a Modern French pavilion with a vast triple portal at the center of the west facade.[334] It was only in 1931-36, however, when John Russell Pope built the New York State Theodore Roosevelt Memorial, that the museum acknowledged the park and belatedly attempted to adapt to what had become a city of Classical monuments.[335]

The short-lived Dutch Revival, a shift from the free, synthetic eclecticism of the 1880s to a purer and frequently more scholarly form of eclecticism, was the first blossoming of the Composite Era in the West End. The location of two great Classical memorials on Riverside Drive—the Grant Memorial at its furthest extremity and the Soldiers' and Sailors' Monument at West Eighty-ninth Street—crystallized the West End's composite stage of development, when the Modern French style became the pervasive mode of the entire West Side of Manhattan.

John H. Duncan's twin houses for Richard Cunningham and Oscar S. Straus (1891) on West Seventy-fourth Street provided a transition between the Cosmopolitan and Composite taste; the new sense of Classical calm was seen in the fenestration and simplified roof line, although the detailed design of the facade harked back to the astylar eclecticism of the 1880s.[336] Duncan's American basement house for Nathan Straus (1896) at 27 West Seventy-second Street carried the Classical impulse further in a facade united by a graceful four-story swell front.[337] The fenestration was framed by a vertical stone band composed of Classical fragments. The facade culminated in a balustraded cornice which carried across the cornice line of the adjacent house and allowed the attic to be slightly set back, understating the scale of the house and restoring a sense of continuity with the rest of the street.

With the development of Morningside Heights just to the north of the West End, a large concentration of Classical townhouses was built from 1899 to 1901 on West 105th to 108th streets between Riverside Drive and West End Avenue.[338] Many of the houses in the new, Classical enclave were the work of Janes & Leo, the firm most representative of the West End's Composite Era. Two recent graduates of Columbia University and the Ecole des Beaux-Arts, their work in the West End approached in scope that of Lamb & Rich in the 1880s. Stylistically, it ranged from a restrained, almost severe Classicism represented by the three American basement houses at 324-328 West 108th Street, to the lush, almost overblown Modern French manner seen in their best known work, the flamboyant Dorilton Apartments built in 1902 at Broadway and Seventy-first Street.

The West 108th Street houses (1898), typical of many in the blocks leading up to Riverside Drive, featured two-story-high bay windows which provided the living room and library of each house with diagonal views of Riverside Park and the Hudson River beyond.[339] In the central house the bay was curved, while those flanking it were polygonal. While the exteriors were distinctly Classical, the interiors indulged in a wide variety of styles ranging from Colonial or Georgian vestibules and drawing rooms to English Gothic dining rooms.

Janes & Leo's four-house group (1899) at 316-322 West 108th Street was more unusual, juxtaposing one house in the Modern French style, Number 322, with three quite restrained examples of the red brick American Georgian style just beginning to gain favor in New York.[340] Though the plans of all four houses were virtually identical, the location of the entrance doors, the handling of the fenestration and, most importantly, the articulation of the front wall to achieve desirable river views yielded a rich but still coherent streetscape.

The most consistent example of the West End's Modern French period was found in a group of rowhouses built between 1899-1901 on 105th and 106th streets between Riverside Drive and West End Avenue. Janes & Leo were the architects of Numbers 302-316 on the south side of 105th Street and 301-307 on the north.[341] The remaining houses on the north side, 309-321, were designed by William E. Mowbray of Mowbray & Umberfield.[342] Mowbray's houses were clearly intended to harmonize with the slightly earlier Janes & Leo rows, restating the gently swelling bays to give the street a gracious rhythm as it sloped down toward the river. The Janes & Leo houses were slight variations on a single type which was then symmetrically disposed to subtly transform the entire row into a unified composition. Their mansion on the north corner of Riverside and 105th Street broke from the rowhouse mold, its mass separated from the rest of the street by a low, glazed conservatory.[343] A heavy balcony supported on vigorous consoles framed the entrance. Above it the windows were united in a three-story panel of metal and glass which provided a dramatic vertical termination to the insistently horizontal lines of Mowbray's rowhouses.

The architects Hoppin & Koen, who designed Numbers 334-336 Riverside Drive (1899), lacked much of the brio of Janes & Leo, but Number 335 was an unusual example in the West End of the Colonial Revival.[344] River Mansion, at the south corner of 106th Street and Riverside Drive, was surely the most distinguished in the group.[345] Designed in 1900 by Robert D. Kohn, it had a facade on the Drive united by a single glazed tripartite bay stretching two stories above the ground floor. Two similar motifs were used on the long 106th Street front, projecting forward from stone quoins embedded in a flat wall of Flemish bond brickwork. Although Kohn gave the house an undeniably French feeling, he brought to River Mansion the same talent for imaginatively abstracted Classicism that he displayed in his better known *Evening Post* and Ethical Culture Society buildings.

By 1899, the editors of the *Real Estate Record and Guide* considered the success of Riverside Drive to be virtually assured. While it had not become a boulevard lined with freestanding villas, it was nonetheless attracting the most enlightened speculative development, and the results seemed commensurate with the investments made by the city in the park and in the very design of the roadway itself: "While 5th Avenue may continue to hold the multi-millionaires, the Riverside Drive seems to house another class wealthy from ordinary standards and distinctly representative of the shrewdness and conservatism of the business world."[346]

The suburban trend which had flourished briefly in the late 1880s and early 1890s enjoyed an incandescent revival at the turn of the century when four splendid freestanding

Mrs. Alfred Corning Clark house, northeast corner of Riverside Drive and Eighty-ninth Street. Ernest Flagg, 1900. View from Eighty-ninth Street. OMH

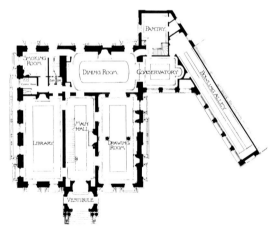

Mrs. Alfred Corning Clark house, northeast corner of Riverside Drive and Eighty-ninth Street. Ernest Flagg, 1900. Plan of ground floor. CU

Isaac L. Rice house, southeast corner of Riverside Drive and Eighty-ninth Street. Herts & Tallant, 1902. View from Riverside Drive. MCNY

houses were erected on the Drive. Unlike their earlier counterparts, these were less villas than great palaces rivaling those of Fifth Avenue. Two of the houses were erected across Eighty-ninth Street from one another, where they commanded sweeping views from a bend in the Drive and formed a gateway to the Hudson River. Appropriately, the first of these was the residence of Mrs. Alfred Corning Clark, whose family had long pioneered the development of the West End.[347] The new Clark mansion was completed in 1900 by Ernest Flagg, later the architect of three office buildings for the family business, the Singer Manufacturing Company. Flagg's design synthesized Modern French detailing with Georgian massing. The house was freestanding except for a one-story glazed loggia containing a bowling alley, which partially masked the blank party wall of the neighboring rowhouse on Eighty-ninth Street. The plan was indebted to Colonial houses; a long, narrow central stairhall, ringed by a gallery upstairs, was flanked by the library and drawing room.

The Isaac L. Rice house across Eighty-ninth Street was completed by Herts & Tallant in 1902.[348] Like the Clark house it was built of red brick and white marble, but Herts & Tallant manipulated the contrasting materials to create a dialogue between the Classical and the vernacular. A Modern French *Serliana* and a broad flight of stairs to Riverside Drive lent grandeur to the otherwise simple facade. On the side street, a swelling brick and marble bay sheltered a *porte-cochère* and gestured across the street to the more elaborate entrance of the Clark house. Together the two houses presented an imposing gateway to the 1902 Soldiers' and Sailors' Memorial. The vivid contrast they offered to the Cyrus Clark and John Matthews mansions one block north gave convincing testimony to the vigor of the new generation of French-trained American architects.

The Maurice Schinasi residence was built in 1909 on the northeast corner of 107th Street. Like the Rice mansion, it was relatively small. The architect, William B. Tuthill, reported: "It was not asked that the structure be either monumental or relatively large; the owner . . . required the building of a 'home' . . . rich in materials and as far as possible faultless in execution. . . . It is what one might call a 'portrait' house, in that the house . . . was designed for his intimate home living and without particular reference to any conventional claim or social function."[349] In response,

Right: Charles H. Schwab house, Riverside Drive and West End Avenue between Seventy-third and Seventy-fourth streets. Maurice Hebert, 1901–07. A view which also shows Riverside Drive with the exposed train tracks at the left. MCNY

Tuthill designed an exquisite French Renaissance jewelbox executed in pristine white marble, with deep-green roof tiles and bronze grills on the balconies and at the main entrance. Schinasi so prized the whiteness of the facades that a special system of pumps was installed to allow every part of the exterior to be cleaned. The rich materials, wood panelling, mosaics and stencil patterns used inside contributed to a precious refinement unsurpassed in the West End, while mirrors and vistas between rooms enhanced the apparent spaciousness of the house.

The Charles M. Schwab mansion was the most lavish of the turn-of-the-century villas on Riverside Drive.[350] Intent on rivalling Andrew Carnegie, his partner in the United States Steel Corporation, Schwab purchased the site of the Orphan Asylum Society encompassing the entire block between West End Avenue and the Drive, Seventy-third and Seventy-fourth streets, for $865,000, an unprecedented sum for a building lot in 1901. Construction began in 1901 and lasted six years.

The French architect Maurice Hébert designed a French Renaissance chateau set in its own landscaped park. The Riverside Drive facade was based on that of Chenonceaux. The rear was a more relaxed composition based on fragments of the chateaux at Blois and Azay-le-Rideau; the rather coldly archaeological feeling of the river facade was somewhat alleviated by the use of brick with stone trim and variegated massing. Inside, a broad two-and-a-half-story hall surrounded by balconies led to a monumental staircase lit from above, creating an effect less like that of a house than of a public building. Provisions for servicing the owner's needs were unprecedented in their complexity and included garages for four cars, a separate receiving lodge for goods, and a service tunnel buried beneath the garden terraces. A belfry with chimes, indoor swimming pool, chapel and roof garden served less practical functions.

Hébert's design of the Schwab house was criticized by the *Architectural Record* as literal, heavy-handed and distinctly less effective than Haight's more "intelligent and effective adaptation" of similar motifs at the Cancer Hospital a decade before.[351] Nonetheless the house was admired as a type, and Schwab regarded as a "pioneer in detecting the true uses of the West Side. . . . Riverside Drive, from the moment of its completion, seemed plainly destined to be a boulevard of palaces, a *rus in urbe* combining the great

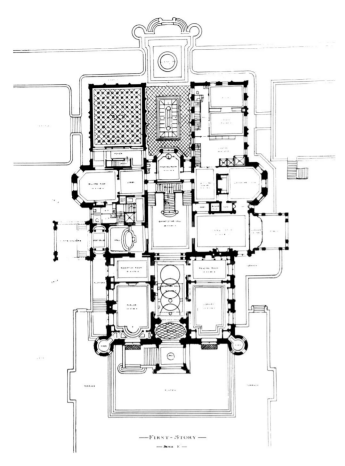

Charles H. Schwab house, Riverside Drive and West End Avenue between Seventy-third and Seventy-fourth streets. Maurice Hebert, 1901–07. Plan of ground floor. CU

Charles H. Schwab house, Riverside Drive and West End Avenue between Seventy-third and Seventy-fourth streets. Maurice Hebert, 1901–07. Transverse section through stairhall. CU

prospect, down, up, across the Hudson, with easy accessibility from the commercial quarters and from stage-land and clubland. Suburban [the houses] should have been, in the sense of being detached and lighted all around."[352]

The removal of the orphanage from the Schwab site sparked a renaissance of building in the side streets off the Drive just above Seventy-second Street, creating a Classical enclave at the southern end of the Drive which balanced the development around 106th Street, near its northern end. Babb, Cook & Willard's townhouses for Mrs. J.O. Hoyt and E.J. Stimson (1897) at 310–312 West Seventy-fifth Street were unusual in that, though similar in design, they were executed in different materials.[353] The Stimson house had a narrow entrance court at its western flank allowing the principal rooms greater privacy and ventilation. The facades were suave, delicate essays in French Baroque.

Herts & Tallant's 1904 remodelling of an 1887 townhouse facade by E.L. Angell at 232 West End Avenue, between Seventieth and Seventy-first streets, was a grandiloquent example of the Modern French style.[354] A broad segmental arch sheltered an outdoor vestibule, creating a theatrical entrance and disguising the off-center position of the doorway in Angell's English basement plan. The floors above were united in a two-story glazed bay set within a rusticated frame, further exaggerating the scale of the house.

While the work of Janes & Leo dominated the upper West End, C.P.H. Gilbert's early career flowered at its southern end. His house (ca. 1899) at Seventy-second Street and Riverside Drive revealed the deft synthesis of Classical massing and plan with late French Gothic and early Renaissance detailing which was his trademark.[355] This was also evident in his 1894–95 design for 330 West Seventy-sixth Street, between West End Avenue and Riverside Drive.[356] Here the combination of delicate stone carving and buff-colored Roman brick lent the house a warmer texture than characterized Gilbert's later stone work on the East Side. The houses of Mrs. Miller and Mrs. McGucken at 307–309 West Seventy-sixth Street were exceptions to the François I mode that dominated Gilbert's career.[357] Perhaps in order to relate to the adjacent Lamb & Rich houses, their red and brown brick facades were delicate, low-relief abstractions of Classical motifs, with iron brackets supporting a deeply projecting wooden cornice.

Rowhouses, 18–52 West Seventy-fourth Street. Percy Griffin, 1902–04. MCNY

Hotel Majestic, southwest corner of Central Park West and Seventy-second Street. Alfred Zucker, 1899. Perspective of the dining room. CU

The tradition of the middle-class townhouse in the West End concluded with appropriate symmetry. In 1902–04 Frederick Ambrose Clark, whose family had crystallized the West Side movement with the construction of the Dakota twenty-five years earlier, constructed a row of American basement houses designed by Percy Griffin at 18–52 West Seventy-fourth Street.[358] These were among the earliest and best expressions in the West End of the newly emerging Georgian sensibility which was far more prevalent on the East Side. The rhythmic sequence of three repeated unit types and the contrapuntal rhythm of pedimented entrance porches provided sufficient variety to keep the street scene lively, while the careful detailing of the red brick and limestone facades and a continuous cornice line established an overall unity.

The Seventy-fourth Street rowhouses were a futile effort to reverse an already inevitable trend. The *Real Estate Record and Guide* described Clark's aim as "to provide a better abode than can be obtained for an equal rent in an apartment hotel; to provide . . . a place where there may be real family life as it used to exist before the city grew to proportions that forced real estate values up so high that now only the wealthy can live in houses."[359] In 1904 the opening of the I.R.T. subway beneath Broadway had already made possible the metamorphosis of the West End, from an area of single-family houses with concentrations of apartments for the affluent along Central Park West and tenements along Columbus Avenue, into a neighborhood increasingly dominated by high-rise construction for the middle classes. The anticipated completion of the subway had brought with it an increase in land values that forever halted construction of townhouses on the West Side.

As early as 1906 the *Real Estate Record and Guide* observed that "people would not pay the increased price for that class of building in that section, but a greater rise in the value of land on the East side actually augmented the demand in that section for private dwellings. . . . The reason, of course, is that in the course of time none but rich people will be able to afford private houses in the central borough of New York City; and it so happens that it is the rich who are or want to be fashionable. Fashion has stamped its approval on the East side, and has passed the West side by."[360] Together with the construction of the Riverside Drive viaduct over the Harlem Valley in 1900, the

Hotel Marie Antoinette, northwest corner of Broadway and Sixty-sixth Street. Julius Munckowitz, 1895. Suite. MCNY

subway signalled the transformation of the West End into the West Side—no longer a discrete neighborhood with a northern boundary but a continuous zone of developmental possibilities stretching as far uptown as Washington Heights.[361] While the fabric of rowhouses along the minor side streets frequently remained intact, the major avenues and crosstown streets underwent a process of rebuilding that continued until World War I, when the river tunnels made daily commuting to the more rural suburbs attractive to those who had originally sought the West End for its approximation of suburban scale.

By 1911 the *Real Estate Record and Guide* could write: "The middle-class man of family seems . . . to be losing his taste for city life. An estimate by a real estate authority is that fifty thousand families have moved off the island this year. A far larger number of newcomers have, of course, taken their place, but the fact remains that many old New York families have found during the last decade that old ties and associations are being broken up, and that things are not as they used to be."[362] Thus, the years between 1900 and 1920 witnessed the departure of the old families from the West End and an influx of newly rich urban types—denizens of the city including actors, politicians and prosperous, newly assimilated immigrants who preferred urban to suburban life.

The transformation of Central Park West and Broadway into a new vertical townscape of apartment buildings had been presaged by an influx of hotel construction in the 1890s. The grandest of these was Alfred Zucker's Hotel Majestic (1889).[363] Rising eleven stories above Seventy-second Street and Central Park West, just opposite the Dakota apartments, it had an inventive plan featuring numerous exterior light courts to maximize light, air and park views for the guests. Its opulent public rooms more than compensated for a relatively bland Classical exterior. The dining room was a vast hypostyle hall whose columns supported Gothic fan vaults and whose every surface was encrusted in a rich Moorish filigree; a tribute to the Cosmopolitan Era's eclecticism and taste for luxury.

Hotels on Broadway in the West End were generally smaller and less elaborate than those of Central Park West. The St. Andrews (1897) at Seventy-second Street was designed by Andrew Craig;[364] the Marie Antoinette (1895) at Sixty-sixth Street was the work of Julius Munckowitz, a

Hotel Marie Antoinette, west side of Broadway between Sixty-sixth and Sixty-seventh streets. Left: Julius Munckowitz, 1895. Right: C.P.H. Gilbert, 1903. View from Broadway. NYHS

Alimar, northeast corner of West End Avenue and 105th Street. Janes & Leo, 1901. CU

little known architect with offices on 125th Street in Harlem.[365] The exterior of the Marie Antoinette was distinguished by delicate and refined detailing which established a tone of elegant domesticity. The interiors were more richly decorated in an elaborate Jacobean mode with dark wood panelling, an eclectic mix of furniture and heavy draperies.

In 1903, the Marie Antoinette was expanded to the north by C.P.H. Gilbert; the two wings of the building offered a juxtaposition as startling as those of the Hotel Renaissance downtown.[366] Gilbert's addition was unusual for his work, a fulsome interpretation of the Modern French style with bulbous mansards and a plethora of dormers. The corner was marked by a rounded bay, but above the ninth story the corner was chamfered, creating a delightful balcony far above Broadway and seemingly sheltered by a vast split pediment in the dormer above.

West End Avenue had developed in the 1880s as a street of private houses for the upper-middle class, defying earlier predictions that it would become the West End's commercial thoroughfare. Within a short time, however, it was completely transformed as the West End's principal apartment house thoroughfare for that same class, a direct reflection of "a change in our method of living rather than in the utilization of the land. This thoroughfare furnishes a striking example of the decline in private house construction and the rise of the huge apartment house in popular form."[367] Between 1907 and 1912, according to the *Real Estate Record and Guide,* approximately half of the avenue's houses were replaced by apartment buildings.[368]

Many of the apartment houses built on West End Avenue around 1900 were architecturally undistinguished. Typical of these tenements for the rich was the Wellesley on the northeast corner of Eighty-first Street, a stiffly composed Italianate design by Little & O'Connor.[369] The Wellesley was originally to have been quadrupled in size so as to cover the entire block. William B. Franke's New Century apartments (1900) on the northwest corner of Seventy-ninth Street was awkwardly proportioned and even less successful at preserving the avenue's distinguished character.[370] Its chief amenity was the provision of an early automobile garage in a two-story annex on the side street.

The Alimar at 925 West End Avenue redeemed somewhat the architecture of that thoroughfare's early apartment houses.[371] It was designed in 1901 by Janes & Leo,

Dorilton, northeast corner of Broadway and Seventy-first Street. Janes & Leo, 1902. View from Sherman Square. CU

whose early career in townhouses expanded to include some of the West End's most stylish apartments. The Alimar was a U-shaped building surrounding a narrow light court euphemistically labelled "Garden" in the architects' plans. Although the bedrooms were strung along long, narrow corridors, the sophisticated arrangement of the principal rooms *en suite* reflected the French influence on the firm's work. The red brick and limestone facade continued the Modern French theme, with a copper mansard and baroque pedimented dormers. The avenue facade was framed by delicate metal and glass oriel windows, while a wrought-iron balcony on the sixth floor related to the height of the adjoining rowhouses on 105th Street.

The rebuilding of West End Avenue eventually robbed it of much of its charm. While its early apartment houses were generally mediocre, they were at least modest in height. By 1910 the scale of development on the West Side increased, transforming what had once been a street of three- or four-story houses lined with broad, tree-lined sidewalks into a barren canyon bereft of sunlight.[372]

The eventual scale of the West End was first evident in a series of far more stylish apartment houses and apartment hotels erected along Broadway.[373] The simultaneous construction of the subway, the Dorilton, and the Ansonia brought the newly rechristened street to its fullest expression as an American *Champs Elysées*.

Janes & Leo's twelve-story Dorilton (1902) at the northeast corner of Broadway and Seventy-first Street was the first of these to be completed and the most stylistically extreme, a highly florid Modern French design of exceptional vigor which developed themes previously explored at the Alimar.[374] The Dorilton's bold massing dominated Sherman Square. A heavily rusticated limestone base supported a bright red brick superstructure and a voluminous three-story mansard of black slate and copper. The entrance was through a south-facing court on Seventy-first Street. A stone arch supported by a steel truss linked the two flanking wings of buildings at the cornice line, transforming the courtyard into a heroically scaled entrance portal. Four stone piers at street level flanked a canopy sprouting cherubs, creating a sense of entrance at a more human scale. The Broadway facade was somewhat less aggressive, its center anchored by a five-story-high, sheet-metal oriel bay, a device echoed at a lesser scale on the two pavilions facing Seventy-

Ansonia Apartment Hotel, Broadway between Seventy-third and Seventy-fourth streets. W.E.D. Stokes and Graves & Duboy, 1899–1904. Broadway elevation with unexecuted central tower. CU

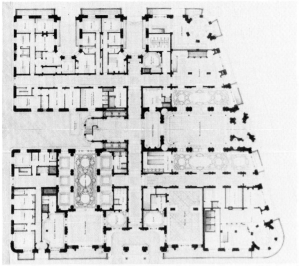

Ansonia Apartment Hotel, Broadway between Seventy-third and Seventy-fourth streets. W.E.D. Stokes and Graves & Du Boy, 1899–1904. Plan of ground floor. CU

Ansonia Apartment Hotel, Broadway between Seventy-third and Seventy-fourth streets. W.E.D. Stokes and Graves & Duboy, 1899–1904. Bedroom of a bachelor's apartment decorated by J.H. Freedlander in 1905. CU

first Street which made delightful spaces of the rooms within, despite a plan riddled with long, narrow corridors. The Dorilton was distinguished by the astonishing voluptuousness of its details. The cartouches, rustication, and the rather Junoesque sculptures seemingly trapped on the fourth-floor balcony were carved with a brio and exhibitionism that led the *Architectural Record* to quote Carlyle: "That all men should see this; innocent young creatures, still in arms, be taught to think this beautiful; and perhaps, women in an interesting situation to look up to it as they pass? I put it to your religious feeling, to your principles as men and fathers of families!"[375] The *Record* ascribed the "incendiary qualities of the edifice . . . to violence of color, then to violence of scale, then to violence of 'thinginess,' to the multiplicity and the importunity of the details. . . . How everything shrieks to drown out everything else!"[376] Nonetheless it was precisely the intricacy and the burly swagger of the Dorilton which was the source of its drama and expressed the optimism of the new century.[377]

The Ansonia was the largest and grandest of all of the New York apartment hotels, rivaling Hiss & Weekes's Gotham Hotel (1905) for the honor of being the most elegant.[378] It was built in 1899–1904 by the developer W.E.D. Stokes and architects Graves & Duboy on a bend in Broadway between Seventy-third and Seventy-fourth streets, a site which allowed it to command vistas northward from Fifty-ninth Street and southward from 105th Street. While Howard & Cauldwell's 1897 addition to the Hotel Renaissance had reproduced the forms of the French Boulevard, the Ansonia transformed Parisian prototypes into a veritable skyscraper. The scale of its eighteen-story mass was diminished by exterior light courts, corner towers, a bulbous mansard and countless delicate wrought-iron balconies. The light courts created symmetrical massing on each facade, but the individual wings were not symmetrical within themselves; the building's composition was originally to have been resolved by a vast *baldachino* rising the equivalent of ten stories above the roof garden, an amazingly extravagant gesture evoking the roofscape of Chambord.

The Modern French bravado of the Ansonia's facades also informed the interior. The main entrances were on the side streets, linked by a robustly decorated through-block gallery to the elevator lobby and the major public rooms: the Assembly Room, the Palm Garden, the Grille Room and, at the center of the Broadway facade, a public restaurant with a glass and metal roof. A swimming pool and a garage were provided in the basement. The individual suites reflected both the exigencies of the oddly shaped lot and an extraordinary variety of room shapes.[379] J.H. Freedlander's decoration of an apartment in the Ansonia for "a bachelor whose tastes are somewhat architectural" was as lavish as the building itself, causing the editors of the *Architectural Review* to remark that "the apartment breathes the spirit of New York very much in the same way that the Hotel St. Regis typifies the love of display and magnificence developed by the people of that city, and we are led to wonder whether there will not soon come a reaction, with a return to extreme simplicity in the city's art and architecture."[380]

The completion of the Ansonia was quickly followed by Mulliken & Moeller's more restrained but far less inventive Spencer Arms apartments (1907) at the southeast corner of Broadway and Sixty-ninth Street,[381] their twin Van Dyck and Severn apartments (1907) which occupied the east side of Amsterdam Avenue from Seventy-second to Seventy-third streets,[382] Hill & Turner's Euclid Hall (1903) on the west side of Broadway between Eighty-fifth and Eighty-sixth streets,[383] and further north, Harry Allan Jacobs's joyously exuberant Hotel Marseilles (1905) at Broadway and 103rd Street.[384] The Marseilles and Emery Roth's Belleclaire (1903) further advanced Broadway's case as America's leading Parisian boulevard. At the Belleclaire, a domed turret marked the corner, and two stacks of bay windows set between continuous pilasters and crowned by arched cornices articulated the Broadway facade, while a deep light court reduced the building's bulk along Seventy-seventh Street.[385]

With the construction of Clinton & Russell's Astor apartments (1905) on the west side of Broadway between Seventy-fourth and Seventy-fifth streets, the same firm's Apthorp (1908) at Seventy-ninth Street, proclaimed the world's largest apartment house, and H. Hobart Weekes's Belnord (1908) at Eighty-sixth Street, also proclaimed the

Ansonia Apartment Hotel, Broadway between Seventy-third and Seventy-fourth streets. W.E.D. Stokes and Graves & Duboy, 1899–1904. Lobby. MCNY

Left: Harperly Hall, northwest corner of Central Park West and Sixty-fourth Street. Henry W. Wilkinson, 1910. Right: Prasada, southwest corner of Central Park West and Sixty-fifth Street. Charles W. Romeyn and Henry R. Wynne, 1900. MCNY

Hotel Belleclaire, southwest corner of Broadway and Seventy-seventh Street. Stein, Cohn & Roth, 1903. View from Broadway. NYHS

Red House, 350 West Eighty-fifth Street. Harde & Short, 1904. CU

world's largest apartment house,[386] the intensely French vision of the *fin de siecle* began to give way to the more generalized, if equally powerful, Classicism which dominated the West End's apartment houses well into the 1920s.

Central Park West also enjoyed a second surge of apartment house construction at the turn of the century. Beginning with Neville & Bagge's Cherbourg (1900) at Ninety-second Street[387] and J.E. Ware & H.S.S. Harde's 348–349 Central Park West (1900),[388] the motley character of the avenue was gradually transformed into a grand boulevard of apartment houses and churches. The Cherbourg and 348–349 Central Park West were part of an almost continuous row of roughly seven-story apartment houses that extended north from 72nd to 110th streets. Many of these were little more than glorified tenements reflecting the last gasps of the Richardsonian Romanesque style and constituted, in Franz K. Winkler's phrase, a "panorama of platitude" only faintly relieved by the crenelated massing of Ardsley Hall at the southwest corner of Ninety-second Street and The Towers at the northwest corner of Ninety-fourth Street.[389]

Mulliken & Moeller's Central Park View (1907), between Eighty-fifth and Eighty-sixth streets, brought a new scale of development to the street; twelve stories high, occupying a full block front, the simplified expression of its red brick and limestone facades gave way on the interior to luxuriously appointed hallways and apartments.[390] While Charles W. Romeyn and Henry R. Wynne's Prasada (1906) at the southwest corner of Sixty-fifth Street[391] and Eliott Lynch's Parkview (1903) at the southwest corner of Eighty-eighth Street attempted a more bravura effect, three other designs, more than any others on Central Park West, returned to the avenue some of the distinction it enjoyed at the time of Hardenbergh's Dakota: Clinton & Russell's Langham (1905), between Seventy-third and Seventy-fourth streets;[392] Henry W. Wilkinson's Harperley Hall (1910) at One West Sixty-fourth Street;[393] and Albert J. Bodker's Turin apartments (1911) at the northwest corner of Ninety-third Street.[394] Clinton & Russell made the best of the Langham's restricted site, wrapping a U-shaped mass around a carriage court. The interior appointments in the public halls and the individual apartments shared a very high level of Modern French detailing. Though the Turin was stylistically less interesting, Bodker's skillful use of numerous exterior courts maximized light and park views for the apartments. The price paid for these was awkwardly planned dwelling units with rather small rooms strung out along narrow corridors.[395]

By 1911, Broadway and West End Avenue were almost completely lined with tall (usually twelve-story) apartment houses. The redevelopment of the West End was in many ways the most dramatic example of the city's capacity to rebuild itself; substantial houses only twenty-five years old gave way to new apartment houses, with scarcely a word said in protest—the restrictive covenants having run out.[396] Janes & Leo's Wellsmore apartments at the southeast corner of Broadway and Seventy-seventh Street was typical of the new buildings.[397] A far cry from their earlier, flamboyant Dorilton, or their low, elegant Alimar, the Wellsmore was a twelve-story red brick and limestone palazzo entered off Broadway via a long hall to the elevators set deep within the building's core.

Significantly, Riverside Drive maintained its status as a street of private houses with only one apartment house—S.B. Ogden's The Turrets (1900) at Riverside Drive and Eighty-fourth Street—erected along its length before the turn of the century, and none replacing the rowhouses until after World War I.[398] With extremely large apartments, ranging from ten rooms and three baths to twenty rooms and six baths, as well as a white marble swimming pool and a fully equipped gymnasium, a billiard room, a large ballroom, a banquet hall, bowling alleys and a basketball court, The Turrets went well beyond any other apartment house of its time in terms of amenities.

While the presence of numerous covenants and municipally enforced height restrictions tended to limit the number of apartment houses on side streets, a few notable examples were built. Harde & Short's Jacobean style Red House (1904) at 350 West Eighty-fifth Street[399] was one of the few to carry forward the spirit of the artistic house into the multiple dwelling.

In keeping with its function as a "city within a city" the

Langham, Central Park between Seventy-third and Seventy-fourth streets. Clinton & Russell, 1905. View from Central Park West. MCNY

Colonial Club, southwest corner of Broadway and Seventy-second Street. Henry F. Kilburn, 1894. An 1894 view from Verdi Square. MCNY

West End included many social and religious institutions that catered to its own residents and not to the city at large. These included a number of clubs such as J.A. Schweinfurth's West Side Republican Club House, on the west side of Broadway between Eighty-third and Eighty-fourth streets.[400] Originally designed as a five-story structure, only three floors were realized in 1897. The elegant, American Georgian design, built of light pink "wash brick" trimmed with Indiana limestone with a delicately proportioned pedimented porch and central *Serliana* that could open in good weather to form a loggia, was closer in spirit to Harvard's club on West Forty-fourth Street than to Tammany's on Fourteenth Street.

The two other clubhouses in the West End more faithfully mirrored its characteristic qualities: Henry F. Kilburn's Colonial Club (1894) at the southwest corner of Broadway and Seventy-second Street, and Louis Korn's Progress Club (1904) at 1 West Eighty-eighth Street. First incorporated in 1889 as "The Occident Club of New York," in the early 1890s the Colonial Club charged Kilburn, a resident of "this West Side City," as *American Architect and Building News* described the West End, with the "amalgamating of their needs and their ideas into a concrete unit."[401]

Kilburn's vaguely Colonial design incorporated a ballroom, dining rooms and bedrooms, as well as a bowling alley and a small concert hall. Significantly, because the Colonial was the first club to admit unescorted ladies, separate dining rooms and bowling alleys were provided for each sex, all ingeniously accommodated on a restricted and awkwardly shaped site. But the Colonial Club was short-lived: by 1906 it had been converted into an office building and renamed the Lincoln Trust Building.[402]

In contrast with the somewhat uncertain Classicism of Kilburn's Colonial Club, Korn's Progress Club reflected the Composite Era's pervasive emphasis on stylistic correctness.[403] Raised on a high, rusticated base, the facade above articulated with engaged columns, the Progress evoked an Italian palazzo in a far more legible way than the members' previous clubhouse by Alfred Zucker.

The Classical monumentality evident in the Progress Club informed a series of new houses of worship erected along Central Park West at the turn of the century. They spoke vividly of the neighborhood's sociological and archi-

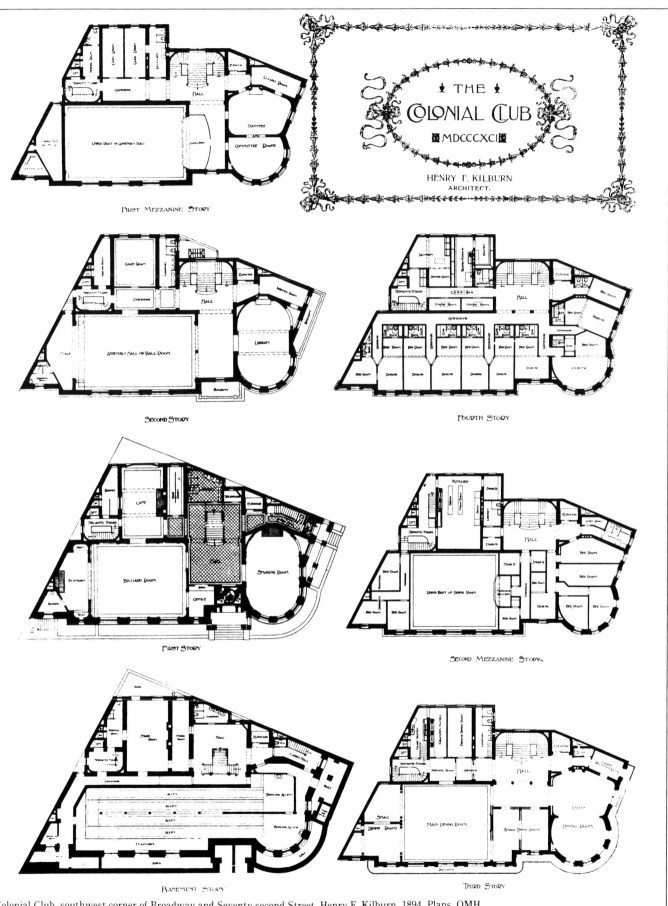

Colonial Club, southwest corner of Broadway and Seventy-second Street. Henry F. Kilburn, 1894. Plans. OMH

Colonial Club, southwest corner of Broadway and Seventy-second Street. Henry F. Kilburn, 1894. View of Ladies' Dining Room. MCNY

Congregation Shearith Israel, southwest corner of Central Park West and Seventieth Street. Brunner & Tryon, 1897. View from Central Park. OMH

tectural transformation. The cosmopolitanism of their denominations reflected the passing of the West End's days as a bastion of Knickerbocker traditions. Together with a number of public buildings they made a chain of monumental gateways along the avenue which rejected the suburban ambience of the 1880s for the urban vision of the City Beautiful.

Carrère & Hastings's Century Theater opened on the southern end of Central Park West in 1909, its setting enhanced by the neighboring Ethical Culture Society buildings on Central Park West between Sixty-third and Sixty-fourth streets. The society's school on the north corner of West Sixty-third Street was intended as a model of educational reform.[404] Designed by Robert D. Kohn and Carrère & Hastings in 1902, its facades were marked by a sophisticated expression of a nonstructural skin. The subtle panelling of the brickwork abstracted the forms of pilasters and rustication, while the steel and glass infill of windows and the openwork metal cornice exploited the potential of new technology without sacrifice of traditional composition.

Kohn was solely responsible for the adjacent Ethical Culture Society Hall, which carried across the base moldings and cornice line of the school building but substituted an appropriately monumental scale. Built in 1911, it was praised by the *Architectural Record* for "the austerity of the treatment in general, the leaving of square arrises in so many cases where one would expect a moulding of transition, the point at which the development of the corbels has been arrested, insomuch that one may also be inclined to say that the fronts are 'en bloc' instead of being finished."[405] The simplification of traditional forms was carried into the interior of the auditorium, covered by a groin vault articulated with simple flat moldings and decorated with an Art Nouveau pattern in the arms of the cross. Kohn's extreme abstraction of traditional forms was held to be appropriate for a religion which "not only deprives itself of spiritual sanction, but denies itself those ritual observances which constitute the data and the material of the ecclesiastical architect."[406]

Congregation Shearith Israel on Central Park West and Seventieth Street, designed by Brunner & Tryon in 1897 in a far more explicitly Classical vein, reflected the desire of established Jewish congregations to disassociate themselves from the Oriental or Near Eastern mode of synagogues typical of the Cosmopolitan Era (represented by the same architects' West End Synagogue on Eighty-second Street between Columbus and Amsterdam avenues).[407] This rush to architectural assimilation was part of a widespread movement to distinguish Western European Jewish traditions from those of the East as large numbers of poorer Jews arrived from Eastern Europe between 1890 and 1914. Congregation Shearith Israel was known as the Spanish and Portuguese Synagogue, a reference to its Sephardic traditions that dated back beyond its founding in the Dutch colony of New Amsterdam to the origins of the group in medieval Spain and Portugal. As if to stress the congregation's venerable age and deep American roots, a small synagogue, in effect a chapel, was built to the side in the Colonial Revival style.[408] Its interior was composed of fragments of the congregation's previous houses of worship.

Shearith Israel presented a boldly scaled temple front with a grand flight of steps to Central Park West. With its prominent location facing Central Park, its scale and glistening whiteness offered a dramatic contrast to the modest brownstone landscape of the west seventies. The centrally placed altar was executed in a cool Roman vocabulary, with the scrolls of the Torah stored in a Classical vault at the west end.

Shearith Israel was soon followed on Central Park West by F.R. Comstock's Second Church of Christ Scientist, built in 1900 on the corner of Sixty-eighth Street.[409] Comstock's design, a densely composite synthesis of historical allusions, was an inventive response to the task of representing a creed with no specific architectural heritage. The side street and avenue facades were of different lengths, but each was a tripartite composition based on a heroically scaled arched window with a pediment above and flanking corner piers. The similarity of the facades reflected the square proportions of the auditorium within, and implied a centralized plan which alluded to the humanism of the Italian Renaissance. The exterior detailing combined fashionable Modern French ornament with the severe proportiuons of the neo-

Center: Church of the Divine Paternity, southwest corner of Central Park West and Seventy-sixth Street. William A. Potter, 1898. Right: the New-York Historical Society, Central Park West between Seventy-sixth and Seventy-seventh streets. York & Sawyer, 1908. View looking south on Central Park West. NYHS

Hall for the Society for Ethical Culture, southwest corner of Central Park West and Sixty-fourth Street. Robert D. Kohn, 1911. View from Central Park West. To the left is the Ethical Culture Society School by Kohn and Carrère & Hastings (1902). CU

First Church of Christ Scientist, northwest corner of Central Park West and Ninety-sixth Street. Carrère & Hastings, 1904. View from Central Park. CU

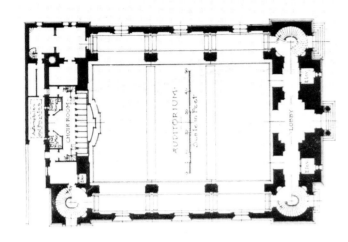

First Church of Christ Scientist, northwest corner of Central Park West and Ninety-sixth Street. Carrère & Hastings, 1904. Plan of ground floor. CU

First Church of Christ Scientist, northwest corner of Central Park West and Ninety-sixth Street. Carrère & Hastings, 1904. Auditorium. CU

Grec. The interior was contrastingly sober; the sparsity of its ornament recalled the frugal London churches of Sir Christopher Wren.

William A. Potter's Church of the Divine Paternity (1898), a Universalist congregation, was one of the few buildings to break from Central Park West's prevailing Classicism.[410] A rather archaeological design in English Gothic, it evaded the issue of representing the particular beliefs of the denomination. Schuyler described the church as "a decent and well-behaved example of Anglican church architecture, without any marks of personality or individuality in the architect, any more than with any recognition of the peculiarity of the problem."[411] Potter's design, particularly in light of his earlier eclectic work, reflected the significance attached to stylistic accuracy in the Composite Era. It stood in sharp contrast to York & Sawyer's equally correct but Classical New-York Historical Society.

Carrère & Hastings's First Church of Christ Scientist, built in 1904 for the city's oldest Christian Science denomination, concluded Central Park West's row of churches at Ninety-sixth Street.[412] The First Church was a far more powerful design than Comstock's effort at Sixty-eighth Street: a major monument of the Composite Era, it was one of the city's most compelling religious structures in the Classical manner. Carrère & Hastings's evocation of the low church architecture of Georgian London and New England set the tone for many subsequent Christian Science churches throughout the northeast.

Carrère & Hastings achieved a remarkable sense of solidity not only through the blocky composition, inspired by the English Mannerist architect Nicholas Hawksmoor, but also through the use of extremely large blocks of a white Concord granite, a stone so hard that it shattered mechanical saws and had to be cut by hand. Inside, the church was less distinctly English in feeling. A gallery wrapped around three sides of the auditorium, and barrel vaults sprang from piers which barely cleared the galleries, creating a powerfully encompassing effect. The room was largely undecorated, except for an elaborate organ case and rich Modern French plasterwork on the ceiling, which also contained rondels of concealed lighting.

Supported above the auditorium arches were the church's offices, reading rooms and extensive Sunday school facilities. Clearly expressed on the exterior, their location reflected a unique solution to the problem of the parochial complex. Owen R. Washburn was correct in his assessment for the *Architectural Record:* "if we may not speak of a cathedral, in this case, we surely possess the metropolitan church."[413]

The monumentality of the public buildings and the splendor of the luxury apartment houses on Central Park West combined to give the avenue a character far different than had once been expected. Its social cachet never successfully rivalled that of patrician Fifth Avenue, but the street's phalanx of upper-middle-class apartments nonetheless created a far more coherent streetwall and a theatrical backdrop for Central Park. In the late 1920s, Central Park West flowered briefly for a final time with the construction of a series of twin-towered skyscraper apartments with romantic silhouettes which became a quintessential part of the New York skyline. The skyscraper apartments completed the metamorphosis of the West End from a suburban enclave into a richer and more heterogeneous urban neighborhood. Lewis Mumford has written of the West End's transformation from a quarter dominated by rowhouses and villas: "Within twenty years this domestic loss was written off by the building of a great palisade of apartment houses for a less choosy economic group; and within another thirty years scarcely a vestige of these suburban palaces remained on Riverside Drive: one of a hundred examples that bear witness to the swift tempo of construction and destruction that has characterized my native city. If someone were to ask me now for directions in the neighborhoods where I lived the first twenty-five years of my life, I could only say, with a helpless smile: 'I'm a stranger here myself.' New Yorkers over fifty are all Rip Van Winkles."[414]

Morningside Heights
We are too eclectic to evolve an academic scheme like the Place de la Concorde, and we are too evilly circumstanced by the rapid development of our cities and the high values of land to lay out in leisurely extravagance the groundwork for a stupendous square like that of San Marco. But we have the basis for as interesting a future as either line of departure could promise . . . in New York at that point in the city where the new Cathedral of Saint John the Divine will soon break the horizon in close company with St. Luke's Hospital and the buildings of Columbia College. We know how to work in the spirit of monumental art, and that means everything. Royal Cortissoz, "Landmarks of Manhattan," Scribner's 18 (November 1895): 531-44.

The name Morningside was one of Frederick Law Olmsted's most felicitous inventions. Olmsted and Calvert Vaux first planned Morningside Park in 1873, but its construction was delayed until 1887.[415] Like Riverside Park, its creation was a result of the intractability of the city grid. The rocky escarpment facing east as it rose above the populous flatlands of Harlem was useless to developers, and its interruption of cross streets defined the area between the two parks, from 110th Street to the Harlem Valley at 125th Street, as a distinct entity. The area's growth was hampered by the lack of public transportation. The Ninth Avenue El, which opened in 1880 and brought the West End to its first flowering, veered eastward at 110th Street before resuming its northward route towards Harlem at Eighth Avenue, and left the Heights comparatively isolated.

Morningside Heights was the site of the Bloomingdale Insane Asylum and the Leake & Watts Orphanage, whose presence at once determined the area's institutional character and prevented further development. The asylum had twice resisted public pressure to relinquish its fifty-acre grounds: in 1880 when Ulysses S. Grant chaired a committee to organize a World's Fair to be held three years later, and in 1888 when New York City sought to host the World's Columbian Exposition of 1892.[416]

In 1889, however, the asylum began to sell off its properties in preparation for its eventual move to more spacious quarters in White Plains.[417] Lots between Broadway and Amsterdam Avenue from 112th to 114th streets were bought by speculators who ultimately erected rowhouses and apartment buildings. Two years earlier, in 1887, the Cathedral of St. John the Divine had announced its purchase of the former site of the orphanage, three full blocks on Morningside Drive between 110th and 113th streets. In 1892, St. Luke's Hospital acquired the block north of the cathedral's site, and Columbia College purchased the asylum grounds between Broadway and Amsterdam Avenue from 116th to 120th streets. Columbia's move to the Heights was eventually "the largest single factor . . . in promoting private real estate and building activity on the plateau."[418] But at first its influence was more sharply felt in the related institutions which were attracted to the Heights: Teachers College bought the block north of Columbia in 1892 and a year later affiliated with Columbia, and Barnard College purchased a site directly west of Columbia in 1896.

By 1897, when the first set of Morningside's new institutions was securely in place, the *Real Estate Record and Guide* noted its transformation from a region "practically empty of houses into an extraordinary nucleus of institutional buildings that classical New Yorkers like to term their acropolis."[419] The concentration of cultural and educational facilities on the "acropolis" reflected both the trend toward institutional consolidation which characterized the Composite Era and the city's long established pattern of migratory growth. It also represented a deliberate attempt to create a monumental quarter of the city along the lines of Vienna's Ringstrasse or London's Kensington Museums site. If Morningside never achieved the cogency of its European models, the reason lay in large part in the artificiality of the attempt, which sought to divorce the quarter from the messy vitality of the city downtown and its democratic exploitation of economic forces. Morningside's first monuments rose in isolated splendor, confronting one another across unpopulated fields, but within twenty years the growth of the city's residential section had enveloped them with apartment buildings.

The construction of the Cathedral of St. John the Divine brought into sharp focus the shift of values between the Cosmopolitan and Composite eras. The project was first broached by Bishop Horatio Potter in 1872, but lay dormant until he was succeeded by his nephew, Henry C. Potter, who saw it as an opportunity to build an American Westminster Abbey—a monument of the metropolis and the entire nation.[420] Potter's vision immediately caught the imagination of the public, despite doubts as to the continuing validity of a cathedral as a religious expression in the modern age. In 1885, Marianna Griswold van Rensselaer observed: "It would be impossible, in this day and land, to build a cathedral that should be such in more than name, that should have the actual, not to speak of the relative, importance of the cathedrals of old—almost as impossible as undesirable. . . . On our soil, would not such a cathedral be an anachronism? We have learned to glorify God in other ways."[421] But a correspondent to the *Real Estate Record and Guide* noted that the idea of a nondenominational monument held wide appeal: "Many people doubt the pressing necessity for the Cathedral from a religious point of view, and it was because Bishop Potter dwelt so strongly on this dual view of the building that his appeal was so well received by all denominations."[422]

The cathedral was also to serve as an ecclesiastical response to the burgeoning scale and luxury of the Cosmopolitan Era. Potter believed that "even the temporary housing of people . . . in huge caravanseries where the marble halls and corridors, the frescos and hangings, and ornaments of every kind, has educated men and women to impatience with modest surroundings, to extravagance, and to wanton and reckless living. . . . But as yet religion waits for its worthy expression in material form."[423]

Two issues were immediately perceived as critical: the new cathedral's site and its style. The first was swiftly resolved, and widely approved, despite some agitation to build in Central Park.[424] Unlike the small city block between Madison and Fifth avenues on which St. Patrick's had been built, the site was extensive enough to allow a church comparable in magnitude to those of Europe. Far removed from the northern edge of the developed city, its location was seen as a far-sighted decision that would prove itself in the years to come. Furthermore, the site's topography was magnificent: a high, rocky outcropping that crowned the cliffs of Morningside Park and offered unobstructed views of the city and its rivers. Its prominence stimulated the project's

A 1908 aerial perspective by H.M. Pettit, looking south, showing Morningside Heights as it would look with a number of its major building projects completed. In the lower left corner are the I.R.T. subway tracks coming above ground at Broadway and 122nd Street. Above them is William A. Potter's Teachers College (1892), with Howells & Stokes's Horace Mann School (1901) on Broadway between 120th and 121st streets. The Columbia University campus is shown with its 1903 revised masterplan complete. Beyond Columbia, the dome of Ernest Flagg's St. Luke's Hospital (1892-96) is visible at 113th Street between Morningside Drive and Amsterdam Avenue. Directly to its south, St. John the Divine is rendered as completed to the designs of Heins & LaFarge. In the center middleground is Charles Rich's unexecuted 1904 masterplan for Barnard College, with Riverside Park extended eastward to Claremont Avenue. At the right, John Duncan's Grant's Tomb (1897) crowns Riverside Drive; above it is Pettit's own design for Columbia Stadium on the Hudson River, and in the far distance Gustav Lindenthal's 1891 project for the Hudson River Bridge. CU

supporters to imagine a boldly silhouetted structure facing south towards an as yet largely ground-hugging city, commanding its skyline as St. Paul's did that of London. Visible from New York Bay and the flatlands of New Jersey, it would serve to "mark the seat of civilization,"[425] an early premonition of Morningside's destiny as an acropolis of learning.

The matter of style, though, was vexing from the first. Many professionals and observers advocated a Gothic design, but Bishop Potter felt that the cathedral called for a more freely conceived, astylar design divorced from any single specific prototype yet sufficiently diverse in its associations to reflect an ecumenical ideal.[426] St. John the Divine would thus stand in sharp contrast to the specifically Roman Catholic, French Gothic forms of St. Patrick's Cathedral and the slightly less precise Orientalism of the synagogues.

The difficulty of the problem produced a widespread demand that the architect be chosen by competition. In the spring of 1888 a competition was announced which paid fourteen firms to participate but which other architects might also enter.[427] Four firms were selected out of the sixty-six entries in May 1889 to further develop their proposals for resubmission in February 1890: Potter & Robertson; William Halsey Wood; George Martin Huss (in association with John H. Buck); and Heins & LaFarge.[428] Potter, Robertson and Buck were established practitioners, but the others were young, inexperienced and comparatively unknown, leading many architects to question the failure to choose well-known entrants such as Richard Morris Hunt; Richard M. Upjohn; McKim, Mead & White; and Carrère & Hastings from among those invited to enter.[429] Others suggested that Potter & Robertson, the only finalists with established reputations for ecclesiastical architecture, had been chosen because William Appleton Potter was the Bishop's half-brother, and predicted that their scheme was sure to win the final commission.[430] The suggestions of impropriety were fueled by the fact that in March 1889, just two months earlier, William Potter had won the competition for the Episcopal Diocese's St. Agnes Chapel on West Ninety-second Street.[431]

The controversy brought demands for a public exhibition of all the entries, but the trustees had pledged not to exhibit the schemes unless all the competitors agreed. In October 1889, with the second stage of the competition still in process, some of the unselected architects broke the agreement by releasing their designs to the press.[432] The following year, thirty-three schemes were exhibited at the Fifth Annual Exhibition of the Architectural League, further heightening the debate.[433] The *Real Estate Record and Guide* expressed an opinion that was widespread at the time of the second competition: "Not one of the drawings is sufficiently superior to the others to enable one to feel that here, in truth, is the Cathedral of St. John the Divine. Neither would one feel in choosing one that others equally as good have not been passed over. More positive results than these should have been obtained in an undertaking of this magnitude."[434]

Examined together, the unpremiated entries and revised submissions of the four finalists offer compelling testimony to what may now be seen as the free spirit of the era, but to many at the time that freedom seemed chaotic. The competition afforded a new generation of young architects an opportunity to design a religious monument free of the constraints of Ruskinian morality which had suffused ecclesiastical architecture in the High Victorian era. Many of the designs provided a vast unobstructed crossing to accommodate a large congregation within hearing distance of the preacher, and elaborated this motif with a precipitously tall tower. In part this reflected the influence of the massing of Richardson's Trinity Church and his unexecuted project for the Albany Cathedral, but the predilection towards mammoth size and vertical proportions led the visiting English architect, Alexander Graham, to doubt "whether national religious sentiment, rather than a craving for a tall cathedral by a people of everyday tall ideas, was the underlying motif in this undertaking."[435]

Nevertheless, the range of proposals was wide. Many of the submissions used English Gothic themes as references to Episcopal traditions, but few did so in an archaeological spirit. Huss & Buck's scheme was among the most stylistically correct entries: its horizontal nave and choir and much of the detail were based on Salisbury Cathedral, but the facade was more French, and the central tower was inflated to a metropolitan scale.[436]

Potter & Robertson's scheme was a more inventive and successful synthesis.[437] Although Gothic in spirit, the scheme employed Romanesque round arches, most spectacularly in a monumentally scaled portico which Schuyler found superior to its prototype, the triple arched portal of Peterborough Cathedral.[438] The absence of towers at the entrance front allowed those at the crossing to provide an almost overwhelming climax to the scheme. Rather than attempting to erect a lantern over the crossing, Potter created a square, vaulted space the full width of the building, inspired by the Cathedral at Gerona, Spain. The vault's weight was buttressed by four towers at its corners. As Schuyler reflected in 1909, Potter's scheme "noted or 'connoted' a very impressive general conception. That quartet of spires would have crowned Morningside Heights very grandly."[439]

William Halsey Wood's entry was the most romantic and eclectic of all the entries. The most extreme example of the Cosmopolitan approach to design, it was reportedly Bishop Potter's favorite.[440] "This fantasia was a melange, if you choose a potpourri, of elements taken from everywhere, from the wings of the front, apparently suggested by Bernini's colonnade at St. Peter's, to the slim towers at the rear, apparently suggested by the minarets of the Cairene mosques," a critic wrote in the *Architectural Record*. "The architecture is not only Gothic, but is nearly as much Mahometan as Christian."[441] The *Real Estate Record and Guide* was more scathing, pronouncing that the scheme "possesses the singular merit of representing a building that is like nothing in heaven above, in the earth beneath, or the water under the earth, and it might therefore without violating the Decalogue serve as an object of worship as well as a place to worship in. It is unnecessary to describe this vast pile, with its 'tower-dome-spire,' its towers, turrets, porches and general immensity."[442]

Wood defended his scheme as a response to both the increasingly vertical cityscape of New York and the ecumenicism of the program: "The new and difficult element I recognize is one of altitude. Under the crush of population and rapidly increasing value of land, construction is driven upward with an irresistible impulse, and with a growing force and daring. . . . Something that should bind past and present in one, that should incorporate the ethnic types of civilization, the pyramid of Egypt, the circle that girdles the landscape, the square of the ancient Temple, the oblong of the Basilica, the Cross of Basilica Church and Cathedral, even the dome itself—type of over-reaching heavens—why should not each and all of these ancient, historic types meet in a spirit of devout eclecticism."[443]

Carrère & Hastings submitted one of the few Classical entries.[444] It was as eclectic as Wood's design, but in response to Bishop Potter's desire for a "modern" cathedral, it drew upon the entire repertoire of Classicism to describe an inherited cultural legacy rather than a specific religious tradition. The architects' description was prophetic for many of the Classical churches soon to be built in Composite New York: "under the general law of development, church-life and church-architecture have moved together in mutual sympathy and correspondence. In modern times the Church has been advancing in its life by keeping what was good in the Reformation, and by correcting its excesses. It has been felt that she should do the same in her architecture. She should strip the Renaissance of its excesses, and keep what is good in it as the basis for an advance to something better. If the church would go back to the medieval in architecture, she must go back to the medieval in life, for she must live as she builds and build as she lives." Their scheme thus strove to "keep the character of the Basilican or first forms of a house of God, and to keep the lofty spirit of the Gothic, but to accept the real advance of the Renaissance. . . . For this reason the 'Transition Renaissance' has been adopted."[445] The attenuated, vertical proportions sought to adapt ecclesiastical motifs to the new context of a city of skyscrapers, while the theatrical system of cascading staircases and ramps at the south facade was among the most successful solutions to the steeply sloping site.

The *American Architect and Building News* was impressed by Carrère & Hastings's proposal:

Cathedral of St. John the Divine competition entry, north side of 110th Street between Morningside Drive and Amsterdam Avenue. Potter & Robertson, 1889. Perspective view from the southeast. CU

[it] must certainly be placed first as a work of art, although we cannot avoid a certain astonishment that any New York architects should have imagined that such an arrangement would commend itself to the Trustees of a Protestant Episcopal Church in this country. The very plan, so masterly in the skill with which a complex group of parts is combined into what appears to be a simple, though rich and artistic scheme, is redolent of incense, and, to the architect, the rows of lateral chapels, and the imposing arrangement of the choir, suggest the clusters of sparkling candles, and the varied life and color of a great Roman Catholic Church, far more than Protestant rectitude and sobriety.[446]

The commission was awarded to Heins & LaFarge in June 1891. Schuyler later observed that of the four entries by Wood, Huss & Buck, Potter & Robertson and Heins & LaFarge, "the real contest was between [Potter & Robertson's scheme] . . . and the design finally selected, the other two being the tamest and wildest of the competition and being for these opposite reasons in effect debarred."[447] Potter & Robertson's design was criticized for the indirect lighting of its central square, which had no overhead lantern, but more importantly, the implication of nepotism led Bishop Potter to actively oppose his half-brother's scheme.[448] Heins & LaFarge's scheme was described as "a domical church in a Gothic shell"; in their own words the interior followed "the architectural tradition of the early Church, the exterior following the architectural traditions of the Church of England."[449] Abjuring any specific prototype, the exterior was characterized by "a gradually increasing verticality of composition proceeding from the chancel toward the facade and culminating in the latter in a strongly marked predominance of vertical lines, thus giving a Norman Romanesque character to the chancel growing into Gothic in the facade."[450] The design was thus meant to capture some of the character of European cathedrals which, executed over long periods of time, contained elements of various styles. Yet the architects displayed a desire to create an organized work of architecture by suggesting a legible process of evolution. From the start they planned to employ new technology: the interior domes and vaults, reminiscent of the Byzantine influenced churches of St. Mark's in Venice or St. Front in Périgueux, were to be constructed with the modern Guastavino tile system.[451]

Cathedral of St. John the Divine competition entry, north side of 110th Street between Morningside Drive and Amsterdam Avenue. Heins & LaFarge, 1889. Perspective view from the southeast. NYHS

Shortly after the competition was decided, Heins & LaFarge's scheme was compromised when the cathedral trustees chose to revert to standard ecclesiastical orientation and face the church west rather than south, forever depriving the building of its intended relationship to the city. Terminating the axis of 112th Street, a minor side street only two blocks long, the cathedral had something of the air of an overscaled parish church, while from below Morningside Park the cathedral's *chevet* crowned the cliff less dramatically than would its long flank.

The magnitude of the project and the difficult site conditions, which required the construction of vast foundations and a crypt, caused the building of St. John the Divine to drag on over a period of decades. By 1911, when the cathedral was formally dedicated, only the choir, the structural armature of the crossing and the vast "temporary" dome over it were complete. Meanwhile, the passage of time had rendered Heins & LaFarge's associationally evocative synthesis of historical forms increasingly at odds with the Composite Era's predilection for stylistic purity. This was despite Heins & LaFarge's revisions in the course of construction, designed to bring the Byzantine interior more into harmony with its Gothic exterior. The cathedral's domes were largely replaced by ribbed vaults, and tracery in the windows was designed in English Perpendicular style. As the original design fell victim to a more conservative stylistic purity, so too did the notion of the cathedral as an ecumenical monument: Heins & LaFarge's revisions expressed "the desire to Anglicanize as much as might be."[452]

Heins died in 1907, and four years later the trustees took advantage of a clause in their contract which allowed them to hire a new architect if either partner should die; Ralph Adams Cram was brought in as consulting architect. The *Architectural Record* observed that Heins & LaFarge's completed choir, "such as it is . . . has been generally acclaimed as an impressive and most interesting building, an architectural success. The only adverse criticism it has encountered in public has been that which begged the entire question involved in the building by denouncing it for not being the 'English Gothic' which, one may say it expertly disclaimed any intention of being, from the point of view of the purists who berated it. The basis of this criticism is the cheerful assumption that every departure from 'Anglican-

Left: Home for Old Men and Aged Couples, northwest corner of Amsterdam Avenue and 112th Street. Cady, Berg & See, 1897. Center: St. Luke's Hospital, north side of 113th Street between Morningside Drive and Amsterdam Avenue, Ernest Flagg, 1892-96. Right: Cathedral of St. John the Divine, east side of Amsterdam Avenue at 112th Street, Heins & LaFarge, 1889-1911. A view showing one of the arches of the cathedral crossing in construction. MCNY

ism' in the design . . . is a proof of ignorance or bad faith."[453]

Ironically, Cram based his revisions on French precedents, proposing a French Gothic nave and west facade which were stylistically inappropriate. Not only had French Gothic and its associations been rejected in the 1889 competition but it was incapable of synthesis with Heins & LaFarge's choir:[454] the *Architectural Record* felt that Cram's work showed "an entire lack of sympathy with what has thus far been done on Morningside Heights."[455] Construction of Cram's designs for St. John the Divine did not begin until the dawn of the Age of Convenience, but their antiquarianism was a product of the Composite Era. The mammoth project was an anachronism in the pragmatic period which followed the war, when ecclesiastical projects such as Bertram Grosvenor Goodhue's proposed Convocational and Office Building were more typically given metropolitan scale through the hybridization of building types.

St. John the Divine was but one of a trio of institutional buildings erected on the Heights by the Episcopal Diocese. In the hope of creating an appropriately institutional context for the cathedral, the diocese flanked it with St. Luke's Hospital (1892-96) and the Home for Old Men and Aged Couples (1896). The artistic ferment of the cathedral competition was also evident in the strongly contrasting styles of the institutions which clustered around it.

St. Luke's had been located on West Fifty-fourth Street and Fifth Avenue since 1858, but by the 1890s its quarters were technologically outmoded and incapable of expansion.[456] In 1892, the trustees of the hospital paid five architectural firms to compete for the design of the new building: Renwick, Aspinwall & Renwick; George E. Harney; Charles W. Clinton; James Brown Lord; and Heins & LaFarge (who had prepared the program and outline specifications for the competition).[457] The competition was also open to any architect who cared to enter; with building activity at a lull, a total of eighty entries were received. Lord's entry was notable for its attempt to harmonize with the cathedral.[458] It was designed in a sympathetic English Gothic style, with the administration building placed at the western end of the site and surmounted by a symbolic belfry. Its wards, however, were strung out inefficiently along 113th Street. The trustees chose, by virtue of its superior functional planning, the design of the young Ernest Flagg, who had started his practice only a year before.[459]

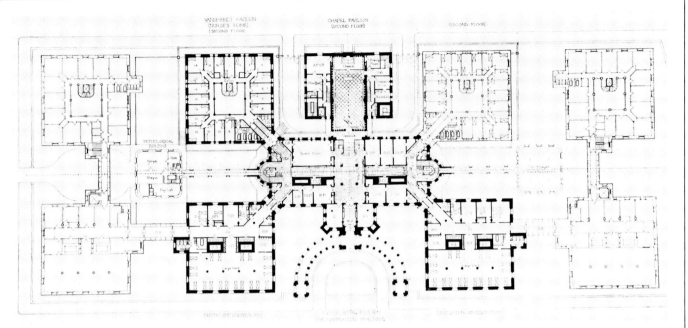

St. Luke's Hospital, north side of 113th Street between Morningside Drive and Amsterdam Avenue. Ernest Flagg, 1892-96. Plan of ground floor with first phase of construction shown in black. CU

Flagg's design, as executed in 1896, accommodated ten pavilions on the constricted site, insuring light and ventilation to the wards.[460] The southern pavilions contained the wards, and were linked by open arcades which served as "fresh air cutoffs," an inspired response to the need to isolate possible infection before the development of more sophisticated mechanical ventilation systems. Two of the northern pavilions contained the nurses' quarters. In each the rooms were grouped around a central glazed courtyard which contained a curvilinear iron staircase and an open cage elevator. For sanitary reasons, the interior spaces were kept bare throughout with no moldings and rounded corners wherever possible. An elaborate system of flues assured the continuous movement of air in both summer and winter.

Flagg's elevations were Modern French interpretations of the French Renaissance. Although indebted to the Palais de Luxembourg in Paris, they brilliantly monumentalized mundane functions. The ventilating shafts were disguised as heroically scaled chimneys, the vertically stacked toilets were expressed as turrets in the corner angles, and the central dome over the administration wing contained the operating theater. Despite the undeniable brio of Flagg's design, St. Luke's failed to establish a convincing relationship to St. John the Divine. In part this was due to the revised siting of the cathedral, which lay too close to the northern edge of its lot, and to the rigidly neutral street grid which made the creation of an architectural ensemble difficult to achieve. Flagg's Modern French Classicism also made an abrupt, if vivid, juxtaposition to Heins & LaFarge's emotive eclecticism.

St. John the Divine and St. Luke's were joined in 1896 by the Home for Old Men and Aged Couples by Cady, Berg & See. Standing on the northwest corner of Amsterdam Avenue and 112th Street, across the street from the cathedral's main entrance, it was a domestically scaled, restrained essay in Victorian Gothic which was stylistically sympathetic to the cathedral. But it was immediately evident that the opportunity for an architectural ensemble had been lost. "The group of buildings in various styles that is taking form at the Morningside Heights promises to make that portion of the city extremely interesting," the *Architectural Review* wrote in 1898. "We cannot but wish that these buildings had been considered in relation to one another, not

St. Luke's Hospital, north side of 113th Street between Morningside Drive and Amsterdam Avenue. Ernest Flagg, 1892-96. View of glazed courtyard in nurse's pavilion. MCNY

in style alone, but in some system of monumental approach. . . . St. Luke's hospital, in white and yellow, fronts the side of the new cathedral of St. John the Divine, in grey; and the street upon which it faces is an unimportant one. All this might easily have been improved—can yet be improved. The site is unsurpassed—the setting of these important buildings upon it very unsteady."[462]

The new building for the Woman's Hospital, which had been founded in 1855 as the first hospital in the world devoted solely to the treatment of women, was located directly to the south on a mid-block site between 109th and 110th streets, and continued the Classicizing French Renaissance mode of St. Luke's.[463] Formerly located on Park and Lexington avenues between Forty-ninth and Fiftieth streets, it was displaced by the enlargement of Grand Central Terminal. The new facility was designed by Allen & Collens in 1904 and completed in 1906. A U-shaped building sheltering a courtyard which opened to the south, its chief distinctions were technological. Allen & Collens explored advanced systems of mechanical ventilation and pioneered new strategies for achieving the flexibility demanded by a rapidly developing technology. A one-foot-wide air space in the outer wall contained all the plumbing, heating and ventilating pipes, as well as electrical conduits and other mechanical services; kitchen and laundry spaces were placed in the attic so that heat and odors could be carried away without affecting the hospital.

Columbia and Teachers College purchased their adjacent sites on Morningside in early 1892, anticipating their formal affiliation by a year. The Teachers College campus was donated by George W. Vanderbilt, a trustee, and designed in a retardataire form of the High-Victorian Gothic by William A. Potter, a former chairman of its Board of Managers.[464] The original buildings were located on a mid-block site between Broadway and Amsterdam Avenue, from 120th to 121st streets. Potter's plans called for three connected buildings surrounding a small courtyard. The picturesque composition and the ragged perimeter created an ambiguous relationship with the surrounding streets. Two buildings were initially constructed: the Main Building, the principal classroom and administrative facility, and Macy Hall, which was devoted to disciplines of arts and crafts only then being introduced into school curricula. A third building, Milbank Memorial Hall, was added in 1897. In 1901 Howells & Stokes rebuilt the Horace Mann School, which the college used for training, on Broadway between 120th and 121st streets. Three years later, Parish & Schroeder designed Thompson Memorial Hall on 121st Street, connecting the school with the Main Building. These last two additions succeeded in tying the complex into the street grid while closely emulating Potter's High Victorian Gothic style. Its Gothic architecture established collegiate associations with Oxford and Cambridge, and Potter and the trustees probably expected Columbia to erect its new campus in a similar style. Ironically, however, Charles Follen McKim was about to transform Columbia into the city's greatest monument of the American Renaissance.

Columbia's previous campus, like Potter's Teachers College, had reflected the ideals of the Cosmopolitan Era.[465] Located on East Forty-ninth Street between Park and Madison avenues, it was a loosely organized cluster of buildings surrounding a garden. Most of the buildings were designed by Charles Coolidge Haight in a sober Ruskinian Gothic which related both to the neighboring St. Patrick's Cathedral and the Oxbridge tradition. Unlike the Gothic of the English universities, however, Haight's campus achieved no sense of collective expression; it lacked a grand open court or a particularly strong attitude toward the block pattern of the city. Nonetheless, its very randomness seemed to express a romantic, introverted conception of scholarship divorced from the public life of the city. As Schuyler observed, "The air of seclusion and repose has been as completely attained on a bustling New York avenue as in the sleepiest of university towns."[466]

Since the 1860s the college had added affiliated professional schools and pre-professional programs, but as Schuyler succinctly put it: "Columbia waned while New York waxed."[467] By 1890, when Haight's midtown campus had been outgrown, its cloistral associations were no longer attractive. Seth Low, a former mayor of Brooklyn and future mayor of Greater New York, was elected president of the college in 1890, and masterminded both its move to

Columbia University, Broadway and Amsterdam Avenue between 114th and 120th streets. McKim, Mead & White, 1893-1913. A view from the southwest, showing, in center, Arnold W. Brunner's School of Mines (1904) and, right of center, McKim's Low Library (1895-98) and the tiled dome of Howells & Stokes's St. Paul's Chapel (1907). In the center foreground is Heins & LaFarge's 116th Street I.R.T. Subway Kiosk; north of Columbia is the Teachers College Campus. NYHS

Morningside Heights and its simultaneous transformation into a university. "That a man of the character and training of Mr. Seth Low has been placed at the head of New York's leading educational institution is a matter of much more than local significance," the *Century* said in 1890. "President Low has an inspiring opportunity, in his new position, of making his mark upon this community and the country at large. Those who have pondered on the needs of New York have dreamed of a time—which Mr. Low can, and we believe will, do much to hasten—when Columbia College will be the center, and our various museums, libraries, and other institutions more or less formal and official parts, of 'the great metropolitan university.'"[468]

In 1892, the college trustees invited Richard Morris Hunt, Charles Follen McKim and Charles Coolidge Haight to serve as a commission, advised by Professors William Robert Ware and William P. Trowbridge, to lay out the new campus on the former site of the Bloomingdale Asylum, from 116th to 120th streets between Broadway and Amsterdam Avenue.[469] The three architects were unable to agree on a joint proposal, and in April of 1893 each submitted an independent scheme. Haight and Hunt favored cloistral plans with continuous buildings defining secluded open spaces. Haight located the entrance on the east and favored a continuation of the Collegiate Gothic tradition. Hunt, who suggested an entrance at the west, proposed "facades preferably of stone, as being more monumental, say, in the Italian Renaissance style."[470] McKim favored a southern approach leading to "two separate planes or platforms . . . the southern occupying about two blocks of the whole area, the northern one about one third . . . 15 feet or so below the other . . . [with elevations of] pure classical forms, as expressing in the simplest and most monumental ways the purposes to which the buildings are devoted."[471]

Unable to decide among the alternatives, the trustees asked Frederick Law Olmsted to collaborate on a proposal that would combine "the large accommodation and open external courts of Mr. Hunt's scheme, and the practical convenience and ample provision for lecture rooms shown in Mr. Haight's, with the symmetry and monumental disposition of Mr. McKim's."[472] The new plan was for a campus entered from the south and comprised of continuously linked buildings opening around smaller courts at the edges.

None of the architects were willing to work on the basis of the proposal by Ware and Olmsted, but they agreed to collaborate on a set of guidelines for the selection of an architect. Influenced by the Ware and Olmsted plan and the spirit of McKim's proposal, these guidelines set in motion the campus design ultimately built. Especially significant was the suggestion that the campus be composed of individual buildings or "pavilions" instead of the continuous one initially proposed by all three architects—a practical recognition of the fact that the plan would not be realized at once. In addition, it was noted that "few architects today can express themselves with fluency in the Gothic . . . [a] larger and increasing number of architects have devoted themselves" to Classicism which "will appeal most strongly to secure an imposing architectural effect." Any attempt at Gothic was seen as an imitation of "the English universities, and shall thereby suggest a comparison which can scarcely fail to be unfavorable to us."[473]

After extensive politicking, McKim was hired in December 1893 and his masterplan approved in 1894.[474] The choice of McKim depended more on questions of image than practicality. His solution for the steeply sloping site was to create two terraces; the higher one dominated by the library in the center of a south-facing quadrangle, the lower on the north left as a garden. The classroom buildings were located in two rings along the avenues, tying the campus to the street grid while establishing a university precinct with a distinct ambience. The plan was thus, as the committee had requested, "appropriate to the municipal character of the situation,"[475] although others argued that the neighborhood was so isolated from the path of the city's development that Morningside could easily have become a cloistered precinct.[476] The orientation of the complex towards the south acknowledged a relationship with the public life of the city, while McKim's monumental Classicism established a deeper connection with the public realm. Its carefully modulated ensemble represented in miniature form the urban ideals of the City Beautiful movement.

Following immediately upon the public success of the

Columbia University, Broadway and Amsterdam Avenue between 114th and 120th streets. McKim, Mead & White, 1893–1913. A view from 116th Street showing McKim's Low Library and the dome of Howells & Stokes's St. Paul's Chapel. MCNY

Columbia University, Broadway and Amsterdam Avenue between 114th and 120th streets. McKim, Mead & White, 1893–1913. Low Library. McKim, Mead & White, 1895–98. View of the reading room. CU

World's Columbian Exposition, the Columbia campus was perhaps the clearest permanent expression of the American Renaissance, rendering lithic the plaster and lath scenography of Chicago. Schuyler regretted the complete obliteration of the Gothic architectural traditions of Columbia: "Anglicisms supplied precisely what had for generations been recognized as the most appropriate and attractive architecture for a place of education for English-speaking mankind."[477] Yet McKim's design must also be seen as an evocation of Columbia's more distant heritage. The hybrid and vernacular Classicism looked back to pre-industrial America and recalled Columbia's colonial status as King's College. Through the invocation of the Classical ideal, seen in its purest form in the library and in more compromised versions in the classroom buildings, McKim responded to both contemporary conditions and historical continuity.

The principal focus of McKim's plan was the Low Library, constructed with Seth Low's gift of one million dollars, reportedly a third of his fortune, as a monument to his father. Despite its grandeur, the rigidly planned building never functioned successfully as a working library, as the compartmentalized organization conflicted with the rapid and uneven expansion of the different departments within the collection. Schuyler mockingly observed that a French friend of his may well have been correct that Low was "a library de luxe and not de books."[478]

The library's design revealed McKim's study of recent precedents including Smithmeyer & Pelz's Library of Congress (whose more specifically Classical portions were the work of Edward Pearce Casey), Hunt's Administration Building at the World's Columbian Exposition and John Duncan's Grant's Tomb, each of which contributed to a synthesis expressive of the building's combined functions of library, administration building and memorial. The *parti* also belonged to a tradition extending from Serlio to Ledoux and countless proposals for the Prix de Rome.[479] By associating the library's design with these well known precedents, McKim was able to place Columbia in a public context. Yet the individual references were entirely synthesized in the new building at the heart of an ensemble without any direct parallel. Low Library's chaste Classicism, correctness and play of large masses contrasted with the unarticulated, stolidly rectangular brick and stone classroom buildings with their debased Italo-French details.[480] Before it, graced by two fountains and Daniel Chester French's statue of *Alma Mater,* the plaza was conceived of as a significant break in the wall of buildings expected to line both sides of 116th Street, a wide cross-town street like Thirty-fourth or Forty-second streets downtown. Iron gates set between stone pylons were to have continued the line of the street and marked the transition to the academic precinct. The library, seen diagonally at this point, would have loomed up powerfully, the subtle curvature of the plaza steps correcting normal perspectival distortion and giving it a more active sculptural presence. Although side staircases led to the more private realm of the campus, the plaza steps were so broad and shallow that they could be traversed easily only on the diagonal, guiding the visitor almost inexorably through the outer portico and vestibule into the domed main reading room of the library. As the *New York Times* observed in 1897, the terraces and library together formed "one great approach of stone, broken here and there, but unmistakably leading to an object, and the object worthy of the approach."[481]

Royal Cortissoz was among the first critics to acclaim the campus as a landmark, writing in 1895, when construction was still underway: "It is apparent . . . that the buildings will continue, from 110th Street to 120th Street, to establish a special and monumental standard for that part of New York . . . the essential character of the streets west of Morningside Park is bound to be fixed by the presence of such monuments." Cortissoz saw the Columbia campus as part of a new monumental quarter of the city, predicting that "the friction of daily life will smooth off the roughness and vulgarities" of something so grand and so new, and replace them with "the gentle offices of culture. . . . Modifying slowly but surely all the characteristics of the vicinity, the buildings at Morningside Park [will] do more than anything we have yet brought forth to place the Metropolis on a level with the capital cities of the Old World. In one way we shall surpass Haussman, though at times we may suffer from the absence of that power to pull down as well as to

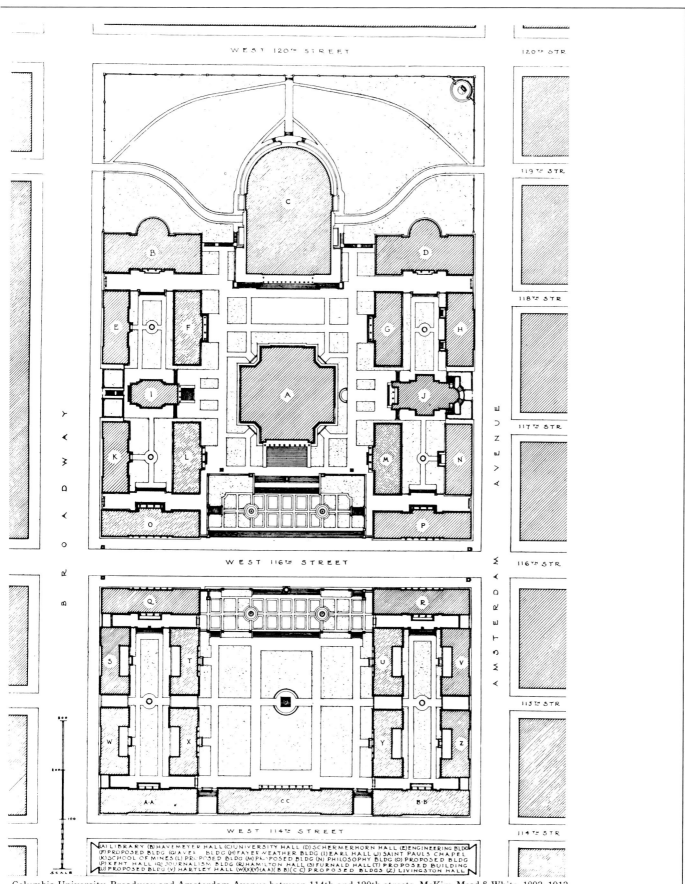

Columbia University, Broadway and Amsterdam Avenue between 114th and 120th streets. McKim, Mead & White, 1893-1913. The top of the plan represents the original 1893 masterplan; the lower half was added in 1903. CU

Columbia University, Broadway and Amsterdam Avenue between 114th and 120th streets. McKim, Mead & White, 1893–1913. St. Paul's Chapel. Howells & Stokes, 1907. View from the northwest. MCNY

Columbia University, Broadway and Amsterdam Avenue between 114th and 120th streets. McKim, Mead & White, 1893–1913. St. Paul's Chapel. Howells & Stokes, 1907. View of crossing and chancel. NYHS

build up, which was one of the chief sources of his success. We shall have the knowledge that while our picturesque Renaissance uptown is largely a matter of topography, of architecture, it springs first and last from the deep inner growth of the people."[482]

But in 1910, when the library, the plaza and some of the classroom buildings were complete, Montgomery Schuyler was less impressed. He was particularly critical of the "homelier and more idiomatic handling" of the classroom buildings, which he regarded as "a contradiction in terms. Brick fronts simply do not become specimens of classical architecture because you plaster little porticoes against them, nor because you erect them on Cyclopean bases of huge slabs of pink granite, with a swaggering half-round by way of base moulding, as the badge of your 'style.' . . . The group of Columbia, in so far as it is carrying out of the special intention, is a failure. One might take it for a hospital, for a group of official buildings, for almost anything but what it is. You may admit that it is 'municipal.' You cannot possibly maintain that it is 'collegiate.'"[483]

In the design of two buildings placed on the cross axis of the library McKim attempted to synthesize the uncompromising Classicism of the library and the more vernacular character of the classroom buildings. Earl Hall, a student center on the west side of Low Library, combined the centralized form of a Renaissance church with a Greek temple front.[484] Its counterpart across the campus, St. Paul's Chapel, was designed by Howells & Stokes; the chapel and Arnold W. Brunner's School of Mines were the only buildings on the original campus not designed by McKim.[485] Earl Hall was rather cheaply built and crudely detailed, but St. Paul's was a finely crafted, intricately conceived example of brick architecture that took full advantage of the Guastavino vaulting systems to support a great dome without steel construction, thereby achieving a sense of traditional weight without resorting to excessive structure. A hybrid mixture of Byzantine and Renaissance motifs, St. Paul's was a departure from the secular character of the campus which managed not to appear eccentric or to violate the *parti* established by Earl Hall.

The chapel was the only building on the campus to win Schuyler's affections: "the one building . . . which shows an earnest and intelligent and most interesting effort to combine the effects of what we have called the architecture of formula with those proper to the architecture of craftsmanship."[486] While Schuyler felt that the exterior suffered from the need to conform to the Greco-Roman character of the campus, he admired the way the interior captured the character of a church without explicitly resorting to the classic or Gothic styles: "The thing is so clearly and unmistakably made out of its own elements that there is not a detail which seems to have been 'lugged in.' . . . The result is that refreshing sense of reality of which we commonly have to mourn the absence. The interior is one of those rare architectural successes which, being of no style, yet unmistakably have style. . . . This interior is a distinct and rare architectural success, with an air as 'original,' as home-bred and vernacular, as that of a shingled suburban cottage."[487]

By 1914, the original campus plan was as fully developed as it was to be until after World War II. Avery Hall, containing the School of Architecture and the Avery Library, was built in 1912[488] and Kent Hall (1914) for the Law School.[489] Avery was the only one of McKim's proposed inner-row of buildings to be realized.

In 1903 the university acquired the two blocks south of 116th Street between Broadway and Amsterdam Avenue, designating them the South Field.[490] As early as 1898, President Low had recognized the need for the university to attract a more national student body than it had, but it was unable to without the construction of dormitories for which no space was provided in the original campus plan.[491] Nor had any space been provided for athletics. McKim planned for the South Field to be devoted largely to undergraduate classroom and athletic facilities and rows of dormitories along the east and west edges of the site, forming two quadrangles and a large "campus" at the center. He abandoned the diagonal orientation of the entrance plaza and made an axial approach to Low Library possible for the first time. Because the South Field was below the level of the original terraces, McKim was able to raise the new buildings on high bases and thereby produce buildings that, though taller, did not break the established cornice line. The

Barnard College, 119th Street between Broadway and Claremont Avenue. Lamb & Rich, 1895-97. Perspective view from Broadway, and plans of first and second floors of Milbank, Brinkerhoff and Fiske halls. OMH

Barnard College, Broadway and Claremont Avenue between 116th and 120th streets. Charles A. Rich, 1904. Aerial perspective view of proposed masterplan showing Teachers College and Columbia University in the background and the Riverside Park expansion in the foreground. CU

first phase of the South Field plan to be executed included two dormitories, Hartley and Livingston halls, and a classroom building, Hamilton Hall, which ran parallel to 116th Street and closed the northern end of the east quadrangle. Together with Kent Hall, its mirror opposite to the north, Hamilton Hall established the eastern "gateway" to the campus and reinforced 116th Street's function as a monumental cross axis linking Riverside Park with Morningside Park, where Jacob Wrey Mould's heroic flights of stairs cascaded from the Heights to the flats below.

In response to Columbia's refusal to admit women, Barnard College was founded in 1889. After a series of temporary accommodations it followed Columbia to Morningside in 1895, acquiring a site at 119th Street between Broadway and Claremont Avenue. Milbank, Fiske and Brinkerhoff halls were designed by Lamb & Rich as one mass which defined three sides of a courtyard.[492] Schuyler found their style "Jacobean . . . a picturesque degeneration of the Gothic . . . a mode of classic" which, by contrast with the "irrelevant grandiosity" of the adjacent Columbia campus, allowed "the expression of a place of education which is a place of residence as well as instruction" to approach the "ideal of a 'college.'"[493]

In 1904 Mrs. A.A. Anderson donated funds to extend the Barnard campus southward to 116th Street. Charles Rich sought to establish a connection with the river and prepared a masterplan which extended Riverside Park across the Drive to Claremont Avenue.[494] Rich conceived of the campus as a raised terrace open to the west, with a U-shaped complex of four new Modern French buildings dominated by a domed administration block. The library was on the south side of 119th Street. Its vaulted reading room was raised above an arcade to connect the new campus with the earlier quadrangle. All of the buildings were to be linked by intimately scaled cloisters, while the main quadrangle was to be treated as a romantic garden populated by antique statuary and architectural fragments. Its romanticism was an intensification of the studied naturalism of Olmsted's Riverside Park. Rich's masterplan was abandoned when the Claremont Avenue site was developed with apartment buildings. Barnard Hall, the principal administration and classroom building built by Brunner & Tryon in 1917, was a pallid attempt to relate to the Columbia classroom buildings.

Barnard College dormitory, west side of Amsterdam Avenue between 120th and 121st streets. Bruce Price. 1901. View from the northeast. CU

Barnard's first dormitories predated Columbia's. In 1901, before purchasing the additional land on Broadway, the college completed a massive dormitory on the west side of Amsterdam Avenue between 120th and 121st streets.[495] Designed by Bruce Price and A.M. Darroch in a castellated Gothic style which harmonized with the adjacent buildings at Teachers College, it featured deep courtyards facing east to maximize sunlight in the students' rooms. A continuous one-story base containing shops ran across the building; finished in smooth limestone, it reiterated the high base of McKim's Columbia campus across the street.

The National Academy of Design considered a formal alliance with Columbia University and planned to move to Morningside Heights, but neither arrangement materialized. Founded in 1826, the academy constructed a building in 1865, designed by Peter B. Wight, on the northwest corner of Fourth Avenue and Twenty-third Street which was perhaps the most important example of Ruskinian Gothic architecture in the United States.[496] Although known as the "American Ecole des Beaux Arts," the academy differed from the Ecole in that its instruction was largely limited to painting.[497] An affiliation with Columbia's School of Architecture was proposed in the mid-1890s reflecting the American Renaissance ideal of allied arts. The prominent muralist Will H. Low described the need to transform the institution into "what it is in name—an academy of design . . . which would comprise within its ranks men of all arts . . . standing before our public as a homogeneous whole."[498] Although many older academicians objected to any surrender of its autonomy, in 1897 the academy acquired a large site on the east side of Amsterdam Avenue between 109th and 110th streets facing the grounds of St. John the Divine. Carrère & Hastings were commissioned to design the new building, and proposed plans which focused on a glazed sculpture court indebted to Felix Duban's Palais des Etudes at the Ecole des Beaux-Arts in Paris. The academy, however, decided that the prestigious commission should be awarded through a closed competition. Although McKim, Mead & White declined their invitation, entries were submitted by: Carrère & Hastings; Babb, Cook & Willard; Edward Pearce Casey; Ernest Flagg; Henry J. Hardenbergh; and George B. Post.[499] The distinguished jury included the architects Charles F. McKim, John Galen Howard, Robert Swaine Peabody and four Academicians.

Union Theological Seminary, Broadway to Claremont Avenue between 120th and 121st streets. Allen & Collens, 1910. View from Claremont Avenue looking north. NYHS

Carrère & Hastings won the competition with a more developed version of their earlier, rejected scheme.[500] The facade was articulated as a central pavilion with an attic and hipped roof flanked by lower wings. Its rusticated base with arched windows supported a two-story blind arcade of paired Ionic columns. The galleries behind were lit by skylights, and the windowless facade served as a foil for sculpture. Flagg's entry infused similar motifs with an exuberant interpretation of neo-Grec decoration and an even more extensive use of metal and glass.[501] His plans were notable for dynamic half-level changes and the decision to incorporate the sculpture court into a processional circulation route.

Although a more central location next to the Fine Arts Society on West Fifty-seventh Street had been rejected as too costly, many members of the academy regretted the proposed move to Morningside, as the site seemed too remote to attract the public to its semi-annual exhibitions. Moreover, the academy still lacked the funds to construct a building of the magnitude called for in the competition, and a temporary building was erected on the southwest corner of the site in 1899.[502] In 1915, when negotiations with Columbia had finally broken down, the academy left Morningside for new headquarters on Fifth Avenue and Eighty-ninth Street.

The Institute of Music, located at the northeast corner of 122nd Street and Claremont Avenue and designed by Donn Barber in 1910, was far more delicately scaled than the typical Morningside building; it reflected the growing taste for a more refined and canonical form of French Classicism than the Modern French which had flourished in the late 1890s.[503] The Union Theological Seminary, founded in 1836, established a campus in 1882 on the west side of Park Avenue between Sixty-ninth and Seventieth streets, where it commissioned buildings from William A. Potter and James Brown Lord.[504] After deciding in 1907 to move to Morningside, the seminary invited four architectural firms to submit designs in an open competition for a new campus that would extend along the west side of Broadway from 120th to 122nd streets.[505] The competition was won by the Boston firm of Allen & Collens with an English Perpendicular Gothic design which evoked the collegiate architecture of Oxbridge, introducing to Morningside an atmosphere entirely opposite to that achieved by McKim on the Colum-

A ca. 1905 view looking east from the New Jersey shore toward Morningside Heights showing the original relationship of Morningside's institutions to the Hudson River. From left to right: the Riverside Drive viaduct over the Harlem Valley, Grant's Tomb, Teachers College, Barnard College, Columbia University, St. Luke's Hospital and St. John the Divine under construction. NYHS

bia campus.

Allen & Collens's original proposal had two courtyards, fulfilling the seminary's desire for a scheme that could be realized in two stages, but the final design filled the entire site with a perimeter-block building surrounding a verdant courtyard. A continuous cloister arcade on the ground level connected dormitory space at the north end of the site, a chapel at 121st Street whose tower was rather unceremoniously devoted to an infirmary, and a memorial tower prominently located at Broadway and 120th Street.

The seminary reflected the transformation of the generally accepted urban ideal which had taken place in the twenty years since the close of the Cosmopolitan Era. The perimeter block reinforced the urban fabric of the street grid and established a communal place within the courtyard. Even though the stylistic language of the seminary was Gothic, the composition and the attitude to the urban context were securely rooted in the academic traditions of the Beaux-Arts and the American Renaissance.

Allen & Collens believed "that the natural development of collegiate and ecclesiastical Gothic in England reached its climax in the Perpendicular, and that any deviation from the established forms is a new type and should go under a new name just as 'Classical Architecture' has grown into what is called 'Modern French.'" Their scholarly use of Perpendicular Gothic was a deliberate attempt to inculcate in the students a sense "of the best period of English Gothic" so that they might "work toward the betterment of ecclesiastical architecture throughout the parishes."[506]

By the turn of the century the expected completion of the I.R.T. subway sparked widespread speculation in real estate on the Heights, and it was increasingly clear that Morningside's institutions, clustered on the highest ground of the plateau rather than along its cliffs, would soon be hemmed in from both Riverside and Morningside parks by continuous walls of apartment buildings. Charles Rich's 1904 plan for the Barnard campus was the first of a series of projects which sought to relate the institutional acropolis to the riverfront, and in 1906 Architecture reported that a "movement is now on foot" to carry out Rich's proposal to extend the Park eastward to Claremont Avenue between 116th and 121st streets.[507] In the same year H.M. Pettit made a sketch proposal for a "water gate" on the river bank at 116th Street, which would complement the park extension

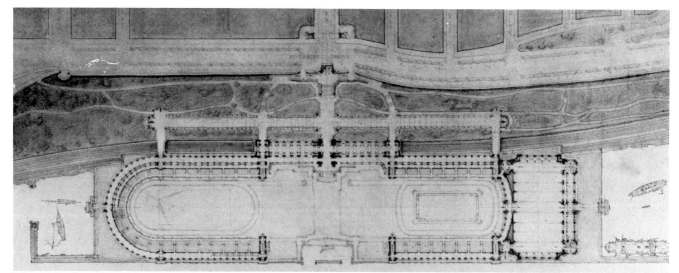

Columbia Stadium, Naval Reserve, Public Recreation Pier and Water Gate, between 112th and 120th streets on the Hudson River. Palmer & Hornbostel, 1907. Plan. CU

and serve as the city's official reception point for dignitaries visiting the city.[508] Pettit's multi-level facility included a much needed sports stadium and recreational fields for Barnard College. In 1907 Palmer & Hornbostel expanded this scheme to visionary proportions in their design for a "Columbia Stadium, Naval Reserve, Public Recreation Pier and Water Gate."[509] The project extended from 112th to 120th streets along the Hudson River. A triumphal arch and loggia on the axis of 116th Street bridged the railroad tracks and served as a monumental backdrop to a vast public plaza flanked by two stadia built over the water. Water gates at the north and south ends provided quai-side loading for large ships. Palmer & Hornbostel's Modern French facades reduced Classical vocabulary to a simplified system of panelling which suggests that they intended to explore the use of poured concrete as an inexpensive way of constructing such a vast project. The abstraction of traditional forms also lent the scheme a monumental scale commensurate with the view of the Palisades.

Of all the attempts to provide Morningside with a monumental entrance, the competition for the Robert Fulton Memorial seemed the most likely to succeed.[510] It was organized in 1909 by the Robert Fulton Memorial Association, whose members included prominent citizens such as Cornelius Vanderbilt, to mark the three hundredth anniversary of Hendrik Hudson's exploration of New York Harbor and the one hundredth anniversary of the launching of Robert Fulton's first successful steamboat, the *Clermont*. The complexity of the program for the site in Riverside Park between 114th and 116th streets recalled earlier schemes: the memorial was to include Fulton's tomb, a naval museum, a reception hall for official visitors, docks and promenades. It was to be a working monument typical of the Composite Era: "To the foreign visitor it will be not merely the gateway of the city but of a new world, and his greeting should be urbane and dignified and his first impression of serene majesty,"[511] but it was also to function like one of the city's downtown recreation piers for neighborhood apartment dwellers.

H. Van Buren Magonigle's winning scheme was a peristyle along Riverside Drive linking the museum and reception hall at either end to a central pavilion sheltering Fulton's catafalque. A monumental staircase as broad as the peristyle covered the railroad tracks and descended to a boat landing framed by colonnaded piers. The insistent horizontality of Magonigle's scheme was intended to contrast with the jagged skyline of apartment houses already appearing along the Drive and achieve "a height of simplicity and pure beauty which McKim, Mead & White alone have hitherto attained."[512] By comparison, Albert Kelsey and Paul Cret's third-prize scheme was skillfully composed but overblown. Ripley, Clapp & Faelton's second-prize submission was out of scale with its surroundings but had lighthouses at the ends of sea walls extending into the river which promised the visitor a more intimate relationship with the water.

The Fulton Memorial was never fixed in the public imagination, and funds were never realized for its construction.[513] But the profession acclaimed the competition as a great artistic success. Even the losers were so satisfied with its conduct that they organized a dinner on April 28, 1910, to honor Vanderbilt, L.C. Holden (the professional advisor) and the jury (which included Thomas Hastings, George B. Post, and Robert Fulton Cutting). The project's significance lay in its illustration of the high level of skill among the generation of French-trained architects, and the achievement of a remarkable stylistic consensus. The *American Architect and Building News* observed:

Our dependence on European tradition has not yet become a yoke; it is still a staff and the wisdom of retaining it as such until we no longer as a people, need it has been abundantly vindicated.... We are not ripe for the indigenous art of which a few forerunners have given us many remarkable and few really meritorious examples. There are still too many apparently incongruous elements in our national system that need adjusting before assimilation is possible, and without a thorough assimilation of important material and intellectual factors there can be no real progress in art. The development of art involves the establishment of a tradition founded on such a settled state of mind as cannot yet exist in this country.[514]

Morningside had first flowered in a period of transition.

Columbia Stadium, Naval Reserve, Public Recreation Pier and Water Gate, between 112th and 120th streets on the Hudson River. Palmer & Hornbostel, 1907. Perspective view looking north. CU

Robert Fulton Memorial competition entry, Riverside Park between 114th and 116th streets. H. Van Buren Magonigle, 1910. Perspective view from the Hudson River. CU

Alpha Club, 434 Riverside Drive. Wood, Palmer & Hornbostel, 1903. CU

The competition for St. John the Divine summed up the passing of the Cosmopolitan Era, and the institutions which followed it exhibited, in their diversity of styles and their failure to relate to one another, the divergent strains of thought which marked the early 1890s. The competition for the Fulton Memorial came too late; the decorum and stylistic uniformity of its entries summed up the vision of the City Beautiful just as a new and more pragmatic sense of urban design was being fostered by the gradual replacement in the planning process of architects by professional planners. The growth of Morningside Heights thus charted the course of the American Renaissance in New York—just as McKim's Columbia campus was one of its first, seminal manifestations, the failure to construct Magonigle's project pointed to its exhaustion. By 1910 the conflict between the ideals of the City Beautiful and the realities of the commercial marketplace could be seen in the vivid contrast between the institutional architecture of the Heights and the mediocre apartment houses that had sprung up in its wake to remind one of the commercial origins of the wealth that had made Morningside possible and would ensure its continuing vitality.

Despite the grandeur of the institutions on Morningside Heights, its character as a monumental enclave was challenged almost from the first by pressures of residential development. Because the highlands along the Hudson River above 110th Street (of which Morningside was the southern gateway) had been bypassed by the El in the Cosmopolitan Era, they remained Manhattan's last developmental frontier.[515] By 1898 the construction of the I.R.T. subway beneath Broadway was a virtual certainty, and a boom in residential and commercial construction was inevitable.

Only a few rowhouses were built on the Heights. The first, built by the developer David Kennedy on the north side of 117th Street between Amsterdam Avenue and Morningside Drive, "fixed the standard for that class of improvements in the section."[516] Townhouses were also built on Riverside Drive and along the south side of 114th Street, facing what would soon become Columbia's South Field.[517] These were all routine examples of the vaguely Classical American basement houses erected by speculative developers in the 1890s, with none of the flair of contemporary rowhouses ten blocks to the south along the West End's northern edge. The only comparable townhouses in Morningside were built to house college fraternities. The first of these was the Alpha Club (1903) on Riverside Drive just south of 116th Street, designed by Wood, Palmer & Hornbostel.[518] Its red brick and limestone Modern French facade was remarkably rich, with a series of superimposed balconies culminating in a pediment which broke through the cornice line to shelter a cartouche bearing the fraternity's insignia. A narrow light court above the first floor on the northern edge of the lot increased views of the river and enhanced the building's singularity in an already dense urban context.

In 1907 Thomas Nash designed the Delta-Phi Clubhouse around the corner on 116th Street.[519] The four-story building was hemmed in by giant apartment houses on either side and terminated the axis of Claremont Avenue. In response to the context Nash enhanced the building's scale with a vigorous order of engaged columns on the second-floor balcony and a two-story, steeply pitched mansard roof. Both strategies gave an appearance of greater size to what might otherwise have been an unexceptional essay in late eighteenth-century Classicism.

In 1912 Columbia University erected its President's House on Morningside Drive at the other end of 116th Street.[520] William Kendall of McKim, Mead & White designed a freestanding red brick and limestone villa which synthesized the monumentality of McKim's Columbia campus with a domestic ambience. From his acropolis of learning, the president could survey the city below as it grew.

The turn of the century saw the construction of townhouses in Manhattan coming to a halt except in the Billionaire District of the East Side. The late start of Morningside's residential growth deprived it of the historical stratum of middle-class rowhouses which, juxtaposed with later apartments, animated the West End's streetscape. By 1906 the *Real Estate Record and Guide* found the Heights had been transformed from "a wilderness of confusing possibilities" into an area that, despite the presence of its institu-

Sethlow Bachelor Apartments, 509 West 121st Street. Emery Roth, 1911. Perspective. CU

Hendrik Hudson, Riverside Drive between Cathedral Parkway and 111th Street. William L. Rouse, 1907. View from Riverside Drive. MCNY

tions, was becoming "probably the most distinctive high class apartment house quarter in the city."[521] Five years later the *Record and Guide* observed of Morningside: "It would seem as if some law had been passed against any other kind of a house than a great multi-family palace."[522]

Despite the *Record and Guide*'s boosterism, most of the apartment houses along the side streets between 110th and 114th streets were mediocre efforts, offering cramped, ill-lit accommodation to the lower strata of the middle class. Schwartz & Gross's Heathcote Hall, at 609 West 114th Street,[523] and Lawlor & Haase's somewhat more elegantly planned 521 and 523 West 112th Street[524] were somewhat better than the typical side street apartment house which, in the aggregate, presented a continuous, monotonous wall to the street. The Britannia apartments at 515 West 110th Street, completed in 1909 by Waid & Willauer, were instantly lauded as an ingenious alternative solution for a mid-block apartment house.[525] Its broad light court fronted on the street and was lined with rippling bay windows which maximized exterior exposure. The brick and stone English Gothic facades complemented the nearby cathedral and exuded an air of domesticity.

Emery Roth's Sethlow bachelor apartments, at 509 West 121st Street, were named in honor of Columbia's former president and expanded on the arrangement of the Britannia.[526] The *Real Estate Record and Guide* found its shallow, arcaded entrance court to have a "scholastic appearance" appropriate to its intended clientele; its three- and four-room kitchenette apartments and duplex studios were designed for professors and the "wealthier students" of the university.[527] Roth's limestone and tapestry brick facades synthesized influences from the Modern French school and progressive Viennese Classicism, while their broad eaves and tiled roofs evoked an Italian villa, alluding to a rustic, bucolic imagery as an antidote to Morningside's densely urban fabric.

A series of more opulent and fashionable apartment houses was built along Broadway, Riverside Drive and Columbia Grounds, the southern end of Claremont Avenue. The first lavish apartment house on the Heights was the Hendrik Hudson; at the time of its construction (1906-07) it was one of the largest in the city.[528] Located on a bend in Riverside Drive between 110th and 111th streets, its site commanded sweeping views of the park and river. According to its architect, William L. Rouse, "the question of design is entirely submerged by the exigencies of the plan," and the individual apartments were indeed undistinguished, with long hallways and eccentrically shaped rooms.[529] Light courts along the side streets ventilated the back apartments while the facade along the Drive was an unbroken wall of apartments taking in the river view and defining the edge of the park with its cliff-like mass. Despite the pragmatism of the plan, the Riverside facade was a spirited tour de force. The broad eaves of the red tiled roof were carried on bronze brackets and evoked a Tuscan villa, an association made explicit by the *Serlianas* in the rooftop pavilions. A rhythmic pattern of balconies extended the exuberance of the design, and added "an air of domesticity"[530] to an otherwise monumental conception. As Rouse admitted, "On an ordinary street this scheme would be looked upon as somewhat overdone,"[531] but the Hendrik Hudson was scaled to dominate the view from the Drive as it passed some five hundred feet away. In 1908 the building was extended eastward along Cathedral Parkway to Broadway.[532] The addition was four stories taller and somewhat confused in its massing, with a bracketed cornice line interrupted by heroically scaled terra-cotta pylons sporting nautical trophies in tribute to the building's namesake.

The Hendrik Hudson set the tone for many of the later apartment buildings on the Heights, which combined routine planning with bravura facades. In H.W. Frohne's words, they were marked by "much superficial pretense, little substantial fulfillment. The hand of the speculator is again in evidence, and . . . the extent to which he can trade on popular credulity is much greater in these expensive projects."[533] In contrast to the patrician palazzos being erected on the East Side, Morningside's apartments carried forward the lively Modern French tradition of the West End's Dorilton and Ansonia, but frequently with a greater degree of inventive abstraction and a knowledge of the more advanced strains of the Art Nouveau.

Eton and Rugby halls, 29 and 35 Claremont Avenue. Gaetan Ajello, 1910. Elevation. CU

Ardelle, 527 Riverside Drive. Radcliffe & Kelley, 1910. MCNY

George & Edward Blum's apartment house (1909) at the northwest corner of Broadway and 113th Street rivalled the Hendrik Hudson in terms of the lavish size of its apartments.[534] A twelve-story Modern French palazzo crowned by a boldly projecting copper cornice, its facades were articulated by stacks of oriel windows which suggested a giant order of columns and established the traditional tripartite organization at colossal scale. As in the Hendrik Hudson extension, the street level along Broadway was given over to shops.

George F. Pelham's Fowler Court (1909) at the northeast corner of 112th Street and Riverside Drive was perhaps the finest Modern French apartment house on Morningside.[535] Its carefully composed facades of red brick and limestone rose only seven stories and were enlivened by ornamental dolphins and seashells.

At the same time, the block west of Barnard College between Claremont Avenue and Riverside Drive, which Charles Rich had hoped to develop as an extension of the Park to connect the campus to the river, was developed with apartments around 1909. A number of these were designed by Gaetano Ajello, who built some fifty apartments in Morningside and the Upper West Side in the next twenty years. Among Ajello's spacious but stylistically naive Italianate palazzos were the Mira Mar (1909) at 452 Riverside Drive, the Peter Minuit (1910) at 25 Claremont Avenue, and Eton and Rugby halls (1910), two adjacent buildings which shared a continuous facade at 29 and 35 Claremont Avenue.[536] H.W. Frohne characterized Ajello's glistening white terra-cotta and glazed brick facades as merely "the 'appearance of more appearance.' . . . The show of the front is but poorly supported by the planning of the apartments."[537] Far more inventive was George and Edward Blum's Oxford Hall (1911) at 454 Riverside Drive.[538] Its three vertical groups of paired windows terminated in gables whose rich white terra-cotta ornamentation looked for inspiration to the Glasgow School of Art Nouveau.

Farther north, Radcliffe & Kelley designed The Ardelle at 527 Riverside Drive opposite Grant's Tomb. The interiors were compactly planned and included only two apartments on each floor. Frohne described the facade as "architectural features worked for all they are worth, but with a questionable result."[539] Nonetheless the architects matched the bravura eclecticism of Roth's Sethlow apartments, framing the richly patterned brick facade with continuous vertical stacks of bay windows culminating in twin pediments which broke through the heavily bracketed cornice of the tile roof.

Within little more than twenty years, Morningside had been transformed from a bypassed wilderness into a world famous acropolis of learning, only to have the vision of a monumental quarter of the city challenged by the more mundane realities of a comfortable bourgeois neighborhood. To some extent the apartments served the academic community of the neighborhood's institutions, but they more clearly reflected the trend towards the development of the entire west side of Manhattan—a development which blurred the distinctions between individual neighborhoods and imposed a new, uniformly dense urbanism of elevator apartments. Rather than commanding the bluffs of Morningside and Riverside parks, the individual components of the acropolis on the Heights were left as isolated oases in the urban grid; even from within the Columbia campus, McKim's ensemble was compromised by the sight of apartment buildings which overtopped its cornice line. But by 1910, when residential construction in the neighborhood was at its most intense, it was already evident to some that "the increasing exodus into the suburbs and within a commuting distance of City Hall is the beginning of a mighty revolt of which the city real estate market will ultimately have to bear the brunt."[540]

Suburbs
Long Island . . . Staten Island . . . the coast of New Jersey, and . . . Westchester County . . . already . . . are becoming the seats of villages, built by capital from the city, and occupied by a teeming population from the city, who continue to spend their hours of business in the great metropolis. Here too, in every direction, are springing up the suburban villas of the more opulent citizens, who seek beyond the din and dust of the city proper, the quiet that is denied them. The New York of 1900 will probably be a much less compactly built city than that which now occupies the southern extremity of Manhattan Island. . . . Fifty years hence a city of cottages with gardens, and villas with parks and pleasure grounds, and clusters of dwellings among cultivated fields and miniature groves will cover a circular area of fifty miles diameter, centering at the present site of the City Hall. Daniel Curry, *New-York: A Historical Sketch of the Rise and Progress of the Metropolis* (New York: Carlton & Phillips, 1853), 337-38.

The growth of New York City has been controlled at every stage by the nature of public transportation available to its citizens. When transportation was limited to horses and walking, New York was limited to a small area on the southern tip of the island that combined the residential and commercial sections in one. But as early as 1814, when Robert Fulton began scheduled steam-ferry service between Brooklyn and Manhattan, workers from the Battery started commuting across the river to Brooklyn Heights, where developers quickly built a residential community that is sometimes called America's first suburb.[541] Ferry service to New Jersey was soon started, and a new housing pattern developed as the population of the city grew: those who were rich enough to afford horses and carriages lived uptown above Washington Square, the very poor huddled in tenements along Manhattan's eastern bulge at Corlears Hook, and the middle class, unable to afford the rising land prices, moved off the island.[542]

Several types of suburbs grew up around Manhattan. The earliest, like Brooklyn Heights, was built with Victorian rowhouses lining a gridiron of streets. But as the number of ferries multiplied and the amount of land easily accessible to Manhattan grew, land values decreased, and middle-class families were able to afford freestanding houses on individual lots. By 1831, when the New York State Legislature granted its first charter to the New York & Harlaem Railroad to run from Twenty-third Street through what was still open countryside to the village of Harlaem, the New York *Morning Courier and Enquirer* could speculate that Harlem would soon become a suburb where commuters would be able to enjoy a comfortable house on an acre or two of land with "a garden, orchard, dairy, and other conveniences."[543] Five years later the text of a prospectus for the speculative development of New Brighton on Staten Island made it clear that New Yorkers were familiar with this new type of suburb,[544] which *Harper's Monthly* called "the country enlivened by the intelligence of the city."[545]

Begun as a matter of economic expediency, the suburb quickly became an ideal housing type. As America's industrial age grew and her cities boomed, many needed to work in the city but no longer wanted to live there. Because of the spread of modern transportation across the country, the landscape architect Andrew Jackson Downing wrote in 1853, "hundreds of thousands, formerly obliged to live in the crowded streets of the cities, now find themselves able to enjoy a country cottage, several miles distant—the old notion of time and space being half annihilated."[546]

The early suburbs in Brooklyn and on the New Jersey shore of the Hudson River were planned with a gridiron of streets almost identical to those in Manhattan. But as the suburb developed as an ideal American neighborhood, prominent architects and planners like Downing and Frederick Law Olmsted became interested in its design and introduced a more romantic style of plan with curvilinear streets that evoked the image of the winding country lane.

Olmsted was particularly fascinated by the suburb as a planning type: in 1868 he wrote that though many of the burgeoning suburbs were

as yet little better than rude over-dressed villages, or fragmentary half-made towns, it can hardly be questioned that, already, there are to be found among them the most attractive,

Manhattan Beach Estates, Coney Island, Brooklyn. A view showing the Manhattan Beach and the Oriental hotels and the early development of Manhattan Beach Estates. NYHS

the most refined and the most soundly wholesome forms of domestic life, and the best application of the arts of civilisation to which mankind has yet attained. It would appear then, that the demands of suburban life, with reference to civilised refinement, are not to be a retrogression from, but an advance upon, those which are characteristic of town life, and that no great town can long exist without great suburbs. It would also appear that whatever element of convenient residence is demanded in a town will soon be demanded in a suburb, so far as is possible for it to be associated with the conditions which are the peculiar advantage of the country, such as purity of air, umbrageousness, facilities for quiet out-of-door recreation, and distance from the jar, noise, confusion, and bustle of commercial thoroughfares.[547]

To improve on the "fragmentary half-made towns" Olmsted and other suburban planners concentrated perhaps most of all on the issue of imagery. In addition to curving streets, the new suburbs were given rules governing lot size, building placement, property rights and design controls—standards which gave them a unified sense of community.

The first suburb designed to these standards was Llewellyn Park, New Jersey, built in 1853 by a pharmaceuticals importer named Llewellyn Haskell, and advertised as an ideal residential community only "twelve miles west of Fifth Avenue."[548] But Llewellyn Park was almost a rural environment, with craggy topography, medieval imagery (many of the original houses and the gate lodge were designed in an American Gothic style by Alexander Jackson Davis), curving, unpaved streets, a fifty-acre park known as The Ramble, and a consistent vision of nature that was only slightly manicured to meet the needs of upper-middle-class domesticity.

Approximately twenty-five years later in nearby Milburn, New Jersey, a window shade manufacturer named Stewart Hartshorn constructed a new station on the Erie & Lackawanna line and started a suburb he called Short Hills Park.[549] Hartshorn had made enough money to retire from business in 1874 and pursue his boyhood dream of founding an ideal town: by 1879 he had acquired sixteen hundred acres of land and hired McKim, Mead & White to design a model house that could be built for five thousand dollars and a community center known as the Music Hall. Hartshorn laid out the rest of the town himself and picked his customers carefully—he said he wished to attract nature-loving people to his community as he found such people had taste and initiative—although he reserved the right to review all plans after selling the land. Even so, the highly eclectic group of houses expressed each buyer's individuality and exemplified the spirit of the Cosmopolitan Era.

Other model suburbs were built on Long Island—Garden City, by the New York merchant Alexander T. Stewart in 1869[550]—and Westchester County—Rochelle Park, in New Rochelle (ca. 1885),[551] and Lawrence Park, in Bronxville (1892).[552] But the lessons of these planned communities were also applied in the five counties that became New York City after 1898, where individual pockets were carved out of the omnipresent gridiron to create some of the city's finest neighborhoods. The earliest was built in Brooklyn, spurred on in the 1880s and 1890s by the construction of railroads which fanned out from the New York ferries.

Brooklyn

The first suburban-style developments in Brooklyn were resort communities like Manhattan Beach which grew up around the hotels on Coney Island. One of the last of these was Sea Gate, built in 1898 on the western tip of the island between the Atlantic Ocean and Gravesend Bay.[553] Forty-three square blocks (125 acres) divided into 1,800 lots, Sea Gate was anchored by the American Yacht Club and surrounded by some of the finest beaches in the area. The earliest houses were rambling Colonial and Shingle Style designs, some by the Parfitt Brothers,[554] but Squires & Wynkoop's vernacular stucco houses for H.J. Keiser[555] and J.H. Biggs[556] were typical of later work.

The Brooklyn, Bath & West End Railroad opened in the early 1880s, but because the railroad's terminal was a long walk from the Brooklyn Bridge, the railroad's route to Coney Island was less popular than those of other lines located more conveniently to the bridge.[557] The initiation in 1889 of direct ferry service from Manhattan to its terminal, however, made the small towns served by the Brooklyn, Bath & West End ripe for development. One of the choicest

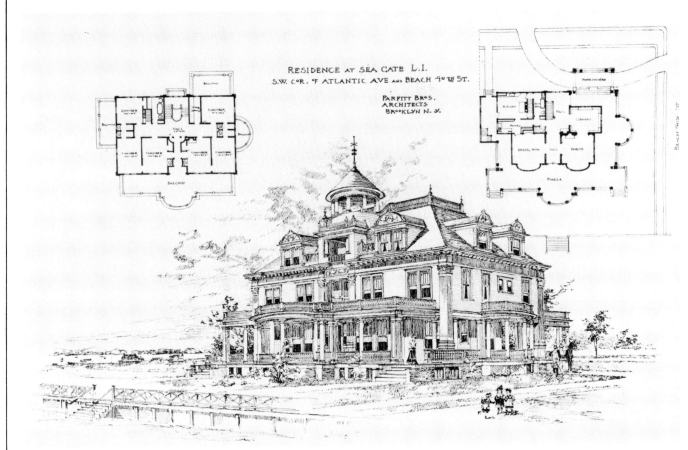

Typical house, southwest corner of Atlantic Avenue and Fortieth Street, Sea Gate, Brooklyn. Parfitt Bros., 1901. Perspective view and plans of first and second floors. CU

locations was a small resort called Bath Beach, which stood on a low, wooded bluff overlooking Gravesend Bay, New York Harbor and Coney Island.[558] A New York real estate developer named James D. Lynch saw the opportunity to expand the village by buying adjoining farm land, but he was blocked by the Benson family, who owned several of the farms and refused to sell. Lynch acquired these last pieces by agreeing to name his section of Bath Beach "Bensonhurst" and to preserve the Benson homestead and land as a park. By the time the railroad arrived he had hired B.S. and G.S. Olmstead (who were no relation to Frederick Law Olmsted) as landscape architects and the Parfitt Brothers as architects, and had two hundred men at work grading the land and laying out streets and sidewalks.

Bensonhurst . . . began to grow like a fairyland . . . twenty miles of young trees had been set out along the sidewalks. Neat palings of blue and green were erected and the land of each block turned into a green lawn, sodded, watered and rolled until it had the aspect of age and maturity. . . . The work of levelling and grading awakened widespread interest and attracted Sunday throngs. Before it was completed thirty villas had been built, and others were building, all contributing to the beauty of the landscape. Strict building laws were enforced. Stores were restricted to certain streets, devoted to business. Other streets were graded to the character of the dwelling houses constructed. Buyers on one street agreed to put up no houses costing less than $10,000. On other streets, the minimum price was fixed at $7,000, while there were streets where one could build for $3,000. Thus everyone could have what he could afford and the symmetry of the neighborhood preserved.[559]

The town plan was not notable, although the Olmsteads did provide a one-hundred-foot-wide boulevard (Twenty-first Avenue) that gave a shorter route from F.L. Olmsted's Ocean Parkway to the sea. Nevertheless, Bensonhurst-by-the-Sea, as it was briefly called, was an almost immediate success: doctors, lawyers and even a brother of Mrs. W.H. Vanderbilt lived there.

Nearby, in the old town of New Utrecht, the City and Suburban Homes Company branched out from their construction of model tenements in Manhattan and built model houses for wage earners: "mechanics, lettercarriers, policemen, firemen, clerks, bookkeepers, in fact the great body of

Brooklyn, Bath & West End Railroad Station, Bensonhurst, Brooklyn. A ca. 1895 view showing the early development of Bensonhurst. NYHS

persons earning from, let us say, $800 to $1,500 a year—these are the ones whose patronage is chiefly sought."[560] Creating 530 lots on both sides of Seventeenth Avenue between Ovington Avenue and Seventy-fourth Street, in 1897 the company hired Percy Griffin to design extremely economical semi-detached and detached houses. In order to keep the costs down, houses were constructed only after groups of one hundred houses had been ordered and individually mortgaged. After construction, 5 percent of the profit was returned to the shareholders of the City and Suburban Homes Company, 1 percent was kept for overhead, and the rest was distributed back to the buyers in the form of low purchase prices. But an even more unusual feature of the program was described by the organization's president:

The City and Suburban Homes Company insists on life insurance as a cardinal feature of its operations. In the first place, no man ought to undertake the purchase of a home or an obligation to pay a large amount of money without assuring his family in the event of his death in the interim. This principle has particular force in the case before us, because the purchaser has so little real capital and must depend upon his monthly earnings to carry out the bargain. Now, if he dies the family is placed in a very unfortunate position. Probably it will not be able to complete the transaction. Therefore, for the sake of the family, as well as for the company's protection, it is wise to insist on a life insurance policy taken out at the time when the original contract is entered into, and covering the purchase price. The City and Suburban Homes Company would never wish to be embarrassed by having to dispossess a widow, and yet such would inevitably happen if life insurance were not provided.[561]

Flatbush, one of the original settlements of what is now Brooklyn, was a sleepy village of Dutch farming families until the late-nineteenth century, when the establishment of mass transportation to the cities of Brooklyn and New York transformed it into a middle-class residential suburb. Richard Ficken's development of the Tennis Court area in 1886 was the first large-scale subdivision in Flatbush of freestanding suburban frame houses.[562] Located on a site bordered by Albermarle Road, Church and Ocean avenues, East Eighteenth and Nineteenth streets, Ficken's development was the beginning of a movement by real estate devel-

Hammersley gate lodge and library, Bath Beach, Brooklyn. Parfitt Bros., 1892-93. Perspective. CU

opers to build suburban enclaves with specific boundaries, where the construction of houses could be carefully controlled. Ficken divided the property into fifty-foot-wide lots, encouraged owners to site their houses behind lawns, and required that the houses cost a minimum of six thousand dollars. He reinforced the sense of his development's identity by constructing brick gate posts at its entrance at Tennis Court and Ocean Avenue, and designed a garden and fountain at the junction of East Nineteenth Street and Tennis Court. In 1897 the Knickerbocker Field Club moved to Ficken's development and built a clubhouse designed by the Parfitt Brothers in the Shingle Style that was their specialty. Though the Tennis Court was architecturally quite coherent, its rather sculpturally modelled, Shingle Style houses seemed slightly out of keeping with the more urban character of the gridiron plan.

Much of the suburban development of Flatbush in the late 1880s and 1890s consisted of freestanding houses built by individual owners. Many of these houses were designed in an urban variation of the Shingle Style. The architects consolidated the size and shape of the houses and employed considerable amounts of Colonial ornament, simultaneously looking back to the vernacular Colonialism of the Cosmopolitan Era and forward to the more academic Georgian that was beginning to play an important role in the Composite Era. Ludlow & Valentine's W.F. Moore residence of 1896[563] and E.G.W. Dietrick & A.M. Stuckert's house for W.A. Porter[564] exemplify the kind of shingled Colonial villas that abounded in Flatbush.

In 1892 Flatbush began to function in earnest as a suburban community when the Vandeveer family's Germania Real Estate and Improvement Company bought forty-three acres of land east of Flatbush Avenue.[565] Their development, Vandeveer Park, was planned as a wage-earner's community specifically aimed at "thrifty and well-to-do mechanics, clerks, etc."[566] Vandeveer Park had inexpensive wood-frame houses that could be purchased on mortgages with lenient payment schedules provided by the developers. While the houses were not architecturally distinguished, they were generously embellished with porches, and occasionally graced with other features such as turrets. Nearly all turned a narrow gable end toward the street and sat behind small front yards. The clear expression of the public responsibility of the street facade made the neighborhood a more unified ensemble than the slightly earlier planned suburbs of the Cosmopolitan Era, although the detailed design of the gardens and the rear and side elevations of the individual houses gave it a measure of individuality as well.[567]

Vandeveer Park houses were large enough for a family and cheap enough for those unable to afford rowhouses in Manhattan or the more substantial and widely spaced villas of Bensonhurst, so the project was a great success. In the late 1890s the developers acquired much more land and extended Vandeveer Park well beyond Flatbush Avenue towards Flatlands, and industry began to settle nearby to take advantage of the large pool of skilled workers.

In 1895 the Brooklyn, Flatbush & Coney Island Railroad began service between Flatbush and the Fulton Ferry. By 1899 the line was electrified and provided direct service to Manhattan via the Brooklyn Bridge, thereby accelerating the area's growth. While some of the development consisted of rowhouses that fostered an urban image for Flatbush, the majority of the new developments continued the suburban character of the 1880s and 1890s.

Prospect Park South was the most important of the planned developments which helped establish Flatbush as a particularly desirable suburban district. Northwest of Flatbush's traditional village center at Church and Flatbush avenues, it was begun in 1899 on former farmland owned by the Dutch Reformed Church.[568] The developer Dean Alvord, the Scottish-born landscape designer John Aiken, and the architect John J. Petit (partner in the firm of Kirby, Petit & Green) transformed Prospect Park South into an exemplar of the spread of the City Beautiful ideal to suburban neighborhoods, establishing a "rural park within the limitations of the conventional city block and the city street."[569] Prospect Park South was more conveniently located than more spacious developments further from the city's core, such as Rochelle Park or Garden City, yet was able to compete with them in terms of amenities by virtue of the unusually elaborate public improvements which Alvord introduced: houses

Japanese house, 131 Buckingham Road, Prospect Park South, Brooklyn. John J. Petit, 1902. CU

were set back thirty feet from the street, and planting strips in the centers of Albermarle and Buckingham roads further enhanced the sense of nature and open space. Two types of trees were planted in regular rows along the sidewalks—Carolina poplars which grew quickly but were short-lived and slower maturing Norway maple trees which would last virtually forever.

Houses at Prospect Park South were available in several domestic styles: Georgian, Tudor, Elizabethan and Swiss chalet were the most common, although there was also a remarkable Japanese-style house completed in 1902 on Buckingham Road.[570] The houses could either be bought from Alvord, who employed Petit to design them, or one could hire Petit directly. Alvord's own Tudoresque house was less imposing than several temple-fronted mansions in the Adam style which provided at a suburban scale the sense of civic spirit found in the mansions of the Billionaire District.

Prospect Park South influenced a number of subsequent suburban enclaves in Flatbush, including Ditmas Park and Ditmas Park West, which were developed after 1902 by Lewis Pounds in a large area stretching from Ocean Avenue to Coney Island Avenue between Newkirk Avenue, Ditmas and Dorchester roads.[571] Pounds, who set out to give his developments a "distinctly suburban effect,"[572] believed he had a moral responsibility to lay out his development properly and select buyers who would cooperate in its improvement. Pounds imposed set-back controls and provided ample planting along the streets and on the individual lots.

While the houses in Ditmas Park were more modest than those of Prospect Park South, several houses designed by the architect Arlington W. Isham and his partner Harry Grattan were interesting. Isham's cluster of thirteen bungalows, built in 1899 on East Sixteenth Street,[573] north and south of Ditmas Road, were fine representations of a type that Gustav Stickley was beginning to proselytize in his magazine the *Craftsman*. These one-and-a-half-story frame structures were individually designed with long shed dormers and porches that provided a lively composition, but they were dominated by a large, single gable sometimes turned parallel to the street to enhance the scale of the house and reinforce the street wall. Ditmas Park also included large houses along Ocean Avenue, a late flowering of the Cosmopolitan spirit in the fine church group built in 1899 by the Flatbush Congregational Church with a remarkably inventive seven-sided Shingle Style rectory designed by Whitefield & King,[574] and a fine example of the sensibility of the Composite Era, a brick and limestone Georgian church designed eleven years later by Allen & Collens in association with Louis Jallade.[575]

Ditmas Park was followed in 1905 by Fiske Terrace, a development for middle-class families who could not afford Prospect Park South but were more affluent than the artisans and wage earners of Vandeveer Park.[576] The developer of Fiske Terrace, the T.B. Ackerman Construction Company, laid out the major streets with central garden malls and brick gateposts with bronze plaques at the entrances to the development. Unlike Alvord, however, he did not build individually designed houses but spread a series of identical houses throughout the area. Based on houses by a number of architects including Isham and John Slee, the designs were usually for two-and-a-half-story villas that combined the bungalow roofs of Ditmas Park with imposing Colonial style detailing that enhanced their self-importance.

A development similar to Fiske Terrace, South Midwood, began in 1899 with the construction of some imposing houses on Ocean Avenue, but did not really get going until 1905, when the John R. Corbin Company began to build houses designed by Benjamin Driesler.[577] Working together for the next five years, Corbin and Driesler filled the new development with houses on fifty-by-one-hundred-foot lots.

By the end of the Composite Era, Flatbush was an established Eden of middle-class fulfillment—a testament to John J. Petit's belief that "A suburban residential section in the broadest interpretation of the term should always define a community combining its appeal to the 'home seeker' efficient transit facilities, churches, congenial society, the gracious gifts of nature, and, above all, attractive and artistic houses."[578]

Dean Alvord house, Albermarle Road, Prospect Park South, Brooklyn. John J. Petit, 1902. CU

Dean Alvord house, Albermarle Road, Prospect Park South, Brooklyn. John J. Petit, 1902. Plans of first and second floors. CU

Queens

Queens developed much more slowly than Brooklyn. Its ocean shore was considerably further than Brooklyn's coast from the business districts of Brooklyn and Manhattan, while northern Queens, before the development of midtown Manhattan, was even more isolated. One of the earliest sections to attract attention from New York City was Far Rockaway, which had a large seaside hotel called the Marine Pavilion.[579] Built in 1833, it was famous enough by 1850 to have attracted Henry Wadsworth Longfellow and Washington Irving. A small suburban-style resort called Wavecrest, similar to those on Coney Island, developed near the hotel in the 1870s.[580]

In 1863 a developer named Dr. Thompson bought most of the land around Rockaway Beach, further to the west, and built a railroad from East New York to Canarsie, where he maintained a steam ferry across Jamaica Bay to Rockaway Beach which began the growth of the area as an amusement resort.[581] Soon, in 1869, a steam railroad was built to Far Rockaway and extended in 1872 to Rockaway Beach. Samuel Wood bought several hundred acres of land located between the Brower's Point railroad station and Jamaica Bay and renamed the area Woodsburgh.[582] He built a large hotel he called the Woodsburgh Pavilion and constructed a few houses, but the land was still largely undeveloped when Wood died in 1878.

In 1877 the New York, Woodhaven & Rockaway Railway Company had built a trestle across Jamaica Bay to provide direct access to Rockaway Beach, and three years later the Brooklyn Rapid Transit Company began running summer service over the bridge. A speculator named William Trist Bailey laid out a small subdivision of Far Rockaway he called Bayswater; the first Rockaway Yacht Club was built there, and the first hunt with hounds on Rockaway started there.[583]

The development of the peninsula was much more concentrated in the 1890s. Robert L. Burton, who had inherited majority control of Woodsburgh in 1878, began its development in earnest.[584] Tearing down most of the old houses, he built a new village center and a restricted residential community which became quite fashionable. In 1892 Frederick J. Lancaster bought a nearby sandy waste with two or three houses and promoted it as New Venice.[585]

The largest development was made by two brothers, Newbold and Alfred Lawrence. Naming the project after themselves, they provided land for the Lawrence railroad station and built the Lawrence Association, which contained a school and a public hall.[586] The new town was so successful that the Rockaway Hunting Club decided to move there from Bayswater and hired Bruce Price to design a new clubhouse.[587]

By 1898, when Queens was incorporated into New York, the Long Island Railroad had started its own service to Rockaway Beach, the Ocean Electric Railway, and the peninsula was firmly tied to the city. Nevertheless in 1915, 1916 and 1917 the local administrations of Far Rockaway and Rockaway Beach attempted to secede, and twice had the necessary bills passed in both houses of the state legislature, only to be vetoed by Mayor John Purroy Mitchel. One of the only early suburban developments in northern Queens was started by a New York lawyer named Albon P. Man, who between 1868 and 1870 bought nearly four hundred acres of farm land surrounding a branch of the Long Island Railroad.[588] Calling the area Richmond Hill, he built a train station and a post office and hired the landscape architect Edward Richmond to lay out and manage the new town.

Development was slow until 1891, when Man died and his son Alrick assumed control of the project. Alrick Man paved the roads and laid sidewalks, as well as building many new roads and houses. But the development of Richmond Hill and northern Queens accelerated even more rapidly after 1906, when the borough's corrupt president, Boss Cassidy, was turned out of office. Elevated service from Manhattan was extended through Brooklyn to Jamaica Avenue and Liberty Avenue, and the Long Island Railroad opened a new line which passed through the northern section of Richmond Hill. Man built another station on the new branch and started a development he called Kew Gardens.[589] The reformed Queens administration responded by installing a sewer system throughout both developments and making telephones and electric street and house lighting universal in the area.

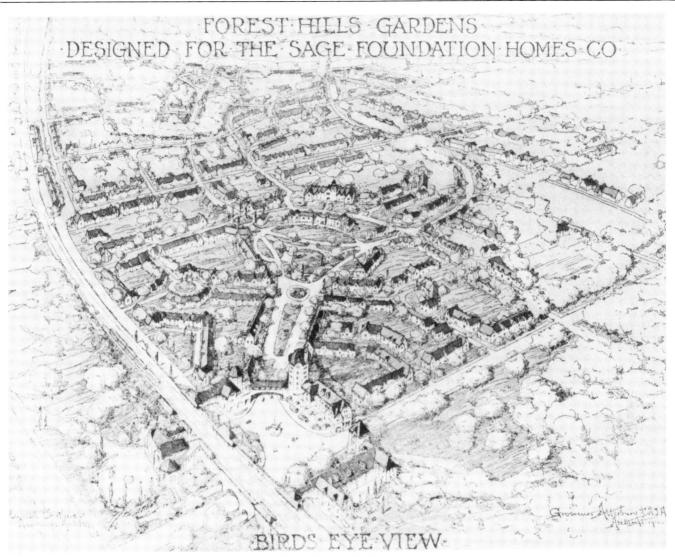

Forest Hills Gardens, Queens. Grosvenor Atterbury and the Olmsted Bros., 1909–12. Aerial perspective drawn in 1910. CU

Station Square and Forest Hills Inn, Forest Hills Gardens, Queens. Grosvenor Atterbury, 1909–12. View from the southwest showing the tower of Forest Hills Inn. CU

The opening of the Steinway Tunnels in 1907, the Queensboro Bridge in 1909 and the Pennsylvania and Long Island railroad tunnels in 1910 spurred the growth of midtown Manhattan and shifted the attention of many developers from Brooklyn to Queens. Typically, the subdivisions were uninspired extensions of the city grid, like the nearly one thousand houses built by the Mathews Brothers on former farmland in Ridgewood.[590] But early in 1909 the Russell Sage Foundation, founded in 1907 with a commitment to the improvement of the physical environment of the masses, purchased two hundred acres of land in Forest Hills, nine miles by train from Pennsylvania Station. They planned the first major project of the foundation, a new suburb called Forest Hills Gardens, and hired the Olmsted Brothers as planners and Grosvenor Atterbury as architect to build a model residential community as a pattern for future development.[591] Its unique combination of city planning and architecture achieved a dense, consolidated image of suburban living that made Forest Hills Gardens the preeminent expression of the suburban ideal of the Composite Era and the most important suburb built in New York, the only one to assume international importance. The foundation's creation was hailed by the journalist-reformer Jacob A. Riis as an opportunity to document the social and economic conditions of the city, and by Professor Edwin Seligman of Columbia as a possible "laboratory of social experimentation."[592]

The Sage Foundation intended Forest Hills Gardens to be a village that mixed middle-class and wage-earner's housing, but its nearness to Manhattan made the land cost too high, and the development established itself as an upper-middle-class enclave soon after it opened in 1912. A number of serious attempts were made to keep the costs down: the highest density development was placed on the costly land nearest the train station, and much of the construction in the early stages utilized prefabricated panels.[593]

The most English of America's planned suburbs, Forest Hills Gardens was clearly dependent on the example of Parker & Unwin's work at Hampstead Garden Suburb outside London, which like Forest Hills Gardens was an aesthetic triumph but a failure at social reform. Station Square was the gateway to the community: the brick-paved plaza was dominated by the tower of the Forest Hills Inn and bordered on one side by the embankment of the railroad

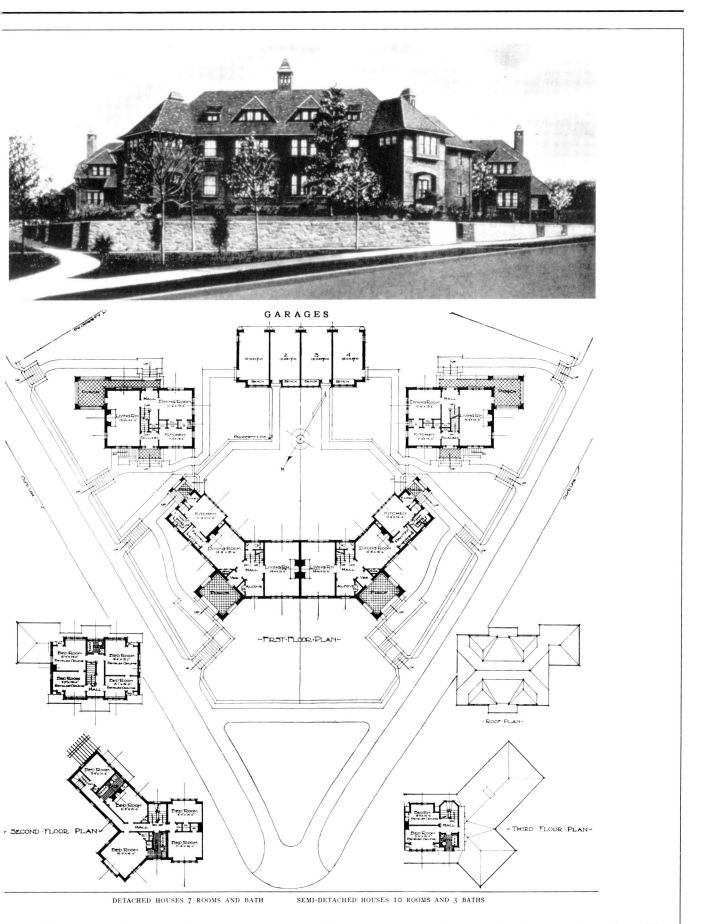

Group XII houses, Forest Hills Gardens, Queens. Grosvenor Atterbury, 1910–12. View from the northwest and plans of the first and second floors. CU

Group houses, Willet Avenue to Middletown Street between Shelton and Colonial Avenues, Jamaica, Queens. Electus D. Litchfield, 1914. A group of seventeen houses. CU

and its station and on the other three sides by a continuously arcaded building that yielded the impression, as Samuel Howe observed, "of a college or cathedral city."[594] Passing under two arches, the principal village streets led from the square to residential neighborhoods intended to contradict earlier, more romantically planned suburbs such as Llewellyn Park. In the prospectus of 1911, the sponsors stated that "fantastically crooked layouts have been abandoned for the cozy, domestic character of local streets, not perfectly straight for too long, but gently curving to avoid monotony."[595] As one moved away from Station Square the urban character became more rural, suggesting a metaphoric journey from town to open country.

Atterbury was responsible for Station Square and some of the loveliest buildings in the Gardens, though other architects, including Wilson Eyre and Albro & Lindeberg, also built there. Atterbury's group house development on Puritan Avenue had three buildings arranged to form a court which was divided into individual gardens. The original design pioneered new strategies permitting individual ownership and communally held open space that became basic criteria for planned suburban development after World War I. Atterbury's group at the fork between Greenway North and Markwood Road had four houses, two of which were combined into a semi-detached unit.[596] His design skillfully adapted the axial composition principals of the City Beautiful to the suburban milieu, simultaneously culminating the axis of Greenway North and providing an interior space that made a virtue of the site's awkward geometry.

Despite the fact that Forest Hills Gardens was an important monument of the Composite Era, its designers were aware that theirs was not purely a project of urban beautification and institutional symbolism. Forest Hills Gardens was to be an ideal model town sponsored by a foundation, but it was also a business proposition. Atterbury was aware in his writings of the problems that this seeming schizophrenia of intentions might bring with it. "It is unfortunate that the somewhat misleading word 'model' must be applied to such an eminently practical scheme as the development of the Russell Sage Foundation," he wrote,

"for the reason that there is a kind of subtle odium which attaches to 'model' things of almost any kind, even when they are neither charitable nor philanthrophic—a slightly sanctimonious atmosphere that is debilitating rather than stimulative of success."[597]

Forest Hills Gardens did serve as a model for future development, however, perhaps most notably in the new towns and large subdivisions that were built during the First World War for munitions workers and shipbuilders.[598] Electus D. Litchfield, who would later design Yorkship Village outside Camden, New Jersey, one of the best of the shipbuilding projects, in 1914 planned a small private development of about ten city blocks in Queens, adapting some of the lessons of Forest Hills to the gridiron and the requirements of speculative, middle-class housing.[599] "The value of the land is such that in order that the house and lot may be sold at a price which will appeal to persons in moderate circumstances," the *Brickbuilder* reported, "the amount of land to be sold with each house must be as small as possible. On the other hand, it was desired to maintain, as far as possible, the suburban character of the neighborhood. For this reason, it was planned to build only a certain number of individual houses, free standing upon moderate sized plots, and to have the majority of the houses semi-detached or in groups of four or five, and in some cases in very extensive groupings."[600]

The largest, in fact, was seventeen houses under one roof. Although Litchfield attempted to balance the large block with three smaller group houses across the street, the sheer size of the group overwhelmed the simple Colonial style details. Yet all the houses worked quite well, particularly considering the modest dimensions of the individual units. Constructed of brick with slate roofs, the houses had custom exterior and interior woodwork. "While the interior finish is extremely simple in its character," the *Brickbuilder* said, "it displays the quiet good taste which appeals to people of refinement."[601]

The Bronx
When New York consolidated the five boroughs in 1898, the borders of the new city encompassed large areas of

Group house, Willet Avenue to Middletown Street between Shelton and Colonial Avenues, Jamaica, Queens. Electus D. Litchfield, 1914. A 1914 view of a typical end unit in a group of four houses. CU

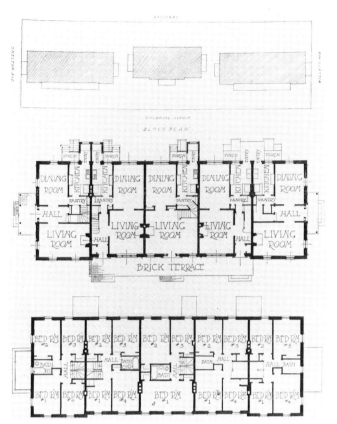

Group houses, Willet Avenue to Middletown Street between Shelton and Colonial Avenues, Jamaica, Queens. Electus D. Litchfield, 1914. Block plan and plans of the first and second floors in a typical grouping of four houses. CU

Advertisement for houses built by Edward Delafield in Fieldston and Riverdale. 1913. CU

Eugene Christian house, West 253rd Street, Riverdale, Bronx. Herbert M. Baer, 1908-09. Watercolor rendering. CU

open country. In Manhattan, central Harlem was developed, but Inwood and Washington Heights lay in comparative isolation to its northwest, without any elevated railroad service. Enormous sections of Brooklyn and Queens were still farmland, although developmental pressures were beginning to press in on them as public transportation improved. But some remote sections of the city were already developed at a low density, suburban scale. The stretch of the Bronx along the Hudson River that included Riverdale and Spuyten Duyvil was the most geographically advantaged of the suburban areas within the new city. Long served by the New York Central Railroad, Riverdale and Spuyten Duyvil had become a section of large country estates which resisted the pressures of urbanization well into the twentieth century. One of the most lavish estates was Giovanni P. Morosini's Elmhurst.[602] Designed by Jardine, Kent & Jardine, the Morosini estate was dominated by a large, rambling red brick and tile house, roofed in tile and surrounded by extensive porches carried on numerous thin Ionic columns. Though not so grand as Elmhurst, Eugene Christian's castle was certainly the most fantastic suburban estate in the city. Designed in 1908 by Herbert M. Baer for a site at 253rd Street in Riverdale, it recalled the Hudson River castles by Alexander Jackson Davis of fifty years before.[603]

The extension of the Broadway subway to Van Cortlandt Park in 1906 made the hitherto relatively isolated communities as accessible to the center of the city as more remote sections served by commuter railroads, such as Bronxville and New Rochelle in Westchester County or Great Neck and Manhasset in Nassau County. The country estate within the city's borders became an anomaly, and relatively modest suburban villas began to proliferate. By 1913, Edward Delafield, a prominent landowner and developer in the Riverdale area, could observe that "if New York can develop a fashionable suburban center, such as has been done in Boston, Philadelphia and Baltimore, the Riverdale section offers the only possibility."[604] Delafield banded together with other landowners in the area to halt the city's plans to extend the street grid, substituting a more picturesque scheme to develop Riverdale and Fieldston, adjacent to Riverdale, with modest houses and streets of great charm. Many of the houses were built by Delafield, who usually hired Dwight James Baum, the architect who reno-

Dwight James Baum house, Fieldston, Bronx. Dwight James Baum, 1915. CU

vated Delafield's family mansion, Fieldston Hill in 1916,[605] and designed the local country club in 1924.[606] Baum's own house in Fieldston had complex hipped roofs, a brick base, and a stucco second floor that made it a convincingly American version of the English Free Vernacular style of C.F.A. Voysey and M.H. Baillie Scott.[607] Albro & Lindeberg stayed close to English precedent in their very modest Nicholas Kelley residence[608] and more rambling Clayton S. Cooper house.[609] Mann & MacNeille designed numerous Fieldston houses in a half-timbered cottage mode,[610] as well as the Barnard School,[611] which together with the Horace Mann and Riverdale schools made the suburb the city's headquarters for the newly fashionable "country-day school."[612]

Staten Island

The introduction of scheduled ferry service to Staten Island in 1817 started an interesting tradition of suburban development in Staten Island. The founder of the first ferry, Daniel D. Tompkins, former vice president of the United States and governor of New York, was also the founder in 1814 of a Staten Island development called Tompkinsville.[613] When he initiated a ferry service from Tompkinsville to Manhattan the route became the main avenue for travel to Philadelphia and Washington, and the town flourished. Within a few years some early suburbanites began commuting back and forth between Tompkinsville and New York, and neighboring planned suburbs sprang up, such as New Brighton, which promised "to men engaged in active business . . . the means . . . of withdrawing from the labors and anxiety of commerce to the quiet of their own families."[614]

Staten Island slept through most of the mid-nineteenth century, but with the growth of the metropolis after the Civil War it became fashionable as a country seat. In the 1890s the architects Ernest Flagg and John Carrère both had country houses on Staten Island, where they each built model suburban houses. Flagg's estate was begun in 1898, the year that Staten Island became part of New York City, and was the most extensive on the island.[615] Over the years, Flagg lined the edges of his property with a series of small houses that he designed and built at his own expense to demonstrate his theories of suburban form and small-house design.[616] The houses were all designed on grid paper to develop a proportioning and dimensioning system Flagg

Semi-detached houses, Vanderbilt Avenue, Clifton, Staten Island. Carrère & Hastings, 1900. CU

House 50, Ernest Flagg Estate, Flagg Place, Staten Island. Ernest Flagg, ca. 1900. CU

thought would be readily understood by the workmen; the proportions of the grid were related to certain theories Flagg had developed concerning the origins of architecture. Constructed of fieldstone, many of the houses appeared to be extensions of the walls which surrounded the estate rather than freestanding objects on the landscape. Flagg devised new strategies for natural ventilation systems for each house, extending his exploration of the possibilities inherent in the use of dormers and traditional roof shapes.

After the turn of the century Flagg was hired as consulting architect for a development called Dongan Hills, built between Flagg's estate on the peak of Todt Hill and the rapid transit railway station at the foot of the hill.[617] The real estate prospectus described the development as a model suburban village "adjacent to the grounds of the Richmond Country Club and . . . 60 to 100 feet above sea level and . . . therefore high and dry commanding a beautiful view of the ocean and lower bay."[618] Lots were fifty by one hundred feet, sold for one thousand dollars, and buyers could choose their own house design from several different models.

In 1900 Carrère & Hastings designed a row of more tightly packed model houses built in Clifton for George W. Vanderbilt.[619] Carrère used the houses in his article "Better Taste in Small Houses" as an example "which shows that distinction can be gained without departing from simplicity in line and ornament."[620] Although the colorful, half-timbered houses with steep, overhanging roofs were far from simple, Carrère would have staggered the orderly row of houses for even more variety.

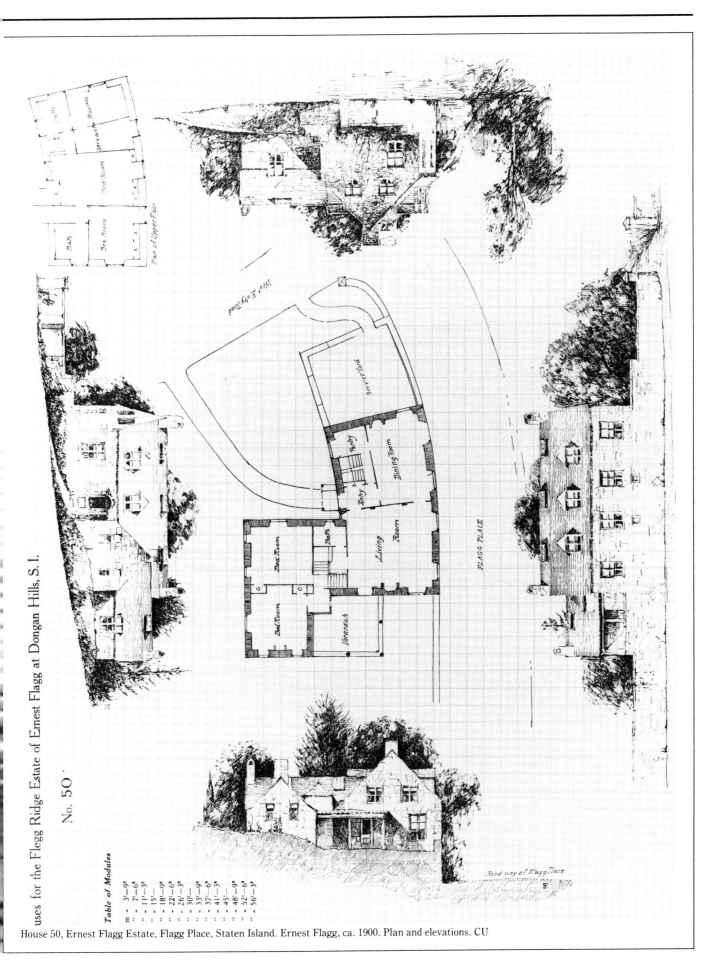

House 50, Ernest Flagg Estate, Flagg Place, Staten Island. Ernest Flagg, ca. 1900. Plan and elevations. CU

An aerial view of midtown Manhattan in 1933. AP

Afterword

The Composite Era drew to a close as the world plunged into the most devastating war in history. Fifteen years after the establishment of Greater New York, the city of three million had grown to one of five million. The high ideals of a balanced metropolitan order that motivated Andrew Haswell Green, Seth Low and others in their efforts to consolidate the scattered cities and villages into a metropolis comparable to London or Paris seemed quite naive and certainly far less attainable, with every municipal service overtaxed and significant elements of the population ill-housed.

The generation of political and architectural idealists who had formulated the structure and the image of the Composite City was no longer alive to see its ideals shattered. Green, the "father of Greater New York," died in 1903, Charles Follen McKim in 1909 and Seth Low in 1916. A new and more pragmatic generation was taking command. It was not without ideals, to be sure, but its idealism was tempered with more realism than in the immediate past, as it applied the architectural techniques of the Composite Era to a set of economic, political and social problems typical of a democratic society. The new generation took as its tasks the amelioration of congestion and the improvement of the everyday environment of the citizen of modest means. Concerns for convenience and efficiency jostled for recognition with beauty and grandeur.

After World War I the values of the American Renaissance were so deeply ingrained in the general architectural value system that a remarkably vital and uniquely American (some might even argue New York-ian) architectural synthesis of pragmatic and poetic ideals seemed to have been permanently established. This synthesis had its vulgar side, resulting in forms which have been characterized as "beautilitarian" by the historian Arnold Lehman.[1] But the synthesis, most explicitly expressed in the sophisticated manipulations of the Modern Classic—a later expression of the exuberant Modern French that combined Classical composition with the syncopated rhythms and sense of streamlined form typical of the arts in general during the interwar years—was part of a fundamental transformation of the conception of architecture from a civic to a commercial art. That, however, takes us ahead of our story. . .

1. Arnold L. Lehman, *The New York Skyscraper: A History of Its Development, 1870-1939* (Ph.D. diss., Yale University, 1970).

Photographic Sources

Photographs have been obtained courtesy of the following institutions:

Amaryllis Press, New York, New York
AP

American Telephone and Telegraph, New York, New York
AT&T

Brown Brothers, Sterling, Pennsylvania
BB

Avery Library, Columbia University, New York, New York
CU

Museum of the City of New York, New York
(including the Byron and Wurtz collections)
MCNY

Metropolitan Museum of Art, New York, New York
MM

Metropolitan Opera, New York, New York
MO

New-York Historical Society, New York, New York
(including the Hall collection)
NYHS

New York Public Library, New York, New York
NYPL

Office for Metropolitan History, New York, New York
OMH

Notes

AGE OF METROPOLITANISM
440
CIVIC STRUCTURE
442
CIVIC GRANDEUR
444
PALACES OF PRODUCTION
454
PALACES OF PLEASURE
462
PALACES FOR THE PEOPLE
466
METROPOLITAN NEIGHBORHOODS
470

AGE OF METROPOLITANISM

1. Thomas Beer, *The Mauve Decade: American Life at the End of the Nineteenth Century* (New York: Knopf, 1926); and Roger Shattuck, *The Banquet Years* (Garden City, N.Y.: Doubleday, 1961). Also see Van Wyck Brooks, *The Confident Years 1885-1915* (New York: Dutton, 1952); Ray W. Ginger, *Age of Excess: The United States from 1877 to 1914* (New York: Macmillan, 1965); and Howard Mumford Jones, *The Age of Energy: Varieties of American Experience, 1865-1915* (New York: Viking Press, 1971). For a somewhat earlier period, see Mark Twain and Charles D. Warner, *The Gilded Age: A Tale of Today* (Hartford, Conn.: American Publishing Co., 1873); and Lewis Mumford, *The Brown Decades: A Study of the Arts in America, 1865-1895*, 2nd rev. ed. (New York: Dover, 1955).
2. Andrew Saint, review of Alastair Service, *London 1900* in *Journal of the Society of Architectural Historians* 39 (December 1980): 327-28.
3. Alejandro Cirici Pellicer, *1900 in Barcelona, Modern Style, Art Nouveau, Modernismo, Jugendstil* (New York: G. Wittenborn, 1967); Franco Borsi and Ezio Godoli, *Paris 1900* (Brussels: Vokaer, 1976); Franco Borsi, *Bruxelles 1900* (Brussels: Vokaer, 1979); Alastair Service, *London 1900* (New York: Rizzoli, 1980); and Gavin Stamp, ed., "London 1900," *Architectural Design* 48 (May-June 1978).
4. John A. Krout, "Framing the Charter," in Allen Nevins and John Krout, eds. *The Greater City: New York, 1898-1948* (New York: Columbia University Press, 1948).
5. Herbert Croly, "New York as the American Metropolis," *Architectural Record* 13 (March 1903): 193-206.
6. John DeWitt Warner, "Matters that Suggest Themselves," *Municipal Affairs* 2 (March 1898): 123.
7. See Vincent Scully, *The Shingle Style and the Stick Style* (New Haven: Yale University Press, 1955); and Richard Guy Wilson, *Charles F. McKim and the Development of the American Renaissance: A Study of Architecture and Culture* (Ph.D. diss., University of Michigan, 1972).
8. Croly, "New York as the American Metropolis": 194.
9. "Editorial, The City Spirit and the Metropolitan," *Scribner's* 37 (March 1905): 378.
10. "Growth of New York," *Real Estate Record and Guide* 19 (May 19, 1877): 395-96.
11. Henry Isham Hazelton, *The Boroughs of Brooklyn and Queens, Counties of Nassau and Suffolk* (New York: Lewis Historical Publishing Co., 1925), 380.
12. Frederick Law Olmsted, quoted by William Alex and Elizabeth Barlow, *Frederick Law Olmsted's New York* (New York: Praeger, 1972), 21.
13. John F. Sprague, *New York the Metropolis* (New York: The New York Recorder, 1893), 36.
14. See Carroll L.V. Meeks, "Wright's Eastern Seaboard Contemporaries, Creative Eclecticism in the United States Around 1900," in *Arts of the Twentieth International Congress of the History of Art* (Princeton: Princeton University Press, 1963), 64-77; Harvey Kantor, *Modern Urban Planning in New York City, Origins and Evolution, 1890-1933* (Ph.D. diss., New York University, 1971), 21-26; and Richard Guy Wilson, "The Great Civilization," in *The American Renaissance: 1876-1917* (New York: Pantheon, 1979), 32.
15. A.D.F. Hamlin, "The Battle of the Styles, I" *Architectural Record* 1 (January-March 1892): 265-75.
16. Montgomery Schuyler, "The Brooklyn Bridge as a Monument," *Harper's Weekly* 27 (May 26, 1883): 326; reprinted in William Jordy and Ralph Coe, eds., *American Architecture and Other Writings* (Cambridge: Harvard University Press, 1961), 331-44; and Alan Trachtenberg, *Brooklyn Bridge: Fact and Symbol* (New York: Oxford University Press, 1965).
17. Marianna Griswold van Rensselaer, "Recent Architecture in America, II, Public Buildings Continued," *Century* 28 (July 1884): 323-34.
18. Moses King, *King's Handbook of New York* (Boston: M. King, 1893; New York: Benjamin Blom, 1973), 590. Also see "The New Music Hall," *Architecture and Building* 12 (May 17, 1890): 234; "Music Hall, 57th St. and Seventh Ave., N.Y. City," *Architecture and Building* 12 (June 7, 1890): plates; and "Music Hall, 57th St. and Seventh Ave., N.Y. City, Entrance Vestibule," *Real Estate Record and Guide* 47 (January 3, 1891): 517.
19. "Tower, Carnegie Music Hall, New York, Wm. B. Tuthill, Architect; Henry J. Hardenbergh, Associate," *Architecture and Building* 20 (February 17, 1894): plate.
20. Croly, "New York as the American Metropolis": 196.
21. Croly, "New York as the American Metropolis": 194.
22. Moses King, *New York: The American Cosmopolis, The Foremost City of the World* (Boston: M. King, 1894). Croly described the city as "the most highly organized and the most distinguished collective expression of American social life." Croly, "New York as the American Metropolis": 199.
23. James W. and Daniel B. Shepp, *Shepp's New York City Illustrated. Scene and Story in the Metropolis of the Western World* (Philadelphia and Chicago: Globe Bible Publishing Co., 1893), 8.
24. Marianna Griswold van Rensselaer, "Picturesque New York," *Century* 23 (December 1892): 164-75.
25. Marianna Griswold van Rensselaer, "People in New York," *Century* 49 (February 1895): 534-48.
26. Croly, "New York as the American Metropolis": 199-200.
27. A partial list of books and articles written on New York history during the period includes: Moses King, *King's Handbook of New York City: An Outline History and Description of the American Metropolis* (Boston: M. King, 1892); Thomas A. Janvier, "The Evolution of New York," *Harper's New Monthly Magazine* 86 (May 1893): 813-29 and (June 1893): 15-19; Thomas A. Janvier, *In Old New York* (New York: Harper & Bros., 1894); Benson J. Lossing, *History of the City of New York*, engravings by George E. Perine (New York: Perine, 1894); Alice Morse Earle, *Colonial Days in Old New York* (New York: Scribners, 1896); Marianna Griswold van Rensselaer, "The Mother City of Greater New York," *Century* 34 (May 1898): 138-46; Maude M. Goodwin, Alice C. Royce, Ruth Putnam, eds., *Historic New York* (New York: G.P. Putnam's Sons, 1898-99); Thomas E.V. Smith, *The City of New York in the Year of Washington's Inauguration, 1789* (New York: A.D.F. Randolph, 1899); Frank Bergen Kelley, ed., *Historical Guide to the City of New York* (New York: City Historical Club of

New York, F.A. Stokes Co., 1909); Marianna Griswold van Rensselaer, *History of the City of New York in the Seventeenth Century* (New York: Macmillan, 1909); Isaac Newton Phelps Stokes, *The Iconography of Manhattan Island, 1848-1909,* 7 vols. (New York: R.H. Dodd, 1915-1928).

28. Montgomery Schuyler, "The Small City House in New York," *Architectural Record* 8 (April-June 1899): 359.

29. Marianna Griswold van Rensselaer, "Fifth Avenue," *Century* 47 (November 1893): 5-18.

30. "Mr. Olmsted protests against the Destruction of the Palisades," *American Architect and Building News* 45 (August 25, 1894): 69; "The Destruction of the Palisades," *American Architect and Building News* 52 (June 20, 1896): 110; F.P. Albert, Letter to the Editor, "A Way to Save the Palisades," *Century* 54 (June 1897): 317-18; "The Destruction of the Palisades," *Architecture and Building* 27 (October 16, 1897): 137; and Frederick Stymetz Lamb, "Planning of Cities, Paper No. 5: On The Embellishment of New York City Waterfronts," *Public Improvements* 2 (December 15, 1899): 75-77.

31. Robert Kerr, "Supplement" to James Ferguson, *History of the Modern Styles of Architecture,* 3rd ed., (London: 1891), 373. Quoted in Wilson, *American Renaissance,* 13.

32. Wilson, *Charles F. McKim and the Development of the American Renaissance,* 339.

33. Hamilton Wright Mabie, "The Genius of the Cosmopolitan City," *The Outlook* 76 (March 5, 1904): 577-93. In his text, Mabie precisely reverses our definitions of "Composite" and "Cosmopolitan."

34. Gabrielle T. Stewart, "Municipal Beauty I," *Architects' and Builders' Magazine* 5 (July 1904): 471-82. Every aspect of municipal life was subjected to artistic consideration, from lamp standards designed for Central Park by Henry Bacon, to street signs, to "Isles of Safety" (traffic islands built in the middle of important intersections such as Twenty-third Street and Fifth Avenue, and in front of the Astor Hotel on Times Square). See "Current Notes on Public Art," *Municipal Affairs* 6 (June 1902): 275-76; Nelson S. Spencer, "Street Signs and Fixtures, *Municipal Affairs* 5 (September 1901): 726-37; and "W.W. Astor's Gift," *Real Estate Record and Guide* 73 (June 1903): 1304.

35. Charles H. Caffin, "Municipal Art," *Harper's* 100 (April 1900): 655-66.

36. Edward Bellamy, *Looking Backward, 2000-1887* (New York: Boston, Ticknor and Co., 1887; New York: World Publishing Co., 1946), 44.

37. "The Point of View," *Scribner's* 7 (March 1890): 396.

38. Van Rensselaer, "People in New York": 545.

39. Quoted in "New York Architecture," *Architecture and Building* 13 (October 25, 1890): 211-12.

40. George Hill, "A Metropolitan Standard of Buildings," *Real Estate Record and Guide* 73 (June 11, 1904): 1395-1427.

41. Hill, "Metropolitan Standard": 1396.

42. Mumford, *The Brown Decades,* 8.

43. "New York: The Color Changes in New York Buildings," *American Architect and Building News* 27 (February 15, 1890): 108-09. Also see An Admirer of Ruskin, Letter to the Editor, "Our Building Material, Stone Versus Iron," *Real Estate Record and Guide* 17 (March 4, 1876): 165; and W.S. Adams, "The Return To Stone," *Architectural Record* 19 (October 1899): 203-09.

44. Richard Longstreth, "Academic Eclecticism in American Architecture," *Winterthur Portfolio* 17 (Spring 1982): 55-82.

45. *The Art Interchange* 2 (May 14, 1879): 81. Quoted in Wilson, *American Renaissance,* 39.

46. A.D.F. Hamlin, "The Battle of the Styles, II," *Architectural Record* 1 (April-June 1892): 405-13.

47. C.H. Reilly, "The Modern Renaissance in American Architecture," *Journal of the Royal Institute of British Architects* 17, 3rd series (June 25, 1910): 630-35.

48. Reilly, "Modern Renaissance": 634.

49. Charles F. McKim, "Memoranda to Edith Wharton," (ca. February 2, 1897), McKim Collection, The Library of Congress, Washington, D.C. Quoted in Wilson, *American Renaissance,* 61.

50. Charles Garnier, *Le Théâtre* (Paris: 1871): 404. Quoted in David Van Zanten, "Architectural Composition at the Ecole des Beaux-Arts from Charles Percier to Charles Garnier," in Arthur Drexler, ed., *The Architecture of the Ecole des Beaux-Arts* (New York: Museum of Modern Art, 1977), 278.

51. For an earlier attempt to clarify the use of the term "Beaux-Arts Baroque" which was sometimes used to describe the Modern French style, see Robert Stern, *George Howe: Toward a Modern American Architecture* (New Haven: Yale University Press, 1975), 23, note no. 9.

52. Quoted by Curtis Channing Blake, *The Architecture of Carrère & Hastings* (Ph.D. diss., Columbia University, 1976), 175.

53. Montgomery Schuyler, "New New York Houses, East Side," *Architectural Record* 10 (November 1911): 451-74.

54. Hamlin, "Battle of the Styles, I": 270. Also see James Philip Noffsinger, *The Influence of the Ecole des Beaux-Arts on the Architecture of the United States* (Washington, D.C.: Catholic University of America Press, 1955); Richard Chafee, "The Teaching of Architecture at the Ecole des Beaux Arts" and "Beaux Arts Buildings in France and America," in Arthur Drexler, ed., *The Architecture of the Ecole des Beaux-Arts,* 69-110, 417-93.

55. Ernest Flagg, "Influence of the French School on Architecture in the United States," *Architectural Record* 4 (October-December 1894): 211-28.

56. Ernest Flagg, "American Architecture as Opposed to Architecture in America," *Architectural Record* 10 (October 1900): 178-80.

57. A.D.F. Hamlin, "Modern French Architecture," *Architectural Record* 10 (October 1900): 153-54.

58. "Chicago Claims Leadership in Architecture," *Real Estate Record and Guide* 77 (March 31, 1906): 570-71.

59. H.W. Desmond, "The Works of Ernest Flagg," *Architectural Record* 11 (April 1902): 8-22.

60. "A Letter by Ernest Flagg, From the Symposium Published in the T-Square Club Catalogue, 1899," *Architectural Annual* 1 (1900): 31-32.

61. Reilly, "Modern Renaissance": 630-35.

62. Quoted by Wilson, *American Renaissance,* 12.

63. Ralph Adams Cram, "The Case Against the Ecole des Beaux-Arts," *American Architect and Building News* 54 (December 26, 1898): 107-09. McKim advocated the foundation of an American Academy in Rome. Although this was modelled on the French Academy, it was a specific attempt to short-circuit contemporary French styles without over-throwing the principles of French pedagogy. Americans would first study at American schools that employed the methods of the Ecole but did not advocate the Modern French forms, and then travel to Rome to further their work surrounded by the authentic models of antiquity and the Renaissance. See Steven M. Bedford and Susan M. Strauss, "History II 1881-1912," in Richard Oliver, ed., *The Making of an Architect 1881-1981* (New York: Rizzoli, 1981), 23-48. So explicit was the criticism of the French situation that the Society of Beaux-Arts Architects withdrew support from the Academy, arguing that Paris, and not Rome, was the true center of modern architectural activity. See Paul R. Baker, *Richard Morris Hunt* (Cambridge: MIT Press, 1980), 440, on which Bedford and Strauss based their work.

64. See Dolores Hayden, *The Grand Domestic Revolution, A History of Feminist Designs for American Homes, Neighborhoods and Cities* (Cambridge: MIT Press, 1981).

65. According to Mumford, the term originated with Patrick Geddes. See Geddes's *Cities in Evolution* (New York: Oxford University Press, 1950); Lewis Mumford, *City Development, Studies in Disintegration and Renewal* (New York: Harcourt, Brace & Co., 1945), 37, 208-12; and Lewis Mumford, *The City in History, Its Origins, Its Transformations, and Its Prospects* (New York: Harcourt, Brace & World, 1961), 525-67.

66. Commission on Building Districts and Restrictions, *Final Report* (New York, 1916); Kantor, *Modern Urban Planning in New York City,* 165-229; and Mel Scott, *American City Planning Since 1890* (Berkeley: University of California Press, 1971), 153-61.

67. Committee on the Regional Plan of New York and Its Environs, *The Graphic Regional Plan, I* (New York, 1929); Thomas Adams, assisted by Harold M. Lewis and Lawrence M. Orton, *The Building of the City II* (New York, 1931); Kantor, *Modern Urban Planning in New York City,* 230-327; Scott, *American City Planning Since 1890,* 261-65, 287-94.

68. See Winston Weisman, "New York and the Problem of the First Skyscraper," *Journal of the Society of Architectural Historians* 12 (March 1953): 13-21; "A New View of Skyscraper History" in Edgar Kaufman, ed., *The Rise of an American Architecture* (New York: Praeger, 1970), 115-60; Arnold L. Lehman, *The New York Skyscraper: A History of Its Development, 1870-1939* (Ph.D. diss., Yale University, 1974); Rosemarie Haag Bletter and Cervin Robinson, *Skyscraper Style: Art Deco New York* (New York: Oxford University Press, 1975); Carl W. Condit, *American Building* (Chicago: University of Chicago Press, 1968), 114-19; Manfredo Tafuri, "New Babylon: Das New York Der Zwanzigerjahre und die Suche nach dem Amerikanismus," *Metropolis 3: Amerikanismus, Skyscraper und Ikonografie, Architese* 20 (1976): 12-24; and Vincent Scully, *American Architecture and Urbanism* (New York: Praeger, 1969).

69. Carol Herselle Krinsky, *Rockefeller Center* (New York: Oxford University Press, 1978); Alan Balfour, *Rockefeller Center, Architecture as Theater* (New York: McGraw-Hill, 1978); and Robert A.M. Stern with Thomas P. Catalano, *Raymond Hood* (New York: Institute for Architecture and Urban Studies, 1982).

70. Robert A. Caro, *The Power Broker* (New York: Knopf, 1974).

71. Robert A.M. Stern, "With Rhetoric: The New York Apartment

House," *VIA* 4 (1980): 78-111.
72. Clarence S. Stein, *Toward New Towns for America* (New York: Reinhold, 1957).
73. Caro, *The Power Broker*, 334-35.
74. "New York Airport," *Architects' Journal* 93 (March 20, 1941): 195-99.
75. *Pencil Points* 22 (July 1941): 44; and Norval White and Elliott Willensky, *AIA Guide to New York City* (New York: Collier, 1978), 435.
76. For Gilbert's project see, "Hudson River Bridge," *American Architect* 131 (February 6, 1927): 169.

CIVIC STRUCTURE

1. Charles Rollinson Lamb, "Civic Architecture from its Constructive Side," *Municipal Affairs* 2 (March 1898): 69-86.
2. Charles H. Caffin, "Municipal Art," *Harper's Monthly* 100 (April 1900): 655-66. Also see Charles H. Caffin, "The Beautifying of Cities," *World's Work* 3 (November 1901): 1429-35.
3. Cited by Harvey A. Kantor, "The City Beautiful in New York," *New-York Historical Society Bulletin* 57 (April 1973): 152.
4. For early city planning in New York see Henry Hope Reed, "The Vision Spurned: Classical New York—The Story of City Planning in New York," *Classical America* 1 (1971): 31-41, 2 (1972): 10-19. Also see Paul R. Baker, *Richard Morris Hunt* (Cambridge: MIT Press, 1980), 295-99; and Mario Manieri-Elia, "Toward an 'Imperial City': Daniel H. Burnham and the City Beautiful Movement," in Giorgio Ciucci et al., *The American City: From the Civil War to the New Deal* (Cambridge: MIT Press, 1979), 1-121.
5. Baker, *Hunt*, 436.
6. Reprinted in *Yearbook of the Art Societies of New York, 1898-1899* (New York, 1899), 94-98.
7. "Public Art in American Cities," *Municipal Affairs* 2 (March 1898): 1-13. Also see Frederick Stymetz Lamb, "New York City of the Future," *House and Garden* 2 (June 1903): 295-310; and *Architectural Review* 3 (June 1894): 9-10.
8. "From Battery to Harlem, Suggestions of the National Sculpture Society," *Municipal Affairs* 3 (December 1899): 616-50. As Greater New York was created in 1898, the Municipal Art Society was itself incorporated with an expanded membership and program, now devoted to sponsoring works to be executed at the city's expense. It also lobbied successfully for the new City Charter's provision for a Municipal Art Commission, with veto power over all public art and, at the mayor's discretion, city buildings and bridges. The society numbered among its members Andrew Carnegie, Robert W. De Forest, Charles R. Lamb, Charles Follen McKim, and Frederick Stymetz Lamb. See John M. Carrère, "The Art Commission of the City of New York and its Origins," *New York Architect* 2 (March 1908): Harvey Kantor, *Modern Urban Planning in New York City: Origins and Evolution, 1890-1933* (Ph.D. diss., New York University, 1971), 40; and Henry Rutgers Marshall, "The Art Commission of the City of New York," *American Architect* 117 (December 24, 1919): 782-83.
9. Julius F. Harder, "The City's Plan," *Municipal Affairs* 2 (March 1898). 24-45.
10. Harder, "The City's Plan": 30. Also see Julius F. Harder, "The Planning of Cities: Paper No. 1," *Public Improvements* 1 (October 15, 1899): 297-300; *Architecture* 10 (August 15, 1904): 114; and Julius F. Harder, "Greater New York's Future," *Public Improvements* 5 (February 1901): 645-50.
11. Kantor, "The City Beautiful in New York": 151.
12. Ernest Flagg, "The Plan of New York, and How To Improve It," in "The Field of Art," *Scribner's* 36 (August 1904): 253-56. Also see Henry James, *The American Scene* (New York: Harper & Bros., 1907; Bloomington: Indiana University Press, 1968), 100-01.
13. Flagg, "Plan of New York": 253.
14. Flagg, "Plan of New York": 255.
15. "A New Plan for Manhattan," *Real Estate Record and Guide* 75 (August 20, 1904): 390.
16. See, for example, Sturgis's "Grass and Trees in Town," *Scribner's* 36 (November 1904): 637-40.
17. The *New York Herald*, for example, asked a number of experts "How Can New York Be Made the City Beautiful?" *New York Herald*, April 29, 1900, cited in Kantor, "The City Beautiful in New York": 152.
18. Mel Scott, *American City Planning Since 1890* (Berkeley and Los Angeles: University of California Press, 1969), 157. The paper's appeal was echoed by the Fine Arts Federation; see *American Architect and Building News* 75 (February 15, 1902): 49.
19. Carrère, "Art Commission."
20. Kantor, "The City Beautiful in New York": 158. See also *American Architect and Building News* 79 (January 17, 1903): 17.
21. *The Report of the New York City Improvement Commission to the Honorable George B. McClellan, Mayor of the City of New York, and to the Honorable Board of Aldermen of the City of New York* (New York, 1904): 2. Also see "Planning for New Street System," *Real Estate Record and Guide* 73 (March 5, 1904): 482-83; Louis E. Jallade, "Proposed Improvements for the City of New York," *House and Garden* 8 (January 1905): 35-45; and M.G. Cunniff, "What a City Might Be," *World's Work* 10 (July 1905): 6353-54.
22. *New York Improvement Commission* (1904): 16.
23. Herbert Croly, "What is Civic Art?" *Architectural Record* 16 (July 1904): 47-52.
24. *The Report of the New York City Improvement Commission to the Honorable George B. McClellan, Mayor of the City of New York, and to the Honorable Board of Aldermen of the City of New York* (New York, 1907). Also see Herbert N. Casson, "New York, The City Beautiful," *Munsey's* 38 (November 1907): 178-86.
25. Lewis Mumford, *Sticks and Stones* (New York: Boni & Liveright, 1924), 18.
26. "City Beautiful," *New York Architect* 5 (March 1911): 95-96.
27. Scott, *American City Planning*: 82.
28. Dr. Herman C. Bumpus, Director of the Museum, was also a founder of the Committee. The exhibition is described in great detail in *Charities and the Commons* 20 (April 4, 1908): 26-53. Also see Kantor, *Modern Urban Planning in New York City*, 116-77; and *Real Estate Record and Guide* 85 (May 14, 1910): 1027.
29. Scott has labeled it the "City Efficient," *American City Planning: 1*.
30. *Charities and the Commons* 18 (1907): 77-78, 191.
31. Kantor, *Modern Urban Planning in New York City*, 132-35.
32. Kantor, *Modern Urban Planning in New York City*, 141-45.
33. Editorial, *New York Architect* 4 (December 1910): 3. A report on the first annual dinner of the Fifth Avenue Association held in November, at which Borough President McAneny spoke. According to the editor Donn Barber, "It is plainly evident that gradually the idea that the great City of New York can be made to meet the tremendous new demands upon it, in an artistic as well as practical way has now come to full maturity and that presently something real will be done. The formation of the Fifth Avenue Association just entering upon its fifth year was the first step in the right direction. Many of its members who are largely property owners consider the architectural future of New York largely in the hands of its prominent architects." Also see Henry Collins Brown, *Fifth Avenue Old and New, 1824-1924* (New York: Fifth Avenue Association, Wynkoop Hallenbeck Crawford Co., 1924).
34. Herbert Croly, "Civic Improvements: The Case of New York," *Architectural Record* 21 (May 1907): 347-52. Also see Charles Mulford Robinson, "Civic Improvements: A Reply," *Architectural Record* 22 (August 1907): 117-20.
35. "Neighborhoods and Nuisances," *Real Estate Record and Guide* 19 (March 24, 1877): 219-20.
36. "Neighborhoods and Nuisances," *Record and Guide*: 220.
37. "Neighborhoods and Nuisances," *Record and Guide*: 220.
38. "The Growth of New York," *Real Estate Record and Guide* 19 (May 19, 1877): 395-96.
39. Scott, *American City Planning*: 153-54.
40. "Effect of the 'Save New York Movement,'" *Real Estate Record and Guide* 99 (February 3, 1917): 23, 25. Also see "Editorial Comment," *Architectural Forum* 32 (February 1920): 94.
41. "New York City's Planning Exhibition," *American City* 9 (December 1913): 504-12. Also see Kantor, *Modern Urban Planning in New York City*, 152-54.
42. "Save New York Movement," *Real Estate Record and Guide*: 25. Also see Scott, *American City Planning*: 154-55.
43. Robert H. Whitten, "The Building Zone Plan of New York City," *Real Estate Record and Guide* 99 (February 3, 1917): 21, 45.
44. Scott, *American City Planning*: 153-56.
45. "New Uses for the Zoning System," *Architectural Review* 6 (April 1918): 66-67.
46. Carl Condit, *The Port of New York: A History of the Rail and Terminal System from the Beginnings to Pennsylvania Station* (Chicago and London: University of Chicago Press, 1980), XV.
47. "Proposed Grand Central Station of New York City," *Inland Architect and News Record* 44 (December 1904): 39; "The New Grand Central Station, New York," *Architects' and Builders' Magazine* 6 (March 1905): 267-71; "The Project of Rapid Transit in Greater New York," *Architects' and Builders' Magazine* 8 (May 1907): 359-60; "Real Estate as an Investment," *Real Estate Record and Guide* 84 (December 18, 1909): 1084-85; "Stairways Eliminated from the Grand Central Terminal," *Real Estate Record and Guide* 86 (July 16, 1910): 108; "The New Grand Central

Terminal," *Architects' and Builders' Magazine* 11 (November 1910): 45-51; Samuel O. Dunn, "The Problem of the Modern Terminal," *Scribner's* 52 (October 1912): 416-42; "Monumental Gateway to a Great City," *Scientific American* 107 (December 7, 1912): 484-87, 499-500; "A Gateway to the Heart of New York: The New Grand Central Station and its Relation to New York Traffic," *Scientific American Supplement* 74 (December 7, 1912): 364-66; "Grand Central Terminal," *Architecture* 27 (March 15, 1913): 45-47; "The Grand Central Terminal," *Real Estate Record and Guide* 92 (July 15, 1913): 29-36; Carroll Meeks, *The Railroad Station* (New Haven and London: Yale University Press, 1965), 129-30; James Marston Fitch and Diana S. Waite, *Grand Central Terminal and Rockefeller Center: A Historic-critical Estimate of Their Significance* (New York: New York State Parks and Recreation, Division for Historic Preservation, 1974); William D. Middleton, *Grand Central, The World's Greatest Railway Terminal* (San Marino, California: Golden West Books, 1977); and Deborah Nevins, ed. *Grand Central Terminal: City Within the City* (New York: Municipal Art Society, 1982).

48. "Grand Central Terminal," *Architecture* 27 (March 15, 1913): 45, 47.

49. While the 1898-1900 renovations were short-lived, it is interesting to note that the architect Bradford L. Gilbert replaced the mansarded towers of John B. Snook's original design with enlarged finials loosely based on the Tempietto, and overlayed the facade with a necessarily inchoate veneer of classical detail. Gilbert's interior designs were never executed; Middleton, *Grand Central*, 39-44. The interiors were remodelled in 1900 by Philadelphia architect Samuel Huckel, Jr.; "Grand Central Station, New York," *Inland Architect* 38 (September 1901): plates.

50. Leland Roth, *Urban Architecture of McKim, Mead & White, 1870-1910* (Ph.D. dissertation, Yale University, 1973), 695-96.

51. Roth, *Urban Architecture of McKim, Mead & White*, 693-98; and Middleton, *Grand Central*, 63.

52. Middleton has ably documented the evolution of the design, from Reed & Stem's initial, ingeniously organized proposal to the final, inspired synthesis of planning and aesthetics. Once Warren and Wetmore were involved, many of Charles Reed's strategies for handling pedestrian and vehicular traffic were abandoned as the architects searched for a more monumental expression, only to return again in the final scheme arrived at in 1909; Middleton, *Grand Central*, 63-79. Also note that Reed was Wilgus's brother-in-law. Nevins, *Grand Central Terminal*, 13-16.

53. Whitney Warren, quoted in "The Grand Central Terminal," *Real Estate Record and Guide* 92 (July 5, 1913): 29-36.

54. "The Park Avenue Viaduct, New York City," *Architecture* 39 (February 1919): 41-44.

55. "New Roadways Around Grand Central Terminal Formally Opened," *Real Estate Record and Guide* 122 (September 15, 1928): 5.

56. The width of the mall was drastically reduced in the late 1920s to accommodate an extra traffic lane in each direction.

57. Middleton, *Grand Central*, 101.

58. "The Pennsylvania's New York Station," *Architectural Record* 27 (June 1910): 519-22. Also see Henry W. Desmond and Herbert Croly, "The Work of McKim, Mead & White," *Architectural Record* 10 (September 1906): 153-246.

59. "A Promising Mercantile Thoroughfare," *Real Estate Record and Guide* 89 (April 13, 1912): 737-38.

60. Condit, *Port of New York*, XIII-XIV.

61. Montgomery Schuyler, "The New Pennsylvania Station in New York," *International Studio* 41 (October 1910): LXXXIX-XCIV.

62. Thomas Wolfe, *You Can't Go Home Again*, (New York: Charles Scribner's Sons, 1940), 247-48.

63. Alexander Cassatt, the President of the Pennsylvania Railroad, wanted a profitable office tower, but McKim prevailed. The decision to build a monumental station rather than an office block sealed the fate of the station. Pennsylvania Station, the culmination of the greatest railroad consolidation in history, only survived fifty years. Roth, *Urban Architecture of McKim, Mead & White*, 700.

64. Quoted in Margaret Clapp, "The Social and Cultural Scene," in Allen Nevins and John Krout, eds. *The Greater City: New York 1898-1948* (New York: Columbia University Press, 1948), 221.

65. Arnold W. Brunner and Frederick Law Olmsted, *Proposed Change of Map for Riverside Drive Extension; Report and Plans* (New York, 1913).

66. "West End Improvement," *Architecture and Building* 13 (November 22, 1890): 294.

67. Milton See, "The Planning of Cities: Paper No. 4," *Public Improvements* (December 1, 1899): 51.

68. "Riverside Drive Extension," *Real Estate Record and Guide* 66 (July 7, 1900): 2.

69. Brunner and Olmsted, *Proposed Change of Map*.

70. Brunner and Olmsted, *Proposed Change of Map*.

71. Robert A. Caro, *The Power Broker: Robert Moses and the Fall of New York* (New York: Alfred A. Knopf, 1974), 525-66.

72. Condit, *Port of New York*, 332-33.

73. See Mel Scott, *American City Planning Since 1890* (Berkeley and Los Angeles: University of California Press, 1969), 221-22.

74. Montgomery Schuyler, "Along the 'Harlem River Branch,'" *Architectural Record* 24 (December 1908): 417-29. Also see Condit, *Port of New York*, 312-32.

75. Schuyler, "Along the 'Harlem River Branch'": 417-25; *Architecture* 31 (April 1915): plates 38-42.

76. By 1937 the line was no longer running, and within a few years it was absorbed into the city's subway system as the Dyre Avenue line of the I.R.T. System. Stan Fischler, *Uptown, Downtown: A Trip Through Time on New York's Subways* (New York: Hawthorn Books, 1976), 150-60.

77. Quoted in Fischler, *Uptown, Downtown*, 154. Also see Lloyd Ultan, *The Beautiful Bronx (1920-1950)* (New Rochelle: Arlington House, 1979), 24, 258.

78. "Some Recent Works of Clinton & Russell," *New York Architect* 3 (September 1909).

79. "Competitive Drawing for Uptown Terminal of the McAdoo Tunnel," *American Architect and Building News* 93 (February 12, 1908): plate.

80. S.D.V. Burr, *Rapid Transit in New York City* (New York: Chamber of Commerce of the State of New York, 1905), 10-11.

81. Alfred H. Thorp, "A Scheme for Rapid Transit for New York City," *Architecture and Building* 14 (February 28, 1891): 103-04. Also see Editorial, *American Architect and Building News* 48 (June 8, 1895): 93.

82. See Editorial cited above as well as *American Architect and Building News* 49 (August 31, 1895): plates.

83. J.J.R. Croes, "Suggestions as to Rapid Transit Routes and Structures," *Architecture and Building* 22 (January 12, 1895): 23-25.

84 *American Architect and Building News* 58 (November 20, 1897): 62.

85. "The Rapid Transit Road," *Public Improvements* 2 (November 1, 1899): 7-8.

86. *Public Improvements* 3 (July 1900): 377; and William Barclay Parsons, "Rapid Transit in New York," *Scribner's* 27 (May 1900): 545-55.

87. *Interborough Rapid Transit. The New York Subway. Its Construction and Equipment* (New York: IRT Company, 1904).

88. The idea was borrowed from the Budapest subway, where, instead of major above-ground terminals, simple open pavilions (kushks in Hungarian) were built to mark the entrances and shelter the steps from rain and snow. See Burr, *Rapid Transit in New York*, 106, 212; and Fischler, *Uptown, Downtown*, 37.

89. The control house at Seventy-second Street was particularly lavish. The West End Association was, however, critical of the design, finding it "not only an offense to the eye, but a very serious danger to life and limb." Landmarks LP 1021, January 9, 1979. Burr (*Rapid Transit in New York*: 139) particularly admired the control house at 116th Street and Broadway.

90. M.G. Cuniff, "The New York Subway," *World's Work* 8 (October 1904): 5346-64.

91. "The Old Rapid Transit and The New," *Real Estate Record and Guide* 74 (October 29, 1904): 896.

92. *Real Estate Record and Guide* 74 (November 5, 1904): 949.

93. Editorial, *American Architect and Building News* 86 (December 1904): 73.

94. "City Hall Station of the New York Subway," *Brickbuilder* 13 (April 1904): 85.

95. Fischler, *Uptown, Downtown*, 134.

96. *American Architect and Building News* 86 (December 3, 1904): 73.

97. *Real Estate Record and Guide* 74 (November 5, 1904): 949-50.

98. Roth, *Urban Architecture of McKim, Mead & White*, 688-93; and "IRT Power Station," *Architecture* 14 (July 1906): plate 51.

99. "New York's First Underground Sidewalk," *Architects' and Builders' Magazine* 6 (October 1904): 27-36.

100. "New York's First Underground Sidewalk": 35, "The continuance of such a subsidewalk over to Broadway, for instance, or its eventual development in connection with subways throughout the business districts of the city, is a dream of the future that may occur in many minds."

101. "The Project of Rapid Transit in Greater New York," *Architects' and Builders' Magazine* 8 (May 1907): 359-60.

102. S.J. Vickers, "Architectural Treatment of Stations on the Dual System of Rapid Transit in New York City," *Architectural Record* 45 (January 1919): 15-20.

103. *New York City Improvement Commission* (1904): 6-8.

104. "The Municipal Ferry Terminals," *Architects' and Builders' Magazine* 9 (May 1907): 397-99; "The City's New Ferry Terminal and Office Building," *Real Estate Record and Guide* 81 (June 6, 1908): 1062; and Edward W. Hudson, "Architectural Design in Steel Work," *Royal Institute*

of British Architects Journal 19, 3rd series (March 9, 1912): 330-39.
105. Charles C. Hurlbut, "Modern Architectural Copper Work," *Architects' and Builders' Magazine* 10 (November 1908): 99-106; and "The Ferry Terminals at the Foot of West Twenty-third Street, New York City," *Architects' and Builders' Magazine* 8 (May 1907): 374.
106. "The New Stapleton Ferry Terminal: Snelling & Potter, Architects," *American Architect and Building News* 94 (August 1908): 98.
107. "Municipal Ferry Terminals," *Architects' and Builders' Magazine* 397-99; "Work of Carrère & Hastings," *Architectural Record* 27 (January 1910): 1-120.
108. "The Chelsea Section Improvement—A Municipal Enterprise," *Architects' and Builders' Magazine* 10 (February 1910): 165-73.
109. *Architecture and Building* 13 (July 5, 1890): 2; Condit, *Port of New York*: 256-58.
110. O.F. Nichols, "The New East River Bridge," *Public Improvements* 1 (May 15, 1899): 21-22; Sharon Reier, *The Bridges of New York* (New York: Quadrant Press, 1977), 31.
111. John De Witt Warner, "Bridges and Art," an address delivered before the National Sculpture Society on December 19, 1899, reprinted in *Public Improvements* 2 (January 1, 1900): 97-99.
112. George Post, "The Planning of Cities," *Public Improvements* 2 (November 15, 1899): 26-27; Montgomery Schuyler, "Bridges and the Art Commission," *Architectural Record* 22 (December 1907): 469-75; Henry F. Hornbostel, "The New East River Bridges," *Architecture* 8 (August 1903): 103-05; "Two Ways: Public Works in Paris and New York," *Real Estate Record and Guide* 66 (September 1, 1900): 261-62; and Montgomery Schuyler, "New York Bridges," *Architectural Record* 18 (October 1905): 243-62.
113. "The Architectural Embellishment of the New Williamsburg Bridge," *House and Garden* 3 (March 1903): 141-45. Also see Reier, *Bridges of New York*, 28-39.
114. Montgomery Schuyler, "Our Four Big Bridges," *Architectural Record* 25 (March 1909): 149-60; and Charles C. Hughes, "Interesting Examples of the Use of Burnt Clay in Architecture," *Brickbuilder* 18 (August 1909): 155-60.
115. Schuyler, "Our Four Big Bridges": 152.
116. Schuyler, "Our Four Big Bridges": 151.
117. Schuyler, "Our Four Big Bridges": 160.
118. *American Architect and Building News* 79 (February 14, 1903): 50; Schuyler, "New York Bridges": 259-62.
119. *American Architect and Building News* 83 (January 16, 1904): 17; *Architecture* 9 (May 1904): 66; *American Architect and Building News* 92 (August 31, 1907): 65; and Curtis Channing Blake, *The Architecture of Carrère & Hastings* (Ph.D. diss., Columbia University, 1976), 310-12.
120. Schuyler, "Our Four Big Bridges": 160.
121. "The New Manhattan Bridge: A Bridge Beautiful as well as Useful," *Architects' and Builders' Magazine* 5 (September 1904): 547-53.
122. "The Borough of Manhattan Approach to Manhattan Bridge No. 3, New York," *American Architect* 102 (August 14, 1912): 61-63.
123. Reier, *The Bridges of New York*, 41-51.
124. Henry F. Hornbostel, "The Queensboro Bridge," *Architecture* 19 (April 15, 1909): 49-53, 57.
125. *New York City Improvement Commission* (1904): 12-14; *New York City Improvement Commission* (1907): 16-18.
126. Reier, *The Bridges of New York*, 58-65.
127. Schuyler, "Bridges and the Art Commission": 472-75; *American Architect and Building News* 92 (August 17, 1907): 50; "What Hell Gate Bridge will do for Queens Borough," *Real Estate Record and Guide* 96 (October 9, 1915): 605; and Condit, *Port of New York*, 332-41.
128. While the Hell Gate crossing and the viaduct over Randalls and Wards Islands formed the principal section of the connecting railway, a second significant segment, designed by Arnold Brunner, carried the railroad across Queens to Sunnyside where it linked up with the Long Island and Pennsylvania systems. Brunner's triple arched bridge over Queens Boulevard is elegant though more explicitly classical than Hornbostel's. The Pelham Parkway Bridge was also a collaboration between Hornbostel and Lindenthal. An early example of reinforced concrete construction, this low, three arched bridge seemed unresolved to Schuyler. H. Hornbostel, "The Queensboro Bridge," *Architecture* 19 (April 1909): 49-53.
129. Marianna Griswold van Rensselaer, "Fifth Avenue," *Century* 47 (November 1893): 5-18.
130. "Stable of C.K.G. Billings, Esq.," *Architectural Review* 4 (September 1902): 223; and *Architecture* 9 (January 15, 1904): 8.
131. "Fifth Avenue Riding School," *American Architect and Building News* 7 (May 1, 1880): 191.
132. "The 'Dakota' Stable," *American Architect and Building News* 17 (June 6, 1885): 270.

133. "The Riding Stable of Frank Gould," *Architectural Record* 12 (June 1902): 228; and "Riding Ring of Frank J. Gould, Esq., New York," *Architectural Review* 4 (September 1902): 221-22.
134. "Revolutionary Ideas in Stable Architecture," *Architects' and Builders' Magazine* 8 (December 1906): 115-24.
135. "The Tichenor-Grand Stable," *Architects' and Builders' Magazine* 8 (January 1907): 163-69.
136. "Stable for the Standard Coach Horse Co.," *American Architect and Building News* 78 (December 27, 1902): plate; and "Standard Coach Horse Building," *Inland Architect and News Record* 43 (February 1904): plate.
137. "Development in Garage Construction," *Real Estate Record and Guide* 81 (April 18, 1908): 703.
138. "House of Mr. Ernest Flagg, Architect," *American Architect and Building News* 89 (May 12, 1906): 163-64; "A New Type of City House," *Real Estate Record and Guide* 80 (August 24, 1907): 287-88; "The Automobile Garage as an Adjunct to the New York City House," *Real Estate Record and Guide* 80 (August 31, 1907): 324-25; "A New Type of City House," *Architectural Record* 22 (September 1907): 177-94; and "New York City Houses," *Brickbuilder* 17 (September 1908): 197.
139. "The Automobile Club of America," *American Architect and Building News* 91 (May 4, 1907): 187, plates.
140. Quoted in David P. Handlin, *The American Home* (Boston: Little, Brown, 1979), 149.
141. Lewis Mumford, "The Roaring Traffic's Boom," *The New Yorker* (1955), quoted in Caro, *The Power Broker*, 915.

CIVIC GRANDEUR

1. Charles Lockwood, *Manhattan Moves Uptown* (Boston: Houghton Mifflin Co., 1976), 1.
2. Lockwood, *Manhattan Moves Uptown*, 1.
3. "Accepted Designs for New Municipal Buildings in the City of New York, Charles B. Atwood, Architect," *Building* 9 (December 29, 1888): plates; and "Tower, New City Hall, N.Y.," *American Architect and Building News* 27 (February 1, 1890): plate.
4. *Building* 11 (September 21, 1889): 92; A.J. Bloor, Letter to the Editor, *Building* 11 (September 28, 1889): 105-6.
5. Quoted in "The Site for the Municipal Building," *Real Estate Record and Guide* 47 (March 21, 1891): 436. Also see "The New Municipal Building," *Real Estate Record and Guide* 47 (March 14, 1891): 390.
6. "Shall the City Hall Be Removed?" *Real Estate Record and Guide* 47 (April 11, 1891): 554-56. In 1891, as the New York *Herald* was planning to relocate uptown, it proposed that a new City Hall should be built on what was soon to be renamed Herald Square. See *Real Estate Record and Guide* 47 (April 4, 1891): 509-10.
7. *Architecture and Building* 23 (October 19, 1895): plates. The action was surprising, since the head of Columbia's architecture program, William Robert Ware, was in favor of the building's removal. See "The City Hall Matter in New York," *American Architect and Building News* 39 (March 18, 1893): 161-62. In 1894, *American Architect and Building News* also published a plate of City Hall; "The City Hall, New York, N.Y., John McComb, Architect," *American Architect and Building News* 44 (June 23, 1894): 139.
8. *American Architect and Building News* 39 (January 28, 1893): 50.
9. "A New Municipal Building for New York," *Architecture and Building* 24 (January 25, 1896): 37.
10. "The City Hall Matter in New York," *American Architect and Building News*: 161-62.
11. The *Record* also proposed that if the new City Hall must be in the park, it should replace the Tweed Courthouse, "a monument of fraud that recalls the most disgraceful period of the city's history." "The New York City Hall Competition—A Protest," *Architectural Record* 3 (October-December 1893): 213-15.
12. Editorial, "The New York Municipal Building Competition," *Architecture and Building* 20 (January 6, 1894): 1-2; *American Architect and Building News* 43 (January 13, 1894): 14; Editorial, "The New York City Hall Competition," *Architecture and Building* 20 (January 27, 1894): 37-38; Editorial, *American Architect and Building News* 44 (May 26, 1894): 81; "A New Municipal Building for New York," *Architecture and Building* 24 (January 25, 1896): 37; and *American Architect and Building News* 51 (February 8, 1896): 58.
13. "Competitive Design for Proposed City Hall, New York, N.Y., Cram, Wentworth & Goodhue, Architects," *American Architect and Building News* 52 (May 9, 1896): plates.
14. "A Prize Competitive Design for the New York City Hall, Gordon, Bragdon & Orchard, Architects," *American Architect and Building News*

444

52 (April 18, 1896): 31, plates.
15. "Competitive Design for Proposed City Hall, Brunner & Tryon, Architects," *American Architect and Building News* 52 (May 9, 1896): plate; The proposals of Dodge & Braun, H. Langford Warren, O. Van Nerta, Eames & Young and Cram, Wentworth & Goodhue are also illustrated in this issue. The proposals of Rankin & Kellogg and T.M. Clark are published in a later issue. Also among the six selected was Edward Pearce Casey's Modern French proposal whose principal interest lay in an elaborate three-story entry hall. *American Architect and Building News* 55 (January 30, 1897): 39, plates.
16. "The Matter of the Over-richness of Interior Work in the New York Hall of Records," *American Architect and Building News* 65 (July 29, 1899): 32; "Proposed Design for the New York Court House on the Chambers Street Site," *Architects' and Builders' Magazine* 5 (April 1904): 332-36; "Hall of Records N.Y.," *Architecture* 10 (December 1904): plate 103; *American Architect and Building News* 88 (July 1, 1905): 1-2; Montgomery Schuyler, "The New Hall of Records," *Architectural Record* 17 (May 1905): 383-87; "The New Hall of Records: New York's Most Beautiful Building," *Architects' and Builders' Magazine* 8 (January 1907): 142-55; and "Rotunda, Hall of Records, N.Y.," *Architecture* 15 (January 1907): plate VIII.
17. "Political and Architectural History of the New York Hall of Records," *American Architect and Building News* 88 (January 1905): 1-2.
18. Schuyler, "The New Hall of Records": 383, 385.
19. Schuyler, "The New Hall of Records": 387.
20. Israels & Harder had also both been employed by Charles Atwood when he prepared his 1888 City Hall competition entry. See "Plans for New County Courthouse," *Real Estate Record and Guide* 73 (January 9, 1904): 49-50; and "Proposed Design for the New York Court House on the Chambers Street Site," *Architects' and Builders' Magazine* 5 (April 1904): 332-36.
21. "A Civic Centre for New York," *Municipal Affairs* 6 (Fall 1902): 478-83; "City Hall Improvement," *Public Improvements* 6 (October 1902): 159-60; and *American Architect and Building News* 79 (January 24, 1903): 26.
22. Herbert Croly, "New York as the American Metropolis," *Architectural Record* 13 (March 1903): 198.
23. *Report of the New York City Improvement Commission to the Honorable George B. McClellan and the Honorable Aldermen of the City of New York* (New York, 1904): 2.
24. George B. Post, "The Planning of Cities, Paper No. 3," *Public Improvements* 2 (November 15, 1899): 26-29.
25. Post, "The Planning of Cities": 27.
26. "Proposed Brooklyn Bridge Terminal and City Offices," *Architects' and Builders' Magazine* 4 (August 1903): 483-89; *American Architect and Building News* 81 (August 15, 1903): 50; "Proposed Layout of City Hall Park in Connection with the New York Terminal of the Brooklyn Bridge, Showing the Campanile and Municipal Buildings on the Left," *Architecture* 8 (August 1903): plate LXII; "Plans for Rebuilding Brooklyn Bridge," *Real Estate Record and Guide* 73 (January 2, 1904): 4; and "The Extension of the Manhattan Terminal of the New York and Brooklyn Bridge," *Architects' and Builders' Magazine* 6 (September 1905): 521-30. The Municipal Art Society proposed a similar, though schematic, solution in 1902. See "Suggested Changes in the City Hall Park, New York," *American Architect and Building News* 77 (August 16, 1902): 49; "A Civic Centre for New York," *Municipal Affairs* 6 (Fall 1902): 478-83; "City Hall Improvement," *Public Improvements* 6 (October 1902): 159-60; and *American Architect and Building News* 79 (January 24, 1903): 26.
27. *American Architect and Building News* 81 (August 15, 1903): 50.
28. "Adoption of a Scheme for a Brooklyn Bridge Terminal Station," *American Architect and Building News* 88 (July 15, 1905): 17; and "The Extension of the Manhattan Terminal of the New York and Brooklyn Bridge," *Architects' and Builders' Magazine*: 521-30.
29. All four entries were published in *American Architect and Building News* 63 (May 27, 1908): plates.
30. Leland Roth, *Urban Architecture of McKim, Mead & White, 1870-1910* (Ph.D. diss., Yale University, 1973), 740-43.
31. "Accepted Competitive Design, Municipal Office Building, New York," *Architecture* 13 (May 1908): plate XXI; William Walton, "The New Municipal Building, New York, and Its Sculpture," *American Architect* 101 (March 20, 1912): 133-38, 140; "Municipal Building, N.Y. City," *Architectural Year Book* 1 (1912): 299; *Architecture and Building* 46 (October 1914): 381-96; "New York Municipal Building," *Architecture* 28 (July 1913): 149, plates 60-63; and *A Monograph of the Works of McKim, Mead & White* (New York: 1915, Benjamin Blom, 1973), 50, 56, plates 320-27.
32. "Architectural Aberrations No. 10, The New Criminal Court Building, New York," *Architectural Record* 3 (April-June 1894): 429-32. Also see "New Criminal Court Building," *Architectural Record* 1 (April-June 1892): 493; "Staircase in the Main Court of the Criminal Courts Building, Corner Centre and Franklin Streets, New York, N.Y.," *American Architect and Building News* 46 (October 27, 1894): plate; and "The New Criminal Court House, Centre Street, From Franklin to White Streets, New York," *Architecture and Building* 21 (December 22, 1895): plate.
33. "Architectural Aberrations No. 10," *Architectural Record*: 432. Haviland's Tombs Prison was built in 1838 and connected to the new courthouse by a "Bridge of Sighs" across Franklin Street. In 1897 it was replaced by a new, castellated prison by the architects Withers and Dickson. See "City Prison, New York," *American Architect and Building News* 56 (April 3, 1897): plates.
34. "The Proposed Encroachment on City Hall Park by New Buildings," *American Architect and Building News* 97 (March 16, 1910): 123; "The Problem of Selecting a Site for New York County Court House," *American Architect and Building News* 97 (March 23, 1910): 139; "The New New York Court House," *Architectural Record* 27 (April 1910): 359-60.
35. "Study for the New York Court House on a Single Block Site," *Architecture* 11 (February 15, 1909): 20-21.
36. "A Tower Building A Thousand Feet High," *Real Estate Record and Guide* 85 (April 30, 1910): 921-22.
37. "A Tower Building A Thousand Feet High," *Real Estate Record and Guide*: 921. At the same time, Ernest Flagg proposed a site at the Battery. See "Why Mr. Flagg Would Build the Court House at the Battery," *Real Estate Record and Guide* 85 (April 26, 1910): 808-09.
38. "New York Court House Story In Brief," *Architectural Record* 36 (July 1914): 77-78.
39. The invited architects were: Arnold W. Brunner; Charles Butler and Charles Morris, associated; Carrère & Hastings; James Riely Gordon; La Farge & Morris; H. Van Buren Magonigle; McKim, Mead & White; Tracy, Swartwout & Litchfield; Trowbridge & Livingston; and York & Sawyer. "Competition for Court House, New York City," *Brickbuilder* 21 (June 1912): 169.
40. "The New York Court House," *Brickbuilder* 22 (April 1913): 97; "First Prize Design, Competition for New York County Courthouse," *American Architect* 103 (April 30, 1913): 214, plates; "The Court House Award," *Architectural Record* 33 (May 1913): 469-71; Montgomery Schuyler, "The New York Court House and Its Site," *Architectural Record* 36 (July 1914): 1-11; Editorial, "The New York Court House," *Architecture* 29 (May 1914): 96-97; and Alanson T. Briggs, "The Conditions of the Court House Problem," *Real Estate Record and Guide* 101 (January 5, 1918): 3, 6, 11-12.
41. "The New York County Courthouse," *American Architect* 116 (December 3, 1919): 681-86.
42. "The City's Court House Problem," *Real Estate Record and Guide* 95 (June 12, 1915): 991.
43. "Sculpture and Decoration for the New York Appellate Courthouse," *American Architect and Building News* 59 (March 5, 1898): 73; "New Court House for the Appellate Division of the Supreme Court," *Architecture and Building* 30 (June 3, 1899): plate; "The Appellate Division Courthouse," *Real Estate Record and Guide* 63 (June 3, 1899): 1042; "Accepted Model and Original Sketch for Pediment Group: Appellate Court House, New York, N.Y.," *American Architect and Building News* 66 (November 4, 1899): plate; "The New Appellate Court Building," *Public Improvements* 2 (January 1, 1900): 102-03; "The New Appellate Courthouse, New York City," *Architectural Record* 9 (April 1900): 429-34 (illus.); "Court House, Appellate Division of the Supreme Court, Twenty-fifth Street and Madison Avenue, New York," *Architecture* 2 (October 1900): 376-77; "Appellate Court House: East 25th St. and Madison Ave., New York, N.Y.," *American Architect and Building News* 70 (December 8, 1900): plate; and Russell Sturgis, "The Field of Art," *Scribner's* 28 (December 1900): 768.
44. "The New Appellate Court Building," *Public Improvements*: 102.
45. "Bronx County Court House, 161st Street and 3d Avenue, New York," *Architecture and Building* 46 (April 1914): 163-66 (illus.).
46. "Gates Avenue Court House, Borough of Brooklyn, New York, N.Y.," *Architectural Review* 10 (December 1903): plates 58-61; and "The Gates Avenue Court House, Borough of Brooklyn," *New York Architect* 3 (April 1909): plates. Also see Crow, Lewis & Wickenhoffer's "Children's Court Building, 137 East 22d Street, New York," *American Architect* 105 (March 4, 1914): plate; and "The Children's Municipal Court, New York City," *Architectural Review* 4 (May 1916): plate XLIV.
47. See a proposal by McKim, Mead & White: Leland Roth, *The Architecture of McKim, Mead & White, 1870-1920: A Building List* (New York: Garland, 1978), 36; and one by Lord, Hewlett & Hull: "Brooklyn Municipal Building," *American Architect and Building News* 93 (February 12, 1908): plate.
48. *Brickbuilder* 16 (January 1907): plates; and Curtis Channing Blake,

The Architecture of Carrère and Hastings (Ph.D. diss., Columbia University, 1976), 275-78. The Hotel-de-Ville in Tours had recently been published. See Georges Gromort, "The Hotel-de-Ville, Tours, France," *Architectural Review* 10 (June 1903): 61-66.

49. Blake, *The Architecture of Carrère & Hastings*, 278-80.

50. "New Fire Engine Houses," *Real Estate Record and Guide* 62 (November 5, 1898): 652-53.

51. See Moses King, *King's Handbook of New York City 1893* (Boston: M. King, 1893; New York: Benjamin Blom, 1972), 530.

52. "Fire Department Headquarters," *Real Estate Record and Guide* 39 (June 18, 1887): 830; "New Fire Engine Houses," *Real Estate Record and Guide:* 652. For Le Brun's work for the Fire Department, see "The Work of N. Le Brun & Sons," *Architectural Record* 27 (May 1910): 365-81.

53. "Engine House and Battalion Headquarters, Elm and White Streets, New York, N.Y.," *American Architect and Building News* 54 (November 7, 1896): 47, plate.

54. "New Fire Engine Houses," *Real Estate Record and Guide:* 652.

55. "New Fire Engine Houses," *Real Estate Record and Guide:* 652. Also see "Fire-Engine House, Forty-third Street, New York, N.Y.," *American Architect and Building News* 60 (June 4, 1898): plate. Hoppin & Koen's design closely resembled Le Brun's Engine House Number Fourteen at 14 East Eighteenth Street. See "Engine House No. 14," *American Architect and Building News* 54 (October 24, 1896): plate.

56. "New Fire Engine Houses," *Real Estate Record and Guide:* 652.

57. "New Fire Engine Houses," *Real Estate Record and Guide:* 652-53; and "Fire-Engine House, Great Jones St., New York, N.Y.," *American Architect* 70 (November 24, 1900): plate. Also see "Engine House, New York City," *Brickbuilder* 6 (May 1897): plate 47; and H.W. Desmond, "Description of the Works of Ernest Flagg," *Architectural Record* 11 (April 1902): 48-49.

58. Edward Pearce Casey's House for an Engine Company on 159th Street (which seems not to have been realized), was an equally bold design with a steeply hipped roof and bold rustication that reflected contemporary English classicism. The bold use of quoining to unify pilasters and the decisiveness with which the dormers were cut into the roof attest to Casey's freshness of approach. "House for an Engine Company. City of New York," *Brickbuilder* 7 (November 1898): plates 85-86. Also see "Engine House, New York City, Edward P. Casey, Architect," *Brickbuilder* 13 (December 1904): 259.

59. "Fire-Engine House, No. 22 East 12th Street, New York, N.Y.," *American Architect and Building News* 64 (November 2, 1901): plate.

60. "Water-Tower No. 3, and Hook and Ladder House No. 24, New York, N.Y.," *American Architect and Building News* 75 (February 8, 1902): plate.

61. "Fire Engine House," *Brickbuilder* 13 (December 1904): plate. Also see Griffin's Tudor style "Fire Engine House, Ogden Avenue, New York City," *Architectural Review* 6 (January 1899): plate V.

62. "Fire Engine House, 232 W. 63d St., New York, N.Y.," *American Architect and Building News* 94 (August 5, 1908): plates; "Hook and Ladder House, New York City," *Brickbuilder* 19 (May 1910): plate 60.

63. "Engine House, New York City," *Brickbuilder* 19 (May 1910): plate 62. Herts & Tallant's partially realized design for the Fire Department's Manhattan Headquarters was totally uncharacteristic of their work: a strict interpretation of a Florentine palazzo. See "New York Fire Department Headquarters, New York City," *Architectural Review* 15 (June 1908): plates 33-34.

64. For a particularly bad example see "Architectural Aberrations, The Twenty-third Precinct Police Station House, New York City," *Architectural Record* 30 (August 1911): 181-84.

65. "Accepted Design for New Police Headquarters," *Real Estate Record and Guide* 73 (January 23, 1904): 165; *Architects' and Builders' Magazine* 10 (January 1910): 123-29; "New Police Headquarters, Centre and Grand Sts., New York," *Architecture* 21 (January 15, 1910): 2-3, 5; and Frank Marshall White, "The Finest Police Headquarters in the World," *Harper's Weekly* 53 (August 14, 1909): 27.

66. *New York Times* (January 1903): 3, quoted in N.Y.C. Landmarks Preservation Commission Report LP-0999 (September 26, 1978).

67. "First Precinct Police Station, Old Slip, New York City," *American Architect and Building News* 93 (February 12, 1908): plate; and "Old Slip, First Precinct Police Station, New York," *American Architect* 104 (December 24, 1913): plate.

68. Edward Pearce Casey, "Concrete Construction Used in the New 13th Precinct Police Station, N.Y.C.," *American Architect* 101 (January 24, 1912): 42-45.

69. Casey, "13th Precinct": 45.

70. "The Forty-first Precinct Police Station," *Architects' and Builders' Magazine* 7 (August 1906): 461-65.

71. "The Forty-first Precinct," *Architects' and Builders' Magazine:* 464-65.

72. "New Custom House Building for New York," *Real Estate Record and Guide* 47 (March 7, 1891): 344; *Architecture and Building* 30 (February 4, 1899): 34; and "The New York Custom House Competition," *Architecture and Building* 30 (May 13, 1899): 149.

73. The submissions of Carrère & Hastings, Trowbridge & Livingston, and Gibson were published in *Inland Architect and News Record* 35 (February 1900): plates; the Shepley, Rutan & Coolidge proposal in "A Competitive Design for the United States Custom House, N.Y.," *American Architect and Building News* 70 (December 1, 1900): plates.

74. *Architectural Review* 7 (May 1900): 58, quoted in Blake, *Architecture of Carrère & Hastings*, 74.

75. Blake, *Architecture of Carrère & Hastings*, 74.

76. "Cass Gilbert's New York Customhouse [sic] Design," *Inland Architect* 35 (February 1900): 6-7. Also see Montgomery Schuyler, "The New Custom House at New York," *Architectural Record* 20 (July 1906): 1-14; "The New York Custom House," *Architects' and Builders' Magazine* 9 n.s. (November 1907): 51-61; "United States Custom House, New York, N.Y.," *American Architect and Building News* 68 (March 24, 1900): plates; *Architectural Review* (Boston) 10 (February 1903): plate 11; and Charles De Kay, "The New York Custom House," *Century* 71 (March 1906): 733-43.

77. "The Ellis Island Immigration Station," *Architects' and Builders' Magazine* 2 (July 1901): 345-52; also see "Main Building, U.S. Immigrant Station, Ellis Island, N.Y. Harbor," *Architecture and Building* 30 (April 1, 1899): plate; "Immigrant Station for the United States Government, Ellis Island, N.Y. Harbor," *Brickbuilder* 11 (July 1902): plates; and "Architectural Appreciations No. III. The New York Immigrant Station," *Architectural Record* 12 (December 1902): 726-33.

78. "Architectural Appreciations No. III," *Architectural Record* 12: 726-33.

79. Henry James, *The American Scene* (New York: Harper & Bros., 1907; Bloomington: Indiana University Press, 1968), 84-85.

80. "New Public School Buildings," *Real Estate Record and Guide* 45 (February 22, 1890): 257-58.

81. See John Beverly Robinson, "The School Buildings of New York," *Architectural Record* 7 (January–March 1898): 359-84; Russell Sturgis, "The Field of Art," *Scribner's* 26 (November 1899): 637-40; "The Unconscious Aesthetic Education," *Scribner's* 29 (February 1901): 251-52; and Adele Marie Shaw, "The True Character of New York Public Schools," *World's Work* 7 (December 1902): 4204-21.

82. Shaw, "True Character of New York Public Schools": 4205.

83. Shaw, "True Character of New York Public Schools": 4205-06.

84. Shaw, "True Character of New York Public Schools": 4205 and *passim.*

85. "C.B.J. Snyder," Obituary, *National Architect* 2 (1946): 34.

86. Schools more than four stories high were built with steel frame construction, "the adoption of the system being due to the building laws, which exact certain thicknesses of wall over and above a specified amount for every 10 per cent. or fraction thereof in which the openings in a bearing wall exceed 25 per cent. of its area. . . . As our window frames are usually 10 ft. 6 ins. . . . by 16 ft. . . . our walls would be 36 ins. or so in thickness in the first story, instead of the 16 ins. permissible under the steel 'skeleton' type of construction. I believe that a schoolroom should be lighted from one single source of light stretching as nearly as may be from the rear to within 4 ft. or so of the front of the room at the left side of the pupils, and not by a series of windows alternating with brick or stone piers, which means light and shadow for each alternate 4 or 5 ft., hence cross lights." Described by Snyder in a letter published by the architect Edmund B. Wheelwright in "The American Schoolhouse, XVI," *Brickbuilder* 8 (March 1899): 45-47. Also see C.B.J. Snyder, "The Lighting of School Rooms," *American Architect* 108 (September 8, 1915): 170-76.

87. Robinson, "School Buildings of New York": 364.

88. "Public School, St. Nicholas Avenue and 117th Street," *Real Estate Record and Guide* 62 (August 20, 1898): 261.

89. Robinson, "School Buildings of New York": 364.

90. Sometimes Snyder worked in a Collegiate Gothic style. At P.S. 166 on West Eighty-ninth Street between Columbus and Amsterdam avenues, he designed a boldly scaled castle keep to mark the building's principal entrance. See "Public School No. 166, New York, N.Y., C.B.J. Snyder, Architect," *American Architect and Building News* 75 (March 29, 1902): plates. In the city's inner core on the Lower East Side of Manhattan, Snyder attempted to evoke a monumental and even militaristic quality instead of the domestic imagery used in other areas. But by the late 1890s more domestic themes predominated, even in tough inner-city facilities, perhaps reflecting an increasingly humanitarian attitude toward the poor. We can hypothesize that Snyder was increasingly concerned with the interrelationship among themes of education, sociology and a sense of the school's potential role as a community facility. Certainly the influence of the work of the London County Council architects can be felt in Snyder's work beginning in the late 1890s, outwardly manifested in the perspective drawings of new school facilities favored by Snyder and his delineator, F. Howard Blackledge. The lettering and overall techniques of these drawings reveal a knowledge of Mackintosh and other artists of the English Art Nouveau.

Snyder's task was formidable. "It must be admitted" he wrote, "that the conditions which we have to confront here in New York are entirely different from those presented by any other city in this or any other country. The density of the population and the number of children coming from the blocks and acres of five-story, four-family tenements in various parts of the city is simply appalling." Quoted by Wheelwright, "American Schoolhouse, XVII," *Brickbuilder* 8 (April 1899): 67-69. For 1890s schools on the Lower East Side, see Robinson, "School Buildings of New York": 366-68.

91. Snyder devised the H plan during a trip to Paris in 1896, while "standing in front of the Hotel Cluny . . . studying the notable features of the huge structure there came the solution of a great problem." The influence of the H plan was far reaching. In 1906 San Francisco constructed its first school following the model, and in the same year a delegation from England visited New York to study its application. See Charles C. Johnson, "The Model School House," *World's Work* 12 (June 1906): 7664-68. Also see "School Planning in New York," *American Architect and Building News* 53 (July 4, 1896): 1-2. For articles on P.S. 165, see Wheelwright, "American Schoolhouse, XVI": 47; Wheelwright, "The American Schoolhouse, XVII": 67-69; and "Public School 165, New York City, C.B.J. Snyder, Architect," *Brickbuilder* 14 (August 1905): 187.

92. Johnson, "Model School House": 7665; "Girls High School, 114th to 115th Streets and Seventh Avenue, New York City, C.B.J. Snyder, Architect," *Architecture and Building* 29 (September 3, 1898): plate; Wheelwright, "American Schoolhouse, XVII": 46-47; and "Public School, New York, T.E. Schneider [sic], Architect," *Inland Architect and News Record* 42 (September 1903): plate.

93. Wheelwright, "American Schoolhouse XVI": 45; and C.B.J. Snyder, "Public School Buildings in the City of New York, Part III," *American Architect and Building News* 93 (March 4, 1908): 75-77, plates 28-43.

94. "Two New High Schools," *Real Estate Record and Guide* 73 (January 2, 1904): 10; "The DeWitt Clinton High School, Tenth Ave. and 59th St., New York, C.B.J. Snyder, Architect," *Architecture* 12 (December 1905): plate CV; "Entrance Loggia, DeWitt Clinton High School, Tenth Avenue., New York, N.Y., C.B.J. Snyder, Architect," *American Architect and Building News* 89 (April 14, 1906): plate; "Two Recent High Schools," *Architects' and Builders' Magazine* 8 n.s. (March 1907): 251-65; "Typical Schools in New York, Chicago and St. Louis," *American Architect and Building News* 93 (January 4, 1908): 9-10; and C.B.J. Snyder, "Public School Buildings in the City of New York, Part I," *American Architect and Building News* 93 (January 25, 1908): 27-30, plates 1-21.

95. "Two Recent High Schools," *Architects' and Builders' Magazine* 251.

96. Morris High was originally intended to be called Peter Cooper High School. See "Preliminary Sketch, High School for Boys and Girls," *Architecture and Building* 39 (August 6, 1898): plate; "Two New High Schools," *Real Estate Record and Guide*: 10; "The Peter Cooper High School, 166th Street and Boston Avenue, Architect, C.B.J. Snyder," *Real Estate Record and Guide* 67 (January 26, 1901): 137; Shaw, "True Character of New York Schools": 4220; "Morris High School, 166th Street and Boston Road, New York, N.Y., C.B.J. Snyder, Architect," *American Architect and Building News* 88 (July 29, 1905): 39-40, plates; and Snyder, "Public School Buildings, I": 30, plate 8.

97. "Competitive Design for Erasmus Hall High School, Brooklyn, N.Y., Mowbray & Uffinger, Architect," *Architecture and Building* 28 (April 23, 1898): plate. Also see F.P. Dinkelberg's, based on a French *hôtel de ville*. "Erasmus Hall High School, Brooklyn, N.Y.," *American Architect and Building News* 59 (February 5, 1898): plate.

98. "Erasmus Hall High School, Brooklyn, N.Y., J.G. Glover, Architect, H.C. Carrell, Associate," *Architecture and Building* 29 (October 8, 1898): plate. For another outer borough school not designed by Snyder, see "School Buildings, Queens, L.I. Boring & Tilton, Architects," *Architecture and Building* 28 (April 23, 1898): plate.

99. "Erasmus Hall High School, Brooklyn, C.B.J. Snyder, Architect," *Architecture* 11 (March 1905): 52. For views of Erasmus Hall as built, see C.B.J. Snyder, "Public School Buildings in the City of New York, Part IV," *American Architect and Building News* 93 (March 11, 1908): 83-85, plates 49-57.

100. "Public School No. 124, Fourth Avenue, Between 13th and 14th Streets, Brooklyn, N.Y., C.B.J. Snyder, Architect," *American Architect and Building News* 74 (November 2, 1901): plate.

101. Snyder, "Public School Buildings, III": plate 33; and Snyder, "Public School Buildings, IV": 85.

102. Snyder, "Public School Buildings, IV": 84, plate 59.

103. Johnson, "Model School House": 7667; and Snyder, "Public School Buildings, I": plates 9-14.

104. C.B.J. Snyder, "Public School Buildings in the City of New York, Part II," *American Architect and Building News* 93 (January 29, 1908): 35-41, plates 15-27.

105. Snyder, "Public School Buildings, II": 38-41; and "Type of Modern School, Public School 66, 88th Street near 1st Avenue, Manhattan," *Real Estate Record and Guide* 83 (January 16, 1909): 95.

106. Snyder, "Public School Buildings, III": plates 37-38.

107. Snyder, "Public School Buildings, I": plate 27.

108. "The Washington Irving High School," *American Architect* 103 (March 19, 1913): 145-49, 155-56, plates. Also see Snyder's Normal College, a late example of his Collegiate Gothic style. Built in 1913 on Lexington Avenue between Sixty-eighth and Sixty-ninth streets, the building later housed the prestigious Hunter High School, a public school open to girls throughout the city through a competitive examination program. "Operations on the Upper East Side," *Real Estate Record and Guide* 88 (April 15, 1911): 682-83. For other Gothic schools see "New Public School No. 170, 111th and 112th Sts., Between Fifth and Lenox Aves., New York, C.B.J. Snyder, Architect and Superintendent of School Buildings," *Architecture and Building* 29 (July 30, 1898): plate; "Public School, Fordham, N.Y., Charles B.J. Snyder, [sic] Architect," *Inland Architect and News Record* 40 (October 1902): plate; and "Public School 172 Brooklyn, N.Y., C.B.J. Snyder, Architect," *Brickbuilder* 22 (August 1913): 177.

109. "Washington Irving High School," *American Architect*: 148.

110. "Washington Irving High School," *American Architect*: 149.

111. "Bushwick High School, New York City, C.B.J. Snyder, F.A.I.A.," *American Architect* 105 (April 29, 1914): 197-201.

112. Snyder, "Lighting of School Rooms": 170-73.

113. "Evander Childs High School, Bronx, New York City," *Architecture* 42 (November 1920): plate CLXI.

114. "Trade School for Girls, Lexington Avenue, New York, C.B.J. Snyder, Architect," *American Architect* 112 (September 19, 1917): plate 112.

115. "Baron de Hirsch Trade School, J.H. Freedlander and Arthur Dillon, Architect," *Architectural Review* 5 (June 10, 1898): plates 25-28; and "Baron de Hirsch Trade School, J.H. Freedlander and Arthur Dillon, Architects," *Architecture and Building* 30 (May 6, 1899): plates.

116. "School of Applied Design for Women, 30th St. and Lexington Ave., New York, Pell & Corbett, Architects," *Architecture* 19 (February 1909): plate XVI; "New York School of Applied Design for Women, Entrance Detail," *Architects' and Builders' Magazine* 10 (April 1909): 313; "New York School of Applied Design for Women, New York, N.Y., Pell & Corbett, Architects," *Brickbuilder* 18 (April 1909): plates 48-49; and "Aberrations and Others," *Architectural Record* 25 (June 1909): 448-49. Also see "Architectural Study for Women," *Architecture and Building* 19 (July 8, 1893): 14. A number of institutions grew up to help those who did not fit in either the public or private schools—orphans, young children of working parents, the handicapped, and the countless numbers of immigrants who needed vocational training in order to enter and survive in the metropolitan work-force. For early trade schools see "An Industrial School," *Real Estate Record and Guide* 42 (December 29, 1888): 1538; "Industrial School, East Eightieth Street, Near Third Avenue, New York City, Fowler & Hough, Architects," *Architecture and Building* 24 (June 20, 1896): plate; "Hebrew Technical Institute, 34 and 36 Stuyvesant Street, New York, Buchman & Deisler, Architects," *Architecture and Building* 28 (February 12, 1898): plate; "Industrial School No. 5, Brooklyn, N.Y., Hough & Deriell, Architects," *Architecture and Building* 28 (March 12, 1898): plate; "Packard Commercial School, Lexington Ave. and 35th St., New York, H.F. Ballantyne, Architect," *Architecture* 24 (October 1911): plate CII; and "Packard Commercial School, Lexington Ave. & 35th St., New York, H.F. Ballantyne, Architect," *Architectural Year Book* 1 (1912): 405. The kindergarten movement met the needs of working-class children, while pioneering new concepts of early learning. The Speyer School, affiliated with Columbia's Teachers College, was one of the most elaborate of the kindergartens. Edgar Joselyn's design provided classrooms and a library for the community as well as a kindergarten for toddlers. The enormous crow-stepped gable on the facade was intended to help an eleomosynary institution to impress its beneficiaries with the heritage of old New York. "The Speyer School, Lawrence Street, New York, N.Y., Edgar A. Josselyn, Architect," *American Architect and Building News* 89 (April 21, 1906): 139, plates. Also see "Boys' Lodging House and Schools, Seventh Av., N.Y., for the New York Childrens' Aid Society, Vaux & Radford, Architects," *American Architect and Building News* 16 (November 29, 1884): plate; "The Hans S. Christian Memorial Kindergarten,

Brooklyn, N.Y., Hough & Deweel, Architects," *Architecture and Building* 29 (November 12, 1898): plate; "The Crippled Children's School, 155 Henry St., New York, Schickel & Ditmars, Architect," *Architecture* 17 (April 1908): plate XXX; "New York Kindergarten Asso., 524 West 42d St., New York, Babb, Cook & Willard, Architects," *Architecture* 17 (May 1908): plate XLV; and "Saint Pascal's Day Nursery, East Twenty-second Street, New York, Reiley & Steinbach, Architects," *American Architect* 115 (August 6, 1919): plate 54.

117. "The Berkeley School, West Forty-fourth Street, New York, N.Y., Messrs. Lamb & Rich, Architects, New York, N.Y.," *American Architect and Building News* 30 (November 1, 1890): 74, plate; "The Berkeley School, West Forty-fourth Street, New York, N.Y., Messrs. Lamb & Rich, Architects, New York, N.Y.," *American Architect and Building News* 35 (February 6, 1892): plate; and "Entrance to Berkeley School, New York, N.Y., Lamb & Rich, Architects," *American Architect and Building News* 35 (March 26, 1892): plate.

118. "The Brearley School, West 44th Street, New York, N.Y., Henry Rutgers Marshall, Architect," *American Architect and Building News* 37 (July 2, 1892): plate; and "Briarley School [sic], 9 and 11 West Forty-fourth Street, New York, Henry Rutgers Marshall, Architect," *Architecture and Building* 22 (March 9, 1895): plate.

119. "Brearley School, Park Ave. and 61st St., New York, McKim, Mead & White, Architects," *Architecture* 27 (April 1913): plate XXXI.

120. See Christopher Gray, "Neighborhood, Private Girls' Schools," *Avenue* 6 (September 1981): 43-48.

121. Gray, "Girls' Schools": 45.

122. "Spence School, West Forty-fifth Street, James B. Baker, Architect," *Architectural Record* 11 (October 1901): 718.

123. Christopher Gray, "Neighborhood, The Private Schooling of Proper Young Men," *Avenue* 6 (October 1981): 61-66.

124. Gray, "Proper Young Men": 63.

125. "St. Stephen's Parish School, R.C., East 28th St., N.Y., Elliot Lynch, Architect," *American Architect and Building News* 64 (June 17, 1899): plate; and "St. James Parochial School [sic], East 28th St., New York," *Architects' and Builders' Magazine* 1 (February 1900): 167. For a non-classical but equally unaccomplished parochial school see "St. John the Evangelist Parochial School, New York, J.V. Van Pelt, Architect," *Architects' and Builders' Magazine* 10 (October 1908): 40-41.

126. "Regis High School, New York, Maginnis & Walsh, Architects," *Architecture* 31 (February 1915): plates V-VIII; Editorial, *Architecture* 31 (February 15, 1915): 63-65; and "St. Regis School, New York, Maginnis & Walsh, Architects," *Architecture and Building* 47 (April 1915): 159-61.

127. Margaret Clapp, "The Social and Cultural Scene" in Allen Nevins and John Krout, eds., *The Greater City: New York 1898-1948* (New York: Columbia, 1948), 196.

128. "Architecture in Brooklyn" *American Architect and Building News* 27 (January 4, 1890): 5-8; and A.D.F. Hamlin, Letter to the Editor, *Architecture and Building* 18 (January 18, 1893): 45-47.

129. A.D.F. Hamlin, Letter to the Editor, *Architecture and Building* 18 (February 11, 1893): 70-71; "Brooklyn Museum Competition," *Architecture and Building* 18 (January 18, 1893): 46-47.

130. Clay Lancaster, *Prospect Park Handbook* (New York: Walton H. Rawls, 1967), 63-66; and Roth, *Urban Architecture of McKim, Mead & White*, 473.

131. Chambers & Cromwell's and Bigelow's schemes are published in "Proposed Museum of Arts and Sciences, Brooklyn," *American Architect and Building News* 41 (August 12, 1893): 100, plates.

132. Roth, *Urban Architecture of McKim, Mead & White*, 473-75. Also see "Brooklyn Institute, Brooklyn, N.Y. Central Pavilion, Eastern Parkway Elevation," *Architectural Review* 6 (December 1899): plate LXXVII; "Brooklyn Institute," *Architects' and Builders' Magazine* 1 (February 1900): 168-69; "Brooklyn Institute of Arts and Sciences," *Architecture* 18 (July 1908): plate 54; *A Monograph of the Works of McKim, Mead & White*, 64, plates 85-91; and Richard Guy Wilson, "The Great Civilization," in *The American Renaissance, 1876-1917* (New York: The Brooklyn Museum, 1979), 6, 58, 98-99.

133. The masterplan was revived in 1909 at which time the central rotunda was heightened; it was now based on Bramante's project for St. Peter's. Construction continued until 1925. Roth, *Urban Architecture of McKim, Mead & White*, 474.

134. King, *King's Handbook*, 303-04; Paul R. Baker, *Richard Morris Hunt* (Cambridge: MIT Press, 1980), 172-76, 441-42.

135. "The Opening of the Metropolitan Museum of Art in New York," *American Architect and Building News* 7 (April 10, 1880): 27; "Enlargement of the Metropolitan Museum of Art, New York. South Elevation. Messrs. Weston and Tuckerman, Architects," *Building* 8 (February 25, 1888): plate; "The Metropolitan Museum of Art," *American Architect and Building News* 25 (February 16, 1889): 77-78; and *American Architect and Building News* 66 (December 30, 1899): 105. Upon Tuckerman's death Joseph Wolf became the architect. Baker, *Richard Morris Hunt*, 442.

136. Calvin Tomkins, *Merchants and Masterpieces, The Story of the Metropolitan Museum of Art* (New York: Dutton, 1970), passim. Also see "Increasing Usefulness of Metropolitan Museum," *American Architect and Building News* 95 (February 3, 1909): 40; and Wilson, *American Renaissance*, 58. After di Cesnola's death, J.P. Morgan chose Sir Caspar Purdon Clarke, then director of the Art Department of the Victoria and Albert Museum, to succeed him. Arthur Hoebber, "A New Era for the Metropolitan," *Munsey's* 33 (May 1905): 179-85.

137. "The Enlargement of the Building of the Metropolitan Museum," *American Architect and Building News* 51 (January 25, 1896): 37; "New Addition to the New York Art Museum," *Public Improvements* 2 (March 15, 1900): 219; "Detail of Fifth Ave. Front: Metropolitan Museum of Art, New York, N.Y.," *American Architect and Building News* 70 (November 17, 1900): plate; "Metropolitan Museum of Art, New York," *Inland Architect and News Record* 38 (September 1901): plate; "The New Metropolitan Museum of Art," *Architectural Record* 12 (August 1902): 304-10; "Grand Entrance Hall, Metropolitan Museum of Art, New York, N.Y.," *American Architect and Building News* 87 (April 22, 1905): plate; Hoebber, "A New Era for the Metropolitan": 179-85; "Main Staircase, From Grand Entrance Hall, Metropolitan Museum of Art, New York, N.Y.," *American Architect and Building News* 87 (May 6, 1905): plate; "The Fiftieth Anniversary of the Metropolitan Museum of Art," *Architecture* 41 (June 1920): 173; Roth, *Urban Architecture of McKim, Mead & White*, 657; and Baker, *Richard Morris Hunt*, 441-49.

138. Paul Goldberger, *The City Observed: New York* (New York: Vintage, 1979), 250.

139. Hoebber, "A New Era for the Metropolitan": 179-85; *American Architect and Building News* 88 (September 23, 1905): 98; and Roth, *Urban Architecture of McKim, Mead & White*, 657.

140. "Hall of Classical Sculpture, Metropolitan Museum of Art, New York," *American Architect* 113 (February 20, 1918): plate; "Hall of Classical Sculpture, Metropolitan Museum of Art, New York, McKim, Mead & White, Architects," *Architectural Record* 44 (July 1918); *A Monograph of the Works of McKim, Mead & White*, 69, plates 251-57, 275 X, 277-79; and Roth, *Urban Architecture of McKim, Mead & White*, 657-59.

141. King, *King's Handbook*, 325-26; Blake, *The Architecture of Carrère & Hastings*, 208-09.

142. Royal Cortissoz, "Charles F. McKim," *Scribner's* 42 (January 1910): 125-28. Also see "The Lenox Library, New York, N.Y., R.M. Hunt, Architect," *American Architect and Building News* 22 (September 1, 1877): 280, plates; King, *King's Handbook*, 326-27; and Baker, *Richard Morris Hunt*, 181-85.

143. Quoted in Blake, *Carrère & Hastings*, 210. Also see M.C.M., "The Columbian Reading Union," *Catholic World* 70 (December 1899): 430-32. Tilden's original bequest of $5 million was challenged by his nephew in extended litigation which reduced the library's portion of the estate to $2 million and 20,000 books.

144. Quoted in Blake *Carrère & Hastings*, 207-08. See Chapter 6, for a full discussion of the early history of the New York Public Library through the completion of the Forty-second Street building in 1911.

145. It was said that Tilden had admired the cruciform configuration of a competition entry for the Library of Congress. Arthur Dillon, "The Proposed Tilden Trust Library," *Architectural Review* 1 (September 12, 1892): 69-72.

146. The ecclesiastical model was favored for libraries by other French-trained architects, such as Frank Furness whose Furness Library at the University of Pennsylvania, completed in 1891, was probably known by Flagg.

147. Dillon, "Proposed Tilden Trust Library": 72.

148. "The Site of a Great Library," *Architecture and Building* 24 (May 23, 1896): 241; and *American Architect and Building News* 52 (June 7, 1896): 90.

149. Blake, *Carrère & Hastings*, 215-26.

150. Board of Trustees' Minutes, New York Public Library, vol. 1L 253-61, quoted in Blake, *Carrère & Hastings*, 216.

151. *American Architect and Building News* 66 (May 29, 1897): 66; Barr Ferree, "In Streets and Papers, the New York Public Library Competition," *Architecture and Building* 26 (May 29, 1897): 262; Barr Ferree, "In Streets and Papers, The Architect of the New York Public Library," *Architecture and Building* 26 (June 12, 1897): 283-84; unsigned, probably Barr Ferree, "In Streets and Papers," *Architecture and Building* 26 (June 19, 1897): 291; *American Architect and Building News* 57 (July 24, 1897): 30; and "An Objectionable Feature in the New York Library Competition Program," *American Architect and Building News* 57 (July 31, 1897): 37-38.

152. *American Architect and Building News* 57 (July 24, 1897): 30.

153. "Competitive Design for the New York Public Library, Brite &

Bacon, Architects," *American Architect and Building News* 57 (October 2, 1897): plate.
154. "Design for the New York Public Library, William W. Knowles, Architect," *American Architect and Building News* 57 (November 20, 1897): plate. Other schemes such as W.H. Symond's Gothic design, "Competitive Design for New York Public Library," *Architecture and Building* 29 (November 12, 1898): plate; W. Geding Beatty's *Architecture and Building* 29 (October 29, 1898): plate; and Francis Marion Wright's "Competitive Design for the New York Public Library, submitted in the Preliminary Competition," *American Architect and Building News* 59 (January 8, 1898): plate were amateurish awkwardly scaled, elaborately ornamented classicizing proposals.
155. "New York Library—Preliminary Competition," *Architecture and Building* 28 (July 31, 1897): 43. In addition to those who survived the second cut, the first twelve selected included: Lord, Hewlett & Hull; Clarence S. Luce; Ross & Weber; C.W. and A.A. Stoughton; Parish, Schroeder & Ellingwood; and James E. Ware & Son. *American Architect and Building News* 57 (August 7, 1897): 46.
156. "Final Competition for the New York Public Library," *Architecture and Building* 57 (August 14, 1897): 61.
157. "Competition Designs for the New York Public Library, Astor, Lenox and Tilden Foundations," *Architectural Review* 4 (December 1, 1897): 68, plates 52-61 illustrates Carrère & Hastings's and Howard & Cauldwell's entries. For Carrère & Hastings's also see *American Architect and Building News* 58 (November 20, 1897): 61-62; *Architecture and Building* 27 (December 11, 1897): plate. For McKim's project, see Charles Moore, *The Life and Times of Charles Follen McKim* (New York: 1929, Da Capo, 1970), plate; Blake, *Carrère & Hastings*, 220-22; Roth, *Urban Architecture of McKim, Mead & White*, 478-79.
158. Blake, *Carrère & Hastings*, 220-23.
159. These entries are published in *Architecture and Building* 28 (April 2, 1898): plates.
160. Blake, *Carrère & Hastings*, 229-43, 248-50.
161. The progress of the design and construction was frequently recorded in the press: "Model of the New York Public Library," *American Architect and Building News* 72 (May 25, 1901): plate; "Details, New York Public Library," *American Architect and Building News* 59 (January 3, 1903): plates; "Details of the Fifth Ave. Front: New York Public Library," *American Architect and Building News* 80 (April 11, 1903): plates; Sidney K. Greenslade, "Libraries in the United States, II; The New York Public Library," *American Architect and Building News* 77 (July 26, 1902): 27-30; Clifford Smyth, "New York's Great New Library," *Munsey's* 34 (February 1906): 517-29; "Details of the New York Public Library," *American Architect and Building News* 92 (November 23, 1907): 167, plates; "Bryant Monument, On Bryant Park Terrace, New York Public Library," *American Architect* 98 (July 20, 1910): plates; A.C. David, "The New York Public Library, The Most Important of the Great American Institutions," *Architectural Record* 28 (September 1910): 144-72; "The Interior of the New York Public Library," *International Studio* 41 (October 1910): XCVIII-CII; "Interior Decoration of the New York Public Library," *American Architect* 98 (November 9, 1910): 153-56, 158, plates; "The Planning of the New York Public Library," *Architects' and Builders' Magazine* 11 (January 1911): 137-56; "Architectural Criticism," *Architecture* 23 (March 15, 1911): 33-34, plates XXII-XXXI; "The New York Public Library," *New York Architect* 5 (May 1911): 73-79; "A Bryant Park Improvement," *Real Estate Record and Guide* 95 (February 6, 1915): 207; "Carved Oak Details in the New York Public Library, New York, N.Y.," *Brickbuilder* 24 (December 1915): 297; and "Illumination of Public Library, Victory Celebration, New York City," *Architectural Forum* 5 (November 1920): frontispiece.
162. A.C. David, "The Work of Messrs. Carrère & Hastings," *Architectural Record* 28 (January 1910): 109.
163. M.C.M., "The Columbian Reading Union": 431.
164. "Professional Comment," *Architecture* 12 (November 15, 1905): 165. Also see "Objections Made to the Appointment of an Architect for the Brooklyn Public Library," *American Architect and Building News* 90 (September 29, 1906): and "A Difference of Opinion Between Borough President Coler and the Trustees for the Brooklyn Public Library," *American Architect and Building News* 90 (October 20, 1906): 121.
165. "McKim Fellowship, Columbia University," *Architecture* 12 (August 15, 1905): 120-21.
166. H.W. Frohne, "The Brooklyn Plaza and the Projected Brooklyn Central Library," *Architectural Record* 23 (February 1908): 97-110. Also see Robert A.M. Stern and Gregory Gilmartin, "Apropos 1900, New York and the Metropolitan Ideal," in Richard Oliver, ed., *The Making of an Architect: 1881-1981* (New York: Rizzoli, 1981), 71.
167. "The Montauk Club," *Architecture and Building* 16 (January 2, 1892): plate; and "The Montauk Club, Brooklyn," *Brickbuilder* 3 (August 1894): 154, 156.
168. "Residence of Guido Pleisner, Plaza and Lincoln Place, Brooklyn, N.Y.," *Architecture and Building* 23 (August 10, 1895): plate.
169. "Residence of Geo. W. Shiebler, Plaza and Union Streets, Brooklyn, N.Y.," *Architecture and Building* 24 (February 22, 1896): plate.
170. *Pencil Points* 22 (July 1941): 44.
171. "Notes of Current Interest," *Building* 7 (September 10, 1887): 88; and Baker, *Richard Morris Hunt*, 291-94.
172. "Aguilar Free Library, New York," *American Architect and Building News* 73 (July 6, 1901): plate; Albert Halstead Moore, "Individualism in Architecture, The Works of Herts & Tallant," *Architectural Record* 15 (January 1904): 55-91.
173. Arthur E. Bostwick, "Carnegie Libraries and Good Reading," in Theodore W. Koch, *A Book of Carnegie Libraries* (White Plains, N.Y.: Wilson, 1917), 42-49; *Criterion Magazine* (February 7, 1903) reprinted.
174. "The New Buildings For The Circulation Branches of the New York Public Library," *Architects' and Builders' Magazine* 6 (December 1904): 97-104; Theodore W. Koch, *A Book of Carnegie Libraries* (White Plains, N.Y.: Wilson, 1917); and Roth, *Urban Architecture of McKim, Mead & White*, 648.
175. "School of Architecture," *Columbia University Quarterly* 4 (March 1902): 209-10.
176. "Andrew Carnegie As An Architectural Educator," Editorial, *Brickbuilder* 10 (March 1901): 45-46.
177. "The New Buildings for the Circulation Branches of the New York Public Library," *Architects' and Builders' Magazine*: 99.
178. "The Carnegie Branches of the New York Public Library," *American Architect and Building News* 74 (November 2, 1901): 30; and "Some Recent American Libraries," *Architects' and Builders' Magazine* 4 (December 1902): 88-120.
179. Walter Cook, "The Architecture of the Manhattan Branches," *Carnegie Libraries*, (ca. 1907): 34-37.
180. "Some recent American Libraries," *Architects' and Builders' Magazine*: 88, 91-93; "East Broadway Branch of the Public Library," *American Architect and Building News* 83 (February 13, 1904): plate; "The New Buildings for the Circulation Branches of the New York Public Library," *Architects' and Builders' Magazine*: 100; *A Monograph of the Works of McKim, Mead & White*, plate 196; Roth, *Urban Architecture of McKim, Mead & White*, 650-51.
181. "Branches of the Public Library, New York," *American Architect and Building News* 87 (April 15, 1905): plate; "Carnegie Branch Library, Rivington Street, New York," *Brickbuilder* 14 (July 1905): plate; and Roth, *Urban Architecture of McKim, Mead & White*, 651.
182. The Tompkins Square Branch at 331 East Tenth Street (1903-05) was the first of a series of simpler schemes. Round arched windows set in smooth ashlar walls lit the two lower floors changing to rectangles at the top story. "The New Buildings for the Circulation Branches of the New York Public Library," *Architects' and Builders' Magazine*: 98; "Branches of the Public Library, New York, N.Y.," *American Architect and Building News*: plate; *A Monograph of the Works of McKim, Mead & White*, plate 198; Roth, *Urban Architecture of McKim, Mead & White*, 649. The branch at 224 East 125th Street was similar, but the third floor windows were treated as tiny squares and supplemented by skylights from above. See "The New Buildings for the Circulation Branches of the New York Public Library," *Architects' and Builders' Magazine*: 98; *A Monograph of the Works of McKim, Mead & White*, plate 196; Roth, *Urban Architecture of McKim, Mead & White*, 649-50.
183. "Branches of the Public Library, New York, N.Y.," *American Architect and Building News*: plate. The heavily rusticated branch at 203 West 115th Street of 1907-08 and the Hamilton Grange Branch at 503-505 West 145th Street with smooth cut ashlar represented the firm's most Florentine efforts, and came closest to their townhouse work of the period. The Hamilton Grange Branch was not only more delicately detailed but also more complexly conceived, with an alternation of large and small windows on the two principal floors that was resolved into 5 equal windows in the attic. *A Monograph of the Works of McKim, Mead & White*, plates 196, 198-99; Roth, *Urban Architecture of McKim, Mead & White*, 650.
184. "Public Library No. 29, 303 East 36th St., New York," *Architecture* 17 (April 1908): plate 32; *A Monograph of the Works of McKim, Mead & White*, plates 196-97; and Roth, *Urban Architecture of McKim, Mead & White*, 649-50.
185. Their branch at 328 East Sixty-seventh Street was crudely proportioned, its austerity only relieved by the intricate patterning of the mullions at the entrance. "New Buildings for the Circulation Branches of the New York Public Library," *Architects' and Builders' Magazine*: 102.
186. "Carnegie Branch Library, 140th Street and Alexander Avenue, New York City," *Brickbuilder* 13 (December 1904): plate.
187. "The New Buildings for the Circulation Branches of the New York

Public Library," *Architects' and Builders' Magazine:* 99, 101. Carrère & Hastings's Riverside branch at 190 Amsterdam Avenue is disappointing. Similar to McKim's Chatham Square branch, it had a more generous intercolumnation but fussy details like the strange triple keystones emerging from otherwise unornamented round arches on the ground floor.
188. "Brooklyn Public Library, Greenpoint Branch," *American Architect and Building News* 88 (July 15, 1905): plate; and "Carnegie Branch Libraries, Greenpoint, N.Y., and Flatbush, N.Y.," *Brickbuilder* 15 (April 1906): plates 48, 51.
189. Lord & Hewlett's Bedford branch was also a lively red brick and marble essay in the Modern French style, with a second floor set beneath a hipped mansard and skylit from above. Set in a park, the spacious site enhanced its potential as a community center. "Bedford Branch, Carnegie Library, New York City," *Brickbuilder* 14 (April 1905): plate. Lord & Hewlett's smaller Far Rockaway branch adapted a similar vocabulary to a one-story pavilion, also set in a parklet. "Far Rockaway Branch, Carnegie Library, New York City," *Brickbuilder* 14 (April 1905): plate. Lord & Hewlett's Flushing branch for the Queens Borough Public Library, on a generous site stretching between Jamaica and Jagger avenues ("Flushing Branch, Queen's Borough Public Library," *American Architect and Building News* 87 (June 10, 1905): plate) was a similarly conceived large facility, but rather stiffly composed.
190. "East Branch: Brooklyn Public Library, Brooklyn, N.Y.," *American Architect and Building News* 87 (May 13, 1905): plate.
191. "The Carroll Park Branch Library, Brooklyn, N.Y.," *American Architect and Building News* 87 (April 29, 1905): plate; and "Carnegie Branch Library, Clinton and Union Streets, Brooklyn, N.Y.," *Brickbuilder* 14 (July 1905): plate. Tubby's hipped-roof pavilion for the De Kalb branch, corner Bushwick Avenue, also explored Modern French themes with considerable style, surrounding doors and windows with boldly rusticated limestone quoining. See "De Kalb Branch: Carnegie Public Library, Brooklyn, N.Y.," *American Architect and Building News* 87 (April 1905): plate. By comparison, Walker & Morris's Williamsburg branch with its modified butterfly plan and red brick and limestone exterior seemed very plodding. "Williamsburg Branch, Brooklyn Public Library," *American Architect and Building News* 87 (April 15, 1905): plate.
192. "The Carnegie Libraries in New York," *Architectural Record* 26 (August 1909): 74.
193. "Library, J. Pierpont Morgan, East 36th St., New York," *Architecture* 9 (February 1904): plate 15; "Library of J.P. Morgan, Esq., New York City," *Architecture* (December 1905): plate 101; "Library of J.P. Morgan, Esq., New York City," *Brickbuilder* 19 (February 1910): plate 23; *A Monograph of the Works of McKim, Mead & White,* 69, plates 241-49; Roth, *Urban Architecture of McKim, Mead & White,* 635-47.
194. Roth, *Urban Architecture of McKim, Mead & White,* 637.
195. Wilson, *American Renaissance,* 70.
196. King, *King's Handbook,* 309-10.
197. Editorial, *American Architect and Building News* 38 (October 29, 1892): 65; *American Architect and Building News* 39 (January 21, 1893): 45-46.
198. "Competitive Designs for the American Fine Arts Society," *Architecture and Building* 14 (January 24, 1891): plates.
199. "Proposed Design for the American Fine Arts Society's Building, New York," *Architectural Review* 1 (February 1892): plate 18.
200. "Doorway from Competition Design for the American Fine Arts Society," *Architectural Review* 1 (July 1892): plate 50. This was even more evident in Edmund B. Welles's "Competitive Drawing for the Proposed Building for the American Fine Arts Society," *American Architect and Building News* 32 (June 6, 1891): plate.
201. "Competitive Drawing for the American Fine Arts Society Building, New York," *American Architect and Building News* 32 (June 6, 1891): plate.
202. "The New Building of the American Fine Arts Society," *American Architect and Building News* 28 (May 31, 1890): 125; "American Fine Arts Society Building, 215 West 57th Street," *Architecture and Building* 18 (May 20, 1893): plate; and Montgomery Schuyler, "Henry Janeway Hardenbergh," *Architectural Record* 6 (January-March 1897): 355-75.
203. "Competitive Design for the New York Historical Society's Building," *American Architect and Building News* 84 (June 4, 1904): plate.
204. "New Home for the Historical Society," *Public Improvements* 5 (November 1901): 871-72; "Building for the New York Historical Society, Central Park West, 76th and 77th Streets," *Architectural Review* 9 (March 1902): plates; "Building of the Moment," *Real Estate Record and Guide* 74 (November 19, 1904): 1081-82; William Walton, "The Museum and Gallery of Art of the New York Historical Society," *Scribner's* 39 (June 1906): 764-68; and "The New Building of the New York Historical Society," *Architectural Record* 21 (January 1907): 76-78.
205. The central portion was completed in 1908. The north and south wings were built in 1938 by Walker & Gillette.
206. Landmarks Preservation Commission, LP-1001, Audubon Terrace Historic District: 1.
207. Landmarks Commission, LP-1001: 1-2.
208. "Hispanic Society's Museum," *Real Estate Record and Guide* 74 (November 26, 1904): 1151; "Hispanic Society of America Building, 156th St. near Broadway, New York," *Architecture* 13 (June 1906): plate XXXVI; "Museum for the Hispanic Society of America, Audubon Park, New York, N.Y.," *American Architect and Building News* 89 (June 30, 1906): 220, plates; Charles P. Huntington, "Architectural Criticism," *Architecture* 19 (March 1909): 34-35; Royal Cortissoz, "The Genius of Spain in New York," *Scribner's* 49 (June 1911): 765-68; and Landmarks Commission, LP-1001: 4-5. Also note "Westerly Entrance Gates, Building of Hispanic Society of America, Broadway and 155th Street, New York," *American Architect* 111 (May 17, 1916): plate.
209. Huntington, "Architectural Criticism": 34-35.
210. Cortissoz, "The Genius of Spain in New York": 768.
211. "Museum for the American Numismatic Society, New York, N.Y.," *American Architect and Building News* 91 (June 29, 1907): plates; "Museum, American Numismatic Society, Broadway & 156th St., New York," *Architecture* 18 (November 1908): plate LXXXIII; Huntington, "Architectural Criticism": 35; Landmarks Commission, LP-1001: 5-6.
212. "Church of Our Lady of Guadalupe, Audubon Park," *American Architect and Building News* 96 (October 20, 1909): 160, plate; L.R. McCabe, "Our Lady of Hope Spanish Church, in New York City," *Architectural Record* 33 (January 1913): 14-20; and Landmarks Commission, LP-1001: 7-8.
213. "American Geographical Society Building, Broadway and 156th St., New York," *Architecture* 24 (October 1911): plate XCVII; "American Geographical Society Building, Broadway and 156th St., New York," *Architectural Yearbook* 1 (1912): 403; and Landmarks Commission, LP-1001: 6-7.
214. "The Architects' Portfolio," *Architectural Record* 11 (January 1902): 84-89; and "Building of the American Geographical Society, New York City," *Inland Architect and News Record* 40 (August 1902): plate.
215. "Museum of the American Indian, Heye Foundation, New York," *American Architect* 110 (October 4, 1916): plate; Landmarks Commission, LP-1001: 8-9.
216. Landmarks Commission, LP-1001: 5.
217. The last components of Audubon Terrace failed to reinforce the sense of an architectural ensemble. The American Academy of Arts and Letters by William Kendall of McKim, Mead & White (1917-23) and Cass Gilbert's National Institute of Arts and Letters (1930) were located at the western end of the terrace on a slightly raised courtyard that ignored the issue of visually terminating the long axis from Broadway and left the view down the terrace dominated by the back wall of an apartment building. See "American Academy of Arts and Letters, West 155th Street, New York City," *American Architect* 111 (February 28, 1917): 143; and Landmarks Commission, LP-1001: 9-10.
218. King, *King's Handbook,* 275-76; Roth, *Urban Architecture of McKim, Mead & White,* 378-82.
219. Schuyler, "Architecture of American Colleges, IV: New York City Colleges," *Architectural Record* 27 (June 1910): 443-69.
220. "Hall of Languages, University of the City of New York," *Architecture and Building* 27 (October 9, 1897): plate.
221. "Gould Dormitory, University of the City of New York," *Architecture and Building* 27 (October 9, 1897): plate. Also see "Chemistry Building, University of the City of New York," *Architecture and Building* 28 (February 19, 1898): plate; and "Hall of Philosophy, New York University," *Architecture* 32 (August 1915): plate.
222. "Library of the New York University, New York, N.Y.," *Brickbuilder* 10 (July 1901): plates; Sidney K. Greenslade, "Libraries in the United States, II. New York University Library," *American Architect and Building News* 77 (July 26, 1902): 29; *A Monograph of the Works of McKim, Mead & White,* 31-32, plates 74-77.
223. "A Hall of Fame for New York University," *American Architect and Building News* 67 (March 17, 1900): 81-82; "A Hall of Fame," *World's Work* 1 (December 1900): 133; "Editor's Easy Chair," *Harper's Monthly* 103 (August 1901): 490-95.
224. Schuyler, "New York City Colleges": 456.
225. Montgomery Schuyler, "The College of the City of New York," *Architectural Record* 21 (March 1907): 167-85.
226. Schuyler, "The College of the City of New York": 168.
227. McKim, Mead & White, Charles C. Haight, John R. Thomas, R.H. Robertson, George B. Post, Cyrus W. Eidlitz, Cady, Berg & See, and William B. Tuthill. *Architecture and Building* 27 (October 30, 1897): 154. George Martin Huss's unsolicited entry is published in "Proposed College

of the City of New York," *Architecture and Building* 21 (July 2, 1898): plates. Also see C.C. Haight's "Competitive Design for Proposed College of the City of New York," *Architecture and Building* 29 (November 5, 1898): plate.
228. *Architecture and Building* 22 (June 29, 1895): 306; "College of the City of New York," *Architecture* 7 (March 15, 1903): 28-30; "The College of the City of New York," *Architectural Review* 12 (December 1905): 305-12; "Entrance From the College Grounds, Sub-Freshman Building, College of the City of New York," *Architecture* 12 (November 1905): plate XCI; "Assembly Hall, College of the City of New York," *Architecture* 15 (April 1907): plate XXXII; Schuyler, "The College of the City of New York": 167-85; Arthur Ebbs Willauer, "The College of the City of New York," *American Architect and Building News* 93 "Part 1" (May 13, 1908): 155-61, plates; "Part 2" (May 20, 1908): 163-68, plates; William Walton, "Mr. Blashfield's Mural Painting in the College of the City of New York," *Scribner's* 44 (July 1908): 125-58; "Assembly Hall, College of the City of New York," *Architecture* 18 (July 1908): plate LII; "The Great Hall of the College of the City of New York," *American Architect and Building News* 95 (March 31, 1909): 110-11; "College of the City of New York," *New York Architect* 3 (June 1909): and Schuyler, "New York City Colleges": 460-65.
229. Schuyler, "The College of the City of New York": 184.
230. Schuyler, "The College of the City of New York": 185.
231. Montgomery Schuyler, "A Great American Architect: Leopold Eidlitz, I, Ecclesiastical and Domestic Work," *Architectural Record* 24 (September 1908): 163-79.
232. Montgomery Schuyler, "Recent Church Building in New York," *Architectural Record* 13 (June 1903): 509-34. Even so ardent a champion of Richardson as Marianna Griswold van Rennselaer nonetheless regarded Trinity as "an intensely individual, not a broadly characteristic, piece of work . . . which stands apart and aside from the most hopeful current of our art." See Marianna Griswold van Rensselaer, "Recent Architecture in America, IV: Churches," *Century* 29 (January 1885): 323-38.
233. A.D.F. Hamlin, Letter to the Editor, "Church Architecture in America," *Century* 52 (August 1896): 635-36.
234. Russell Sturgis, "The Works of McKim, Mead & White," *Architectural Record* (May 1895): reprinted in *Great American Architects Series*: 10-14. Also see *A Monograph of the Works of McKim, Mead & White*, plates 54-55; "American Church Architecture," *Architecture* 46 (December 1922): 18.
235. "Randall Memorial Church, Sailors' Snug Harbor, Staten Island, N.Y.," *American Architect and Building News* 66 (October 7, 1899): plates.
236. "The New Madison Square Church," *Brickbuilder* 15 (December 1906): 271-72. See also Christian Binton, "A Departure in Church Building," *Century* 70 (September 1905): 718-19; "New Madison Square Presbyterian Church, New York, N.Y.," *American Architect and Building News* 7 (July 1906): 8, plate; "The Vanishing of a Church," *Real Estate Record and Guide* 78 (August 11, 1906): 252; "Foyer, Madison Square Presbyterian Church, New York," *Architecture* 17 (January 1907): plate VI; "Interior of the Madison Square Presbyterian Church, Looking Toward the Pulpit," *Architectural Record* 21 (February 1907): 156; "Pediment of Madison Square Presbyterian Church, New York City," *Brickbuilder* 19 (July 1910): 171; "The New Pediment Panel in Dr. Parkhurst's Madison Square Church," *Brickbuilder* 19 (July 1910): 174-75; J. Monroe Hewlett, "Polychrome Terra Cotta in Exterior Architecture," *Brickbuilder* 20 (April 1911): 71-72; *A Monograph of the Works of McKim, Mead & White*, 69, plates 251-57; "The Madison Square Presbyterian Church," *Architectural Review* 9 (August 1919): plate; "The Madison Square That Was, and Is No More," *Architecture* 58 (May 1928): 280; and Baldwin, *Stanford White* (New York: 1931, Da Capo Press, 1971), 232-37.
237. Hewlett, "Polychrome Terracotta": 71.
238. "The Fort Washington Presbyterian Church," *Architecture and Building* 46 (March 1914): 116-117; "West Park Presbyterian Church," *Brickbuilder* 24 (December 1915): plates 168-71; and "The Fort Washington Presbyterian Church, New York City," *American Architect* 111 (June 13, 1917): plate.
239. Montgomery Schuyler, "The Work of Barney & Chapman." *Architectural Record* 15 (September 1904): 203-96.
240. *American Architect and Building News* 53 (August 1, 1896): 38-39. See also Thomas Cusack, "Church Architecture in Materials of Clay," *Brickbuilder* 8 (May 1899): 89-92.
241. Schuyler, "Recent Church Building in New York": 514.
242. "Architectural Criticism," *Architecture* 21 (February 15, 1910): 18-19.
243. Rev. James H. Ross, "The Broadway Tabernacle," *American Architect and Building News* 87 (February 18, 1905): 59-60; see also , "The Broadway Tabernacle," *Architecture* 11 (March 1905): plates 21-22.
244. Bertram Grosvenor Goodhue's Office and Convocational Building projected for Madison Square was surely the most awe inspiring of these;

see Charles Harris Whitaker, Editor, *Bertram Grosvenor Goodhue—Architect and Master of Many Arts* (New York: Press of the American Institute of Architects, 1925), plates CXCVI-CXCVII. Tillion & Tillion's Manhattan Congregational Church was the most confused (the Gothic church related not at all to the office building above); and Henry C. Pelton, Burnham Hoyt, and Allen & Collens's Riverside Church was the only one to achieve a fully resolved synthesis and restate the Gothic at a convincing metropolitan scale.
245. "St. Thomas's Church, and the Houses of W. Seward Webb and H. McK. Twombley, New York, N.Y.," *American Architect and Building News* 21 (April 16, 1887): plate; "Burning of St. Thomas's, New York City," *American Architect and Building News* 88 (August 12, 1905): 51; "St. Thomas's Church, New York, N.Y., After the Fire," *American Architect and Building News* 88 (September 9, 1905): plate.
246. All of the competition entries were published in "St. Thomas' Church Competition," *Architecture* 13 (May 15, 1906): 65, plates 68-98.
247. Montgomery Schuyler, "The New St. Thomas's Church," *Scribner's* 54 (December 1913): 791-94. Also see Theodore Starrett, "Saint Thomas's Church," *Architecture and Building* 46 (March 1914): 97-99; Whitaker, ed., *Goodhue*, plates CXXXVII-CXLV; "St. Thomas's Church," *Architecture* 52 (April 1920): 44.
248. Gerald Allen, "St. Thomas Church: Serving Two Spaces," in Gerald Allen and Charles Moore, *Dimensions: Space, Shape & Scale in Architecture* (New York: Architectural Record Books, 1976), 25-40.
249. Schuyler, "The New St. Thomas's Church": 794.
250. "The Rebuilding of Park Avenue, *Real Estate Record and Guide* 84 (December 4, 1909): 991-93; "The New South Reformed Church on Park Ave.," *Real Estate Record and Guide* 85 (January 8, 1910): 55-56; "Architectural Criticism," *Architecture* 23 (June 15, 1911): 81, 83, plate LVI; "Interior, South Church, Park Ave. and Eighty-fifth Street, New York," *Architecture* 23 (September 1911): plate XCII; "Recent American Churches," *Architecture and Building* 43 (November 1911): 589-626; "South Church, Parish House, and Rectory, Park Ave. and Eighty-fifth Street, New York," *Architectural Year Book* 1 (1912): 541-47; and Whitaker, ed., *Goodhue*, plates CLXV-CLXIX.
251. "Architectural Criticism," *Architecture*: 81.
252. C. Matlack Price, " The Chapel of the Intercession, New York City," *Architectural Record* 35 (June 1914): 526-43. Also see Montgomery Schuyler, "Distinctive American Architecture: Chapel of the Intercession, Trinity Parish New York," *Brickbuilder* 23 (May 1914): 85-90.
253. "The Farragut Monument," *Scribner's* 22 (June 1881): 161-67; "The Farragut Statue," *American Architect and Building News* 9 (June 25, 1881): 301; Marianna Griswold van Rensselaer, "Mr. St. Gaudens's Statue of Admiral Farragut in New York," and "The Farragut Monument," *American Architect and Building News* 10 (September 10, 1881): 119-20, plate; "Intimate Letters of Stanford White," *Architectural Record* 30 (September 1911): 283-48; *A Monograph of the Works of McKim, Mead & White*, 62, plate 15; "Farragut Monument, Madison Square, New York City," *Architecture* 67 (October 1927): 184; Baldwin, *Stanford White*, 126-38; and Wilson, *American Renaissance*, 43, 45.
254. "The Farragut Statue," *American Architect and Building News*: 301.
255. "The Farragut Monument," *American Architect and Building News:* 120.
256. This sentiment was echoed by Marianna Griswold van Rensselaer, "Mr. St. Gaudens's Statue of Admiral Farragut in New York": 119. As late as 1911, Montgomery Schuyler complained that the city's memorials were poorly located: "Stray Statues," *Scribner's* 1 (September 1911): 381-84.
257. Bartholdi's Statue of Liberty," *American Architect and Building News* 14, Part I (September 15, 1883): 126-27; Part 2 (September 22, 1883): 137-38; "Town Talk," *The Manhattan* 3 (January 1884): 94-95, (March 1884): 289-90; Marvin Trachtenberg, *The Statue of Liberty* (New York: Viking Press, 1976); and Baker, *Richard Morris Hunt*, 314-22.
258. "The Monumental Spirit," *Building* 11 (November 9, 1889): 149-50.
259. "*The New York Evening Post* and Our Remarks on Riverside Park," and "The Grant Memorial Should be a Thing of Art, not Cost," *American Architect and Building News* 18 (August 15, 1885): 73-74; *Real Estate Record and Guide* 36 (August 22, 1885): 927; and *Building* 3 (December 1885): 52. The entries in both Grant Memorial Competitions are discussed by David M. Kahn, "The Grant Memorial," *Journal of the Society of Architectural Historians* 41 (October 1982): 212-31.
260. *Real Estate Record and Guide* 41 (February 18, 1888): 260; "The Grant Monument Competition," *American Architect and Building News* 26 (October 12, 1889): 170; "General Grant's Monument," *Architecture and Building* 12 (March 1, 1890): 104; "The Grant Monument Competition," *American Architect and Building News* 27 (March 8, 1890): 145;

"Editorial Notes and Comments," *Architecture and Building* 12 (April 5, 1890): 158; "The New Grant Monument," *American Architect and Building News* 28 (May 3, 1890): 61-62; "Grant's Towering Tomb," *Architecture and Building* 13 (September 13, 1890): 130; "The Grant Monument," *Architecture and Building* 13 (September 20, 1890): 135-36; "The Grant Memorial," *Architecture and Building* 16 (April 23, 1892): 208-09; General Horace Potter, "The Tomb of General Grant," *Century* 53 (April 1897): 839-47. The competition entries of J.A. Schweinfurth, John Ord, C.W. Clinton, John Duncan, and Carrère & Hastings are published in *American Architect and Building News* 30 (October 18, 1890): plates. For Carrère & Hastings, also see "Competitive Design for a Monument to General Grant," *American Architect and Building News* 30 (October 25, 1890): plate; and Blake, *Carrère & Hastings*, 307-08. Their proposal, a robust example of the French academic or Beaux-Arts approach, was spatially complex, with a semi-circular exedra enclosing a forecourt that led to a memorial hall or museum based on Bramante's project for St. Peter's Basilica in Rome. A campanile, set behind the memorial hall, rose above the graves of General and Mrs. Grant. Though this scheme effectively concluded the southern axis of approach from the city, the numerous pavilions in the colonnade surrounding the museum made the design more expensive yet less compelling than the condensed mass of Duncan's scheme.

261. "The Brooklyn Monument," *Real Estate Record and Guide* 42 (December 8, 1888): 1442; *Building* 11 (August 31, 1889): 68; "The Monumental Spirit," *Building*: 149-50; "Approach to Soldiers' and Sailors' Monument, Brooklyn, N.Y., J.H. Duncan, Architect," *Architecture and Building* 10 (February 18, 1893): 75; "The Soldiers' and Sailors' Monument, Brooklyn, N.Y.," *American Architect and Building News* 74 (December 14, 1901): plates; and Lancaster, *Prospect Park Handbook*, 69-70.

262. "New York," *American Architect and Building News* 21 (May 18, 1889): 238-39.

263. *American Architect and Building News* 25 (May 18, 1889): 230; "Washington Memorial Arch," *Architecture and Building* 12 (May 3, 1890): 211; "The Washington Arch in New York," *American Architect and Building News* 28 (June 14, 1890): 157; *Real Estate Record and Guide* 48 (October 15, 1891): 1364; "Washington Memorial Arch, Washington Square, New York City," *Architecture and Building* 23 (November 23, 1895): plate; "Detail of the Washington Arch, Washington Square, New York, N.Y.," *American Architect and Building News* 65 (September 23, 1899): plate; *A Monograph of the Works of McKim, Mead & White*, 63, plates 39-40; and Baldwin, *Stanford White*, 194-98.

264. *Real Estate Record and Guide* 48 (October 15, 1891): 1364.

265. "The Eighth League Exhibition," *American Architect and Building News* 39 (January 21, 1893): 45-46. Also see *Architecture and Building* 17 (October 8, 1892): 178; and Henry Hope Reed, "The Vision Spurned: Classical New York, Part II," *Classical America* 1 (1972): 10-19. The rostral column at Columbus Circle by the sculptor Gaetano Russo was the city's only permanent commemoration of the event. See "The Columbus Monument and the Gates of Central Park, New York," *American Architect and Building News* 35 (March 5, 1892): 145; and "The Columbus Monument, 8th Ave. and 59th St., New York, N.Y., Signor Gaetano Russo, Sculptor," *American Architect and Building News* 46 (December 1, 1894): 95, plate.

266. "The Triumphal Arch for the Dewey Celebration in New York," *American Architect and Building News* 65 (August 12, 1899): 49; J. Wilton Brooks, "The Dewey Arch" *Public Improvements* 1 (September 15, 1899): 189-91; "Proposed Perpetuation of the Dewey Arch," *American Architect and Building News* 66 (October 14, 1899): 9; "The Dewey Arch," *Architects' and Builders' Magazine* 1 (October 1899): 1-8; Russell Sturgis, "The Sculptures of the Dewey Reception in New York," *Scribner's* 26 (December 1899): 765-68; Barr Ferree, "The Dewey Arch," *American Architect and Building News* 67, Part 1 (January 13, 1900): 11-12, plates; Part 2 (January 20, 1900): 19-20; and "Detail of the Dewey Memorial Arch," *American Architect and Building News* 67 (February 10, 1900): plate. J.H. Freedlander's "Triumphal Piers for the Return of a Victorious Army," intended for erection at Madison Square, was an alternate proposal for the Dewey Celebration. See *Architectural Review* 6 (February 1899): plates IX-X.

267. Russell Sturgis, "Points of View: American 'Style,'" *Scribner's* 28 (July-December 1900): 123.

268. "The Dewey Arch," *Architects' and Builders' Magazine* 1 (October 1899): 1-8.

269. "The Destruction of the Dewey Arch," *World's Work* 1 (January 1901): 242-43.

270. "Dewey Arch," *Architectural Annual* 1 (1900): 246-50.

271. *Brickbuilder* 13 (December 1909): 244; and "Prison Ship Martyrs' Monument," *Architects' and Builders' Magazine* 10 (January 1910): 148.

272. "The Maine Memorial," *American Architect and Building News* 103 (May 28, 1913): 251; "National Maine Monument, Central Park, New York," *American Architect* 104 (July 9, 1913): plate; "The National Maine Monument, Central Park West and 59th Street, New York," *Architecture* 28 (July 1913): plate; "The National Maine Monument," *Architectural Review* 8 (October 1901): plate LXIX. Magonigle also designed the Piccirilli Studio Building in the northeast Bronx. "Studio Building for Piccirilli Brothers," *Brickbuilder* 13 (December 1904): plate.

273. *American Architect and Building News* 72 (May 11, 1901): 42; H.W. Desmond, "Description of the Works of Ernest Flagg," *Architectural Record* 11 (April 1902): 4; and "The Architect's Portfolio," *Architectural Record* 14 (August 1903): 145.

274. "The Soldiers' and Sailors' Monument for New York City," *American Architect* 57 (July 3, 1887): 1; "Public Art in American Cities," *Municipal Affairs* 2 (March 1898): 10.

275. *American Architect and Building News* 58 (October 2, 1897): 2.

276. According to the *Architectural Review* 4 (October 1897): 1, the six other entrants also proposed columns embellished by statuary. Stoughton & Stoughton's original prize-winning entry is published in "Model of the Original Design for the Soldiers' and Sailors' Monument, New York, N.Y.," *American Architect and Building News* 70 (November 17, 1900): plate.

277. "The Soldiers' and Sailors' Monument for New York," *American Architect and Building News* 58 (December 4, 1897): 77; "Further Tribulations of the New York Soldiers' and Sailors' Monument," *American Architect and Building News* 59 (January 1, 1898): 1; "The New York Soldiers' and Sailors' Monument," *American Architect and Building News* 59 (January 22, 1898): 25; *American Architect and Building News* 67 (January 13, 1900): 10; "The New York Soldiers' and Sailors' Memorial Monument Site," *American Architect and Building News* 67 (February 3, 1900): 33; and "The Soldiers' and Sailors' Memorial Monument," *Architects' and Builders' Magazine* 5 (October 1903): 1-8.

278. "The Soldiers' and Sailors' Monument, Riverside Park, New York City," *American Architect and Building News* 70 (November 17, 1900): plate; "Soldiers' and Sailors' Monument, New York City," *Inland Architect and News Record* 41 (April 1903): plate; "The Soldiers' and Sailors' Monument, Riverside Park, New York, N.Y.," *American Architect and Building News* 81 (August 22, 1903): 63-64, plates; and "The Soldiers' and Sailors' Memorial Monument," *House and Garden* 5 (January, 1904): 34-36.

279. New York's failure to build Bruce Price's study for a "Monument Commemorative of the Results of the Conflict from the Union, the Federation of the States and the Peace and Prosperity Which Flowed," *American Architect and Building News* 65 (September 30, 1899): plate suggests that even at a late date the city was still uneasy over its role in the Civil War and unwilling to reopen old wounds through a bravura show of northern supremacy.

280. Thomas Hastings, "New York's Altar to Liberty and the Avenue of the Allies," *Architecture* 38 (November 1918): 301-02, plates; "The Victory Arch in New York," *American Architect* 114 (December 4, 1918): 673-74, plates; "Arch of Freedom, Madison Square, New York," *American Architect* 115 (January 15, 1919): plates 18-20; "New York Victory Arch," *Architecture* 39 (April 1919): 101; Thomas Hastings, "New York's Arch of Victory," *Architecture* 39 (April 1919): 56-58; and *American Architect* 115 (April 30, 1919): plates 140-45.

281. "The Arch of Democracy, Brooklyn, New York," *American Architect* 115 (January 15, 1919): 94-95, plate 22.

282. "The Gateway of the Nation," *American Architect* 115 (April 30, 1919): 602-06.

283. In 1918, Otto Eggers and E.H. Rosengarten essentially revived H. Van Buren Magonigle's 1910 Fulton Memorial scheme for Riverside Park. See "A Suggested Design for a Victory Memorial in New York," *American Architect* 114 (December 4, 1918): plates 169-171.

284. Charles Cornelius, "War Memorials, Part II. Community Buildings for Large Cities," *Architectural Record* 47 (January 1920): 39-57. Also see Adeline Adams, "War Memorials in Sculpture," *Scribner's* 65 (March 1919): 381-84; Charles Cornelius, "War Memorials," *Architectural Record* 46 (July 1919): 94-96; and "A Projected War Memorial," *Architectural Record* 45 (March 1919): 288. Armstrong & DeGelleke's grandiose proposal for a 1,000-foot-high obelisk in Central Park was definitely out of touch with the shifting public mood. See "A Design for a National Memorial," *Architecture* 42 (August 1920): 233-34.

285. "New York Delays Action on Victory Memorial," *American Architect* 116 (December 31, 1919): 815; and Cornelius, "War Memorials, Part II": 39-57. Also see Warren & Wetmore's "Proposed Memorial for the Seventy-Seventh Division A.E.F., New York," in "Drawings by John Vincent," *Architectural Review* 9 (September 1919): plate XL.

286. "Proposal to make Mr. Hunt's Central Park Gateway his own Memorial," *American Architect and Building News* 51 (February 22, 1896):

81. Also see "In Streets and Papers," *Architecture and Building* 24 (February 22, 1896): 89; *American Architect and Building News* 55 (March 6, 1897): 74; "Model for the Memorial Monument to Richard Morris Hunt, Architect, New York, N.Y.," *American Architect and Building News* 55 (March 13, 1897): 86; "The Richard M. Hunt Memorial," *Architecture and Building* 28 (February 19, 1898): 71; "Present State of the R.M. Hunt Memorial, Fifth Avenue, New York, N.Y.," *American Architect and Building News* 62 (March 4, 1899): plate; Russell Sturgis, "The Works of Bruce Price," *Architectural Record* (July 1899), reprinted in *Great American Architects' Series* (New York: Da Capo Press, 1977): 25-27; and Baker, *Richard Morris Hunt,* 455-56. When the Hunt Memorial was erected, no architect in America had been similarly honored. After John Merven Carrère was killed in a traffic accident in 1911, his partner Thomas Hastings designed a memorial in Riverside Park at West Ninety-ninth Street. It consisted of a modest pink granite exedra and staircase. See "John Merven Carrère Memorial," *Architectural Forum* 31 (November 1919): 161. In 1920 Lawrence Grant White designed the bronze doors of the Library of New York University's Washington Heights campus as a memorial to his father, Stanford White. See "Stanford White Memorial at New York University," *Architectural Record* 47 (April 1920): 380-81; "The Stanford White Memorial Doors," *Architecture* 42 (January 1922): 10.

287. "Monument to Peter Cooper, Astor Place, New York, N.Y.," *American Architect and Building News* 49 (September 25, 1897): plate; and "Intimate Letters of Stanford White," *Architectural Record* 30 (October 1911): 397-406.

288. *Report of the New York City Improvement Commission* (1907): 32.

289. The competition entries of Carrère & Hastings, McKim, Mead & White, H. van Buren Magonigle, and John Russell Pope are published in *American Competitions* 3 (1913): 132-49, plates 33-34. Also see "Winning Design, The Joseph Pulitzer Memorial, New York City," *Architectural Review* 11 (May 1913): plates XXVI-XXVIII; "The Joseph Pulitzer Fountain, Fifth Avenue, 58th and 59th Streets, New York," *American Architect* 108 (November 17, 1915): plates; and Blake, *Carrère & Hastings,* 312-14.

290. Baker, *Richard Morris Hunt,* 291. Also see Montgomery Schuyler, "The Works of the Late Richard Morris Hunt," *Architectural Record* 5 (October-December 1895): 114.

291. "Lodges at the East Entrance to Greenwood Cemetery," *American Architect and Building News* 4 (August 3, 1878): 40; Edward Streeter, *The Story of Woodlawn Cemetery* (New York: Woodlawn Cemetery), 6-8.

292. Quoted in William Lee Younger, *Old Brooklyn in Early Photographs 1865-1929* (New York: Dover, 1978), 152.

293. King, *King's Handbook,* 515-19; and Streeter, *Woodlawn Cemetery,* 7-9.

294. "A Sketch of the History of All the Cemeteries in and around the cities of New York and Brooklyn," *New York Times* (March 30, 1866) quoted in Streeter, *Woodlawn Cemetery,* 8.

295. 'Mausoleum for Giovanni P. Morosini," *Architecture and Building* 23 (December 7, 1895): 276, plates; and "Mausoleum for G.P. Morosini," *American Architect and Building News* 46 (December 1, 1894): plate.

296. "Mortuary Architecture," *American Architect* 106 (October 14, 1914): 225-30.

297. King, *King's Handbook,* 515-16.

298. "Mausoleum at Woodlawn Cemetery," *Architects' and Builders' Magazine* 5 (August 1904): 541.

299. "Woodlawn Cemetery," *Architects' and Builders' Magazine:* 536.

300. "Mortuary Architecture," *American Architect:* 229-30.

301. "The Work of McKim, Mead & White," *Architectural Record* 22 (September 1906): 195; *A Monograph of the Works of McKim, Mead & White,* plate 217.

302. Herbert Croly, "Recent Works of John Russell Pope," *Architectural Record* 29 (June 1911): 441-511.

303. Croly, "John Russell Pope": 508.

304. "Mortuary Architecture," *American Architect:* 225, 229.

305. L.R. McCabe, "A Revival of French Gothic Architecture," *Architectural Record* 34 (September 1913): 202-12.

306. "Mausoleum, Salem Fields Cemetery," *Architects' and Builders' Magazine* 5 (August 1904): 541.

307. "Salem Fields Cemetery," *Architects' and Builders' Magazine* 5: 542

308. "Mausoleum at New Union Fields Cemetery," *Architects' and Builders' Magazine* 5 (August 1904): 540.

309. "Union Fields Cemetery," *Architects' and Builders' Magazine* 5: 538.

310. *Real Estate Record and Guide* 28 (October 29, 1881): 1005; "The Proposed New Parks," *Real Estate Record and Guide* 35 (March 21, 1885): 287-88; "Trees and Parks in Cities," *Municipal Affairs* 4 (June 1900): 421-22; and George F. Pentecost, "City Gardens," *Architectural Record* 14 (July 1903): 50-61.

311. See Albert Fein's contrast of the political and social attitudes in Edward Bellamy's utopian novel *Looking Backward* which prefigures the City Beautiful movement, and Olmsted's conception of a decentralized society, in his *Frederick Law Olmsted and the American Environmental Tradition* (New York: George Braziller, 1972), 57-61. Also see Frederick Law Olmsted Jr. and Theodore Kimball, editors, *Frederick Law Olmsted: Landscape Architect, 1822-1903* (New York: 1922, Benjamin Blom, 1970), 486-98.

312. Roth, *Urban Architecture of McKim, Mead & White,* 355-56.

313. All four columns are sometimes attributed to White. See, however, "Approach to Soldiers' and Sailors' Monument, Brooklyn, N.Y., J.H. Duncan, Architect," *Architecture and Building* 18 (February 18, 1893): 75; and Lancaster, *Prospect Park Handbook,* 69-70.

314. *A Monograph of the Works of McKim, Mead & White,* 63, plate 20.

315. "The Monumental Spirit," *Building* 11 (November 9, 1889): 149-50; "'Horse-Tamer' Groups: Entrance to the Ocean Parkway, Brooklyn, N.Y.," *American Architect and Building News* 65 (September 16, 1899): plates; French Strother, "Frederick MacMonnies, Sculptor," *World's Work* 11 (December 1905): 6965-6981; *A Monograph of the Works of McKim, Mead & White,* 63, plate 21; Lancaster, *Prospect Park Handbook,* 70, 83.

316. "Croquet Shelter, Prospect Park, Brooklyn, N.Y.," *Brickbuilder* 13 (December 1904): plate.

317. "Shelter, Prospect Park, Brooklyn," *Architecture* 23 (June 1911): plate 52; "Shelter, Prospect Park, Brooklyn," *Architectural Yearbook* 1 (1912): 307, 309.

318. "Boat House, Prospect Park, Brooklyn," *Architecture* 71 (August 1907): plate LXXI; and Lancaster, *Prospect Park Handbook,* 73-74.

319. Richard Morris Hunt, *Designs for the Gateways of the Southern Entrances to the Central Park* (New York: 1866); Baker, *Richard Morris Hunt,* 146-56.

320. Clarence Cook, "Mr. Hunt's Designs for the Gates of the Central Park," *New York Daily Tribune* (August 2, 1865): 8, quoted in Baker, *Richard Morris Hunt,* 152. Also see Fein, *Olmsted and the American Environmental Tradition,* 11-13; and Wilson, *American Renaissance,* 82-83.

321. William J. Hoppin, "Monumental Art in the Central Park: Mr. Hunt's Gateways," *New York Evening Post* (March 29 and April 5, 1866), quoted in Baker, *Richard Morris Hunt,* 152-53.

322. Roth, *Urban Architecture of McKim, Mead & White,* 657-59. Also see Olmsted and Kimball, editors, *Frederick Law Olmsted,* Chapter XII, "Various Encroachments Proposed and Warded Off," 518-32.

323. Bacon's lamp posts were also installed in Prospect Park. Lancaster, *Prospect Park Handbook,* 113.

324. "The Sunken Garden in Central Park, New York," *American Architect* 112 (August 8, 1917): 105-08; "The Sunken Garden in Central Park," *American Architect* 112 (October 17, 1917): 282; "The Sunken Garden Proposed for the Lower Reservoir Basin in Central Park, New York City," *Architectural Review* 5 (November 1917): 244 and plates.

325. Henry Fairfield Osborn, *History, Plan, and Design of The New York State Roosevelt Memorial* (New York: 1928); and George N. Pindar, *The New York State Roosevelt Memorial, Dedicated January 19, 1936* (New York: 1936).

326. Bryant Park was redesigned by Aymar Embury II and Major Gilmore D. Clark. See Robert A Caro, *The Power Broker: Robert Moses and the Fall of New York* (New York: Knopf, 1974), 368-74.

327. Hudson Park was also known as St. John Park. "Improvement of St. John Park, New York City, Messrs. Carrère & Hastings, Architects," *Architectural Review* 5 (December 10, 1898): 88 plate; and "Trees and Parks in Cities," *Municipal Affairs* 4 (June 1900): 421-42.

328. Montgomery Schuyler, "'Formal Gardens' and Small Parks," *Scribner's* 27 (June 1900): 637-40.

329. George F. Pentecost, Jr., "City Gardens," *Architectural Record* 14 (July 1903): 50-61.

330. Edward H. Kendall, "The Recreation Piers," *Public Improvements* 1 (July 1, 1899): 78-79. Also see "The City's Social Policy," *Real Estate Record and Guide* 60 (July 10, 1897): 45-46; and Seth T. Stewart, "Recreation Centers in the City of New York," *Charities and The Commons* 18 (August 3, 1907): 510-12.

331. Kendall, "Recreation Piers": 78-79. Note that Little Italy, the city's principal Italian quarter, was located in what is now East Harlem until around the Second World War.

332. Kendall, "Recreation Piers": 79.

333. See, for example, a description of Public Baths in England; Robert Donald, "Public Baths and Laundries," *Outlook* 53 (February 15, 1896): 285-86. Also see "The City's Social Policy," *Real Estate Record and Guide* 45-46.

334. "The 'Cosmopolitan' Bath Competition," *Architecture and Building* 12 (March 8, 1890): 112.

335. "The 'Cosmopolitan' Public Baths and Laundry Competition," *Architecture and Building* 12 (June 21, 1890): 296; "Design for Public Baths, Submitted by John Galen Howard, New York," and "Cosmopolitan Magazine Competition: Public Laundries, Submitted by Lyman A. Ford," *Architecture and Building* 13 (July 26, 1890): plates.
336. *Architecture and Building* 35 (February 27, 1892): 130. Also see "Movement to provide Public Baths in New York," *American Architect and Building News* 32 (April 25, 1891): 49-50.
337. *American Architect and Building News* 32 (May 9, 1891): 78.
338. "Free Public Baths," *Architecture* 11 (February 1905): 25.
339. Russell Sturgis, "Pavilions in the New York Parks," *Architectural Record* 17 (March 1905): 236-50; "Seward Park Pavilion," *American Architect and Building News* 80 (April 4, 1903): plate; and "Design for Seward Park Pavilion," *Architecture* 17 (April 15, 1903): 47. Also see "Shelter House, Corlears Hook, New York," *Architecture and Building* 27 (November 20, 1897): plate.
340. "The First Free Plunge Bath in New York City," *Architects' and Builders' Magazine* 7 (July 1906): 448-52; "A New York Public Bath," *American Architect and Building News* 90 (August 25, 1906): 71, plates; Harold Werner and August P. Windolph, "The Public Bath, Part III," *Brickbuilder* 17 (April 1908): 70-79.
341. "Free Public Baths," *Architecture* 11: 25, plates; "Free Public Baths, Ave. A., 23d and 24th Sts., New York," *Architecture* 17 (February 1908): plates XIII-XIV; "Public Baths, East Twenty-third Street, New York," *Brickbuilder* 17 (April 1908): plate 5. Aiken may have been the actual designer; Brunner's East Eleventh Street Bath is far more conventionally classical in its character, and therefore more typical of his work. See Werner and Windolph, "The Public Bath": 11
342. "Free Public Baths for the City of New York," *American Architect and Building News* 88 (December 16, 1905): plates; Werner and Windolph, "The Public Bath": 71.
343. "Free Public Baths, 109th Street, New York City," *Brickbuilder* 13 (September 1904): plate.
344. "A New Public Bath," *Real Estate Record and Guide* 84 (July 3, 1909): 9-10.
345. "A Public Bath and Gymnasium in the City of New York," *American Architect* 101 (May 5, 1912): 226, plates; and "Public Bathing Establishments," *Brickbuilder* 24 (January 1915): 13-16.
346. "Public Bathing Establishments," *Brickbuilder* 24 (January 1915): 16. Also see Renwick, Aspinwall & Tucker's "Public Baths, Carmine Street, New York," *Brickbuilder* 17 (November 1908): plate.
347. Norval White and Elliot Willensky, *AIA Guide to New York City* (New York: Collier Books, 1978), 356.
348. *American Architect and Building News* 35 (January 2, 1892): 2, "Bronx Park 'Zoo,'" *Public Improvements* 2 (April 16, 1900): 273-75; and William T. Hornaday, "The New York Plan for Zoological Parks," *Scribner's* 46 (November 1909): 590-606.
349. "Front Elevation, Museum Building, New York Botanical Garden," *Brickbuilder* 7 (August 1908): 171; "Museum Building, New York Botanical Garden," *Architecture and Building* 29 (October 1, 1898): plates; and "Botanical Garden and Museum, Bronx Park," *Public Improvements* 2 (April 16, 1900): 274. Also see Parish & Schroeder's "Competitive Design, Museum Building in Bronx Park, New York Botanical Garden," *Architecture and Building* 28 (February 12, 1898): plates.
350. *American Architect and Building News* 57 (July 31, 1897): 38.
351. Quoted in White & Willensky, *AIA Guide*, 322.
352. Hornaday, "The New York Plan for Zoological Parks": 590-606.
353. *American Architect and Building News* 35 (January 2, 1892): 2; "Bronx Park Zoo," *Public Improvements*: 273-75; "House for Primates, Bronx Park," *Brickbuilder* 11 (April 1902): plate; "Detail of Main Entrance, Lion House," *Brickbuilder* 13 (January 1904): plate; "Main Entrance to Antelope House," *Brickbuilder* 13 (September 1904): plate; "Elephant House, New York Zoological Park," *Architects' and Builders' Magazine* 10 (January 1911): 129-32; and Hornaday, "The New York Plan for Zoological Parks": 590-606.

PALACES OF PRODUCTION

1. See "The New Trinity Building," *Architects' and Builders' Magazine* 6 (June 1905): 383-401. Before the nineteenth century, office space was almost always found in mixed-use buildings, and even well into the century single-use office buildings were usually converted dwellings. For a brief history of the office building see Russell Sturgis, *A Dictionary of Architecture and Building* 3 (New York: Macmillan, 1901-02), columns 11-12. But, as Nikolaus Pevsner says, the office building has never been well documented. See his *A History of Building Types* (Princeton: Princeton University Press, 1976), 213-24.
2. "The New World Building, *Real Estate Record and Guide* 45 (June 14, 1890): 879; Russell Sturgis, "A Review of the Work of George B. Post," *Architectural Record* (June 1898): 1-102, reprinted in *Great American Architects Series* (New York: Da Capo Press, 1977); and Winston Weisman, "The Commercial Architecture of George B. Post," *Journal of the Society of Architectural Historians* 31 (October 1972): 176-203. Also see "Competitive Drawing for Proposed New World Building, R.H. Robertson, Archt," *American Architect and Building News* 25 (February 9, 1889): plate.
3. J. Lincoln Steffens, "The Modern Business Building," *Scribner's* 22 (July 1897): 37-61. Changes to the New York skyline are also discussed by John Beverly Robinson in "Recent Brick and Terra-Cotta Work in New York," *Brickbuilder* 4 (April 1895): 76-79.
4. Steffens, "Modern Business Buildings": 37. Also see "One Mile of New York," *Scribner's* 19 (January 1896): 127-28; Robinson, "Recent Brick and Terra-Cotta Work in New York": 76-79; and "The Rebuilding of New York, A Remarkable Era of Transformation and Improvement, the End of Which is not Yet in Sight," *Dun's Review* 16 (December 1910): 34-35, reprinted as an advertisement in *Architectural Yearbook* 1 (1912).
5. "Thirty Years of Office Building," *Real Estate Record and Guide* 61 (April 9, 1898): 641-42.
6. Montgomery Schuyler, "The 'Skyscraper' Up to Date," *Architectural Review* 8 (January-March 1899): 231-37.
7. Leopold Arnaud, "The Tall Building in New York in the Twentieth Century," *Journal of the Society of Architectural Historians* 11 (May 1952): 15-18.
8. "The Equitable Life Assurance Society," *Scribner's* 3 (June 1890): 21-23. For essays on the beginnings of the modern office building see Carl W. Condit, *American Building Art: The Nineteenth Century* (New York: Oxford University Press, 1960), 39-50; and Winston Weisman, "A New View of Skyscraper History," in Edgar Kaufman, ed., *The Rise of an American Architecture* (New York: Praeger, 1970), 115-60.
9. See Winston Weisman, "New York and the Problem of the First Skyscraper," *Journal of the Society of Architectural Historians* 12 (March 1953): 15-21; Weisman, "New View of Skyscraper History," 120-21; and Weisman, "Commercial Architecture of George Post": 181-82. Also see "The Reconstructed Western Union Building," *Real Estate Record and Guide* 47 (April 25, 1891): 647-48.
10. Paul R. Baker, *Richard Morris Hunt* (Cambridge: MIT Press, 1980), 219-23, 502, 543.
11. *Daily Graphic*, June 3, 1873, cited in Weisman, "New York and the Problem of the First Skyscraper": 18.
12. "Height, the Architectural Feature of the Age," *American Builder* (September 1874), quoted in Weisman, "New York and the Problem of the First Skyscraper": 20.
13. "The Highest Building in the Dry-Goods District," *Real Estate Record and Guide* 36 (September 12, 1885): 996-97. Also see "Some Examples in Good Building," *Real Estate Record and Guide* 45 (May 10, 1890): 688-89.
14. For a comparison of the Produce Exchange to William Le Baron Jenney's Home Insurance Building in Chicago, the first building to have a completely metal structure, see Condit, *American Building Art: Nineteenth Century*, 44-45, 51-54. Also see "The New York Produce Exchange Competition," *American Architect and Building News* 9 (March 12, 1881): 123-24; "Competitive Design for the New York Produce Exchange, Mr. F.C. Withers, Architect, New York, New York," *American Architect and Building News* 9 (April 9, 1881): 174-75, plates; "Competitive Design for the New York Produce Exchange Building, C.B. Atwood, Architect," *American Architect and Building News* 9 (June 11, 1881): plates; "Design for the New York Produce Exchange, R.M. Upjohn, Arch't," *American Architect and Building News* 13 (September 8, 1883): plate; "The Produce Exchange, New York, N.Y., Mr. George B. Post, Architect," *American Architect and Building News* 19 (June 20, 1886): 305-06, plate; "New York Produce Exchange, Broadway and Beaver Street, New York," *Architecture and Building* 19 (August 5, 1893): plate; and Sturgis, "Work of Post": 29-32.
15. Condit, *American Building Art: Nineteenth Century*, 46-48. Also see "The Tower Building," *Real Estate Record and Guide* 43 (February 16, 1889): 207; "The Tower Building," *Architecture and Building* 12 (March 1, 1890): plate; "The First 'Skeleton' Building," *Real Estate Record and Guide* 64 (August 12, 1899): 239; and "New York's First Skyscraper and Its Architect," *Real Estate Record and Guide* 88 (October 21, 1911): 589.
16. Cited by Condit, *American Building Art: Nineteenth Century*, 48.
17. Russell Sturgis, "A Review of the Works of Clinton & Russell," *Architectural Record* 6 (October-December 1897): 1-61.
18. See Montgomery Schuyler, "The Works of R.H. Robertson," *Architectural Record* 6 (October-December 1896): 184-219; William H. Birkmire, "The Planning and Construction of High Office Buildings," *Architecture and Building* 25 (December 5, 1896): 267-71; "The Park

Row," *Real Estate Record and Guide* 62 (August 27, 1898): 287-88; and "Mercantile Building, Nos. 17-21 Park Row," *Architecture and Building* 29 (December 3, 1898): plate. For a good photograph see, "Park Row Syndicate Building, New York," *Brickbuilder* 7 (July 1898): 148.

19. Unlike Carl Condit, Nikolaus Pevsner or Siegfried Giedion, who stress the importance of structural evolution in the development of the office building, or Winston Weisman, who emphasizes the chronological evolution of styles in his histories of the New York skyscraper, we believe that the development of a new typology was the most important factor of this new building type. See Condit, *American Building Art: Nineteenth Century, passim;* Pevsner, *History of Building Types*, 213-24; and Giedion, *Space, Time and Architecture* (Cambridge: Harvard University Press, 1941), 161-275, 333-421. For an interpretation closer to our own, see Cesar Pelli, "Skyscrapers," *Perspecta* 18 (1982): 134-51.

20. "Chicago-Proposed Odd Fellows Temple," *Graphic* 5 (December 19, 1891): 404, cited and reproduced in Donald Hoffman, "The Setback Skyscraper City of 1891, an Unknown Essay of Louis H. Sullivan," *Journal of the Society of Architectural Historians* 29 (March 1970): 181-87.

21. Louis H. Sullivan, "The High Building Question," *Graphic* 5 (December 19, 1891): 405, reprinted in Hoffman, "Setback Skyscraper City of 1891": 184-86.

22. Montgomery Schuyler, "Architecture in Chicago, Part 1, A Critique of the Works of Adler & Sullivan," *Architectural Record* 5 (February 1896): 1-48, reprinted in *Great American Architects Series* (New York: Da Capo Press, 1977).

23. See Lewis Mumford, "New York *vs.* Chicago in Architecture," *Architecture* 56 (November 1927): 241-44; Giedion, *Space, Time and Architecture, passim;* and Colin Rowe, "Chicago Frame," *The Mathematics of the Ideal Villa and Other Essays* (Cambridge: MIT Press, 1976), 89-118.

24. In 1900 the *Real Estate Record and Guide* said that "everyone is aware of the exodus of large industrial corporations from the interior cities of the country to New York. We refer, of course, to their executive offices, not to factories or plants. The movement of corporations . . . to New York is not new. It has accelerated, however, of recent years, and the reasons are not far to seek." The *Record and Guide* cited prestige, the concentration of financial interests, and tax advantages which were particularly favorable in comparison to the tax situation in Chicago. See "Large Corporations Moving to New York," *Real Estate Record and Guide* 67 (December 15, 1900): 822.

25. Montgomery Schuyler, "The Field of Art," *Scribner's* 34 (September 1903): 253-56.

26. "The Union Trust Company's New Building," *Real Estate Record and Guide* 44 (November 16, 1889): 1534; "The Union Trust Company," *Real Estate Record and Guide* 45 (February 1, 1890): 149; "Union Trust Co. Building, 76-80 Broadway, New York, Geo B. Post, Architect, *Architecture and Building* 19 (August 26, 1893): plate; "Union Trust Company's Building, 80 Broadway, New York, N.Y., George B. Post, Architect," *American Architect and Building News* 42 (October 21, 1893): plate; and Schuyler, "The 'Skyscraper' Up To Date": 233-34.

27. Schuyler, "The 'Skyscraper' Up To Date": 233-34.

28. "The Warren Building, New York, McKim, Mead & White, Architects," *Brickbuilder* 3 (November 1884): 226. McKim, Mead & White's design for the seven-story American Safe Deposit Company, built in 1882 on Fifth Avenue at the corner of Forty-second Street, was a bearing-wall structure with a planar expression slightly more unified than the Warren Building. Above a rusticated base, the windows of the middle floors were grouped into vertical strips separated by brick piers which supported an attic floor with a different window treatment. See "Building of the American Safe Deposit Company, New York, N.Y., Messrs. McKim, Mead & White, Architects, New York, N.Y.," *American Architect and Building News* 19 (January 30, 1886): 55, plate.

29. Barr Ferree, "The High Building And Its Art," *Scribner's* 15 (March 1894): 297-318.

30. For a discussion of McKim's attitude toward the tall building, see Leland Roth, *Urban Architecture of McKim, Mead & White, 1870-1910* (Ph.D. diss., Yale University, 1973), 730-42.

31. "Pierce Building, Cor. Franklin & Hudson St's, New York, N.Y., Carrère & Hastings, Arch'ts," *American Architect and Building News* 32 (April 25, 1891): plate; and Curtis Channing Blake, *The Architecture of Carrère & Hastings* (Ph.D. diss., Columbia University, 1976), 322-23.

32. "Architectural Aberrations, The Edison Building," *Architectural Record* 1 (October-December 1891): 133-36. Also see "The Edison Building, New York, N.Y., Messrs. Carrère & Hastings, Architects," *American Architect and Building News* 30 (December 6, 1890): plate; "The Edison Building, 42 Broad St., New York, N.Y.," *Architecture and Building* 14 (September 19, 1891): plate; "The Edison Building, 42 Broad Street, New York, Carrère & Hastings, Architects, New York, N.Y.," *American Architect and Building News* 42 (October 7, 1893): plate; and Blake, *Carrère & Hastings,* 323-25.

33. Schuyler, "The 'Skyscraper' Up To Date": 233.

34. "Architectural Aberrations, the Edison Building," *Architectural Record:* 134.

35. "Building for the Mail and Express, New York City, Carrère & Hastings, Architects," *Architectural Review* (November 2, 1891): plate I; "The Mail and Express Building, New York, Messrs. Carrère & Hastings, Architects, 44 Broadway, New York," *Architecture and Building* 15 (October 3, 1891): 163-64; "Detail of Broadway Front, Mail and Express Building, New York, Carrère & Hastings, Architects," *Architecture and Building* 18 (February 18, 1893): plate; Francis Swales, "Architecture in the United States, II, The Commercial Buildings," *Architectural Review* (England) 24 (August 1908): 61-68; "The Work of Messrs. Carrère & Hastings," *Architectural Review* 27 (January 1910): 1-120; and Blake, *Carrère & Hastings,* 325-29. Also see Francis Swales, "Architecture in the United States, I, The Commercial Buildings," *Architectural Review* (England) 24 (August 1908): 61-68.

36. For a transcript of the speech see Thomas Hastings, "High Buildings and Good Architecture," *American Architect and Building News* 46 (November 17, 1894): 67-68. Also see an untitled summary in the *Architectural Review* 3 (September 1894): 33-38. Carrère & Hastings's Life Building (19-21 West Thirty-first Street, 1893-94) was a special case, because it housed not only the magazine's offices but also a number of apartment suites in the upper floors that were intended for the use of the writers. Given this unusual mix, it is not surprising that the three-bay Modern French brick and limestone facades should seem so much more like those of a typical Parisian apartment house than of a New York office building. The editors of *Architectural Review* were taken with the building's unusual character: "In the fierce battle which is now raging as to the right or wrong use of precedent, the design of the 'Life' building may well come in to disarm the criticism which would make every new building the unadorned expression of practical wants; for it so perfectly satisfies all rational requirements, and gives besides so much that has real and associated charm that it were crass perversity not to welcome it most cordially." "Scale Drawings of the Facade of the 'Life' Building," *Architectural Review* 2 (May 1893): 36, plates XXV-XXVII. Also see "Life Building, New York City," *Architectural Review* 2 (August 1894): 30-31; "Work of Carrère & Hastings," *Architectural Record:* 16, 18; and Blake, *Carrère & Hastings,* 132-34.

37. Swales, "Architecture in the United States, II": 124-25.

38. Birkmire, "Planning and Construction of High Office Buildings": 269; Montgomery Schuyler, "The Works of Kimball & Thompson," *Architectural Record* 7 (April-June 1898): 479-578; and Swales, "Architecture in the United States, II": 119, 123, 125.

39. "Home Life Insurance Building, Broadway, New York, N.Y., N. Le Brun & Sons, Architects," *American Architect and Building News* 55 (March 20, 1897): plate; and Montgomery Schuyler, "The Works of N. Le Brun & Sons," *Architectural Record* 27 (May 1910): 365-81.

40. "The Work of George Edward Harding & Gooch," *Architectural Record* 7 (July-September 1897): 104-17. Also see "Commercial Cable Building, Broad Street, New York, Geo. E. Harding & Gooch, Architects," *Architecture and Building* 27 (November 13, 1897): plate; and "Commercial Cable Building, Broad Street, New York, Geo. E. Harding & Gooch, Architects," *American Architect and Building News* 57 (December 11, 1897): plate.

41. "A Mammoth Office Building, 60-62 Wall Street, New York, Clinton & Russell, Architects," *Architects' and Builders' Magazine* 6 (July 1905): 429-36; and "Sixty Wall Street Office Building, New York, Clinton & Russell, Architects," *Architecture* 16 (July 15, 1907): 124. Also see Bruce Price's tall and narrow Century Building, built in 1903 between the Union Trust and Manhattan Life buildings, in "The Mercantile Buildings," *Real Estate Record and Guide* 73 (June 11, 1904): 1429, 1433.

42. Sturgis, "Clinton & Russell": 8-10. In the same article, see the Franklin Building (9-15 Murray Street), the Stokes Building (47 Cedar Street), the Rhinelander Building (232-38 William Street), the Fabrys Building (54 Maiden Lane), the Samson Building (63-65 Wall Street), and the Continental Insurance Company Building (46 Cedar Street).

43. "Lawyers Title Insurance and Trust Co., 160 Broadway, New York, Clinton & Russell, Architects," *Architecture* 16 (July 15, 1907): 110-11.

44. "Entrance Detail, Van Cortlandt Building," *Inland Architect and News Record* 43 (February 1904): plate; Ferree, "Art of High Building": 463-65; and "Mercantile Buildings," *Real Estate Record and Guide:* 1429.

45. Ferree, "Art of High Building": 463. Also see "The Next Fourth Avenue Building," *Real Estate Record and Guide* 86 (July 2, 1910): 5.

46. See "The 'H' Plan for Office Buildings," *Real Estate Record and Guide* 84 (August 7, 1909): 254. Also see "Getting Daylight into a Skyscraper," *Architectural Record* 33 (March 1913): 279.

47. The Bayard Building was named for William Bayard, first president of the Bank for Savings, which had occupied the site until a fire destroyed its building and the bank's offices were moved to new headquarters on Fourth Avenue. The building was renamed the Condict Building. "Brick and Terra-Cotta Work In American Cities, and Manufacturers' Department," *Brickbuilder* 7 (June 1898): 127-28; "The Bayard Building," *Real Estate Record and Guide* 62 (October 15, 1898): 531-32; "Condict Building, 65 Bleecker St., New York, L.H. Sullivan, Architect," *Architecture* 1 (April 15, 1900): 146; "The Condict Building, Bleecker St., New York, N.Y., L.H. Sullivan & L.P. Smith, Associated Architects," *American Architect and Building News* 70 (October 6, 1900): plates; and "Entrance to the Condict Building, Bleecker St., New York, N.Y., L.H. Sullivan & L.P. Smith, Associated Architects," *American Architect and Building News* 70 (October 13, 1900): plate.

48. Louis Sullivan, "The Tall Building Artistically Considered," *Lippincott's Magazine* 57 (March 1896): 403-09, reprinted in Louis Sullivan, *Kindergarten Chats and Other Writings* (New York: George Wittenborn, Inc., 1947), 202-13.

49. Russell Sturgis, "Good Things in Modern Architecture," *Architectural Record* 8 (July-September 1898): 92-110.

50. "Bayard Building," *Real Estate Record and Guide:* 531.

51. Schuyler, "The 'Skyscraper' Up To Date": 255-57. Though the editors of *Architecture* considered the profession to be "almost a unit in its approval," they rhetorically asked their readers if anyone among them had ever heard an ordinary layman say that he admired it, replying that the "educated designer, although knowing the past of his art, understands also the conditions which created it—and . . . is therefore rejoiced to see a . . . designer adapt old traditions to modern methods in a logical manner . . . the lay public (at least the educated part) are also familiar with the visible evidence of the past, but beyond that visible evidence they have not penetrated and all of their vague ideas of architectural beauty are centered around these monuments of past methods, which to them are the standard by which all future work must be judged." "Professional Comment," *Architecture* 2 (October 15, 1910): 369.

52. H.W. Desmond, "A Rational Skyscraper," *Architectural Record* 15 (March 1904): 275-84; and Alan Burnham, "Forgotten Pioneering," *Architectural Forum* 106 (April 1957): 116-21.

53. An early design by Richard Morris Hunt for a building on Broadway also anticipated Flagg's dialogue between frame and curtain wall. "Iron Front on Broadway," *American Architect and Building News* 1 (June 10, 1876): plate.

54. Desmond, "Rational Skyscraper": 279-83.

55. "The New Evening Post Building," *Architects' and Builders' Magazine* 8 N.S. (September 1907): 569-73; and "Building for the Evening Post, New York City, Robert D. Kohn, Architect," *Architectural Review* 15 (September 1908): 143, plate.

56. Montgomery Schuyler, "Some Recent Skyscrapers," *Architectural Record* 22 (September 1907): 161-76.

57. "The Blair Building, Broad St. and Exchange Pl., New York, N.Y.," *American Architect and Building News* 78 (November 8, 1903): plate; "The Blair Building, Broad Street, New York, Carrère & Hastings, Architects," *Architectural Review* 5 (October 1903): 161-62; "Blair Building, New York," *Inland Architect and News Record* 42 (November 1903): plate; H.W. Desmond, "A Beaux Arts Skyscraper, The Blair Building, New York City," *Architectural Record* 14 (December 1903): 436-43; "Skyscrapers, the November Meeting of the Architectural League of New York," *Architects' and Builders' Magazine* 5 (December 1903): 113-22; Claude Bragdon, "Architecture in the United States, III, The Skyscraper," *Architectural Record* 26 (August 1909): 51-96; "Work of Carrère & Hastings," *Architectural Record:* 75-76; and Blake, *Carrère & Hastings,* 336-41.

58. Ferree, "Art of the High Building": 463.

59. Desmond, "Beaux Arts Skyscraper": 437.

60. Desmond, "Beaux Arts Skyscraper": 439.

61. Bragdon, "Architecture in the United States, III": 94.

62. Desmond, "Beaux Arts Skyscraper": 443.

63. "Building of the United States Rubber Company," *American Architect* 102 (July 10, 1912): 14, 16, plates; and Blake, *Carrère & Hastings,* 342-44.

64. "Office Building, S.W. Cor. Fifth Ave. and Twenty-second St., New York, Robert Maynicke, Architect," *Architecture and Building* 28 (February 26, 1898): plate.

65. "High Buildings," *Scribner's* 19 (March 1896): 389-90; "The Most Modern Instance," *Real Estate Record and Guide* 59 (June 5, 1897): 962-65; "Porch of the St. Paul Building, New York, N.Y., George B. Post, Architect, Karl Bitter, Sculptor," *American Architect and Building News* 66 (October 7, 1899): plate; and Weisman, "Commercial Architecture of George Post": 197. J. Graham Glover and Henry C. Carrel's proposal for the *Herald* Building, which may have been intended for the same site, was a more advanced expression of verticality. Glover & Carrell engaged a corner turret crowning the tower with a full dome on a colonnaded drum. "Proposed Design for *Herald* Building," *American Architect and Building News* 61 (August 6, 1898): plate.

66. Schuyler, "The 'Skyscraper' Up To Date": 236.

67. "Atlantic Building, Wall Street, New York, Clinton & Russell, Architects," *Inland Architect and News Record* 38 (March 1901): plate; "Over the Draughting Board, Opinions Official and Unofficial, The Design of Our Tall Buildings—The Latest Phase," *Architectural Record* 11 (October 1901): 705-16; and "The Atlantic Building, Wall and William Streets, New York, N.Y., Clinton & Russell, Architects," *American Architect and Building News* 75 (January 4, 1902): plates. Also see "Recent Brick and Terra-Cotta Work in New York," *Brickbuilder:* 78-79; "The Woodbridge Building, William, Platt and John Streets, New York City, Clinton & Russell, Architects," *Architectural Record* 6 (April-June 1897): 467; Sturgis, "Clinton & Russell": *passim;* "Battery Park Building, State Street from Pearl to Bridge Street," *Real Estate Record and Guide* 66 (February 10, 1900): 239; "Battery Park Buildings, New York, Clinton & Russell, Architects," *Architecture* 1 (March 15, 1900): 106; and "Wall Street Exchange Building, Clinton & Russell, Architects," *Architects' and Builders' Magazine* 4 (May 1903): 340-42.

68. "East River Savings Bank Building, Broadway and Reade St., New York, Clinton & Russell, Architects," *Architecture* 23 (May 1911): plate LI.

69. "The Broadway Chambers, New York, N.Y., Mr. Cass Gilbert, Architect, St. Paul, Minn.," *American Architect and Building News* 67 (February 24, 1900): 63, plate; "The Broadway Chambers," *Architects' and Builders' Magazine* 33 (October 1900): 45-52; "Upper Stories, Broadway Chambers, New York, N.Y., Cass Gilbert, Architect," *Brickbuilder* 10 (February 1901): plate; "Broadway Chambers, Broadway and Chambers St., New York, N.Y., Cass Gilbert, Architect," *American Architect and Building News* 72 (May 18, 1901): plates; "Building Skyscrapers, Described by Cass Gilbert, Architect," *Real Estate Record and Guide* 66 (June 23, 1900): 1085-86.

70. "Building for the Knickerbocker Trust Company, New York," *Architectural Review* 9 (March 1902): plate 11; "The Knickerbocker Trust Co. Building 34th St. and 5th Ave., New York," *Architecture* 9 (March 1904): plate; "The Knickerbocker Trust Company, New York City," *Architectural Review* 12 (February 1905): 82-83; Montgomery Schuyler, "A 'Modern Classic,'" *Architectural Record* 15 (May 1904): 431-44; and Talbot Faulkner Hamlin, "The Columbia Trust Company Building," *Architecture* 41 (January 1920): 17.

71. "Architectural Criticism," *Architecture* 20 (July 15, 1909): 98, plates LX-LIX; "Downtown Building, Knickerbocker Trust Company, New York, McKim, Mead & White, Architects," *American Architect and Building News* 99 (May 3, 1911): plates.

72. "Architectural Criticism," *Architecture:* 98.

73. "Astor Trust Building, Fifth Ave. and 42d St., New York, Montague Flagg, Architect," *Architecture* 36 (July 1917): 121.

74. "Royal Insurance Company's Building, William Street and Maiden Lane, New York, N.Y., Messrs. Howells & Stokes, Architects," *American Architect and Building News* 92 (August 31, 1907): 72, plates. For Howells & Stokes's Hilliard Building at 55 John Street, see "Two New York Office Buildings," *Architecture and Building* 43 (September 1911): 506-10.

75. "The Washington Life Building," *Real Estate Record and Guide* 61 (April 30, 1898): 778-79.

76. Schuyler, The 'Skyscraper' Up To Date: 246. In the original design for the Chesebrough Building, built in quite a different form on the corner of Pearl and State streets, Clinton & Russell attempted to get the same sense of verticality by combining the structural expression of the Bayard Building with more conventional Classicism. The attempt was not very successful; the later decision to cover the entire wall in rustication negated the sense of infill panels and made the vertical bays superfluous. Sturgis, "Works of Clinton & Russell": 4; "Chesebrough Building, Battery Park, New York City," *Brickbuilder* 8 (July 1899): 145, plate; and "Improvement at Apex of Manhattan," *Real Estate Record and Guide* 95 (January 16, 1915): 91.

77. "Germania Life Insurance Building, Fourth Ave. and 17th St., New York, D'Oench & Yost, Architects," *Architecture* 23 (May 1911): plate L; and "Comparative Types in Office and Loft Buildings," *Architecture and Building* 43 (July 1911): 425-26. Also see "Corn Exchange Bank Building, Corner of Beaver and South William Streets, New York, N.Y., Mr. R.H. Robertson, Architect," *American Architect and Building News* 38 (October 22, 1892): plate; "American Tract Society's Building, Corner Nassau and Spruce Streets, New York, N.Y., Mr. R.H. Robertson, Architect, New York, N.Y.," *American Architect and Building News* 44 (May 26, 1894): 92, plate; "Cushman Building, Corner Maiden Lane and Broadway, New York, C.P.H. Gilbert, Architect," 29 (September 3, 1898): plate; and

"The Vincent Building," *Real Estate Record and Guide* 63 (February 18, 1899): 285-86. Post's Vincent Building was built on the southeast corner of Broadway and Duane Street.

78. "Design for Proposed Sun Building, City Hall Square, New York City, Bruce Price, Architect," *Architectural Record* 1 (July-September 1891): 75; and Swales, "Architecture in the United States, I": 66. For early examples by other architects see "Building for the Postal Telegraph Cable Company, New York, N.Y., Geo. Edw. Harding and Gooch, Architects," *American Architect and Building News* 36 (May 14, 1892): plate; "Morris Building, N.W. Corner Broad & Beaver Streets, New York, Youngs & Cable, Architects," *Architecture and Building* 18 (May 27, 1893): plate; "Fulton Building, Nassau Street, New York City, De Lemos & Cordes, Architects," *Architectural Record* 3 (July-September 1893): 82; "Scott & Bowne Building, Junction of New Chambers, Pearl & Rose Streets, New York, Wm. Schickel & Co., Architects," *Architecture and Building* 19 (November 11, 1893): plate; "The Townsend Building, Broadway, N.W. Corner of 25th Streets," *Real Estate Record and Guide* 59 (April 3, 1897): 555; "The Central Bank Building, Broadway and Pearl Street, New York City, John T. Williams, Architect," *Architectural Record* 6 (April-June 1897): 466; and "Queen Insurance Company Building, Broadway, New York City, Geo. Edw. Harding & Gooch, Architects," and "Dunn Building, Broadway, New York City, Geo. Edw. Harding & Gooch, Architects," *Brickbuilder* 6 (September 1897): 208-09.

79. "American Surety Building, Bruce Price, Architect," *American Architect and Building News* 48 (May 18, 1895): plates; "American Surety Building, Pine Street and Broadway, New York," *Brickbuilder* 4 (October 1895): 222; "High Buildings," *Scribner's*: 389-90; and "American Surety Building, Broadway, New York, Bruce Price, Architect," *American Architect and Building News* 53 (August 15, 1896): plate.

80. Swales, "Architecture in the United States, II": 67-68. Carrère & Hastings took a quite different tack with their entry to the competition, designing restless elevations reflecting a struggle to adopt the elements of the Classical language to the demands for a unified vertical composition of great height. Piling up several distinct parts to mask the repetitive nature of the office building, the architects combined seven floors behind a unified glass and spandrel treatment which rushed the eye upward. A slender and elaborate cupola topped the building, simultaneously recalling the tower at McKim, Mead & White's Madison Square Garden and looking forward to the base and cupola formula of later New York skyscrapers. "Competitive Design for the American Surety Building, New York, N.Y., Messrs. Carrère & Hastings, Architects, New York," *American Architect and Building News* 44 (February 17, 1894): plate. Also see "Competitive Scheme for Proposed Building for American Surety Company, New York, N.Y., Submitted by Mr. George Martin Huss, Architect, New York, N.Y.," *American Architect and Building News* 44 (May 5, 1894): 53, plate; and "Competitive Scheme for Proposed Building for American Surety Company, New York, N.Y., Submitted by Mr. John R. Thomas, Architect, New York, N.Y.," *American Architect and Building News* 44 (May 5, 1894): 54, plate.

81. "The St. James Building," *Architectural Record* 6 (April-June 1897): 460; and "St. James Building, New York, N.Y.," *American Architect and Building News* 81 (August 1, 1903): plate. Also see "Architectural Additions to New York, No. 1, International Banking and Trust Co.'s Building, Northwest Corner Broadway and Cedar Street, Bruce Price, Architect," *Real Estate Record and Guide* 66 (January 13, 1900): 51; "Critiques on Current Buildings, No. 1, 137 Broadway, the International Banking and Trust Co.'s Building," *Architectural Record* 9 (April 1900): 424-28; "The Latest Office Building, Novelty in Design, the International Banking and Trust Co.'s Building," *Real Estate Record and Guide* 66 (April 14, 1900): 626-27; "International Banking & Trust Co.'s Building," *American Architect and Building News* 81 (August 1, 1903): plate; and "Bank of the Metropolis, Bruce Price, Architect," *Architects' and Builders' Magazine* 4 (April 1903): 292-94.

82. "The Third Tallest Tower," *Real Estate Record and Guide* 85 (April 23, 1910): 864; "The Bankers Trust Company Building," *Architecture* 6 (May 1912): 241-47; and "Bankers Trust Company Building," *Architecture and Building* 44 (June 1912): 232-43. The Bankers Trust Building replaced the thirteen-year-old, twenty-one story Gillender Building, the first tall building of significant size to be demolished.

83. "Recent Brick and Terra-Cotta Work in New York," *Brickbuilder* 76-78; and Montgomery Schuyler, "A Picturesque Skyscraper," *Architectural Record* 5 (January-March 1896): 299-302. Also see "Wolfe Building, Maiden Lane, Corner of William Street, New York, H.J. Hardenbergh, Architect," *Architecture and Building* 23 (July 13, 1895): plate; and Montgomery Schuyler, "Henry Janeway Hardenbergh," *Architectural Record* 6 (January-March 1897): 335-75.

84. "Sketch for a New York Office Building, Bruce Price, Architect," *American Architect and Building News* 81 (August 1, 1903): plate.

85. "The Beaver Building, Clinton & Russell, Architects," *Architects' and Builders' Magazine* 5 (August 1904): 514-22.

86. "Seligman Building," *New York Architect* 2 (March 1908); and Schuyler, "Some Recent Skyscrapers": 174-76.

87. "German American Insurance Building," *Real Estate Record and Guide* 81 (January 4, 1908): 25; "German American Ins. Co. Bldg., Maiden Lane and Liberty St., New York, Hill & Stout, Architects," *Architecture* 17 (June 1908): plates XLIX-LI; Frederick P. Hill, "A Criticism," *Architecture* 19 (February 1909): 19; and "New York Skyscraper Architecture, Old and New," *Architectural Record* 26 (August 1909): 122.

88. F.C. Gordon, "The 'Sky-scraper,'" *American Architect and Building News* 46 (December 8, 1894): 100-01, plate.

89. Russell Sturgis, "Experiment in Color: The Whitehall Building," *Architectural Record* 14 (July 1903): 70-73; and Barr Ferree, "The Art of the High Building": 445-66.

90. "The New Whitehall Building," *New York Architect* 5 (February 1911); "The Enlarged Whitehall Building," *Architecture and Building* 43 (April 1911): 295-306; "The Whitehall Building Extension," *Architectural Record* 27 (May 1910): 430; and "Improvement at Apex of Manhattan," *Real Estate Record and Guide*: 91.

91. "Skyscraper Builders in Gigantic Race, Work Being Rushed by Rival Owners of Huge Structures in the Downtown District," *Real Estate Record and Guide* 77 (June 30, 1906): 1237; "Detail, West Street Building, New York," *Architecture* 15 (May 1907): plate XL; "Modern Office Buildings," *Architects' and Builders' Magazine* 8 (June 1907): 413-39; "The West Street Building," *Architectural Record* 22 (August 1907): 102-09; and "West Street Building, New York," *Architecture* 16 (September 1907): plate LXXV.

92. "The West Street Building," *Architectural Record:* 108. Schuyler marveled at "the pinnacle diadem of the West Street Building, which the uninteresting building beneath lifts into the empyrean to become the cynosure of a justified imagination." Montgomery Schuyler, "The Evolution of the Skyscraper," *Scribner's* 46 (September 1909): 257-71. The Emmet Building, built in 1912 by J. Stewart Barney and Stockton B. Colt at the corner of Madison Avenue and Twenty-ninth Street, was a two-sided, corner infill building covered in an emphatically vertical Gothic shell. "The Emmet Building, New York City," *Brickbuilder* 21 (December 1912): 325-27.

93. "Competition for Figure to Surmount Fulton Street Tower, New Western Union Building, New York City," *American Architect* 106 (September 2, 1914): plates; "Telephone and Telegraph Building, New York," *Architecture* 34 (December 1916): 268-69, plates CLXXXI-CXC; and "The Telephone and Telegraph Building, N.Y. City," *Architecture and Building* 49 (January 1917): cover, 1-10.

94. "New York Life Building, Broadway and Leonard Street, New York, McKim, Mead & White, Architects," *Architecture and Building* 27 (October 2, 1897): plate; and "New York Life Insurance Company's Building, New York, N.Y., McKim, Mead & White, Architects," *American Architect and Building News* 79 (January 31, 1903): plates.

95. Swales, "Architecture in the United States, II": 117-19.

96. "The New Trinity Building," *Real Estate Record and Guide* 73 (June 11, 1904): 1436; "New Trinity Building, Francis H. Kimball, Architect," *Architects' and Builders' Magazine* 6 (June 1905): 383-401; "Trinity Building, 111 Broadway, New York, N.Y.," *American Architect and Building News* 88 (July 29, 1905): plates; and "Trinity and United States Realty Building," *New York Architect* 2 (March 1908). Also see the "Empire Building, Broadway and Rector Street, New York, N.Y., Kimball & Thompson, Architects," *American Architect and Building News* 88 (October 5, 1898): plate.

97. "Modern Office Buildings," *Architects' and Builders' Magazine* 447; "The City Investing Building, New York, N.Y.," *American Architect and Building News* 93 (February 12, 1908): plate; Donn Barber, Editorial, *New York Architect* 2 (May 1908); and Francis H. Kimball, "The City Investing Building," *New York Architect* 2 (May 1908). One of the most notable features of the City Investing Building was a large arcade connecting Broadway with the elevated railroad on Church Street and introducing to the New York office building a measure of spatial grandeur and public convenience that would continue as an increasingly important feature throughout the Metropolitan Era.

98. "Accepted Competition Design, Municipal Office Building, New York," *Architecture* 13 (May 1908): plate XXI; William Walton, "The New Municipal Building and Its Sculpture," *American Architect* 101 (March 20, 1916): 133-38; "Municipal Building, N.Y. City," *Architectural Year Book* 1 (1912): 299; "Municipal Building, New York," *Architecture and Building* 46 (October 1914): 381-96; "New York Municipal Building," *Architecture* 28 (July 1913): 149, plates 60-63; "*A Monograph of the Works of McKim, Mead & White, 1879-1915*" (New York: Architectural Book Publishing Co., 1915; Benjamin Blom, 1973), 50, 56; plates 320-27; and Roth, *Urban*

Architecture of McKim, Mead & White, 1870-1910 (Ph.D. diss., Yale University, 1973): 740-43.
99. "'The Flat-Iron,' 23d St. and Broadway, New York, N.Y., Messrs. D.H. Burnham & Co., Architects, Chicago, Ill.," *American Architect and Building News* 77 (September 27, 1902): 103, plates; "Architectural Appreciations, No. 11, The 'Flatiron' or Fuller Building," *Architectural Record* 12 (October 1902): 528-36; and Thomas S. Hines, *Burnham of Chicago* (New York: Oxford University Press, 1974), 289-90.
100. Paul Goldberger, *The Skyscraper* (New York: Alfred A. Knopf, 1981), 38-39.
101. "The Times Building," *Architects' and Builders' Magazine* 4 (September 1903): 531-37; Schuyler, "The Evolution of a Skyscraper": 329-44; "The New Times Building," *Architects' and Builders' Magazine* 6 (March 1905): 241-60; and "The 'Times' Building," *American Architect and Building News* 87 (June 3, 1905): 179-80, plates. For the earlier *Times* Building see "The 'Times' Building," *Real Estate Record and Guide* 43 (January 12, 1889): 32-33; "The New York Times Building, Printing House Square, George B. Post, Architect," *Building* 9 (October 6, 1888): plate; and Weisman, "Commercial Architecture of Post": 192-93.
102. Schuyler, "Works of Barney & Chapman": 204-08.
103. Desmond, "Works of Ernest Flagg": 34.
104. Schuyler, "The 'Skyscraper' Up To Date": 240-41.
105. "Arguments for and Against Tall Buildings," *Architecture and Building* 24 (January 18, 1896): 30, 33. See also, Ernest Flagg, "The Dangers of High Buildings," *The Cosmopolitan* 21 (May 1896): 70-79; and "The Question of Height Limit in Buildings," *Architecture and Building* 24 (May 16, 1896): 229-30.
106. "Discussion of the High-Building Bill," *Architecture and Building* 24 (May 23, 1896): 250-51. John M. Carrère, Thomas Hastings, Ernest Cordes, Arnold Brunner, William B. Tuthill and William A. Boring among others also spoke in favor of the legislation. Support for height and bulk controls came from many quarters, such as from the Chamber of Commerce, which considered a resolution limiting the height of buildings to a proportion of the width of the streets they faced and restricting to 80 percent of the site the coverage of buildings over eighty-feet tall, a rule similar to that then pertaining to tenements. Discussed in Barr Ferree, "In Streets and Papers," *Architecture and Building* 24 (January 11, 1896): 20; and "The Tall Building Controversy," *Architecture and Building* 24 (January 18, 1896): 25.
107. "The Most Modern Instance," *Real Estate Record and Guide* 59 (June 5, 1897): 962-64.
108. See Montgomery Schuyler, "The New National Park Bank," *Architectural Record* 17 (April 1905): 318-28.
109. A.C. David, "Private Residences for Banking Firms," *Architectural Record* 14 (July 1903): 13-18.
110. Montgomery Schuyler, "The Skyscraper Problem," *Scribner's* 34 (September 1903): 253-56. Also see "Skyscrapers, The November Meeting of the Architectural League of New York," *Architects' and Builders' Magazine* 5 (December 1903): 113-22.
111. Charles Rollinson Lamb, "Civic Architecture From Its Constructive Side," *Municipal Affairs* 2 (March 1898): 46-72.
112. "The Invasion of New York City By Darkness," *Real Estate Record and Guide* 81 (June 6, 1908): 1056-57.
113. Ernest Flagg, "The Limitation of Height and Area of Buildings in New York," *American Architect and Building News* 93 (April 15, 1908): 25-26.
114. Schuyler, "The 'Skyscraper' Up To Date": 131.
115. Schuyler, "The 'Skyscraper' Up To Date": 131. See also "The 'Skyscraper' Problem," *Real Estate Record and Guide* 59 (June 5, 1897): 961-65.
116. Henry James, *The American Scene* (New York: Harper & Bros., 1907; Bloomington: Indiana University Press, 1968), 76-77.
117. Quoted by Goldberger, *The Skyscraper*, 10. Flagg also proposed that development rights be transferable so that owners of small lots would not suffer undue economic hardships. D. Knickerbocker Boyd's proposal was in some ways even closer than Flagg's to the ordinance eventually adopted in 1916. Boyd, a Philadelphian, suggested that the height of buildings be governed in one of two ways: either an architect could terrace his building from the edge of its property line or set back a specified distance from the property line and rise uninterruptedly. Discussed in Winston Weisman, "A New View of Skyscraper History," *The Rise of An American Architect,* 115-60.
118. Montgomery Schuyler, "To Curb the Skyscraper," *Architectural Record* 24 (October 1908): 300-02. Behind the formula was Sullivan's projected Fraternity Temple, which the *Real Estate Record and Guide* pointed out "was of value not alone as an example of architectural design, but as an illustration of how, under proper conditions, even this towering altitude might be attained in a commercial building without doing injury to the neighbors. . . . The scheme sufficed to show that the thing could be done, if done on a scale large enough. If the owner of the skyscraper owns all the ground upon which its shadow can fall, he is within his rights," "Most Modern Instance," *Real Estate Record and Guide:* 963.
119. Flagg, "Dangers of High Buildings": 70.
120. Quoted in "Arguments for and Against Tall Buildings," *Architecture and Building* 24 (January 18, 1896): 32-33. Also see "A Rejoinder," *Architecture and Building* 24 (February 1, 1896): 57-58.
121. "Realm of Building, Proposed Singer Tower Building," *Real Estate Record and Guide* 77 (March 3, 1906): 368; "Singer Building Addition, Broadway and Liberty Street, New York, N.Y.," *American Architect and Building News* 90 (September 22, 1906): plates; "Main Entrance Hall, Singer Building, Broadway, New York," *Architecture* 18 (August 1908): plate LXIV; and Burnham, "Forgotten Pioneering": 116-21.
122. W. Parker Chase, *New York, The Wonder City* (New York: Wonder City Publishing Co., 1931), 184.
123. Flagg's Produce Exchange Bank Building, an office building across from Post's Produce Exchange, consisted of brick sheathed piers alternating with ornamental iron work and terra-cotta panels framing the window bays that rose from the fourth to the tenth story where an iron balcony carried on small iron brackets ran around the entire building front. Above the twelfth floor, pairs of larger brackets carried a metal cornice embellished by lion's heads. "The Future Produce Exchange Bank, Corner Broadway and Beaver Street, Ernest Flagg, Architect," *Real Estate Record and Guide* 73 (May 7, 1904): 1042; "Produce Exchange Bank Building, 10 Broadway, New York, Ernest Flagg, Architect," *Architecture* 12 (October 1905): plate LXXXIV; and "The New York Produce Exchange Bank Building, Ernest Flagg, Architect," *Architects' and Builders' Magazine* 7 n.s. (October 1905): 3-8.
124. Nathan Silver, *Lost New York* (New York: Schocken, 1967), 212-13.
125. "The Metropolitan Life Building," *New York Architect* 3 (July 1909); and "Architectural Criticism, Metropolitan Life Tower," *Architecture* 20 (September 15, 1909): 129-31, plates LXXXI-LXXXIV. For the lower building see "The Metropolitan Life Insurance Building, New York, N.Y., N. Le Brun & Sons, Architects, New York, N.Y.," *American Architect and Building News* 38 (October 15, 1892): 47, plate; "Main Staircase in the Metropolitan Life Building, No. 1 Madison Avenue," *American Architect and Building News* 46 (December 22, 1894): 131, plate; "Metropolitan Life Insurance Co. Building," *Architecture* 10 (October 1904): plate; and "The Metropolitan Building, New York City," *Architects' and Builders' Magazine* 6 (January 1905): 145-56.
126. Schuyler, "Work of Le Brun": 380.
127. "The Newest Thing In 'Skyscrapers,'" *Real Estate Record and Guide* 77 (March 24, 1906): 512.
128. "Skyscraping Up To Date," *Architectural Record* 23 (January 1908): 74-75.
129. New York *Herald,* May 13, 1906, quoted in Rem Koolhaas, *Delirious New York* (New York: Oxford University Press, 1978), 73.
130. "The Newest Thing In 'Skyscrapers,'" *Real Estate Record and Guide:* 512.
131. "Perspective of the New Equitable Office Building," *Architecture and Building* 46 (January 1914): 34; "The Equitable Building," *Architecture and Building* 47 (May 1915): 165-83; and "Equitable Building, 120 Broadway, New York," *Architecture* 31 (June 1915): plate LX.
132. "Daylight Is the Only Cure for Over-Building," *Real Estate Record and Guide* 88 (October 21, 1911): 593-94.
133. "Limiting Heights of Buildings In New York," *American Architect* 104 (October 1, 1913): 130, 132.
134. "Highest Building in the World," *Real Estate Record and Guide* 86 (May 6, 1911): 844-45; "Sketch for the Woolworth Building," *Architectural Year Book* 1 (1912): 419; "Woolworth Building," *Architecture* 27 (January 1913): plate I; Montgomery Schuyler, "The Towers of Manhattan, and Notes on the Woolworth Building," *Architectural Record* 33 (February 1913): 99-122; "Woolworth Building," *American Architect* 103 (March 26, 1913): plates; "Architectural Criticism," *Architecture* 27 (June 1913): 119, plates LV-LVI; and Twells Brex, "A Poem of Skyscrapers," *Architecture and Building* 46 (June 1914): 237-39.
135. The base appeared solid from most vantage points, but was actually a U-shaped court that opened to the west.
136. Schuyler, "Towers of Manhattan": 111.
137. Edwin A. Cochran, *The Cathedral of Commerce,* with a foreword by S. Parkes Cadman (New York, 1920).
138. Gilbert was quoted by Francisco Mujica, *History of the Skyscraper* (Paris: Archaeology and Architecture Press, 1929; Da Capo Press, 1977), 34. Yet for Claude Bragdon, the Woolworth Building was "a notable example of the complete coordination between the structural framework and its envelope and falls short of ideal success only in the employment of an archaic and alien ornamental language, used however, let it be said,

458

with a fine understanding of the function of ornament." Claude Bragdon, "Architecture and Democracy, Part I, Before the War," *Architectural Record* 44 (July 1918): 75-84.
139. "West Street Building," *Architectural Record:* 109.
140. One more project of Kimball's threatened to surpass the Woolworth Building in height and in civic importance: in 1913 plans were filed for an 894-foot-high Pan American Association Tower containing offices, exhibit spaces as well as a grand rotunda covering 35,000 square feet to be donated by Brazil. While Kimball and his sponsor, Hudson Maxim, never settled on a site, the scheme was interesting in that, rising behind a broad plaza, was the first unbroken, fully freestanding tower proposed for New York. "Will Be The World's Highest Skyscraper," *Real Estate Record and Guide* 92 (October 4, 1913): 613; and "The Highest Office Building," *American Architect* 105 (January 14, 1914): 19-20.
141. "Modern Architecture," *Real Estate Record and Guide* 88 (December 16, 1911): 920.
142. "The New York Skyscraper," *Architecture* 27 (March 1913): 53, 59, 65.
143. "The Threatened City," quoted in Stephen Zoll, *Superville: New York—Aspects of Very High Growth* (Amherst: Massachusetts Review, 1973), 449.
144. David, "Private Residences for Banking Firms": 13-28. Also see King, *King's Handbook*, 691-97.
145. Montgomery Schuyler, "A Great American Architect: Leopold Eidlitz, Part 2, Commercial and Public Work," *Architectural Record* 24 (October 1908): 277-98.
146. Weisman, "Commercial Architecture of George Post": 183-84.
147. David, "Private Residences for Banking Firms": 18.
148. "Accepted Design for Bleecker Street Savings Bank," *Architectural Record* 2 (October-December 1892): 209; "Bank for Savings, City of New York, S.W. Corner Fourth Avenue and Twenty-second Street," *Architecture and Building* 22 (January 5, 1895): plate; and Montgomery Schuyler, "C.L.W. Eidlitz," *Architectural Record* 5 (April-June 1896): 411-35.
149. Schuyler, "C.L.W. Eidlitz": 427-28. Robert W. Gibson's Greenwich Savings Bank, at the northwest corner of Sixth Avenue and Sixteenth Street, went further toward an explicit Classicism, although its restless skyline and combination of Classical motifs with Richardsonian rough-faced stonework seemed old-fashioned when it was completed in 1892. The interior was grand despite its lingering Victorianism, with Corinthian columns raised on high bases supporting a coved ceiling lit from above by domed skylights. "Greenwich Savings Bank, Sixth Avenue and West Sixteenth Street, New York, N.Y.," *American Architect and Building News* 61 (August 20, 1893): plates; and King, *King's Handbook*, 775. Another example of the Cosmopolitan Era's sensibility in savings banks was "North River Savings Bank, 266 West 34th Street, New York," *Architecture and Building* 19 (October 28, 1893): plate.
150. "Brooklyn Savings Bank, Corner Pierrepont and Clinton Streets, Brooklyn, N.Y.," *Architecture and Building* 21 (September 15, 1894): plate; and "Brooklyn Savings Bank, Brooklyn, New York," *American Architect and Building News* 62 (February 11, 1899): plate. Also see Freeman's "Title Guarantee and Trust Co.'s Building, Brooklyn," *Architects' and Builders' Magazine* 8 (September 1907): 606-09.
151. See Montgomery Schuyler, "The Romanesque Revival in New York," *Architectural Record* 1 (October-December 1891): 151-98.
152. "The Bowery Savings Bank, New York, N.Y.," *American Architect and Building News* 64 (October 12, 1901): plates; "Bowery Front: Bowery Savings Bank, New York, N.Y.," *American Architect and Building News* 64 (October 19, 1901): plate; *A Monograph of the Works of McKim, Mead & White*, plates 66-68; and Roth, *Urban Architecture of McKim, Mead & White*, 665-66.
153. "The New York Savings Bank, New York, N.Y., Robertson & Potter, Architects," *Architectural Review* 12 (January 1905): 66.
154. "Illustrations of Recent Work: Greenpoint Savings Bank," *Architects' and Builders' Magazine* 10 (December 1908): 122-26
155. "Accepted Design, Union Square Savings Bank, New York," *Architecture* 12 (December 1905): 186; and "Union Square Savings Bank, Union Sq., New York," (May 1907): plate XLI.
156. With even less frontage, C.E. Birge's North River Savings Bank (1905) slid into a narrow site on West Thirty-fourth Street between Fifth and Sixth avenues. Its coolly composed white marble facades consisted of paired Doric columns lifted on bases supporting a simple cornice and attic above. Inside, a skylight helped make explicit the architect's conception of the banking hall as the atrium of a Roman house. "The North River Savings Bank," *Architects' and Builders' Magazine* 7 (March 1906): 266-70.
157. "Dime Savings Bank of Brooklyn, New York," *Architecture* 19 (February 1909): plate XI; and "The Dime Savings Bank, Brooklyn, N.Y.," *Architects' and Builders' Magazine* 10 (January 1909): 135-38.
158. "Design for Franklin Savings Bank, New York City," *Architecture and Building* 30 (June 17, 1899): plate.
159. "The Franklin Savings Bank, New York, N.Y.," *Architectural Review* 12 (January 1905): 62-63; "Entrance Front: Franklin Savings Bank, 42nd Street and Eighth Ave., New York, N.Y.," *American Architect and Building News* 72 (June 29, 1901): plate; and "Franklin Savings Bank, New York," *Inland Architect and News Record* 38 (September 1901): plate. York & Sawyer enlarged the building in 1924. See "Franklin Savings Bank to Enlarge Home on Eighth Ave.," *Real Estate Record and Guide* 115 (December 13, 1924): 9.
160. Alfred H. Taylor's Union Dime Savings Bank at the northwest corner of Sixth Avenue and West Fortieth Street was simpler still, with tapering rusticated piers at the corner and rusticated surrounds at the arches. "Union Dime Savings Bank," *Architecture* 21 (March 1910): plate XXVI. Also see York & Sawyer's Broadway Savings Institution (1906) on Park Place with a severe central hall capped by a top-lit coffered dome. "Broadway Savings Institution, New York City," *Architectural Review* 13 (June 1906): plate XXXVI; and "Broadway Savings Institution, Park Place, New York," *Architecture* 15 (June 1907): plate LVIII.
161. David, "Private Residences for Banking Firms": 13-14.
162. Schuyler, "The New National Park Bank": 318-28.
163. "The Most Modern Instance, *Real Estate Record and Guide* 59 (June 5, 1897): 962-65.
164. David, "Private Residences for Banking Firms": 14, 16.
165. David, "Private Residences for Banking Firms": 13-28; and "Bank Building, Speyer & Co., 24 Pine Street, New York," *Architecture* 8 (December 1903): plate.
166. David, "Private Residences for Banking Firms": 21.
167. "Elevations of Office Building for the Bush Company, Limited, New York, N.Y.," *American Architect and Building News* 87 (January 7, 1905): 7-8, plate; "Dutch Art Revival in Old Town," *Real Estate Record and Guide* 76 (September 9, 1905): 395; and "Offices, Bush Terminal Co., Broad and Pearl Sts., New York," *Architecture* 12 (October 1905): plate LXXXI.
168. "Dutch Art Revival," *Real Estate Record and Guide:* 395.
169. "Offices of Messrs. Chubb & Son, South William St., New York, N.Y.," *American Architect and Building News* 89 (April 7, 1906): 129; "Office for an Insurance Company, South William Street, New York," *Brickbuilder* 16 (August 1907): plate 114; and Blake, *Carrère & Hastings*: 335-36. The *American Architect and Building News* misattributes the building to Kirby, Petit & Green.
170. "Interior, National Park Bank, New York," *Architecture* 9 (April 1904): plate XXXIII; J.M. Bowles, "Business Buildings Made Beautiful," *World's Work* 9 (November 1904): 5499-5508; "National Park Bank, New York, N.Y.," *Architectural Review* 12 (January 1905): 98-99; Schuyler, "The New National Park Bank": 318-28; "The Newest Banking Room," *Real Estate Record and Guide* 76 (July 1, 1905): 8; and "National Park Bank, Broadway, Ann and Fulton Streets, New York, N.Y.," *American Architect and Building News* 88 (October 21, 1905): plate.
171. Schuyler, "The New National Park Bank": 325.
172. Schuyler, "The New National Park Bank": 328.
173. Schuyler, "The New National Park Bank": 328.
174. "Chemical National Bank, New York," *Architecture* 15 (May 1907): 76, plates XLV-XLVII; "The Chemical National Bank," *Architects' and Builders' Magazine* 8 n.s. (June 1907): 415-18, plates; and "Notes and Comments: The New National Chemical Bank," *Architectural Record* 21 (July 1907): 61.
175. "Banking House, J.P. Morgan & Co., New York," *Architecture* 30 (December 1914): 275-76, plate CLXVI; "Banking House of J.P. Morgan and Company," *Architecture and Building* 47 (January 1915): 5-14; and John J. Klaber, "Some Recent Bank Plans: The Work of Thomas Bruce Boyd," *Architectural Record* 37 (February 1915): 96-115. Also see a similar design by Cross & Cross. Charles Over Cornelius, "The Sixtieth Street Branch of the Guaranty Trust Company of New Company," *Architectural Record* 43 (June 1918): 491-504.
176. "The Mutual Bank, New York," *American Architect* 99 (February 22, 1911): plates; and "Architectural Criticism," *Architecture* 27 (April 1913): 70-71, plates XXXVII-XXXVIII.
177. Mowbray & Uffinger's work for the People's Trust Company reflects McKim's impact on this type of building. Their earliest facility, in Brooklyn, employed a Classical vocabulary and was simply embellished with cartouches and swags and by a corner turret in an effort to look modern and French. "People's Bank, Brooklyn, N.Y.," *Architecture and Building* 30 (April 8, 1899): plate. Their subsequent branch for the same bank on Montague Street (1903) is more explicitly Classical with a tetrastyle Ionic temple front leading to a large banking hall lit from above by a coved skylight. "People's Trust Company's Building, Montague Street,

Brooklyn, N.Y.," *American Architect and Building News* 90 (July 28, 1906): plates; and "The People's Trust Company," *Architects' and Builders' Magazine* 7 (September 1906): 524-29.

178. "Eighty-sixth Street Branch, Corn Exchange Bank, New York," *Architecture* 32 (September 1915): plate CVIII.

179. "Bronx Branch, Corn Exchange Bank, New York," *Architecture* 32 (November 1915): plate CXXXI. Also see S. Edson's Gage's "Corn Exchange Bank, Branch, 311 Lenox Avenue, New York," and "Branch, 12 West 28th Street, New York," *Architecture* 43 (March 1921): plate XXXIX.

180. "Thirty-fourth Street National Bank, New York," *Architectural Review* 12 (February 1905): 43.

181. "Provident Loan Society of New York, New York," *Architecture* 19 (June 1909): plate LIII; and "The Provident Loan Society of New York," *Architects' and Builders' Magazine* 10 (June 1909): 337-38. Also see Renwick, Aspinwall & Tucker's more conventional "Dollar Savings Bank, Willis Avenue, New York," *American Architect* 116 (August 27, 1919): plates 74-75.

182. "The Bank Number," *Architectural Record* 25 (January 1909): 1-67.

183. See note 70 this chapter.

184. Hamlin, "Columbia Trust": 17.

185. "American Bank Note Co. Building, 70 Broad St., New York," *Architecture* 17 (May 1908): plate 44; "Elevations, Office Building, American Bank Note Company, New York City," *Architectural Review* 15 (June 1908): plate XXXV; and "The American Bank Note Company," *Architects' and Builders' Magazine* 10 (October 1908): 21-24.

186. "Importers' & Traders' Nat'l Bank, New York," *Architecture* 18 (September 1908): plate LXVII; "Importers' and Traders' National Bank," *Architects' and Builders' Magazine* 10 (November 1908): 45-56; H.W. Frohne, "A New Type of Bank Building," *Architectural Review* 24 (November 1908): 387-94; and "The Bank Number," *Architectural Record* 26-27.

187. "The New Building for the Guaranty Trust Company of New York City," *Architectural Review* 2 n.s. (July 1913): 207-09, 214-15, plate; Klaber, "Some Recent Bank Plans": 96-115; and "The Guaranty Trust Company Building, New York," *Architecture* 28 (August 1913): 167, 169, plates 77-78. The Guaranty Trust Company was the model for Ludlow & Peabody's "The People's Trust Co. Building, Brooklyn, N.Y.," *Architecture* 41 (May 1920): plate LXXVI. Among York & Sawyer's later works were the Greenwich Savings Bank, at Broadway and Thirty-sixth Street, the Central Savings Bank, on the north side of Sherman Square, and the Federal Reserve Bank Building, on Liberty Street. See "Work Started on New Building for Greenwich Savings Bank," *Real Estate Record and Guide* 109 (May 13, 1922): 585; "The Greenwich Savings Bank," *Architecture* 50 (August 1924): 272-73, plates; "Central Savings Bank to Cost $2,500,000," *Real Estate Record and Guide* 119 (June 4, 1927): 7; and "Competition for Federal Reserve Bank Building in New York," *American Architect* 116 (November 12, 1919): plates 162-68.

188. "The Old New York Custom House and the New City Bank," *Architectural Record* 34 (November 1908): 441-45.

189. "The Old New York Custom House," *Architectural Record*: 441-43.

190. "National City Bank, New York," *Architecture* 19 (January 1909): plate 2; Pendleton Dudley, "National City Bank of New York," *New York Architect* 2 (February 1909): 1-3; "National City Bank, New York City," *Architects' and Builders' Magazine* 10 n.s. (February 1908): 117-91; "America's Largest Banking Institution in its New Quarters," *Architectural Record* 25 (February 1909): 137-40; "Architectural Criticism," *Architecture* 21 (March 15, 1910): 33, 35, 37, plate XXIV; and Roth, *Urban Architecture of McKim, Mead & White*, 670-73.

191. "The Old New York Custom House," *Architectural Record*: 442-43.

192. "America's Largest Banking Institution," *Architectural Record*: 140.

193. King, *King's Handbook*, 700-02.

194. "Competitive Design for the New York Clearing House," *Architectural Review* 3 (October 1894): plates XXIX-XXX.

195. King, *King's Handbook*, 690D; and "The New Clearing House," *Architectural Record* 4 (July-September 1894): 34.

196. Henry Hope Reed, "Drawings by Nicholas Solovioff," *Classical America* 1 (1971): 12-14.

197. Ivy Lee, "The New Centre of American Finance," *World's Work* 5 (November 1902): 2772-75.

198. Heins & LaFarge's and Gibson's entries are published in "Competitive Designs for the New York Stock Exchange," *Architecture* 1 (February 15, 1900): 48, 52.

199. Percy C. Stuart, "The New York Stock Exchange," *Architectural Record* 11 (July 1901): 526-52; Lee, "The New Centre of American Finance": 2772-75; Edmund Clarence Stedman, "Life 'On the Floor,'" *Century* 67 (November 1903): 1-20; "The New York Stock Exchange,"

Architects' and Builders' Magazine 4 (June 1902): 389-96; Russell Sturgis, "The Pediment of the New York Stock Exchange," *Scribner's* 36 (September 1904): 381-84; Russell Sturgis, "Facade of the New York Stock Exchange," *Architectural Record* 16 (November 1904): 465-82; Schuyler, "Some Recent Skyscrapers": 161-76; and "The New York Stock Exchange," *New York Architect* 3 (June 1909): plate. Trowbridge & Livingston built a twenty-three story addition to the north in 1920. "Addition to New York Stock Exchange," *Architectural Record* 48 (September 1920): 192.

In 1907 the Consolidated Stock and Petroleum Exchange built a new headquarters, no doubt inspired to do so by the example of its rival, the New York Stock Exchange. Clinton & Russell's four-story facades were screened by an Ionic colonnade carrying a chaste cornice and an unembellished attic. The exchange room, entered by expansive steps from Broad Street, was an ample, simply detailed room rising the building's full height to a saucer dome with a glazed oculus. The design was thus tinged with irony: the architects based their design on Rogers's Merchants Exchange at the very moment of its transformation by McKim, Mead & White, providing the fledgling institution with a monument that harked back to the Greek Revival.

200. "The New Chamber of Commerce Building," *Real Estate Record and Guide* 67 (May 4, 1901): 787; A.C. David, "New York's Great Commercial Institution," *Architectural Record* 13 (January 1903): 55-69; "New Chamber of Commerce, Liberty Street, New York," *Architects' and Builders' Magazine* 4 (January 1903): 191; "The Chamber of Commerce Building," *Real Estate Record and Guide* 73 (June 11, 1904): 1425; and "Sculptured Groups on the Chamber of Commerce Building, New York, N.Y.," *American Architect and Building News* 87 (March 18, 1905): plate.

201. Reginald Pond, *Selfridge: A Biography* (London: 1960), 107. Quoted by Gunther Barth, *City People, The Rise of Modern City Culture in Nineteenth Century America* (New York: Oxford University Press, 1980), 129, 110-47.

202. "All Kinds of a Store," *Architectural Record* 12 (August 1902): 286-303; Winston Weisman, "Commercial Palaces of New York: 1845-1875," *Art Bulletin* 36 (December 1954): 285-302; and Barth, *City People*, 110-11, 125-28.

203. Allan Nevins, *The Diary of Philip Hone* (New York: Dodd, Mead & Co., 1936), 2, 272.

204. "A.T. Stewart as a Real Estate Operator," *Real Estate Record and Guide* 17 (April 1, 1876): 237.

205. See Weisman, "Commercial Palaces": *passim*.

206. "Stern Brothers Building, Nos. 32 to 46 West 23rd Street, New York," *Architecture and Building* 19 (October 7, 1893): plate. Also see Richard Mercer's equally eclectic "Sachs Building, Mercer St., from 4th St. to Washington Place, New York," *Architecture and Building* 21 (August 18, 1894): plate; and "Store Building, 14th Str. betw. 5th Ave. & B'way, for Mrs. Mary S. Van Beuren, D'Oench & Simon, Architects," *American Architect and Building News* 32 (April 11, 1891): plate.

207. "All Kinds of a Store," *Architectural Record*: 81-82.

208. "All Kinds of a Store," *Architectural Record*: 286-303. Also see John Tauranac, *Essential New York* (New York: Holt, Rinehart and Winston, 1979), 82-83.

209. "All Kinds of a Store," *Architectural Record*: 302; and Clay Lancaster, *Photographs of New York Interiors at the Turn of the Century* (New York: Dover, 1976), 153, plate 122.

210. "Department Store for the Adams Dry Goods Company," *Architects' and Builders' Magazine* 2 (June 1901): 310-14; and "All Kinds of a Store," *Architectural Record*: 293-98.

211. "A New Prospect for Herald Square," *Real Estate Record and Guide* 67 (April 27, 1901): 739; "Store of R.H. Macy & Co., 'Herald Square,' New York, N.Y.," *American Architect and Building News* 76 (May 10, 1902): plate; "The R.H. Macy Department Store Building," *Public Improvements* 6 (June 1902): frontispiece; "All Kinds of a Store," *Architectural Record*: 287, 292-303; "The New Macy Store," *Architects' and Builders' Magazine* 4 (October 1902): 1-10; and Frank Owen Payne, "Notable Decorative Sculptures of New York Buildings," *Architectural Record* 47 (January 1920): 99-116. Macy's was expanded in 1922 by Robert D. Kohn. See "Contract Awarded for $5,000,000 Addition to Macy's Store," *Real Estate Record and Guide* 109 (February 18, 1922): 211; "Addition to Department Store of R.H. Macy & Co., New York City," *American Architect and Architectural Review* 125 (June 4, 1924): 531-37, plates; and G.H. Edgell, *The American Architecture of To-day* (New York: Scribner's, 1928), 308-09.

212. "All Kinds of a Store," *Architectural Record*: 292.

213. "The New Wanamaker Store," *Architects' and Builders' Magazine* 7 (June 1906): 362-72.

214. "Some Interesting Facts About the Gimbel Building," *The New York Architect* 4 (June 1910); and "The Gimbel Store," *Architects' and*

Builders' Magazine 43 (November 1910): 71-72.
215. "The Newest Uptown Department Store," *Real Estate Record and Guide* 92 (August 30, 1913): 391-94.
216. "Sale of the Altman Sixth Avenue Store," *Real Estate Record and Guide* 77 (April 21, 1906): 7; "Altman Building, B. Altman & Co., Fifth Ave. and 35th St., New York," *Architecture* 14 (November 1906): plate LXXX; A.C. David, "The New Fifth Avenue," *Architectural Record* 30 (July 1907): 1-14; "Future of the Wholesale and Retail Districts," *Real Estate Record and Guide* 78 (July 7, 1906): 2; and Francis Swales, "Architecture in the United States, Part IV—The Commercial Buildings—The Shops," *Architectural Review* (London) 25 (February 1909): 82-91.
217. David, "The New Fifth Avenue": 12.
218. "The New Fifth Avenue," *Real Estate Record and Guide* 74 (December 17, 1904): 1346.
219. "The McCreery Building. A Feat in Rapid Construction," *Real Estate Record and Guide* 8 (January 1907): 156-62. McCreery's was known for its "model" rooms displaying Craftsman-style furniture.
220. "First Picture of W. & J. Sloane's Store," *Real Estate Record and Guide* 86 (May 6, 1911): 845; and "W. & J. Sloane's New Store," *Architect* 6 (April 1912): 237.
221. "Middle Fifth Avenue, The Evolution of the New Piccadilly," *Real Estate Record and Guide* 67 (April 20, 1901): 694.
222. "Middle Fifth Avenue," *Real Estate Record and Guide:* 694. Also note two taxpayers by Hoppin & Koen, "Mercantile Building, Northwest Corner Broadway and Thirty-seventh Street, New York," *Architecture and Building* 27 (November 20, 1897): plate; and one on Broadway and Sixty-eighth Street, "Suggestions for a 'Taxpayer,'" *Real Estate Record and Guide* 81 (March 28, 1908): 546, 550.
223. Charles Warren Hastings, "The Lord & Taylor Building," *Architecture and Building* 46 (March 1914): 118-27; and "Architectural Criticism," *Architecture* 24 (April 1914): 77-79, plates XLII-L.
224. "Brooks Brother Building, New York, LaFarge & Morris, Architects," *Architecture and Building* 47 (August 1915): 304-05.
225. "Abercrombie & Fitch Building, Madison Avenue and 45th Street, New York," *American Architect* 112 (July 11, 1917): 33-36.
226. Reed & Barton, a third major jeweler, moved to Fifth Avenue at Thirty-second Street in a building designed by Robert Maynicke that was less a palace than an office or loft building. "Commercial Palaces," *Architects' and Builders' Magazine* 7 (February 1906): 177-92.
227. C. Matlack Price, "A Renaissance in Commercial Architecture, Some Recent Buildings in Uptown New York," *Architectural Record* 31 (May 1912): 449-69.
228. T.P. O'Connor, "Impressions of New York," *Munsey's* 37 (June 1907): 387-91.
229. "The New Tiffany Building, Fifth Ave. and 36th St., New York, N.Y.," *American Architect and Building News* 87 (April 1, 1905): plate; Henry Olmsted, Jr., "Essentials and Costs of a Modern Jewelry Store–The Tiffany Building," *Architecture* 12 (August 15, 1905): 119, 126, plate LXI; "Commercial Palaces," *Architects' and Builders' Magazine*: 178-85; H.W. Desmond and Herbert Croly, "Work of McKim, Mead & White," *Architectural Record* 22 (September 1906): 219-21; and *McKim, Mead & White Monograph:* plates 261-64.
230. "Commercial Palaces," *Architects' and Builders' Magazine:* 185-86.
231. "The Gorham Building, Fifth Ave. and 36th St., New York," *Architecture* 12 (August 1905): plate LXII; "Commercial Palaces," *Architects' and Builders' Magazine:* 186-90; Desmond and Croly, "Work of McKim, Mead & White": 214-15; and *McKim, Mead & White Monograph:* plates 234-40. Also see McKim, Mead & White's interior for the Havanna Tobacco Company, A.C. David, "The Finest Store in the World," *Architectural Record* 17 (January 1905): 43-49.
232. "The Wetzel Building, East 44th Street, New York City," *Brickbuilder* 14 (November 1905): plate; "Wetzel Building, 4 East 44th St., New York," *Real Estate Record and Guide* 76 (December 2, 1905): 866; "The Wetzel Building, 2 and 4 East 44th Street, New York, N.Y.," *American Architect and Building News* 88 (December 30, 1905): plates; and "Wetzel Building, 4 East 44th St., New York," *Architecture* 33 (June 1916): plates. The Peerless Motor Car Company and A.T. Demarest & Company buildings, both designed by Francis Kimball in 1909, were similarly contextual. They were located on the east side of Broadway between Fifty-sixth and Fifty-seventh streets, adjoining Barney & Chapman's Broadway Tabernacle, and Kimball's designs echoed the church's Gothic style. "Two Buildings for Automobile Trade, To Rise on the Same Block and Be Similar in Architectural Style," *Real Estate Record and Guide* 83 (February 20, 1909): 333.
233. Francis Swales, "The Shops": 84-85.
234. David, "The New Fifth Avenue": 11.
235. Alfred H. Taylor, "Reconstructed Business House Fronts in New York," *Architectural Record* 16 (July 1904): 13-25.
236. "Studio Building, 382 Fifth Avenue," *Architecture* 7 (February 1904): plate XVIII; and Taylor, "Reconstructed Business House Fronts": 14-15.
237. Taylor, "Reconstructed Business House Fronts": 14, 16, 18.
238. "Elevation of Premises, West 33rd Street, New York City," *Brickbuilder* 10 (October 1901): plate.
239. "Building of Theodore A. Kohn & Son," *Architectural Record* 17 (June 1905): 522; David, "The New Fifth Avenue": 5, 8-10; and Henry L. Walters, "Modern Store Fronts," *Architectural Review* (Boston) 14 (June 1907): 153-68.
240. Walters, "Modern Store Fronts": 162. Also see "Modern Shopkeeping Methods," *American Architect* 107 (March 17, 1915): 181, 188, plate; Paul Vibert, "Shop Fronts and Windows," *Architecture* 32 (July 1915): 171-73; "Shop Fronts," *American Architect* 110 (December 20, 1916): 383-88; and "Shop at 630 Fifth Avenue, Starrett & Van Vleck, Architects," *Architecture* 34 (November 1924): 357-58.
241. David, "The New Fifth Avenue": 1.
242. David, "The New Fifth Avenue": 1.
243. David, "The New Fifth Avenue": 2.
244. Price, "Renaissance in Commercial Architecture": 459, 462; "Building for Messrs. Black, Starr & Frost, Fifth Avenue, N.Y.," *American Architect* 102 (November 27, 1912): plates; and Blake, *Carrère & Hastings,* 347-48.
245. "New Fifth Avenue Building," *Real Estate Record and Guide* 80 (October 19, 1907): 609; "Fifth Avenue Shop Architecture," *New York Architect* 5 (September 1911): 183-84, plates; Price, "Renaissance in Commercial Architecture": 453-54; "Building of Dreicer & Co., Fifth Avenue, New York," *Architectural Year Book* 1 (1912): 371-73; "Dreicer Building, Fifth Avenue, New York," *Brickbuilder* 23 (June 1914): 127; and Rawson W. Haddon, "Some Recent Salesroom Interiors," *Architecture* 36 (July 1917): 125-29.
246. "Fifth Avenue Shop Architecture," *New York Architect:* 183-84, plates; "Store of Theodore B. Starr, Inc., New York," *Architectural Year Book* 1 (1912): 367-69.
247. Price, "Renaissance in Commercial Architecture": 459. Also see "Portfolio of Current Architecture," *Architectural Record* 30 (December 1911): 540.
248. "Building at 556 Fifth Avenue for M. Knoedler & Co.," *Architecture and Building* 44 (November 1912): 445-46; Price, "Renaissance in Commercial Architecture": 451, 459; "Shop of M. Knoedler & Co., New York," *Architectural Forum* 40 (June 1924): plate 94; and Blake, *Carrère & Hastings,* 346.
249. "Duveen Brothers, Inc., New York," *Architectural Forum* 40 (June 1924): plate 94; and Henry Hope Reed, *The Golden City* (New York: W.W. Norton, 1970), 40. The commission was originally Lucien E. Smith's, whose drawings, as well as those of Sargent and a model of the building, are in Avery Library at Columbia University.
250. "Some Current Work of Harry Allan Jacobs, Architect," *New York Architect* 5 (August 1911): 165-68, plates; "Portfolio of Current Work," *Architectural Record* 30 (December 1911): 541; and "Hardman Peck & Co's. Building, New York," *Architectural Year Book* 1 (1912): 437.
251. Tauranac, *Essential New York,* 115-16.
252. "The Architect. What He Has Done Recently and Why He Has Done It: Transforming a Fifth Avenue House," *Real Estate Record and Guide* 81 (May 30, 1908): 1007-08. Also see "New York's Shopping District and the Shifting of Trade Centers," *American Architect* 110 (December 20, 1916): 386-88.
253. "Scribner Building, 597 Fifth Ave., New York," *Architecture* 28 (August 1913): 178, 180.
254. "The Scribner Building, Nos. 153 to 157 Fifth Avenue, New York," *Architects' and Builders' Magazine* 2 (November 3, 1894): plate. Flagg also designed the Scribner Press factory on West Forty-third Street. See "The Business of a Great Publishing House," *Scribner's* 43 (June 1908): 129-38.
255. Swales, "The Shops": 85.
256. Aymar Embury II, "'From Twenty-third Street Up.' The Architectural Development of Fifth Avenue and Intersecting Streets in New York City," *Brickbuilder* 25 (October 1916): 255-60. Also see a polychromed store by Shape & Bready, "The Edison Shop, Fifth Avenue, New York," *American Architect* 106 (November 25, 1914): plate; "The Edison Shop, 473 Fifth Ave., New York," *Architecture* 30 (November 1914): 273; Berlinger & Moscowitz's "Marceau Building, 624 Fifth Ave., New York," *Architecture* 33 (June 1916): 130-32; and a store and office building by William Welles Bosworth, "John D. Rockefeller, Jr., To Build Adjoining St. Thomas's Church," *Real Estate Record and Guide* 98 (July 29, 1916): 163.
257. Aymar Embury II, "'From Twenty-third Street Up'": 255-60.
258. "Woolworth Store for Fifth Avenue," *Real Estate Record and Guide* 100 (July 28, 1917): 120.

PALACES OF PLEASURE

1. The most comprehensive treatment of New York theaters, though not an architectural study, is Mary Henderson, *The City and The Theater* (Clifton, New Jersey: James T. White & Co., 1973). The term "Great White Way" was in use by 1911; see "The Folies Bergère, New York, *New York Architect* 5 (June 1911): 119-20.
2. William H. Birkmire, "The Planning and Construction of American Theaters: Part I," *Architecture and Building* 21 (October 13, 1894): 175-79. Carrère & Hastings remodelled the auditorium of the Metropolitan Opera House ten years later, in 1903; see Curtis Channing Blake, *The Architecture of Carrère & Hastings* (Ph.D. diss., Columbia University, 1976): 301-2.
3. Charles C. Baldwin, *Stanford White* (New York: Dodd, Mead & Co., 1931; Da Capo Press, 1971), 199-212. Also see "Architectural Competitions," *Building* 6 (November 5, 1886): 166; "The New Madison Square Garden," *Real Estate Record and Guide* 40 (July 2, 1887): 923; "Our Future Buildings," *Building* 7 (November 12, 1887): 157; "The Madison Square Garden Project," *Real Estate Record and Guide* 41 (March 10, 1888): 297; "The Madison Square Garden," *Real Estate Record and Guide* 45 (July 28, 1890): 944-45; "The Madison Square Garden Tower,"*Architecture and Building* 23 (July 12, 1890: 16; *Architectural Review* 1 (May 2, 1892): 41; *American Architect and Building News* 37 (July 16, 1892): pl. 864; *American Architect and Building News* 40 (May 27, 1893): 125; Marianna Griswold van Rensselaer, "The Madison Square Garden," *Century* 47 (March 1894): 732-47; "Madison Square Garden," *American Architect and Building News* 43 (March 10, 1894): 115; "The Future of Madison Square Garden," *Architecture and Building* 26 (March 20, 1897): 133; *Real Estate Record and Guide* 65 (March 3, 1900): 953; "Architectural Exposition Next Fall," *Real Estate Record and Guide* 81 (April 25, 1908): 757; "The Madison Square Garden in New York," *Architectural Record* 25 (January 1909): 65; "Madison Square Garden, New York," *American Architect* 99 (March 15, 1911): 3; "The Madison Square Garden," *American Architect* 100 (December 13, 1911): 254; "Buys Madison Square Garden," *Real Estate Record and Guide* 97 (January 6, 1917): 14; "World's Largest Amusement Building for Eighth Avenue," *Real Estate Record and Guide* 113 (June 21, 1924): 7; "Architectural Cannibalism," *Architecture* 50 (August 1924): 309; "New Sites Suggested for Madison Square Tower and Diana," *Real Estate Record and Guide* 115 (December 27, 1924): 8; and "Preliminary Work Begins on New Madison Square Garden," *Real Estate Record and Guide* 115 (January 17, 1925): 9.
4. Marianna Griswold van Rensselaer, "The Madison Square Garden": 758.
5. William H. Birkmire, "The Planning and Construction of American Theaters, Part I"; also Part II, *Architecture and Building* 22 (March 16, 1895): 127-30. For the Empire, also see *Architecture and Building* 20 (March 24, 1894). The interior of the Empire was remodelled by Carrère & Hastings in 1903; "Alterations in the Empire Theater, New York, N.Y.," *Architectural Review* 10 (November 1903): plate.
6. Montgomery Schuyler, "The Works of Francis H. Kimball and Kimball and Thompson," *Architectural Record* 7 (April-June 1898): 479-518.
7. Schuyler, "Kimball": 497.
8. Schuyler, "Kimball": 494, 496. Also see *American Architect and Building News* 18 (August 27, 1885): 102; James Taylor, "The History of Terra Cotta in New York City," *Architectural Record* 2 (October-December 1892): 136-48; and Lloyd Morris, *Incredible New York: High Life and Low Life of the Last Hundred Years* (New York: Bonanza, 1951), 189, 267.
9. "Examples of Recent Architecture at Home," *Real Estate Record and Guide* 47 (February 21, 1891): 270; "Harrigan's Theater," *Architecture and Building* 15 (October 24, 1891): plate; "Harrigan's Theater," *American Architect and Building News* 34 (November 14, 1891): plate; and William H. Birkmire, "The Planning and Construction of American Theaters: Part VI," *Architecture and Building* 22 (March 16, 1895): 127-30. The facade of Harrigan's served as the prototype for V. Hugo Koehler's Lyric Theater on Forty-third Street west of Broadway; "Lyric Theater," *Architects' and Builders' Magazine* 5 (February 1904): 217-21; and "The Lyric Theater, New York City," *Brickbuilder* 13 (January 1904): plate. Kimball's New Fifth Avenue Theater was much more exuberant than Harrigan's; see "Examples of Recent Architecture at Home," *Real Estate Record and Guide* 47 (May 30, 1891): 864; William H. Birkmire, "The Planning and Construction of American Theaters: Part V," *Architecture and Building* 22 (February 10, 1895): 81-85; also "Part VI," *Architecture and Building* 22 (March 16, 1895): 127-30.
10. "Olympia Theater," *Architecture and Building* 26 (June 26, 1897): plate; and William H. Birkmire, "The Planning and Construction of American Theaters: Part X," *Architecture and Building* 23 (December 28, 1895): 305-7.
11. "The Harlem Auditorium," *Architects' and Builders' Magazine* 5 (February 1905): 223-27.
12. "The New York Hippodrome," *Architects' and Builders' Magazine* 6 (August 1905): 489-99. Also see "Building the Hippodrome," *Real Estate Record and Guide* 74 (December 24, 1904): 1420-21; George De Forest Barton, Letter to the Editor, "Old-Time Hippodromes," *Real Estate Record and Guide* 74 (December 31, 1904): 1491; "The New York Hippodrome," *American Architect and Building News* 87 (May 13, 1905): 156; and *American Architect and Building News* 87 (May 20, 1905): 163-64.
13. "Manhattan Opera House," *Architectural Record* 21 (February 1907): 148-52; and "The Manhattan Opera House," *Architects' and Builders' Magazine* 8 (February 1907): 227-31.
14. Abbott Halstead Moore, "Individualism in Architecture: The Works of Herts & Tallant," *Architectural Record* 15 (January 1904): 58-91.
15. The same basic facade scheme—the three story arch— was adopted by Herts & Tallant in 1904 at the Liberty Theater (234 West Forty-second Street), built for the Rogers Brothers, a popular musical-comedy team. The miniature front, in a kind of eclectic Flemish Gothic, achieved a lacelike delicacy, its every surface panelled and patterned. See Mary Henderson, *The City and the Theater*, 249.
16. Moore, "Herts & Tallant": 68. Also see "The New Amsterdam Theater," *Architecture* 8 (December 1903): plate; and "The New Amsterdam Theater," *Architects' and Builders' Magazine* 5 (February 1904): 186-92.
17. Moore, "Herts & Tallant": 68. Also see "The Lyceum Theater," *Architecture* 8 (December 1903): plate 82; "Lyceum Theater, New York City," *Brickbuilder* 13 (January 1904): plate; "The Lyceum Theater," *Architects' and Builders' Magazine* 5 (February 1904): plate, 193-98; and "Lyceum Theater," *American Architect and Building News* 88 (July 29, 1905): plate 1544.
18. See Montgomery Schuyler, "A Great American Architect: Leopold Eidlitz," *Architectural Record* 24 (September 1908): 365-78 for the old Academy of Music; for the Brooklyn Academy of Design, also known as The Academy of Science, see Montgomery Schuyler, "The Works of Cady, Berg and See," *Architectural Record* 6 (April-June 1897): 517-52.
19. "The Brooklyn Academy of Music," *Architects' and Builders' Magazine* 7 (December 1905): 92-97 illustrates the competition entry. Also see "Brooklyn Academy of Music," *American Architect and Building News* 90 (November 10, 1906): 150, 152, pl. 1611; "The New Academy of Music," *Architecture* 18 (October 1908): 159, 166-68, pl. 75-82; and "The New Brooklyn Academy of Music," *Brickbuilder* 17 (October 1908): 233-38.
20. "Professional Comment," *Architecture* 18 (August 1908): 121.
21. H.W. Frohne, "The German Theater in New York," *Architectural Record* 24 (December 1908): 409-16; and "The Decoration of the New German Theater," *Architects' and Builders' Magazine* 10 (December 1908): 89-93.
22. "Gaiety Theater," *Brickbuilder* 17 (October 1908): plate 119.
23. "The Folies Bergère, New York," *New York Architect* 5 (June 1911): 119-20; *Architecture and Building* 93 (May 1911): 361-65; and *Architectural Yearbook* 1 (1912): 381, 383.
24. "Shubert Theater," *American Architect* 104 (November 19, 1913): plates; and "The Booth and the Shubert Theaters," *Architecture* 28 (November 1915): 259, 267-68, 270.
25. *American Architect and Building News* 89 (May 5, 1906): 150; *Architectural Review* 13 (June 1906): 89; *American Architect and Building News* 90 (July 21, 1906): pl. 1595; *American Architect and Building News* 96 (December 8, 1909): pl. 1772; "Beautiful New Theater in Central Park West," *Real Estate Record and Guide* 83 (November 6, 1909): 809; *New York Architect* 3 (November 1909); *Architecture* 20 (December 1909): 178-79; "The New Theater: Its Aim and Success," *The Outlook* 94 (March 5, 1910): 514-15; and Blake, *Architecture of Carrère & Hastings:* 295-303.
26. "Globe Theater," *Architecture* 21 (April 1910): plate 38; "Globe Theater," *American Architect and Building News* 18 (July 20, 1910): plates; and Blake, *Architecture of Carrère & Hastings:* 302-3.
27. "Maxine Elliott's Theater, New York," *American Architect and Building News* 95 (February 1909): 33-34, pl. 1728. Thomas Lamb's Cort Theater was an even more refined essay in French Classicism; its delicate detail seemed more domestic than public. But for Aymar Embury only Murphy and Dana's Punch and Judy Theater "has any real quality of modernity and gaiety . . . where the facade is of the simplest possible description, relieved by a couple of color decorations and some decorative lines." See Aymar Embury II, "From Twenty-third Street Up, Part 2: 42nd Street to 59th Street," *Brickbuilder* 25 (November 1916): 281-91.
28. Charles Over Cornelius, "The Henry Miller Theater, New York City," *Architectural Record* 44 (August 1918): 112-24. F.B. Hoffman was originally to have collaborated with Allen and Ingalls but entered government service during the war.

29. "The Little Theater," *The Architect* 6 (April 1912): 232-34. Also see *The Architectural Yearbook* 1 (1912): 507-13; and "The Little Theater," *American Architect* 101 (April 17, 1912): plates.
30. "The Little Theater," *The Architect*: 232.
31. "New Broadway Theater," *Real Estate Record and Guide* 92 (October 18, 1913): 705; P.R. Pereira, "The Development of the Moving Picture Theater," *American Architect* 106 (September 23, 1914): 177-82; and Ben M. Hall, *The Golden Age of the Movie Palace* (New York: Clarkson N. Potter, Inc., 1961), 37-41.
32. Madison Square Garden was most likely the second roof garden in New York, and Koster & Bial's the third. Robert H. Montgomery, "The Roof Gardens of New York," *Indoors and Out* 2 (August 1906): 214-19.
33. Baldwin, *Stanford White*: 201.
34. The Victoria was built in 1899 by J.B. McElfatrick & Co. Robert H. Montgomery, "Roof Gardens": 215; Mary Henderson, *The City and the Theater*, 279.
35. F.X. Tambour, "Roofs for Winter Use," *Indoors and Out* 1 (March 1906): 296-97.
36. Tambour, "Roofs for Winter Use": 297.
37. Montgomery, "Roof Gardens"; 217-18.
38. "A Sale of Historical Properties," *Real Estate Record and Guide* 65 (April 21, 1900): 677; "Delmonico's, New York," *American Architect and Building News* 61 (July 16, 1898): plates; "The Palm-Garden, Delmonico's," *American Architect and Building News* 61 (October 15, 1898): plate; "Delmonico's," *Architecture and Building* 29 (October 22, 1898): plate; F.S. Lawrence, "On the Passing of Old Delmonico's, An Architectural Landmark," *Architecture* 52 (November 1925): 419-21.
39. "Delmonico's Downtown Restaurant," *American Architect and Building News* 42 (November 25, 1893): plate.
40. "Sherry's," *American Architect and Building News* 62 (January 21, 1899): plates.
41. Robert Shaplen, "Delmonico: I—The Rich New Gravy Faith," *The New Yorker* 32 (November 10, 1956): 189-210.
42. Lloyd Morris, *Incredible New York*: 256; and Kate Simon, *Fifth Avenue: A Very Social History* (New York: Harcourt Brace Jovanovich, 1978), 116-18; Virginia Lee Warren, "Sherry's To Open Again," *New York Times*, (July 24, 1966): 56.
43. Amy Lyman Phillips and Others, "Famous American Restaurants, and Some of the Delicacies for Which They Are Noted," *Good Housekeeping* 48 (January 1909): 22-31.
44. "Murray's Roman Gardens," *Architects' and Builders' Magazine* 8 (September 1907): 574-79; "Interiors for Dining and Dancing," *Architectural Review* 10 (January 1920): 19-23; *New York Plaisance—An Illustrated Series of New York Places of Amusement* 1 (New York: New York Plaisance Co., 1908); Rem Koolhaas, *Delirious New York* (New York: Oxford University Press, 1978), 82-87. Erkins was also architect of the Cafe de l'Opera.
45. "Murray's Roman Gardens," *Architects' and Builders' Magazine*: 575.
46. Phillips, "Famous American Restaurants": 24.
47. Phillips, "Famous American Restaurants": 24.
48. Phillips, "Famous American Restaurants": 23.
49. Phillips, "Famous American Restaurants": 23-24.
50. *American Architect and Building News* 93 (January 19, 1910): 31. Also see, Edwin C. Hill, "Ghosts of a Gayer Broadway," *North America Review* 229 (May 1930): 544-52; and Benjamin De Casseres, "Mouquin's," *American Mercury* 25 (March 1932): 363-71.
51. Clay Lancaster, *Photographs of New York Interiors at the Turn of the Century* (New York: Dover, 1976), 96.
52. "Cafe Savarin," *Architecture and Building* 47 (December 1915): 458-59; "The New Cafe Savarin in the Equitable Building," *Architecture* 32 (December 1915): 314-15; and "Mural Decorations in the Ladies' Restaurant, Cafe Savarin," *Architecture* 33 (March 1916): 65.
53. Henry J. Davison, "The Bankers' Club of America—An Art Achievement," *Architecture* 32 (September 1915): 221-24.
54. Cleveland Moffett, "Mid-Air Dining Clubs," *Century* 62 (September 1901): 643-52.
55. Moffett, "Dining Clubs": 644.
56. "The Lawyers' Club, New York," *Architecture and Building* 44 (October 1912): 418-22; and "The New Lawyers' Club of New York City," *Architectural Record* 32 (November 1912): 393-404.
57. "The New Lawyers' Club," *Architectural Record*: 393.
58. "The Union League Clubhouse Competition," *American Architect and Building News* 5 (April 26, 1879): 133-34; Potter & Robertson, *American Architect and Building News* 5 (May 31, 1879): 173, plates; McKim, Mead & Bigelow, *American Architect and Building News* 5 (June 7, 1879): 180, plates; E.E. Raht, *American Architect and Building News* 5 (June 14, 1879): 189, plates; Gambrill & Ficken, *American Architect and Building News* 5 (June 21, 1879): plates; G.E. Harney, *American Architect and Building News* 6 (June 28, 1879): plates; Richard Morris Hunt, *American Architect and Building News* 6 (July 5, 1879): 4, plates; S.D. Hatch, *American Architect and Building News* 6 (July 12, 1879): 12, plates; Thorp & Price, *American Architect and Building News* 6 (August 23, 1879): 60, plates; Peabody & Stearns, *American Architect and Building News* 6 (September 20, 1879): 92, plates; James Renwick, *American Architect and Building News* 6 (October 11, 1879): 117, plates; West & Anderson, *American Architect and Building News* 6 (October 18, 1879): 124, plates. Also see "The Union League Clubhouse," *American Architect and Building News* 5 (May 3, 1879): 141.
59. Anne W.D. Henry, *The Building of a Club: Social Institution and Architectural Type* (Princeton: School of Architecture and Planning, Princeton University, 1976) gives an overview of the American club.
60. "The Union League Competition," *American Architect and Building News* 5: 133.
61. Harry Loomis Nelson, "The Clubs of Boston," *Harper's Weekly* 34 (1890): 57-60; "Some New York Clubs," 34 (1890): 193-96, 211; "The Clubs of Philadelphia," 34 (1890): 569-79; "The Clubs of Chicago," 36 (1890): 806-08.
62. Because these rooms did not take up the whole second floor, the remaining area was usually divided into two floors of lower height which contained offices and apartments.
63. "First Accepted Design for the New York Athletic Club, H. Edwards Ficken, Archt.," *American Architect and Building News* 19 (April 10, 1886): plates.
64. "The Manhattan Athletic Club's New Building," *Real Estate Record and Guide* 42 (July 14, 1888): 888. The competition was won by P.J. Lauritzen. See *Real Estate Record and Guide* 45 (March 8, 1890): 12; and Moses King, *King's Handbook of New York* (Boston: Moses King, 1893; New York: Benjamin Blom, 1972), 564-68. Also see "The New Manhattan Athletic Club," *Real Estate Record and Guide* 36 (November 14, 1885): 1250.
65. "Clubhouse of the New York Athletic Club, 59th Street and Sixth Ave., New York, N.Y., W.A. Cable, Architect," *American Architect and Building News* 64 (May 6, 1899): plate; and "Entrance to the New York Athletic Club, W.A. Cable, Architect," *American Architect and Building News* 64 (May 13, 1899): plate. Also see Duncan Edwards, "Life at the Athletic Clubs," *Scribner's* 18 (July 1895): 5-23; *King's Handbook*, 565; and "The Crescent Athletic Clubhouse, Brooklyn, Frank Freeman, Architect," *Architects' and Builders' Magazine*, n.s. 8 (February 1907): 197-207.
66. "The Grolier Clubhouse, 29 East 32d St., New York, N.Y., Messrs. Romeyn & Stever, Architects, New York, N.Y.," *American Architect and Building News* 48 (June 1, 1895): plates. The original Grolier Club was decidedly old-fashioned even when it was built in 1895, although the attempt at a Serliana on the second floor and the use of Corinthian columns in the third floor frieze suggest an attempt to be up to date.
67. "Grolier Club, 47 East 60th St.," *Architecture* 37 (June 1918): 101-02.
68. "Accepted Design for the Caledonian Club, 846 Seventh Avenue, New York, Alfred H. Taylor, Architect," *Architects' and Builders' Magazine* 28 (June 11, 1898): plate.
69. "The Building Trades Clubhouse, West 126th Street, New York, John P. Leo, Architect," *Architects' and Builders' Magazine* 30 (February 4, 1899): plate.
70. "The Catholic Clubhouse, No. 120 West 59th Street, New York, N.Y., Messrs. Wm. Schickel & Co., Architects, New York, N.Y.," *American Architect and Building News* 48 (June 15, 1895): 112, plates.
71. "The Colonial Club, Boulevard and Seventy-second Street, New York, N.Y., Mr. Henry F. Kilburn, Architect," *American Architect and Building News* 38 (December 10, 1892): 170-71; "The Colonial Club, New York, N.Y.," *American Architect and Building News* 46 (December 29, 1894): 135, 140, plates; and *King's Handbook*, 550.
72. "Mendelssohn Glee Club Building, New York, N.Y., R.H. Robertson, Archt.," *American Architect and Building News* 33 (September 19, 1891): plates; and "Mendelssohn Glee Club, No. 113 to 119 West Fortieth Street, New York, N.Y., R.H. Robertson, Architect," *Architects' and Builders' Magazine* 19 (November 18, 1893): plate. Also see "A Decorative Painting by Robert Blum," *Scribner's* 19 (January 1896): 4-9.
73. "Bohemian Club, East Seventy-third Street, New York, Wm. C. Frohme, Architect," *Architects' and Builders' Magazine* 27 (October 16, 1897): plate.
74. "The Growth of Clubs in New York City," *Real Estate Record and Guide* 45 (March 8, 1890): 1-13; "Progress Club—Fifth Avenue and Sixty-third Street," *Real Estate Record and Guide*, 45 (May 3, 1890): 11; "Progress Club, 1 East Sixty-third Street, New York, N.Y., Alfred Zucker, Architect," *American Architect and Building News* 45 (December 6, 1890): plate; and *King's Handbook*, 551. Zucker was selected as the result of a

competition. See "Important Buildings Projected and Under Way," *Real Estate Record and Guide* 41 (April 28, 1888): 529. The previous Progress Clubhouse, at Fourth (Park) Avenue and Fifty-ninth Street, was also won in competition. Designed by Rafael Guastavino in a Moorish style, the work was carried out in collaboration with Henry Fernbach, a member of the selection committee. See George R. Collins "The Transfer of Thin Masonry Vaulting from Spain to America," *Journal of the Society of Architectural Historians* 27 (October 1968): 176-201. In 1901 the club held a third competition, for their new site on the northwest corner of Central Park West and Eighty-eighth Street. Louis Korn beat six other competitors with a compact classical design of four stories. The limestone building had a rusticated base, a two-story order uniting the main public rooms, and an attic story with a smaller applied order. See "New Home for Progress Club," *Public Improvements* 6 (February 1902): 23; and "Fireproofing Progress Club" (advertisement), *Real Estate Record and Guide* 75 (March 11, 1905): 523.

75. "The Montauk Club, Lincoln Place and Eighth Avenue, Brooklyn, N.Y., Francis H. Kimball, Architect," *Architects' and Builders' Magazine* 16 (January 2, 1892): plate; and "The Montauk Club, Brooklyn," *Brickbuilder* 2 (August 1894): 154-56. "The Montauk Club House furnished still another opportunity for taking advantage of the facility which the use of terra cotta furnishes the designer. The name of the club gave an Indian significance to the design which the architect made use of, and the result is an ensemble of Indian trophies and implements utilized in decorative features that are both pleasing and suggestive, while the sculptured friezes enabled the architect to record in a durable material many incidents of Indian life and customs which makes this structure an object of interest to the general public." See James Taylor, "The History of Terra Cotta in New York City," *Architectural Record* 2 (October-December 1892): 136-48.

76. "The Engineer's House," *Real Estate Record and Guide* 60 (December 11, 1897): 903-04; and "Club-House of the American Society of Civil Engineers, 220 W. Fifty-seventh Street, New York, N.Y., C.L.W. Eidlitz, Architect," *American Architect and Building News* 61 (August 30, 1898): plate. Also see "House for Am. Soc. C.E. (Competitive Design), W.B. Bigelow and F.E. Wallis, Architects, Townsend Building, New York," *American Architect and Building News* 66 (December 16, 1899): plate.

77 "Growth of Clubs," *Real Estate Record and Guide:* 7.
78. Baldwin, *Stanford White.*
79. "A New Club House," *Real Estate Record and Guide* 41 (June 9, 1888): 731. Also see "The Central Turnverein," *Real Estate Record and Guide* 44 (September 14, 1889): 1233-34; and "The Arion Society Building," *Real Estate Record and Guide* 39 (June 11, 1887): 196; and *King's Handbook,* 319, 551.
80. "Deutscher Verein," *Architects' and Builders' Magazine* 19 (August 18, 1893): plate. Also see "Growth of Clubs," *Real Estate Record and Guide:* 3-4; and Russell Sturgis, "The Works of McKim, Mead & White," *Architectural Record* 8 (May 1895): 18-19.
81. "The Century Club," *Century* 41 (March 1891): 673-89; "The Century Club, West 43 Street, New York City, McKim, Mead & White, Architects," *Architectural Record* 11 (July-September 1891): 98; "The Century Club-House, West Forty-third Street, New York, N.Y., McKim, Mead & White, Architects," *American Architect and Building News* 36 (May 21, 1892): plate; "Century Club-House, New York, N.Y., McKim, Mead & White, Architects, Messrs. McKim, Mead & White," *Architectural Review* 1 (September 12, 1892): 77-78, plate 63; "The Century Club-House, New York, N.Y.," *American Architect and Building News* 47 (February 23, 1895): 87; Sturgis, "McKim, Mead & White": 3-10; *King's Handbook,* 548; and *McKim, Mead & White Monograph:* plates 27-29. Also see a view of West Forty-third Street in 1891 in *American Architect and Building News* 36 (June 18, 1892): plate.
82. Although Schuyler characterized the clubhouse as "a piece of quite free and modern architecture, for which the architect has taken whatever suggestions seemed suitable for his purpose from whatever source he could find them without troubling himself about incongruities that were only scholastic and not aesthetic incongruities, and it exhibits also an individual inventiveness." See his "Romanesque Revival in New York." The many clubs on West Forty-third and Forty-fourth streets clearly served the new business district which sprang up following the completion of the first Grand Central Terminal in 1871. But the reason behind the choice of those two blocks between Fifth and Sixth avenues has been lost. See "In West Forty-third Street," *Real Estate Record and Guide* 47 (March 28, 1891): 467-68; "Detail of the Racquet Club, West 43rd Street, New York, N.Y., C.L.W. Eidlitz, Architect"; and *King's Handbook,* 566.
83. In *The American Scene* (Bloomington: Indiana University Press, 1968), 165.
84. See Henry, *The Building of a Club:* 31-33. Also see Nelson, *Harper's Weekly:* passim; E.S. Nadal, "London and American Clubs," *Scribner's* 9 (January-June 1891): 289-305; "As Seen by Him," *Vogue* 1 (January 21, 1873): 84-85; and Robert Stewart, "Clubs and Club Life in New York," *Munsey's* 22 (October 1899): 105-22.
85. Stewart, "Clubs and Club Life in New York": 119.
86. "Metropolitan Club-House, Fifth Avenue and Sixtieth Street, New York, N.Y., Messrs. McKim, Mead & White, Architects, New York, N.Y.," *American Architect and Building News* 50 (May 5, 1894): plates; "Metropolitan Club-House, Fifth Avenue and Sixtieth Street, New York, N.Y., Messrs. McKim, Mead & White, Architects, New York, N.Y.," *American Architect and Building News* 51 (January 11, 1896): plate; "Fireplace in the South Lounging Room of the Metropolitan Club House, Fifth Avenue and Sixtieth Street, New York, N.Y., Messrs. McKim, Mead & White, Architects, New York, N.Y.," *American Architect and Building News* 51 (February 8, 1896): plates; "Fireplace in the Main Card-Room: Metropolitan Club-House, New York, N.Y., Messrs. McKim, Mead & White, Architects, New York, N.Y.," *American Architect and Building News* 53 (September 26, 1896): plate; "Staircase of the Metropolitan Club-House, New York, N.Y., Messrs. McKim, Mead & White, Architects, New York, N.Y.," *American Architect and Building News* 55 (February 13, 1897): plates; and *McKim, Mead & White Monograph:* plates 57-61.
87. Stewart, "Clubs and Club Life in New York": 119. "Club-House of the University Club, New York, N.Y., McKim, Mead & White, Architects," *American Architect and Building News* 65 (July 29, 1899): plates; "Club-House of the University Club, New York, N.Y., McKim, Mead & White, Architects," *American Architect and Building News* 65 (August 12, 1899): plates; "Lounging Room, University Club, New York, N.Y., McKim, Mead & White, Architects," *American Architect and Building News* 65 (August 26, 1899): plates; "Club-House of the University Club, 54th St. and 5th Ave., New York, N.Y., McKim, Mead & White, Architects," *American Architect and Building News* 65 (August 29, 1899): plates; "University Club, New York, N.Y.," *American Architect and Building News* 65 (September 16, 1899): plates; "The University Club." *Architects' and Builders' Magazine* 1 (October 1899): 18-19; "University Club, New York City," *Brickbuilder* 19 (February 1910): plate 24; and *McKim, Mead & White Monograph:* plates 130-140C. Also see Leland Roth, *Urban Architecture of McKim, Mead & White, 1870-1910* (Ph.D. diss. Yale University, 1973): 461-65. For the unrelated and more mundane Women's University Club see "Women's University Club, 106 East 52d St., New York, Nelson & Van Wagenen, Architects," *Architecture* 30 (September 1914): plate 115.
88. "The Metropolitan Club," *Harper's Weekly* 38 (1894): 226.
89. Roth, *Urban Architecture of McKim, Mead & White:* 463.
90. Roth, *Urban Architecture of McKim, Mead & White:* 464.
91. Royal Cortissoz, "The Field of Art, H. Siddons Mowbray, American Mural Painter,"*Scribner's* 83 (May 1928): 650-58. Richard Guy Wilson, "The Great Civilization": 61; and Richard N. Murray, "Statements of Culture: Painting and Sculpture": 187, in *The American Renaissance: 1876-1916* (New York: The Brooklyn Museum, 1979).
92. C.H.C., New York *Evening Post* (April 26, 1899), cited by *American Architect and Building News* 65 (August 26, 1899): 71.
93. "Notes From New York," *Brickbuilder* 10 (October 1901): 215; and "Union Club, 5th Avenue and 51st Street, New York City, John Du Fais and Cass Gilbert, Architects," *Real Estate Record and Guide* 73 (June 11, 1904): 1455.
94. "A Competitive Design for the Club-House of the Union Club, New York, N.Y., Donn Barber, Architect," *American Architect and Building News* 72 (June 8, 1901): plates.
95. "Competitive Design for Union Club, New York, Wood, Palmer & Hornbostel, Architects," *Architecture* 3 (March 15, 1901): 80; "Competition for the Union Club-House, New York City, Palmer & Hornbostel, Architects," *Architectural Review* 8 (March 1901): plates 20-21; and "The Exhibition of the Architectural League of New York," *Brickbuilder* 10 (March 1901): 53-57.
96. "A Competitive Design for the Club House of the Union Club, New York, N.Y., Barney & Chapman, Architects," *American Architect and Building News* 70 (October 6, 1900): plates.
97. "Racquet and Tennis Club, Park Avenue, New York, McKim, Mead & White, Architects," *Architecture* 38 (August 1918): plates 124-32; and *McKim, Mead & White Monograph:* plates 398-99A.
98. "Current Building Operations," *Real Estate Record and Guide* 96 (October 23, 1915): 708; and "Colony Club, Park Avenue and 62nd St., New York, Delano & Aldrich, Architects," *Architecture* 33 (April 1916): plates 59-61.
99. "The Colony Club, 122 Madison Avenue, New York, McKim, Mead & White, Architects," *Architecture* 14 (April 1907): plate 34; Florence Finch Kelly, "A Club-Women's Palatial Home," *Indoors and Out* 4 (May 1907): 77-82; "Club Houses for Women," *Architects' and Builders' Magazine* 8 (July 1907): 490-95; Anna McClure Sholl, "The Colony Club," *Munsey's* 37 (August 1907): 544-601; and *McKim, Mead & White Mono-*

graph: 280-82. Also see Roth, *Urban Architecture of McKim, Mead & White:* 602-03. For the Cosmopolitan Club, another women's club, see Leon V. Solon, "The Cosmopolitan Club, New York, Edward C. Dean, Architect," *Architectural Record* 46 (July 1919): 19-28; and "The Cosmopolitan Club, New York, Thomas Harlan Ellett, Architect," *American Architect* 143 (May 1933): 21-30.
100. Quoted by Roth, *Urban Architecture of McKim, Mead & White:* 602.
101. "Club Women's Palatial Home," *Indoors and Out:* 77.
102. "Club Women's Palatial Home," *Indoors and Out:* 79.
103. "The Harvard Club, 27 West Forty-fourth Street, New York, N.Y., McKim, Mead & White, Architects," *American Architect and Building News* 49 (July 20, 1895): 31; "Elevation, 45th Street, Addition to Harvard Club, New York, McKim, Mead & White, Architects," *Architecture* 11 (March 1905): plate 23; "Rear Facade, Harvard Club, 45th Street, New York, N.Y., McKim, Mead & White, Architects," *American Architect and Building News* 89 (April 7, 1906): plate; Herbert Croly, "The New Harvard Club House," *Architectural Record* 19 (March 1906): 194-98; John Taylor Boyd, Jr., "The Addition to the New York Harvard Club, McKim, Mead & White, Architects," *Architectural Record* 38 (December 1915): 615-30; and *McKim, Mead & White Monograph:* 340-45. Also see Roth, *Urban Architecture of McKim, Mead & White:* 527, 600-01.
104. "Harvard Club, New York, McKim, Mead & White, Architects," *Architecture* 32 (November 1915): plates 132-134.
105. Clay Meredith Greene, "A Unique New York Club," *Munsey's* 33 (July 1905): 431-35; "The Lambs' Club, 128-130 West 44th Street, McKim, Mead & White, Architects," *Architecture* 12 (September 1905): plate 71; "The Lambs' Club, New York City, McKim, Mead & White, Architects," *Brickbuilder* 14 (September 1905): plate; and *McKim, Mead & White Monograph:* 225-26. Also see Roth, *Urban Architecture of McKim, Mead & White:* 601.
106. "Current Building Operations," *Real Estate Record and Guide* 96 (October 23, 1915): 708.
107. "Accepted Design for the New York Yacht Club Building, Whitney Warren & Charles D. Wetmore Architects," *Architectural Review* 6 (April 1899): plates 22-23; and "Current Periodicals," *Architectural Review* 8 (June 1901): 72-73. Also see "New York Yacht Club, 37 West Forty-fourth Street, New York," *Architecture* 3 (March 1901): 66-75; "Some Recent American Designs," *Architectural Record* 10 (April 1901): 406-24; "Club-House of the New York Yacht Club, 44th Street, New York, N.Y., Warren & Wetmore, Architects," *American Architect and Building News* 72 (April 20, 1901): plates; "Club-House of the New York Yacht Club, 44th Street, New York, N.Y., Warren & Wetmore, Architects," *American Architect and Building News* 72 (April 27, 1901): plates; "Club-House of the New York Yacht Club, 44th Street, New York, N.Y., Warren & Wetmore, Architects," *American Architect and Building News* 72 (May 11, 1901): plates; and "The New York Yacht Club, Warren & Wetmore, Architects," *Architects' and Builders' Magazine* 3 (January 1902): 117-24.
108. "Competition Design for the New York Yacht Club Building, Howard, Cauldwell & Morgan, Architects," *Architectural Review* 6 (April 1899): plate 24; and "Current Periodicals," *Architectural Review* 8 (June 1901): 72-73. Also see a note on the competition in *Brickbuilder* 7 (October 1898): 261; and "A Competitive Design for Club-House of the New York Yacht Club, R.H. Robertson, Architect," *American Architect and Building News* 66 (December 30, 1899): plates.
109. "Current Periodicals," *Architectural Review:* 72. The grill room, designed like a ship's hold, continued the nautical theme.
110. "Harmonie Club, 10 East 60th St., New York, McKim, Mead & White, Architects," *Architecture* 13 (February 1906): plate 10; "The New Harmonie Clubhouse," *Real Estate Record and Guide* 77 (March 17, 1906): 472; "The New Home of the Harmonie Club, A German Organization of New York, McKim, Mead & White, Architects," *Indoors and Out* 2 (April 1906): 22-28; Herbert Croly, "The Harmonie Club House," *Architectural Record* 19 (April 1906): 237-43; and *McKim, Mead & White Monograph:* 228-29. Also see Roth, *Urban Architecture of McKim, Mead & White:* 602.
111. "Lotus [sic] Club, 110 West 57th St., New York, Donn Barber Architect," *Architecture* 16 (November 15, 1907): 180-81; "Lotus [sic] Club Building, 110 West Fifty-seventh Street, New York, N.Y., Mr. Donn Barber, Architect," *American Architect and Building News* 92 (December 14, 1907): plates; "Lotos Club, 110 West 57th St., New York, Donn Barber, Architect," *Architecture* 19 (February 1909): plate 15; "The Lotos Club, New York," *Brickbuilder* 18 (February 1909): 39, plates; "The New Home of the Lotos Club," *New York Architect* 3 (March 1909); "New Lotus [sic] Club, 110 West 57th St., New York, Mr. Donn Barber, Architect," *American Architect and Building News* 95 (March 24, 1909): plates; and "The Lotos Club, New York, 110 West Fifty-seventh Street, Donn Barber, Architect," *Architects' and Builders' Magazine* 41 o.s. (April 1909): 265-77.
112. "Exhibition Architectural League": 55; and "The Yale Club House, by Tracy & Swartwout, Architects," *Architects' and Builders' Magazine* 3 (December 1901): 77-82.
113. Marion Wilson, "The Yale Club's New House," *Architectural Record* 38 (September 1915): 310-43.
114. "Republican Club, New York City, York & Sawyer, Architects," *Brickbuilder* 13 (May 1904): plates 32-34.
115. "The New York Club's Projected Building (From the Architect's drawing), West 40th Street, near 5th Avenue, H.J. Hardenbergh, Architect," *Real Estate Record and Guide* 77 (April 14, 1906): 675; "New York Club, 20 West Fortieth Street, New York, H.J. Hardenbergh, Architect," *Architecture* 16 (March 1907): 43; and "The New York Club, H.J. Hardenberg [sic], Architect," *Architects' and Builders' Magazine* 8 (July 1907): 502-05. For earlier clubhouses, see *King's Handbook,* 546; and "Alterations for New York Club Building, R.H. Robertson and A.J. Manning, Associated Architects," *American Architect and Building News* 25 (June 1, 1899): plate.
116. "Competitive Designs, Engineers' Club Building, New York," *Architecture* 10 (August 15, 1904): 113-18; "The Engineering Building and Engineers' Club," *Architects' and Builders' Magazine* 38 o.s. (March 1906): 225-35; Notes, *American Architect and Building News* 89 (June 2, 1906): 182; "Engineer's Club, 32 West Fortieth Street, New York, N.Y., Whitfield & King, Architects," *Architectural Review* 13 (December 1906): plates 6-7; "Engineering Building–39th Street View," *Real Estate Record and Guide* 74 (January 26, 1907): 148; "The Engineer's Club, West 40th Street, New York, N.Y., Messrs. Whitfield & King, Architects, New York, N.Y.," *American Architect and Building News* 91 (April 20, 1907): 152, plates; "Engineer's Club, West Fortieth Street, New York, N.Y.," *American Architect and Building News* 91 (May 25, 1907): plates; and "Engineers' Club, 32 West 40th St., New York," *Architecture* 16 (May 1907): plate 39. Also see "The Engineering Societies Building, New York," *American Architect and Building News* 91 (April 13, 1907): 139-40, plates.
117. "Masonic Hall, 46-54 West 24th St., New York, H.P. Knowles, Architect," *Architecture* 20 (August 1909): 114, plate 68; and "Masonic Temple, New York, H.P. Knowles, Architect," *Architecture* 20 (November 15, 1909): 161, 163, plates 95-104.
118. "Masonic Temple," *Architecture:* 161.
119. "New York Lodge No. 1. Benevolent Protective Order of Elks, James Reily Gordon, Architect," *Architects' and Builders' Magazine* 43 (December 1911): 633-49.
120. "Young Women's Christian Association Building, New York, N.Y., Donn Barber, Architect," *Architectural Forum* 32 (January 1920): 25-26, plates 7-10. Also see "Headquarters Building of the National Board of the Young Women's Christian Associations of the United States of America," *American Architect* 103 (February 26, 1913): plates.
121. "Young Women's Christian Association Building, No. 7 East 15th Street, R.H. Robertson, Architect," *American Architect and Building News* 17 (June 13, 1885): plate.
122. "West Side Branch—Y.M.C.A. Building, New York, Parish & Schroeder, Architects," *Architects' and Builders' Magazine* 27 (September 4, 1897): plates. Also see "The Hudson River Branch Y.M.C.A.," *Real Estate Record and Guide* 40 (August 20, 1887): 1079-80; "Young Men's Hebrew Association, 91st St. and Lexington Avenue, New York, A.W. Brunner, Architect," *Architects' and Builders' Magazine* 2 (April 1901): 245; "Railroad Branch, Y.M.C.A., New York, Warren & Wetmore, Architects," *Architects' and Builders' Magazine* 46 (August 1914): 307-11; and "Y.W.C.A. Building, Colored Women's Branch, 179 West 137th Street, New York, J.J. Pettit, Architect," *Architects' and Builders' Magazine* 52 (April 1920): 46-47.
123. "Young Women's Hebrew Association, New York, Louis Allen Abramson, Architect," *Architects' and Builders' Magazine* 47 (January 1915): 21-25; and "Young Women's Hebrew Association Building, New York, N.Y., Louis Allen Abramson, Architect," *Brickbuilder* 24 (February 1915): 51, plate 22.
124. "A New Y.M.C.A. Building, The Eastern District Branch, Brooklyn, New York, Boring & Tilton, Architects," *Architects' and Builders' Magazine* 7 (May 1906): 341-44. Also see "Competition Design for the Naval Branch of the Y.M.C.A., Brooklyn, N.Y.," *Architectural Review* 8 (April 1903): plate 29; and "Central Branch Y.M.C.A., Brooklyn, N.Y., Trowbridge & Ackerman, Architects," *Architectural Record* 45 (May 1917): 434-35.
125. "Elks' Club House, Brooklyn, N.Y., H. Van Buren Magonigle, A.W. Ross, Architects," *Brickbuilder* 24 (March 1915): plates 37-38; and "Elks' Lodge Brooklyn, H. Van Buren Magonigle, Architect," *Architects' and Builders' Magazine* 47 (May 1915): 199-202.
126. "Brooklyn Masonic Temple, Lord & Hewlett, Architects," *Brickbuilder* 14 (July 1905): 156-57, plates; "Masonic Temple, Brooklyn, N.Y., Lord & Hewlett, Architects, Pell & Corbett, Associated Architects," *Brickbuilder* 18 (June 1909): plates 90-95; "Masonic Temple, Brooklyn, N.Y., Lord & Hewlett, Architects," *Architecture* 20 (July 15, 1909): 97, plate

61; C. Howard Walker, "Masonic Temple, Brooklyn, N.Y.," *Brickbuilder* 18 (July 1909): 148-50; and "The Masonic Temple for the Brooklyn Masonic Guild, Lord & Hewlett, Architects," *Architects' and Builders' Magazine* 41 o.s. (August 1909): 435-40.
127. "Masonic Temple," *Architecture:* 97.
128. Julian Ralph, "Coney Island," *Scribner's* 20 (July 1896): 3-20. For general histories of Coney Island, see Oliver Pilat and Jo Ransom, *Sodom By The Sea* (New York: Doubleday, 1941); Edo McCullough, *Good Old Coney Island* (New York: Charles Scribner's Sons, 1957); and Rem Koolhaas, *Delirious New York* (New York: Oxford University Press, 1978).
129. "Hotel Brighton, Coney Island, N.Y.," *American Architect and Building News* 4 (September 7, 1878): plate.
130. Schuyler, "Kimball": 488-89.
131. Ralph, "Coney Island": 15-16.
132. Ralph, "Coney Island": 10.
133. William Lee Younger, *Old Brooklyn in Early Photographs: 1865-1929* (New York: Dover, 1978), 126-27; and John Grafton, *New York in the Nineteenth Century* (New York: Dover, 1977), 129.
134. Lindsay Denison, "The Biggest Playground in the World," *Munsey's* 33 (August 1905): 557-66.
135. "Fireproof Recreation Building," *Real Estate Record and Guide* 81 (April 4, 1908): 598.
136. Albert Bigelow Paine, "The New Coney Island," *Century* 68 (August 1904): 528-38.
137. Frederic Thompson, "Amusement Architecture," *Architectural Review* 16 (July 1909): 85-90.
138. Paine, "The New Coney Island": 535.
139. Barr Ferree, "The New Popular Resort Architecture: Dreamland, Coney Island," *Architects' and Builders' Magazine* 5 (August 1904): 499-513.
140. Ferree, "Resort Architecture": 499.

PALACES FOR THE PEOPLE

1. Cited by Jefferson Williamson, *The American Hotel* (New York: Alfred A. Knopf, 1930), 124.
2. In the *Temple Bar Magazine* 2. Cited by Williamson, *American Hotel:* 48.
3. See William Hutchins, "The New York Hotels, Part I, The Hotels of the Past," *Architectural Record* 12 (October 1902): 459-71.
4. Cited by Charles Lockwood, *Manhattan Moves Uptown* (Boston: Houghton Mifflin, 1976), 150.
5. Lockwood, *Manhattan Moves Uptown,* 150.
6. Lockwood, *Manhattan Moves Uptown,* 150.
7. Lockwood, *Manhattan Moves Uptown,* 150-51. Also see Hutchins, "New York Hotels I": 465-69.
8. Hutchins, "New York Hotels I": 469-70. Also see Robert Stewart, "The Hotels of New York," *Munsey's* 22 (November 1899): 281-95.
9. Moses King, *King's Handbook of New York City* (Boston: Moses King, 1893; New York: Benjamin Blom, 1972), 226. Also see Hutchins, "New York Hotels I": 470; and Stewart, "Hotels of New York": 283-84. In 1896, Alfred Zucker built a Venetian Gothic addition; see "The Ball-Room: Hoffman House, New York, N.Y.," *American Architect and Building News* 72 (June 22, 1901): plate. For a later addition, see "New Addition to Hoffman House, Broadway, between 24th and 25th Streets, Barney & Chapman, Architects," *Real Estate Record and Guide* 74 (July 16, 1904): 123.
10. *King's Handbook,* 218. Also see Hutchins, "New York Hotels I": 470.
11. *King's Handbook,* 226. Also see Hutchins, "New York Hotels I": 470. For the later addition, see "Addition to the Buckingham Hotel, New York City, R.W. Gibson, Architect," *Architectural Record* 3 (April-June 1894): 433-35; and "Buckingham Hotel Annex, 615 Fifth Avenue, New York, R.W. Gibson, Architect," *Architecture and Building* 23 (August 17, 1895): plate.
12. *Real Estate Record and Guide* 43 (January 26, 1899): 105.
13. Hutchins, "New York Hotels I": 459.
14. Cited by William Hutchins, "New York Hotels, Part II, The Modern Hotel," *Architectural Record* 16 (November 1902): 621-35.
15. "The New Astor Hotel, northwest corner Fifth Avenue and Thirty-second Street [sic], H.J. Hardenburg [sic], Architect," *Real Estate Record and Guide* 47 (March 28, 1891): 491; "Hotel Waldorf, H.J. Hardenburgh [sic], Architect," *Architecture and Building* 14 (June 6, 1891): plate; "Hotel Waldorf, Fifth Avenue and 33d Street, New York City, Henry J. Hardenbergh, Architect," *Architectural Record* 1 (April-June 1892): 414; "The Hotel Waldorf, Fifth Avenue, New York, N.Y., H.J. Hardenbergh, Architect," *American Architect and Building News* 42 (October 14, 1893): plate; "The New Astoria Hotel," *Architecture and Building* 28 (February 5, 1898): 51-56, plates; "The Hotel Waldorf-Astoria, New York," *American Architect and Building News* 60 (April 2, 1898): 3-4; "Hotel Waldorf-Astoria," *American Architect and Building News* 60 (April 2, 1898): plates; "Hotel Waldorf-Astoria, New York, N.Y.," *American Architect and Building News* 60 (June 18, 1898): plates; "Hotel Waldorf-Astoria, New York, N.Y.," *American Architect and Building News* 61 (August 27, 1898): plates; "Hotel Waldorf-Astoria, New York, N.Y.," *American Architect and Building News* 61 (September 10, 1898): plate; and Stewart, "Hotels of New York": 284-86. Also see Montgomery Schuyler, "Henry Janeway Hardenbergh," *Architectural Record* 6 (January-March 1897): 335-75; and Richard F. Bach, "Henry Janeway Hardenbergh," *Architectural Record* 44 (July 1918): 91-93.
16. Schuyler, "Hardenbergh": 363.
17. Schuyler, "Hardenbergh": 364.
18. Hutchins, "New York Hotels II": 635.
19. "The New Astoria Hotel," *Architecture and Building:* 51-56.
20. Stewart, "Hotels of New York": 284-85.
21. Stewart, "Hotels of New York":.291-92.
22. Albert Bigelow Paine was very impressed by the organization required. See his "The Workings of a Modern Hotel," *World's Work* 5 (March 1903): 3171-85.
23. Henry James, *The American Scene* (New York: Harper & Bros., 1907; Bloomington: Indiana University Press, 1968), 105.
24. "A special feature of each [room] is an electric indicator by which a guest, without waiting for a bell-boy, may signal direct to the office for any of 140 various articles. This indicator, known as the Herzog Teleseme . . . is the most perfect of all signalling systems. It comprises a dial sunk into the wall, and connected by electricity with the office; upon this dial is printed 140 articles at times needed by travellers, and the guest has only to move the pointer until it points at the desired object, and then press an electric button, whereupon the clerk in the office thus apprised, will send up without further instructions or delay, the desired newspaper, or bottle, or food, or servant, or any other needed thing." *King's Handbook,* 224. Also see Stewart, "Hotels of New York": 288.
25. *King's Handbook,* 224.
26. "Editorial Notes and Comment," *Architecture and Building* 16 (June 25, 1892): 318; *King's Handbook,* 220-21; and Stewart, "Hotels of New York": 284-85.
27. "The New Netherlands Hotel, Fifth Avenue and Fifty-ninth Street, W.H. Hume, Architect," *Real Estate Record and Guide* 47 (March 28, 1891): 470; *King's Handbook,* 218-19; and Stewart, "Hotels of New York": 289.
28. "The 'Plaza' Apartment House, New York, N.Y.," *American Architect and Building News* 16 (July 5, 1884): 445, plate. There is some confusion, however, as to the precise history of the early Plaza. According to Landau, W.A. Potter was engaged by the Rev. Jared B. Flagg to design the Fifth Avenue Plaza Apartments in 1883. The developer's son, the young Ernest Flagg, was to provide the interior plans. The Flaggs were unable to arrange financing for the cooperative venture. See Sarah Bradford Landau, *Edward T. and William A. Potter: American Victorian Architects, 1855-1901* (Ph.D. diss., New York University, 1978): 428-29; also "The Prospect for Apartment Houses," *Real Estate Record and Guide* 32 (October 24, 1883): 830.
29. *King's Handbook,* 222-23.
30. H.W. Frohne, "Designing a Metropolitan Hotel, The Plaza," *Architectural Record* 22 (November 1907): 349-64. Also see "Plaza Hotel, New York, H.J. Hardenbergh, Architect," *Architecture* 16 (June 1907): plate LII; "The Plaza Hotel," *American Architect and Building News* 92 (October 26, 1907): 134-36, plates; "New Plaza Hotel," *Architecture* 16 (November 15, 1907): 179, 187, plates XCI-V; and "Hotel Plaza, New York City, H.J. Hardenbergh, Architect," *Architectural Review* 11 (April 1908): 64-65.
31. "New Plaza Hotel," *Architecture:* 179.
32. Stewart, "Hotels of New York": 285.
33. "The New Metropolitan Hotels," *Real Estate Record and Guide* 74 (September 3, 1904): 478.
34. Arthur C. David, "The Best Type of Metropolitan Hotel," *Architectural Record* 15 (June 1904): 552-63. Also see "Astor Apartment House," *Real Estate Record and Guide* 67 (February 9, 1901): 227; C.H. Israels, "New York Apartment Houses," *Architectural Record* 11 (July 1901): 476-508; "The Hotel St. Regis, New York," *Architecture* 9 (June 15, 1904): 81-91, plates XLII-L; and "St. Regis Hotel, New York City, Trowbridge & Livingston, Architects," *Architectural Review* 11 (April 1913): 62-70.
35. "Ritz-Carlton Hotel and Carlton House, New York City," *Architecture* 23 (January 15, 1911): 1-2, plates VII-VIII; "Concerning the Ritz-Carlton Hotel," *New York Architect* 5 (January 1911): plates; "Ritz-Carlton Hotel, Warren & Wetmore, Architects," *Architects' and Builders' Magazine* 11 (February 1911): 197-208; "The Ritz-Carlton Hotel, New York, Warren & Wetmore, Architects," *American Architect* 99 (February 1, 1911): 45-48, plates; "Ritz-Carlton Hotel," *Architectural Yearbook* 1 (1912): 363; and "Ritz-Carlton Hotel, New York City, Warren & Wetmore, Architects," *Architectural Review* 11 (April 1913): 109-11. Also see Warren & Wetmore's Adamesque "Hotel Chatham, Vanderbilt Ave., 48th to 49th Sts.," *Architecture* 6 (December 1917): plates CCVI-CCIX.

36. "The Hotel Imperial, Broadway and 32nd Street, New York, N.Y., McKim, Mead & White Architects," *American Architect and Building News* 30 (October 25, 1890): plate. For a later addition, see "Addition to the Hotel Imperial, New York City (Tallest Building of the Block), Warren & Wetmore, Architects," *Brickbuilder* 14 (January 1905): plate.
37. "Hotel Renaissance, New York City, Clarence Luce, Architect," *Brickbuilder* 3 (December 1894): 250.
38. "Hotel Manhattan, Madison Avenue and Forty-second Street, New York, H.J. Hardenbergh, Architect," *Architecture and Building* 26 (March 6, 1897): plates; "Manhattan Hotel, New York, N.Y., H.J. Hardenbergh, Architect," *American Architect and Building News* 66 (October 14, 1899): plates; "Office Fireplace, Hotel Manhattan, New York, N.Y., H.J. Hardenbergh, Architect," *American Architect and Building News* 66 (November 4, 1899): plate; "The Office, Hotel Manhattan, 42nd St. and Madison Ave., New York, N.Y., H.J. Hardenbergh, Architect," *American Architect and Building News* 66 (December 2, 1899): plate; and "Dining Room, Hotel Manhattan, New York, N.Y., H.J. Hardenbergh, Architect," *American Architect and Building News* 75 (March 1, 1902): plate. Also see Hardenbergh's Martinique Hotel on West Thirty-third Street, with a later addition on the northeast corner of Broadway and West Thirty-second Street. Israels, "New York Apartment House": 506; "Hotel Martinique Addition, New York City," *Architects' and Builders' Magazine* 11 (February 1911): 190-194; and "Hotel Martinique," *Architectural Review* 11 (April 1913): 76-77.
39. "Hotel Navarre, Seventh Avenue and Thirty-eighth Street, New York," *Architecture* 2 (December 15, 1900): 463; "Hotel Navarre, 37th Street and Seventh Ave., New York, Barney & Chapman, Architects," *Architects' and Builders' Magazine* 2 (May 1901): 289; and Montgomery Schuyler, "The Works of Messrs. Barney & Chapman," *Architectural Record* 16 (September 1904): 203-296.
40. "The Hotel Renaissance, New York, Howard & Cauldwell, Architects," *Architectural Review* 4 (May 1897): plates XXIX-XXXI; "The New Hotel Renaissance," *Real Estate Record and Guide* 60 (November 22, 1897): 811-12; "Hotel Renaissance, Southwest corner Forty-third St., and Fifth Ave., New York, Howard & Cauldwell, Architects," *Architecture and Building* 29 (August 6, 1898): plate; and "Extension of the Hotel Renaissance, Fifth Ave. and Forty-third St., New York, N.Y.," *American Architect and Building News* 66 (December 30, 1899): plate.
41. "New Hotel Renaissance," *Real Estate Record and Guide*: 811.
42. "New Hotel Renaissance," *Real Estate Record and Guide*: 812.
43. "A New Landmark on Broadway," *Real Estate Record and Guide* 93 (June 11, 1904): 1428; "Hotel Astor, Longacre Square, New York, Clinton & Russell, Architects," *Architecture* 10 (September 1904): plate LXVII; "The Hotel Astor," *Architects' and Builders' Magazine* 6 (November 1904): 49-71; "The Ball-Room, Hotel Astor, Broadway, Between 44th and 45th Streets, New York, N.Y.," *American Architect and Building News* 87 (May 13, 1905): plate; "Entrance Hall, Hotel Astor, Broadway, Between 44th and 45th Streets, New York, N.Y.," *American Architect and Building News* 87 (May 27, 1905): plate; "The Orangery, Hotel Astor, New York, N.Y., Clinton & Russell, Architects," *American Architect and Building News* 87 (June 17, 1905): plate; and "Hotel Astor, Longacre Square, New York, Clinton & Russell, Architects," *Architecture* 16 (July 15, 1907): 122-25. For the development of Times Square as a hotel district, see "Changes in Longacre Square," *Real Estate Record and Guide* 80 (November 16, 1907): 799; "Hotel Saranac at Auction," *Real Estate Record and Guide* 80 (November 16, 1907): 800; and Allen E. Beals, "The New York Hotel and Its Mission," *Real Estate Record and Guide* 87 (May 13, 1911): 898-901.
44. T.J. George, "Hotel Astor," *New York Architect* 3 (December 1909); and "New Addition to Hotel Astor, New York, Messrs. Clinton & Russell, Architects," *American Architect and Building News* 97 (January 19, 1910): plates.
45. Hutchins, "New York Hotels II": 630-33; "The Opening of the Knickerbocker Hotel," *Real Estate Record and Guide* 78 (October 27, 1906): 675; "The Hotel Knickerbocker, Trowbridge & Livingston, Architects," *Architects' and Builders' Magazine* 8 n.s. (December 1906): 89-102; "Knickerbocker Hotel, Broadway and 42d St., New York, Marvin & Davis, Architects, Bruce Price, Consulting Architect, Trowbridge & Livingston, Architects of Interior," *Architecture* 14 (December 1906): plate XCIII; and H. Toler Booraem, "The Significance of Architectural Form," *Architectural Record* 25 (March 1909): 193-202.
46. "The Hotel Rector, New York, D.H. Burnham & Co., Architects," *American Architect* 99 (January 18, 1911): 25-29, plate; "Hotel Rector, Broadway and 44th St., New York, D.H. Burnham & Co., Architects," *Architecture* 23 (February 1911): 19-21, plate XXI; "The Hotel Rector," *New York Architect* 5 (February 1911), "Hotel Rector, New York, D.H. Burnham & Co., Architects," *Architectural Year Book* 1 (1912): 393-95; and "Hotel Rector, New York City, D.H. Burnham & Co. Architects," *Architectural Review* 11 (April 1913): 93.
47. "Hotel Rector," *American Architect*: 27.

48. "Hotel Belmont, Park Ave. and 42d St., New York," *Architecture* 12 (September 1905): plate LXXII; "The Hotel Belmont, Warren & Wetmore, Architects," *Architects' and Builders' Magazine* 7 n.s. (May 1906): 319-35; "Hotel Belmont, New York, Warren & Wetmore, Architects," *Architecture* 13 (June 1906): plates XXVII-XL; and Henry Frohne, "The Hotel Belmont," *Architectural Record* 20 (July 1906): 63-70. Warren & Wetmore, with Reed & Stem, also designed the Grand Central Palace, a combined exhibition hall and hotel planned as part of the Grand Central "Terminal City." See "Entrance, Grand Central Palace, Lexington Ave. and 46th St., New York. Reed & Stem and Warren & Wetmore, Architects," *Architecture* 24 (August 1911): plate 83; and "Grand Central Palace, Lexington Ave. and 46th St., New York," *Architectural Year Book* 1 (1912): 375.
49. "Vanderbilt Hotel, Park Ave., New York, Warren & Wetmore, Architects," *Architectural Year Book* 1 (1912): 357-61; "The Vanderbilt Hotel, Warren & Wetmore, Architects," *Architecture and Building* 44 (January 1912): 144-52; "The Vanderbilt Hotel, Warren & Wetmore, Architects," *New York Architect* 6 (January-February 1912): 209-10; Samuel Howe, "The Vanderbilt Hotel, Warren & Wetmore, Architects," *American Architect* 101 (February 14, 1912): 69-73; Samuel Howe, "Della Robbia Room, Hotel Vanderbilt, Warren & Wetmore, Architects," *Brickbuilder* 21 (February 1912): 43-46; and Walton H. Marshall, "The Vanderbilt Hotel, Messrs. Warren & Wetmore, Architects," *Architectural Review* 11 (April 1913): 66-70.
50. "The Biltmore Hotel, New York, Warren & Wetmore, Architects," *Architecture* 1 (February 1914): 33-36, plate XXIV; "The Biltmore Hotel, New York, Messrs. Warren & Wetmore, Architects," *American Architect* 105 (February 11, 1914): 53-57, plates; Theodore Starrett, "The Biltmore Hotel Building," *Architecture and Building* 46 (February 1914): 48-50; "The Biltmore, Warren & Wetmore, Architects," *Architects' and Builders' Magazine* 46 (February 1914): 53-69; Montgomery Schuyler, "The Biltmore Hotel, Madison Avenue, New York, Warren & Wetmore, Architects," *Brickbuilder* 23 (February 1914): 37-40; and Walter S. Schneider, "The Hotel Biltmore, The Newest Addition to New York's Palatial Hotels, Warren & Wetmore, Architects," *Architectural Record* 35 (March 1914): 222-45.
51. Starrett, "Biltmore": 48.
52. "The Commodore, A New Hotel on Pershing Square, New York, Warren & Wetmore, Architects," *American Architect* 115 (March 5, 1919): 337-38, plates 69-76; and "The Hotel Commodore, New York, Warren & Wetmore, Architects," *Architecture* 39 (April 1919): 98-99, plates XLVII-LI.
53. David E. Tarn, "New York's Newest Hotel, Notes on the Hotel McAlpin, F.M. Andrews & Company," *Architectural Record* 33 (March 1913): 231-41. Also see "Hotel McAlpin, 33d to 34th Streets and Broadway, New York," *Architects' and Builders' Magazine* 11 (February 1911): 209; "Hotel McAlpin, F.M. Andrews & Company, Architects," *Architectural Year Book* 1 (1912): 449; "The Hotel McAlpin, Frank M. Andrews, Architect," *Architecture* 27 (February 1913): 33-39, plate XIX; "A Terra Cotta Grill Room, the Café of the New McAlpin Hotel, New York City, by F.M. Andrews & Co., Architects," *Brickbuilder* 22 (March 1913): 63-66; and "Hotel McAlpin, New York City, F.M. Andrews & Co., Inc., Architects," *Architectural Review* 11 (April 1913): 82-85, 93, 109-11, 132-33.
54. Tarn, "New York's Newest Hotel": 240.
55. "The Hotel Pennsylvania, New York," *American Architect* 105 (February 26, 1919): 297-306. Also see "Hotel Pennsylvania, New York," *Architecture and Building* 51 (March 1919): 21-22, plates 41-43, 52-53, and frontispiece; and "Hotel Pennsylvania, New York, McKim, Mead & White, Architects," *Architecture* 39 (April 1919): LIII-LVII.
56. See "Apartment Hotels," *Real Estate Record and Guide* 19 (January 20, 1877): 42; "The Apartment Hotel," *Real Estate Record and Guide* 64 (August 12, 1899): 240; and "The Hotel Beresford," *Real Estate Record and Guide* 44 (September 21, 1889): 1263.
57. See Charles H. Israels, "The Metropolitan Apartment House and Hotel," *Real Estate Record and Guide* 73 (June 11, 1904): 1464-73.
58. E.T. Littell, "Club Chambers and Apartment Houses," *American Architect and Building News* 1 (February 19, 1876): 59-60.
59. Littell, "Club Chambers": 59.
60. Israels, "Metropolitan Apartment House": 1465, 1470; and "The Warrington, 161 Madison Ave., New York," *Architecture* 11 (January 1905): 6.
61. "The Devon, 70 West 55th Street, New York," *Architecture* 11 (January 1905): 13, plate VII.
62. "The Arlington, 25th Street, near Broadway, New York, Israels & Harder, Architects," *Architectural Review* 5 (June 1903): 119; and Walter H. Kilham, "The Planning of Apartment Houses, IV," *Brickbuilder* 13 (January 1904): 323-28.
63. "The Holland, 66 and 68 West 46th Street, New York, Israels & Harder, Architects," *Architectural Review* 5 (June 1903): 118; and "Apartment House, West 46th Street, New York, N.Y.," *American Architect and Building News* 88 (July 5, 1905): plates.
64. "Iroquois Apartment Hotel, H.B. Mulliken, Architect, New York

467

City," *Architectural Record* 14 (July 1903): 74.
65. "Hotel Somerset, 150 West 47th Street," *Architecture* 11 (January 1905): 8-9.
66. "New Architectural Additions to New York, Nos. 9 and 11 East 39th Street," *Real Estate Record and Guide* 66 (July 21, 1900): 77; Charles H. Israels, "New York Apartment Houses," *Architectural Record* 11 (July 1901): 476-508; and Israels, "Metropolitan Apartment House": 1473.
67. "The Mansfield (Bachelor Apartments), New York, Renwick, Aspinwall & Owen, Architects," *Architectural Review* 5 (June 1903): 127.
68. "The Prince George Hotel," *Architectural Record* 18 (December 1905): 470-80; and "The Prince George Hotel, Howard Greenley, Architect," *Architects' and Builders' Magazine* 7 n.s. (April 1906): 273-82.
69. "Entrance to Hotel Seymour, West 45th St., New York, N.Y.," *American Architect and Building News* 80 (May 9, 1903): plate; "Hotel Seymour, New York, Ludlow & Valentine, Architects," *Architectural Review* 5 (June 1903): 114-15; and Kilham, "Apartment Houses": 4-5.
70. "Batchelor [sic] Apartment Building, New York, Lienau & Nash, Architects," *Inland Architect and News Record* 41 (June 1903): plate; and "Bachelor Apartments, 15 East 48th Street, New York, Lienau & Nash, Architects," *Architectural Review* 5 (June 1903): 123.
71. "The Hermitage Hotel, Robert D. Kohn, Architect," *Architectural Review* 5 (June 1903): 132; and "The Hermitage—Detail of Base," *Real Estate Record and Guide* 80 (November 9, 1907): 744.
72. M.S., "An Interesting Skyscraper," *Architectural Record* 22 (November 1907): 365-68.
73. "Hotel Cumberland, Broadway and 54th Street," *Architecture* 11 (January 1905): 11, 14.
74. "Hotel Seville, Madison Avenue and 29th Street," *Architecture* 11 (January 1905): 12, plate IV; and "Some Current Work of Harry Allan Jacobs," *New York Architect* 5 (August 1911): 165-68.
75. "The Carlyle Chambers, Fifth Ave., and 38th St., New York, N.Y., Herts & Tallant, Architects," *American Architect and Building News* 73 (September 21, 1901): plate.
76. "Hotel Essex, Madison Avenue and Fifty-sixth Street, New York," *Architecture* 4 (November 15, 1901): 311; and "The Essex, New York, Howard, Cauldwell & Morgan, Architects," *Architectural Review* 5 (June 1903): 126.
77. Hutchins, "New York Hotels II": 622-24; "The Hotel Gotham," *Architects' and Builders' Magazine* 7 n.s. (November 1905): 45-56; "Hotel Gotham, Fifth Ave. and 55th St., New York, Hiss & Weekes, Architects," *Architecture* 11 (June 1905): plate XLV; "Main Doorway, Hotel Gotham, Fifty-fifth Street and Fifth Avenue, New York, N.Y., Hiss & Weekes, Architects," *American Architect and Building News* 89 (May 12, 1906): 49; and "Hotel Gotham, New York City, Hiss & Weekes, Architects," *Architectural Review* 11 (April 1913): 85.
78. "Mills House Number One, New York City, Ernest Flagg, Architect," *Architectural Review* 6 (January 1889): plates VI-VIII; and H.W. Desmond, "The Works of Ernest Flagg," *Architectural Record* 11 (April 1902): 11-104. Mills House No. 2, also published in "The Works of Ernest Flagg," was less than half the size of Mills House No. 1.
79. "A Palace at Twenty Cents a Night," *Scribner's* 20 (July 1896): 129-30.
80. Andrew Alpern, "In the Manor Housed," *Metropolis* 1 (March 1982): 11-15.
81. Andrew Alpern, *Apartments for the Affluent* (New York: McGraw-Hill, 1975), 12-13. Alpern suggests that the Stuyvesant may have been a reconstruction of several older houses. Also see Montgomery Schuyler, "The Works of the Late Richard M. Hunt," *Architectural Record* 5 (October-December 1895): 110-11; Israels, "New York Apartment Houses": 476; "The Apartment Houses of New York, With an Example from Berlin in Comparison," *Real Estate Record and Guide* 85 (March 26, 1910): 644-46; R.W. Sexton, *Apartment Houses, Hotels, and Apartment Houses of Today* (New York: Architectural Book Publishing Co., 1929), 3; Anthony Jackson, *A Place Called Home* (Cambridge: MIT Press, 1976), 86; Lockwood, *Manhattan Moves Uptown*, 294; and Paul R. Baker, *Richard Morris Hunt* (Cambridge: MIT Press, 1980), 204-07.
82. Many were young couples with small families who considered the apartments particularly suited to their needs. Among the earliest tenants were Colonel W.C. Church, editor of *The Galaxy*, G.P. Putnam, the publisher, and even Calvert Vaux, F.L. Olmsted's partner. Baker, *Hunt*, 205.
83. "The New Homes of New York, A Study of Flats," *Scribner's* 3 (March 1874): 76.
84. *King's Handbook*, 242-43.
85. Chas. F. Wingate, "Apartment Houses," *Building* 5 (September 25, 1886): 152-53.
86. "The Problems of Living in New York," *Harper's Monthly* 65 (November 1882): 922.
87. In the following year, 1872, Hunt's Stevens House (Broadway and Twenty-seventh Street) was designed with an elevator. Schuyler described the building as "perhaps the most Parisian in effect of anything of its period or its author." It was soon converted, however, into the Victoria Hotel. See Schuyler, "Richard M. Hunt": 111; Israels, "New York Apartment Houses": 476; and Baker, *Hunt*, 208-13.
88. Wingate, "Apartment Houses": 152.
89. "Architecture in Apartment Buildings," *American Architect and Building News* 2 (October 21, 1893): 36-37; "The Modern Apartment House in Paris," *Architectural Record* 2 (January–March 1893): 324-31; and Helene Lipstadt, "Housing the Bourgeoisie: Cesar Daly and the Ideal Home," *Oppositions* 8 (Spring 1977): 33-47.
90. Sarah Gilman Young, *European Modes of Living, or, The Question of the Apartment House* (New York: Putnam, 1881) is reviewed in "A Book of Apartment-Houses," *American Architect and Building News* 9 (February 12, 1881): 78. Also see "Apartment Houses: Part 2," *American Architect and Building News* 30 (November 15, 1890): 97-101; Hubert, Pirsson & Hoddick, "New York Flats and French Flats," *Architectural Record* 2 (July–September 1892): 55-64; "The Modern Apartment House in Paris" and Fernand Mazade, "How and Where to Live in Paris on $3,000 a Year," *Architectural Record* 13—Part 1 (April 1903): 349-57, Part 2 (May 1903): 423-32, Part 3 (June 1903): 548-54; and Jean Shopfer, "City Apartments in Paris," *Architectural Review* 10 (July 1903): 91-97. In addition, general articles on the apartment house usually included comparative French examples. See, for example, Irving K. Pond, "Architecture of Apartment Buildings," *Brickbuilder* 7—Part 1 (June 1898): 116-18, Part 2 (July 1898): 139-41, Part 3 (December 1898): 249-52.
91. "The March of Improvement," *Real Estate Record and Guide* 20 (September 15, 1877): 709-11.
92. "Apartment Houses," *Real Estate Record and Guide* 17 (April 1876): 237-38. By 1900, as Albert Bigelow Paine observed, the word "tenement" was no longer popular. "We hear of 'flats' and 'apartments' now, of rentals as high as six thousand and even ten thousand dollars a year, but the law makes no distinction. Every house, however big and expensive, which contains layers of inhabitants, all duly recorded, labeled and pigeonholed, is a 'tenement.'" "The Flat Dwellers of a Great City," *World's Work* 5 (April 1903): 3281-94.
93. "The Berkshire," *American Architect and Building News* 14 (August 4, 1883): 53-54, plates.
94. "The 'Hoffman Arms,'" *American Architect and Building News* 17 (January 24, 1885): 43, plates.
95. "The Osborne," *Real Estate Record and Guide* 17 (June 3, 1876): 428; "The Osborne," *Real Estate Record and Guide* 18 (September 23, 1876): 704-5; Alpern, *Apartments for the Affluent*, 22-23; and Alpern "In the Manor Housed": 12.
96. H.W. Fabian, "Evolution of the New York Dwelling-House," *Building* 5 (July 31, 1886): 56-57. Also see "Interesting Talks on High Apartment Houses," *Real Estate Record and Guide* 41—Part 1 (February 4, 1888): 141-42, Part 2 (February 18, 1888): 208.
97. Jackson, *A Place Called Home*, 55; and Baker, *Hunt*, 262.
98. Alfred T. White, *Improved Dwellings for the Laboring Classes* (New York: Improved Model Dwelling Co.); Louis H. Pink, *The New Day in Housing* (New York: John Day, 1928), 9; Edith Elmer Wood, *Recent Trends in American Housing* (New York: Macmillan, 1931), 11; Jackson, *A Place Called Home*, 55; and Charles Lockwood, "Quintessential Housing of the Past: Tenements Built for the Poor," *New York Times*, July 23, 1978, section 8: 1.
99. Jackson, *A Place Called Home*, 41.
100. Alfred T. White, *The Riverside Buildings of the Improved Model Dwelling Co.* (New York: Improved Model Dwelling Co., 1890).
101. "The Dakota Apartment House," *Real Estate Record and Guide* 35 (March 7, 1885): 232; "The Dakota Apartment House," *American Architect and Building News* 20 (July 24, 1886): plate; Alpern, *Apartments for the Affluent*, 20-21; and Montgomery Schuyler, "Henry Janeway Hardenbergh": 337-40. One large apartment house complex contemporaneous with the Dakota explored the lessons of the courtyard plan on an even larger scale. In 1882, the firm of Hubert, Pirsson & Hoddick designed the Central Park Apartments, or Spanish Flats, as they came to be known. Eight twelve-story apartment buildings located on a 200 by 425 foot site at the west side of Seventh Avenue between Fifty-eighth Street and Central Park South, the Central Park Flats were originally planned as a cooperative venture, but when the financing could not be arranged, they were built on a conventional rental basis by a developer named J. Jennings McComb. Constructed from Hubert, Pirsson & Co.'s plans, the buildings surrounded a long narrow courtyard that was more of an alleyway than a public space. Flamboyantly eclectic in design, with a complex roofline, the Central Park Flats were as notable a feature of the skyline as the Dakota. See "The Central Park Apartments," *Building* 2 (December 1883): 32, plate; "The Central Park Apartment Houses," *Real Estate Record and*

Guide 37 (March 21, 1886): 350; "The Duplex Apartment House: A Comparison of the Newest Buildings of this Type," *Architectural Record* 29 (March 1911): 326-34; C. Matlack Price, "A Pioneer in Apartment House Architecture: Memoir on Philip G. Hubert's Work," *Architectural Record* 36 (July 1914): 74-76; "Street That Has Maintained Its Character. Central Park South, Where Some of the First Apartment Houses Were Erected, Still Retains Its Hold As a Residential Center," *Real Estate Record and Guide* 96 (August 7, 1915): 225; Alpern: *Apartments for the Affluent,* 16-17.

102. "Evolution of the New York Dwelling House, Part 4," *Building* 5 (July 24, 1886): 46-47.

103. The courtyard of Hardenbergh's earlier Vancorlear Apartment House on Seventh Avenue (1879) was by contrast reserved for tradespeople. See "The Vancorlear, New York," *American Architect and Building News* 7 (January 20, 1880): plates; "Apartment Houses," *Real Estate Record and Guide* 27 (January 15, 1881): 46-47; "Apartment Houses: Part 4," *American Architect and Building News* 31 (January 17, 1891): 37-39; and Schuyler, "Henry Janeway Hardenbergh": 336.

104. Hubert, Pirsson & Hoddick, "New York Flats and French Flats": 55-64.

105. Hubert, Pirsson & Hoddick, "New York Flats and French Flats": 58.

106. Hubert, Pirsson & Hoddick, "New York Flats and French Flats": 63.

107. "The Duplex Apartment House," *Architectural Record:* 326; Price, "Memoir on Philip G. Hubert's Work": 75; Alpern, *Apartments for the Affluent,* 14-15. A more interesting early duplex building, because of its more intricate cross section, was the Dalhousie. Built in 1884 at 40-48 West Fifty-ninth Street, it had alternating duplex and simplex apartments, so that the duplexes had living and dining rooms with 15½-foot ceilings facing Central Park, and bedrooms, baths and kitchens grouped at the rear under ten-foot ceilings. *The Dalhousie, Elegant Apartment House* (New York, 1884); and "Fifty Seven Years of Progress in Apartment Building," New York *Herald Tribune,* June 29, 1941: 1-2.

108. Israels, "New York Apartment Houses": 481-86.

109. Gwendolynn Wright, *Building the Dream* (New York: Pantheon, 1981), 123.

110. Ernest Flagg, "The New York Tenement House Evil and its Cure," *Scribner's* 16 (July 1894): 108-17. In the late 1880s architects such as E.T. Potter and J.P. Putnam had begun to publish carefully researched arguments demonstrating the benefits of grouped planning. Potter's proposals for paired apartments on seventy-five-foot lots, though they were never adopted in New York where high rise construction soon led to a larger lot module, in many ways anticipated the plans developed in the Chicago suburbs by Myron Hunt and others in the late 90s. E.T. Potter, "Plans for Apartment-Houses," *American Architect and Building News* 22 (October 15, 1887): 177; and 23 (May 5, 1888). See Sarah Bradford Landau, *Edward T. and William A. Potter: American High Victorian Architects, 1885-1901* (Ph.D. diss., New York University, 1978): 393-409; and Handlin, *American Home: Architecture and Society, 1815-1915* (Boston: Little Brown & Co.), 207-09. Putnam on the other hand convincingly argued in behalf of the apartment house as a palace block with many hotel facilities including restaurants. J.P. Putnam, "The Apartment House," *American Architect and Building News* 27 (January 4, 1890): 3-8.

111. Handlin, *The American Home,* 204.

112. "Model Apartment Houses," *Architecture and Building* 26 (January 2, 1897): 7-10; H.W. Desmond, "The Works of Ernest Flagg," *Architectural Record* 11 (April 1902): 11-104.

113. Desmond, "Ernest Flagg": 38-39.

114. "Model Apartment Houses," *Architecture and Building:* 7-10; Jackson, *A Place Called Home,* 107-09.

115. The New Law's provisions are described in Elisha Harris Janes, "The Development and Financing of Apartment Houses in New York—1," *Brickbuilder* 17 (December 1908): 276-78. At the same time, the wider lots gave the traditional dumbbell a new lease on life, Grosvenor Atterbury's Rogers Model Dwellings on West Forty-fourth Street offered a particularly interesting variation. By combining two lots, Atterbury was able to provide two separate units, one at the front, the other at the back connected at the ground floor by a small hall and a perambulator storage area and at the second floor by a skylit reading room. Roof space was devoted to clothes drying facilities as well as an open-air playground for children. "Rogers Model Dwellings," *American Architect* 104 (October 29, 1913): plates.

116. "Building For Health: Sensible and Hygienic House Plans Are One Significant Result of the Present Campaigning Against Disease," *The Craftsman* 19 (March 1910): 552-61; Henry Atterbury Smith, "Open-Stair Apartments: A New Development in City Architecture," *The Craftsman* 20 (July 1911): 364-71; "Prize Winning Houses," *Real Estate Record and Guide* 89 (February 24, 1912): 386-87; "The Shiveley Sanitary Tenements, New York," *American Architect* 101 (February 28, 1912): plates; H.A. Smith, "Some Facts and Figures About Some Successful Housing Schemes," *Architecture* 37 (March 1918): 72-74; and Handlin, *American Home,* 204-05.

117. "What a Tenant Gets for $10,000," *Real Estate Record and Guide* 84 (November 6, 1909): 807-09.

118. *Architecture* 21 (February 15, 1910): 18. See also "What a Tenant Gets for $10,000," *Real Estate Record and Guide:* 807-08; "Alwyn Court," *Architects' and Builders' Magazine* 10 (June 1910): 336-40; and Alpern, *Apartments for the Affluent,* 54-55.

119. "Apartments for Millionaires," *Real Estate Record and Guide* 86 (August 3, 1910): 272; *American Architect* 98 (August 24, 1910): 67; *American Architect* 100 (November 29, 1911): plates; "No. 998 Fifth Avenue," *Architecture and Building* 42 (February 1912): 91-102; "The Multiple Dwelling: No. 998 Fifth Avenue," *Architect* 6 (March 1912): 221-23; "Century Holding Co. Apartment House, 998 Fifth Avenue," *Architectural Year Book* 1 (1912): 293; Leland Roth, *Monograph of the Works of McKim, Mead & White 1879-1925* (New York: Benjamin Blom, 1973), 50, 71, plates; and Alpern, *Apartments for the Affluent,* 74-75.

120. Israels, "New York Apartments": 490-91; Charles H. Israels, "The Metropolitan Apartment House and Hotel," *Real Estate Record and Guide* 73 (June 11, 1904): 1464-73; and Alpern, *Apartments for the Affluent,* 26-27.

121. "Largest in the World," *Real Estate Record and Guide* 77 (January 13, 1906): 51-52; "The Apthorp," *American Architect and Building News* 91 (January 5, 1907): plates; "What a Tenant Gets for $6,000 A Year," *Real Estate Record and Guide* 82 (July 4, 1908): 20-21; "The Apthorp Apartments—The Largest in the World," *Architecture* 18 (September 1908): 130-31; "The Apthorp," *Architects' and Builders' Magazine* 9 (September 1908): 531-33; "The Apthorp Apartments," *American Architect* 98 (January 19, 1919): plates; and Alpern, *Apartments for the Affluent,* 52-53.

122. "The Belnord To Have Interesting Features," *Real Estate Record and Guide* 132 (November 7, 1908): 873-75; "The Belnord," *Real Estate Record and Guide* 82 (December 9, 1908): 1215; "Apartment Houses of Duplex and Studio Plan": 248-49; "The Belnord Apartment House," *Architects' and Builders' Magazine* 42 (November 1909): 111-13.

123. "Astor Court," *Architecture and Building* 49 (March 1916): plates; "Astor Court Apartments," *Architecture* 34 (September 1916): plates; "The Latest High Class Apartment House" (advertisement), *Real Estate Record and Guide* 98 (September 16, 1916): 395; "The Development of the Apartment House," *American Architect* 110 (November 29, 1916): 331-36; and "A Half Century of Progress in the Development of Distinctive Types of Buildings in the United States," *American Architect* 129 (January 5, 1926): 73-95.

124. Elisha Harris Janes, "The Development of Duplex Apartments—3. Residential Type," *Brickbuilder* 21 (August 1912): 203-06.

125. "Studio Apartment at 70 Central Park West, New York City," *Architectural Review* 27 (February 1920): 33-34.

126. Allan L. Benson, "The Spread of the 'Own-Your-Own-Home' Movement," *New York Times* (July 29, 1909): 27. Ranger would, of course, have known Richard Morris Hunt's Tenth Street Studios, built in 1858 at 51 West Tenth Street, but only a few of those studios had bedrooms, so the Studio Building was not generally considered an apartment house. See Baker, *Hunt,* 93-107. In addition, an unsigned article in the *Brickbuilder* states that the first cooperative apartment house "was the 'Rembrandt Studios' built on West 57th Street by Jared Flagg and a number of artists in 1880. Within three years ten others were built. After the conspicuous failure of the 'Navarro Flats' (owing to the error of building on leased ground), construction lagged until 1898, when Harry [sic] Ranger, heading a syndicate of artists revived the idea." "Cooperative Apartment House," *Brickbuilder* 18 (November 1909): 237. However, most accounts credit Hubert, Pirsson & Co. with the first cooperative apartment building in New York.

127. A.C. David, "A Cooperative Studio Building," *Architectural Record* 14 (October 1903): 232-54.

128. "Sixty-Seventh Street Atelier Building, New York," *American Architect and Building News* 91 (January 5, 1907): plates; "Some Interesting Studio Apartments in the Atelier Building, 33 W. 67th St., N.Y.," *Architectural Record* 21 (May 1907): 385-88; and "Atelier Building," *Architecture* 15 (April 4, 1907): plate 37.

129. "Projected Buildings," *Real Estate Record and Guide Quarterly* (1904): 682.

130. "Projected Buildings," *Real Estate Record and Guide Quarterly* (1905): 905.

131. "Projected Buildings," *Real Estate Record and Guide Quarterly* (1906): 107.

132. "A Painter's Studio in the Hotel des Artistes, New York," *Architectural Review* 9 (October 1919): plate LXIV; "A Studio in the Hotel des Artistes, New York City," *Architectural Review* 9 (December 1919): plates

XCV-XCVI; and Alpern, *Apartments for the Affluent,* 90-91.

133. "Bryant Park Studios," *Architects' and Builders' Magazine* 3 (May 1902): 317-25; "Bryant Park Studio Building," *American Architect and Building News* 64 (October 5, 1901): plates; and "Bryant Park Studio Building," *American Architect and Building News* 109 (January 19, 1916): plates.

134. Under its twelfth-floor balcony, the Arts Club had gargoyles similar to those at Post's City College buildings. "The National Arts Club Building, East 19th Street, New York, N.Y., Messrs. George B. Post & Sons, Architects," *American Architect and Building News* 40 (November 17, 1906): 159, plates.

135. The Studio Building was distinguished by its exceptionally lofty studios supplemented by living rooms and its gingerbread Gothic ornament in terra cotta, which caused the *Architectural Record* to cite it in the monthly "Architectural Aberations," *Architectural Record* 25 (June 1909): 434-37. Also see "Studio Apartment House," *Architects' and Builders' Magazine* 10 n.s. (October 1909): 379-82.

136. "Gainsborough Studios, 222 Central Park South, New York, C.W. Buckham, Architect," *Architecture* 35 (December 1908): 199, plate XC; and "The Gainsborough Studios, Central Park South, New York, Mr. Charles W. Buckham, Architect," *American Architect and Building News* 6 (December 22, 1909): plates.

137. "36 Central Park South, C.W. Buckham, Architect," *Real Estate Record and Guide* 89 (May 11, 1912): 1003; "Plaza Home Club Apartments, Central Park South, New York, Mr. C.W. Buckham, Architect," *American Architect* 100 (November 29, 1911): plates; and "The Plaza Home Club, C.W. Buckham, Architect," *Architectural Review* 11 (April 1913): 133.

138. "Apartment Studio Building, No. 200 West 57th Street, Cass Gilbert Architect," *American Architect* 113 (January 9, 1918): 38, plates. Also see Claude Bragdon, "Architecture and Democracy, Part III, After the War," *Architectural Record* 44 (September 1918): 253-58.

139. Including "Studio Apartments, 130 West 57th Street, New York, Pollard & Steinam, Architects," *Architecture* 19 (March 1909): plate XXVI.

140. Richard Morton, "An Essay on Duplex Apartments in General and Those at 471 Park Avenue in Particular," *Apartment Houses of the Metropolis* (New York: Hesselgren, 1908), 5-6; "Apartment Houses of Duplex and Studio Plan in New York City": 222-23; and Charles W. Buckham, "Duplex Co-Operative Apartment Houses," *American Architect and Building News* 96 (December 22, 1909): 266-67.

141. A.C. David, "A Co-Operative Apartment House in New York Designed by Charles Platt," *Architectural Record* 24 (July 1908): 1-18; "What A Cooperative Apartment Is," *Real Estate Record and Guide* 82 (July 4, 1908): 7; "Studio Apartments, 131 and 135 East 66th Street, New York City," *Architectural Review* 67 (March 1930): 220-21; "131 and 135 E. 66th St., N.Y.," *Architectural Review* 16 (February 1909): 19-20, plates 13-14, 16-20.

142. A.C. David, "A Co-Operative Apartment House": 15.

143. See "The Duplex Apartment House," *Architectural Record*: 326; and Price, "Memoir on Philip G. Hubert's Work": 75. Also see "All About Home Clubs," *Real Estate Record and Guide* 30 (December 30, 1882): 147; "Joint Stock Apartment Houses in New York," *American Architect and Building News* 13 (April 28, 1883): 193; "The Cooperative Apartment Craze of a Score of Years Ago, The Present Rage for Syndicate Building," *American Architect and Building News* 76 (June 28, 1902): 97; and "Principles of Co-Operative Building," *Real Estate Record and Guide* 86 (September 24, 1910): 485-86.

144. "Newest Forms of Residential Construction," *Real Estate Record and Guide* 84 (October 23, 1909): 719-20.

145. "The Duplex Apartment House," *Architectural Record* 29 (April 1911): 327-34.

146. "Apartment Houses," *American Architect* 8 (November 29, 1911): 229-30.

147. Benson, "Own Your Own Home": 27. For the Gramercy Park Apartments see "About Some Apartment Houses," *Real Estate Record and Guide* 35 (April 18, 1883): 428.

148. "Apartment House Upon a Cooperative Plan," *Real Estate Record and Guide* 83 (January 2, 1909): 5-6; "Newest Form of Residential Construction," *Real Estate Record and Guide* 84 (October 23, 1909): 719-20; and "Studio Apartments, 24 Gramercy Park, New York, Herbert Lucas, Architect," *Architecture* 21 (January 1910): plate 9.

149. "Newest Form of Residential Construction," *Real Estate Record and Guide* 720; and "Gramercy Park Club Apartments, Gramercy Park, New York," *Architecture* 21 (May 1910): 67, plate XLVI.

150. "Number One Lexington Avenue," *Real Estate Record and Guide* 85 (May 21, 1910): 1085.

151. "The Home Club, 11-15 East 45th Street, New York, N.Y., Messrs. Gordon, Tracy & Swartout [sic], Architects," *American Architect and Building News* 90 (October 20, 1906): 128, plates; "Home Club Building, 11-15 East 45th St., New York, Gordon, Tracy & Swartwout, Architects," *Architecture* 17 (February 1907): plate XII; and Egerton Swartwout, "Architectural Criticism," *Architecture* 19 (January 15, 1909): 1-2.

152. "The El Nido Apartments," *Architects' and Builders' Magazine* 33 (October 1900): 59-63; and Israels, "New York Apartment Houses": 481. The El Nido was an early project by Neville & Bagge. For other early apartment houses see "Apartment House, Northwest Corner 152nd Street and St. Nicholas Avenue, New York City, Neville & Bagge, Architects," *Architecture and Building* 25 (August 8, 1896): plate; the Cherbourg in Israels, "New York Apartment Houses": 489; and an apartment hotel, "Stratford House, No. 11 East 32d Street, Neville & Bagge, Architects," *Architects' and Builders' Magazine* 5 (November 1903): 60-61.

153. Israels, "New York Apartment Houses": 479. For a brief discussion of the improvement of the tenement, see "The Modern Flat," *Architecture and Building* 24 (April 25, 1896): 193-94.

154. "The Netherlands, 86th Street near Riverside Drive, New York," *Architecture and Building* 42 (January 1910): 152.

155. "Reed House, N.E. Cor. Broadway and 121st St., Neville & Bagge, Architects," *Real Estate Record and Guide* 75 (June 3, 1905): 1259; and "Reed House, Neville & Bagge, Architects," *Real Estate Record and Guide* 79 (March 28, 1908): 567.

156. "Apartment House, 590 West End Avenue, New York, Neville & Bagge, Architects," *Architecture and Building* 48 (December 1916): 77-78.

157. "Apartment House, 789 West End Avenue, New York City, Neville & Bagge, Architects," *Architecture and Building* 48 (December 1916): 81-82.

158. "Two Broadway Corner Improvements," *Real Estate Record and Guide* 87 (April 17, 1909): 752.

159. "The Dorchester, New York, Neville & Bagge, Architects," *Architecture and Building* 11 (June 1910): 339-40.

160. Alpern, *Apartments for the Affluent,* 64-65. Also see "Diversity of Planning in Apartment House Design, Work of Schwartz & Gross, Architects," *Architects' and Builders' Magazine* 11 n.s. (December 1910): 95-112.

161. "The Apartment Houses of New York," *Real Estate Record and Guide* 85 (March 26, 1910): 644.

162. Alpern, *Apartments for the Affluent,* 58-59.

163. Alpern, *Apartments for the Affluent,* 80-81.

164. Alpern, *Apartments for the Affluent,* 82-83.

165. "New York Apartment Houses," *Architects' and Builders' Magazine* 8 (April 1907): 316-23. Also see "The Wyoming Apartments, Seventh Ave. and 55th St., New York," *Architecture* 23 (March 1907): 45, plate XXVII.

166. "A Riverside Drive Apartment House," *Real Estate Record and Guide* 85 (March 12, 1910): 538.

167. "Three-Seventy-Five Park Avenue," *Real Estate Record and Guide* 92 (October 25, 1913): 751-54.

168. See, for example, "Apartments, 178 East 70th St., New York, Wm. L. Rouse and L.A. Goldstone, Architects," *Architecture* 31 (May 1915): plate XLVII; "Apartments, 226 West 70th St., New York, Wm. L. Rouse and L.A. Goldstone, Architects," *Architecture* 31 (May 1915): plate L; "Apartments, 302 West 87th St., New York, Wm. L. Rouse and L.A. Goldstone, Architects," *Architecture* 31 (May 1915): plate XLIX; and "Apartment House, 45 East 62nd Street, New York City, Rouse & Goldstone, Architects," *Architectural Review* 5 (October 1917): plate LXVI. Also see Aline L. and Harmon H. Goldstone, *Lafayette A. Goldstone, A Career in Architecture* (New York: 1964).

169. "The Sumner Apartments, 31 West Eleventh St., New York, Browne & Almiroty, Architects," *Architecture* 24 (July 1911): 104.

170. "Studio Apartments, 144 East 40th St., New York, Walker & Gillette, Architects," *Architecture* 23 (May 1911): 68.

171. "Studio Apartments and Plans, 132 East 19th St., New York, F.J. Sterner, Architects," *Architecture* 23 (May 1911): plates.

172. "Astor Apartments, 305 West 45th St., New York, Tracy & Swartwout, Architects," *Architecture* 31 (June 1915): 162, plate 67.

173. "The Development of the Apartment House," *American Architect* 110 (November 29, 1916): 331-36, plates.

METROPOLITAN NEIGHBORHOODS

1. See Joy Wheeler Dow, "Lower Fifth Avenue," *Architectural Review* 4 (January 1902): 61-64.

2. "The Fifth Avenue," *Real Estate Record and Guide* 21 (June 15, 1878): 515-16.

3. See Mariana Griswold van Rensselaer, "Fifth Avenue," *Century* 47 (November 1893): 5-18.

4. Van Rensselaer, "Fifth Avenue": 7.

5. Moses King, *King's Handbook of New York* (Boston: Moses King,

1893; New York: Benjamin Blom, 1972), 352-54.
6. *King's Handbook,* 336-39.
7. *King's Handbook,* 391-94. Many institutions were also in the area. Columbia College was still at Madison Avenue and Fiftieth Street, the Women's Hospital of the State of New York was a few blocks over, on Fiftieth Street between Fourth (Park) and Lexington avenues, and the Nursery and Child's Hospital was on Lexington at Fifty-first Street. The Catholic Female Orphan Asylum was on the corner of Madison Avenue and Fifty-third Street, the Catholic Male Orphan Asylum was on Madison Avenue between Fifty-first and Fifty-second streets, and St. Luke's Hospital was on Fifth Avenue between Fifty-fourth and Fifty-fifth streets. Eventually the need for larger facilities and the increasing value of their midtown sites led the institutions to migrate far beyond the boundary of the settled city, particularly to Morningside Heights.
8. Nathan Silver, *Lost New York* (New York: Schocken, 1971), 124. In 1869-70 Rebecca Jones, sister of Mary Jones, built the Colford Jones Block on the same side of Fifth Avenue, just to the south between Fifty-fifth and Fifty-sixth streets. The eight houses were designed by Detlef Lienau.
9. Edith Wharton, *The Age of Innocence* (New York: D. Appleton Co., 1921), 24-25.
10. William C. Shopsin and Mosette Glaser Broderick, *The Villard Houses, Life Story of a Landmark* (New York: Viking Press, 1980), 46.
11. Broderick, *Villard Houses,* 46. Also see Montgomery Schuyler, "Recent Buildings in New York, V, The Vanderbilt Houses," *Real Estate Record and Guide* 9 (May 21, 1881): 243-44; "Dwelling House for C. Vanderbilt, Esq.," *American Architect and Building News* 9 (May 21, 1881): plates; "Novelties in City Architecture," *Real Estate Record and Guide* 30 (July 8, 1882): 659; and "House of Cornelius Vanderbilt, Esq., 58th St. and Fifth Ave., New York, N.Y., Mr. George B. Post, Architect, New York, N.Y.," *American Architect and Building News* 45 (August 4, 1894): plates.
12. Broderick, *Villard Houses,* 46-47.
13. Broderick, *Villard Houses,* 47.
14. Schuyler, "Vanderbilt Houses": 243.
15. Schuyler, "Vanderbilt Houses": 243-44; "Mr. Wm. K. Vanderbilt's House," *Real Estate Record and Guide* 38 (June 12, 1886): 770; "Mr. Wm. K. Vanderbilt's House," *Real Estate Record and Guide* 38 (July 3, 1886): 856-57; "American Construction Through British Eyes," *American Architect and Building News* 28 (August 29, 1891): 132; A.A. Cox, "The Residence of Mr. W.K. Vanderbilt, New York," *American Architect and Building News* 33 (August 29, 1891): 132; Montgomery Schuyler, "The Works of the Late Richard M. Hunt," *Architectural Record* 5 (October-December 1895): 97-180; Barr Ferree, "Richard Morris Hunt, His Art and Work," *Architecture and Building* 23 (December 7, 1895): 274; John Vredenburgh Van Pelt, *A Monograph of the William K. Vanderbilt House* (New York: J.V. Van Pelt, 1925); and Arthur W. Colton, "The Architect's Library: A Monograph of the William K. Vanderbilt House," *Architectural Record* 58 (September 1925): 295-99.
16. "Like an Oriental Dream," *New York Herald* (March 27, 1883): 3. Cited by Paul Baker in *Richard Morris Hunt* (Cambridge: M.I.T. Press, 1980), 284.
17. Baker, *Richard Morris Hunt,* 284, 286. Hunt came as Cimabue, the painter whom Dante chose to symbolize the transience of fame.
18. Schuyler, "Vanderbilt Houses": 244.
19. According to an anecdote that Daniel Burnham liked to tell. Charles Moore, *Daniel H. Burnham, Architect, Planner of Cities* (Boston: Houghton Mifflin, 1921), Vol. 1: 116.
20. Royal Cortissoz, "Leaders in American Architecture," *Art and Common Sense* (New York: Charles Scribner's Sons, 1913), 396.
21. Herbert Croly, "The Work of Richard Morris Hunt," *Architectural Record* 59 (January 1926): 88-89. Baker calls the house "the most highly praised" of all Hunt's works and cites other articles. Baker, *Richard Morris Hunt,* 286-87.
22. Baker, *Richard Morris Hunt,* 293, 295-96. Also see "Residence of Mr. H.G. Marquand, 68 [sic] Madison Ave., N.Y., Mr. R.M. Hunt, Architect," *American Architect and Building News* 19 (June 26, 1886): plate; "The House of Mr. Henry G. Marquand, New York City," *American Architect and Building News* 22 (December 3, 1887): 261-62; "American Construction Through English Eyes, III, the Marquand Residence, New York," *American Architect and Building News* 33 (August 29, 1881): 131-32; and Schuyler, "Works of Richard Morris Hunt": 131, 165.
23. "Handsome East Side Residence Under Way," *Real Estate Record and Guide* 36 (October 24, 1885): 1159-60; "House for Charles L. Tiffany, Esq., on Seventy-second, New York, N.Y., Messrs. McKim, Mead & White, Architects, New York, N.Y.," *American Architect and Building News* 20 (July 17, 1886): 80, plate; "An Interior in the House of C.L. Tiffany, Esq., New York, N.Y., Messrs. McKim, Mead & White, Architects, New York, N.Y.," *American Architect and Building News* 22 (December 10, 1887): 278, plate; Russell Sturgis, "The Works of McKim, Mead & White," *Architectural Record* (May 1895), reprinted in *Great American Architect Series* (New York: Da Capo Press, 1977): 1-111; "The Tiffany House," *Architectural Record* 10 (October 1900): 191-202; *A Monograph of the Works of McKim, Mead & White, 1879-1915* (New York: Architectural Book Publishing Co., 1915; New York: Benjamin Blom, 1973), plates 5-6; Leland Roth, *Urban Architecture of McKim, Mead & White 1870-1910* (Ph.D. diss., Yale University, 1973), 186-88; and Broderick, *Villard Houses,* 45.
24. Sturgis, "Works of McKim, Mead & White": 55.
25. "Handsome East Side Residences," *Real Estate Record and Guide:* 1159.
26. Broderick, *Villard Houses,* 45.
27. "Tiffany Houses," *Architectural Record:* 191.
28. "The New York House of the Future," *Real Estate Record and Guide* 28 (December 1881): 1208; "Interior of the Villard House," *Real Estate Record and Guide* 36 (November 14, 1885): 1247-48; "Fireplace in House Built for Henry Villard, Esq., New York, N.Y., McKim, Mead & White, Architects," *American Architect and Building News* 22 (December 24, 1887): plate; "Two Dwellings," *Real Estate Record and Guide* 42 (July 28, 1888): 944-45; "East End of Dining Room in the House of the Hon. Whitelaw Reid, New York, N.Y., McKim, Mead & White, Architects," *American Architect and Building News* 26 (December 21, 1889): plate; *McKim, Mead & White Monograph,* plates 7-11; and Broderick, *Villard Houses, passim.*
29. Villard bought the site in several parcels. See Broderick, *Villard Houses,* 24.
30. "The New York House of the Future," *Real Estate Record and Guide:* 1208.
31. Henry Russell Hitchcock suggests that Villard, born in Speyer, Germany, developed the concept from the palace of the Princes von Thurn und Taxis in Frankfurt-am-Main. See Broderick, *Villard Houses,* 30-31.
32. Charles Moore, *The Life and Times of Charles Follen McKim* (Boston and New York: Houghton Mifflin, 1929), 47-48.
33. Broderick, *Villard Houses,* 38.
34. *King's Handbook,* 152. See "House for Mr. Robert Goelet, S.E. corner of 5th Avenue and 48th St., New York, Edward H. Kendall, Architect," *American Architect and Building News* 10 (July 9, 1881): plate; "House for O. Goelet, Esq., Fifth Ave., New York, E.H. Kendall, Arch't.," *American Architect and Building News* 9 (June 11, 1881): plate; "Residence of C.P. Huntington, Esq., Southeast corner Fifth Avenue and Fifty-seventh Street, New York City, Geo. B. Post, Architect," *Architectural Record* 1 (April-June 1892): 270; "A Bay Window in New York," *American Architect and Building News* 40 (June 24, 1893): 189; "Carriage Entrance to House of C.P. Huntington, Esq., 57th St., New York, N.Y., Mr. George B. Post, Architect," *American Architect and Building News* 45 (July 14, 1894): plate; and "Residence of C.P. Huntington, Fifth Avenue, corner of Fifty-seventh Street, New York," *Architecture and Building* 23 (October 5, 1895): plate; and "Two Miles of Millionaires," *Munsey's* 19 (June 1898): 345-61.
35. Norval White and Elliott Willensky, *AIA Guide to New York City* (New York: Macmillan, 1978), 168. Another intrusion was the Bolkenhayn Apartment House. Designed by Alfred Zucker, it was built in 1895 at the northeast corner of Fifty-eighth Street and Fifth Avenue and was the first apartment house in the district. To Zucker must also be attributed the apartment's improbable name, that of a small town in Silesia, "Bolko Burg," whose venerable castle was closely allied with the fortunes of the Hohenzollerns. Despite the vaguely Italianate style of the exterior, similar in spirit to Zucker's Progress Club five blocks further uptown, every effort was made to emphasize the Imperial German connection. Not only was the lobby floor emblazoned with the coats of arms of the provinces of the Prussian Kingdom, but each apartment, instead of being numbered, was named after a famous member of the Hohenzollern family. "Bolkenhayn," *Architectural Record* 3 (April-June 1894): 434; and "The Bolkenhayn," *Architecture and Building* 23 (November 2, 1895): 211-14, plate. Also see "Middle Fifth Avenue: The Evolution of the New Picadilly," *Real Estate Record and Guide* 67 (April 20, 1901): 694.
36. "The Fashionable Residential District, No. 1," *Real Estate Record and Guide* 76 (December 16, 1905): 950-51; *Real Estate Record and Guide* 77 (February 10, 1906): 229; *Real Estate Record and Guide* 78 (October 27, 1906): 677; *Real Estate Record and Guide* 85 (January 8, 1910): 51; "Passing of 'Last Vacant Corner': Parcel Recently Sold Site for Tall Office Building—Only Unimproved Fifth Avenue Corner Between 42nd and 59th Streets," *Real Estate Record and Guide* 96 (October 9, 1915): 603; and John Tauranac, *Essential New York* (New York: Holt, Rinehart & Winston, 1979), 115-16.
37. "Residence for Morton F. Plant," *Real Estate Record and Guide* 97 (January 15, 1916): 113.
38. Cited by Charles Lockwood, *Manhattan Moves Uptown* (Boston: Houghton Mifflin, 1976), 305. Also see "The Fifth Avenue," *Real Estate*

Record and Guide 515-16; "Fashion as an Element of Value," *Real Estate Record and Guide* 18 (October 21, 1876): 779-80; "Central Park Lots," *Real Estate Record and Guide* 18 (November 18, 1876): 851-52; "The March of Improvement," *Real Estate Record and Guide* 20 (September 15, 1877): 709-11; "East Side and West Side," *Real Estate Record and Guide* 20 (October 13, 1877): 785-86; "The New Fashionable Quarter," *Real Estate Record and Guide* 24 (September 20, 1879): 737; Montgomery Schuyler, "Recent Building in New York, III, Dwellings, I," *American Architect and Building News* 9 (April 23, 1881): 196-97; "Dwellings, II," (April 30, 1881): 207-08; "The Future of Fifth Avenue," *Real Estate Record and Guide* 30 (December 30, 1882): 143-44; "Fifth Avenue East of Central Park," *Real Estate Record and Guide* 43 (June 15, 1889): 1159-60; "The Fashionable Residential District, No. 2," *Real Estate Record and Guide* 76 (December 23, 1905): 997-98; "No. 3," (December 30, 1905): 1004-05; "No. 4," (January 6, 1906): 5; "No. 5," (January 13, 1906): 52; and "No. 6," (January 20, 1906): 102.

39. "The New Fashionable Quarter," *Real Estate Record and Guide*: 737.

40. Marianne Griswold van Rensselaer, "People in New York," *Century* 49 (February 1895): 534-48.

41. By 1890 the area was overbuilt and overcrowded, with almost as many social problems as those that existed below Fourteenth Street. (The "Lower East Side" was quickly becoming home to immigrants from Italy and Eastern Europe.) The usually boosterish *Record and Guide* labelled it "a disgrace to the people of this city . . . row succeeds row here without disclosing a trace of beauty or charm—streets of cheerless buildings that cannot be looked at without ennui . . . the city has undertaken to see that buildings are erected so as to be safe and healthy. One is almost tempted to wish that this authority might be extended to the aesthetic parts of buildings." "East Side Architecture—Fifth Avenue," *Real Estate Record and Guide* 45 (May 3, 1890): 640-41.

42. See Lockwood, *Manhattan Moves Uptown*, 310-13.

43. "Fifth Avenue, East of Central Park, A Contrast to Central Park West," *Real Estate Record and Guide* 43 (June 15, 1889): 836-37. Among these was Anthony Mowbray's McCreery mansion on the northeast corner of Fifth Avenue and Seventy-fourth Street. "A Newly Completed Fifth Avenue House," *Real Estate Record and Guide* 40 (October 1, 1887): 1228. Also see "On the East Side," *Real Estate Record and Guide* 41 (June 23, 1888): 799; "East Side Number," *Real Estate Record and Guide* 45 (May 3, 1890): 1-13; "East Side Number," *Real Estate Record and Guide* 47 (May 30, 1891): 1-16, 24; and "Upper Fifth Avenue: Features of the Building Movement on this Important Thoroughfare," *Real Estate Record and Guide* 66 (September 22, 1900): 349-50.

44. Wanderer, "A Group of East Side Residences," *Real Estate Record and Guide* 37 (February 27, 1886): 25. Also see "The Frontier for Millionaires' Homes," *Real Estate Record and Guide* 92 (September 27, 1913): 571-72.

45. This was the Graham, on the southwest corner of Madison Avenue and Eighty-ninth Street. John Livingston built a six-story apartment house, the Prospect Hill, on the southwest corner of Madison Avenue and Ninety-first Street. "East Side Number," *Real Estate Record and Guide*: 1-16, 24. Also see W.B. Franke's "The Lenox Hill Apartment House," *Real Estate Record and Guide* 37 (March 6, 1886): 283; and "Some East Side Houses," *Real Estate Record and Guide* 45 (February 15, 1890): 220.

46. Herbert Croly, "The Contemporary Metropolitan Residence," *Real Estate Record and Guide* 73 (June 11, 1904): 1447-62.

47. "Two Miles of Millionaires," *Munsey's*: 348.

48. Herbert Croly, "The Contemporary New York Residence," *Architectural Record* 12 (December 1902): 705-22. For views of Fifth Avenue see *Both Sides of Fifth Avenue* (New York: J.F.L. Collins, 1910); and *Fifth Avenue From Start to Finish* (New York: Welles & Co., 1911).

49. "East Side Architecture—Fifth Avenue," *Real Estate Record and Guide* 45 (May 3, 1890): 640-41.

50. For examples of Fifth Avenue mid-block houses in the Cosmopolitan Era, see "Dwelling to be Built on Fifth Avenue, New York, N.Y., Mr. R.H. Robertson, Architect," *American Architect and Building News* 9 (March 12, 1881): 127, plate; "House on Fifth Ave., New York, N.Y., W.H. Beers, Arch't.," *American Architect and Building News* 26 (July 6, 1889): plate; and "No. 589 Fifth Avenue, New York, N.Y., J.G. Prague, Architect," *American Architect and Building News* 33 (July 11, 1891): plate. Also see "Houses in East 67th St. for E. Doying, Esq., 1880: James E. Ware, Architect," *American Architect and Building News* 8 (September 18, 1880): plate; and "The East Side Number," *Real Estate Record and Guide*: 1-16, 24.

51. Russell Sturgis, "The Works of George B. Post," *Architectural Record* (June 1898), reprinted in *Great American Architects Series* (New York: Da Capo Press, 1977): 2-102. Sturgis also describes Post's Collis P. Huntington house, diagonally across Fifth Avenue from the original C. Vanderbilt II house. For the Vanderbilt house, also see "Porte Cochère to House of Cornelius Vanderbilt, Esq., 58th St., New York, N.Y., Mr. George B. Post, Architect," *American Architect and Building News* 45 (August 4, 1894): plate; and Baker, *Richard Morris Hunt*, 286, 523, 548.

52. Sturgis, "Works of George B. Post": 56.

53. "House of Elbridge T. Gerry, Esq., Fifth Ave., New York, N.Y., Mr. R.M. Hunt, Architect, New York, N.Y.," *American Architect and Building News* 45 (August 25, 1894): 76, plate; "House of Elbridge T. Gerry, Esq., Fifth Avenue, New York, N.Y., R.M. Hunt, Architect," *American Architect and Building News* 48 (June 1, 1895): plate; "Residence of Elbridge T. Gerry, No. 2 East Sixty-first Street, New York, Richard M. Hunt, Architect," *Architecture and Building* 22 (June 29, 1895): plate; Barr Ferree, "Richard Morris Hunt, His Art and Work," *Architecture and Building* 23 (December 7, 1895): 274; "Porte-Cochère, House of E.T. Gerry, Esq., Sixty-first Street and Fifth Avenue, New York, N.Y., R.M. Hunt, Architect," *American Architect and Building News* 56 (April 3, 1897): plate; and Baker, *Richard Morris Hunt*, 340-45.

54. Schuyler, "Works of Richard M. Hunt": 131.

55. "Astor Residence," *American Architect and Building News* 48 (June 22, 1895): plates; "Residence of John Jacob Astor, Esq., Northeast Corner of Sixty-fifth Street and Fifth Avenue, New York, Richard M. Hunt, Architect," *Architecture and Building* 23 (December 7, 1895): plate; "House of John Jacob Astor, Esq., Fifth Avenue and Sixty-fifth Street, New York, N.Y.," *American Architect and Building News* 57 (August 7, 1897): plate; Herbert Croly, "Notes and Comments: The Work of Richard Morris Hunt," *Architectural Record* 59 (January 1926): 88-89; and Baker, *Richard Morris Hunt*, 345-48. The interior was very ornate: Mrs. Astor's social position required lots of entertaining. The ballroom, for example, was large enough to hold 1,200 guests. When Mrs. Astor died in 1908, her son had Carrère & Hastings remodel the house to serve just his family and provide even more rooms for entertainment. "The Residence of Col. John Jacob Astor," *Architectural Record* 27 (June 1910): 469-82.

56. Designed by McKim, Mead & White in 1881. Montgomery Schuyler, "Recent Building in New York, Part III: Dwellings, Part I," *American Architect and Building News* 9 (April 23, 1881): 196-97.

57. Richard Howland Hunt collaborated on the "Schmid Residence," *American Architect and Building News* 49 (September 7, 1895): plate; "Residence of Mrs. Josephine Schmid, Sixty-second Street and Fifth Avenue, New York, Richard H. Hunt, Architect," *Architecture and Building* 24 (January 11, 1896): plate; and Baker, *Richard Morris Hunt*, 547.

58. Richard Howland Hunt collaborated on the "Residence of W.V. Lawrence, Seventy-eighth Street and Fifth Avenue, New York, N.Y., Richard H. Hunt, Architect," *Architecture and Building* 24 (February 29, 1896): plate; Baker, *Richard Morris Hunt*, 340, 342, 547.

59. "A Fifth Avenue House," *Real Estate Record and Guide* 41 (April 7, 1888): 420-21; "House of Isaac V. Brokaw, Esq., Fifth Avenue and 79th Street, New York, N.Y., Messrs. Rose & Stone, Architects, New York, N.Y.," *American Architect and Building News* 32 (June 13, 1891): 170, plates; "Modern Residences No. 1," *Architectural Record* 1 (October-December 1891): 127-31; and Christopher Gray, "Neighborhood, Demolished Mansions," *Avenue* 5 (July-August 1981): 50-57. An even more distinctly Richardsonian design was the "Residence of H.O. Havemeyer, N.E. Corner 5th Ave. and 66th Street, New York, Charles C. Haight, Architect," *Architecture and Building* 20 (May 19, 1894): plate. Also see Montgomery Schuyler, "The Romanesque Revival in New York," *Architectural Record* 1 (July-September 1891): 7-38; and Montgomery Schuyler, "A Review of the Work of Charles C. Haight," *Architectural Record* 1 (July 1899): 1-82.

60. "Mrs. Waldo's House, 728 [sic] Madison Ave., Kimball & Thomson [sic] Architect," *American Architect and Building News* 49 (September 11, 1897): plate; and Montgomery Schuyler, "The Works of Francis H. Kimball and Kimball & Thompson," *Architectural Record* 7 (June 1898): 479-518. Also see "House of Louis Stern, Esq., 993 Fifth Ave., New York, N.Y., Schickel & Ditmars, Architects," *American Architect and Building News* 67 (February 17, 1900): plate; and "Residence, Louis Stern, New York," *Architecture* 3 (May 15, 1901): 147.

61. "House of Mr. W.K. Vanderbilt, Jr., 666 Fifth Avenue, New York, N.Y., McKim, Mead & White, Architects," *American Architect and Building News* 92 (November 2, 1907): plates; "Notes and Comments: An Architectural Comparison," *Architectural Record* 23 (May 1908): 409-12; and *McKim, Mead & White Monograph*, plates 259-60.

62. For an unbuilt medieval, primarily Alsatian design see "Combined House and Office, C.P.H. Gilbert, Architect," *American Architect and Building News* 72 (May 18, 1901): 55, plate.

63. "House of I.D. Fletcher, Esq., New York, N.Y., C.P.H. Gilbert, Architect," *American Architect and Building News* 67 (March 31, 1900): plates; and "Residence, Isaac D. Fletcher, Fifth Ave. and Seventy-ninth

St., New York," *Architecture* 1 (January 15, 1900): 14.

64. "Residence, F.W. Woolworth, Fifth Avenue and Eightieth Street, C.P.H. Gilbert, Architect," *Architecture* 4 (November 15, 1901): 304-06; "The Modern American Residence," *Architectural Record* 16 (October 1904): 297-405; and Schuyler, "Billionaire District": 693-95.

65. "A Fifth Avenue Home," *Real Estate Record and Guide* 80 (December 28, 1907): 1059; "Three Fifth Avenue Mansions," *Real Estate Record and Guide* 83 (May 1, 1909): 852; and *Felix Warburg Residence*, portfolio of photographs in the collection of Avery Library, Columbia University.

66. "A Fifth Avenue Home," *Real Estate Record and Guide:* 1059.

67. "House of F.E. [sic] Converse, West [sic] 78th Street, New York, C.P.H. Gilbert, Architect," *Architects' and Builders' Magazine* 1 (January 1900): 127; and "House of E.C. Converse, Esq., 3 East Seventy-eighth Street, New York, N.Y., C.P.H. Gilbert, Architect," *American Architect and Building News* 67 (February 24, 1900): plate. The small house he built for Mrs. Allene Teid Nichols was more vigorously composed with a full-width, four-story bay and central elliptically arched entrance. Landmarks Preservation Commission, City of New York, *Upper East Side Historic District Designation Report* (New York: 1981), 183.

68. "House of Edward Thaw, Esq., East 89th Street, New York, N.Y., Israels & Harder, Architects," *American Architect and Building News* 87 (April 22, 1905): plate.

69. Shiras Campbell, "An Excellent Gothic Residence, A Carefully Studied Solution of the Problem Presented by the Limitations of a City Lot," *Architectural Record* 29 (April 1911): 289-90, plates.

70. Herbert Croly, "Rich Men and their Houses," *Architectural Record* 12 (May 1902): 27-32.

71. Croly, "Rich Men and their Houses": 30-31. Also see C. Matlack Price, "The City House Palatial: A Study in Architectural Evolution," *International Studio* 54 (January 1915): LXXXII-LXXXVI; and "Current Architectural Press," *American Architect* 107 (February 10, 1915): 91-93.

72. Herbert Croly and Henry W. Desmond, "The Work of Messrs. McKim, Mead & White," *Architectural Record* 20 (September 1906): 153-246. Also see Gordon S. Parker, "The Work of Three Great Architects," *World's Work* 12 (October 1906): 8051-66; and Royal Cortissoz, "Some Critical Reflections on the Architectural Genius of Charles F. McKim," *Brickbuilder* 19 (February 1910): 26-37.

73. "Residence for Henry C. Taylor, 3 East Seventy-first Street, New York, McKim, Mead & White, Architects," *Architecture and Building* 28 (March 19, 1898): plate; and *McKim, Mead & White Monograph*, plates 80-82.

74. Desmond and Croly, "The Work of Messrs. McKim, Mead & White": 228; Gordon S. Parker, "The Work of Three Great Architects": 8051-66; "Lest We Forget, The Kane House," *Architecture* 62 (September 1930): 171; *McKim, Mead & White Monograph*, plates 285-88; and Roth, *Urban Architecture of McKim, Mead & White*, 582.

75. "After the residence had been designed," Gordon Parker reported, "a search was made for some stone closely resembling the Roman travertine of which the Colissum, St. Peter's, and the Farnese are built." Parker, "Three Great Architects": 8059.

76. "Residence, Joseph Pulitzer, 9 E. 73d St., New York," *Architecture* 7 (February 1903): plate XVI; "Residence of Joseph Pulitzer, Nos. 7-15 East 73d St., New York City," *Architectural Record* 14 (November 1913): 328; *McKim, Mead & White Monograph*, plates 180-82; and Roth, *Urban Architecture of McKim, Mead & White*, 574-77.

77. Leland Roth, "McKim, Mead & White Reappraised," *McKim, Mead & White Monograph* (1973), 10-57.

78. William Adams Delano, "No. 100 East Seventieth Street," *New York Architect* 2 (June 1908). George Brewster built a palazzo designed by Trowbridge & Livingston one block away at the northwest corner of Park Avenue and Seventy-first Street. "Some New Townhouses in Manhattan," *Real Estate Record and Guide* 88 (September 16, 1911): 383.

79. Delano, "No. 100 East Seventieth Street."

80. "Residence, Payne Whitney, 972 Fifth Avenue, New York, McKim, Mead & White, Architects," *Architecture* 21 (April 1910): 52-53, plates XXXIII-XXXVII; and *McKim, Mead & White Monograph*, plates 289-92. Also see "Residence of Wm. C. Whitney, New York, McKim, Mead & White, Architects," *Architects' and Builders' Magazine* 2 (June 1901): 321-25; "Some Recent American Designs," *Architectural Record* 10 (April 1901): 406-24; and *McKim, Mead & White Monograph*, plates 144-45.

81. "House of E.J. Berwind, Esq., East 64th St. and Fifth Avenue, Nathan C. Mellon [sic], Architect," *American Architect and Building News* 65 (July 1, 1899): plates. Also see Mellen's "Residence, New York City, Carrère & Hastings [sic] Architects," *Inland Architect and News Record* 37 (June 1901): 48, plate. Another Italianate design was "Residence of Mrs. Thompson, Madison Avenue and 41st Street, New York City, Montrose W. Morris, Architect," *Architectural Record* 19 (January 1900): 324.

82. "Residence of Mrs. James E. Martin, 803 Fifth Avenue, Henry F. Kilburn, Architect," *Architecture and Building* 22 (February 23, 1895): plate; "Residences of Wm. V. Brokaw and Mrs. H. Bramhall Gilbert, Nos. 825 and 826 Fifth Avenue," *Architecture and Building* 24 (February 8, 1896): plate; and "Residence of Mrs. Catherine L. Kernochan, 824 Fifth Avenue," *Architecture and Building* 25 (August 29, 1896): plate. 826 Fifth Avenue was next to the Berwind house.

83. "Residence, No. 9 East Sixty-eighth Street," *Architecture and Building* 26 (June 5, 1897): plate. This is actually Number 5, built for John J. Emery in 1894-96. *Upper East Side Historic District*, 368-69. Number 8 was built by the same architects for Anna S. Colby in 1892-93. *Upper East Side Historic District*, 403.

84. "Two Houses, Nos. 6 and 8 East 76th Street," *Architecture and Building* 29 (October 15, 1898): plate.

85. "House of Mr. Isaac Stern, Schickel & Ditmars, Architects," *Architects' and Builders' Magazine* 3 (May 1902): 357-68. Also see "No. 6 East 79th Street, New York, N.Y., Barney & Chapman, Architects," *American Architect and Building News* 72 (April 13, 1901): plate; "House, 6 East 79th Street, New York City, Barney & Chapman, Architects," *Brickbuilder* 10 (April 1901): plate; "House of D.C. Blair, Esq., 6 East 61st St., New York, N.Y.," *American Architect and Building News* 74 (October 5, 1901): plate; "The Dwelling of A. Lanfear Norrie, No. 15 East 84th Street, New York City, Renwick, Aspinwall & Owen, Architects," *Architectural Record* 14 (December 1903): 453-61; and "Residence, New York City, Grosvenor Atterbury, Architect," *Inland Architect and News Record* 42 (January 1904): plate.

86. "House for Hon. Levi P. Morton, Fifth Avenue, New York, N.Y., McKim, Mead & White, Architects," *Brickbuilder* 11 (January 1902): plate; and Roth, *Urban Architecture of McKim, Mead & White*, 450-51.

87. "An Astor House," *Real Estate Record and Guide* 79 (June 1, 1907): 1061; "Residence, 844 Fifth Avenue, New York, *Architectural Record* 21 (June 1907): 468-72; "House at 844 Fifth Avenue," *Architectural Review* 17 (March 1910): plate; *Monograph of the Work of Charles A. Platt* (New York: Architectural Book Publishing Co., 1913), 166-67; and Keith Morgan, "Charles A. Platt, The Artist as Architect" (an unpublished ms.): 87.

88. Morgan, "Charles Platt": 87. Platt's Mrs. James Roosevelt house (47-49 East Sixty-fifth Street, 1907) was Italian Renaissance with English influence. *Monograph of the Works of Charles A. Platt*, 163-64; and Morgan, "Charles Platt": 85-86.

89. "Residence, John S. Phipps, 6 E. 87th St., New York, Grosvenor Atterbury, Architect," *Architecture* 9 (January 1904): plate IV; and "Residence at 6 E. 87th St., N.Y.C." *New York Architect* 3 (August 1909): plate.

90. "House, 14 East 71st Street, New York, Messrs. York & Sawyer, Architects," *American Architect* 105 (March 4, 1914): plate; and *Upper East Side Historic District*, 537.

91. "Portfolio of Current Architecture," *Architectural Record* 39 (February 1916): 163-67; and *Upper East Side Historic District*, 707.

92. Ralph M. Calder, "Sgraffito, A Modern Revival of an Ancient Art," *American Architect* 106 (September 9, 1914): 145-48; "Art Gallery, Thos. F. Ryan, 3 East 67th Street, New York," *Architecture* 32 (August 1915): plate XCVIII; and Curtis Channing Blake, *The Architecture of Carrère & Hastings* (Ph.D. diss., Columbia University, 1976): 182.

93. "House of Thomas Newbold, 15 E. 79th Street, N.Y., McKim, Mead & White, Architects," *American Architect* 113 (March 6, 1918): plate 77; "Residence of Thomas Newbold, New York, McKim, Mead & White, Architects," *Architectural Record* 46 (August 1919): 166-68; "House of Thomas Newbold, 15 East 79th Street, New York, McKim, Mead & White, Architects," *American Architect* 116 (December 10, 1919): plates 196-98; and *McKim, Mead & White Monograph*, plates 397-97A.

94. Leon V. Solon, "The Residence of Otto H. Kahn, Esq., New York, J. Armstrong Stenhouse, Architect," *Architectural Record* 46 (August 1919): 99-114.

95. Herbert Croly, "The Contemporary New York Residence," *Architectural Record* 712.

96. Schuyler, "Billionaire District": 683.

97. "Preliminary Sketch for the Facade of House of Richard Hoe," *Architectural Review* 1 (August 1892): plate LXI; "Elevation of House for Richard M. Hoe, Esq., New York," *Architectural Review* 2 (February 13, 1893): 20, plate XII; "House of R.M. Hoe, Esq., 11 East 71st St., N.Y.," *American Architect and Building News* 47 (March 2, 1895): plate 1001; "The Work of Messrs. Carrère & Hastings," *Architectural Record* 27 (January 1910): 1-112; and Blake, *Carrère & Hastings*, 175-77.

98. "House for Dr. C.A. Herter," *American Architect and Building News* 39 (February 25, 1893): plate; "Residence of Dr. C.A. Herter, 819 Madison Avenue, New York," *Architecture and Building* 22 (January 26, 1895): plate; "Work of Carrère & Hastings," *Architectural Record* 34; and Blake, *Carrère & Hastings*, 177.

99. "Principal Facade, Carrère & Hastings Architects," *American*

Architect and Building News 42 (November 18, 1893): plate; "Part Elevation of House for H.T. Sloane, Esq., New York, Messrs. Carrère & Hastings, Architects," *Architectural Review* 3 (August 1894): plate; "Residence of Henry T. Sloane, 9 East Seventy-second Street, New York, Carrère & Hastings, Architects," *Architecture and Building* 26 (April 10, 1897): plates; "House, Formerly of Mrs. Sloane, Seventy-second Street, New York, N.Y., Carrère & Hastings, Architects," *American Architect and Building News* 64 (April 15, 1899): plate; Herbert Croly, "The Contemporary Metropolitan Residence," *Real Estate Record and Guide* 73 (June 11, 1904): 1447-62; "Work of Carrère & Hastings," *Architectural Record*: 35; and Blake, *Carrère & Hastings*, 177-79.

100. "Editorial," *Architectural Review* 4 (November 1, 1897): 49.

101. "Residence for Mrs. Ernesto G. Fabbri, New York City, Haydel & Shepard, Architects," *Architectural Review* 6 (February 1899): plate XII; "Residence, Mrs. Ernesto G. Fabbri, 11 E. 62nd St., New York, Haydel & Sheppard [sic], Architects," *Architecture* 1 (June 15, 1900): 217; and "Residence of Mrs. E.G. Fabbre [sic], Haydel & Shepard, Architects," *Inland Architect and News Record* 37 (June 1901): plate.

102. "Residence of M. Newborg, Esq., New York, N.Y., J.H. Freedlander, Architect," *Architectural Review* 10 (April 1903): plates XXIII-XXIV; and "A New York House of Today, The Residence of Mr. M. Newborg, J.H. Freedlander, Architect," *Architectural Record* 17 (May 1905): 401-09.

103. "Stable and Artist Studio, 121-123 East 63rd Street, New York, Trowbridge & Livingston, Architects," *Architectural Record* 11 (October 1901): 721. Also see "Stable for M.J. Sullivan, New York, Trowbridge & Livingston, Architects," *Inland Architect and News Record* 41 (February 1903): plate; "The Riding Stable of Frank Gould, 57th Street, New York City, York & Sawyer, Architects," *Architectural Record* 12 (June 1902): 228; "Stable, New York City, Warren & Wetmore, Architects," *Inland Architect and News Record* 42 (November 1903): plate; and "The Ver Meer Studios, 111 E. 66th St., New York City, E.R. Bossage, and Butler & Rodman, Associated Architects," *Brickbuilder* 21 (March 1912): plate 31.

104. "77th St. Elevation, Residence, Hon. W.A. Clark, 77th St. and Fifth Ave., New York, Lord Hewlett & Hull and K.M. Murchison, Jr., Associated Architects," *Architecture* 9 (May 1904): plate XXXV-XLI; "Preliminary Study of Billiard and Smoking Room," *Architectural Record* 11 (July 1904): plate XLI; Charles De Kay, "The Future of Metals in Decoration, Part 3," *Architectural Record* 16 (August 1904): 142-47; "Architectural Aberration No. 21, The House of Senator Clark," *Architectural Record* 19 (January 1906): 27-30; and "The Clark Residence," *Architecture* 16 (September 15, 1907): 157, 159, plates LXXVI-LXXX.

105. "House of Senator Clark," *Architectural Record*: 30.

106. "House of Senator Clark," *Architectural Record*: 30.

107. "Clark Residence," *Architecture*: 16. C.P.H. Gilbert's J.R. De Lamar residence, though not in the Billionaire's District but on Murray Hill, at the northeast corner of Thirty-seventh Street and Madison Avenue, was smaller, less elaborate, but an equally robust Modern French palace. Unlike the Clark mansion, the De Lamar house had a careful composition of belt courses and cornices which maintained a degree of civility toward the brownstone rows which flanked it. "The Residence of J.R. De Lamar, Madison Avenue and 37th Street, C.P.H. Gilbert, Architect," *Architectural Record* 17 (June 1905): 508. Bruce Price designed a Modern French interpretation of the château. "Design for a City House, Bruce Price, Architect," *American Architect and Building News* 81 (August 1, 1903): plate. Also see "Residence of Dr. Lawrence, New York City, Wm. Albert Swasey, Architect, St. Louis," *Inland Architect and News Record* 40 (December 1902): plate.

108. "Current Periodicals," *Architectural Review* 8 (September 1901): 108-10. Also see "Residence of E.K. Dunham, New York City, Carrère & Hastings, Architects," *Inland Architect and News Record* 38 (July 1901): plate; "The Architect's Portfolio of Recent American Architecture," *Architectural Record* 11 (October 1901): 723; "House of E.K. Dunham, Esq., 35 East 68th St., New York, N.Y.," *American Architect and Building News* 83 (January 23, 1904): plate; and Blake, *Carrère & Hastings*, 180-81.

109. "Architect's Portfolio," *Architectural Record*: 723.

110. "Residence, L.H. Lapham, 15 West 56th St., Carrère & Hastings, Architects," *Architecture* 7 (March 1903): plate XVIII.

111. "Residence, 8 E. 83rd St., New York, Janes & Leo, Architects, Jas. A. Frame & Sons, Builders," *Architecture* 7 (February 1903): plate XV. Another speculative house is described in "The New Mansion, No. 991 Fifth Avenue," *Real Estate Record and Guide* 66 (December 22, 1900): 865-66. Also see "Entrance to House of H.T. Haggin, Esq., 441 Madison Ave., N.Y.," Janes & Leo, Architects," *American Architect and Building News* 72 (June 22, 1901): plate.

112. "Residence, George Q. Palmer, 1 East 73rd Street, New York, Palmer & Hornbostel, Architects," *Architecture* 9 (April 1904): plate XXVIII.

113. "Residence, Stuart Duncan, 1 East 75th St., New York, C.P.H. Gilbert, Architect," *Architecture* 10 (September 1904): plate LXIX; and "House of Stuart Duncan, Esq., 1 East 75th Street, New York, N.Y., C.P.H. Gilbert, Architect," *American Architect and Building News* 89 (June 9, 1906): 90-91. Also see "Residence, 85th Street, New York City, Howard & Cauldwell, Architects," *Brickbuilder* 7 (October 1898): plate 77; "Residence, George Crocker, Fifth Avenue and Sixty-fourth St., New York, Brite & Bacon, Architects," *Architecture* 1 (January 15, 1900): 19; "House of F.L. Stetson, Esq., 4 E. Seventy-fourth Street, New York, N.Y., Alexander M. Welch, Architect," *American Architect and Building News* 67 (March 3, 1900): plate; "No. 32 East 36th Street, New York, N.Y., George A. Freeman, Architect," *American Architect and Building News* 70 (November 10, 1900): plate; "Residence for B.A. Williams, New York City, Van Vleck & Goldsmith, Architects," *Inland Architect and News Record* 42 (September 1903): plate; "Residence, New York City, Van Vleck & Goldsmith, Architects," *Inland Architect and News Record* 43 (February 1904): plate; "House of Mrs. C.J. Coulter, 6 West 48th Street, New York, N.Y., C.I. Berg, Architect," *American Architect and Building News* 83 (March 26, 1904): plate; and "The Town House of a Physician, Lord & Hewlett, Architects," *Indoors and Out* 1 (January 1906): 202.

114. "Residence, Mrs. Fred'k Edey, 10 West 56th St., Warren & Wetmore, Architects," *Architecture* 7 (March 1903): plate XIX.

115. "Residence, G.H. Warren, 924 Fifth Avenue, New York, Warren & Wetmore, Architects," *Architecture* 11 (May 1905): plate XLI. For other Modern French designs by Warren & Wetmore, see "Residence of William Pendleton, New York City, Warren & Wetmore, Architects," *Inland Architect and News Record* 38 (July 1901): plates; and "Residence, New York, Warren & Wetmore, Architects," *Inland Architect and News Record* 42 (November 1903): plate.

116. "Residence, O.G. Jennings, 7 East Seventy-second St., New York, Ernest Flagg and W.B. Chambers, Architects," *Architecture* 2 (August 15, 1900): 292; "The Residence of O.G. Jennings, Esq., 7 East 72d Street, New York City, Architects, Ernest Flagg and Walter B. Chambers," *Architectural Record* 10 (October 1900): 213-24; and H.W. Desmond, "The Works of Ernest Flagg," *Architectural Record* 11 (April 1902): 11-104.

117. *Upper East Side Historic District,* 346. Flagg's nearby Cortlandt F. Bishop house at 15 East Sixty-seventh Street (1907) had severe rectilinear details relieved by only a few decorative touches including a cartouche above the entrance and swag panels at the windows and roof. "House No. 15 East Sixty-seventh Street, New York, N.Y.," *American Architect and Building News* 89 (June 2, 1906): 188, plate; and *Upper East Side Historic District,* 332.

118. "Front Elevation, Residence for Charles Scribner, Esq., Ernest Flagg, Architect," *Architectural Year Book* 1 (1912): 259; and *Upper East Side Historic District,* 279.

119. Hunt's Schieffelin house was a more robust example of the Modern French taste. Hunt treated the three-bay facade as quite flat except for the elaborate brackets supporting a second-story balcony and the lushly modelled carving between the pedimented dormers. The continuation of limestone and red brick rendered an otherwise grand composition more intimate. "Nos. 5 and 7 East Sixty-sixth Street," *Real Estate Record and Guide* 64 (October 28, 1899): 633-35; "House No. 5 East Sixty-sixth Street, New York, N.Y.," *American Architect and Building News* 71 (February 23, 1901): 63, plates; and *Real Estate Record and Guide* 73 (June 11, 1904): 1451.

120. "Works of Carrère & Hastings," *Architectural Record*: 109; and Blake, *Carrère & Hastings*, 180-81.

121. "Residence, 32 East 51st Street, New York City, Architects, Charles Brendon & Co.," *Architectural Record* 11 (January 1902): 95.

122. "39 East Seventy-seventh Street, Charles Brendon, Architect," *American Architect and Building News* 81 (September 17, 1903): plate; and *Upper East Side Historic District,* 851.

123. "Residence, Albert Gould Jennings, 2 East 82d St., New York, Ernest Flagg, Architect," *Architecture* 7 (March 1903): plate XVII. Albert Gould Jennings's relation to Oliver Gould Jennings is unknown. According to the Office for Metropolitan History, records at the New York City Department of Buildings and other sources indicate that the house was designed not by Flagg but rather William Schickel or Welch, Smith & Provot.

124. "Residence of Mrs. Charles H. Senff, New York City, Carrère & Hastings, Architects," *Architectural Review* 8 (August 1901): 104; "Works of Carrère & Hastings," *Architectural Record*: 64; and Blake, *Carrère & Hastings*, 185-86.

125. Flagg's R. Fulton Cutting house on the southwest corner of Madison Avenue and Sixty-seventh Street, built in 1897, was a limestone interpretation of the late French Renaissance. "Residence for R. Fulton Cutting, Esq., 67th Street and Madison Avenue, New York City, Ernest Flagg, Architect," *Brickbuilder* 6 (October 1897): 233, plates 85-87; and "Residence of Mr. R. Fulton Cutting, Southwest Corner Sixty-seventh

Street and Madison Avenue, New York, Ernest Flagg, Architect," *Architecture and Building* 28 (March 12, 1898): plate. Also see "Residence, Upper Fifth Avenue, New York City, Janes & Leo, Architects," *Architecture and Building* 30 (June 24, 1899): plate.

126. "An Epoch Making Mansion," *Real Estate Record and Guide* 67 (supplement to March 9, 1901); and "A House of Jacob H. Schiff, Esq., 96 [sic] Fifth Ave., New York, N.Y., Charles C. Thain, Architect," *American Architect and Building News* 83 (January 23, 1904): plate; "The House of Jacob H. Schiff," *Architectural Record* 18 (July 1905): 33-39; and "The House of Mr. Jacob H. Schiff," *Real Estate Record and Guide* 76 (July 1, 1905): 3.

127. "An Epoch Making Mansion," *Real Estate Record and Guide.*

128. "House of J.F.D. Lanier, Esq., 123 East 35th St., New York, N.Y., Hoppin, Koen & Huntington, Architects," *American Architect and Building News* 86 (December 24, 1904): plates; and "Some Country and City Residences by Hoppin & Koen, Architects," *New York Architect* 5 (July 1911): 149-56.

129. "Residences by Hoppin & Koen," *New York Architect:* 152. Also see "A House on Fifty-seventh Street, New York City, Hoppin, Koen & Huntington, Architects," *Architectural Review* 13 (July 1906): plate XLVI; and "R.T. Wilson, Jr., 15 East 57th St., New York, Hoppin, Koen & Huntington, Architects," *Architecture* 15 (April 1907): plate XXXV.

130. "Residences by Hoppin & Koen," *New York Architect:* 152.

131. "The 'Marble Twins,' 645-647 Fifth Ave., New York, Hunt & Hunt, Architects," *Architecture* 11 (June 1905): plate XLIX.

132. "The Residence of Mr. Geo. L. Rives, Carrère & Hastings, Architects," *Architectural Record* 26 (August 1909): 107-12. Also see "House for George L. Rives, Esq., New York, N.Y.," *American Architect and Building News* 93 (May 6, 1908): plate; and "A Residential Facade Worthy of Imitation," *Real Estate Record and Guide* 81 (August 21, 1909): 342.

133. "Residence, M. Orme Wilson, 3 East 64th St., New York," *Architecture* 10 (July 1904): plate LV.

134. "Residence, J.A. Burden, 7 East 91st St., New York, Warren, Wetmore & Morgan, Architects," *Architecture* 11 (May 1905): plate XL.

135. Blake, *Carrère & Hastings,* 182. Also see "House for Mrs. J.H. Hammond, East 91st Street, New York," *Architectural Review* 9 (May 1902): plate XXII; "Residence, John H. Hammond, 9 East 91st Street, New York, Carrère & Hastings, Architects," *Architecture* 9 (January 1904): plate II; and Blake, *Carrère & Hastings,* 186-89.

136. Blake, *Carrère & Hastings,* 53.

137. "Work of Carrère & Hastings," *Architectural Record:* 91, 96.

138. "Work of Carrère & Hastings," *Architectural Record:* 2.

139. "Work of Carrère & Hastings," *Architectural Record:* 12.

140. "Residence, E.S. Harkness, Cor. Fifth Ave. and 75th St., New York, Hale & Rogers, Architects," *Architecture* 19 (March 1901): plate XXV; "A Fifth Avenue Mansion," *Architectural Record* 27 (May 1910): 382-400; "A Dignified Type of City House Residence No. 1 East 75th Street, New York, James Gamble Rogers (of Hale & Rogers) Architect," *New York Architect* 5 (March 1911): plates; and "Residence, No. 1 East 75th Street, New York, James Gamble Rogers (of Hale & Rogers), Architect," *Architectural Year Book* 1 (1912): 101-03. For a more Italian design see "Proposed House for Mr. J.B. Haggin, New York, City, Copeland & Dole, Architects," *Architectural Review* 13 (March 1906): plate XI. This house on the former site of the Progress Club was never built. Haggin's estate sold the lot to the architect Goldwin Starrett, who built a large apartment house. See Lawrence B. Elliman, "Many Large Transactions on Fifth Avenue," *Real Estate Record and Guide* 99 (February 3, 1917): 53, 76.

141. "Residence, Henry Phipps, Fifth Ave. and 87th St., New York, Trowbridge & Livingston, Architects," *Architecture* 12 (December 1905): plate CII; and "Phipps Residence, 5th Avenue and 87th Street, N.Y. City," *The Architects and Their Work* 1 (November 7, 1908): plate VIII.

142. "A Dignified Type of City Residence," *New York Architect.*

143. "New Palaces on Fifth Avenue," *Real Estate Record and Guide* 85 (June 4, 1910): 1194-95. Also see "Mr. Gary's New House on Fifth Avenue," *Real Estate Record and Guide* 86 (October 1, 1910): 522. Rowhouses were rarely built in the Modern Renaissance style. See, however, "The City House To Date, The Residence of J.W. Herbert, Esq., Harry Allan Jacobs, Architect," *Architectural Record* 33 (March 1913): 205-16; later published as "The Residence of Mrs. Frederick Lewisohn, Harry Allan Jacobs, Architect," *Architecture* 41 (January 1920): 9, plates X, XII; and John Taylor Boyd, "Residence of William McNair, Esq., H. Van Buren Magonigle, Architect," *Architectural Record* 41 (May 1917): 387-402. The Herbert/Lewisohn house was at 835 Fifth Avenue, and the McNair house at 5 East Seventy-ninth Street.

144. "Residence, Edwin Gould, 936 Fifth Avenue, New York, Carrère & Hastings, Architects," *Architecture* 23 (April 1911): plate XXXV.

145. "Three Fifth Avenue Mansions," *Real Estate Record and Guide* 83 (May 1, 1909): 852; and "Residence, George J. Gould, Fifth Ave. and 67th St., New York, Horace Trumbauer, Architect," *Architecture* 20 (October 1909): 145-46, plates XCI-XCII.

146. "Residence, George J. Gould," *Architecture:* 145-46.

147. "New Palaces on Fifth Avenue," *Real Estate Record and Guide:* 1194-95; "Residence, J.B. Duke, 1 East 78th St., New York, Horace Trumbauer, Architect," *Architecture* 27 (April 1913): plates XXXV-VI; and "House at Seventy-eighth Street and Fifth Avenue, New York, Mr. Horace Trumbauer, Architect," *American Architect* 107 (April 7, 1915): plates.

148. "Henry Clay Frick Residence, New York City, Thomas Hastings, Architect," *Architecture* 30 (November 1914): 251-52, plates CXXV-CXXIX; and Blake, *Carrère & Hastings,* 195-200.

149. In 1935, John Russell Pope rebuilt the house as a museum and research center, remodelling the rooms of the house and adding the Frick Art Reference Library at 10 East Seventy-first Street. Blake, *Carrère & Hastings,* 199-200.

150. "House, C. Ledyard Blair, 2 East 70th St., New York," *Architecture* 35 (January 1917): plates IV-VI; and Blake, *Carrère & Hastings,* 200-02.

151. Carrère & Hastings resisted the Modern Renaissance trend in Manhattan residential design when they revived the polychrome French Renaissance style in the William Starr Miller house, built in 1913 on the southeast corner of Fifth Avenue and Eighty-sixth Street. The facades were Beaux-Arts interpretations of the Pavilion du Roi in the Place Royal, designed by Jean Robelin in 1605. The brick and stone house had lost the Cartouche style ornament of Hastings's earlier Charles Senff house, but the almost equal ratio of window opening to wall surface, the busy quoin pattern that framed those windows, and the polychromatic contrast between vertical and horizontal elements combined to form an elevation which was unusually active for the decade. Blake, *Carrère & Hastings,* 193-94.

152. "Architectural Criticism," *Architecture* 24 (October 15, 1911): 145.

153. Charles Moore, *The Life and Times of Charles Follen McKim* (New York: Houghton Mifflin, 1929; Da Capo Press, 1973), 41.

154. *McKim, Mead & White Monograph,* plate 16.

155. *McKim, Mead & White Monograph,* plate 121.

156. "Near the New University Club," *Real Estate Record and Guide* 61 (January 22, 1898): 142-43; "House for James J. Goodwin, Esq., 54th Street, New York, McKim, Mead & White, Architects," *Brickbuilder* 7 (May 1898): plate 34; Russell Sturgis, "The Art Gallery of the New York Streets," *Architectural Record* 10 (July 1900): 95-112; *McKim, Mead & White Monograph,* 120-21; Philip Lippincott Goodwin, *Rooftrees, or the Architectural History of an American Family* (Philadelphia: J.B. Lippincott & Co., 1933); and Roth, *Urban Architecture of McKim, Mead & White,* 456.

White built the Prescott Hall Butler house on the corner of Park Avenue and Thirty-fifth Street in 1895-97. The Butler house was a variation of McKim's John F. Andrews house on the corner of Commonwealth Avenue and Hereford Street in Boston (1883-88) which in turn was based on the double-bowed Women's Club by Alexander Parris (1818). Both McKim, Mead & White houses had oval bays well suited to corner sites on Commonwealth and Park avenues. Coincidentally, the Butler house was converted to the Women's City Club in 1919. "House for Prescott Hall Butler, Esq., New York City," *Brickbuilder* 7 (April 1898): plates 29-30; "House of Mr. Butler and Mr. Guthrie, Park Avenue, New York, N.Y.," *American Architect and Building News* 64 (June 10, 1899): plate; "The Women's City Club, 22 Park Avenue, New York," *Architecture* 39 (June 1919): plates LXXXVI-LXXXIX; and Roth, *Urban Architecture of McKim, Mead & White,* 449-50. Also see "Residence of J. Hamden Robb, 23 Park Avenue, Corner Thirty-fifth Street, New York City, McKim, Mead & White, Architects," *Architecture and Building* 25 (July 4, 1896): plate; and "Residence of Mrs. William B. Ogden, No. 266 Madison Avenue, New York, Peabody & Stearns, Architects," *Architecture and Building* 25 (August 8, 1896): plate.

157. Sturgis, "Art Gallery of the New York Street": 96.

158. "House of Andrew Carnegie, Esq., New York, N.Y., Babb, Cook & Willard, Architects," *American Architect and Building News* 66 (December 16, 1899): plates; "Residence of Andrew Carnegie, New York City, Babb, Cook & Willard, Architects," *Inland Architect and News Record* 40 (December 1902): plates; "Residence, Andrew Carnegie, Fifth Avenue and 91st Street, New York, Babb, Cook & Willard, Architects," *Architecture* 7 (January 1903): 6-7; plates I-VII; and "House of Andrew Carnegie, Esq., Fifth Ave., New York, N.Y., Babb, Cook & Willard, Architects," *American Architect and Building News* 81 (July 18, 1903): plates.

159. Schuyler, "Billionaire District": 683.

160. Paul Goldberger, *The City Observed: New York* (New York: Vintage Books, 1979), 256.

161. "The New Residence of Hon. Elihu Root," *Indoors and Out* 1 (March 1906): 250-86. Also see "Residence, Elihu Root, 733 Park Ave., New York," *Architecture* 13 (February 1906): plate; and Blake, *Carrère & Hastings,* 189-91.

162. "New Residence of Hon. Elihu Root," *Indoors and Out:* 286.

163. "A Residence at the Southwest Corner of Madison Avenue and Seventy-eighth Street, New York City, Designed by McKim, Mead & White, Architects," *House & Garden* 1 (November 1901): 10-12; Herbert Croly, "Renovation of the Brownstone District," *Architectural Record* 13 (June 1903): 555-71; "No. 28 East Seventy-eighth Street, Corner Madison Avenue, New York, N.Y., McKim, Mead & White, Architects," *American Architect and Building News* 89 (May 12, 1906): plate; and *McKim, Mead & White Monograph*, 162-63.

164. See Montgomery Schuyler, "The New New York House," *Architectural Record* 19 (February 1906): 83-103. For the Davis house see "Residence, John W.A. Davis, 65th Street and Lexington Avenue, New York, E. Outwater, Architect," *Architecture* 10 (December 1904): plate CII.

165. "Residence, Mrs. Willard Straight, 1130 Fifth Avenue, New York, Delano & Aldrich, Architects," *Architecture* 41 (March 1920): plates XXXIII-XXXVIII.

166. Schuyler, "New New York House": 89.

167. Schuyler, "New New York House": 86.

168. See A.C. David, "Recent Brickwork in New York," *Architectural Record* 13 (February 1903): 144-56.

169. "Residence, Robert McA. Lloyd, 133 East 62nd Street, New York, Foster, Gade & Graham, Architects," *Architecture* 9 (January 1904): plate VIII. Also see "Residence, G.L. McAlpin, 9 East 90th Street, New York, Geo. Keister, Architect," *Architecture* 9 (February 1904): plate XVI; "Residence, R.D. Graham, 153 East 64th St., New York, Foster, Gade & Graham, Architects," *Architecture* 10 (September 1904): plate LXX; and "31, 33 and 35 East 51st Street, York & Sawyer, Architects, New York City Houses," *Brickbuilder* 17 (September 1908): 195.

170. Schuyler, "New New York House": 89. A number of the larger Georgian townhouses bypassed American precedents in favor of English models, resulting in grandly Edwardian compositions that would have been at home in Bloomsbury or parts of Belgravia. Clinton & Russell's pair of houses at 18 and 20 East Eighty-fourth Street, and their similar but not identical house next door at Number 16, epitomize the English approach with their sunken areaways, continuous iron balconies at the parlor floor and extremely flat detailing. "Houses at 16, 18 and 20 East 84th Street, Clinton & Russell, Architects," *Brickbuilder* 10 (October 1901): plate. Charles Platt replaced two brownstone houses with a Georgian house for F.S. Lee at 125 East Sixty-fifth Street of 1904-05 that Schuyler found less old New York than a transplant from Philadelphia. The high iron fence of the Lee house and its batteries of wooden window shutters caused Schuyler to waggishly remark that the front looked as though it was "impregnable against a street mob." Schuyler, "New New York Houses, East Side," *Architectural Record* 30 (November 1911): 451-74. Also see "The House of Mr. Frederick S. Lee, New York City," *Architectural Record* 20 (November 1906): 427-36; "125 East 65th Street, Charles Platt, Architect," *Brickbuilder* 17 (September 1908): 190; and Morgan, "Charles Platt," 82-85.

171. "House, John T. Pratt, 7 East 61st Street, Chas. A. Platt, Architect," *Architecture* 35 (June 1917): plates XCV-CI; and Morgan, "Charles Platt," 8.

172. "House of P.L. Ford, Esq., 37 East 77th Street, New York, N.Y., Henry Rutgers Marshall, Architect," *American Architect and Building News* 75 (March 22, 1902): plates; "Great American Houses: Residence of Mrs. Paul Leicester Ford, New York City, Henry Rutgers Marshall, Architect," *Architectural Record* 14 (July 1903): 62-69; and *Upper East Side Historic District,* 850. Also see "House, 5 East 63rd Street, New York City, Heins & La Farge, Architects," *Brickbuilder* 11 (May 1902): plate; and "New York City Houses," *Brickbuilder* 17 (September 1908): 158.

173. "A City Residence, Robertson & Potter, Architects," *American Architect and Building News* 78 (December 27, 1902): plate; "Residence, Hugh D. Auchincloss, 33 East 67th Street, New York, Robertson & Potter, Architects," *Architecture* 9 (January 1904): plate VII; and *Upper East Side Historic District,* 343. Their much narrower Elizabeth S.C. Potter house of 1903-04 at 123 East Seventy-third was more richly detailed and more confidently Georgian. "Residence, R. Burnside Potter, 123 E. 73d St., New York City, R. Burnside Potter, Architect," *Architecture* 11 (March 1905): 42-44.

174. "Residence, Charles Dana Gibson, 127 East 73rd Street, New York, McKim, Mead & White, Architects," *Architectural Record* 15 (February 1904): 172-79, plate; "Residence, Charles Dana Gibson, 127 East 73d St., New York," *Architecture* 9 (March 1904): 43; Desmond and Croly, "McKim, Mead & White": 207; *McKim, Mead & White Monograph*, 191-92; and Roth, *Urban Architecture of McKim, Mead & White*, 588-89. McKim, Mead & White's Thomas B. Clarke House boasted a two-story oriel window reminiscent of Richard Norman Shaw's New Zealand Chambers. "No. 22 East 35th Street, New York, N.Y.," *American Architect and Building News* 87 (February 4, 1905): plate.

175. See "66 East 81st Street, Pickering & Walker, Architects," *Brickbuilder* 17 (September 1908): 207; and *Upper East Side Historic District:* 210 for the Ellen W. Turnbull house at 127 East Sixty-fourth Street. Also see "House of Joseph W. Burden, Esq., 108 East 78th Street, New York," *American Architect* 100 (October 4, 1911): plate.

176. "House for J. Langdon Erving, Esq., 62 East 80th Street, New York, N.Y., Messrs. Albro & Lindeberg, Architects," *American Architect and Building News* 93 (May 6, 1908): plates; and Schuyler, "New New York Houses, East Side": 474.

177. For Ruth L. Sterling at 19 East Seventy-seventh Street, see Schuyler, "New New York Houses, East Side," and *Upper East Side Historic District,* 845.

178. For R.I. Jenks at 54 East Sixty-fourth Street, see *Upper East Side Historic District,* 177.

179. "5 East 51st Street, Percy Griffin, Architect," *Brickbuilder* 17 (September 1908): 199.

180. "Residence, 22 East 63rd Street, New York, Charles W. Romeyn, Architect," *Architecture* 1 (April 1900): 130. Also see "115 East 40th Street, George E. Wood, Architect," *Brickbuilder* 17 (September 1908): 192.

181. For Sarah J. Robbins at 33 East Seventy-fourth Street. Croly admired the Robbins house for its flatness, its picturesque contrast with its neighbors, and its four, as opposed to the more usual five, stories. Herbert Croly, "The Renovation of the New York Brownstone District": 562, 565. Also see "Residence, J.W. Robbins, 33 East 74th Street, New York, Grosvenor Atterbury, Architect," *Architecture* 9 (January 1904): plate VI; *Real Estate Record and Guide* 73 (June 11, 1904): 1459; "33 East 74th Street, Grosvenor Atterbury, Architect," *Brickbuilder* 17 (September 1908): 200; and *Upper East Side Historic District,* 722.

182. "House of Allen Wardwell, Esq., 127 E. 80th St., N.Y., Messrs. Delano & Aldrich, Architects," *American Architect* 107 (March 10, 1915): plates.

183. "House of Marshall J. Dodge, Esq., No. 37 E. 68th Street, N.Y., Messrs. Delano & Aldrich, Architects," *American Architect* 107 (March 10, 1915): plates.

184. "House of Howard Gardner Cushing, Esq., 121 E. 70th St., N.Y., Messrs. Delano & Aldrich, Architects," *American Architect* 107 (March 10, 1915): plates.

185. "House of Miss Marion Hague, No. 161 E. 70th St., N.Y.," *American Architect* 107 (March 10, 1915): plates.

186. "House No. 1 East 76th Street, New York City, Brite & Bacon, Architects," *Brickbuilder* 8 (July 1899): 143, plate 50; "House of C.I. Hudson, Esq., No. 1, East Seventy-sixth Street, New York, N.Y., Brite & Bacon, Architects," *American Architect and Building News* 67 (February 24, 1900): plate; and *Upper East Side Historic District,* 800. Also see the Martin Erdmann house, which Schuyler called German Renaissance. "Residence, Martin Erdmann, 57 E. 55th Street, New York, Taylor & Levi, Architects," *Architecture* 20 (October 1909): plate LXXXV; and Schuyler, "New New York House, East Side": 459.

187. "House of Irving T. Bush, Esq., 28 East 64th Street, New York, N.Y., Kirby, Petit & Green, Architects," *American Architect and Building News* 87 (January 7, 1905): plates; "Residence, Irving T. Bush, 28 East 64th Street, New York, Kirby, Petit & Green, Architects," *Architecture* 13 (June 1906): plate 41; and "New York City Houses: 28 East 64th Street, Kirby, Petit & Green, Architects," *Brickbuilder* 17 (September 1908): 194. Kirby, Petit & Green's Bush office building was also in the Gothic style. See "Dutch Art Revival in Old Town," *Real Estate Record and Guide* 76 (September 9, 1905): 395.

188. Montgomery Schuyler, "The New New York House": 98. Kirby, Petit & Green's H.B. Gilbert house (1910) was more completely Gothic, with a facade sheathed in the same bluish stone preferred by Hunt, relieved by elaborate ornament. But the Gothic theme was only partially continued in the principal rooms. Some, like the library, were more closely related to the Gothic Revival of Charles Eastlake than to the Middle Ages. The dining room was a Modern French version of 18th century work. See Shiras Campbell, "An Excellent Gothic Residence," *Architectural Record* 29 (April 1911): 289-90, plates. Also see "House of Edward Thaw, Esq., East 89th Street, New York, N.Y., Israels & Harder, Architects," *American Architect and Building News* 87 (April 22, 1905): plate; and "Residence, H.H. Flagler, 32 Park Ave., New York, Little & O'Connor, Architects," *Architecture* 15 (January 1907): plate V.

189. Schuyler, "New New York Houses, East Side": 473.

190. Schuyler, "The New New York House": 83-85; and "New New York Houses, East Side": 451-52. A few of the houses used the English Basement Plan. See "Types of Private Residences," *Real Estate Record and Guide* 74 (July 2, 1904): 4; "The Residence of Mr. Geo. L. Rives," *Architectural Record:* 107; and John A. Gade, "The City Home of the Prosperous American, I, The City House as a Domestic Establishment," *Indoors and Out* 3 (October 1906): 19-25.

191. Herts & Tallant's Philip S. Henry residence at 1053 Fifth Avenue was one of the earliest artistic houses to be built in the Billionaire District. Labelled "a masterpiece of the American craftsman" by the *Architects' and Builders' Magazine,* it had a vaguely Gothic facade freely composed in brick trimmed with stone. Its interiors revealed that sophisticated synthesis between traditional composition and Art Nouveau detail that characterized Herts & Tallant's best theaters of the period. "A Masterpiece of the American Craftsman," *Architects' and Builders' Magazine* 5 (May 1904): 354-63. Also see Abbott Halstead Moore, "Individualism in Architecture: The Work of Herts & Tallant," *Architectural Record* 15 (January 1904): 58-91. Herts & Tallant also worked in a highly florid Modern French style. See a set of interior designs for "A City Residence," *Architectural Review* 6 (July 18, 1899): plates XLII-XLVI; "Design for a Dining Room," *Architectural Review* 6 (September 1899): plate LXII; and "Decoration for a Ball Room," *Architectural Review* 6 (October 1899): plate LXIX.

192. "New York City Houses, 59 East 77th Street," *Brickbuilder* 17 (September 1908): 198; "Remodeled House for E.T. Cockcroft, Esq., No. 59 East 77th St., Albro & Lindeberg, Architects," *American Architect and Building News* 94 (April 21, 1908): plate; and *Upper East Side Historic District,* 853. Also see "House, No. 124 East 55th St., New York, Albro & Lindeberg, Architects," *American Architect* 97 (May 4, 1910): plate.

193. "House and Plans, 53 East 61st., New York, Walker & Gillette, Architects," *Architecture* 21 (February 1910): plate XV; and Schuyler, "New New York Houses, East Side": 470. York & Sawyer designed a more formal version, in a cross between freestyle and Modern French. "House at 14 East 76th Street, New York, N.Y.," *Brickbuilder* 23 (June 1914): plate 90.

194. Schuyler, "New New York Houses, East Side": 470.

195. "House at No. 139 E. 19th Street, New York, Mr. F.J. Sterner, Architect," *American Architect and Building News* 95 (February 24, 1909): 67, plates; "Artistic Development Near Gramercy Park," *Real Estate Record and Guide* 86 (July 9, 1910): 60-61; and "House at 135 East 19th Street, New York City, Frederick Junius Sterner, Architect," *Brickbuilder* 19 (December 1910): plate 162.

196. "Editorial: The Development of East Sixty-third St., New York, By Mr. Sterner," *Architecture* 31 (April 1915): 117, plates XXXIII-XXXVII; and "Office and Residence of Frederick Sterner, New York City," *Architectural Forum* 37 (October 1922): plates 57-61. Also see "A City House Facade, New York, N.Y., Frederick J. Sterner, Architect," *Architectural Forum* 31 (July 1919): 21; "House of Maurice Brill, New York City," *Architectural Forum* 40 (January 1924): plates 10-13; and Edgell, *American Architecture,* 144-45.

197. "Houses, 105 & 107 East 73d St., New York, Grosvenor Atterbury, Architect," *Architecture* 13 (January 1906): plate VIII; "105 and 107 East 73d Street, Grosvenor Atterbury, Architect," *Brickbuilder* 17 (September 1908): 189; and "Architectural Criticism," *Architecture* 21 (February 15, 1910): 17-18.

198. "Architectural Criticism," *Architecture:* 17-18.

199. Schuyler, "The New New York House": 92.

200. "The Residence of Bertram G. Goodhue," *Architectural Review* 16 (June 1909): 75-80. Donn Barber's own house, though more modestly conceived, was equally free of hackneyed motifs. The nominally ornamented brick facade was interrupted on the second and third floors by a largely glazed shallow curving bay relieved by elegantly carved panels in relief. "House of Mr. Donn Barber, New York City, Donn Barber, Architect," *Brickbuilder* 22 (January 1913): plate 14.

201. Schuyler, "The New New York House": 99.

202. For the former Columbia site see "Residences on the Old Columbia University Site," *Architects' and Builders' Magazine* 1 (November 1899): 55-58; "Very Desirable New Residences," *Real Estate Record and Guide* 64 (December 9, 1899): 881; "Modern Dwellings," *Real Estate Record and Guide* 66 (November 24, 1900): 698; "Three Ideal Town Houses, Built by Charles Buek on the Columbia College Site," *Real Estate Record and Guide* 67 (January 12, 1901): 45; "House, 47 East 49th Street, New York, N.Y., Barney & Chapman, Architects," *Brickbuilder* 10 (April 1901): plate; and "Residence of Mrs. Douglas Henry, East 49th St., Barney & Chapman, Architects," *Architects' and Builders' Magazine* 2 (May 1901): 290.

203. "Near the University Club," *Real Estate Record and Guide* 61 (January 22, 1898): 142-43.

204. Russell Sturgis, "The Art Gallery of New York Streets," *Architectural Record* 10 (July 1900): 92-112.

205. Sturgis, "Art Gallery of New York Streets": 93-94.

206. Sturgis, "Art Gallery of New York Streets": 95-96. York & Sawyer's 9 East Fifty-fourth Street was another essay in the Modern French mode. See "The Architect's Portfolio," *Architectural Record* 12 (December 1902): 752-58. Also see Herbert Croly, "Renovation of the Brownstone District."

207. Sturgis, "Art Gallery of New York Streets": 96-98.

208. "18 East Fifty-fourth Street, Palmer & Hornbostel, Architects," *Brickbuilder* 17 (September 1908): 208.

209. "26 East Fifty-fourth Street, C.P.H. Gilbert, Architect," *Brickbuilder* 17 (September 1908): 204.

210. Sturgis, "Art Gallery of New York Streets": 103-04. Also see Roth, *Urban Architecture of McKim, Mead & White,* 573.

211. Sturgis, "Art Gallery of New York Streets": 105-06. For numbers 16 and 26 East Fifty-fourth Street see "New York City Houses," *Brickbuilder* 17 (September 1908): 204, 208.

212. "New York City Houses," *Brickbuilder* 17 (September 1908): 199.

213. "Residence, Mrs. Chas. D. Dickey, 27 East 51st Street, New York, Wm. Strom, Architect," *Architecture* 9 (April 1904): plate 27; "A Series of Views of the Residence of Chas. D. Dickey, Esq., New York City, Wm. Strom, Architect," *Architects' and Builders' Magazine* 7 (July 1906): 425-31; and "25 and 27 East 51st Street, William Strom, Architect," *Brickbuilder* 17 (September 1908): 196.

214. "New York City Houses," *Brickbuilder* 17 (September 1908): 195. Also see "House of J.W. Henning, Esq., No. 50 W. 52nd St., N.Y.," *American Architect and Building News* 41 (August 26, 1893): plate; "House, 23 West 52nd Street, New York City, C.P.H. Gilbert, Architect," *Brickbuilder* 11 (April 1902): plate; "House of H.G. Trevor, Esq., Fifth Avenue and Fifty-second Street, New York, N.Y., A.N. Allen, Architect," *American Architect and Building News* 89 (May 5, 1906): plate; "Three Houses on a Fifty-Foot Lot, 50-54 East Fifty-second Street, Charles Brendon, Architect," *Real Estate Record and Guide* 77 (June 2, 1906): 1047; "Residences, 45 & 47 East 53rd St., New York, S. Edson Gage, Architect," *Architecture* 7 (March 1903): plate XX; "New York City Houses, 45 and 47 East 53d Street, S. Edson Gage, Architect," *Brickbuilder* 17 (September 1908): 209; "House on 55th St., Near 5th Ave., New York City," *Building* 5 (October 9, 1886): plate; "Four Houses in West 55th St., N.Y., for C.T. Barney, Esq., Jas. Brown Lord, Architect, 121 East 23rd Street, N.Y.," *American Architect and Building News* 22 (October 1, 1887): plate; and "House of Mr. Sherman, 8 W. 55th Street, New York, N.Y., R.H. Robertson, Architect," *American Architect and Building News* 65 (August 5, 1899): plate.

215. "New York City Houses," *Brickbuilder* 17 (September 1908): 206. Also see "The New Houses Along Madison Avenue, Fifty-fifth and Fifty-sixth streets," *Real Estate Record and Guide* 21 (April 27, 1878): 360.

216. "Residence, H.B. Holland [sic], New York City, McKim, Mead & White, Architects," *Inland Architect and News Record* 38 (June 1901): plate; "Residence, H.B. Hollins, 12 West Fifty-sixth Street, McKim, Mead & White, Architects," *Architecture* 4 (November 15, 1901): 310; and "12 West 56th Street, McKim, Mead & White Architects," *Brickbuilder* 17 (September 1908): 187. Also see "Residence of L.L. Benedict, Esq., No. 125 East 56th Street, New York, J.H. De Sibour, Architect," *Architectural Review* 12 (April 1905): 126-27, plate XXVI; and "72 East 56th Street, Foster, Gade & Graham, Architects," *Brickbuilder* 17 (September 1908): 202.

217. Henry Hope Reed, *The Golden City* (New York: W.W. Norton & Company, 1959), 40.

218. Croly, "Contemporary New York Residence," *Architectural Record* 12 (December 1902): 705-27. Also see "Two Grand Houses on Fifty-seventh Street," *Real Estate Record and Guide* 26 (October 2, 1880): 851; "In West Fifty-seventh Street," *Real Estate Record and Guide* 36 (September 13, 1885): 992-93; "House of Mr. W. Zinsser,, 119 West 57th Street, New York, De Lemos & Cordes, Architects," *Architecture and Building* 20 (January 13, 1894): plate; "A Skillful Piece of Remodelling," *Architecture and Building* 20 (April 7, 1894): 163-65; "House of Adolph Lewisohn, Esq., New York, N.Y., Arnold W. Brunner, Architect," *American Architect and Building News* 65 (July 22, 1899): plate; "Residence of Adolph Lewisohn, Esq., New York City," *New York Architect* 3 (January 1909); and "Russell Sturgis's Architecture," *Architectural Record* 25 (June 1909): 405-10.

219. See Christopher Gray, "Neighborhood, New York's Most Elegant Sidestreet," *Avenue* 6 (April 1982): 49-58. Also see *Upper East Side Historic District,* 456-532.

220. See Gray, "Most Elegant Sidestreet": 50. The destruction of Hunt's Lenox Library building to make way for Henry Clay Frick's house was controversial. Frick's offer to rebuild it stone for stone on the Arsenal site in Central Park, though generous, merely substituted the destruction of one monument so that another could be saved; moreover, public sentiment against any new buildings in the park, a sentiment Frick may well have anticipated, called the sincerity of his offer into question. "The Lenox Library Building," *American Architect* 101 (June 12, 1912): 259-60.

221. "Residence, Dave H. Morris, 19 East 70th St., New York, Thornton Chard, Architect," *Architectural Yearbook* 1 (1912): 105; "Some Recent Interiors by Thornton Chard," *Architectural Record* 37 (February 1915): 177-86; and Landmarks Preservation Commission, *19 East Seventieth Street House Designation Report* (LP-0849), prepared by Ellen W. Kramer, (New York, City of New York, July 23, 1974). Although Frick bought his lot in 1908, the other lots on the north side of Seventieth between Fifth and

Madison avenues were not sold until 1909. Other houses of the period include the Cornelius Luyster house (11 East Seventieth Street, John Duncan, 1909-10), the John Chandler Moore house (15 East Seventieth Street, Charles I Berg, 1909-10), the Alvin W. Krech house (17 East Seventieth Street, Arthur C. Jackson, 1909-11) and the Gustav Pagenstrecher house (21 East Seventieth Street, William J. Rogers, 1918-19). See *Upper East Side Historic District,* 457-70.

222. "Current Building Operations," *Real Estate Record and Guide* 95 (May 8, 1915): 800.

223. "The Expanding Residential District on the East Side," *Real Estate Record and Guide* 77 (March 31, 1906): 562-63.

224. See note 78 this chapter.

225. "Old Union Seminary Coming Down," *Real Estate Record and Guide* 86 (July 2, 1910): 4-5.

226. Gray, "Most Elegant Sidestreet": 53.

227. "Perspective, Residence, S.C. Clark, East 70th St., New York, F.J. Sterner, Architect," *Architecture* 24 (October 1911): 153; and "Residence, S.C. Clark, New York, F.J. Sterner, Architect," *Architecture* 27 (February 1913): 42.

228. In 1928 he added a third house, 725 Park Avenue, to make one of the most unprepossessing large houses in the city. See Gray, "Demolished Mansions": 56-57.

229. One exception was the Laura K. Bayer house (32 East Seventieth Street, Taylor & Levi, 1910-12). *Upper East Side Historic District,* 475.

230. Gray, "Most Elegant Sidestreet": 55; and *Upper East Side Historic District,* 508.

231. Gray, "Most Elegant Sidestreet": 56; and *Upper East Side Historic District,* 511. Other houses of the period on the block included the remodelled Elizabeth Cochran house (110 East Seventieth Street, Robertson & Potter, 1905), the Grace Lathrop Luling house (118 East Seventieth Street, Trowbridge & Livingston, 1900-01), the Clinton H. Crane house (120 East Seventieth Street, Gay & Nash, 1903-05), the remodelled T.J. McLaughlin house (128 East Seventieth Street, Clement B. Brun, 1905-06), the Julius Goldman house (132 East Seventieth Street, Herbert M. Baer, 1914), the A. Leo Everett house (134 East Seventieth Street, Walker & Gillette, 1914), and a house for the Century Realty Investment Co. (111 East Seventieth Street, William Adams, 1911-12). All in *Upper East Side Historic District,* 485-511.

232. Gray, "Most Elegant Sidestreet": 57; and *Upper East Side Historic District,* 518.

233. *Upper East Side Historic District,* 524.

234. "Residence, Stephen H. Brown, 154 East 70th St., New York, Edw. Pearce Casey, Architect," *Architecture* 19 (February 1909): 30, plate XVII.

235. *Upper East Side Historic District,* 519.

236. *Upper East Side Historic District,* 526.

237. *Upper East Side Historic District,* 527. Also see *Real Estate Record and Guide* 77 (June 30, 1906): 1233. Remodelled houses of the period included the Lydia Laurence Blagden house (176 East Seventieth Street, Walker & Hazard, 1911), the Prof. Munroe Smith house (169 East Seventieth Street, Augustus N. Allen, 1910), and the Georgiana H. Stevens house (171 East Seventieth Street, George B. de Gersdorff, 1911).

238. See note 161 this chapter.

239. John M. Carrère built his own house earlier in the year, in a remodelled brownstone at 101 East Sixty-fifth Street, on the northeast corner of Park Avenue and Sixty-fifth Street. "Plans, Residence, Mr. John Carrère, 101 East 65th Street, New York," *Architecture* 7 (April 15, 1903): 46.

240. *Real Estate Record and Guide* 77 (April 21, 1906): 711. Also see "Fourth Avenue," *Real Estate Record and Guide* 20 (December 15, 1877): 965-66; "Fourth Avenue, What Will The Near Future Do For It?" *Real Estate Record and Guide* 67 (October 20, 1900): 486; "Madison Avenue," *Real Estate Record and Guide* 78 (September 15, 1906): 436; and "Park Avenue and Murray Hill," *Real Estate Record and Guide* 80 (November 30, 1907): 887-88.

241. Francis S. Bancroft, "Residential Improvements on Park Avenue Assure Future," *Real Estate Record and Guide* 99 (February 3, 1917): 71. Also see "The Rebuilding of Park Avenue, To Exemplify Modern Ideals for Residential Planning in a Great City, Giant 'Club' Apartment Houses and Individual Mansions," *Real Estate Record and Guide* 84 (December 4, 1909): 991-93; and "Park Avenue Apartment Activity, Two Multi-Family Structures Add to Already Long Chain of High Class Buildings, Demand Still in Excess of Supply," *Real Estate Record and Guide* 97 (February 19, 1916): 289.

242. Bancroft, "Residential Improvements on Park Avenue": 71. Bancroft was referring to 540 Park Avenue. See "Apartments, Five Hundred and Forty Park Ave., New York, Wm. A. Boring, Architect," *Architecture* 17 (January 1908): plate XIX; "Apartment House, Park Avenue and 61st Street, New York, William A. Boring, Architect," *Brickbuilder* 17 (June 1908): plates 82-83; and H.W. Frohne, "The Planning of Fireproof Apartment Houses in New York," *American Architect* 100 (November 29, 1911): 213-18, plates. Also see "Private Apartment House, No. 520 Park Avenue, Corner 60th Street, New York, Mr. William A. Boring, Architect," *American Architect* 100 (November 29, 1911): plate. In 1887 McKim, Mead & White began designs for the Yosemite Apartment House. It was constructed from 1888 to 1890 on the southeast corner of Park Avenue and Sixty-second Street, but Bancroft, who was the secretary of Pease & Elliman, apparently did not consider it a "high-class" building. See "East Side Number," *Real Estate Record and Guide* (1890): 1, 3, 57; Sturgis, "Works of McKim, Mead & White": 49-51; and Roth, *Urban Architecture of McKim, Mead & White,* 273.

243. "Architectural Criticism," *Architecture* 24 (October 15, 1911): 145-46, plates; "Residence, Percy R. Pyne, Park Ave. and 68th St., New York, McKim, Mead & White, Architects," *Architectural Yearbook* 1 (1912): 33-35; and *McKim, Mead & White Monograph,* plates 349-51A.

244. Roth, *Urban Architecture of McKim, Mead & White,* 589.

245. "Architectural Criticism," *Architecture:* 45-46.

246. "Residence, Henry P. Davison, 690 Park Avenue, New York, Walker & Gillette Architects," *Architecture* 39 (May 1919): plates LXXXVI-LXXXII.

247. *Upper East Side Historic District,* 1099. Also see G.H. Edgell, *The American Architecture of Today* (New York: Charles Scribner's Sons, 1928), 143-44.

248. *Upper East Side Historic District,* 1065-66. For other Georgian houses on Park Avenue see "Architectural Criticism," *Architecture* 21 (March 1910): 35, plate XXVII; *Real Estate Record and Guide* 88 (September 16, 1911): 383; "Residence, J. Frederic Kernochan, 862 Park Avenue, New York, Cross & Cross, Architects," *Architecture* 30 (July 1914): plate XCII; "Residence, Henry P. Davison, 690 Park Avenue, New York," *Architecture* 39 (May 1919): plates 76-82; Edgell, *American Architecture,* 144-45; and Gray, "Park Avenue Mansions": 61.

An apartment house designed by Emery Roth to complete the blockfront occupied by the Colonial style Colony Club was "similar in general character and the idea of architectural harmony was carried out to such an extent that the marble work on the first two stories is identical in design.... A notable feature... is... that the westerly and southerly walls... which overlook the adjoining buildings, have been treated exactly the same as the front of the project." "Apartments near Colony Club," *Real Estate Record and Guide* 47 (March 25, 1916): 487. Also see "Park Avenue Apartment Activity," *Real Estate Record and Guide* 97 (February 19, 1916): 289.

249. "House for Geraldyn Redmond, Esq., Messrs. McKim, Mead & White, Architects," *American Architect* 107 (March 3, 1915): plate; and *McKim, Mead & White Monograph,* 392-93.

250. "The City Residence of Arthur Curtiss James, Park Ave. and 69th Street, New York, Allen & Collens, Architects," *Architecture* 35 (March 1917): 53, plates XXXVIII-LI; and "Current Building Operations, Colony of Residences in the Park Avenue Section Being Augmented by New Home for Commodore Arthur Curtiss James," *Real Estate Record and Guide* 97 (January 15, 1916): 112-13.

251. "House, Park Avenue, New York City, John Russell Pope, Architect," *Brickbuilder* 22 (June 1913): plates 81-83; and "Portfolio of Current Architecture: Residence of Reginald de Koven, Esq., New York City, John Russell Pope, Architect," *Architectural Record* 42 (August 1917): 153-62. On the same block at the corner of Eighty-fifth Street was the Lewis G. Morris house, an unusually picturesque design by Ernest Flagg. Vaguely Queen Anne in style, the brick house had a U-shaped plan with interesting circulation. An exterior stair ran across the central bay to the main entrance on the second floor of the Park Avenue wing. The stepped window pattern of the central bay clearly marked the position of the interior stair, which ran counter to the entry steps.

252. "House, Sherman Hoyt, Park Ave. and 79th St., New York, I.N. Phelps Stokes, Architect," *Architecture* 36 (July 1917): plate; and Gray, "Demolished Mansions": 52-53. Also see "Residence, 891 Park Avenue, New York, Alfred Bussele, Architect," *Architecture* 21 (March 1910): plate XXVII; and "Town House of Henry James, Esq., Park Avenue, N.Y., Mr. Frederick Sterner, Architect," *American Architect* 110 (December 20, 1916): plates.

253. "House, Eighty-fifth Street and Park Avenue, New York City, Hunt & Hunt, Architects," *Brickbuilder* 19 (March 1910): plates 41-42. For another Modern Renaissance house by Hunt & Hunt see "House on Madison Avenue, New York, Messrs. Hunt & Hunt, Architects," *American Architect* 103 (February 12, 1913): plate; and "No. 477 Madison Avenue, Messrs. Hunt & Hunt, Architects," *American Architect* 104 (October 8, 1913): plates.

254. "House to be Built for Oakleigh Thorne," *Real Estate Record and Guide* 86 (May 13, 1911): 901; C. Matlack Price, "Some Recent Work of

Albert Joseph Bodker," *Architectural Record* 33 (May 1913): 381-420. For another Modern Renaissance house by Bodker see "Operations on the Upper East Side," *Real Estate Record and Guide* 87 (April 15, 1911): 682-83; and "Residence of Robert A. Chesebrough, 870 Madison Ave., New York, A.J. Bodker, Architect," *Architectural Year Book* 1 (1912): 265-67.

255. Price, "Recent Work of Bodker": 417.
256. Schuyler, "New New York Houses, East Side": 454. Also see "The Rebuilding of Park Avenue," *Real Estate Record and Guide* 84 (December 4, 1909): 991-93; and *Upper East Side Historic District,* 1080.
257. Schuyler, "New New York Houses, East Side": 454.
258. Schuyler, "New New York Houses, East Side": 454.
259. "Rebuilding of Park Avenue," *Real Estate Record and Guide:* 991.
260. "Apartments, 925 Park Ave., New York, Delano & Aldrich, Architects," *Architecture* 19 (January 1909): 12, plate IX; "Apartment Building, 925 Park Avenue, New York City, Delano & Aldrich, Architects," *Architectural Review* 6 (July 1909): plates; and "Cooperative Apartments, 925 Park Ave., New York, Messrs. Delano & Aldrich, Architects," *American Architect and Building News* 96 (December 22, 1909): plates.
261. "The Duplex Apartment House, A Comparison of the Newest Buildings of this Type," *Architectural Record* 29 (April 1911): 327-34; and "563 Park Avenue, New York, Walter B. Chambers, Architect," *Architect* 6 (April 1912): plate.
262. In 1908 Taylor had completed 471 and 863 Park Avenue. Charles W. Buckham designed 471. See Richard Morton, "An Essay on Duplex Apartments In General and Those at 471 Park Avenue in Particular," *Apartment Houses of the Metropolis* (New York: Hesselgren, 1908), 5-6; and Charles W. Buckham, "Duplex Co-Operative Apartment Houses," *American Architect and Building News* 96 (December 22, 1909): 266-67. Pollard & Steinam, who also designed three of Taylor's cooperative studio buildings on West Sixty-seventh Street, were the architects for 863 Park Avenue. See Pease & Elliman, *Pease & Elliman's Catalog of East Side New York Apartment Plans* (New York: 1925), 173. Taylor also built 823 (Schwartz & Gross), 925 (Delano & Aldrich), and 969 (Tickery & Wells) Park Avenue. See Pease & Elliman, *Catalog of Apartment Plans,* 167, 180-81, 190.
263. "Apartments, Park Ave. and 79th St., New York, Warren & Wetmore and Robt. T. Lyons, Architects," *Architecture* 28 (July 1913): 152-53; and Tauranac, *Essential New York,* 132-34.
264. "Apt. H, No. 640 Park Avenue, New York, J.E.R. Carpenter, Architect," *American Architect-Architectural Review* 121 (March 29, 1922): 264, plate; and Andrew Alpern, *Apartments for the Affluent* (New York: McGraw-Hill, 1975), 84-85.
265. "Apartment House, 960 Park Avenue, New York, N.Y., D. Everett Waid and J.E.R. Carpenter, Associated Architects," *Brickbuilder* 25 (November 1916): plate 175; and Alpern, *Apartments for the Affluent,* 86-87. Also see Wilfred W. Beach, "Some Recent New York Apartment Houses From the Work of J.E.R. Carpenter, Architect," *Architectural Forum* 30 (May 1919): 127-36.
266. Beach, "Recent Apartment Houses from Carpenter": 131-33; and "Apartments, Fifth Avenue and 72nd St., New York, J.E.R. Carpenter, Architect," *Architecture* 35 (April 1917): 71, plate LXVIII.
267. "270 Park Avenue, The Largest of Apartment Houses," *Architecture* 37 (May 1918): 143, plates.
268. "East Side and West Side," *Real Estate Record and Guide* 20 (October 13, 1877): 785-86. Also see "Fashion as an Element of Value," *Real Estate Record and Guide* 18 (October 21, 1876): 779-80; "Capabilities of the West Side," *Real Estate Record and Guide* 21 (January 12, 1878): 23-24; "The Fate of the West Side," *Real Estate Record and Guide* 24 (December 13, 1874): 1004; and "The East Side and the West Side," *Real Estate Record and Guide* 27 (May 14, 1881): 489-90.
269. Edward Clark, "The City of the Future," *Real Estate Record and Guide* 24 (December 27, 1879): 1056. Also see Slawson & Hobbs, "The Upper West Side," letter of December 21, 1906 to the editor, *Real Estate Record and Guide* 79 (January 26, 1907): 157-58.
270. "City Cottages," *Real Estate Record and Guide* 17 (December 23, 1876): 960-61. The article noted that "the majority of our readers have had occasion to make the acquaintance of West Philadelphia during the past year" while visiting the Centennial Celebration. It was also recognized that this suburban ambience would involve a rejection of the uniform architectural style of the brownstone era. The *Real Estate Record and Guide* predicted in 1876 that "a taste will be developed for roomy and spacious houses, detached and isolated, commanding unobstructed views and distinguished by peculiar architectural types and forms." See "City Chateaux or Villas," *Real Estate Record and Guide* 18 (December 23, 1876): 942. Also see "The West Side Association," *Real Estate Record and Guide* 24 (December 20, 1879): 1029-30.
271. Montgomery Schuyler, "The Small City House in New York," *Architectural Record* 8 (April-June 1899): 357-88.
272. "Our West Side," *Real Estate Record and Guide* 24 (December 27, 1879): 1055.
273. Sarah Bradford Landau, "The Row Houses of New York's West Side," *Journal of the Society of Architectural Historians* 34 (March 1975): 19-36. Before 1880, transportation was limited to the omnibus line on the Boulevard and, after 1875, the Eighth Avenue Railroad. "Capabilities of the West Side," *Real Estate Record and Guide:* 23.
274. "West Side Buildings," *Building* 6 (March 26, 1887): 1; "The Architecture of the West Side," *Real Estate Record and Guide* 40 (September 10, 1887): 1150.
275. Edith Wharton, *A Backward Glance* (New York: D. Appleton, 1934), 44-45.
276. "West of the Park," *Real Estate Record and Guide* 36 (November 7, 1865): 1215-16. Also see "The Improvement on the West Side," *Real Estate Record and Guide* 37 (May 8, 1886): 597-98.
277. Schuyler, "The New New York House": 84.
278. In 1879 the *Real Estate Record and Guide* observed a "growing spirit of veneration for our ancestors and a desire to cultivate the antique in such mild forms as it is possible in a new country to present it." "New and Old Houses," *Real Estate Record and Guide* 23 (March 1, 1879): 166.
279. Schuyler, "Small City House": 376.
280. Schuyler, "Small City House": 375.
281. Landau, "Row Houses": 20; and "Houses and Grounds," *Real Estate Record and Guide* 24 (December 13, 1879): 1004. Calvert Vaux objected to the standard lot as "destructive of any opportunity to afford that display which our people actually like." He also advocated polychromy and restrictive convenants in future house construction. See "The Size of Building Lots," *Real Estate Record and Guide* 24 (December 6, 1879): 979.
282. Robert Stewart, "The Hotels of New York," *Munsey's* 22 (November 1899): 281-95.
283. "East Side Architecture—Fifth Avenue," *Real Estate Record and Guide* 45 (May 3, 1890): 640-41.
284. Schuyler, "Small City House": 373.
285. The speculator-built rows of the 1880s, typified by W.J. Merritt's two houses on West Seventy-fifth Street between West End Avenue and Riverside Drive and W.E.D. Stokes's row of houses on West End Avenue between Seventy-fourth and Seventy-fifth streets, reflect Schuyler's observation that "what the public now demanded was variety." Each was a clear expression of the Cosmopolitan spirit with its emphasis on individuality within the context of the group. "West of the Park," *Real Estate Record and Guide:* 1215; "Two Houses, Cor. 75th Street West of Boulevard, New York City, W.J. Merritt, Arch't," *Building* 5 (November 13, 1886): plate; "The West Side Illustrated," *Real Estate Record and Guide* 38 (November 20, 1885): 1418; and Schuyler, "Small City House": 376.
286. "Our West Side," *Real Estate Record and Guide:* 1055.
287. Montgomery Schuyler, "The Romanesque Revival in New York," *Architectural Record* 1 (October-December 1891): 151-98. Also see "Riverside Drive," *Real Estate Record and Guide* 35 (April 25, 1885): 461; "The Riverside Drive and Future City Construction," *Building* 7 (August 27, 1887): 65; and "Around One Hundred and Fourth Street, West," *Real Estate Record and Guide* 47 (January 17, 1891): 86. Also note Gilbert & Thompson's design for a unique mansion on Broadway; "New Residence and Stable, West Boulevard, New York City," *American Architect and Building News* 15 (May 10, 1884): plate.
288. "Residence of Mr. Cyrus Clark," *Building* 11 (Supplement, November 23, 1889): plate. A number of estates were located in the area before Riverside Drive was constructed. See "Old Mansions Once on Bloomingdale's Riverside," *Real Estate Record and Guide* 85 (January 22, 1910): 159. General Egbert Viele, the chief engineer of Central Park, built a late Victorian mansion at Riverside Drive and Eighty-eighth Street which has been attributed to Leopold Eidlitz. For Viele's role in the West End's development, see Landau, "Row Houses": 20.
289. "Residence of Mr. John Matthews, Riverside Drive and Ninetieth Street," *American Architect and Building News* 35 (January 2, 1892): plate; "Residence of Mr. John Matthews, Riverside Drive and Ninetieth St., New York," *Architectural Record* 1 (April-June 1892): 478; "Residence of Mr. John Matthews, Riverside Drive, New York," *Architecture and Building* 18 (April 22, 1893): plate; and "Residence of John Matthews, Riverside Drive, New York—Side View," *Architecture and Building* 18 (May 6, 1893): plate.
290. Bayne, President of the Seaboard National Bank, erected another villa by Freeman on the northeast corner of Riverside Drive and 108th Street. Schuyler observed in 1891 that the Drive's suburban development "is specially fortunate since among the villas already erected, which are for the most part decorous and dull, with one or two exceptions which are highly indecorous and even duller, it has given opportunity to Mr. Freeman to put up two villas, on the opposite corners of 108th Street, which are not only by far the most artistic examples of the Richardsonian Romanesque in our domestic architecture, but are among the most artistic of our

dwellings in any style. Without being grouped, each enhances the effect of the other." Schuyler, "Romanesque Revival": 8, 36. Also see "Residence on Riverside Drive, New York City," *Architecture and Building* 16 (April 23, 1892): plate; and King, *King's Handbook*, 743, 818.

291. Clarence True, *A True History of Riverside Drive* (New York: Unz & Co., 1899). Also see "Literary Notes," *Architecture and Building* 29 (October 14, 1893): 191.

292. "Improvements on Riverside Drive Showing Four Blocks of Dwelling Houses," *Architecture and Building* 28 (June 11, 1898): plate.

293. The houses were 337 West Seventy-sixth Street, 40-41 and 44-46 Riverside Drive, and 334-338 West Seventy-seventh Street. Landau, "Row Houses": 28-29. The double-width Gothic house at 42 Riverside Drive was built by the rival developer-architect Charles Buek, whose houses were typically less Classical and less suave than True's. "A New Riverside Drive Mansion," *Real Estate Record and Guide* 62 (October 8, 1898): 490. Also by Buek, see "Houses on the Riverside Drive, New York, N.Y.," *American Architect and Building News* 37 (September 10, 1892): plate.

294. Landau, "Row Houses": 28-29.

295. "Four Houses on Riverside Drive," *Architecture and Building* 18 (April 1, 1893): plate; and Landau, "Row Houses": 27-28.

296. In 1894, James E. Ware built the four adjacent houses on the northern corner of Seventy-seventh Street and Riverside Drive. Ware's ashlar masonry and more literal interpretation of French Renaissance chateaux contrasted strongly with the Lamb & Rich row. "Block of Houses, Riverside corner of 75th Street, New York," *Architecture and Building* 21 (November 17, 1894): plate.

297. The row included 301-305 West Seventy-sixth Street, 343-357 West End Avenue, and 302-306 West Seventy-seventh Street. "West End Ave. and 76th St.," *American Architect and Building News* 34 (October 17, 1891): plates; "Entrance Hall, No. 303 W. 76th St., Lamb & Rich, Architects," *American Architect and Building News* 34 (November 21, 1891): plate; "Corner West End Ave. and 77th St., Lamb & Rich, Architects," *American Architect and Building News* 37 (August 20, 1892): plate; and "House at the Corner of West 76th Street and West End Avenue, New York, N.Y.," *American Architect and Building News* 44 (June 30, 1894): plate. "No. 243 West End Avenue, Lamb & Rich," *American Architect and Building News* 37 (July 23, 1892): plate, seems to show 343 West End Avenue. Also see Landau, "Row Houses": 28. Also by Lamb & Rich, see "House on 11th Ave. near 75th St., New York City," *Building* 5 (September 11, 1886): plate; "House on 11th Ave. and 75th St., New York City," *Building* 5 (September 18, 1886): plate; "Corner, Seventy-fourth St. and Tenth Avenue," and "Corner 75th Street and West End," *American Architect and Building News* 21 (May 21, 1887): plate; and "House on West Seventy-first St.," *American Architect and Building News* 22 (November 5, 1887): plate.

298. "West of the Park," *Real Estate Record and Guide:* 1215; "In West Seventy-second Street," *Real Estate Record and Guide* 40 (September 17, 1887): 1172-73; Montgomery Schuyler, "Henry Janeway Hardenbergh," *Architectural Record* 6 (January–March 1897): 335-75; Slawson & Hobbs, "The Upper West Side": 157; and Landau, "Row Houses": 20-21.

299. Schuyler, "Hardenbergh": 357. For other houses on West Seventy-third Street, see "Some West Side Houses," *Real Estate Record and Guide* 40 (November 26, 1887): 1472. In 1887 the builder D. Willis James and architect John G. Prague employed strategies similar to Hardenbergh's in their rowhouse development on the south side of Eighty-seventh Street and both sides of Eighty-sixth Street between Columbus and Amsterdam avenues. Although uniform in style, Prague's individual houses were rather busy examples of the Queen Anne taste, and the streets hence lacked much of the unity achieved by Hardenbergh. Lynx, "Model Streets," *Real Estate Record and Guide* 40 (December 10, 1887): 1542; and "Houses on 86th St., New York," *American Architect and Building News* 33 (September 19, 1891): plate. Cyrus L.W. Eidlitz built a far more successful pair of Romanesque townhouses on West Eighty-sixth Street. See "Two Residences, Nos. 341 and 343 West Eighty-sixth Street, New York City," *Architecture and Building* 24 (June 13, 1896): plate; and Montgomery Schuyler, "Cyrus L.W. Eidlitz," *Architectural Record* 5 (April–June 1896): 411-35. Hardenbergh's rowhouses seem to have directly influenced a development by the builder James T. Hall on the south side of Seventy-fifth Street between Central Park West and Columbus Avenue: "A Handsome West Side Improvement," *Real Estate Record and Guide* 45 (April 12, 1890): 517.

300. "West of the Park," *Real Estate Record and Guide:* 1215-16. In 1879 Clark may have considered erecting his own mansion on the Dakota site. "The West Side Association," *Real Estate Record and Guide* 24 (December 20, 1879): 1029-30.

301. "In West Seventy-second Street," *Real Estate Record and Guide:* 1172-73; "The Seventy-second Street Improvement Assured," *Real Estate Record and Guide* 41 (May 26, 1888): 670. Also see "The Adrian Apartment House," *Real Estate Record and Guide* 43 (April 27, 1889): 383; "The 'West Side' Illustrated," *Real Estate Record and Guide* 44 (Supplement to November 16, 1889): 1-6; and Observor, "West Seventy-second Street: The Parkway," *Real Estate Record and Guide* 44 (December 14, 1889): 1668. The Parkway was an early apartment house on the street built by Charles Buek.

302. "In West Seventy-second Street," *Real Estate Record and Guide:* 1172-73. Among the specific houses described were five houses by Charles Buek at the northwest corner of Columbus Avenue, and another group to their west by Thom & Wilson, later the architects of the Criminal Court Building. See "The Improvement of Seventy-second Street," *Real Estate Record and Guide* 38 (December 18, 1886): 1554. Only near its western termination, where Seventy-second Street crossed West End Avenue, was its character redeemed by a row of houses designed by Lamb & Rich (1889) which reflected the new sense of balance between individuality and orderliness. Schuyler, "Romanesque Revival": 23, 36; and Landau, "Row Houses": 27.

303. Schuyler, "Small City House": 376.

304. "The Improvement on the West Side," *Real Estate Record and Guide:* 597-98.

305. "Residences, New York City," *Brickbuilder* 7 (March 1898): 65; Schuyler, "Small City House": 384-85; and Landau, "Row Houses": 22.

306. Schuyler, "Small City House"; 384-85. McKim, Mead & White also explored the Dutch Renaissance in their Goelet offices at 8 West Seventeenth Street. The *Real Estate Record and Guide* described its style as that which "prevailed in old Amsterdam when new Amsterdam was colonized, and which offers a means of swearing one's self onto the original settlers, which it is rather surprising has not been more frequently adopted in domestic architecture." See "Bits of Street Architecture," *Real Estate Record and Guide* 40 (July 9, 1887): 920.

307. "Dwellings that Combine Comfort with Style," *Real Estate Record and Guide* 38 (October 23, 1886): 294; "A Block of Eight Houses, Cor. 78th St. and West End Ave., New York City," *Building* 5 (November 27, 1886): plates; "The 'West Side' Illustrated," *Real Estate Record and Guide:* 3; and Landau, "Row Houses": 22-24. Also see a particularly subtle example of the Dutch Revival designed by Babb, Cook & Willard: "House of Theodore L. DeVinne, W. 76th St. and West End Ave., New York, N.Y.," *American Architect and Building News* 64 (June 24, 1899): plate; and Russell Sturgis, "The City House: The East and South," *Scribner's* 7 (June 1890): 693-715.

308. "Dwellings that Combine Comfort with Style," *Real Estate Record and Guide:* 294.

309. "Collegiate Reformed Dutch Church," *Architecture and Building* 17 (October 29, 1892): 217, plate; and "Recent Brickwork in American Cities, New York," *Brickbuilder* 3 (June 1894): 106-08.

310. "The Best Yet," *Real Estate Record and Guide* 64 (October 7, 1889): 501. Also see "House on West End Avenue, New-York, N.Y., With Detail of Doorway," *American Architect and Building News* 93 (May 6, 1908): plate.

311. See "Recent Brickwork in American Cities," *Brickbuilder:* 106-08; and "Dwellings in New York City," *Brickbuilder* 7 (February 1898): 41. Both sources credit the houses to Frank Miles Day & Bro. They were also published as the work of Wilson Eyre; see "Group of Houses, West End Ave. and 85th St., New York," *Architecture* 10 (November 1904): plate. The same block was later attributed to Clarence True; see "Detail of Block of Houses on West End Avenue, Between 84th and 85th Streets, New York, N.Y.," *American Architect and Building News* 87 (May 20, 1905): plate, and (June 17, 1905): 195.

312. The same brand of associational eclecticism that contributed to the Dutch Revival can be seen in the exotic Spanish-Mooresque rowhouses built by the Catalan-born architect Rafael Guastavino on West Seventy-eighth Street, just west of Manhattan Square. As Landau points out, Guastavino's Moorish style was largely patronized by the city's Jewish community; an adopted vocabulary evocative of the Near East, it compensated for the lack of a specifically Hebraic architectural tradition. Guastavino's houses, built in 1885-86, were characterized by lobed arches, an extensive use of decorative corbelling and fields of brick patterning in low relief. This Mudéjaresque repertoire was combined with classicizing details around the projecting second-story bay windows—an eclectic combination of historical allusions that marked this a late example of Cosmopolitan taste. Landau, "Row Houses": 23-25.

313. Landmarks LP 1021, January 9, 1979.

314. Schuyler, "Romanesque Revival": 17.

315. "Churches on the West Side," *Real Estate Record and Guide* 41 (May 12, 1888): 599-600.

316. The other competitors were C.C. Haight, H.M. Congdon, F.C. Withers, R.M. Hunt, William Halsey Wood, and McKim, Mead & White. Sarah Bradford Landau, *Edward T. and William A. Potter: American Victorian Architects, 1885-1901* (Ph.D. diss., New York University, 1978):

204-09. Also see "Churches on the West Side," *Real Estate Record and Guide:* 599; Schuyler, "Romanesque Revival": 18-20; and "St. Agnes Chapel, 92nd St. Bet. Columbus & Amsterdam Avenues, New York," *Architecture and Building* 19 (October 21, 1893): plate.
317. Schuyler, "Romanesque Revival": 20.
318. Schuyler, "Romanesque Revival": 20.
319. "Trinity School Building, Ninety-first Street, New York, N.Y.," *American Architect and Building News* 45 (September 15, 1894): plate; "Trinity School, West Ninety-first Street between Columbus and Amsterdam Avenues, New York," *Architecture and Building* 23 (November 30, 1895): plate; and Christopher Gray, "The Private Schooling of Proper Young Men," *Avenue* 6 (October 1981): 61-66; Also see "St. Agatha School, Eighty-seventh Street and West End Avenue, New York, William A. Boring, Architect," *Brickbuilder* 17 (November 1908): plate 129.
320. "Churches on the West Side," *Real Estate Record and Guide:* 599; "West Side Churches," *Real Estate Record and Guide* 45, "No. 1," (April 19, 1890): 559-60; "No. 2," (May 17, 1890): 731; Schuyler, "Romanesque Revival": 21-23; and Montgomery Schuyler, "The Works of R.H. Robertson," *Architectural Record* 6 (October-December 1896): 184-219.
321. "West Side Churches, No. 1," *Real Estate Record and Guide:* 559-60; Schuyler, "Romanesque Revival": 20-21; and White and Willensky, *AIA Guide, 189.*
322. "West End Presbyterian Church, Amsterdam Ave. and 105th Street, New York, N.Y.," *American Architect and Building News* 39 (January 7, 1893): plate; and King, *King's Handbook,* 370-71.
323. "Churches on the West Side," *Real Estate Record and Guide:* 600; "Entrance to Park Presbyterian Church, Amsterdam Avenue and 86th Street, New York, N.Y.," *American Architect and Building News* 33 (July 25, 1891): plate; and King, *King's Handbook,* 370-71.
324. J.C. Cady's St. Andrew's Methodist-Episcopal Church on West Seventy-sixth Street near Columbus Avenue adapted a similar strategy to a narrow side street lot. "St. Andrew's Methodist Episcopal Church," *American Architect and Building News* 26 (December 28, 1889): plate; King, *King's Handbook,* 375-76; and Montgomery Schuyler, "The Works of Cady, Berg & See," *Architectural Record* 6 (April-June 1897): 517-52. Cady also designed the Grace Methodist Episcopal Church on 104th Street near Columbus Avenue. "Grace Methodist Episcopal Church, New York, N.Y.," *American Architect and Building News* 28 (April 5, 1890): 14, plate. Also see "Catholic Church, 107th Street, West of Amsterdam Avenue, New York, Schickel & Ditmars, Architects," *Architecture and Building* 27 (September 25, 1897): plate.
325. Schuyler, "R.H. Robertson": 210, 212, 214; "St. Paul's Methodist Episcopal Church, Eighty-sixth Street and West End Avenue, New York," *Architecture and Building* 29 (November 5, 1898): plates; "St. Paul's Methodist Episcopal Church, West End Ave. and 86th St., New York, N.Y.," *American Architect and Building News* 64 (June 24, 1889): plates; "South Porch: St. Paul's Methodist Episcopal Church, West 86th St., New York, N.Y.," *American Architect and Building News* 65 (July 8, 1899): plate; and "Southeast View: St. Paul's Methodist Episcopal Church, West End Avenue and West 86th Street, New York, N.Y.," *American Architect and Building News* 87 (February 18, 1905): plate. Two West End Churches dealt ingeniously with corner sites by setting the auditorium on the diagonal. See J.B. Snook & Son's "All Angels' Church, West End Avenue and 81st Street, New York, N.Y.," *American Architect and Building News* 40 (April 1, 1893): 14, plate; and George Keisler's First Baptist Church at the Northwest Corner of Broadway and Seventy-ninth Street (1892). White and Willensky, *AIA Guide,* 193.
326. Schuyler, "R.H. Robertson": 212-16.
327. Schuyler, "R.H. Robertson": 214.
328. Schuyler, "R.H. Robertson": 214.
329. "The New York Cancer Hospital," *Building* 8 (Supplement, March 31, 1888): plate; "New York Cancer Hospital," *Building* 8 (April 7, 1888): 113; "American Construction Through English Eyes—II: The 'Cancer Hospital', New York," *American Architect and Building News* 33 (August 8, 1891): 86-87; and Schuyler, "Haight": 61-64.
330. King, *King's Handbook,* 441-42; and Baker, *Richard Morris Hunt,* 298-99.
331. King, *King's Handbook,* 306-08.
332. R.H. Robertson's competition entry for the south facade was quite close to the Cady, Berg & See design actually built. "Competitive Design for the Proposed New Centre Pavilion on South Side, American Museum of Natural History," *American Architect and Building News* 26 (July 27, 1889): plate. Also see "East Wing, Museum of Natural History, Central Park West, New York City," *Architecture and Building* 24 (January 4, 1896): plate; Schuyler, "The Works of Cady, Berg & See": 534-37; Frank M. Chapman, "Natural History for the Masses," *World's Work* 5 (November 1902): 2762-70; William Walton, "Mural Decoration in the American Museum of Natural History," *Scribner's* 45 (February 1909):

253-56; Hermon C. Bumpus, "A Great American Museum," *World's Work* 15 (March 1908): 10027-36; and Albert Fein, "The American City, The Ideal and the Real," in Edgar Kaufmann, ed., *The Rise of an American Architecture* (New York: Praeger, 1970), 51-111.
333. Schuyler, "Cady, Berg & See": 535.
334. "How the Central Park Facade of the Museum of Natural History Will Look," *Real Estate Record and Guide* 86 (May 20, 1911): 945. Charles Volz had constructed the Columbus Avenue wing in 1908. Trowbridge & Livingston constructed sections of the Central Park West facade in 1924-26, and the Hayden Planetarium in 1933.
335. Pope won the competition in 1925, the other entrants being H. Van Buren Magonigle, Edward Green & Sons, Helmle & Corbett, Gordon & Kaelber, Trowbridge & Livingston, York & Sawyer, and J.H. Freedlander. The competition entries are published in *American Architect* 128 (July 1, 1925): 14, plates 168-78. Also see "John Russell Pope Appointed Architect of the New York State Roosevelt Memorial," *Architecture* 52 (July 1925): 257-58; *The Architecture of John Russell Pope* (New York: William Helburn, 1925), 2, plates 37-44; Henry Fairfield Osborn, *History, Plan and Design of the New York State Roosevelt Memorial* (New York: 1928); George N. Pinder, *The New York State Roosevelt Memorial, Dedicated January 19, 1936* (New York: 1936); and Robert A.M. Stern and Gregory Gilmartin, "Apropos 1900: New York and the Metropolitan Ideal," in Richard Oliver, ed., *The Making of an Architect, 1881-1981* (New York: Rizzoli, 1981), 49-85.
336. "Houses of Richard Cunningham, Esq. and Hon. Oscar S. Straus, West 74th Street, New York, N.Y.," *American Architect and Building News* 33 (August 15, 1891): plate. Equally transitional was Boring & Tilton's unexecuted Italianate design for "Block of Eleven Houses for E. Kilpatrick, Esq., West End Ave. from 97th to 98th Sts., New York City," *Real Estate Record and Guide* 47 (March 7, 1891): 347; and "Design for a Group of Houses on Eighty-sixth Street, New York, N.Y., George E. Wood, Architect," *American Architect and Building News* 51 (January 11, 1896): plate. Brunner & Tryon's Seligman house was far more confidently Classical than their West End Avenue scheme. See "Residence of Professor Seligman, 324 West Eighty-sixth Street, New York," *Architecture and Building* 29 (November 19, 1898): plate.
337. "Residence of Hon. Nathan Straus, 27 West Seventy-second Street, New York City," *Architecture and Building* 24 (January 27, 1896): plate; and "House of Nathan Straus, Esq., 27 West 72nd St., New York, N.Y.," *American Architect and Building News* 64 (November 30, 1901): plate.
338. "Fine West Side Dwellings," *Real Estate Record and Guide* 67 (March 9, 1901): 400.
339. "Joseph A. Farley's New and Artistic Dwellings," *Real Estate Record and Guide* 62 (November 5, 1898): 656.
340. "Joseph A. Farley's New 108th Street Residences," *Real Estate Record and Guide* 64 (September 2, 1899): 335-36. Janes & Leo also seem to have designed Nos. 303-317 on the north side of 106th Street, as 322 West 108th Street was almost identical to 311 and 317 West 106th Street. See "Up-to-Date Dwellings: A Block of Eight on West 106th St., near Riverside Drive," *Real Estate Record and Guide* 65 (May 12, 1900): 811-12. These are also published as "Houses, Riverside Drive," *Brickbuilder* 10 (September 1901): 196. Also by Janes & Leo, see "Block of Residences, Riverside Drive, New York," *Brickbuilder* 10 (October 1901): 219.
341. Landmarks Preservation Commission, *Riverside-West 105th Street Historic District* (New York: 1973), 5-7; and Landau, "Row Houses": 30-31.
342. Landmarks, *105th Street:* 5, 7.
343. "Houses for James Farley, New York City," *Inland Architect and News Record* 40 (December 1902): plate; Landmarks, *105th Street:* 7-8.
344. "Houses, New York City," *Inland Architect and News Record* 41 (February 1903): plate; and Landmarks, *105th Street:* 7-8.
345. "Houses, New York City," *Inland Architect and News Record:* plate; "House at the Corner of 106th Street and Riverside Drive, New York, N.Y.," *American Architect and Building News* 80 (April 4, 1903): plate; "Current Periodicals," *Architectural Review* 5 (April 1910): 47-48; and Landmarks, *105th Street:* 9. A number of Gothic houses served as an antidote to the prevailing Classicism. See "Studio Residence of the Late Olin L. Warner, 467 Central Park West, New York, Barney & Chapman, Architects," *Architecture and Building* 27 (October 16, 1897): plate; and "No. 918 West End Ave., New York, N.Y., Horgan & Slattery, Architects," *American Architect and Building News* 76 (April 12, 1902): plates. The shift toward Classicism nonetheless pervaded the work even of builder-architects such as A.B. Kight. Among Kight's houses, see "No. 304 West 76th St.," *Real Estate Record and Guide* 59 (February 27, 1897): 331; "No. 306 West 76th St.," *Real Estate Record and Guide* 59 (April 17, 1897): 649; "Two of a Group of Three High-Class Houses, Just Completed on Riverside Drive, South Corner of 104th Street," *Real Estate Record and Guide* 61

(February 19, 1898): 321; "A Riverside Drive Mansion, The South Corner of 104th Street," *Real Estate Record and Guide* 61 (March 19, 1898): 501; "No. 41 West 72nd Street," *Real Estate Record and Guide* 63 (February 11, 1899): 242; and "Dwellings of Up-to-Date Construction, near Riverside Drive, Nos. 313 to 323 West 86th Street," *Real Estate Record and Guide* 65 (January 20, 1900): 99.

346. "The Riverside Drive," *Real Estate Record and Guide* 64 (September 2, 1899): 334. Also see "The Riverside Drive," *Real Estate Record and Guide* 61 (March 12, 1898): 453-54.

347. "House for the Clark Estate, New York City," *Real Estate Record and Guide* 30 (March 18, 1899): plate; "Residence, Mrs. Alfred Corning Clark, Riverside Drive and Eighty-ninth St., New York," *Architecture* 2 (July 15, 1900): 250-52; "House for the Clark Estate," *American Architect and Building News* 70 (December 22, 1900): plates; and H.W. Desmond, "The Works of Ernest Flagg," *Architectural Record* 11 (April 1902): 11-104.

348. Abbott Halstead Moore, "Individualism in Architecture: The Works of Herts and Tallant," *Architectural Record* 15 (January 1904): 55-91; and "Residence, Isaac L. Rice, Riverside Drive and Eighty-ninth Street, New York," *Architecture* 7 (May 1903): plates XXXVIII-XXXIX.

349. William Burnett Tuthill, "Residence of M. Schinasi, Esq.," *New York Architect* 3 (July 1909). Also see "Residence of Maurice Schinasi," *Architects' and Builders' Magazine* 10 (August 1909): 442-50; and "A Portrait House," *Real Estate Record and Guide* 84 (August 21, 1909): 340.

350. "American Residence Series: The Residence for Mr. Charles M. Schwab," *Architectural Record* 12 (October 1902): 538-47; "Mr. Schwab's Mansion," *Real Estate Record and Guide* 73 (May 7, 1904): 1043; "Residence, Chas. M. Schwab," *Architecture* 11 (March 1905): plates XIX-XX; "House of Chas. M. Schwab, Esq.," *American Architect and Building News* 88 (November 4, 1905): plates; "Mr. Schwab's Great House Nearly Finished," *Real Estate Record and Guide* 77 (February 17, 1906): 288; and "Chateau Schwab," *Architectural Record* 21 (February 1907): 96-102.

351. "Chateau Schwab," *Architectural Record*: 96, 98.

352. "Chateau Schwab," *Architectural Record*: 100.

353. "Houses of Mrs. J.O. Hoyt and E.J. Stimson, Esq., 310-312 West 75th St., New York, N.Y.," *American Architect and Building News* 65 (July 1, 1899): plate. A similar strategy was employed by Carrère & Hastings in their John Hammond House on East Ninety-first Street.

354. "232 West End Avenue," *Brickbuilder* 17 (September 1908): 205; and White and Willensky, *AIA Guide,* 190.

355. "Some Designs of Charles P.H. Gilbert," *Architectural Record* 9 (October 1899): 165-73.

356. "Some Designs of Charles P.H. Gilbert," *Architectural Record*: 170; Landau, "Row Houses": 34-35. Gilbert's early work was more synthetic; see a design for a large corner house combining Dutch and Gothic allusions: "Examples of Recent Architecture At Home: Residence to be erected on the West Side," *Real Estate Record and Guide* 47 (February 23, 1891): 306. Also see an abstracted Gothic design by J.H. Freedlander: "House on West Seventy-fifth Street, New York," *American Architect and Building News* 95 (February 3, 1909): plates.

357. "Houses of Mrs. Miller and Mrs. McGucken, West 76th Street, New York, N.Y.," *American Architect and Building News* 45 (July 7, 1894): plate; and Landau, "Row Houses": 35-36.

358. "A Residence Block," *Architectural Record* 20 (June 1906): 405; "A Block of Real Homes," *Real Estate Record and Guide* 79 (Janury 26, 1907): 211; "Two Houses in Block 18 to 52 West 74th Street, With Typical Plans," *Brickbuilder* 17 (September 1908): 203; and Landau, "Row Houses": 30, 32.

359. "A Block of Real Homes," *Real Estate Record and Guide*: 211.

360. "Residences of the West Side," *Real Estate Record and Guide* 78 (November 10, 1906): 760. Also see "Private Dwellings vs. Flats in North New York," *Real Estate Record and Guide* 73 (April 2, 1904): 726.

361. See "The Riverside Drive Viaduct," *Public Improvements* 2 (February 15, 1900): 176-77.

362. "Changing City Life," *Real Estate Record and Guide* 88 (December 16, 1911): 923.

363. "Grand Hall, Hotel Majestic," *Architectural Record* 1 (July-September 1891): 70; "Hotel Majestic, New York, Alfred Zucker, Architect," *Architecture and Building* 15 (September 5, 1891): plate.

364. "St. Andrews Hotel, Corner Boulevard and Seventy-second Street, New York," *Architecture and Building* 26 (January 23, 1897): plate.

365. "Hotel Marie Antoinette, Sixty-sixth Street and W. Boulevard, New York," *Architecture and Building* 22 (June 1, 1895): plate; and Albert Bigelow Paine, "The Flat Dwellers of a Great City," *World's Work* 5 (April 1903): 3281-94.

366. "Hotel Marie Antoinette, New York," *Inland Architect and News Record* 42 (December 1903): plate; Paine, "Flat Dwellers": 3290.

367. "The Real Estate Boom in West End Avenue," *Real Estate Record and Guide* 89 (June 29, 1912): 1393-94. Also see "Is Apartment-Hotel Construction to be Revived?" *Real Estate Record and Guide* 86 (August 6, 1910): 232; "The Reconstruction of West End Avenue," *Real Estate Record and Guide* 89 (June 12, 1912): 1359; and "Straus Square Section in Healthy State," *Real Estate Record and Guide* 99 (February 3, 1917): 63.

368. "The Real Estate Boom in West End Avenue," *Real Estate Record and Guide*: 1393.

369. "Wellesley Apartment House, N.E. Corner West End Ave. and Eighty-first St., New York," *Architecture and Building* 27 (October 23, 1897): plate; and C.H. Israels, "New York Apartment Houses," *Architectural Record* 11 (July 1901): 476-508.

370. Israels, "New York Apartment Houses": 482; and Alpern, *Apartments for the Affluent,* 24-25.

371. "The Alimar, 925 West End Avenue, New York; Janes & Leo, Architects," *Architectural Review* 5 (June 1903): 120; and Elisha Harris Janes, "The Development and Financing of Apartment Houses in New York—I," *Brickbuilder* 17 (December 1908): 276-78.

372. For apartment houses typical of West End Avenue's later development, see Rouse & Goldstone's, "The Allendale Apartments," *Real Estate Record and Guide* 85 (January 1, 1910): 6; "Many New Buildings in the West End Section," *Real Estate Record and Guide* 86 (March 25, 1911): 531; Neville & Bagge's "Apartment House, 789 West End Avenue, New York City," and "Apartment House, 590 West End Avenue, New York City," *Architecture and Building* 48 (December 1916): 77-78, 81-82; Arthur Louis Harmon's "Apartment House at 78th Street and West End Avenue," *American Architect* 115 (May 21, 1919): plates 166-69; Gaetan Ajello's "New Project for West End Ave. Appraised at $1,103,500," *Real Estate Record and Guide* 113 (February 2, 1924): 11; Rosario Candelas "New West End Avenue Project Appraised at $1,831, 650," *Real Estate Record and Guide* 113 (March 8, 1924): 11; and "West End Improvements are Steadily Increasing," *Real Estate Record and Guide* 113 (June 28, 1924): 11.

373. See "Broadway, West of Central Park," *Real Estate Record and Guide* 67 (April 6, 1901): 587-88.

374. Paine, "Flat Dwellers": 3283; "Architectural Aberrations No. 19: The Dorilton," *Architectural Record* 12 (June 1902): 221-26; Israels, "New York Apartment Houses": 502; "The Dorilton Apartments, 71st Street and Broadway, New York," *Architectural Review* 5 (June 1903): 116; "Dorilton Apartments, 71st St. & Broadway," *New York Architect* 2 (January 1908): plates; Janes, "Development and Financing of Apartment Houses in New York": 277; and Alpern, *Apartments for the Affluent,* 28-29.

375. "Architectural Aberrations No. 19," *Architectural Record*: 226.

376. "Architectural Aberrations No. 19," *Architectural Record*: 225.

377. The robust Modern French of the Dorilton was echoed around the corner at the Hargrave, where Frederick Browne adapted its basic strategy to a mid-block site. "The Hargrave, 104 West 72nd Street, New York; Frederick C. Browne, Architect," *Architectural Review* 5 (June 1903): 122. A Modern French apartment hotel projected nearby was not built. See "Apartment Hotel, 204-6 West 72nd St., New York, N.Y.," *American Architect and Building News* 78 (November 22, 1902): plate.

378. Paine, "Flat Dwellers": 3291; "The Ansonia, New York," *Architectural Review* 5 (June 1903): 128; "The Ansonia, Broadway, 73rd and 74th Streets, New York, N.Y.," *Architectural Review* 11 (March 1904): plates XV-XVII; "A Bachelor Apartment in the Ansonia, New York," *Architectural Review* 12 (April 1905): 124-25; Slawson & Hobbs, "The Upper West Side": 157; T.M. Clare, "Apartment-Houses," *American Architect and Building News* 91 (January 5, 1907): 3-11; and Alpern, *Apartments for the Affluent,* 30-31.

379. Ernest Flagg was very critical of the Ansonia: "The plan is complicated and the lighting can hardly be called good. Many of the rooms facing the recessed courts are not well lighted, and there is a good deal of interior space which is practically not lighted at all. Most of the rooms are irregular in shape, without symmetry or beauty of form. A person who understood the principles of planning could have seen at a glance that the plan was wasteful. Such mistakes could hardly have been made by a professional planner. In this case the owner was his own architect. Perhaps the pleasure he derived from the work was more than equivalent for the money which might have been saved by a more skillful planner. It is a peculiar fact that most people, no matter how ignorant they may feel as regards other branches of knowledge, account themselves fully qualified to plan a building. Few realize how much may be saved or lost by a plan." *Architectural Review* (Boston) 1902, quoted by Andrew Alpern, "In the Manor Housed," *Metropolis* 1 (March 1982): 11-15.

380. "Bachelor Apartment," *Architectural Review*: 125.

381. "Spencer Arms Apartments," *New York Architect* 2 (January 1908): plates.

382. "The Severn and The Van Dyck Apartments," *Architecture* 15 (March 1907): 42, plate 20; "The Van Dyck and Severn Apartments," *Architects' and Builders' Magazine* 9 (July 1907): 508-10.

383. "Euclid Hall, New York," *Inland Architect and News Record* 41 (March 1903): plate; and "Euclid Hall, Broadway, 85th to 86th Streets, New York: Hill & Turner, Architects," *Architectural Review* 5 (June 1903): plate.
384. "The Marseilles, Broadway and 103rd St., New York," *Architecture* 11 (January 1905): plates.
385. "The Hotel Belleclaire," *Architects' and Builders' Magazine* 4 (January 1903): 164-65.
386. "Belnord," *Architecture* 35 (December 1908): 192-93.
387. "The Cherbourg," *Real Estate Record and Guide* 66 (November 10, 1900): 619; and C.H. Israels, "New York Apartment Houses," *Architectural Review* 11 (July 1901): 476-508.
388. "Apartment House in Central Park West, New York, N.Y.," *American Architect and Building News* 70 (December 22, 1900): plate; and Franz K. Winkler, "Recent Apartment House Design: Central Park West, New York City," *Architectural Record* 11 (January 1902): 98-109. Also see an apartment house by Neville & Bagge on the northwest corner of Central Park West and Sixty-seventh Street. "Chatham Court Apartment House, New York City," *Inland Architect and News Record* 40 (August 1902): plate.
389. Winkler, "Recent Apartment House Designs": 106-09. Also see "El Dorado Apartment Building, New York City, Neville & Bagge, Architects," *Inland Architect and News Record* 43 (January 1904): plates.
390. "New York Apartment Houses," *Architects' and Builders' Magazine* 8 (April 1907): 315-24; and "Central Park View Apartments," *New York Architect* 2 (January 1908): plate.
391. "The Central Park West Section," *Real Estate Record and Guide* 78 (August 4, 1906): 210-11; and Alpern, *Apartments for the Affluent,* 46-47.
392. "The Langham Apartments, Central Park West and 73d St., New York," *Architecture* 16 (July 15, 1907): 116-17; "The Central Park West Section," *Real Estate Record and Guide* 78 (August 4, 1906): 210-11; and Alpern, *Apartments for the Affluent,* 38-39.
393. "Harperly Hall—An Apartment House," *Architects' and Builders' Magazine* 11 (November 1910): 85-86.
394. "Architectural Criticism," *Architecture* 23 (April 15, 1911): 49-50, 62-63, plate XL; C. Matlack Price, "Some Recent Work by Albert Joseph Bodker," *Architectural Record* 33 (May 1913): 381-420; and Alpern, *Apartments for the Affluent,* 56-57.
395. "Architectural Criticism," *Architecture:* 49-50, 62-63, plate 40; and Alpern, *Apartments for the Affluent,* 56-57.
396. "Many New Buildings in the West End Section," *Real Estate Record and Guide* 86 (March 25, 1911): 531.
397. "Wellsmore Apartments, New York City," *American Architect* 100 (November 29, 1911): 53. Also see "Manhasset Apartment-House, Broadway between 108th and 109th Streets, New York, N.Y., Messrs. Joseph Wolf and Janes & Leo, Architects," *American Architect and Building News* 87 (May 6, 1905): plates.
398. "The Apartment Houses of New York," *Real Estate Record and Guide* 85 (March 26, 1910): 644-46.
399. "The Red House Apartments, 350 West 85th St., New York," *Architecture* 10 (November 1904): plate 94. Mulliken & Moeller's Lombard Apartments was a much larger essay in Venetian Gothic, with none of the Red House's cozy scale. "The Lombard, 260 West 76th St., New York," *Architecture* 16 (December 1907): plate CIX.
400. "West Side Republican Club-House, New York, N.Y.," *American Architect and Building News* 57 (December 4, 1897): 82, plate; and "West Side Republican Club House, Boulevard, Between 83d and 84th Sts., New York City," *Brickbuilder* 7 (May 1898): plate 33.
401. "The Colonial Club-House, New York, N.Y.," *American Architect and Building News* 38 (December 10, 1892): plate; and "The Colonial Club, New York, N.Y.," *American Architect and Building News* 46 (December 20, 1894): 135, 139-40, plates.
402. Slawson and Hobbs, "The Upper West Side": 157-58; and "West 72nd Street in Transition State," *Real Estate Record and Guide* 96 (October 23, 1915): 685.
403. "New Home for Progress Club," *Public Improvements* 6 (February 1902): 23; "Fireproofing the Progress Club" (advertisement), *Real Estate Record and Guide* 75 (March 11, 1905): 523.
404. "Ethical Culture Society Building, Central Park West and 63d St., New York," *Architecture* 10 (September 1904): plate 81; "Building for Ethical Culture Society, 63rd Street and Central Park West, New York City," *Brickbuilder* 13 (September 1904): plate; and Blake, *Carrère & Hastings,* 78-79. Blake neglects to mention Kohn's collaboration. Carrère & Hastings probably received the commission through the influence of Hendon Chubb, a prominent Ethical Culturalist for whom they had already built the Chubb Building on South William Street in 1899-1900. Also see "The Grand Circle and Its Future," *Real Estate Record and Guide* 78 (September 1, 1906): 364-65.

405. "Architectural Appreciations: Hall of the Society of Ethical Culture," *Architectural Record* 30 (August 1911): 175-80.
406. "Hall of the Society of Ethical Culture," *Architectural Record:* 176.
407. See "West End Synagogue (Congregation Shaaray Tefila), Eighty-second Street, between Columbus and Amsterdam Aves., New York," *Architecture and Building* 23 (September 21, 1896): plate. Also see a virtually identical design by George F. Pelham, address unknown: "Jewish Synagogue, New York City," *Inland Architect and News Record* 43 (February 1904): plate. For Shearith Israel, see "Synagogue, Congregation Shearith Israel, Seventieth Street and Central Park West, New York," *Architecture and Building* 27 (August 14, 1897): plate; "Synagogue, Shearith Israel, Seventieth Street and Central Park West, New York, N.Y.," *American Architect and Building News* 57 (October 30, 1897): plate; "Temple Shearith Israel, Central Park West and 70th St., New York, N.Y.," *American Architect and Building News* 70 (November 24, 1900): plate; and Bernard Postal and Lionel Koppman, *Jewish Landmarks in New York* (New York: Hill and Wang, 1964), 130.
408. Postal and Koppman, *Jewish Landmarks in New York,* 131.
409. "Second Church of Christian Scientist," *Architectural Record* 10 (July 1900): 84; "Second Church of Christ," *Real Estate Record and Guide* 66 (September 15, 1900): 320; "Church of Christ Scientist," *Inland Architect and News Record* 37 (June 1901): plate; and "Second Church of the Christian Scientists," *Architectural Record* 12 (June 1902): 231-32.
410. "Church of the Divine Paternity, Corner Seventy-sixth Street and Central Park West," *Architecture and Building* 28 (April 30, 1898): plates; "Nave and Chancel: Church of the Divine Paternity, New York, N.Y.," *American Architect and Building News* 64 (May 27, 1899): plate; and Schuyler, "Potter": 194-95. Also see Heins & LaFarge's somewhat less archaeological exploration of similar motifs: "Fourth Presbyterian Church, West End Ave., Cor. 91st St., New York," *Architecture and Building* 21 (October 20, 1894): plate.
411. Schuyler, "Potter": 194-95.
412. "First Church of Christ, Scientist, New York," *Inland Architect and News Record* 42 (September 1903): plates; Owen R. Washburn, "The Architecture of a Christian Science Church," *Architectural Record* 15 (February 1904): 158-70; "The First Church of Christ, Scientist, New York City," *Architectural Review* 12 (September 1905): 254-55; and "First Church of Christ, Scientist," *American Architect and Building News* 88 (July 1, 1905): plates. Hunt & Hunt's Colonial style house for Mrs. A.E. Stetson at 7 West Ninety-sixth Street attempted rather unsuccessfully to mediate between the blocky massing of the church and the planar rowhouses to the west. "Residence, Mrs. A.E. Stetson, 7 W. 96th St., New York," *Architecture* 14 (September 1904): plate LXVII. The new church stood opposite William H. Hume's Romanesque "Scotch Presbyterian Church, Southwest Corner Ninety-sixth Street and Central Park West, New York," *Architecture and Building* 22 (June 15, 1895): plate. Also see "Lecture Hall on 95th St., Near Central Park West, New York; for the Scotch Presbyterian Church," *Architecture and Building* 19 (December 30, 1893): plate; and King, *King's Handbook,* 365.
413. Washburn, "The Architecture of a Christian Science Church": 158-70.
414. Lewis Mumford, *Sketches from Life: The Early Years* (New York: The Dial Press, 1982), 8.
415. "Morningside Park as It Will Be," *Real Estate Record and Guide* 30 (supplement to October 7, 1882): plates; "Morningside Park," *Real Estate Record and Guide* 30 (October 14, 1882): 23-24; "Active Interest Manifested in Morningside Park," *Real Estate Record and Guide* 39 (January 29, 1887): 131; and Elizabeth Barlow and William Alex, *Frederick Law Olmsted's New York* (New York: Praeger, 1972), 47-50, 114-15.
416. For the proposed 1889 Fair, see "International Exhibition, New York, 1883, W.G. Preston, Architect," *American Architect and Building News* 7 (March 13, 1880): plates; *American Architect and Building News* 8 (September 18, 1880): 134; "The Site for the Exhibition of 1883," *American Architect and Building News* 8 (November 6, 1880): 218; "The Site for the World's Fair for 1883 Selected," *American Architect and Building News* 8 (November 20, 1880): 242; "The World's Fair An Assured Success," *Real Estate Record and Guide* 27 (January 15, 1881): 46; and "The World's Fair," *Real Estate Record and Guide* 27 (March 26, 1881): 273. For the movement to hold the Columbian Celebration in New York, see "Proposed Exhibition by the Three Americas," *American Architect and Building News* 25 (June 8, 1889): 265; "Exposition of 1892," *Building* 11 (July 13, 1889): 9; "The Project for a World's Fair in 1892," *American Architect and Building News* 26 (July 20, 1889): 22; John Mullaly, "The Topic of the Hour—The Exposition," *Real Estate Record and Guide* 44 (August 24, 1889): 1155-56; "The Site for the Exposition of 1882," *Building* 11 (August 31, 1889): 67; "The Use of Central Park Bad Policy," *Building* 11 (September 28, 1889): 99; *Real Estate Record and Guide* 44 (November 2, 1889): 1466; and "Building Prospects," *Architecture and Building* 12 (January 11, 1890): 14.

417. "The Bloomingdale Asylum to Move," *Real Estate Record and Guide* 41 (February 18, 1888): 206; "The Bloomingdale Asylum's Removal," *Real Estate Record and Guide* 41 (May 26, 1888): 670; and "Morningside Plateau," *Real Estate Record and Guide* 60 (October 16, 1897): 542-43.
418. "Morningside Plateau," *Real Estate Record and Guide*: 542.
419. "Morningside Plateau," *Real Estate Record and Guide*: 542.
420. *Real Estate Record and Guide* 39 (June 4, 1887): 763; Robert Ellis Jones, "A Great American Cathedral," *World's Work* 13 (July 1906): 7754-66; and George Macculloch Miller and George F. Nelson, *Cathedral Church of St. John the Divine* (New York: St. Bartholomew's Press, 1916).
421. Marianna Griswold van Rensselaer, "Recent Architecture in America, Part IV: Churches," *Century* 29 (January 1885): 323-38.
422. Letter to the Editors, "The New Cathedral," *Real Estate Record and Guide* 40 (November 12, 1887): 1412.
423. Henry C. Potter, "An American Cathedral," *Munsey's* 19 (May 1898): 242-49. Also see Russell Sturgis, "The Revival of Cathedral Buildings," *Munsey's* 37 (May 1907): 186-95.
424. See two letters to the editor, "The New Cathedral," and "The Purchase of the Cathedral Site," *Real Estate Record and Guide* 40 (November 12, 1887): 1412-13; and "Is The Cathedral Possible?" *Real Estate Record and Guide* 40 (December 31, 1887): 1644.
425. "The Purchase of the Cathedral Site," *Real Estate Record and Guide*: 1413.
426. "What Architects Say About the Proposed Cathedral," *Real Estate Record and Guide* 39 (June 11, 1887): 798-99; "The New Cathedral," *Real Estate Record and Guide*: 1412; "New York: Some Difficulties Attending the Designing of the Proposed Episcopal Cathedral," *American Architect and Building News* 23 (February 18, 1888): 77-78; John Beverley Robinson, Letter to the Editors, "How to Approach the Designing of the New York Cathedral," *American Architect and Building News* 23 (March 10, 1888): 19; *American Architect and Building News* 23 (May 5, 1888): 206; and "The New York Cathedral Competition," *American Architect and Building News* 25 (March 16, 1889): 121.
427. The invited entrants were J.C. Cady & Co.; C.C. Haight; F.C. Withers; R.H. Gibson; H.M. Congdon; R.M. Hunt; Carrère & Hastings; Renwick, Aspinwall & Russell; McKim, Mead & White; R.H. Robertson; Henry Vaughan; Van Brunt & Howe; W. Halsey Wood; and Frank Furness. Landau, *Edward T. and William A. Potter*, 210-11.
428. "The New York Cathedral Competition," *American Architect and Building News* 25 (May 25, 1889): 241. Heins & LaFarge were associated with W.W. Kent and General William Sooy Smith. See "A Charge of Suppressing Information," *American Architect and Building News* 25 (June 1, 1889): 253. The premiated entries were published in "The Cathedral of St. John the Divine," *Real Estate Record and Guide* 47, Part 1 (April 11, 1891): 552-53; Part 2 (April 18, 1891): 603-04; "The Cathedral of St. John the Divine, The Second Competition," *American Architect and Building News* 32 (May 9, 1891): 78, 81-92, plates; and "The Cathedral of St. John the Divine, New York City," *Architectural Record* 30 (August 1911): 185-92.
429. "New York: The Protestant Cathedral Competition," *Real Estate Record and Guide* 25 (May 18, 1889): 238-29; "Exhibition of the New York Cathedral Plans Impossible," *American Architect and Building News* 25 (June 1, 1889): 253; A Non-Competitor, Letter to the Editors, May 31, 1889, "The New York Cathedral Competition," *American Architect and Building News* 25 (June 8, 1889): 275; "The Cathedral Competition," *Building* 10 (June 8, 1889): 181-82; "New York: The Late Competition of the Cathedral of St. John the Divine," *American Architect and Building News* 25 (June 22, 1889): 296-97; and Landau, *Edward T. and William A. Potter*, 212-13.
430. *Real Estate Record and Guide* 47 (March 14, 1891): 383; and Landau, *Edward T. and William A. Potter*, 212-13.
431. Landau, *Edward T. and William A. Potter*, 599.
432. See the unpremiated entries of W.S. Fraser and Carrère & Hastings: *American Architect and Building News* 26 (October 5, 1889): 158-59, plates; R.W. Gibson and Peabody & Stearns: *American Architect and Building News* 26 (October 19, 1889): 182-83, plates; H.M. Congdon and Van Brunt & Howe: *American Architect and Building News* 26 (November 2, 1889): 206, plate; L.S. Buffington (Harvey Ellis, designer), Renwick, Aspinwall & Russell, and Parfitt Bros.: *American Architect and Building News* 26 (November 23, 1889): 242-43, plates; Glenn Brown: *American Architect and Building News* 27 (January 4, 1890): plate; B.G. Goodhue and Messrs. Cram & Wentworth: *American Architect and Building News* 27 (February 8, 1890): 110, plates; and Herter Bros.: *Real Estate Record and Guide* 44 (October 12, 1889): 1366. For Harvey Ellis's scheme, see also Francis Swales, "Master Draftsmen, III: Harvey Ellis (1852-1907)," *Pencil Points* 5 (July 1924): 49-55, 79. Also see James Park Morton, "Resurrections," *Metropolis* 1 (January-February 1982): 12-15.
433. Among those architects exhibited were: Parfitt Bros.; Edward Pearce Casey; Carrère & Hastings; R.W. Gibson; and two proposals by Cram & Wentworth. A Layman, "The Architectural League Exhibition" *Real Estate Record and Guide* 45 (January 11, 1890): 359; "The League Exhibition," *American Architect and Building News* 27, Part I (January 18, 1890): 40-41; Part II (January 25, 1890): 57-58.
434. "Cathedral of St. John the Divine: No. I," *Real Estate Record and Guide*: 552-53.
435. Alexander Graham, "Cathedral for New York," *American Architect and Building News* 26 (December 7, 1889): 267.
436. "The Cathedral of St. John the Divine," *American Architect and Building News* 32 (May 9, 1891): 87-89, plates; "The Cathedral of Saint John the Divine," *Architectural Record*: 190; and Landau, *Edward T. and William A. Potter*, 214.
437. "The Cathedral of St. John the Divine," *American Architect and Building News*: 81-89; Schuyler, "Potter": 191-93; "The Cathedral of St. John the Divine," *Architectural Record*: 190; and Landau, *Edward T. and William A. Potter*, 217-20.
438. Schuyler, "Potter": 193.
439. Schuyler, "Potter": 193.
440. "Cathedral of St. John the Divine, The Second Competition," *American Architect and Building News*: 81-91, plates; "The Cathedral of Saint John the Divine," *Architectural Record*: 190-91; and Landau, *Edward T. and William A. Potter*, 214-15.
441. "The Cathedral of St. John the Divine, New York City," *Architectural Record*: 190.
442. "The Cathedral of St. John the Divine: No. 1," *Real Estate Record and Guide*: 552-53.
443. "Cathedral of St. John the Divine, The Second Competition," *American Architect and Building News*: 81-91. Also see Wood's scheme for St. Agnes Chapel, "Competitive Design for Church, Clergy-House and Schools for Trinity Corporation," *American Architect and Building News* 25 (May 11, 1889): plate.
444. "Competitive Design for the Cathedral of St. John the Divine, New York, N.Y.—Messrs. Carrère & Hastings, Architects," *American Architect and Building News* 26 (October 5, 1889): 158-59, plates; and "The Work of Messrs. Carrère & Hastings," *Architectural Record*: 24-25.
445. "Competitive Design—Messrs. Carrère & Hastings," *American Architect and Building News*: 158-59, plates.
446. "The League Exhibition—I" *American Architect and Building News*: 40.
447. Schuyler, "Potter": 192.
448. Landau, *Edward T. and William A. Potter*, 212-13.
449. "The Cathedral of St. John the Divine," *American Architect and Building News* 32 (May 9, 1891): 89; and "The Cathedral of Saint John the Divine," *Architectural Record*: 185-86, 191-92.
450. "The Cathedral of St. John the Divine," *American Architect and Building News*: 90.
451. For the Guastavino tile system, see George R. Collins, "The Transfer of Thin Masonry Vaulting from Spain to America," *Journal of the Society of Architectural Historians* 27 (October 1968): 176-201. Also see "America's Largest Dome, Erected Without Scaffolding or Falsework Support Two Hundred Feet Above the Ground," *Architecture* 21 (January 1910): 12-13.
452. "The Cathedral of St. John the Divine, New York City," *Architectural Record*: 192. For the evolution of Heins & LaFarge's design, see "The Cathedral of St. John the Divine," *Architectural Record* 2 (July-September 1892): 44-64; Robert Ellis Jones, "A Great American Cathedral," *World's Work* 12 (July 1906): 7754-66; C. Grant LaFarge, "The Cathedral of St. John the Divine," *Scribner's* 41 (April 1907): 385-401; "The Cathedral Church of St. John the Divine," *American Architect* 99 (April 19, 1911): 145-50, 152, plates; and William H. Goodyear, "Temperamental Architecture," *New York Architect* (April 1911): 41-53.
453. "The Cathedral of St. John the Divine," *Architectural Record*: 185. Also see "The Death of G.L. Heins, Architect," and "The Architectural Future of the Cathedral of St. John the Divine," *American Architect and Building News* 92 (October 5, 1907): 105-06.
454. "Design Proposed for the Completion of the Cathedral of St. John the Divine, Mr. Ralph Adams Cram, Consulting Architect," *American Architect* 104 (December 17, 1913): plates; "Notes and Comments: The Truth About the Cathedral Plans," *Architectural Record* 35 (March 1914): 269; *Cathedral Church of St. John the Divine* (New York: Cathedral League, St. Bartholomew's Press, 1916); Ralph Adams Cram, "The Nave of the Cathedral of St. John the Divine, New York," *Architecture* 36 (August, 1917): 144-50; A.D.F. Hamlin, *A Study of the Designs for the Cathedral of St. John the Divine* (New York: 1924); "Contract Let for Nave of Cathedral of St. John the Divine," *Real Estate Record and Guide* 115 (January 31, 1925): 7, 10; and "Cathedral of St. John the Divine, New York City, Cram & Ferguson, Architects, March 1926," *Architecture* 53 (June 1926): 163. Also

see "The Whiting Memorial Chapel of the Cathedral of St. John the Divine, New York, Messrs. Carrère & Hastings, Architects," *American Architect* 102 (July 10, 1912): plates; "Synod House, St. John the Divine, New York, Messrs. Cram, Goodhue & Ferguson (Boston office)" *American Architect* 104 (December 17, 1913): plate; and "St. James Chapel, Cathedral of St. John the Divine, Henry Vaughan, Architect," *Architectural Forum* 33 (October 1920): 121-22, plates 58-60.

455. "The Cathedral of St. John the Divine," *Architectural Record:* 185.
456. King, *King's Handbook,* 471-73.
457. "St. Luke's Hospital Competition," *Architecture and Building* 16 (April 30, 1892): 222.
458. "Proposed Design for St. Luke's Hospital, South Front," *American Architect and Building News* 41 (August 26, 1893): plate.
459. Henry F. and Elsie R. Withey, *Biographical Dictionary of American Architects (Deceased)* (Los Angeles: Hennessey & Ingalls, 1970), 211-12. For Flagg's competition entry, see "Accepted Design for St. Luke's Hospital," *Architecture and Building* 17 (December 24, 1892): plates. It consisted of eight four-story, hipped-roof pavilions and a domed administration wing. The latter fronted an entrance courtyard, while two small staff residences acted as gatehouses.
460. "St Luke's Hospital, New York," *Brickbuilder* 5 (February 1896): plates 7-12; "St. Luke's Hospital, Bloomingdale Heights, New York, N.Y.," *American Architect and Building News* 62 (February 25, 1899): plates; Katherine Hoffman, "A Model Hospital," *Munsey's* 22 (January 1900): 487-96; and Desmond, "Flagg": 13-22. Also note "St. Luke's Emergency Hospital," *American Architect* 112 (September 12, 1917): 181-83.
461. Schuyler, "Cady, Berg & See": 533.
462. *Architectural Review* 5 (January 20, 1898): 8.
463. "Architectural Additions to New York: Woman's Hospital," *Real Estate Record and Guide* 67 (June 2, 1900): 965; "Womans' [sic] Hospital in the State of New York, 110th Street, New York, N.Y.," *American Architect and Building News* 83 (February 20, 1904): plates; and "The New Woman's Hospital, New York," *Architectural Record* 21 (April 1907): 282-94.
464. "The New York College for the Training of Teachers," *American Architect and Building News* 37 (August 27, 1892): plates; King, *King's Handbook,* 293; "New Buildings for the Teachers College, New York, N.Y.," *American Architect and Building News* 40 (April 15, 1893): 46, plates; "The Teachers College, 120th and 121st Streets, between Amsterdam Avenue and the Boulevard, New York," *Architecture and Building* 21 (October 13, 1894): plates; Schuyler, "Potter": 104; Landau, *Edward T. and William A. Potter,* 338-42; and White and Willensky, *AIA Guide,* 258-59. Potter's campus for Teachers College closely resembled his 1882-84 design for the Union Theological Seminary on Park Avenue between Sixty-ninth and Seventieth streets.
465. Marianna Griswold van Rensselaer, "Recent Architecture in America. Public Buildings I," *Century* 6 (May 1884): 48-67; "Notes of Current Interest," *Building* 6 (April 16, 1887): 148; "Columbia College Improvements," *Building* 11 (September 28, 1889): 108; Schuyler, "Haight": 4-12; Montgomery Schuyler, "Architecture of American Colleges, Part IV: New York City Colleges," *Architectural Record* 27 (June 1910): 443-69; and Francesco Passanti, "The Design of Columbia in the 1890s. McKim and His Client," *Journal of the Society of Architectural Historians* 36 (May 1977): 69-84.
466. Schuyler, "Haight": 8.
467. Schuyler, "New York City Colleges": 443. Also see "Columbia College Centennial," *Building* 6 (April 16, 1887): 142; and "Columbia University and Its New Buildings," *Architects' and Builders' Magazine* 33 (October 1900): 11-19.
468. "The New President of Columbia College," *Century* 34 (February 1890): 635. Also see "Editorial Notes and Comments," *Architecture and Building* 15 (October 10, 1891): 170; and "Columbia College," *Century* 43 (March 1892): 790-91.
469. "Editorial Notes and Comments," *Architecture and Building* 16 (May 28, 1892): 270; and Passanti, "Columbia": 70-71.
470. Quoted in Passanti, "Columbia": 71.
471. Quoted in Passanti, "Columbia": 71-72.
472. Quoted in Passanti, "Columbia": 72.
473. Quoted in Passanti, "Columbia": 73.
474. "Personal," *Architecture and Building* 29 (December 9, 1893): 287; and Passanti, "Columbia": 73-75.
475. Quoted in Schuyler, "New York City Colleges": 445.
476. Schuyler, "New York City Colleges": 447.
477. Schuyler, "New York City Colleges": 447.
478. Schuyler, "New York City Colleges": 447.
479. According to the *Record and Guide* a close precedent was M. Rumpf's 1816 design for a church illustrated in *Les Grande Prix d'Architecture, 1804 a 1831; Real Estate Record and Guide* 60 (July 3, 1897): 2; "American Architects as Imitators," *American Architect and Building News* 57 (July 24, 1897): 30. Also see Passanti, "Columbia": 78-82.
480. See Passanti, "Columbia": 81; "Main Reading Room: Library of Columbia University, New York, N.Y.," G.A. Suter, "The Heating and Ventilating of Columbia University," *American Architect and Building News* 62 (October 8, 1898): 12-16, plates; William H. Goodyear, "Horizontal Curves in Columbia University," *Architectural Record* 9 (January 1899): 82-93; "Library—Columbia University, New York City," *Architecture and Building* 30 (January 7, 1899): plates; Albert Winslow Cobb, "New York's Architectural Problems," *Architecture and Building* 30 (April 1, 1899): 99-100; "Columbia University and its New Buildings," *Architects' and Builders' Magazine* 33 (October 1900): 11-19; Sidney K. Greenslade, "Libraries in the United States, II, Columbia University Library," *American Architect and Building News* 77 (July 26, 1902): 28-29; "The New Flag Staff at Columbia University," *Architects' and Builders' Magazine* 8 (November 1906): 77-78; and Robert H. Moulton, "A Granite Ball as a Sun-Dial," *Architectural Record* 43 (January 1918): 96.
481. *New York Times* (November 7, 1897): Sunday Magazine, 2 quoted in Passanti, "Columbia": 82.
482. Royal Cortissoz, "Landmarks of Manhattan," *Scribner's* 18 (November 1895): 531-44.
483. Schuyler, "New York City Colleges": 448-49.
484. "Earl Hall, Columbia University, New York City," *Inland Architect and News Record* 40 (August 1902): plate, "Earl Hall, Columbia College," *Architects' and Builders' Magazine* 4 (January 1903): 86; and "Students Hall, Columbia University, New York City," *Architectural Review* 8 (April 1901): plates XXVI-XXVIII.
485. "St. Paul's Chapel: Columbia University, New York, N.Y.," *American Architect and Building News* 87 (March 25, 1905): plate; "St. Paul's Chapel: Columbia University, New York, N.Y.," *American Architect and Building News* 89 (June 30, 1906): plate; "The New Buildings of Columbia University," *Architects' and Builders' Magazine* 7 (February 1906): 193-205; "St. Paul's Chapel, Columbia University," *Architecture* 14 (August 1906): plate 52; and Russell Sturgis, "St. Paul's Chapel," *Architectural Record* 21 (February 1907): 83-95. Also see "School of Mines, Columbia University, New York, N.Y.," *Architectural Review* 11 (December 1904): plate LXV; and "Entrance Front, School of Mines, Columbia University," *Architecture* 12 (November 1905): plate XCVIII.
486. Schuyler, "New York City Colleges": 450.
487. Schuyler, "New York City Colleges": 452.
488. "Avery Library Building, Columbia University, New York," *American Architect* 102 (November 20, 1912): plate; and C. Matlack Price, "The Design of the Avery Architectural Library," *Architectural Record* 33 (June 1913): 534-49.
489. "Detail, Kent Hall, Columbia University, New York," *American Architect* 105 (March 4, 1914): plate.
490. "Professional Comment," *Architecture* 13 (April 1906): 50; "The New Buildings of Columbia University," *Architects' and Builders' Magazine:* 193-205. Also see "Hamilton Hall, Columbia University," *Architecture* 15 (March 1907): plate XXIII; "School of Journalism, Columbia University, New York," *American Architect* 104 (August 27, 1913): plate.
491. Seth Low, Annual Report to the Trustees, 1898, quoted in *American Architect and Building News* 32 (October 8, 1898): 15. Also see "Hartley and Livingston Halls, Columbia University," *Architecture* 12 (November 1905): plate.
492. "Barnard College, New York City," *Brickbuilder* 8 (August 1899): 142. Also see "Barnard College," *Architecture and Building* 24 (April 25, 1896): 193-94.
493. Schuyler, "New York City Colleges": 450.
494. "Barnard College," *Architecture* 10 (November 1904): 172-75, plate.
495. "Dormitory, Barnard College, New York," *Brickbuilder* 11 (July 1902): plate; and "Dormitories of Barnard College, New York City," *Inland Architect and News Record* 40 (August 1902): plate.
496. *National Academy of Design: Photographs of the New Building, with an Introductory Essay and Description by Peter Bennett Wight* (New York: 1866), in the collection of Avery Library, Columbia University.
497. King, *King's Handbook,* 308.
498. "Editorial Notes and Comments," *Architecture and Building* 25 (July 4, 1896): 2. Also see "Editorial Notes and Comments," *Architecture and Building* 21 (October 6, 1894): 159-60; and "The National Academy of Design," *Architecture and Building* 28 (January 1, 1898): 1.
499. "Editorial Notes and Comments," *Architecture and Building* 26 (May 8, 1897): 222; "The Academy of Design Competition," *Architecture and Building* 27 (October 2, 1897): 125-26; and "The Jury for the Academy of Design Competition," *American Architect and Building News* 58 (October 9, 1897): 9.
500. "The National Academy of Design, New York," *Architecture and Building* 28 (January 1, 1898): plates; "National Academy of Design, New

York," *Architectural Review* 5 (January 20, 1898): plates I-VI; "The New National Academy of Design," and "The Museum, Nantes, France," *Architectural Record* 7 (January-March 1898): 387-88; and Carroll Beckwith, "The National Academy of Design," *Public Improvements* 2 (December 15, 1899): 73-74.

501. "Competitive Design for the National Academy of Design, New York," *Architecture and Building* 28 (January 1, 1898): plates; and "National Academy of Design, New York," *Architectural Review:* plates VIII-X.

502. Carroll Beckwith, "The National Academy of Design": 73-74; and "A Site for the National Academy," *American Architect* 99 (January 11, 1911): 17.

503. "The Institute of Musical Art, Donn Barber, Architect," *American Architect and Building News* 97 (May 25, 1910): 208; "Institute of Musical Art, Claremont Avenue, New York," *American Architect and Building News* 98 (November 2, 1910): plates; "Institute of Musical Art," *Architects' and Builders' Magazine* 11 (December 1910): 119-22; "The Institute of Musical Art of the City of New York, Claremont Avenue and 122nd Street, New York," *Architectural Yearbook* 1 (1912): 301-05; and "Institute of Musical Art Erecting Four-Story Extension," *Real Estate Record and Guide* 114 (July 5, 1924): 10.

504. See Schuyler, "Potter": 190-91; "Old Union Seminary Coming Down," *Real Estate Record and Guide* 86 (July 2, 1910): 4-5.

505. The competition documents were prepared by Professor Warren P. Laird of the University of Pennsylvania. Three other designs were mentioned: Howells & Stokes; Carpenter, Blair & Gould; and Pell & Corbett. "Professional Comment," and "Competition for the Union Theological Seminary," *Architecture* 15 (January 15, 1907): 1-8. Also see "The New Union Theological Seminary Buildings," *American Architect and Building News,* 95 Part 1 (January 20, 1909): 17-20, plates, Part 2 (January 27, 1909): 28-30, plates; "New Buildings of Union Seminary," *Real Estate Record and Guide* 85 (June 4, 1910): 1197; "The Union Theological Seminary Group in New York as Executed," *American Architect and Building News* 98 (October 12, 1910): 128, plates; and "Union Theological Seminary," *Architects' and Builders' Magazine* 11 (October 1910): 1-12.

506. Quoted in "The New Union Theological Seminary Buildings," *American Architect and Building News:* 18.

507. *Architecture* 13 (April 1906): 50. Also note Milton See's early proposal for a watergate to the Heights. Milton See, "The Planning of Cities: Paper No. 4," *Public Improvements* 2 (December 1, 1899): 51.

508. Herbert N. Casson, "New York, The City Beautiful," *Munsey's* 38 (November 1907): 178-86.

509. "Columbia Stadium, Naval Reserve, Public Recreation Pier and Water Gate, 112th Street to 120th Street, on the Hudson, New York," *Architecture* 16 (August 15, 1907): 140-41.

510. "Dinner Given by the Competitors in the Robert Fulton Memorial Competition, to the President of the Committee, Professional Advisor and Jury," *American Architect and Building News* 97 (May 25, 1910): 3-4; H. Van Buren Magonigle, "The Robert Fulton Memorial," *American Architect and Building News* 97 (June 15, 1910): 225-26; "Some Aspects of the Robert Fulton Memorial Competition," *American Architect and Building News* 97 (June 15, 1910): 226-27; "Accepted Competitive Design, Robert Fulton Memorial, New York," *Architecture* 21 (June 1910): 82-83, 90; "An Impression of Mr. H. Van Buren Magonigle," and "A Notable Architectural Exhibition: Display of Drawings for Fulton Memorial an Impressive Collection" *New York Architect* 4 (June 1910); "The Robert Fulton Memorial Competition," *Architectural Review* 1 (January 1912): 1-6; and "Need for a Civic Forum," *American Architect* 105 (May 27, 1914): 270.

511. H. Van Buren Magonigle, "The Robert Fulton Memorial," *American Architect and Building News:* 225-27.

512. "Accepted Competitive Design, Robert Fulton Memorial, New York," *Architecture:* 83.

513. The idea of a water gate to Morningside Heights nonetheless persisted among architects. See Donn Barber, "Suggestion for a War Memorial on Riverside Drive, New York," *American Architect* 114 (September 11, 1918): plate 81; and Charles Over Cornelius, "War Memorials, Part II: Community Buildings for Large Cities," *Architectural Record* 47 (January 1920): 39-47.

514. "Some Aspects of the Robert Fulton Memorial Competition," *American Architect and Building News:* 226.

515. The area around City College grew up simultaneously with Morningside, although Washington Heights and Inwood did not become established neighborhoods until the 1920s and 1930s, respectively.

516. "Morningside Heights," *Real Estate Record and Guide* 63 (March 25, 1899): 520.

517. "New Riverside Drive Mansions," *Real Estate Record and Guide* 62 (November 12, 1898): 701; "New Dwellings on Cathedral Heights," *Real Estate Record and Guide* 62 (November 12, 1898): 704; and "Morningside Heights," *Real Estate Record and Guide:* 520.

518. "Selections from the Detroit Architectural Club Exhibition of 1900," *Inland Architect* 35 (May 1901): plate; and "Alpha Club, Riverside Drive, New York," *Architecture* 8 (September 1903): plate LXVIII.

519. "Delta-Phi Club-house, West 116th Street, New York, N.Y.," *American Architect and Building News* 91 (April 20, 1907): plates.

520. "The President's House, Columbia University, New York City," *Brickbuilder* 21 (November 1912): plate 145; "The President's House, Columbia University," *Architecture* 27 (February 1913): 24; and *Monograph of the Works of McKim, Mead & White,* plates 352-53.

521. "Transformation of Morningside Heights," *Real Estate Record and Guide* 78 (August 11, 1906): 255.

522. "A Unique Contrast on Cathedral Parkway," *Real Estate Record and Guide* 86 (March 11, 1911): 437.

523. Alpern, *Apartments for the Affluent,* 82-83.

524. "Apartments, 521 and 523 West 112th St., New York," *Architecture* 23 (April 1911): 63, plate 41.

525. Arthur E. Willauer, "The Modern Home in New York," *American Architect and Building News* 96 (December 22, 1909): 261-65, plates; "The Britannia Apartments, 515 West 110th St., New York," *Architecture* 20 (December 1909): plate CX; "Points About Prize Winning Houses," *Real Estate Record and Guide* 86 (February 11, 1911): 251-53; "A Unique Contrast on Cathedral Parkway," *Real Estate Record and Guide:* 437; and "A Typical Apartment House District," *Real Estate Record and Guide* 88 (September 16, 1911): 377-78.

526. "A House for Columbia Professors and Students," *Real Estate Record and Guide* 85 (June 18, 1910): 1300; and "Sethlow Bachelor Apartments, 509 West 121st Street," *Real Estate Record and Guide* 86 (May 27, 1911): 1006.

527. "A House for Columbia Professors and Students," *Real Estate Record and Guide:* 1300.

528. William L. Rouse, "Architectural Criticism," *Architecture* 19 (March 15, 1909): 33; H.W. Frohne, "Contemporary Apartment Buildings in New York City," *Architectural Record* 28 (July 1910): 61-70; "Points About Prize Winning Houses," *Real Estate Record and Guide:* 250-51; "A Unique Contrast on Cathedral Parkway," *Real Estate Record and Guide* 437; and Alpern, *Apartments for the Affluent,* 42-43.

529. Rouse, "Architectural Criticism": 33.

530. Rouse, "Architectural Criticism": 33.

531. Rouse, "Architectural Criticism": 33.

532. "Addition to Hendrik Hudson Apartments, 110th St. and Broadway, New York," *Architecture* 18 (December 1908): plate XCVIII; and Alpern, *Apartments for the Affluent,* 42-43.

533. Frohne, "Contemporary Apartment Buildings": 62.

534. "George F. Johnson's Latest Operation," *Real Estate Record and Guide* 84 (November 20, 1909): 903.

535. "Building on Cathedral Heights," *Real Estate Record and Guide* 83 (March 13, 1909): 487-88.

536. For the Mira Mar, see "New Thoughts in Planning Apartments," *Real Estate Record and Guide* 83 (June 26, 1909): 1239; for the Peter Minuit, "New Apartments on Columbia Grounds," *Real Estate Record and Guide* 85 (January 15, 1910): 109; and "The Peter Minuit, 25 Claremont Ave., New York," *Architecture and Building* 44 (December 1912): 482; for Eton and Rugby halls, "New Apartments on Columbia Grounds," *Real Estate Record and Guide* 85 (May 14, 1910): 1032. Also see Frohne, "Contemporary Apartment Buildings": 61-70; and White & Willensky, *AIA Guide,* 258.

537. Frohne, "Contemporary Apartment Buildings": 63, 70.

538. "A Riverside Drive Operation," *Real Estate Record and Guide* 88 (September 2, 1911): 318.

539. Frohne, "Contemporary Apartment Buildings": 64. Also see an advertisement for the Atlantic Terra Cotta Company, *American Architect and Building News* 100 (November 29, 1911): 52.

540. Frohne, "Contemporary Apartment Buildings": 70.

541. See Clay Lancaster, *Old Brooklyn Heights, New York's First Suburb* (New York: Dover, 1979), *passim*; and Christopher Tunnard and Henry Hope Reed, *American Skyline* (New York: New American Library, 1956), 62.

542. See "A Suburban Exploration," *Real Estate Record and Guide* 35 (May 9, 1885): 517-18; and "New Jersey Suburbs Fast Growing," *Real Estate Record and Guide* 77 (June 30, 1906): 1235-36.

543. Cited by William Middleton, *Grand Central, The World's Greatest Railway Terminal* (San Marino, Cal.: Golden West, 1977), 12.

544. George A. Ward, *Description of New Brighton on Staten Island Opposite the City of New York* (New York: New Brighton Association, 1836), 6. The prospectus is at the Staten Island Institute of Arts and Sciences.

545. Cited by Edward K. Spann, *The New Metropolis, New York City, 1840-1857* (New York: Columbia University Press, 1981), 181.

546. Andrew Jackson Downing, *Rural Essays* (New York: George B. Putnam & Co., 1853). Cited by Spann, *New Metropolis*, 194.
547. See S.B. Sutton, ed., *Civilizing American Cities, A Selection of Frederick Law Olmsted's Writings on City Landscape* (Cambridge: MIT Press, 1971), 294-95. On the value of curvilinear streets as a planning strategy, also see Charles W. Leavitt, "The Making of a Residence District in Semi-Urban Districts," *Real Estate Record and Guide* 66 (November 10, 1900): 614-17.
548. Cited by Christopher Tunnard, "The Romantic Suburb in America," *Magazine of Art* 40 (May 1947): 184-87. Also see Andrew Jackson Downing, *A Treatise On The Theory And Practice Of Landscape Gardening, Adapted To North America. . . . With Remarks On Rural Architecture*, 6th ed. (New York: A.O. Moore, 1859), 567-73; Samuel Swift, "Llewellyn Park, West Orange, Essex Co., New Jersey, The First American Suburban Community," *House & Garden* 3 (June 1903): 326-35; Jane B. Davies, "Llewellyn Park in West Orange, New Jersey," *Antiques* 107 (January 1975): 142-58; and Richard Guy Wilson, "Idealism and the Origin of the First American Suburb," *American Art Journal* 11 (Fall 1979): 79-90.
549. "An American Park," *American Architect and Building News* 16 (July 12, 1884): 15-16; Montgomery Schuyler, "Some Suburbs of New York, I—New Jersey," *Lippincott's Magazine* 8 (July 1884): 9-23; "Villa Communities," *Architecture and Building* 14 (March 21, 1891): 137-38; Cora L. Hartshorn, "A Little History of the Short Hills Section of Millburn Township, N.J., developed by Stewart Hartshorn," manuscript dated July 31, 1946, in the Millburn Public Library; Marian Keefe Meisner, "A History of Millburn Township, N.J.," manuscript dated 1957 in the Millburn Public Library; *Millburn: 1857-1957* (Millburn: Millburn Centennial Committee, 1957); Roth, *Architecture of McKim, Mead & White: 1870-1900 (A Building List):* plates 37, 789; and Robert A.M. Stern and John Montague Massengale, *The Anglo-American Suburb* (London: Academy Editions, 1981), 26, also published as "AD Profile 37," *Architectural Design* 51 (October-November 1981).
550. M., "A Millionaire's Cathedral City," *American Architect and Building News* 6, Part 1 (September 20, 1879): 91-92, Part 2 (September 27, 1879): 102-03; *Garden City* promotional brochure (Garden City: Garden City Company, *ca.* 1910) in Avery Library, Columbia University; "Group of Houses, Franklin Court, Garden City, L.I., Ford, Butler & Oliver, Architects," *Architecture* 32 (November 1915): 305-06; Harriet Sisson Gillespie, "An English Cottage Group," *House Beautiful* 46 (August 1919): 74-76; Henry Isham Hazelton, *The Boroughs of Brooklyn and Queens, Counties of Nassau and Suffolk, Long Island, New York 1699-1924* (New York: Lewis Historical Publishing Company, 1925), 865-69; Donald L. Richards, "A History of Garden City, N.Y.," *Yesteryears* 8 (December 1964): 90-95; and Stern and Massengale, *Anglo-American Suburb*, 25. Mumford states that Ebenezer Howard called the form of town he was proposing the "garden city, a name he may have picked up from A.T. Stewart's Garden City experiment, on Long Island, during the few years he spent in America, though Chicago, which he also knew, had been called, once upon a time, the Garden City." Lewis Mumford, *The Highway and the City* (New York: Harcourt Brace & World, 1963), 63.
551. Samuel Swift, "American Suburban Communities IV: Community Life at Rochelle Park," *House and Garden* 4 (May 1904): 235-43; Montgomery Schuyler, "Study of a New York Suburb, New Rochelle," *Architectural Record* 25 (April 1909): 235-48; Frank E. Sanchis, *Westchester County, New York: Colonial to Contemporary* (New York: North River, Croton-on-Hudson, 1977), *passim*; and Stern and Massengale, *Anglo-American Suburb*, 30.
552. "House at Lawrence Park: Bronxville, N.Y., W.W. Kent, Arch't," *American Architect and Building News* 43 (January 6, 1894): plate; "The Casino, Lawrence Park, Bronxville, N.Y., W.A. Bates, Architect," *American Architect and Building News* 70 (October 27, 1900): plate; Theodore Tuttle, "A Picturesque American Suburb," *Architectural Record* 16 (September 1904): 167-77; "Hotel Gramatan, Bronxville, N.Y., W.A. Bates and A.E. Barlow, Associate Architects," *American Architect and Building News* 91 (June 1, 1907): plates; "Hotel Gramatan, Bronxville, N.Y., *Architectural Review* 11 (April 1913): 146; "House of Franklin T. Root, Esq., Bronxville, N.Y., Messrs. Delano & Aldrich, Architects," *American Architect* 109 (February 9, 1916): plate; "Exteriors and Plans, Oak Court Terrace Cottages, Bronxville, N.Y., Bates & How, Architects," *Architecture* 35 (April 1917): 76; and "Apartment House, Bronxville, N.Y., Bates & How, Architects," *Architecture* 43 (June 1921): plates LXXVII-LXXIX. For further sources beyond the scope of this book, see Stern and Massengale, *Anglo-American Suburb*, 31.
553. "The Evolution of an Ideal Suburb—Sea Gate," *Public Improvements* 6 (June 1902): 93, 102.
554. "Residence at Sea Gate, L.I., S.W. Cor. of Atlantic Ave. and Beach 40th St., Parfitt Brothers, Architects, Brooklyn, N.Y.," *Architects' and Builders' Magazine* 2 (April 1901): 246.
555. "House for H.J. Keiser Esq., Sea Gate, New York, Messrs. Squires & Wynkoop, Architects," *American Architect and Building News* 96 (August 11, 1909): plates.
556. "House for J.H. Biggs, Esq., Sea Gate, New York, Squires & Wynkoop, Architects," *American Architect and Building News* 96 (August 11, 1909): plate.
557. Hazelton, *Long Island,* 1090.
558. "A Unique Suburb. Where a Large Part of New York's Population Gravitates To—Thoughts for Real Estate Investors," *Real Estate Record and Guide* 44 (August 17, 1889): 1132-33; and Hazelton, *Long Island,* 1087-91. Also see "Gate Lodge and Hammersley Library. Sea Side Home, Bath Beach, N.Y., Parfitt Bros., Architects," *American Architect and Building News* 38 (November 12, 1892): plate.
559. Hazelton, *Long Island,* 1089.
560. Dr. E.R.L. Gould, President City and Suburban Homes Company, "Homewood, A Model Settlement," *American Monthly Review of Reviews* 16 (July 1897): 43-51. The article is summarized in "Homewood, A Model Suburban Settlement," *Municipal Affairs* 1 (September 1897): 565-66.
561. Gould, "Homewood": 47-48.
562. Andrew Scott Dolkart, *Suburbanization of Flatbush* (Master's Thesis, Columbia University, 1977).
563. "House for W.F. Moore, Esq., Flatbush, L.I.," *Architecture and Building* 24 (January 18, 1896): plate.
564. "House at Flatbush for W.A. Porter, L.I.," *Building* 6 (April 16, 1887): plate. Also see Philemon Tillion, "Possibilities in Detached Houses," *Real Estate Record and Guide* 83 (February 13, 1909): 287-88.
565. Henry A. Meyer, *Vandeveer Park: Reminiscences of Its Growth* (Brooklyn, 1901): *passim*; and Dolkart, *Flatbush*, 13-15.
566. Meyer, *Vandeveer Park,* 12.
567. Dolkart, *Flatbush,* 14-15.
568. Herbert F. Gunnison, *Flatbush To-day* (Brooklyn, 1908), 37. Also see Paul Thurston, "Some Well Designed Suburban Houses," *American Homes and Gardens* 3 (November 1906): 296-99; "Prospect Park South," *Architects' and Builders' Magazine* 3, Part 1 (February 1902): 134-40, Part 2 (February 1902): 176-80; "Residence of Dr. Geo. U. Watson," and "Residence of T.M. Valleau," *Architects' and Builders' Magazine* 3 (September 1902): 454; "Residence, Wm. J. Harrison, Prospect Park South, Brooklyn, N.Y.," *Architects' and Builders' Magazine* 4 (November 1902): 78; Dolkart, *Flatbush*, 19-20; Marcia Chambers, "Metropolitan Baedeker, Flatbush," *New York Times* (May 7, 1978): C-4; Marge Blaine and Roberta Intrater, "The Grandeur That Is Flatbush," *New York* 14 (August 14, 1978): 42-46; and New York City Landmarks Preservation Commission, *Prospect Park South: Historic District Designation Report* (New York, 1979).
569. Dean Alvord, quoted in Dolkart, *Flatbush,* 20.
570. Clay Lancaster, "The American Bungalow," *Art Bulletin* 40 (September 1958): 239-53; and Dolkart, *Flatbush,* 34-35.
571. Dolkart, *Flatbush,* 40-45.
572. Quoted by Gunnison, *Flatbush of To-day,* 93; and Dolkart, *Flatbush,* 40.
573. Dolkart, *Flatbush,* 40.
574. Dolkart, *Flatbush,* 43-44.
575. Dolkart, *Flatbush,* 45.
576. Dolkart, *Flatbush,* 45-47.
577. Dolkart, *Flatbush,* 46-47.
578. Quoted in Dolkart, *Flatbush,* 49.
579. Hazelton, *Long Island,* 1011-12; and Benjamin R. Allison, *The Rockaway Hunting Club* (New York: Rockaway Hunting Club, 1952), 6.
580. Allison, *Rockaway Club,* 6.
581. Hazelton, *Long Island,* 1013-14.
582. Allison, *Rockaway Club,* 10.
583. Hazelton, *Long Island,* 1013; and Allison, *Rockaway Club,* 10.
584. Allison, *Rockaway Club,* 10.
585. Hazelton, *Long Island,* 1013.
586. Allison, *Rockaway Club,* 9-10.
587. Allison, *Rockaway Club,* 11.
588. Hazelton, *Long Island,* 997-1003.
589. Hazelton, *Long Island,* 1001-03.
590. See "Demand for Water Front Homes in Queens," *Real Estate Record and Guide* 99 (February 3, 1917): 93; and Hazelton, *Long Island,* 982-83.
591. "Group of Inexpensive Homes at Forest Hills," *American Homes and Gardens* 7 (June 1909): 244-47; John A. Walters, "A Model Town in America, Development of a Suburban Town After the Ideals of Architect, Landscape Architect and the Sage Foundation," *Arts and Decoration* 1 (January 1911): 118-20; Edward Hale Brush, "A Garden City for the Man of Moderate Means," *Craftsman* 19 (January 1911): 445-51; Grosvenor Atterbury, "Model Towns in America," *Scribner's* 52 (July 1912): frontis-

piece, 20-35; Samuel Howe, "Forest Hills Gardens," *American Architect* 102 (October 30, 1912): 153-58, plates; "The Sage Foundation at Forest Hills," *American Architect* 102 (October 30, 1912): 159-61; "Forest Hills Gardens, Long Island: An Example of Collective Planning, Development, and Control," *Brickbuilder* 21 (December 1912): 317-18, plates 155-64; W.F. Anderson, "Forest Hills Gardens—Building Construction," *Brickbuilder* 21 (December 1912): 319-20; *Forest Hills Gardens*, (New York: Russell Sage Foundation, 2nd edition, 1913) in Avery Library; Mary Eastwood Knevels, "What the Suburban Dweller May Learn from a Model Town," *American Homes and Gardens* 12 (February 1915): 39-45; "The Architect's Scrap Book—Houses at Forest Hills, Long Island," *Architecture* 32 (August 1915): 210-12, and (September 1915): 234-36; "Recent Houses at Forest Hills Gardens, Long Island, From the Work of Grosvenor Atterbury, Architect, and Eugene Schoen, Architect," *Brickbuilder* 25 (June 1916): 139-42; "Two Houses Designed by Albro & Lindeberg, Architects. At Forest Hills Gardens in Long Island, N.Y.," *Brickbuilder* 25 (June 1916): 149-50; Charles C. May, "Forest Hills Gardens from the Town Planning Viewpoint," *Architecture* 34 (August 1916): 161-72, plates CXIX-CXXVII; "Two Modern Apartments for City and Country," *Architecture* 38 (October 1918): 286-89, plate CLXX; "The Church in the Gardens at Forest Hills, N.Y.," *Architectural Review* 9 (August 1919): 37-40, plate XXIV; "Portrait of Grosvenor Atterbury," *Country Life* 107 (October 1920): 947-52; "Arbor Close, Forest Hills, L.I., Robert Tappan, Forest Hills, Architect," *Architect* 6 (August 1926): plates CXXI-CXXIV; Frank Chouteau Brown, "Some Recent Apartment Buildings," *Architectural Record* 63 (March 1928): 193-272; Lewis Mumford, "Mass Production and the Modern House," *Architectural Record* 67 (January 1930): 13-20, (February 1930): 110-16; Grosvenor Atterbury, *The Economic Production of Workingmen's Homes* (New York: Russell Sage Foundation, 1930); Grosvenor Atterbury, *Bricks Without Brains* (New York: Charles Scribner's Sons, 1936); "A Problem of Resources in Planning," *Architectural Record* 95 (January 1944): 87-92; Christopher Tunnard, "The Romantic Suburb in America": 184-87; Francesco Dal Co, "From Parks to the Region, Progressive Ideology and the Reform of the American City," in Giorgio Ciucci et al, *The American City, From the Civil War to the New Deal* (Cambridge: MIT Press, 1979), 143-291; and David P. Handlin, *The American Home, Architecture and Society, 1815-1915* (Boston: Little, Brown and Co., 1979), 285-88.

592. "The Russell Sage Foundation," *Charities and the Commons* 18 (1907): 77-78, 191.
593. Grosvenor Atterbury, *Workingmen's Homes, passim*.
594. Howe, "Forest Hills Gardens": 155.
595. Quoted in Tunnard, "The Romantic Suburb in America": 317-18.
596. May, "Forest Hills Gardens from the Town Planning Viewpoint": 170.
597. Quoted in "Forest Hills Gardens, Long Island," *Brickbuilder* 21 (December 1912): 317-18.
598. See, for example, Yorkship Village, built by the New York Shipbuilding Company in 1918. Electus D. Litchfield was the architect. Richard S. Childs, "The First Emergency Government Towns for Shipyard Workers, I, 'Yorkship Village' at Camden, N.J.," *AIA Journal* 6 (May 1918): 237-44, 249-51, frontispiece; Marcia Mead, "The Architecture of the Small House," *Architecture* 37 (June 1918): 145-54; Electus D. Litchfield, "Recent Government Housing Developments, Yorkship Village, Camden, N.J.," *Housing Problems in America* (Washington, D.C.: National Conference on Housing, 1918), 82-93; and Edith Elmer Wood, *Recent Trends in American Housing* (New York: Macmillan, 1931), 66-69.

Also see government housing in Bridgeport, Connecticut, an infill project by planner Arthur A. Shurtleff and architect R. Clipston Sturgis. "The Workman and His House," *Architectural Record* 44 (October 1918): 302-25; Sylvester Baxter, "The Government Housing at Bridgeport, Connecticut," *Architectural Record* 45 (February 1919): 123-41; and *Report of the United States Housing Corporation* (Washington, D.C.: Government Printing Office, 1919).
599. "A Suburban Development, A Study in Housing," *Architectural Record* 34 (October 1913): 349-52; "Houses, Jamaica, Long Island," *Architecture* 29 (January 1914): 18-24; and Garrett H. Irving, "Architectural Design as an Aid to Real Estate Promotion. Principles of Group Planning Applied to Small Suburban Houses by Electus D. Litchfield, Architect," *Brickbuilder* 23 (December 1914): 295-96, plates.
600. Irving, "Architectural Design as an Aid to Real Estate Promotion": 295-96.
601. Irving, "Architectural Design as an Aid to Real Estate Promotion": 296.
602. "Elmhurst, Residence of Giovanni P. Morosini, Riverdale, New York City," *Architecture and Building* 19 (October 7, 1893): plates. Also see "The Residence of D.P. Kinsey, Esq., Riverdale, New York," *American Homes and Gardens* 2 (March 1906): 169-72.
603. "Innovations for a Riverdale Residence," *Real Estate Record and Guide* 81 (April 11, 1908): 650-53.
604. Edward C. Delafield, "A Fashionable Suburban Section," *Real Estate Record and Guide* 92 (November 22, 1913): 939-40.
605. Dwight James Baum, "Making Old Homes New," *Architecture* 38 (December 1918): 333-41.
606. "Country Club, Fieldston, New York, Dwight James Baum, New York, Architect," *Architect* 3 (October 1924): plates X-XII.
607. "Portfolio of Current Architecture," *Architectural Record* 35 (May 1914): 455-62; Carleton Van Valkenburg, "An Interesting Group of Houses," *American Homes and Gardens* 11 (October 1914): 331-35; and "House of Dwight James Baum, Riverdale [sic], N.Y., Mr. Dwight James Baum, Architect," *American Architect* 57 (June 2, 1915): plate. Baum also had a studio in Spuyten Duyvil, in the southwest corner of the Bronx below Riverdale. See "Architectural Studio, Dwight James Baum, Spuyten Duyvil Parkway, New York," *Architect* 3 (November 1924): plate XXVII. For additional works by Baum in Riverdale, see "House and Plans, J.B. Quinn, Fieldston, Riverdale-on-Hudson, N.Y.," *Architecture* 41 (April 1920): 118-19; "Designs for Double and Single Houses for Robert Fein, Riverdale-on-Hudson, N.Y.," *Architecture* 43 (May 1921): plates LXIX-LXXI; "Detail, House, Mr. B.L. Winchell, Riverdale, N.Y.," *Architect* 2 (April 1924): plate XXIII; "House, Mr. William P. Hoffman, Fieldston, N.Y.," *Architect* 2 (May 1924): plates XXXVI-XXXVIII; "House, Mrs. L. Duncan Bulkley, Riverdale, N.Y.," *Architect* 2 (May 1924): plates XLI-XLII; "House, Mr. Robert Fein, Riverdale, N.Y.," *Architect* 2 (May 1924): plates XLV-XLVI; "House, Judge Nash Rockwood, Fieldston, N.Y.," *Architect* 2 (June 1924): plate LXIX; and "House, Estate of Mr. Cleveland H. Dodge, Riverdale, N.Y.," *Architect* 2 (June 1924): plates LXX-LXXII.
608. "Portfolio of Current Architecture," *Architectural Record*: 460; and Valkenburg, "Interesting Group of Houses": 331-33. Also see Carlton Van Valkenburg, "A Picturesque Hillside Home," *American Homes and Gardens* 11 (December 1914): 416-17.
609. "Portfolio of Current Architecture," *Architectural Record*: 462.
610. "Portfolio of Current Architecture," *Architectural Record*: 455-56, 459.
611. "Portfolio of Current Architecture," *Architectural Record*: 462.
612. Delafield, "Fashionable Suburban Section": 940.
613. J.J. Clute, *Annals of Staten Island, From Its Discovery to the Present Time* (New York: Vogt, 1877), 318. Staten Islander Cornelius Vanderbilt started his fortune by working on and later buying Tompkin's ferry line.
614. Quoted from the New Brighton prospectus, George A. Ward, *Description of New Brighton on Staten Island Opposite the City of New York* (New York: New Brighton Association, 1836). Also see an exhibition catalog prepared by Shirley Zavin and Barnett Shepherd, *Staten Island, An Architectural History* (New York: Staten Island Institute of Arts and Sciences, 1979), 5; and Stern and Massengale, *Anglo-American Suburb*, 18-19. The prospectus was published in 1836, shortly before the founding of several other Staten Island suburbs such as Clifton, built by the Staten Island Association in 1837, and Elliotville, founded near New Brighton by Dr. Samuel McKenzie Elliot in 1839.
615. "County House, Ernest Flagg, Dongan Hills, Staten Island," *Architecture* 11 (January 15, 1901): 24-25.
616. Flagg's houses are published in his book *Small Houses, Their Economic Design and Construction* (New York: Charles Scribner's Sons, 1922).
617. See *Dongan Hills, Where It Is, What It Is, and All About It* (New York: Dongan Hills Realty Company, ca. 1916), a prospectus at the New-York Historical Society.
618. *Dongan Hills*, no pagination.
619. John M. Carrère, "Better Taste in Small Houses: Suburban Development Has Been Too Rapid, It is High Time That We Paused To Contemplate Our Awful Achievement, Some Constructive Suggestions," *Country Life in America* 20 (May 15, 1911): 18-21; and "Works of Carrère & Hastings," *Architectural Record*: 63.
620. Carrère, "Better Taste in Small Houses": 21.

Index

Numbers in italic indicate pages bearing illustrations. The letter "n" indicates the numbered reference note

A

Abbey's Theatre, 206
Abercrombie & Fitch, *196*
Abramson, Louis Allen, 245
Academy of Medicine, 232
Academy of Music, 203, 209
Ackerman, T.B., Construction Company, 425
Adam style, 267, 333, 425
Adams, Henry, 11
Adams Dry Goods store (Adams & Company), 192
Aerial Theater, 212, 222
Aguilar, Grace, 98
Aguilar Free Library, 98, *99*
Aiken, John, 424
Aiken, William Martin, 139
Ajello, Gaetan, 303, *419*
Albro & Lindeberg, 346, 348, 349, 430, 433
Alimar apartments *382-83*, 388
Allaire's (restaurant), 225
Allen, A.N., 351
Allen, Paul R., 219
Allen & Collens, 116, 355, 404, 412, 413
Almirall, Raymond F., 98, 153, 165
Alpha Club, *416,* 417
Altar of Liberty (proposed), 128
Altman, Benjamin, 194, 312
Alvord, Dean, 424, 425
   house, 425, *426*
Alwyn Court, 290
American Adam style, 342
American Bank Note Company, *184*
American basement plan, 348, 364, 373, 417
   houses at 18-52 West Seventy-fourth Street, *378-79,* 380
   houses at 324-328 West 108th Street, 373
American Fine Arts Society, 103-04, *106,* 412
American Geographical Society, *107*
American Georgian style, 373, 390
American Gothic style, 421
American Hispanic Society, 105-*07*
American Institute of Architects
   1894 convention, 150
   Eighth Annual Convention, 275
   Gold Medal from, 358
American Institute of Architects, New York Chapter, 61, 168
   Committee on Civic Improvements, 68
American Institute of Electrical Engineers, 243
American Museum of Natural History, 13, 32, 87, 298, 360, 363, 370-73, *371*
American Numismatic Society, *107*
American Renaissance, 18, 21, 22, 34, 62, 87, 105, 110, 113, 123, 177, 192, 219, 228, 250, 303, 342, 404, 406, 411, 413, 417
American Safe Deposit and Columbian Bank Building, 307
American Society of Civil Engineers, 231
American Society of Mechanical Engineers, 243
American Society of Mural Painters, 123, 126
American Surety Building, *151, 158*-59, *174*
American Telephone and Telegraph Building, 162, 165
American (Theater) Roof Garden, *220,* 222
American Yacht Club, Brooklyn, 421
Ames, Winthrop, 220
Anderson, A.A., 298
Anderson, Mrs. A.A., 410
Andrew, F.M. & Company, 272
Angell, E.L., 377
Anglo-American Georgian style, 113, 303, 316, 321, 333, 341-48
Ansonia Apartment Hotel, 304, *368, 384,* 385, *386,* 418, 482n379
Apartment hotels, 279-79, *273, 274, 275, 276, 277, 278,* 312, *313,* 384, 385, *386,* 388
Apartment house, Broadway and 113th Street, 419
Apartments, 279-304, *280, 281, 284-85,* 381, *382-88, 383, 387, 388, 389, 418-19*
   club buildings, 299-303, *300, 301*
   courtyard, 282-83, *286,* 287-95, *288, 289, 290, 291, 292, 293,* 468n101
   duplex and studio, *294,* 295-99, *296, 297, 298,* 469n107, 469n126
   tenement, improvement of, *300, 302,* 303-04

Appellate Courthouse (Appellate Division, New York State Supreme Court), 67, 68, *71,* 110, *172*
Apthorp apartments, 295, *368,* 385
Arch of Democracy (proposed), 128
Arch of Freedom (proposed), 125
Architectural League of New York, 104, 128
   Fifth Annual Exhibition, 398
Ardelle apartments, *419*
Ardsley Hall apartments, 388
Arlington Hotel, 275
Armour Mausoleum, *130,* 131
Armstrong, Helen Maitland, 131
Arnold Constable Building, 68
Art Nouveau, 46, 54, 130, 132, 141, 209, 211, 216, 239, 266, 269, 278, 418
Art Students League, 104
Arts and Crafts style, 316, 348-50
Associated Banks Building. *See* New York Clearing House Association Building
Association for Improving the Condition of the Poor, 138
Association for the Improved Condition of Deaf Mutes, home of, 314
Association Residence for Aged Respectable Indigent Females, 370
Astor, Caroline Webster Schermerhorn. *See* Astor, Mrs. William
Astor, John Jacob, 255
Astor, Colonel John Jacob, IV, 316
   house of, *317*
Astor, Mrs. William, 310, 316-21
   house of, *317*
Astor, William Waldorf, 255, 316-21
Astor apartments, 304, 385
Astor Building, 145
Astor Court, *293,* 295, 304
Astor family, 295
Astor Hotel, *167,* 222-23, 266, *267*-69
   American Indian Grill Room, 269
   Art Nouveau suite, *266*
   Hunt Room, 269
   Old New York Lobby, 269
   Roof Garden, *222-23,* 269
Astor House (hotel), *165,* 253-55

Astor Library, 91
Astor Trust Building, 157
Astoria Hotel, 255-56, 261
Atelier Building, 295
Atlantic Building, 156, 157
Attendorfer Branch library, 98
Atterbury, Grosvenor, 32, 324, 325, 346, 348, 351, 427, 428, 429
 house, 351
Atwood, Charles B., 61, 309
Auchincloss, Hugh D., house, 345
Audubon, John James, 105
Audubon Park, 105
Audubon Terrace, 105, *107*
Automobile Club of America, 58, *59*

B

Babb, Cook & Willard, 101, 104, 342, 343, 377, 411
Bache, Jules S., stables of, 353
Bacon, Henry, 135, 178
Baer, Herbert M., 432
Bailey, William Trist, 426
Baker, James B., 87, 188, 189
B. Altman & Company, *193,* 194-95, 196
Bank for Savings, *177*-78
Bank of Manhattan Building, 25
Bankers' Club, 226
Bankers Trust Building, *144,* 159, *174,* 176
Banking and commerce, 177-90
Barber, Donn, 180, 181, 182, 183, 237, 239, 243, 245, 412
Barnard, George Gray, 211
Barnard College, 396, *397,* 410-11, *413,* 414
 Barnard Hall, 410
 Brinckerhoff Hall, *410*
 dormitory, *411*
 Fiske Hall, *410*
 Milbank Hall, *410*
Barnard School, 433
Barney & Chapman, 113, 114, 115, 116, 117, 168, 169, 237, 267
Barnum, P.T., 203, 330
 museum, 156
Baron de Hirsch Trade School, 86
Baroque style, 73, 161
Bartholdi, Frédéric Auguste, 118
Bartlett, Paul Wayland, 189
Bassett, Edward M., 33
Bath Beach, Brooklyn, 422
 Hammersley gate lodge and library, *424*
Battery Park, 161
Baum, Dwight James, 432-33
 house, *433*
Bayard Building, *153,* 155, 176
Bayne, Samuel G., house, *362,* 363
Beach, Alfred Ely, 45
Beaux-Arts Baroque, 46, 142, 243, 329
Beaux-Arts rationalism, 170
Beaver Building, *159*-61
Belasco, David, 208
Belcher, John, 73, 157
Bellamy, Edward, 19
Belle Epoque, 304
Belmont, August, 46, 307
Belmont, O.H.P., Mausoleum, 131, *133*
Belmont Avenue (Bronx) combined firehouse, 73
Belnord apartments, *292,* 295, 385

Benevolent Protective Order of Elks, Lodge Number 1, 243
 Lodge Room, 243
Bennett, Arnold, 42
Bennett, Edward H., 32
Bensonhurst, Brooklyn, 422, *423,* 424
Berg, Charles I., 131, 194, 195, 275, 312
Berg, Louis De Coppet, 88
Berkeley School, *86*
Berkshire apartments, 282
Berlage, H.P.A., 177
Bernstein & Bernstein, 139
Berwind, Edward J., house, 324
Best, George E., 51, 64
Big Stores. *See* Department stores
Bigelow, John, 94
Bigelow, William B., 88, 342
Biggs, J.H., 421
Billings, C.K.G., 224
Billings, John S., 94, 95
Biltmore Hotel, *270, 271,* 272
Bitter, Karl, 68, 75, 130
Black, Starr & Frost, *200*
Blackwell's Island, 31
Blair, C. Ledyard
 house, *340*-41, 351
 stable and artist's studio, *329*
Blair Building, *144,* 153, *155*-56, 171
Blachfield, Edwin H., 28, 68, 256
Bloomingdale Insane Asylum, 396, 405
Blum, George & Edward, 419
Blumenthal, George, house, 351, 353
Bodker, Albert Joseph, 356, 388
Bohemian Club, 231
Booth Theater, 217
Borglum, Gutzon, 154
Boring, William A., 354, 458n106
Boring & Tilton, 75, 78, 245
Borough Hall (Brooklyn), 69
Bosworth, William Welles, 162
Bourke Mausoleum, *131*
Bowery Savings Bank, 178, *179,* 183, 184
Bowling Green, 146, 185
Bragdon, Claude, 156
Branch library (Clinton and Union streets, Brooklyn), 102
Branch library (Forty-second Street: Catherine Bruce), 98
Branch library (135th Street), 101
Brearley School, 86-*87*
Brendon, Charles, 333
Brewster, Robert S., house, *324,* 351
Bridge Plaza, 31, *32*
Bridges, 49-*55, 51, 52, 53, 54, 56. See also* individual bridges by name
Brighton Beach Racetrack, 248
Britannia apartments, 418
Brite & Bacon, 94, 346, 347
Broad Street, *144*
Broadway Chambers, *156,* 157, 159, 162
Broadway Tabernacle, *115*-16, *117*
Brokaw, Isaac, residence, 321
Bronx, suburban, 430-*33, 432*
 Fieldston, 432-33
 Riverdale, *432*
 Spuyten Duyvil, 432
Bronx Borough Courthouse, 68
Bronx Park, 141
Bronx Zoo, 141-42, *143*
Brooke, Rupert, 145, 146

Brooklyn, Bath & West End Railroad, 421
 Bensonhurst station, *423*
Brooklyn, Flatbush & Coney Island Railroad, 424
Brooklyn Academy of Arts and Sciences, 212
Brooklyn Academy of Design, 212
Brooklyn Academy of Music, 212, *214, 215,* 216
Brooklyn Bridge, 12, 13, *15,* 25, 31, 49, 50, 64, 145, 421, 424
 Terminal, *60, 64, 65,* 165
Brooklyn Heights, 420
Brooklyn Institute of Arts and Sciences (Brooklyn Museum), 87, 88, *89, 90, 91*
Brooklyn Municipal Center, 31
Brooklyn Public (Central) Library, 25, 88, 95-*98*
Brooklyn Rapid Transit Company, 426
Brooklyn Savings Bank, *178*
Brooks Brothers, 196
Brown, Stephen H., house, 353
Browne, Frederick, 274-75
Browne & Almiroty, 304
Bruce, Catherine, 98
Brunner, Arnold W., 44, 138, 139, 405, 409, 445n39, 458n106
Brunner & Tryon, 62, 392, 410
Bryant Park, 94, 95, 135-37, 192, 240, 244
Bryant Park Studios, *294,* 298
Buck, John H., 398
Buck, Leffert L., 50
Buck, R.S., 51, 54
Buckham, Charles, 296, 298
Buckingham Hotel, 255
Builders' League (club), 231
Building Districts and Regulations, Commission on, 33
Bulkeley, Jonathan, house, 356-57
Burden, James A., 334
 house, *325, 334,* 338
Burges, William, 163, 226
Burnham, Daniel H., 32, 36, 164, 173
Burnham, D.H., & Company, 166, 167, 192, 269
Burton, Robert L., 426
Bush, Irving T., 181
 house, *346*-48
Bush Terminal Company Building, 181
Bushwick Bay Ridge High School, 86
Butler, Charles, 445n39
Byzantine style, 116, 409

C

Cadman, Reverend S. Parkes, 176
Cady, Berg & See, 370, 371, 402, 403
Cady, J.C., & Company, 484n427
Cady, Josiah Cleveland, 13, 14, 15, 87, 109, 138, 212, 363, 370
Cafe Boulevard, 225
Cafe Martin, 224
Cafe Savarin, 226
Caffin, Charles, 27
Caledonian Club, 231
Calumet Club, 307
Carlyle Chambers, *276,* 278
Carnegie, Andrew, 98, 203, 240, 339, 376, 442n8
 residence of, 315, 342, *343*
Carnegie Hall, 13, 15, 87
Carnegie Library, 101
Carpenter, J.E.R., 358
Carpenter, Blair & Gould, 486n505

Carpenter & Blair, 116
Carrell, H.C., 80
Carrère, John M., 88, 95, 98, 325, 433, 434, 453n286, 458n106
Carrère & Hastings, 17, 30, 49, 51-52, 53, 64, 65, 66, 69, 74, 75, 94, 95, 96, 97, 101, 113, 129-30, 135-37, 136, 144, 150, 152, 155, 156, 171, 181, 200, 218, 219, 325, 326, 327, 330, 333, 334, 338, 339, 341, 342, 344, 351, 392, 394, 395, 398, 399, 411, 412, 434, 445n39, 484n427, 484n433
Cartier's, 200, 312, 314
Cartouche Architecture, 22, 316, 329, 333, 338
Casey, Edward Pearce, 74, 353, 406, 411, 484n433
Casino Roof Garden, 221
Casino Theater, 206-07, 220-21
Cassidy, Boss, 426
Castle, Irene and Vernon, 222
Cathedral of St. John the Divine, 15, *16, 17,* 396-*402, 397, 400, 401,* 403, 404, 411, *413,* 417
Cathedral Parkway, 509, 304
Catholic Club, 231
Catholic Female Orphan Asylum, 350
Caughey & Evans, 25
Centennial Arch, 121, 122-23, 125. *See also* Washington Memorial Arch
Central Park, 12, 30, 31, 55, 61, 88, 91, 129, 132, 134-35, 137, *284-85,* 296, 308, 314, 341, 360, 362, 365, 370, 373, 392, 395, 396
 Bethesda Fountain and Terrace, 365
 Mall, 365
 reservoir, 135, *314*
Central Park South, 36, 298
Central Park Studios, 295
Central Park View apartments, 388
Central Park West
 55 Central Park West, 304
 101 Central Park West, 304
 348-349 Central Park West, 388
Century (Association) Club, 27, 42, 231-32, 237, 267
Century Holding Company, 307
Century (New) Theater, 217-19, *218,* 392
Chamber of Commerce of the State of New York, *188,* 189-90
Chambers, Walter B., 71, 330, 331, 346, 357, 358
Chambers, W.B. & J.M. Cromwell, 88
Chandler, Duncan, 131
Chapel of the Intercession, 116
Chapman, C.T., 269
Chapman, Henry Otis, 201
Chard, Thornton, 351, 353
Chateau style, 311, 316-21
Chateau Square Branch library, 101, *102*
Chelsea piers, 49, *50*
Chemical National Bank, *183*
Cherbourg apartments, 388
Cherokee Flats (apartments). *See* East River Houses
Cherry Blossom Grove, 221-22
Chicago School, 148
Childs (restaurant), 225-*26*
Christ Church, 369
Christian, Eugene, castle, Riverdale, Bronx, *432*
Chrysler Building, 25, 225
Chubb Building, 181
Church of Our Lady of Esperanza, 107, *108*
Church of the Ascension, 307

Church of the Divine Paternity, *393,* 395
Churches, 109-16, *111, 112, 113, 114, 115, 117, 118, 119, 120, 121,* 307, 308, *366,* 368-70, *369,* 392-95, *393, 394,* 398, *405, 406, 408, 409,* 425. *See also* individual churches by name
Cities Service Building, 25
City and Suburban Homes Company, 283, 287, 290, 422-23
City Beautiful movement, 18, 19, 24, 27, 29, 30, 31, 32, 34, 40, 43, 91, 135, 139, 250, 360, 392, 405, 417, 424, 430
City Club, 231
City Convenient, 32
City Hall, 31, 61-*62, 63*-64, 67, *152,* 314, 420
City Hall Park, 61, 63, *64,* 67-68, *147, 156,* 158, *165,* 176, 184
 proposed courthouse for, 67-*68*
City Hall Post Office, 146, *165*
City Improvement Commission Plan (1907), 98
City Investing (Company) Building, *164,* 168, 170, *171,* 173, *174,* 176
City planning, 27-34, *35,* 42-44
City Planning Exhibition, 33
Civic Center, 61-68, *64*
Clark, Mrs. Alfred Corning, house, *374,* 375
Clark, Cyrus, house, 363, 375
Clark, Edward S., 360, 364, 370
Clark, Frederick Ambrose, 380
Clark, Stephen C., house, 351
Clark, Senator William A., house, *306,* 329-30, 333, 338
Classicism, 18-19, 21, 22, 27, 41, 55, 58, 62, 67, 69, 80, 86, 87, 88, 91, 95, 101, 108, 109, 110, 113, 116, 122, 123, 128, 130, 131, 134, 135, 137, 141, 148, 150, 154, 156, 157, 170, 177, 178, 181, 183, 187, 191-92, 198, 201, 207, 211, 212, 228, 231, 240, 243, 250, 256, 261, 262, 267, 272, 278, 307, 312, 315, 316, 321, 326, 342, 358, 364, 370, 373, 377, 388, 390, 395, 399, 405, 406, 409, 417
Cleopatra's Needle, 91
Clifton, Staten Island, *434*
Clinton, Charles W., 187, 402
Clinton & Russell, 45, 48, 64, 152, 153, 156, 157, 159, 162, 167, 222, 225, 266, 267, 269, 290, 291, 295, 368, 385, 388, 389
Club Buildings, 299-303, *300, 301*
Clubs, *226*-45, *227, 229, 230, 232, 233, 234, 235, 236, 238, 239, 240, 241, 242, 243, 244,* 307, *350, 390, 391, 392*. *See also* individual clubs by name
Cobb, William R., 141
Cockcroft, E.T., house, *348-*49
College fraternity townhouses, *416,* 417
College (Collegiate) Gothic style, 356, 368
College of the City of New York, 108-*09*
Collegiate Dutch Reformed Church, 79, 110, 308, *366*
Collegiate School, 86, 87
Colonial Club, 231, *368, 390, 391,* 392
Colonial Revival style, 355, 373, 392
Colonial style, 79, 220, 237, 269, 303, 341, 375, 421, 424, 425, 430
Colony Club, *236,* 237, 238
Colosseum, *302, 303,* 304
Columbia Presbyterian Hospital, 25
Columbia Stadium, Naval Reserve, Public Recreation Pier and Water Gate (projected), 413-*14, 415*

Columbia Stadium (projected), *397*
Columbia University, 27, 30, 43, 61, 87, 108, 109, 304, 350, *397,* 404-10, *405, 406, 407, 408, 409, 410,* 411, *412, 413,* 417
 Avery Hall, 409
 College of Physicians and Surgeons, 87
 Columbia College, 108, 312, 396
 Earl Hall, 409
 Hamilton Hall, 410
 Hartley Hall, 410
 Kent Hall, 409, 410
 Livingston Hall, 410
 Low Library, 22, *405, 406,* 409
 McKim Fellowship Competition, 98
 President's House, 417
 St. Paul's Chapel, *405, 406, 408, 409*
 School of Architecture, 95, 411
 School of Mines, *405,* 409
 South Field, 409, 417
 Teachers College, 80, 396, *397,* 404, 405, *410,* 411, *413*
Columbus Arch (temporary), 123
Columbus Circle, 125, 360
Commercial Cable Building, *144, 152, 155*
Commissioners' Plan of 1811, 307, 314, 315, 370
Commodore Hotel, 37, 272
Composite City, 131, 303
Composite Era, 12, 13, 17-24, 25, 32, 34, 43, 44, 48, 49, 51, 55, 68, 69, 74, 78, 86, 87, 88, 101, 103, 104, 105, 107, 108, 116, 118, 121, 122, 123, 128, 129, 131, 139, 141, 146, 148, 156, 157, 176, 178, 183, 185, 191, 192, 196, 203, 206, 207, 209, 223, 225, 228, 231, 232, 240, 245, 250, 255, 256, 275, 287, 295, 310, 311, 312, 324, 333, 354, 367, 368, 370, 373, 390, 395, 396, 399, 401, 402, 414, 424, 425, 428, 430
Comstock, F.R., 392, 395
Condit, Carl, 34
Coney Island, 209, *246-47, 248-*50, *249, 251,* 421
Congdon, Henry, 212, 484n427
Congestion of Population in New York, Committee on, 32, 33
Congestion Show, 32
Congregation Shaaray Tefila, 110
Congregation Shearith Israel (Spanish and Portuguese Synagogue), *392*
Convenience, Era of, 12, 24-25, 55, 58, 148, 171, 176, 192, 196, 272, 402
Converse, E.C., residence, 321
Convocational and Office Building (proposed), 402
Cook, Clarence, 134
Cook, Walter, 98, 101
Cook, William A., house, 325
Coolidge, Shepley, Bulfinch & Abbott, 25
Cooper, Clayton S., house, 433
Cooper, Peter, monument to, 129
Cooperative Studio Building, *294,* 295, 299
Corbett, Harrison & Macmurray, 25
Corbin, John R., Company, 425
Cordes, Ernest, 458n106
Corn Exchange Bank
 Bronx branch, 184
 East Eighty-sixth Street branch, 184
Cornelius, Charles, 128
Cornwall apartments, *300,* 304
Cortissoz, Royal, 91, 107, 311, 396, 406
Cosmopolitan City, 18, 303

Cosmopolitan Era, 12-17, 20, 21, 27, 34, 49, 57, 67, 78, 86, 87, 88, 109, 116, 118, 121, 129, 130, 131, 177, 203, 206, 212, 222, 225, 228, 231, 255, 256, 272, 282, 283, 310, 311, 315, 324, 360, 363, 364, 366, 367, 369, 370, 373, 381, 392, 396, 404, 413, 417, 424, 425
Cosmopolitan magazine public baths competition entry, *137*
Cosmopolitanism, 12, 13, 15, 17, 367
Coster Mausoleum, 131
Court of Honor (Manhattan Bridge), 52, *53*
Coutan, Jules-Alexis, 37
Cox, Kenyon, 68, 233
Craig, Andrew, 368, 381
Cram, Goodhue & Ferguson, 116, 118, 119
Cram, Ralph Adams, 401, 402
Cram, Wentworth & Goodhue, 62
Cram & Wentworth, 484n433
Crane, Walter, 211
Cret, Paul, 414
Criminal Courts Building, 67
Croes, J.J.R., 46
Croly, Herbert, 11, 17-18, 23, 31, 32, 63, 131, 311, 315, 321-23, 325-26
Cultural centers, 87-109
Cuniff, M.G., 46
Cunningham, Richard, house, 373
Curry, Daniel, 420
Cushing, Howard Gardiner, house, 346, 351-53, *352*
Cutting, Robert Fulton, 414

D

Dakota apartments, 283, *284-85,* 360, 364, *365,* 370, 380, 388
Dakota Stable, 57
Daly, Augustin, 208
Damrosch, Walter, 15
Darroch, A.M., 411
Daus, R.L., 101
David, Arthur C., 95, 168, 177, 181, 194, 196-200, 267
Davis, Alexander Jackson, 108, 432
David, John W., house, 344
Davison, Henry P., 355
Day, Frank Miles, 367
De Forest, Robert W., 442n8
de Gersdorff, George B., 346
De Kalb Branch library, *103*
de Koven, Reginald, house, 356
De Lemos & Cordes, 181, 190, 191, 192
de Wolfe, Elsie, 237
Deglane, Henri, 306, 329
Delafield, Edward, 432
  Fieldston Hill (house, Fieldston), 433
Delano & Aldrich, 25, 198, 237, 238, 316, 323-24, 344, 346, 351, 352, 353, 355, 357, 359
Delmonico, Ludivico, 224
Delmonico's, 222, 223, *224*
Delta-Phi Clubhouse, 417
Department stores, 109-96, *191, 193*
Desmond, Henry W., 23-24, 154, 155
Deutscherverein, 231
Devon Hotel, 275
Dewey Arch (temporary), 123-25, *126*
DeWitt Clinton High School, 80, *81, 82-83*
di Cesnola, Louis Palma, 88
Dickey, Mrs. Charles, house, 350

Dietrick, E.G.W., 424
Dillon, Arthur, 86, 94
Dime Savings Bank (Brooklyn), 178
Dodge, Marshall J., house, 346
Dodge, William Leftwich, 212, 217, 269
D'Oench, A.F., 137
D'Oench & Yost, 158
Dongan Hills, Staten Island, 434
Donnelly & Ricci, 177
Dorchester apartments, 304
Dorilton apartments, 304, *368, 373, 383-85,* 388, 418
Downing, Andrew Jackson, 420
Dreamland, Coney Island, 249, 250, *251*
  Creation, *251*
Dreicer & Company, 200
Driesler, Benjamin, 425
Dry Dock Savings Bank, *177*
du Fais, John, 236, 237
Duboy, Paul E.M., 125, 128
Duke, James B., house, 339
Duncan, John H., 88, 121-22, 132-34, 372, 373, 397, 406
Duncan, Stuart, house, 330
Dunham, E.K., house, *330*
Dupont, T. Coleman, 173
Duryea & Potter, 198
Dutch Colonial style, 79, 80, 85, 110, 181, 365, 366, 367, 373
Dutch Renaissance style, 69, 159, 364
Dutch Revival. *See* Dutch Colonial style
Duveen, Joseph, 339
Duveen Brothers (building), 200, 351

E

East Branch library, 102
East Fifty-fourth Street Bath House, 73
East River Houses, *286,* 287-90, *288, 289*
East River Savings Bank Building, *156,* 157
Ecole des Beaux-Arts, 22-23, 25, 75, 321
Edey, Mrs. Frederick, house, *330,* 351
Edison, Thomas, 12
Edison Building, 150
Edwardian Baroque, 157
Eidlitz, Cyrus L.W., 94, 167, 177, 178, 181, 183, 231, 232, 269
Eidlitz, Leopold, 43, 109, 177, 196, 212, 307
Eidlitz & MacKenzie, 167
Eiffel, Gustav, 54
El Nido apartments, 303
Elevated railroads, 12, *28,* 45, 46, *191, 192, 209,* 314, 315, 351, 360, 365, *371,* 396, 417, 426, 457n97
Eliot residence, 315
Elizabethan style, 356, 425
Elks Clubhouse (Brooklyn), 245
Elliman, Douglas L., 295
Elliot, Maxine, 219
Ellis Island, 75
Elm Street Station (firehouse), 69, *71*
Elmhurst (Morosini estate, Riverdale), 432
Embury, Aymar, II, 25, 201
Emerson, William, 139, 353
Emigrant Savings Bank Building, 153, *165*
Empire State Building, 25
Empire Theater, 206
Engine Company Number 33 firehouse, *71,* 72
Engine Company Number 35 firehouse, 73

Engine Company Number 65 firehouse, 69-72
Engine Company Number 72 firehouse, 72
Engineer's Club, 240, *244, 245*
English Baroque, 62, 85
English Collegiate Gothic, 80
English Free Vernacular style, 433
English Gothic style, 395, 398, 402, 413, 418
English Mannerist style, 113
English Perpendicular Gothic style, 412, 413
English Regency style, 342
English Renaissance style, 295, 355
Enlightenment, 55
Eno, Amos F., 253
Equitable (Life Assurance) Building, 145, 158, 164, 173-76, *174,* 226
Erasmus Hall High School, 80-85
Erie (Lackawanna) Ferry House, 49, *50*
Erkins, Henry, 224, 225
Escoffier, 267
Ethical Culture Society
  Hall, 219, 373, *387,* 392, *393*
  school, 392
Eton and Rugby halls, *419*
Euclid Hall apartments, 385
Evander Childs High School, 86
Eyre, Wilson, 104, 430

F

Fabbri, Mrs. Ernesto G., house, *328,* 329
Fabian, H.W., 282, 283
Far Rockaway, Queens, 426
  Bayswater, 426
  Marine Pavilion, 426
  Wavecrest, 426
Farley, John T. and James A., 333
Farragut Memorial, 118, *122,* 129
Federal buildings, *74-78, 75, 76, 77*
Federal style, 220, 342, 345, 353, 355, 365
Felheimer & Long, 44
Fenner, Burt, 90
Fernbach, Henry, 109
Ferree, Barr, 148-50, 153, 155, 250
Ferry service, 420, 421, 424, 426, 433
Ferry terminals, *48,* 49
Ficken, H. Edwards, 228-31
Ficken, Richard, 423
Field, William L., & Sons, 282-83
Fieldston and Riverdale, advertisement for houses in, *432*
Fifth Avenue, 307-09, *308,* 314, 354, 373
  382 Fifth Avenue, 198
  463-467 Fifth Avenue, 198
  844 Fifth Avenue, 324-25
  907 Fifth Avenue, 358
  998 Fifth Avenue, *290-95,* 307, 354
Fifth Avenue Association, 33, 442n33
Fifth Avenue Hotel, *126,* 253, *255*
  Amen Corner, 253
Fifth Avenue Presbyterian Church, 307, 308, *309, 313*
Fifth Avenue Riding School, 57
Filey, Oliver D., house, 355
Firehouse (113 West Thirty-third Street), *72-73*
Firehouse (157 East Sixty-seventh Street), 69
Firehouses, 69-73, *71, 72*
First Church of Christ, Scientist, 110, 113, *394, 395*
First (Police) Precinct House, 74

493

Flagg, Ernest, 23, 24, 29-30, 58, 59, 71, 80, 94, 95, 125, 128, 131, 153-54, 168, 169, 170-71, 174, 187, 200, 201, 278, 279, 287, 330, 331, 333, 346, 374, 375, 397, 402, 403, 404, 411, 412, 433-34, 482n379
    estate, Staten Island, 433-34, *435*
Flagg, Montague, 157
Flagler, Henry M., 312
Flatbush, Brooklyn, 423-25
    Ditmas Park, 425
    Ditmas Park West, 425
    Fiske Terrace, 425
    Knickerbocker Field Club, 424
    Prospect Park South, 424-*25*
    South Midwood, 425
    Tennis Court area, 423-24
    Vandeveer Park, 424
Flatbush Branch library, 101
Flatbush Congregational Church, 425
Flatiron Building, 164-67, *166, 173*
Fletcher, Isaac D., house, 321
Florentine Renaissance style, 290, 324
Flushing High School, 86
Folies Bergère, 216-*17*
Ford, George B., 31, 33
Ford, Henry, 58
Ford, Lyman A., 137
Ford, Paul Leicester, house, *345*
Forest Hills Gardens, Queens, 32, *427, 428*
    houses in, *429*
Forest Hills Inn, Forest Hills, Gardens, Queens, *428*
Forty-first (Police) Precinct House, 74
Fowler Court, 419
François I, style of, 192, 262, 377
Francophilia, 267
Franke, William B., 382
Franklin Savings Bank, 178
Freedlander, Joseph H., 86, 94, 95, 184, 185, 329, 385, 481n335
Freeman, Frank, 13, 98, 178, 362, 363
French, Daniel Chester, 68, 75, 88, 129, 190, 192, 233, 406
French, H.Q., 131
French Academic traditions, 169
French Baroque style, 377
French Classical style, 61, 62, 412
French Gothic style, 115, 131, 303, 310, 316, 321, 364, 365, 370, 377
French Renaissance, 48, 62, 69, 104, 184, 269, 290, 311, 316, 321, 330, 333, 355, 376, 377, 403, 404
French School, 23
Freundschaft Club, 231
Frick, Henry Clay, 339, 351, 477n220
    Art Reference Library, 340, 475n149
    mansion, 129, 315, 339-*40, 341*, 351
Frohne, H.W., 262, 418, 419
Frohne, William C., 231
Fuller (Flatiron) Building, 164-67, *166, 173*
Fulton Ferry, 424
Furness, Frank, 484n427

G

Gaiety Theater, 216
Gainsborough Studios, *296, 298*
Gambrill & Ficken, 228

Garden City, Long Island, 421, 424
Garnier, Charles, 22, 63
Garvin, Michael J., 68
Gates Avenue Courthouse (Brooklyn), 68
Gateway of the Nation (proposed), 128
Geddes, Patrick, 24
General Post Office, 40, 272
George Washington Bridge, 25, 50
Georgian Classicism, 196
Georgian Revival style, 342
Georgian style, 237, 238, 278, 304, 348, 350, 351, 375, 380, 424, 425
German American Insurance Building, *160, 161*
German Hospital, 314
German Renaissance style, 256, 262, 269, 311
German Theater, 212-*16*
Germania Life Building, 158
Germania Real Estate and Improvement Company, 424
Gerry, Elbridge, mansion, *232*, 316
Gibson, Charles Dana, house, *345*
Gibson, R.H., 484n427
Gibson, Robert W., 79, 110, 116, 117, 141, 187, 366, 484n433
Gilbert, Bradford L., 36, 146, 148
Gilbert, Cass, 25, 44, 74, 76, 77, 156, 157, 162, 163, 164, 165, 174, 175, 176, 177, 185
Gilbert, C.P.H., 316, 321, 325, 330, 350, 351, 353, 377, 382
Gilbert, Mrs. H.B., residence, 321, 476n188
Gilbert & Taylor, 104
Gilder, Richard Watson, 303
Giles, Jame H., 191
Gimbel Brothers (department store), 45, 192
Githens & Keally, 98
Gladstone, William, 19
Glasgow School, 216, 419
Globe Theater, 219
Glover, J.G., 80
Gmelin, Paul, 104
Godley & Fouilhoux, 25
Goelet, Robert, 312
Goelet, Mausoleum, 131
Goldenberg, Joel, Mausoleum, *132*
Goodhue, Bertram Grosvenor, 113, 116, 120, 121, 231, 350, 402
    house, *350*
Goodwin, James J., double house for, 342, *343, 350*
Goodyear, Professor W.H., 88
Gordon, Bragdon & Orchard, 62
Gordon, James Riely, 67, 68, 243, 303, 445n39
Gordon, Tracy & Swartwout, 301
Gordon & Kaelber, 481n335
Gorham Company Building, 64-67, 196, *198*, 200
Gotham Hotel, 278-79, 312, *313*, 385
Gothic concept, 54, 79, 110, 115, 116, 131, 162, 163-64, 176, 201, 226, 308, 316, 405
Gothic Revival style, 108, 109, 130, 212
Gottlieb, A.S., 200, 312
Gould, Edwin, house, 339
Gould, George, houses, 339
Gould, Jay, 108, 312
    Mausoleum, 130-31
Grace Church, 113
    Mission Chapel and Dispensary, *113*
Gracie, Archibald, house, 315
Graham, Anderson, Probst & White, 174
Graham, Ernest R., 173, 226

Graham, Thomas, 315
Graham Court, *290, 291,* 295
Grahm & Goodman's garage, 57-58
Gramercy Park, 24, 298, 300, 303
Gramercy Park apartments, 303
Grand Army Plaza (Brooklyn), 88, *98,* 122, 132, *134*
Grand Army Plaza (Manhattan), 125, 130, 232, *252, 256,* 258, 261, 308, 312, *313*
Grand Central Palace, 40
Grand Central Terminal, 31, 33, 34-40, *36, 37, 38, 39,* 41, 58, 64, 240, 272, 307, 353, 358, 404
Grant, Mayor, 61
Grant, Ulysses S., 396
Grant's Tomb, 121-22, *123,* 373, *397,* 406, *413*
    temporary tomb, *122*
Grattan, Harry, 425
Graves & Duboy, 368, 384, 385, 386
Gravesend Bay, 421, 422
Gravesend Racetrack, 248
Greek Revival style, 74, 177, 185, 253, 303, 355
Green, Bernard, 94
Green, Edward, & Sons, 481n335
Greenley, Howard, 275
Greenpoint Branch library, 101
Greenpoint Savings Bank (Brooklyn), 178
Greenwood Cemetery (Brooklyn), 130
Griffin, Percy, 73, 346, 350, 423
Grolier Club, 231
Gron, Neils, 27
Group houses, Jamaica, Queens, *430, 431*
Guaranty Trust Company, 185
Guerin, Jules, 303
Guernsey Building, 311
Guggenheim, Solomon, 262, 312
Guggenheim Mausoleum, 131
Guimard, Hector, 46

H

Hague, Marion, house, 346, 353
Hahnemann Hospital, 314
Haight, Charles Coolidge, 80, 94, 116, 220, 368, 369, 370, 376, 404, 405, 484n427
Haight, Dr. David H., 280
Hale & Rogers, 195
Hall of Records, *60, 62-63,* 64, 68, *165*
Hamilton Square, 314
Hamlin, A.D.F., 13, 21, 22-23, 88, 95-98, 109
Hammerstein, Oscar B., 207, 208, 209, 221
Hammond, Mrs. John Henry, house, 334-38
Hampshire House, 25
Harde, H.S.S., 388
Harde & Short, 290, 297, 388
Hardenbergh, Henry J., 15, 104, 106, 159, 161, 162, 240, 242, 252, 254, 255, 256, 257, 258, 262, 267, 269, 283, 284, 307, 364-65, 372, 388, 411
Harder, Julius, 28-29
Harding, George Edward, 152
Harding & Gooch, 144, 155, 261
Hardman Peck Company, 200
Harkness, Charles, 312
Harkness, Edward S., 338
    house, 338, 339
Harkness, Mary Stillman, 338
Harlem Auditorium, 208
Harlem River Speedway, 57

Harmonie Club, 239, 240
Harney, George E., 402
Harperly Hall apartments, *387,* 388
Harrigan & Hart's Theater, 206
Harrigan's Theater, 207
Hartshorn, Stewart, 421
Harvard Club, 101, 237-38, 240, 290
    Harvard Hall, *238*
Haskell, Llewellyn, 421
Hastings, Thomas, 125-28, 135, 150, 155, 325, 326, 338, 340, 414, 458n106
Haviland, John, 67
Haydel & Shepard, 94, 95, 328, 329
Hazelton, Henry Isham, 12
Heathcote Hall, 304, 418
Hébert, Maurice, 376, 377
Heins & LaFarge, 46, 47, 142, 143, 187, 367, 368, 397, 398, 400-01, 402, 403, 405
Hell Gate Bridge, 45, 52, 54-55, *56*
Helmle & Corbett, 128, 481n335
Helmle & Huberty, 134, 135, 178
Hendrik Hudson apartments, *418,* 419
Henry Hudson Parkway, 44
Henry Miller Theater, 219-20
Herald Building, *190*
Herald Square, 192, 194
Hermitage Hotel, *273, 278*
Herter, Albert, 183
Herter, Dr. Christian A., house, *326,* 329, 333, 334
Herter Brothers, 272, 309
Herts, Henry B., 123, 128, 212, 217
Herts & Robertson, 139
Herts & Tallant, 73, 98, 99, 131, 132, 141, 206, 209-11, 210, 211, 212, 213, 214, 215, 216, 217, 222, 239, 276, 278, 375, 377
Herzog Teleseme, 466n24
Hewitt & Bottomley, 325
Hewlett, J. Monroe, 98, 110-13
Hewlett & Hull, 306
High Renaissance style, 240
High Victorian Gothic style, 134, 404
High Victorian style, 228
Hill & Stout, 57, 160, 161, 196, 197
Hill & Turner, 385
Hispanic Society Library, 107
Hispanic Society of America, 105-07
Hiss & Weekes, 183, 184, 278, 385
Hitchcock, Hiram, 203
Hoe, Richard M., house, *326,* 330
Hofbrau House, 225
Hoffman, F. Burrall, 220
    house, 333
Hoffman Arms, *280, 281,* 282
Hoffman House, 222, *255*
Hoffstatter & Freres buildings, 201
Holden, L.C., 414
Holland Hotel, 275
Holland House (hotel), 261
Hollins, H.B., house, 351
Holy Trinity Church, 113, *114*
    St. Christopher's house, 113
Home Buildings (Brooklyn), 283
Home Club, *301,* 303, 357
Home for Old Men and Aged Couples, *402,* 403
Home Life Insurance Building, *152*
Hone, Philip, 191
Hood, Raymond, 25
Hook and Ladder Company Number 35, 73
Hooper, Professor Franklin, 88

Hope, Henry Reed, 187
Hoppin, William J., 134-35
Hoppin & Koen, 69, 73, 333, 373
Horace Mann School, *397,* 404
    Riverdale campus, 433
Horgan & Slattery, 57, 62, 63, 72, 165
Hornbostel, Henry F., 51, 52, 54, 55, 56, 64
Hornbostel, Wood & Palmer, 94
Horowitz, Louis, 173
Hotel Belleclair, 385, *388*
Hotel Belmont, *268, 272*
Hotel Brighton, Coney Island, 248, 249
Hotel Cumberland, 278
Hotel des Artistes, 295-98
Hotel Essex, *277,* 278
Hotel Imperial, *265,* 267
Hotel Majestic, *365, 380,* 381
Hotel Marie Antoinette, *381-82*
Hotel Marseilles, 385
Hotel Navarre, 267
Hotel Pennsylvania, 272
Hotel Rector, *167,* 269
Hotel Renaissance, *264,* 267, 275, 278, 382, 385
Hotel Seville, 278
Hotel Somerset, *274,* 275
Hotel Touraine, 275
Hotels, 253-72, 313
    Astor, *167, 222-23, 266,* 267-69
    Astor House, *165,* 253-55
    Astoria, 255-56, 261
    Belmont, *268,* 272
    Biltmore, *270, 271,* 272
    Brighton (Coney Island), 248, 249
    Buckingham, 255
    Commodore, 37, 272
    Fifth Avenue, *126,* 253, *255*
    Hampshire House, 25
    Hoffman House, 222, *255*
    Holland House, 261
    Imperial, *265,* 267
    Knickerbocker, 269
    McAlpin, 272
    Majestic, *365, 380,* 381
    Manhattan, 267, 269
    Manhattan Beach (Coney Island), *248,* 421
    Marie Antoinette, *381-82*
    Marine Pavilion (Far Rockaway), 426
    Mt. Pleasant, 315
    Navarre, 267
    New Netherland, 125, 255, 261
    Oriental (Coney Island), *248, 421*
    Pennsylvania, 272
    Plaza, *252, 256, 258-59,* 261-62, 267
    Rector, *167,* 269
    Renaissance, *264,* 267, 275, 278, 382, 385
    Ritz-Carlton, 200, *262, 263,* 267, 272
    St. Andrews, *368,* 381
    St. Regis, 23, *260, 261,* 262-67, 269, 278, 312, 385
    Savoy, 125, 255, 261
    Vanderbilt, 272
    Waldorf, 255-56, 261, 316
    Waldorf-Astoria, 194, 200, *254,* 255-61, *257,* 262, 267, 283
    Waldorf-Astoria (new), 25
    Windsor, 195, 255
Hotels, apartment. *See* Apartment hotels
Howard, Cauldwell & Morgan, 238, 277, 278
Howard, John Galen, 137, 138, 411
Howard & Cauldwell, 94, 95, 264, 267, 275, 385

Howe, Samuel, 430
Howells & Stokes, 45, 64, 67, 105, 107, 157, 397, 405, 406, 409, 486n505
Hoyt, Burnham, 116
Hoyt, Mrs. J.O., house, 377
Hoyt, John Sherman, house, 356
Huber, H.F., 198
Hubert, Pirsson & Company, 287
Hubert Home Clubs, 287, 299
Hudson, Charles, house, *346, 347*
Hudson Building, 152
Hudson Park, *136,* 137
Hudson River Bridge (projected), *397*
Hudson Terminal, 45
Hume, William H., 261
    & Son, 192
Hunt, Richard Howland, 88, 90, 333
Hunt, Richard Morris, 11, 23, 27, 61, 67, 88, 91, 92, 93, 94, 95, 98, 118, 128-29, 130, 134, 135, 137, 145, 147, 148, 178, 228, 229, 232, 279, 282, 309-10, 311, 313, 316, 317, 318, 319, 321, 370, 398, 405, 406, 484n427
Hunt & Hunt, 73-74, 131, 133, 332, 333, 356
Hunting, Walter C., 104
Huntington, Anna Hyatt, 107
Huntington, Archer M., 105-07
Huntington, Charles Pratt, 107, 108
Huntington, Collis P., 312
Huss, George Martin, 398
Huss & Buck, 398, 400
Hutchins, William, 255
Hyde, James Hazen, 224

I

Importers' and Traders' National Bank, 184, *185*
Improved Dwelling Council, 287
Ingalls, Harry Creighton, 219, 220
Institute of Mining Engineers, 243
Institute of Music, 412
International Congress of Engineers, 177
Iroquois Hotel, 275
Irving, Washington, 426
Isham, Arlington W., 425
Israels, Charles H., 304
Israels & Harder, 63, 275, 321
Issing, St. John, 212
Italian Renaissance style, 101, 107, 167, 184, 195-96, 256, 261, 278, 290, 304, 312, 316, 321-25, 333, 334, 338, 339, 342, 345, 351, 370, 392
Italianate Mannerism, 217, 219, 345

J

Jacobean style, 79, 351, 364, 382, 388, 410
Jacobs, Harry Allan, 200, 278, 385
Jacobson, John C., 104
James, Arthur Curtiss, house, *355*
James, Henry, 75-78, 169, 232, 253, 261
James, Dr. W.B., house, 351, 353
James McCreery (department store), 195
Janes & Leo, 330, 368, 373, 377, 382-83, 388
Japanese house, Prospect Park South, Flatbush, Brooklyn, *425*
Jardine, Kent & Jardine, 130, 432
Jefferson, Thomas, 108

Jennings, Albert Gould, residence, 333
Jennings, Oliver Gould, house, 330, *331*
Joass, John James, 73, 157
John Jay Park, 290
John Wolfe Building, *159*
Jones, Mrs. Mary Mason, 308
Joseph Building, 201
J. Pierpont Morgan Library, 90, 102-03, *104, 105*
Judson Memorial Church, 110, *111, 124,* 370

K

Kahn, Otto H., 217
   mansion, *325*
Kane, John Innes, house, *322, 323*
Keally, Francis S., 25
Kean, Van Cortlandt & Company Building, 153, 181
Keiser, H.J., 421
Kelley, Nicholas, residence, 433
Kellum, John, 156, 165, 191
Kelsey, Albert, 414
Kendall, Edward H., 136, 137
Kendall, William, 64-67, 90, 101, 164, 354, 355, 417
Kennedy, David, 417
Kew Gardens, Queens, 426
Kilburn, Henry F., 231, 324, 363, 369, 390, 391, 392
Kimball, Francis H., 98, 161, 163, 164, 171, 174, 206, 207, 208, 226, 231, 248
Kimball & Thompson, 151, 152, 321
Kimball & Wisedell, 206, 207
King, Moses, 18, 190
Kiosks, subway, 46, *47,* 367, *368, 405,* 443n88
Kirby, Petit & Green, 181, 184, 250, 251, 321, 346, 424
Knickerbocker Club, 238, 307
Knickerbocker Hotel, 269
Knickerbocker Trust Building, 156, 157, 178, *184*
Knight, Charles B., 142
Knoedler, M., & Company, 200
Knowles, H.P., 243
Knowles, William W., 94
Kohn, Estelle Rumbold, 154
Kohn, Robert D., 154, 155, 198, 219, 273, 278, 372, 373, 387, 392, 393
Kohn, Theodore, jewelry store, 198
Korn, Louis, 390
Koster & Bial's Theater, 217

L

Ladies' Baptist Home Society, home of, 314
Ladies Mile, 191, 192, 194
LaFarge, John, 11, 68, 316
LaFarge & Morris, 196, 445n39
Laird, Professor Warren P., 486n505
Laloux, Victor, 41, 69
Lamb, Charles Rollinson, 27, 123, 126, 169, 442n8
Lamb, Frederick Stymetz, 442n8
Lamb, Thomas, 220
Lamb & Rich, 86, 87, 361, 364, 373, 377, 410
Lambs' Club, 238
Lancaster, Frederick J., 426

Lane, Wolcott G., house, 325
Langham apartments, 388, *389*
Lanier, J.F.D., house, 333
Lapham, L.H., house, 330, 351
Lawlor & Haase, 418
Lawrence, Newbold and Alfred, 426
Lawrence Park, Bronxville, New York, 421
Lawrence residence (969 Fifth Avenue), 321
Lawrie, Lee, 116
Lawyers' Club, 163, *226*
Lawyers Title Insurance and Trust Company Building, 153
Le Brun, Napoleon, 61, 69, 72, 121
   & Sons, 71, 152, 171, 172, 173
Le Brun, Pierre, 171
Leake & Watts Orphanage, 396
Lee, Ivy, 187
Leeds, William Bateman, Mausoleum, 131, *132*
Lenox Hill, 314, 339, 351, 354
Lenox Library, 67, 91, *94,* 129, 321, 339, 351, 477n220
Lenox Lyceum Theater, 212
Leo, John P., 231
Levi, Julian C., 161
Lexington Avenue, One, *300, 303*
Liberty National Bank, 181, 183
Libraries, 91-103, *94, 95, 96, 97, 98, 99, 100, 101, 102, 103, 104, 105,* 107, 212
Lienau & Nash, 274, 275, 278
Lincoln Trust Building, 390
Lindeberg, Harrie T., 183-84
Lindenthal, Gustav, 50, 51, 52, 54, 55, 56, 64, 397
Lippi, Annibale, 103
Litchfield, Electus D., 430
Littell, E.T., 275
Little & O'Connor, 382
Little Singer Building, 153-54, *155,* 171
Little Theater, 219, 220
Llewellyn Park, New Jersey, 421, 430
   The Ramble, 421
Long Island Railroad, 426
Longacre Square (Times Square), 167, 203, 208. *See also* Times Square
Longfellow, Henry Wadsworth, 426
Longman, Evelyn Beatrice, 162
Lord, Hewlett & Hull, 329
Lord, James Brown, 67, 68, 71, 98, 100, 101, 172, 223, 224, 402, 412
Lord and Burnham Company, 141
Lord & Hewlett, 116, 217, 243, 245
Lord & Taylor, 191, *195*-96
Lotos Club, 239
Louis XVI style, 219, 316, 333, 339, 340
Low, Seth, 30, 50, 404-05, 406, 409, 418
   house, *346*
Low, William H., 316, 411
Low Library, Columbia University, 22, *405, 406,* 409
Lowell, Guy, 57, 68, 69, 70, 312
Lucas, Herbert, 300, 303
Luce, Clarence, 264, 267
Lüchow, August, 225
Lüchow's, 225
Ludlow & Valentine, 57, 278, 424
Luna Park, Coney Island, 209, *246-47, 249-*50, *251*
Lyceum Theater, 211, 212, *213*
Lynch, Elliot, 87, 388
Lynch, James D., 422

M

Mabie, Hamilton Wright, 19
McAdoo Tunnels ("Hudson Tubes"), 45, 49, 192, 272
   entry for proposed uptown terminal, *45*
   Hudson Terminal, 45
McAllister, Ward, 224
McAlpin Hotel, 272
McClellan, Mayor George, 51
MacCracken, Henry M., 108
McElfatrick, John B., 167, 203, 208
   & Son, 206, 207, 208
McGraw-Hill Building, 25
Mack, Andrew, 250
Mackay, William, 131
McKim, Charles F., 11, 22, 24, 30, 36, 41, 42, 43, 64, 67, 87, 88, 90-91, 95 98, 101, 103, 108, 116, 150, 164, 178, 185, 198, 231, 232, 233, 237, 238, 278, 311, 312, 323, 324, 338, 342, 350, 354, 404, 405, 407, 409, 411, 412, 417, 419, 442n8
McKim, Mead & Bigelow, 228
McKim, Mead & White, 10, 21, 26, 27, 36, 40, 41, 42, 43, 60, 64, 67, 87, 88, 89, 90, 91, 92, 93, 94, 95, 101, 102, 103, 104, 105, 108, 110, 111, 112, 116, 122, 124, 125, 129, 131, 132, 134, 135, 147, 148, 157, 163, 164, 165, 172, 173, 178, 179, 184, 185, 186, 187, 190, 195, 198, 201, 202, 204, 205, 206, 223, 224, 225, 231, 232, 233, 234, 235, 236, 237, 238, 261, 265, 267, 272, 278, 287, 290, 307, 310, 311, 312, 316, 320, 321, 322, 323, 324, 325, 338, 341, 342, 343, 344, 345, 350, 351, 354, 355, 365, 367, 398, 405, 406, 407, 408, 409, 411, 414, 417, 421, 445n39, 484n427
McKinley, William, 255
MacMonnies, Frederick, 122, 125, 134, 135
McQuade, Walter, 177
Macy, R.H., & Company (Macy's), *190,* 192
Madison Square, 118, 123, 126, 135, 167, 171, *172, 173,* 191, 203, *255,* 307
Madison Square Garden, 10, 15, 64, 67, *71,* 122, 171, *172,* 202, 203, *204, 205, 206,* 207-08, 209, 212, 287
   roof garden, *202,* 221
Madison Square Presbyterian Church, 110, *112, 172, 173*
Madison Square Theater, 206
Maginnis & Walsh, 87
Magonigle, H. Van Buren, 68, 125, 127, 245, 414, 415, 417, 445n39, 481n335
Maher, George, 23, 73
Mail and Express Building, *150*-51
Mali Estate, 108
Man, Albon P., 426
Man, Alrick, 426
Manhattan Athletic Club, 228
Manhattan Beach Amphitheater, Coney Island, *248*
Manhattan Beach Estates, Coney Island, *421*
Manhattan Beach Hotel, Coney Island, *248, 421*
Manhattan Bridge, 31, 50, *51-52, 53*
   Court of Honor, 52, *53*
Manhattan Congregational Church, 116
Manhattan Hotel, 267, 269
Manhattan Life Insurance Building, *151,* 152
Manhattan Opera House, 209
Manhattan Square, 297, 298, 360, 370, *371,* 373

496

Manhattan Trade School for Girls, 86
Mann & MacNeille, 433
Mansfield Hotel, 275
Marble Collegiate Church, 307
Marble Row, 200, *308,* 309, 310
Marble Twins, *332,* 333
Marc Antony apartments, 304
Marine Air Terminal, 25
Marine Pavilion (hotel), Far Rockaway, Queens, 426
Marquand, Henry G., houses for, 311, 315-16
Marsh, Benjamin C., 32, 33
Marshall, Henry Rutgers, 86, 87, 345
Marshall & Fox, 219
Martiny, Philip, 63
Masonic Hall, 243
Masonic Temple (Brooklyn), *243,* 245
Mathews Brothers, 428
Matthews, John, house, *361,* 363, 375
Maxine Elliott Theater, 219
Mayers, Murray & Philip, 121
Mayfair, The, *298*
Maynicke, Robert, 156
Maynicke & Franke, 199, 200
Mead, William, 342
Medievalism, 113
Megalopolis, 24
Mellen, Nathan C., 324
Menagerie (Central Park), 25
Mendelssohn Glee Club, 231
Mercantile Building, 48
Mercantile Library, 212
Merchants Association, 33
Merchants' Exchange Building, 74, 185
Metropolitan Age, 11, 12-25, 49, 132, 177, 190, 253, 267, 303, 307, 360
  Era of Convenience, 12, 24-25, 55, 58, 148, 171, 176, 192, 196, 272, 402
  Composite Era, 12, 13, 17-24, 25, 32, 34, 43, 44, 48, 49, 51, 55, 68, 69, 74, 78, 86, 87, 88, 101, 103, 104, 105, 107, 108, 116, 118, 121, 122, 123, 128, 129, 131, 139, 141, 146, 148, 156, 157, 176, 178, 183, 185, 191, 192, 196, 203, 206, 207, 209, 223, 225, 228, 231, 232, 240, 245, 250, 255, 256, 275, 287, 295, 310, 311, 312, 324, 333, 354, 367, 368, 370, 373, 390, 395, 396, 399, 401, 402, 414, 424, 425, 428, 430
  Cosmopolitan Era, 12-17, 20, 21, 27, 34, 49, 57, 67, 78, 86, 87, 88, 109, 116, 118, 121, 129, 130, 131, 177, 203, 206, 212, 222, 225, 228, 231, 255, 256, 272, 282, 283, 310, 311, 315, 324, 360, 363, 364, 366, 367, 369, 370, 373, 381, 392, 396, 404, 413, 417, 424, 425
Metropolitan Life Building, 48, 171, *172, 173*
Metropolitan Life Tower, 67, 110, 146, 171, *172, 173,* 176
Metropolitan (Millionaire's) Club, 231, *232-33,* 237, 239
Metropolitan Museum of Art, 13, 87, 88-91, *92, 93, 95,* 134, 135, 178, 314, 338, 370
Metropolitan Opera Company, 13, 87
Metropolitan Opera House, *14,* 15, 87, 203, 209, 217-19
Metropolitanism, 11-25, 31, 32, 44, 67, 116, 366
Milburn, New Jersey, 421
Millbank Memorial, 131
Milliken, Gerrish, 353
  house, 351
Mills, Darius O., 279

Mills House Number One, *278, 279*
Mira Mar apartments, 419
Mitchel, Mayor John Purroy, 426
Modern French style, 22-24, 37, 45, 49, 51, 54, 55, 57, 58, 68, 69, 72, 73, 74, 75, 79, 85, 86, 87, 95, 103, 105, 107, 131, 137, 139, 141, 153, 155, 157, 170, 176, 178, 181, 183, 185, 187, 192, 198, 209, 212, 237, 238, 250, 267, 269, 275, 316, 325-34, 338, 342, 350, 351, 357, 367, 373, 375, 382, 383, 385, 388, 392, 395, 403, 410, 412, 413, 414, 417, 418, 419, 474n107, 474n117, 474n119
Modern Renaissance style, 334-41, 344, 351, 356
Montana apartments, 304, *305*
Montauk Club, 98, 231
Monument Commission, 125
Monuments and memorials, 118-32, *122, 123, 124, 125, 126, 127, 128, 129, 130, 131, 133,* 135, 373, 375, 414
Mook, Robert, 308
Moore, Abbott Halstead, 211
Moore, W.F., residence, 424
Moore, William H., residence, 350
Moravian Cemetery, Staten Island, 130
Morgan, J.P., & Company (bank building), 183
Morgan, J. Pierpont, 90, 102-03, 203, 232, 239, 339
Morningside Heights, 351, 373, 396-419, *397, 405, 411, 413,* 417-18
Morningside Park, 43, 396, 401, 406, 410, 413, 419
Morosini, Giovanni P.
  Elmhurst (estate, Riverdale), 432
  Mausoleum, *130*
Morris, Charles, 445n39
Morris, Dave Hennen, house, 351, *353*
Morris, William, 211
Morris High School, 80, *84,* 85
Morse, George L., 88
Morsieff, Leon, 51, 52
Mortimer Building, 145
Morton, Levi P., house, 324
Moser, John, 161, 164
Moses, Robert, 25, 44
Mott Haven Branch library, 101
Mould, Jacob Wrey, 88, 122, 370, 410
Mount Pleasant. *See* Prospect Hill
Mt. Pleasant Hotel, 315
Mount Sinai Hospital, 314
Mouquin's (2 restaurants), 225
Mowbray, H. Siddons, 68, 233
Mowbray, William E., 373
Mowbray & Uffinger, 80, 178
Mowbray & Umberfield, 373
Mucha, Alphonse, 216
Mullett, A.B., 61, 165
Mulliken, H.B., 275
Mulliken & Moeller, 278, 385, 388
Mumford, Lewis, 31, 58, 61, 395
Munckowitz, Julius, 381-82
Municipal Art Commission, 30, 50, 55, 68
Municipal Art Society, 27-28, 30, 125, 129, 177, 442n8
Municipal Building, *60,* 64, *65, 66, 67, 147,* 164, *165*
Municipal Building (Brooklyn), 69
Municipal Building Commission, 61
Murchison, Kenneth, 49, 50
Murray Hill, 307, 333
Murray's Roman Gardens, 224, *225*

Museum of Natural History. *See* American Museum of Natural History
Museum of the American Indian, *107*
Mutual Bank, 183

N

Nash, Thomas, 417
National Academy of Design, 411-12
National Arts Club, 298
National City Bank, *185, 186, 187*
National Maine Memorial, 125, *127*
National Park Bank, *180,* 181-83, *182*
National Sculpture Society, 28, 123, 126
Naturalism, romantic, 134
Naval Arch (proposed), 125, 128
Neihaus, Charles E., 68
Nelson, Harry Loomis, 228
Neoclassical style, 131
Neo-Grec style, 178, 187, 321, 392-95
Neo-Palladian style, 134
Nesbit, Evelyn, 206, 221
Netherlands apartments, 304
Neville & Bagge, 300, 303, 304, 388
New Amsterdam Theater, *210,* 211-12, 222
New Brighton, Staten Island, 420, 433
New Century apartments, 382
New Fifth Avenue Theater, 207
New Law (1901), 287, 295, 303, 304
New Netherland Hotel, 125, 255, 261
New New York House, 348
New Theater. *See* Century Theater
New Union Fields Cemetery, 131, 132
New Utrecht, Brooklyn, 422-23
New York, New Haven & Hartford Railroad, Morris Park Station, *44*
New York, Woodhaven & Rockaway Railway Company, 426
New York American Tower (proposed), 168, *169*
New York & Harl(a)em Railroad, 314, 315, 420
New York Athletic Club, 228-31
New York Botanical Garden, 141, 142
New York Cancer Hospital, *370,* 376
New York Central Building, 40
New York Central Railroad, 44, 353, 432
  Bridge (proposed), 44
New York City Buildings Department, 309
New York City Improvement Commission, 19, 28, 29, 30, 32, 33, 34, 45
  Report of (1904), 49, 63-64
New York City Improvement Plans (1904 and 1907), 129
New York Clearing House Association (Associated Banks) Building, 185-87, *189*
New York Club, 240, *242*
New York Connecting Railway's bridge, 45. *See also* Hell Gate Bridge
New York County Courthouse, 63, *67-68, 69, 70*
New York Crystal Palace Exhibition, 145
New York *Evening Post* Building, 153, *154-55,* 373
New York Federation of Fine Arts, 125
New York Fireproof Tenement Association, 287
New York Free Circulating Library, 98
New York Hippodrome, *208-09,* 249
New York Hospital, 25
New York Life Insurance Building, *163*
New York Life Insurance Company, 261

New York Produce Exchange Bank Building, 171
New York Public Library, 31, 33, 87, 91-95, *96,*
   97, 98, 137, 194, 240, 242
New York Reform Club, 28
New York Savings Bank, 178
New York Stock Exchange, *144,* 145, *155,*
   187-89
New York *Sun* Building (proposed), *158,* 171
New York Theater, 221
New York *Tribune* Building, 145, *147,* 148, 169
   original 156
New York University, 80, 107-*08*
   Gould Memorial Library, *108*
   Hall of Fame, *108*
   Hall of Languages, 108
New York Yacht Club, 37, 231, 238-39, *240,*
   241, 278
New York Zoological Park, 141-*42, 143*
Newbold, Thomas, house, 325
Newborg, M., house, *329*
New-York Historical Society, 18, 87, 104-05, 314,
   393, 395
Normal College, 314, 447n108
North River Bridge Company, 50
Numbered streets, addresses on:
   Thirty-third Street, 53 West, 198
   Forty-eighth Street, 15 East (bachelor
      apartments), *274, 275,* 278
   Fifty-first Street, 5 East, 350
   Fifty-first Street, 32 East, 333
   Fifty-fourth Street, 7 West, *350*
   Fifty-fourth Street, 18 East, 350
   Fifty-fourth Street, 19 East, 350
   Fifty-fourth Street, 26 East, 350
   Fifty-fourth Street, 46 West, 350
   Fifty-sixth Street, 17 West, 351
   Fifty-seventh Street, 200 West, 298
   Sixty-first Street, 53 East, 349
   Sixty-second Street, 133 East, 345
   Sixty-fifth Street, 7 East, 325
   Sixty-sixth Street, 131-135 East, 298-*99*
   Sixty-seventh Street, 29-33 West, 295
   Sixty-seventh Street, 35 West (never built), 295
   Sixty-seventh Street, 130-134 East, 298-99
   Seventieth Street, 164 East, 353
   Seventy-sixth Street, 307-309 West, houses
      at, 377
   Seventy-sixth Street, 330 West, 377
   Seventy-seventh Street, 39 East, 333
   Seventy-ninth Street, 63 East, 345
   Eighty-third Street, 8 East, 330
   Eighty-sixth Street, 19 East, 345
   108th Street, 316-322 West, houses at, 373
   112th Street, 521 and 523 West, 418

O

Ocean Electric Railway, 426
O'Connor, T.P., 196
Odd Fellows Temple (not built), 148
Office and Convocational Building, 116
Office building, Bruce Price sketch for, *158,* 159
Ogden, S.B., 388
Old Slip Enginehouse, 69
Olmstead, B.S. and G.S., 422
Olmsted, Frederick Law, 12, 31, 42, 43, 55-57,
   88, 130, 132, 134, 137, 362, 396, 405, 420-21,
   422
Olmsted, Frederick Law, Jr., 32, 44

Olmsted & Vaux, 314
Olmsted Brothers, 427, 428
Olympia Theater, *167, 207-08,* 221
Oriental Hotel (Coney Island), 248, *421*
Orphan Asylum Society, 376
Osborn, Mausoleum, 131
Osborne apartments, 282
Ottendorfer Branch library, 98
Outwater, Edwin, 344
Oxford Hall, 419

P

Paine, Albert Bigelow, 249
Palmer, George Carnegie, 330
Palmer, George Q., house, 330
Palmer & Hornbostel, 50, 95, 237, 330, 350, 414,
   415
Paradise Roof Garden, *221,* 222
Parfitt, Albert E., 88
Parfitt Brothers, *421, 422,* 424, 484n433
Parish & Schroeder, 116, 245, 324, 404
Park Avenue, 353-58
   270 Park Avenue, 358
   540 Park Avenue, 354
   563 Park Avenue, 357, *358*
   635 Park Avenue, *358*
   829 Park Avenue, 357
   903 Park Avenue, *357, 358*
   925 Park Avenue, 357, *359*
   929 Park Avenue, 357
   960 Park Avenue, 358
   1185 Park Avenue, 304
Park Presbyterian Church, 369-70
Park Row Building, 146, 147, 152, *165,* 167
Parker & Unwin, 428
Parkhurst, Dr., 110
Parks, Department of, 137
Parks Commission, 135
Parkview apartments, 388
Parrish, Maxwell, 269
Parsons, Samuel, Jr., 141
Parsons, William Barclay, 46
Partridge, William Ordway, 131
Patriarchs, the, 224
Peabody, Robert Swain, 88, 411
Peabody & Stearns, 94, 227, 228, 324
Pelham, George F., 419
Pelham Bay Park, 132, 139
Pell & Corbett, 86, 87, 486n505
Pelton, Henry C., 116
Pennsylvania and Long Island railroad tunnels,
   428
Pennsylvania Station, 22, *26,* 31, 34, *40-42, 41,*
   43, 58, 95, 272, 428
Pentecost, George F., Jr., 137
Peter, Reverend Absalom, 130
Peter Minuit apartments, 419
Petit, John J., 226, 424, 425, 426
Pettit, H.M., 55, 397, 413-14
Pfeiffer, Carl, 57, 261, 282
Phipps, Henry, house, *336-37,* 338-*39*
Phipps, John S., house, *324,* 325, 342
Phyfe & Campbell, 261
Piccirilli, Attilio, 88, 125, 127
Pickering & Walker, 346, 357
Pierce Building, 150
Piers, 49
Pine, John B., 303

Pite, Arthur Beresford, 73
Plant, Morton F., 312
Platt, Charles, 293, 295, 298, 299, 304, 324, 325,
   345, 348
Platt, R.G., 367
Platt, Senator Thomas, 253
Players Club, 231
Plaza Hotel, *252, 256, 258-59,* 261-62, 267
   Men's Cafe, *256,* 262
   Tea Room, *258-59,* 262
Plecnik, Josef, 278
Pleisner, Guido, 98
Police buildings, *73*-74
Police Department Central Headquarters, *73*
Pollard, George Mort, 295
Pollard & Steinam, 295, 298
Pope, John Russell, 131, 132, 135, 356, 373
Port Richmond Branch library, 101
Porter, W.A., house, 424
Post, George B., 27, 64, 68, 69, 88, 94, 108, 109,
   116, 117, 121, 144, 145, 146, 147, 148, 149,
   151, 155, 156, 158, 164, 165, 168, 173, 177,
   184, 187, 189, 309, 313, 316, 411, 414
   & Sons, 298
Potter, Edward Tuckerman, 362
Potter, Henry C., 396
Potter, Bishop Horatio, 396, 399
Potter, William A., 13, 80, 109, 368, 369, 393,
   395, 397, 398, 399, 404, 412
Potter & Robertson, 398, 399, 400
Potter Building, 145
Pounds, Lewis, 425
Power station, I.R.T., 48
Prague, John G., 248
Prasada apartments, *387,* 388
Pratt, John T., house, 345
Presbyterian Hospital, 351
Price, Bruce, 129, 151, 158-59, 171, 174, 411, 426
Price, C. Matlack, 116, 196, 200, 356
Price, H. Brooks, 107
Prince George Hotel, 275-78
Prince Humbert apartments, 304
Prison Ship Martyrs' Monument, *125*
Proctor, A.B., 142
Produce Exchange Building, 146, 150, *184*
Progress Club, *230,* 231, 390
Prospect Hill, *314,* 315
Prospect Park, 31, 88, 132, *134,* 135
   Boathouse on the Lullwater, 134, *135*
   Croquet Shelter, *134*
   Memorial Arch, *134*
   Tennis House, 134
Provident Loan Society of New York, 184
Public baths, 137-39
   Avenue A., *139*
   competition entry, *137*
   East 54th Street, 139, *140, 141*
   Sixtieth Street, *138-39*
Public school (Edgecombe Avenue and 140th
   Street), 79
Public School (St. Nicholas Avenue and 117th
   Street), 79
P.S. 3 (West Village), 86
P.S. 21 (Mott Street), 85
P.S. 34 (Staten Island), 86
P.S. 66 (88th Street), 85
P.S. 124 (Brooklyn), 85
P.S. 130 (Brooklyn), 85
P.S. 137 (Brooklyn), 85
P.S. 153 (Bronx), 80

P.S. 157 (St. Nicholas Avenue), 84
P.S. 165 (108th Street), *80*
Public service buildings, 69-74
Pulitzer, Joseph, 129
  residence, *323*
Pulitzer Building, 145, 146, *147*, 148
Pulitzer Fountain, *129*-30
Pulitzer Memorial, 131
Putnam, J. Pickering, 248
Pyne, Percy, house, *354*-55

Q

Queen Anne style, 206, 228, 261
Queens, 426-30
  Far Rockaway, 426
  Forest Hills Gardens, *427, 428*
  Jamaica, *430, 431*
  Kew Gardens, 426
  Lawrence, 426
  New Venice, 426
  Richmond Hill, 426
  Ridgewood, 428
  Rockaway Beach, 426
  Woodsburgh, 426
Queensboro Bridge, 31, 33, *34,* 50, 51, *52-54, 55,* 428

R

Racquet & Tennis Club, 231, *232,* 237
Radcliffe & Kelley, 419
Radio City Music Hall, 25
Radio Corporation of America Building, 25
Railroads, 34-45, 192, 314, 315, 351, *376,* 420, 421, 426, 432, 434
  local stations, *44-45, 423,* 426
  tunnels, 428
  see also Grand Central Terminal; Pennsylvania Station
Ralph, Julian, 248
Ramée, Jean Jacques, 108
Randall Memorial Church, 110
Ranger, Henry W., 295
Rapid Transit Commission, 46
Real Estate Exchange, 189
Recreation, 132-42
Recreation piers, 137
  East Third Street, *136*
  projected Hudson River, *414, 415*
Rector Restaurant, 269
Red House apartments, *388*
Redmond, Geraldyn, house, 355
Reed & Stem, 34, 36, 37, 38, 39, 40
Reed House, 304
Regional Plan Association, 32
Reid, Daniel G., stables of, 353
Reilly, Charles H., 21-22, 24
Reinhard & Hofmeister, 25
Renaissance style, 195, 338, 369, 409
Renwick, James, Jr., 108, 109, 116, 228
Renwick, Aspinwall & Owen, 130, 131, 275
Renwick, Aspinwall & Renwick, 402
Renwick, Aspinwall & Russell, 484n427
Renwick, Aspinwall & Tucker, 184
Republican Club, 240
Restaurants, 222-26
Reynolds, Senator J.R., 250

Rhind, J. Massey, 192
Rice, Isaac L., 139-41
  house, *375*
Rice Memorial Stadium, 139-41
Rich, Charles, 294, 298, 410, 413, 419
Richardson, H.H., 11, 23, 44, 69, 86, 87, 101, 109, 115, 130, 321, 363, 367, 368, 388, 398
Richardson, W. Symmes, 90, 157, 237
Richmond, Edward, 426
Richmond Borough Hall, 69
Richmond Country Club, 434
Richmond County Courthouse, 69
Richmond Hill, Queens, 426
Riis, Jacob A., 135, 428
Ripley, Clapp & Faelton, 414
Ritz Hotel Adam style, 267
Ritz Tower, 25
Ritz-Carlton Hotel, 200, *262, 263,* 267, 272
River House, 25
River Mansion, *372, 373*
Riverdale School, 433
Riverside buildings (Brooklyn), 283
Riverside Church, 116
Riverside Drive, 360, 362, *363,* 373, *376*
  Clarence True houses on, 364
  memorials on, 373
  viaduct, *123,* 362, 380, *397, 413*
  35-38 Riverside Drive, 364
  440 Riverside Drive, 304
Riverside Park, 43, 44, 121, 125, 132, 360, 396, *397, 410,* 413-14, 419
Rives, George L., house, 333-34
Riviera apartments, 304
Rivington Street Branch library, 101
Robert Fulton Memorial (projected), 43, 414, *415,* 417
Robertson, R.H., 109, 147, 165, 232, 245, 368, 369, 370, 484n427
Robertson, T. Markoe, 128
Robertson & Potter, 178, 345
Robinson, John Beverly, 79
Rochelle Park, New Rochelle, New York, 421, 424
Rockaway Beach, Queens, 426
Rockaway Hunting Club, 426
Rockaway Yacht Club, 426
Rockefeller, John D., 312
  house, 351
Rockefeller Center, 25
Rockefeller family, 18
Roebling, John A., 15
Roebling, Washington, 15, 50, 54
Rogers, Isaiah, 74, 185, 253
Rogers, James Gamble, 25, 240, 338, 339, 353, 356
  house, 353
Roine, G.E., 68
Rollins, Philip A., house, 344
Roman Classicism, 24, 73
Romanesque style, 69, 101, 104, 109, 110, 116, 130, 131, 148, 150, 178, 231, 245, 261, 363, 365, 367-68, 369, 370, 388
Romeyn, Charles W., 346, 387, 388
  & Company, 57, 280, 281, 282
Romeyn & Stever, 231
Roof gardens, 220-22, 463n32
Roosevelt, Governor Theodore, 253
Root, Senator Elihu, 295, 342-44, 353
  house, 342, *344,* 354
Rose & Stone, 321, 369

Roth, Emery, 358, 385, 418, 419
Rouse, William L., 418
Rouse & Goldstone, 304, 305, 358
Rouse & Sloan, 304, 305
Rowhouses
  first on Morningside Heights, 417
  Fifty-first Street, 31, 33, 35 East, *350-51*
  Seventy-third Street, 105-107 East, *348, 349*-50
  Seventy-third Street, West, 360, 364, *372*
  Seventy-fourth Street, 18-52 West, *378-79,* 380
  105th and 106th Streets, West, 373
  West End Avenue and Seventy-sixth Street, *364*
  West End Avenue and Eighty-third Street, 365-66, *367*
  West End Avenue, Eighty-fourth to Eighty-fifth Streets, *367*
Royal Insurance Company Building, *157*
Ruppert house, *314,* 315
Ruskinian Gothic style, 88, 370, 404, 411
Russell, Henry E., Mausoleum, 131, *132*
Russell, Lillian, 206
Russell Sage Foundation, 32, 428
Ruszits Building, 201
Rutgers Presbyterian Church, *368,* 369
Ryan, Thomas Fortune, art gallery, *325*

S

Sage, Russell, 312
Sailors' Snug Harbor, Staten Island, 110
Saint, Andrew, 11
St. Agatha's School, 87
St. Agnes Chapel, 368, *369,* 398
St. Andrews Hotel, *368,* 381
St. Bartholomew's Church, 113, *120, 121*
  Community House, 116
St. Gabriel's Branch library, 101, *103*
St. George Ferry Terminal, Staten Island, *49,* 69
St. James Building, 159
St. James's Church, 113
St. John the Divine. *See* Cathedral of St. John the Divine
St. Luke's Hospital, 312, 350, 396, *397, 402-03, 404, 413*
St. Nicholas Club, 86
St. Nicholas Park, 108
St. Patrick's Cathedral, 17, 109, 116, 308, 396, 404
St. Paul Building, 146, 156, 162, *165,* 168
St. Paul's Chapel, *146, 165*
St. Paul's Chapel (Columbia University), *405, 406, 408, 409*
St. Paul's Methodist Episcopal Church, 370
St. Regis Hotel, 23, *260, 261, 262-67,* 269, 278, 312, 385
  Palm Room, 267
St. Regis School, *87*
St. Stephen's Parish School, 87
St. Thomas Church, 116, *117, 118, 119,* 201, 308, *309,* 313
Saint-Gaudens, Augustus, 11, 30, 118, 122, 129, 130, 316
Sala, George Augustus, 253
Salem Fields Cemetery, 131, 132
San Remo apartments, 25
Sant' Elia, Antonio, 45

Sargent, Rene, 200
Satterlee, Louisa, house, 103
Save New York Committee, 33
Savoy Hotel, 125, 255, 261
Schickel, William, & Co., 192, 231
Schickel & Ditmars, 324
Schieffelin, William J., house, 333
Schiff, Jacob, 321
    house, *333*
Schinasi, Maurice, residence, 375-76
Schmid, Mrs. Josephine, house, *318, 319,* 321
Schnitzer Mausoleum, 131-*32*
School of Applied Design for Women, *86*
Schools, 78-*87, 79, 80, 81, 82-83, 84, 85, 86-87,* 392, 433, 447n116
Schuman, F., 57
Schumann's Sons, *199,* 200
Schuyler, Montgomery, 22, 23, 41, 51, 52, 63, 108, 109, 113, 115, 116, 137, 145, 148, 150, 152, 153, 154-55, 156, 157-58, 159, 161, 162, 168-70, 171, 176, 178, 181, 183, 184, 206, 207, 232-33, 255-56, 278, 307, 309, 310, 315, 316, 326, 342, 344-45, 346-48, 349, 350, 356-57, 360, 362, 365, 367-68, 370, 395, 399, 400, 404, 406, 409, 410
Schwab, Charles H., mansion, 315, *376-77*
Schwartz & Gross, 302, 303, 304, 418
Schweinfurth, J.A., 390
Scientific Eclecticism, 21, 22, 23, 24
Scribner, Arthur, house, 333
Scribner, Charles, house, 333
Scribner buildings, 200-*01*
Sea Gate, Brooklyn, 421
    typical house in, *422*
Second Church of Christ, Scientist, 110, 392
Second Empire style, 61
Second National Bank, 184
See, Milton, 43, 61
Seligman, Professor Edwin, 428
Seligman, Henry, house, 351
Seligman Building, *161*
Semi-detached houses (Clifton, Staten Island), *434*
Senff, Mrs. Charles H., mansion, 333
Sethlow (bachelor apartments), *418,* 419
Seventieth Street, East, 351-53
Seventy-second Street and Riverside Drive
    house at, 377
Severn apartments, 385
Sewell, Robert Van Vorst, 267
Seymour Hotel, 278
Shaw, Adele Marie, 78-79
Shean, Charles M., 250
Shepard, Elliot F., house, *309*
Shepard, Helen Gould, 108
Shepley, Rutan & Coolidge, 74
Shepp, Daniel B., 18
Shepp, James W., 18
Sherman, General, statue of, 130
Sherman Square, *368,* 383
Sherry, Louis, 223-24
Sherry's, 223-*24, 225*
Shiebler, George B., 98
Shingle style, 228, 362, 363, 421, 424, 425
Shonncer Tomb, 132
Short Hills Park, New Jersey, 421
Shubert Alley, 217
Shubert brothers, 208
Shubert Theater, 217
Siegel Cooper (department store), *191,* 192

Simmons, Edward, 68
Simonson, Pollard & Steinam, 295
Simpson, Spicer, 131
Simpson Crawford store, 192
Singer Manufacturing Company headquarters, 168, 170
Singer Tower, 146, *170-71,* 173, *174,* 176
Sisters of Mercy
    home of, 314
    industrial school, 314
Sixtieth Street Public Bath, *138-*39
Skyscrapers, 25, 177, 459n140
Slee, John, 425
Sloane, H.T., house, 326-29, *327,* 330, 334
Sloane, William D., 334
    house, *309,* 355
Small & Schumann, 46
Smith, Henry Atterbury, 286, 288, 289, 290
Smith, Lucien E., 98
Smith, Lyndon P., 153
Smith, W. Wheeler, 94
Smithmeyer & Pelz, 406
Snelling & Potter, 49, 57
Snook, John B., 194, 195, 309
Snyder, C.B.J., 79, 80, 81, 82, 84, 85, 86, 87, 368, 446n90
Soldiers' and Sailors' Memorial (Brooklyn), 88, 121, 122, 134
Soldiers' and Sailors' Monument (Riverside Drive), 125, *128,* 373, 375
South Church, 116
Specialty stores, *195, 196-201, 197, 198, 199,* 200
Spence School, 87
Spencer Arms apartments, 385
Speyer & Company (bank building), 181, 183
Sprague, John F., 13
Squires & Wynkoop, 421
Stable Building & Auction Mart (Fiss, Doerr & Carroll), 57
Stable of C.K.G. Billings, *57*
Stable (Riding Ring) of Frank J. Gould, 57, *58*
Stables, *57, 58,* 353
Standard Coach Horse Company, 57
Standard Oil Company Building, 145
Stapleton Ferry Terminal, 49
Starrett, Theodore, 173, 272
Starrett & Van Vleck, 195, 196
Staten Island, 433-*34, 435*
    Clifton, *434*
    Dongan Hills, 434
    New Brighton, 420, 433
    Tompkinsville, 433
Station Square, Forest Hills Gardens, Queens, *428-*30
Stations
    elevated railroads, *28*
    railroads, *44-*45
    subway, 46-48, *47*
    see also Grand Central Terminal; Pennsylvania Station
Statler Company, 272
Statue of Liberty, 118-21
Steeplechase Park, Coney Island, 249
Steffens, J. Lincoln, 145
Steichen, Edward, 167
Steiglitz, Alfred, 167
Stein, Clarence, 25
Stein, Cohn & Roth, 388
Steinam & Simonson, 295

Steinway Tunnels, 428
Stem, Allen H., 44
Stenhouse, J. Armstrong, 325
Stern Brothers (department store), 192-94
Sterner, Frederick J., 304, 346, 349, 351
    house, *349*
Stevens, Mrs. Paran, 310
Stewart, A.T., 130, 191, 421
    house of, 307, 309
Stewart, Gabrielle T., 19
Stewart, Robert, 256-61
Stewart's (department store), 191, 192
Stick style, 248
Stickley, Gustav, 425
Stillman, James, 185
Stimson, E.J., house, 377
Stokes, I.N. Phelps, 356
Stokes, W.E.D., 368, 384, 385, 386
    house, 351
Stoughton & Stoughton, 74, 125, 128, 139
Straight, Willard, house, *344,* 346
Strand Theater, 220
Straus, Nathan, house, *372,* 373
Straus, Oscar S., house, 373
Strom, William, 350
Stuckert, A.M., 424
Studio Apartments (132 East Nineteenth Street), 304
Studio Apartments (144 East Fortieth Street), 304
Studio Building, *297, 298*
Sturgis, Russell, 23, 30, 110, 123, 147, 152, 153, 311, 316, 342, 350
Sturgis & Simonson, 294, 295
Stuyvesant, Rutherford, 279
Stuyvesant Apartments, 279, 280, 282
Stuyvesant High School, 85, *86*
Suburbs, 420-35
    Bronx, 430-33, *432*
    Brooklyn, *421-*25, *422, 423, 424, 426*
    model, 421, 430
    Queens, *426-*30, *427, 428, 429, 431*
    Staten Island, 433-34, *435*
Subways, 45-49, 167, 192, 380, 381, 383, *397,* 413, 417, 432, 443n76
    kiosks, 46, *47,* 367, *368,* 405, 443n88
    stations, 46-48, *47*
Sullivan, Louis, 22, 148, 153, 155, 176
Sumner apartments, 304
Swales, Francis, 152, 158-59, 163, 196, 200-01
Sweeney, Peter B., 43
Swiss chalet style, 425
Symonds, John Addington, 21

T

Tammany Hall, 62, 225, 390
Taylor, Alfred H., 198, 231
Taylor, H.A.C., 354
Taylor, William J., 295, 357
Tchaikovsky, Peter Ilyich, 15
Teachers College, 80, 396, *397,* 404, 405, *410,* 411, *413*
    Macy Hall, 404
    Main Building, 404
    Milbank Memorial Hall, 404
    Thompson Memorial Hall, 404
Teleseme, Herzog, 466n24
Temple Emanu-El, 109, 196, 307

Temples and synagogues, 109, 110, 196, 307, *392*
Tenement House Law (1879), 280
    Dumbbell Plan, 280
Tenements, 279, 280, 282, 287
Terminal City, 40, 41. *See also* Grand Central Terminal
Thain, Charles C., 333
Thaw, Edward, house, 321
Thaw, Harry K., 221
Theaters, 203-20
    Abbey's, 206
    Aerial, 212, 222
    Booth, 217
    Brooklyn Academy of Music, 212, *214, 215,* 216
    Casino, 206-*07,* 220-21
    Century (New), 217-19, *218,* 392
    Empire, 206
    Folies Bergère, 216-*17*
    Gaiety, 216
    German, 212-*16*
    Globe, 219
    Harlem Auditorium, 208
    Harrigan & Hart's, 206
    Harrigan's, 207
    Henry Miller, 219-20
    Koster & Bial's, 217
    Lenox Lyceum, 212
    Little, 219, 220
    Lyceum, 211, 212, *213*
    Madison Square, 206
    Maxine Elliot, 219
    New Amsterdam, *210, 211*-12, 222
    New Fifth Avenue, 207
    New York, 221
    New York Hippodrome, 208-*09*
    Olympia, *167,* 207-*08,* 221
    Shubert, 217
    Victoria, 221
    Wallack's, 203
Theodore Roosevelt Memorial, New York State, 135, 373
Third Church of Christ, Scientist, 237
Thirteenth (Police) Precinct House, 74
Thirty-Fourth Street National Bank, *183,* 184
Thom, Wilson & Schaarschmidt, 67
Thomas, Andrew Jackson, 25
Thomas, Griffith, 163
Thomas, John R., 61, 62, 63, 165
Thompson, Frederic, 208, 209, 249-50, 251
Thorne, Oakleigh, house, 356
Thorp, Alfred H., 45-46
Tichenor-Grand Stable, 57, *58*
Tiffany, Charles L., house, *310,* 311-12, 315
Tiffany, Louis Comfort, 311-12
Tiffany & Company, *195,* 196, 200
Tilden, Samuel, 91
Tilden Trust, 91-94
    proposed library, *94, 95*
Tillion & Tillion, 116
Tilyou, George, 249
Times Square, *167,* 203, 206, 267, 269. *See also* Longacre Square
Times Tower, *167,* 269
Tombs, the, 67
Tompkins, Daniel D., 433
Tompkinsville, Staten Island, 433
Tottenville Branch library, 101
Tower Building, *146,* 148
Tower apartment complex (Brooklyn), 283

Towers, The, apartments, 388
Towle, Hubert Ladd, 58
Town, Ithiel, 108
Town & Davis, 74
Townsend, Ralph S., 261
Tracy, Swartwout & Litchfield, 445n39
Tracy & Swartwout, 240, 303, 304
Transportation, 34-58, 420
    automobiles, coming of, 55-58
    bridges, 49-*55, 51, 52, 53, 54, 56*
    elevated railroads, 12, *28,* 45, 46, *191,* 192, *209,* 314, 315, 351, 360, 365, *371,* 396, 417, 426, 457n97
    ferry service, 420, 421, 424, 426, 433
    ferry terminals, *48, 49*
    garages, 57-58
    piers, 49, *50*
    railroads, 34-45, 192, 314, 315, 351, *376,* 420, 421, *423,* 426, 432, 434
    stables, *57, 58*
    subways, 45-49, 167, 192, 367, *368,* 380, 381, 383, *397,* 405, 413, 417, 432, 443n76
    tunnels, 428
    see also Grand Central Terminal; Pennsylvania Station; individual bridges by name
Trinity Building, 145, 163, *164, 174,* 176
Trinity Cemetery, 105, 116
Trinity Church, 145, *146,* 158, *174,* 176, 398
Trinity School, 86, 87, 368
Trollope, Anthony, 314
Trowbridge, Samuel, 353
    house, *352,* 353
Trowbridge, Professor William P., 405
Trowbridge & Livingston, 74, 144, 159, 174, 183, 193, 194, 260, 261, 267, 269, 278, 329, 336, 338, 339, 351, 352, 373, 445n39, 481n335
True, Clarence, 363-64, 367
Trumbauer, Horace, 200, 339, 351
Tubby, J.T., 98
Tubby, Willliam B., 88, 102, 103
Tucker, Carll, 358
Tuckerman, Arthur, 88
Tudor style, 353, 356, 425
Tunnels, 428
Turin apartments, 388
Turrets, The, apartments, 388
Tuthill, William B., 15, 375-76, 458n106
Tweed Courthouse, *60,* 61, 67, *165*

U

Union Club, 228, 231, 232, 233-37, *236,* 307
Union League Club, *227,* 228, *229,* 231, 232
    Art Committee, 88
    Building Committee, 228
Union Square, 135, 203, 307
Union Square Savings Bank, 178
Union Theological Seminary, *324,* 351, 355, *412*-13
Union Trust Company Building, 148, *149, 151,* 152
U.S. Custom House, *74-75, 76, 77,* 185
U.S. Immigration Station (Ellis Island), 74, 75, *78*
United States Realty Building, 163, *164,* 226
    Lawyer's Club, 163
United States Rubber Building, 156, 200
University campuses, 107-*09, 108. See also* Columbia University

University Club, 231, 232, 233, *234, 235,* 237, 278, *350*
University Heights, 108
Untermeyer residence, 315
Upjohn, Richard, Sr., 116, 145, 307, 308
Upjohn, Richard M., 130, 398

V

Van Alen, Willliam, 225
Van Brunt & Howe, 484n427
Van Dyck apartments, 385
van Rensselaer, Marianna Griswold, 15, 18, 20, 203, 314, 396
Van Wyck, Mayor, 46
Vanderbilt, Cornelius (Commodore), 137, 203, 272, 309
Vanderbilt, Cornelius, II, 309, 310, 316, 324
    house for, 309, 312, *313,* 315, 316
Vanderbilt, Cornelius, III, 414
Vanderbilt, George W., 98, 404, 434
Vanderbilt, William Henry, 130, 287, 309, 312
    house of, *309,* 339
Vanderbilt, Mrs. William K., 290, 310
    house of, *320*
Vanderbilt, Mrs. William K., Jr., house for, 321
Vanderbilt, William Kissam, 37, 309, 312-14, 321
    house of, *309*-10
Vanderbilt family, 308-09
Vanderbilt Hotel, 272
Vanderbilt Mausoleum, 130
Vanderbilt Row, 233, 309, 312, 321, 323
    rowhouses, 350-51
Vaughan, Henry, 484n427
Vaux, Calvert, 88, 134, 135, 141, 370, 396
Venetian Gothic style, 196
Verdi Square, *368,* 390
Victoria Theater, 221
Victorian Gothic style, 177, 403
Victory Memorial (proposed), 128
Viennese Classicism, 418
Viennese Secessionist style, 154
Villard, Henry, 312
Villard houses, 21, 27, 104, 231, *311, 312,* 323, 325, 342
Villars, Countess de Langier, house, 355
Vincent Astor Estate Office, 324
Viollet-le-Duc, Eugène-Emanuel, 22, 23, 52, 109, 154

W

Wadleigh High School for Girls, 80
Wagner, Otto, 278
Waid & Willauer, 418
Waldo, Gertrude Rhinelander, house, 321
Waldorf Hotel, 255-56, 261, 316
Waldorf-Astoria Hotel, 194, 200, *254,* 255-61, *257,* 262, 267, 283, 321
    Astor Gallery, 256
    Peacock Alley, 256, *257*
Waldorf-Astoria Hotel (new), 25
Walker & Gillette, 304, 349, 355
Walker & Morris, 48, 49, 94, 95, 102
Wall Street, 60-62, 152
Wallack's Theater, 203
Wanamaker's (department store), 192

W. & J. Sloane & Company, 195
Warburg, Felix, residence, 321
Ward, John Quincy Adams, 189
Wardwell, Allen, house, 346
Ware, James E., 121, 282, 287, 388
  & Son, 198
Ware, Professor William Robert, 61, 94, 121, 187, 405
Ware & Metcalfe, 128
Warner, John DeWitt, 11, 27, 50
Warren, G.H., house, 330
Warren, H. Langford, 104
Warren, Whitney, 37, 94, 95, 103, 239
Warren & Wetmore, 34, 37, 38, 39, 40, 49, 50, 153, 196, 200, 224, 238, 239, 240, 241, 262, 263, 267, 268, 270, 271, 272, 330, 333, 334, 335, 338, 351, 357, 358
Warren Building, 148
Warrington Hotel, 275
Washburn, Owen R., 395
Washburn, William, 255
Washington Heights, 351, 381
Washington Irving High School, 86
Washington Life Building, *157*-58
Washington Memorial Arch, *124*
  temporary, *125*
  see also Centennial Arch
Washington Square, 18, 67, 107, 108, 111, 122, 125, 307, 420
Washington Square Park, 110
Webb, Sir Aston, 88
Weekes, H. Hobart, 292, 295, 385
Weinman, Adolph A., 67, 125, 164
Wellesley apartments, 382
Wells, Joseph Morrill, 312
Wellsmore apartments, 388
Werner & Windolph, 73, 138, 139, 140, 141
Wertheim, Henri P., stables of, 353
Wessells Building, 164
West End, 360-95
  metamorphosis, 380-81, 395
  street-name changes, 360
West End Avenue:
  232 West End Avenue, 377
  590 West End Avenue, 304
  789 West End Avenue, 304
  801 West End Avenue, 304
West End Presbyterian Church, 369
West End Synagogue, 392
West Park Presbyterian Church, 113
West Side Association, 360
West Side Improvement Project, 42-44
West Side Republican Club House, 390
West Street Building, 162, *163,* 176
Western Union Building, 307
Western Union Telegraph Building, 145, *146,* 148, 169
Weston, Theodore, 88, 92
Wetmore, Charles D., 37
Wetzel & Company, 196, *197*
Wharton, Edith, 11, 22, 279, 287, 308, 360
White, Alfred T., 282-83
White, Frederick B., 366
White, Lawrence G., 107
White, Stanford, 11, 15, 36, 48, 67, 80, 88, 107, 108, 110, 118, 120, 122, 129, 134, 157, 178, 183, 184, 196, 203, 207, 221, 223, 224, 231, 232, 237, 238, 239, 240, 267, 311, 312, 321, 323, 324, 342, 345, 370, 452n286
Whitehall Building, 161-62

Whitehall Ferry Terminal, *48,* 49
Whitfield & King, 240, 244, 245, 425
Whitney, Harry Payne, 217, 312
  residence, 324, 339
Whitney, William C., 324
Whitten, Robert H., 33
Whyte's Restaurant, 225
Wight, Peter B., 212, 411
Wilgus, William J., 36, 40
Wilkinson, Henry W., 387, 388
Williamsburg Bridge, *31,* 50-51
Williamsburg Savings Bank (Brooklyn), 177
Wilson, Mrs. M. Orme, house, 334, *335*
Wilson, R.T., house, 333
Windsor Arcade, *194,* 195, 312
Windsor Hotel, 195, 255
Wingate, Chas. F., 280-82
Winkler, Franz K., 388
Winthrop, H.R., 217
Wisedell, Thomas, 206
Withers, F.C., 484n427
Wolfe, Thomas, 41-42
Woman's Hospital, 404
Wood, Palmer & Hornbostel, 416, 417
Wood, Samuel, 426
Wood, William Halsey, 16, 95, 398, 399, 400, 484n427
Woodlawn Cemetery, 130, 131, 132, 133
Woodsburgh, Queens, 426
  Woodsburgh Pavilion, 426
Woolner Mausoleum, 131, *132*
Woolworth, Frank W., 177
  residence for, 321
Woolworth Building, 25, 146, *165, 174, 175,* 176-77
Woolworth Company office building and store, 201
Wren, Sir Christopher, 62, 113, 164, 356, 395
Wright, Frank Lloyd, 22
Wynne, Henry R., 387, 388
Wyoming apartments, 304, *305*

#

Yale Club, 240
Yale University, Scientific School, 80
York & Sawyer, 57, 105, 131, 139, 178, 185, 240, 325, 350, 351, 393, 395, 445n39, 481n335
Yorkville Branch library, 98, *100, 101*
Y.M.C.A.
  East Fifteenth Street, 245
  Eastern District (Brooklyn), 245
  West Side, 245
Young Women's Christian Association, Central Branch, 243-45
Y.W.H.A., Central, 245

Z

Ziegfeld, Florenz, 208
Zoning Resolution (1916), 176
Zucker, Alfred, 230, 231, 365, 381, 390